D0607785

# THE FINAL FOUR *of* EVERYTHING

**A celebration of all that's great, surprising, or silly in America using the foolproof method of bracketology* to determine what we love or hate – and why. The arguments begin here.**

*A knockout tournament format made famous by the NCAA's March Madness basketball tournament, now applied to everything but basketball.

Edited by
**Mark Reiter and Richard Sandomir**

Designed by **D.W. Pine**

Simon & Schuster Paperbacks
New York London Toronto Sydney

Simon & Schuster Paperbacks
A Division of Simon & Schuster, Inc.
1230 Avenue of the Americas
New York, NY 10020

Copyright © 2009 by Mark Reiter and Richard Sandomir

All rights reserved, including the right to reproduce this book or portions thereof in any form whatsoever. For information address Simon & Schuster Paperbacks Subsidiary Rights Department, 1230 Avenue of the Americas, New York, NY 10020.

First Simon & Schuster Paperbacks edition May 2009

SIMON & SCHUSTER PAPERBACKS and colophon are registered trademarks of Simon & Schuster, Inc.

For information about special discounts for bulk purchases, please contact Simon & Schuster Special Sales at 1-866-506-1949 or business@simonandschuster.com.

The Simon & Schuster Speakers Bureau can bring authors to your live event. For more information or to book an event, contact the Simon & Schuster Speakers Bureau at 1-866-248-3049 or visit our website at www.simonspeakers.com.

Designed by D.W. Pine

Manufactured in the United States of America

"Final Four" is a registered trademark of the National Collegiate Athletic Association and is used herein with permission of the NCAA.

10 9 8 7 6 5 4 3 2 1

Library of Congress Cataloging-in-Publication Data has been applied for.

ISBN-13: 978-1-4391-2608-0
ISBN-10: 1-4391-2608-9

# THE FINAL FOUR *of* EVERYTHING

# Contents

## The Brackets

**Introduction** *by Mark Reiter*

### AMERICANA

1 **Magical Numbers** *by Richard Sandomir*
2 **American Guns** *by Stephen Hunter*
3 **Jim Henson Creations** *by Michael Davis*
4 **American Products** *by Lee Eisenberg*
5 **Cars That Made a Difference** *by Phil Patton*
6 **Protestant Hymns** *by Nancy Gibbs*
7 **License Plates** *by Tom Vanderbilt*
8 **State Birds** *by Scott Mowbray*
9 **Pseudonyms** *by Stanley Bing*
10 **Iconic Photographs** *by James Danziger*
11 **Ridiculous Celebrity Auctions** *by Leila Dunbar*
12 **Board Games** *by Stefan Fatsis*
13 **Magic Tricks** *by Joshua Jay*
14 **Roller Coasters** *by Scott Rutherford*
15 **SAT Success Strategies** *by Laura Wilson*
16 **Screen Cowboys** *by Neil Amdur*
17 **A New National Anthem** *by Richard Sandomir*

### HISTORY AND POLITICS

18 **Vestiges of the 20th Century** *by Kurt Andersen*
19 **Conservative Texts** *by Mary Matalin*
20 **First Ladies** *by Gail Collins*
21 **Panic Attacks** *by Jack Hitt*
22 **Memorable Speech Lines** *by Jeff Shesol*
23 **Innovators** *by Harold Evans*
24 **Supreme Court Decisions** *by Adam Liptak*
25 **Presidential Pardons** *by P.S. Ruckman, Jr.*
26 **Military Heroes** *by Richard Goldstein*
27 **Enduring One-Liners** *by Jan Van Meter*
28 **Financial Villains** *by Joe Nocera*
29 **Political Rivalries** *by Adam Clymer*
30 **Presidential Speeches** *by Curt Smith*
31 **Influential Radicals and Extremists** *by David Oshinsky*
32 **Biographies** *by James McGrath Morris*

### PEOPLE

33 **Astronauts** *by Jeffrey Kluger*
34 **Supermodels** *by Crystal Renn and Marjorie Ingall*
35 **Celebrity Mugshots** *by Willie Geist*
36 **Mary** *by Mary C. Curtis*
37 **Bald Guys** *by Richard Sandomir*
38 **Geniuses** *by Peter Richmond*
39 **Celebrity Baby Names** *by Linda Rosenkrantz and Pamela Redmond Satran*
40 **Untimely Deaths** *by Mark Reiter*
41 **David** *by David Fisher*
42 **Celebrity Memoirs** *by Charles Leerhsen*
43 **Lousy Husbands** *by Kari Boyer*
44 **William et. al.** *by William/Bill Geist*
45 **Disappearing Acts** *by Franz Lidz*
46 **Richard vs. Dick** *by Richard Sandomir*
47 **American Pinups** *by Gregory Curtis*
48 **Pundits** *by Franklin Foer*
49 **Great Brother Acts** *by Mark Reiter*
50 **Tom vs. Thomas** *by Tom Chiarella*
51 **Immigrants** *by Tony Quinn*

### SPORTS

52 **Olympic Athletes** *by David Maraniss*
53 **NFL Team Logos** *by D.W. Pine*
54 **Dallas Cowboys** *by Jeff Pearlman*
55 **Jewish Baseball Players** *by Daniel Okrent*
56 **All-Time Fantasy Sports Performances** *by Matt Pitzer*
57 **21st-Century Sports Books** *by Will Leitch*
58 **Ringless Athletes** *by Dick Friedman*
59 **Donald Ross Courses** *by Bob Carney*
60 **American Hockey Players** *by Nick Paumgarten*
61 **Steroid-Era Moments** *by Shaun Assael*
62 **Sports Clichés** *by Steve Rushin*
63 **Instant Replays** *by Alan Schwarz*
64 **Sexually Inadequate Nicknames** *by Hart Seely*
65 **Baseball Moments** *by John Thorn*
66 **Absurd College Nicknames** *by Richard Sandomir and Pete Thamel*
67 **Toughest Golf Holes** *by Chris Millard*
68 **Dubious Sports Achievements** *by Richard Hoffer*
69 **From Athlete to Actor** *by Mark Reiter*
70 **Sportscasters** *by Richard Deitsch*
71 **SEC Athletes** *by Steve Eubanks*
72 **Pound-for-Pound Fighters** *by Steve Farhood*
73 **Field Goals and PATs** *by Stefan Fatsis*
74 **Golf Books** *by John Garrity*

75 **New York Athletes** *by George Vecsey*
76 **Boston Athletes** *by Dan Shaughnessy*
77 **Sportswriters** *by Glenn Stout*
78 **Advertising Icons** *by Bryan Curtis*
79 **Greatest Sports Year** *by Mike Vaccaro*

## POP CULTURE

80 **Movie Gunfights** *by Stephen Hunter*
81 **YouTube Videos** *by Virginia Heffernan*
82 **Soul Songs** *by John Leland*
83 **Paul Newman Roles** *by Mark Reiter*
84 **Sitcom Dads** *by Steven Reddicliffe*
85 **Sitcom Moms** *by Richard Sandomir*
86 **Talk-Show Graveyard** *by Bill Carter*
87 **Children's Books** *by Jon Scieszka*
88 **Cinematic Interrogatories** *by John Steinbreder*
89 **Comic Strips** *by R.C. Harvey*
90 **High School Movies** *by Rick Staehling*
91 **Stunt Scenes** *by Kevin Conley*
92 **Impressionists** *by Richard Sandomir*
93 **Literary Heroes** *by B.R. Myers*
94 **Comedy Routines** *by Bill Scheft*
95 **Worst Movies by Great Directors** *by A.O. Scott*
96 **George Carlin Hunks** *by Kelly Carlin-McCall*
97 **Cop Movies** *by Lorenzo Carcaterra*
98 **Reality TV Stars** *by Bob Boden*
99 **Fictional Lawyers** *by Thane Rosenbaum*
100 **Good Imus vs. Evil Imus** *by Richard Sandomir*
101 **Steve Earle Songs** *by Mark Reiter*
102 **Most American Superhero** *by Peter Coogan*
103 **Gangster Films** *by Lorenzo Carcaterra*
104 **Disney Animated Films** *by Richard Corliss*
105 ***Honeymooners*** *by Peter Crescenti*
106 **You Call This Acting?** *by Will Reiter*
107 **Talk Radio Hosts** *by David Hinckley*
108 **Child Actors** *by Griffin Miller*
109 **Detroit Celluloid** *by Kevin Conley*
110 **Girl Singers** *by Tom Moon*
111 **Cathartic Movie Deaths** *by David Edelstein*
112 **Game-Show Hosts** *by Steve Leblang*
113 **Grateful Dead Songs** *by John Steinbreder*
114 **Romance Novels** *by Isabel Swift*
115 **TV Catchphrases** *by Robert J. Thompson*
116 **Jazz Solos** *by Nick Trautwein*
117 **Romantic Comedies** *by David Denby*
118 **Cats and Dogs** *by Lon Tweeten*
119 **Clint Eastwood Films** *by Manohla Dargis*
120 **Comedy Teams** *by Robert Wuhl*
121 **Comic Book Superpowers** *by Peter Coogan*

## NATURE

122 **Fears and Phobias** *by Roz Chast*
123 **National Parks** *by Scott Kirkwood*
124 **Dangerous Animals** *by Chris Jenkins*
125 **Best Ski Runs** *by Steve Cohen*
126 **Nothing but the Tooth** *by James Hudson, D.M.D.*
127 **Fish Tales** *by Peter Kaminsky*
128 **Energy Alternatives** *by Gwyneth Cravens*
129 **My Prized Feathers** *by Luke Dempsey*
130 **Looking Younger** *by David Leffell, M.D.*

## WORDS

131 **Fatherly Advice** *by Jancee Dunn*
132 **Motherly Advice** *by Mark Reiter*
133 **Acronyms** *by Stefan Fatsis*
134 **Lazy Wit** *by Adi Ignatius*
135 **Texas Sayings** *by Anne Dingus*
136 **Seductive Foreign Accents** *by Asif Eydohno*
137 **Yogi Berra Wisdom** *by Dave Kaplan*
138 **Fortune Cookies** *by Jennifer 8. Lee*
139 **All-Purpose Banalities** *by Joe Queenan*
140 **Deadly Sins of Emailing** *by David Shipley and Will Schwalbe*
141 **Politically Correct Terms** *by Henry Beard and Christopher Cerf*
142 **Woody Allen Wisdom** *by Eric Lax*

## FOOD AND DRINK

143 **It's Better with Bacon** *by Peter Kaminsky*
144 **Cocktails** *by Jonathan Miles*
145 **Breakfast Cereals** *by Drew Magary*
146 **Domestic Beers** *by Maureen Ogle*
147 **Artisan Cheeses** *by Max McCalman and David Gibbons*
148 **Regional Soda Pop** *by Bob Roe*
149 **American Wines** *by Joseph S. Ward*
150 **Classic Cookbooks** *by Katie Workman*

**Blank bracket**
**Acknowledgments**

# Introduction

**By Mark Reiter**

## Here's how to enjoy this book.

Stop reading this introduction and start flipping through the pages. Pause at the first page that catches your eye. It might be a picture that grabs you (e.g., **Nick Nolte's mugshot**). Or a name (Otis Redding). Or a song title ("God Bless America"). Or a fortune cookie ("Do or do not. There is no try"). Or a pairing of proper nouns you never expected to be linked together (**Michael Jordan** vs. John Glenn).

If you're engaged by the page, you'll start nodding your head in agreement. Or shaking it in violent disagreement. You might not agree that Paul Newman's best role was in *Absence of Malice,* or that **Mary Tyler Moore** is the greatest American named Mary – ever! Or that Crunch Berries is the best breakfast cereal and **Mark Twain** had the best pseudonym and that a brew from Louisiana named **Turbodog** is America's best beer. Or that **Maine** has the most stylish license plate and "This Land Is Your Land" is the best choice to replace our current national anthem. Or that 1941 was the greatest sports year (I prefer 2008) and **Scrabble** is a better board game than Monopoly.

If you regard any of the above opinions as fighting words, then you're already enjoying this book in the way we intended. In these pages we are celebrating everything good, surprising, and silly about America – which means that (a) it's a happy, optimistic book that (b) is designed to generate arguments. If you want to have livelier conversations over family dinner, place this book at the head of the table.

On the other hand, you might have questions, such as: What does "bracketology" mean? Did you make it up? Why don't you just make a list? Who are all these people with their firm opinions? Who died and made them boss? And of course, how can I do this stuff at home?

My job here is to answer those questions.

The bracket concept is not new. It's a unique way of organizing information that dates back to the rise of the knockout (or single elimination) tournament. Its origins are not precisely known. It's possible that the first bracket was drawn by a master of jousts at a medieval jousting tournament or by an enterprising member of a Scottish golf club in the 16th century as a way of determining the club champion. We do not know, because the crude chart informing jousters and golfers whom they would face in the next round does not survive. But there was genius in the bracket design and it hasn't changed much over the years. By 1849 in London, Henry Buckle was winning the first modern chess tournament and adhering to the bracket format. Tennis, bridge, soccer, rowing, and other sports followed soon enough.

You, of course, may be familiar with the bracket format via the NCAA basketball tournament pairings each March. If you've ever watched ESPN or participated in a March Madness office pool, you know the guiding concept behind this book. All we've done here is take the knockout format and apply it to every category except basketball. In areas where taste, judgment, and hard-earned wisdom really matter, we've set out to determine (as the book's cover modestly announces) the Final Four of Everything.

A bracket is not a list, nor does it aspire to be one. The world already has enough lists. To us, a list is a crude, invidious, one-dimensional device. It ranks things from best to worst, but that's all it does. It doesn't explain. It doesn't pit one item against another, allowing the two to rub together and create friction to determine the superior player.

A bracket is a more dynamic way of understanding personal preferences. The practice of parsing people, places, and things into discrete one-on-one matchups works because it's simple and the face-off happens right in front of you – in real time. In that sense, a bracket invests your opinions with a narrative of how you decided something. Thus, when ***Annie Hall*** and *The Front Page* go at each other in David Denby's Romantic Comedies bracket (#117), you are forced to compare the two films' merits and debits. Isn't a champion more interesting when you know who or what it had to beat to get to the top?

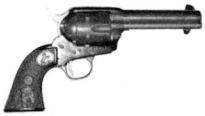

As for the term "bracketology," it is one of those cute neologisms deployed by obsessive fans to inject greater significance into a familiar sports phenomenon – for example, threepeat or SABRmetrics or bouncebackability. I first heard bracketology used by the co-editor of this book, Richard Sandomir, in a March 2006 *New York Times* sports column, in reference to ESPN's saturation coverage of March Madness. The term was new to me (clearly, I do not watch enough ESPN), but its meaning (technically, the study of the brackets) did not sail over my head. I knew it referred to Americans' annual debate over whether the NCAA created a gross miscarriage of justice in, say, seeding Gonzaga (with their 26-3 record and a defeat early in the season of top-ranked Duke) third in the Midwest regional. So crisp and clean was the phrase, creating such a vivid picture of American men devoting their analytical powers to guessing the outcome of a series of basketball games over three long weekends in March, that I wondered, "What if that cranial energy, that heat and obsession, were placed at the service of a better, higher purpose?"

That's when I knew that bracketology could be used to establish our preferences in . . . well, everything.

We do not claim authorship of the concept. One of the earliest non-sporting uses of brackets can be found in the December 1989 issue of *Spy* magazine. But we like to think that in this book, we have taken the concept to its logical extreme.

In celebrating America, we've tried to capture the nation's greatness and glory and occasional foolishness in 150 self-contained two-page spreads of brackets. Our subject matter includes sports, of course, but ventures deeply into history, nature, people, food and drink, popular culture, and miscellaneous issues such as the most seductive foreign accent for speaking English.

We didn't do this all by ourselves. We approached experts and celebrated authorities to render the verdict of what is good, better, and best in America. Thus, you will find bestselling thriller writer (and firearm aficionado) Stephen Hunter bracketizing on **American guns.** And *New York Times* columnist Gail Collins on First Ladies. And Kelly Carlin-McCall on her father **George Carlin's** best comedy routines. And Pulitzer Prize–winning historian David Oshinsky on **extremists and radicals.** And Bill Geist on notable **Williams** and Bills.

One of the underappreciated miracles here is how a bracket can provide an essential nitroglycerine tablet of information on the most complicated topics. In Harry Evans's **Innovators** bracket (#23), you'll find an instant summary of America's most durable business breakthroughs. In Pulitzer Prize–winner David Maraniss's **Olympic Athletes** bracket (#52), you get a memory-jog about our gold-medal heroes – all adding up to what could have been a two-hour documentary. Adam Liptak's **Supreme Court** Decisions (#24) is a cheat sheet for what we will still be arguing about in decades to come. In Stefan Fatsis's **Acronyms** (#133), you get the story of the last 100 years via our shorthand. In Richard Sandomir's Magical Numbers (#1), you'll find a stealth history of the United States through the numbers that we embrace. Each in two pages.

A bracket also displays great versatility as a communications tool. In her **Fatherly Advice** bracket (#131), writer Jancee Dunn accumulates all the pearls of wisdom – solicited or not – that she has heard from her father in her lifetime. Take away the bracket format and I doubt that Dunn would ever have gathered these nuggets in one place at the same time, let alone have them compete to determine that "when you meet someone, shake their hand firmly and look them right in the eye" is the best advice her father has ever given her. Absent the bracket, she might never have known how much she values that advice – and neither would her father.

In that sense, Dunn's bracket could literally serve as her Father's Day card this year – which suggests another use for brackets: *you can do them at home.* (That's why we've provided a blank template at the end of this book.) Facing a dilemma of personal choice, don't fall back on the usual list of dos and don'ts. Draw up a bracket of one-on-one items that gives structure and depth to your many options. The process is simple: fill in the first round with any idea that pops into your mind. Then let this jumble of competing notions play out in a tournament of the mind until a clear winner emerges.

More than anything, though, a bracket can function as a decision-making engine. It lets us confirm what we're really thinking and, as a result, provides us with an incremental gain in self-knowledge. Not long ago I was at a wedding reception in upstate New York. It was a beautiful sunny day as I sipped champagne with a professor of Irish literature and a local attorney. Surveying the lovely scene and stunning weather, the professor said, "James Joyce believed that the two loveliest words in the English language are 'summer afternoon.'"

"That's nice," said the attorney, clasping his flute of champagne. "But I'm partial to 'open bar' myself."

It depends on who you are, I thought. To a schoolkid, the two happiest words might be "snow day"; to a job hunter, "You're hired"; to a childless couple, "We're pregnant"; to a cancer patient, "in remission"; to a defendant, "not guilty." And so on. Curious to know what my happiest two words were, I made a bracket that looked like this:

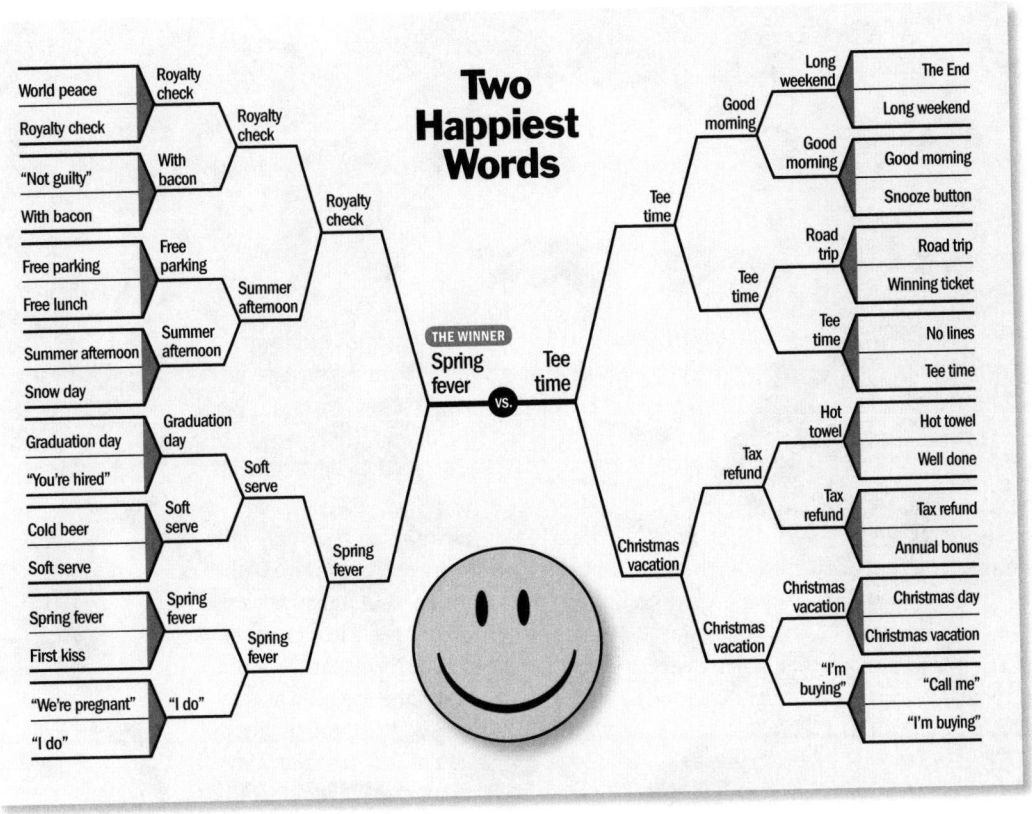


If you study this bracket closely, you could come to a few reliable conclusions about my demons and desires. (Which is why I encourage you to have everyone in your immediate family fill out a similar bracket, if only for mental-health reasons.)

Frankly, I was surprised that "Tee time" reached the finals. I didn't know that playing golf made me happier than earning a living ("Royalty check"). This is particularly shocking if you've seen my golf game. As for the penumbra of happy thoughts surrounding the words "Spring fever," that's much more understandable. It takes me back to my schoolboy years, sitting in a classroom on a gorgeous day in May, scorched by a fizzy restless yearning to be anywhere outdoors. Spring fever reminds me of baseball, of graduation, of putting warm woolens away for another year. It reminds me that summer is not far away – and that golf season is beginning again. So much of what I enjoy is wrapped up in the promise contained within the words "spring fever" that I know its position as champion in my bracket is true. That's something worth discovering.

In this book, we have gathered 150 brackets about something worth discovering in the great land that we live in. You may be glad or disappointed or furious about some of the conclusions drawn here (and we appreciate that; when it comes to brackets, disagreement is music to our ears). But what we're really doing here is turning opinion into a sport.

Now so can you.

# AMERICANA

**Magical Numbers** *by Richard Sandomir* 1
**American Guns** *by Stephen Hunter* 2
**Jim Henson Creations** *by Michael Davis* 3
**American Products** *by Lee Eisenberg* 4
**Cars That Made a Difference** *by Phil Patton* 5
**Protestant Hymns** *by Nancy Gibbs* 6
**License Plates** *by Tom Vanderbilt* 7
**State Birds** *by Scott Mowbray* 8
**Pseudonyms** *by Stanley Bing* 9
**Iconic Photographs** *by James Danziger* 10
**Ridiculous Celebrity Auctions** *by Leila Dunbar* 11
**Board Games** *by Stefan Fatsis* 12
**Magic Tricks** *by Joshua Jay* 13
**Roller Coasters** *by Scott Rutherford* 14
**SAT Success Strategies** *by Laura Wilson* 15
**Screen Cowboys** *by Neil Amdur* 16
**A New National Anthem** *by Richard Sandomir* 17

# Magical Numbers

**By Richard Sandomir**

Richard Sandomir was born on 9/4, nearly 2 score and 12 years ago, files an annual 1040, has a 401(k) account, has read *Catch-22* (but not *Mila 18*), and has never watched *Beverly Hills: 90210.*

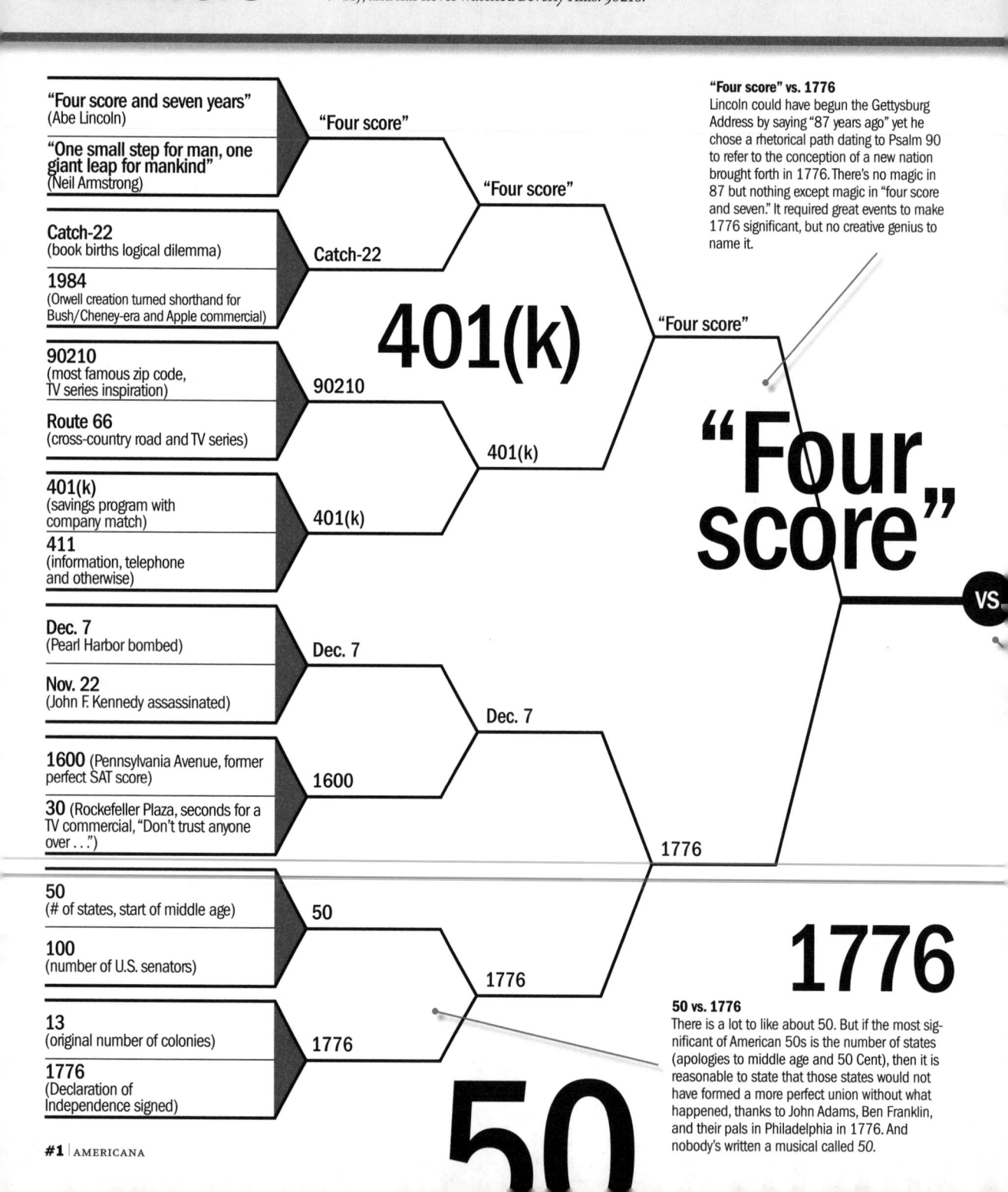


**"Four score" vs. 1776**
Lincoln could have begun the Gettysburg Address by saying "87 years ago" yet he chose a rhetorical path dating to Psalm 90 to refer to the conception of a new nation brought forth in 1776. There's no magic in 87 but nothing except magic in "four score and seven." It required great events to make 1776 significant, but no creative genius to name it.

**50 vs. 1776**
There is a lot to like about 50. But if the most significant of American 50s is the number of states (apologies to middle age and 50 Cent), then it is reasonable to state that those states would not have formed a more perfect union without what happened, thanks to John Adams, Ben Franklin, and their pals in Philadelphia in 1776. And nobody's written a musical called *50.*

IN DAILY LIFE AND HISTORY, certain numbers slice into our subconscious, cling to our chromosomes, and alter our national language. Their magic and linguistic rightness can be sensed in an instant (the way 9/11 evokes the 2001 terror attacks) or only after repetition (the way the 401(k) section of the tax code now represents a deferred savings retirement account). If they are magical, these numbers endure, whether they spring from eloquence, snappiness, bureaucratic necessity, or just a day of the week.

# American Guns

**By Stephen Hunter**

Raconteur, war hero, gourmet chef, champion ballroom dancer. Hunter is none of those things. But he knows a lot about guns.

**Colt Peacemaker**
Star of the West

**"Sawed off" double-barrel shotgun**
De rigeur for stagecoaches

**Colt Peacemaker**

**Colt Detective Special**
Every detective's and every mobster's choice, 1930-1970

**Colt Official Police**
Faster than a speeding bullet

**Colt Detective Special**

**Colt Peacemaker**

**Colt Pocket automatic**
It nailed Colonel Strasser

**Smith & Wesson N-frame .44 Magnum**
Do you feel lucky, punk?

**Smith & Wesson .44 Magnum**

**Smith & Wesson N-frame .357 Magnum**
Original "most powerful handgun ever made"

**Glock**
In every modern cop holster

**Smith & Wesson .357 Magnum**

**Smith & Wesson .44 Magnum**

**Colt Peacemaker**

**Philadelphia Derringer**
Other than that, how did you enjoy the play, Mrs. Lincoln?

**Ruger Mk1 .22**
Gun for the masses

**Ruger Mk1 .22**

**Winchester Lever Guns**
They won the West, carried by everyone from the Duke to Ennis Del Mar

**Winchester Model 70**
American beauty

**Winchester Lever Guns**

**Winchester Lever Guns**

**Colt Peacemaker**

**Springfield**
Doughboy's choice

**Remington 700**
Two generations of snipers can't be wrong

**Remington 700**

**Garand Rifle**
GI's choice

**M-1 Carbine**
GI's second choice

**Garand Rifle**

**Garand Rifle**

**Colt Peacemaker vs. Winchester Lever Guns**
With apologies to Winchester aficionados, yes, it is a crime to squash the Henry, the Model 1866, the Model 1873, the Model 1886, the Model 1892, and the Model 1894 (and that's only the 19th century!) into a generic mishmash called "Winchester lever guns." But do you honestly think this unyielding bracket format could sustain the differences between, say, the '92 and the '94?

**Smith & Wesson N-frame .357 Magnum vs. Glock**
Glocks are cheap, reliable, easy to maintain, ergonomic, and plastic, at least through the frame. That, plus aggressive marketing, has made them the cutting edge of modern police and gang-bang culture. They have a generic look, like the automatics the Beagle Boys carried to rob Uncle Scrooge. Entirely Austrian designed, they have so taken over American hand-gunning that they can be safely categorized as American. In fact, all American handgun makers now sell a version of the Glock.

**Winchester Lever Guns**

**Colt Peacemaker**

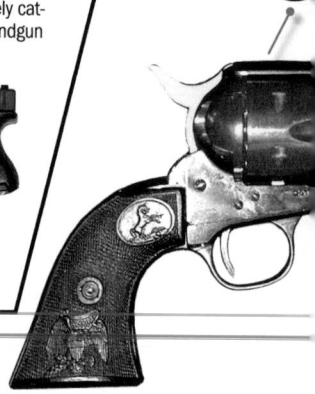

THE WINNER

**Colt Peacemaker**

VS

**Colt Peacemaker vs. Government Model 1911**
Hardly a long shot, this dream of firearm perfection has been delighting people since 1873, then jumped back to life in '50s TV Westerns, and today dominates in the growing sport of Cowboy Western shooting. It's not the best gun even for its time, with that loading gate and one-at-a-time removal and one-at-a-time replacement of cartridges, tough to do with the Clantons closing in from all sides. But as an orchestration of line, symmetry, and ergonomics, as an icon of the century, as a font of popular art, as a reliable tool for tough scrapes, you can't top Colonel Colt's equalizer.

TOOL, DEMON, ERGONOMIC MASTERPIECE, CRUSHER OF DREAMS. That's the American firearm. The criterion here is something indefinable, a memorable orchestration of lines and symmetry that compels the object to memory. History also counts for half. The entries are mostly all-American, though we include two European gizmos that have left their mark within our shores. Guns made famous by movies are favored over guns useful to history, probably because I prefer movies to history. Calibers aren't given because so many were manufactured in multiple calibers.

**Thompson vs. Greasegun**
America's two pre-eminent wartime subguns go head to head. The Greaser is strictly a wartime improvisation, designed for cheapness and ease of manufacture as opposed to the Thompson's more demanding manufacturing requirements. But for a piece of junk, it served well in many conflicts the globe over. Still, the Thompson's classicism rules in its many guises, first as the Zeitgeist of the '30s mob and FBI era, then as the war raiders' reliable buddy in Marine and Airborne hands, then in every cop movie made in the '50s. An American masterpiece.

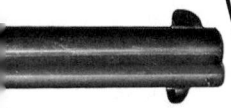

**.50 Browning vs. Government Model 1911**
Both of these guns were designed by the American genius John M. Browning, and both, 80-odd years after his death, are in combat use today. The .50 Browning fires a hugely heavy bullet that is accurate beyond a mile and will blow through anything short of a tank. The grunts say: Ma Deuce (its military designation is M-2) rules. As for the 1911, even though it was replaced by the Beretta some time ago, old soldiers and most elite strike forces (Marine Recon, Delta, SEALs) carry it. That says it all.

- **overnment Model 1911**
  - **Thompson**
    - **M-16**
      - **M-16**
        - **BAR** — Squad's choice
        - **M-16** — Grunt's choice
      - **Marlin 39-A**
        - **Marlin 39-A** — Every boy's dream .22
        - **Mannlicher-Carcano** — Piece of crap became fulcrum of tragedy
    - **Thompson**
      - **Thompson**
        - **Kentucky Rifle** — Frontiersman's choice
        - **Thompson** — Beloved by gangsters and paratroopers alike
      - **Greasegun**
        - **Greasegun** — Looks like it cost $15 but always worked
        - **.30 Watercooled Browning** — The ideal image of the machine gun
  - **Government Model 1911**
    - **.50 Browning**
      - **.50 Browning**
        - **M-60** — Design stolen from Germans, not beloved
        - **.50 Browning** — Ma Deuce rules the battlefield still after 75 years of service
      - **Remington 870**
        - **Remington 870** — Every cop's best friend
        - **.30 Aircooled Browning** — Yeoman service in a batch of wars
    - **Government Model 1911**
      - **Winchester Model 12 Pump**
        - **Browning Over/Under** — Elegance in steel on a workingman's budget
        - **Winchester Model 12 Pump** — Bird hunters' creed: If it flies, it dies
      - **Government Model 1911**
        - **Parker Double-Barreled shotgun** — Elegance in steel on an aristocrat's budget
        - **Government Model 1911** — The ubiquitous .45 auto, almost a century old, still in service

# Jim Henson Creations

**By Michael Davis**

Michael Davis is the author of *Street Gang: The Complete History of Sesame Street.* Not surprisingly, hectoring balcony critics Statler and Waldorf mocked it, Oscar the Grouch trashed it, but Elmo, who can't read, loved it.

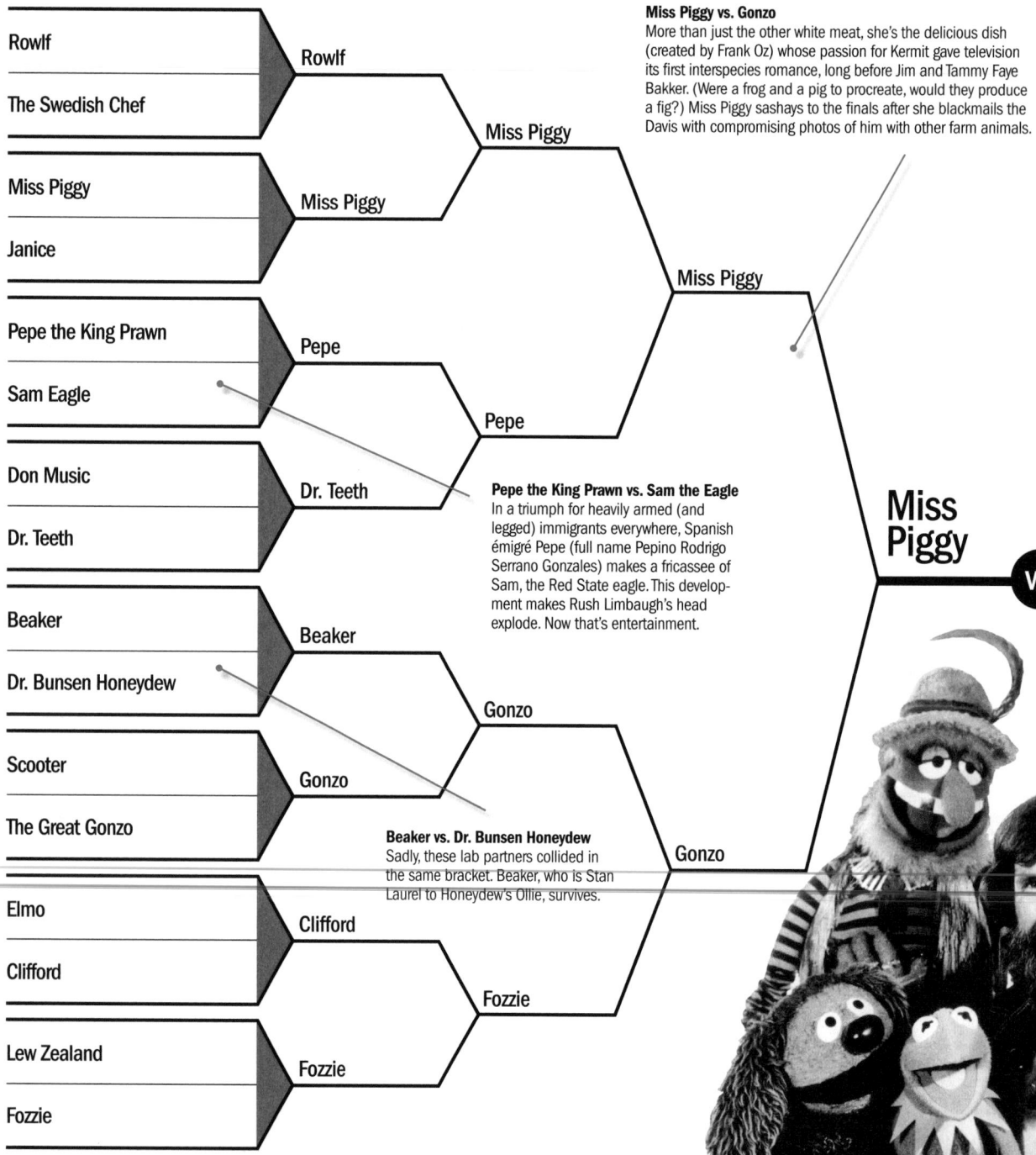


**Miss Piggy vs. Gonzo**
More than just the other white meat, she's the delicious dish (created by Frank Oz) whose passion for Kermit gave television its first interspecies romance, long before Jim and Tammy Faye Bakker. (Were a frog and a pig to procreate, would they produce a fig?) Miss Piggy sashays to the finals after she blackmails the Davis with compromising photos of him with other farm animals.

**Pepe the King Prawn vs. Sam the Eagle**
In a triumph for heavily armed (and legged) immigrants everywhere, Spanish émigré Pepe (full name Pepino Rodrigo Serrano Gonzales) makes a fricassee of Sam, the Red State eagle. This development makes Rush Limbaugh's head explode. Now that's entertainment.

**Beaker vs. Dr. Bunsen Honeydew**
Sadly, these lab partners collided in the same bracket. Beaker, who is Stan Laurel to Honeydew's Ollie, survives.

HEREWITH, A MUPPET MATRIX pitting the late Jim Henson's sneakily subversive commentators on the human condition against one another for the first time, a puppet popularity contest to pick the top dog, frog, pig, bird, rodent, or bear. Let the fur fly!

**Miss Piggy vs. Kermit**
Long before Howard Stern, Kermit was king of all media. He conquered television (hosting the *Tonight* show), the movies (opposite Orson Welles in one of the great denouements in cinema history), and theme park attractions. There's even a Kermit balloon in the Macy's Thanksgiving Day Parade, this culture's highest accolade! Only a brute would hog this amiable amphibian's spotlight.

**Animal vs. Cookie Monster**
It's Id versus Id in this battle between the Electric Mayhem's libidinous stadium-rock drummer and *Sesame Street*'s serial nosher. Both are working through their problems with obsession, but how can you look into Cookie's hypnotically googly eyes and not move him on to Round III?

**Big Bird vs. La Choy Dragon**
This battle of walk-around puppets pits an 8-foot canary from public television against a fire-breathing agent of clever commercialism from the mid-1960s. Big Bird moves on to the next round when the dragon suddenly realizes he's extinct.

**Kermit vs. Ernie**
His split-personality bracket features the two projections of Henson's ego, Kermit, the wry observer who is wary of the fray, and Ernie, the mischievous buddy boy. One could argue that Kermit was proto-observational comic. It wasn't easy bein' green, but he never worked blue.

THE WINNER

# Kermit

- Kermit
  - Cookie
    - Animal
      - Sweetums
      - Animal
    - Cookie Monster
      - Two-Headed Monster
      - Cookie Monster
  - Big Bird
    - Big Bird
      - Big Bird
      - La Choy Dragon
    - Hoots
      - Roosevelt Franklin
      - Hoots
  - Kermit
    - Oscar
      - The Trash Heap
        - The Trash Heap
        - The Mighty Favog
      - Oscar the Grouch
        - Oscar the Grouch
        - Grover
    - Kermit
      - Ernie
        - Bert
        - Ernie
      - Kermit
        - Kermit
        - Rizzo

# American Products

**By Lee Eisenberg**

Lee Eisenberg is the bestselling author of *The Number: A Different Way to Think About the Rest of Your Life* and (next) *Shoptimism: A Journey Through the Heart and Mind of the American Consumer.*

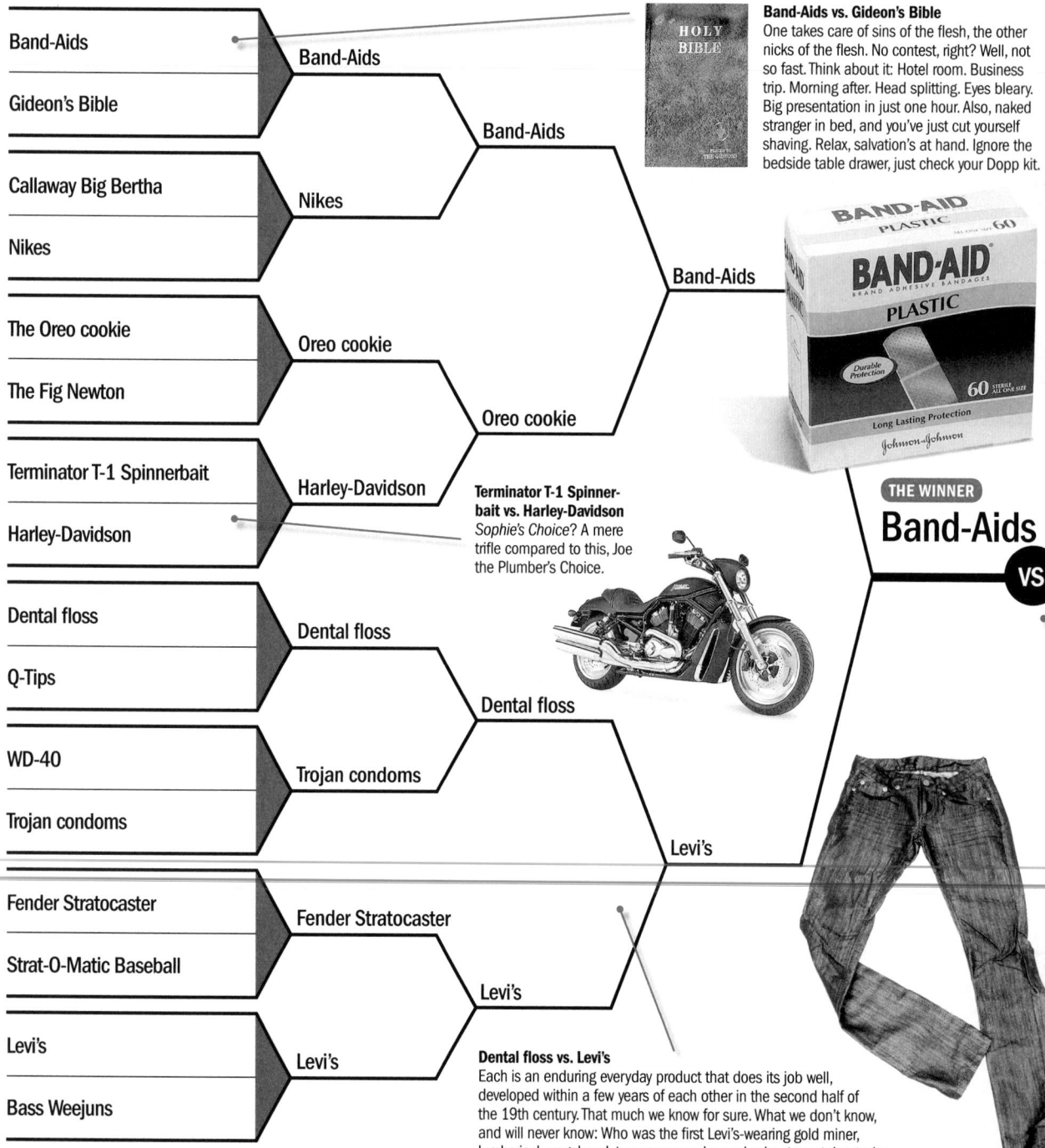


**Band-Aids vs. Gideon's Bible**
One takes care of sins of the flesh, the other nicks of the flesh. No contest, right? Well, not so fast. Think about it: Hotel room. Business trip. Morning after. Head splitting. Eyes bleary. Big presentation in just one hour. Also, naked stranger in bed, and you've just cut yourself shaving. Relax, salvation's at hand. Ignore the bedside table drawer, just check your Dopp kit.

**Terminator T-1 Spinnerbait vs. Harley-Davidson**
*Sophie's Choice*? A mere trifle compared to this, Joe the Plumber's Choice.

**Dental floss vs. Levi's**
Each is an enduring everyday product that does its job well, developed within a few years of each other in the second half of the 19th century. That much we know for sure. What we don't know, and will never know: Who was the first Levi's-wearing gold miner, lumberjack, vagabond, trapper, cowpoke, or riverboat roustabout who actually used dental floss? Floss gets tossed; the jeans keep walking.

IN 1890, the psychologist William James said that "a man's self is the sum total of all that he can call his . . . his clothes and his house . . . his reputation and works, his lands, and yacht and bank-account." He wasn't creating an excuse for materialism. He meant that our true temperament and values are not reflected in the mirror, but in all that's stashed in our garages, kitchens, and bathrooms. In other words, the quintessential All-American product that wins here most reflects who we are.

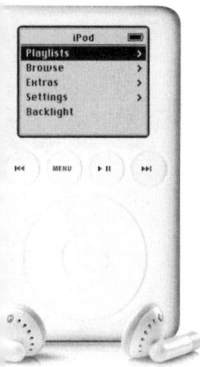


iPod

iPod
- iPod
  - iPod
    - iPod
    - The LP
  - Spanx pantyhose
    - Spanx pantyhose
    - Gore-Tex
- TiVo
  - TiVo
    - TiVo
    - The View Master
  - Microwave popcorn
    - Microwave popcorn
    - The Big Mac

Toilet paper
- Coca-Cola
  - Coca-Cola
    - Coca-Cola
    - Tang
  - Wonder Bread
    - Spam
    - Wonder Bread
- Toilet paper
  - Toilet paper
    - Rolled, perforated toilet paper
    - The Swiffer Sweeper
  - *Playboy*
    - *Reader's Digest*
    - *Playboy* magazine

**iPod vs.TiVo**
One revolutionized the music business, the other changed how we watch television. TiVo loses on a TKO: while it can zap commercials (perhaps too well), it can't erase product placements.

**Band-Aids vs. iPod**
Band-Aids – which come in a variety of shapes, sizes, and ethnically inspired colors and are decorated in designs that range from Hello Kitty to camouflage – possess the power to heal. They apply, indeed they adhere, to skinned knees, schoolyard booboos, annoying hangnails, fingers sliced in kitchen mishaps, and small furry animal bites (including bats). Band-Aids also possess the power to cushion and protect. Apply to back of heel in case of ill-fitting footwear. Finally, Band-Aids possess the power to hide any tell-tale superficial flaw, natural or man-made, including evidence of minor cosmetic surgery, hickeys, and not to be gross, the zits your mother told you not to pick at. Band-Aids have got all of us covered.

# Cars That Made a Difference

**By Phil Patton**

Phil Patton is the author of a dozen books on design and culture and writes about automobiles for the *New York Times, ID, Met Home,* and other publications.

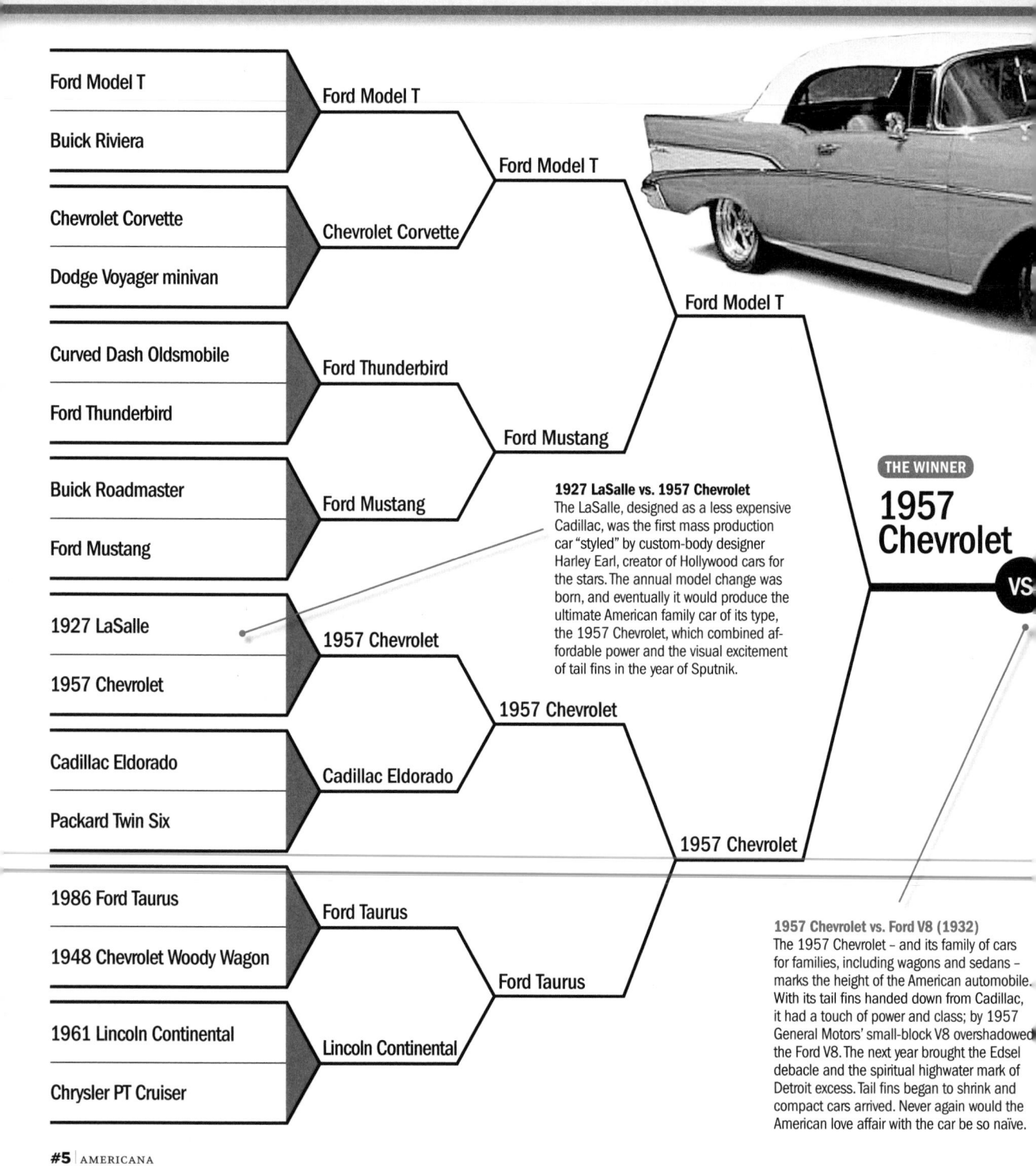


**1927 LaSalle vs. 1957 Chevrolet**
The LaSalle, designed as a less expensive Cadillac, was the first mass production car "styled" by custom-body designer Harley Earl, creator of Hollywood cars for the stars. The annual model change was born, and eventually it would produce the ultimate American family car of its type, the 1957 Chevrolet, which combined affordable power and the visual excitement of tail fins in the year of Sputnik.

**1957 Chevrolet vs. Ford V8 (1932)**
The 1957 Chevrolet – and its family of cars for families, including wagons and sedans – marks the height of the American automobile. With its tail fins handed down from Cadillac, it had a touch of power and class; by 1957 General Motors' small-block V8 overshadowed the Ford V8. The next year brought the Edsel debacle and the spiritual highwater mark of Detroit excess. Tail fins began to shrink and compact cars arrived. Never again would the American love affair with the car be so naïve.

IN A COUNTRY CONQUERED BY THE MACHINE, the car became a perfect avatar for four-wheeled fantasies of speed, size, empowerment, and mobility. Some figured as versions of the cowboy's horse and some as versions of Cinderella's coach. Some carried ideas, like the Model T Ford, which popularized the wild and crazy notion that every family should own at least one car, while others, from Packards to Corvettes, suggested the car as a work of art, an esthetic object compounded by metal, glass, and speed.

# Ford V8
(1932)

- Ford V8 (1932)
  - Ford V8 (1932)
    - Ford V8 (1932)
      - Ford V8 (1932)
      - Ford Falcon
    - Dodge Challenger
      - Dodge Challenger
      - Chrysler 300
  - Pontiac GTO
    - Pontiac GTO
      - Tucker Torpedo
      - Pontiac GTO
    - Studebaker
      - Chevrolet El Camino
      - Studebaker Starliner Coupe
- Jeep Wrangler
  - Lincoln Zephyr
    - Lincoln Zephyr
      - Oldsmobile Rocket 88
      - Lincoln Zephyr
    - Chrysler Airflow
      - Chrysler Airflow
      - Hudson Hornet
  - Jeep Wrangler
    - Jeep Wrangler
      - Cadillac Sixty Special
      - Jeep Wrangler
    - International
      - Stutz Bearcat
      - International Harvester Scout

**Ford V8 (1932) vs. Pontiac GTO**
The adolescent desire for extra power produced classic muscle cars like John DeLorean's Pontiac GTO. But the V8 engine that Henry Ford introduced in 1932, with its cheap horsepower, set the pattern for every one that followed and set Americans thinking they could have power under the hood. Two of its earliest fans, Bonnie and Clyde, lived and died in a V8 Ford.

**Jeep Wrangler vs. Ford V8 (1932)**
It is off-road versus racetrack, a battle of two traditions of American culture. One tradition believes in the rugged basic tool and the mythology of the frontier, the other in technology as the source of show biz and excitement. The Jeep Wrangler is the spiritual ancestor of every SUV since. But the Ford V8 was more fundamentally important and the granddaddy of every hot rod ever born.

**Chrysler Airflow vs. Lincoln Zephyr**
The 1934 Chrysler Airflow was billed as the wonder of the age, the first car shaped and engineered like an airplane. But its face was ugly, with a grille like a toothbrush mustache. The Lincoln Zephyr, introduced two years later, was just as functionally sleek, but was visually graceful as well. Its sales success provided a parable for the victory of style over innovation.

# Protestant Hymns

**By Nancy Gibbs**

Nancy Gibbs is an essayist and editor at large at *Time* magazine, and co-author, with Michael Duffy, of *The Preacher and the Presidents: Billy Graham in the White House.*

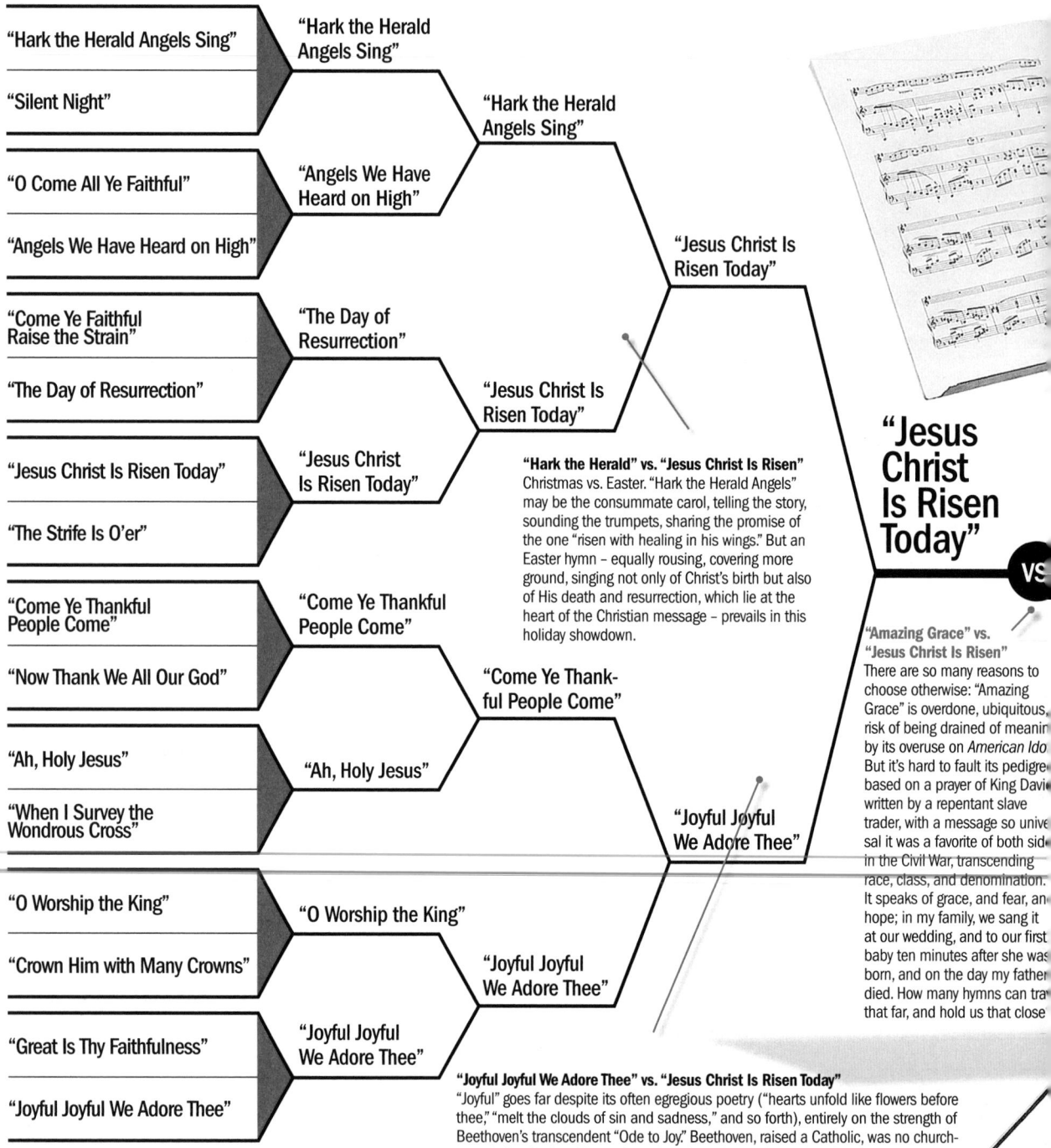

THE PROTESTANT HYMNAL HAS SURVIVED as a thing of musical and spiritual beauty, despite mighty efforts to politically correct it. I'll leave it to others to rank Christian pop, Gospel rap, the megachurch's evangelical praise music, and the black church's roof-raising spirituals (none of which you'll find here). We start with 32 "greatest hits" from the mainline hymnal in its present incarnation – Christmas carols, Easter hymns, Good Friday dirges, joyful hymns of praise, and ceremonial music that carried the country through its 9/11 mourning and recovery. Victory goes to that one that manages to lift the soul toward praise and peace.

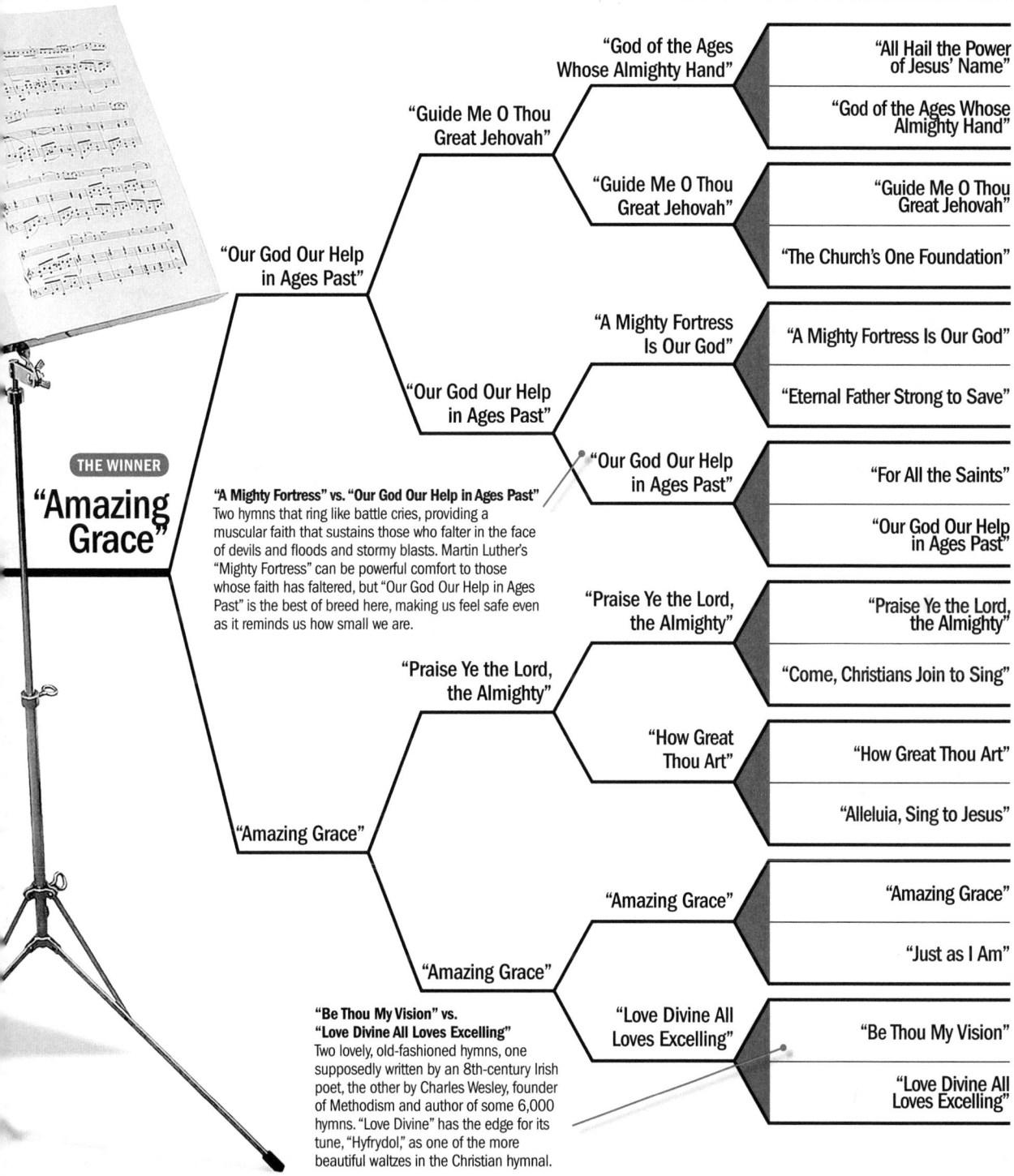

# License Plates

**By Tom Vanderbilt**

Tom Vanderbilt, author of the bestselling *Traffic: Why We Drive the Way We Do (and What It Says About Us),* lives in Brooklyn with his wife, Jancee Dunn (where he receives a lot of second-hand father-in-law advice; see bracket #31).

Colorado

South Carolina

Delaware

Idaho

Washington

Rhode Island

South Dakota

Nebraska

Oklahoma

North Carolina

Maine

Wisconsin

Utah

Oregon

Montana

Iowa

Colorado

Delaware

Rhode Island

Nebraska

North Carolina

Maine

Oregon

Iowa

Colorado

Rhode Island

Maine

Oregon

Colorado

Maine

**Delaware vs. Idaho**
Elegant blue and gold, one undivided string of characters, and slightly retro fonts, Delaware gets points for simplicity. It hasn't changed its design since the Nixon administration. When your motto is "The First State," what more do you need?

THE WINNER

**Maine**

VS

**Rhode Island vs. Nebraska**
No contest. Rhode Island's plate has a soothing, Zenlike balance, a perfect color scheme, and a lovely typeface to boot. Nebraska, lamentably, uses the one-dimensional 3M digital printing technology, which may make things easier on the manufacturing end but removes all the art, like a boring coin with a flat surface.

**Oklahoma vs. North Carolina**
Oklahoma loves symbolism. The icon in the middle of the plate contains a multitude of meaning, from the Osage shield, to the seven feathers standing for the original counties of Oklahoma Territory, the five stars representing the "Five Civilized Tribes" brought to the state in the 19th century, and a crossed calumet and olive branch for harmony between whites and Native Americans. By the time you read this, though, there will be a new tag on Oklahoma roads, depicting Allan Houser's "Sacred Rain Arrow" sculpture. So North Carolina advances by default (clever how "First in Flight" avoids a tussle with Ohio's "Birthplace of Aviation").

LICENSE PLATES ARE MARKERS of identity in the otherwise anonymous world of traffic. There's a curious power in seeing a fellow resident's plate far from home, or some rare species sighting like Hawaii tags on the mainland. Once bearing nothing more than the state's name and a few letters and numbers on a slab of porcelain, the tags increasingly function as touristic come-ons or mobile billboards for civic virtue. In Ohio they can identify you as a repeat drunk driver. But one thing is constant: U.S. plates are still largely manufactured in prisons.

**Maine vs. New Mexico**
Whenever I see a Maine plate in front of me, I feel as if I'm no longer breathing car exhaust but the fragrance of the pines stretching across the plate's bottom, hearing not the motor but the complex call of the black-capped chickadee. I want to follow it home, this stirring postcard in stamped metal, to that magical *Vacationland*, italicized for dreamy emphasis.

**New Mexico**

**Mississippi vs. Minnesota**
Mississippi's plate won New Plate of the Year in 2007 from the Automobile License Plate Collectors Association, but I'm not feeling it. Featured is the Biloxi lighthouse, which withstood Hurricane Katrina, but that rather slights the noncoastal rest of the state: What's the Magnolia State without its magnolia? Whither the Delta? Also, that "Mississippi," with its big swirly-bottomed "S" is a little too Ye Olde Riverboat Queen-ish. Points go to Minnesota for its unforgettable slogan (Land of 5,000 Lakes just doesn't cut it), the graceful white-blue fade, and its ingenious use of the state shape as a number/letter divider.

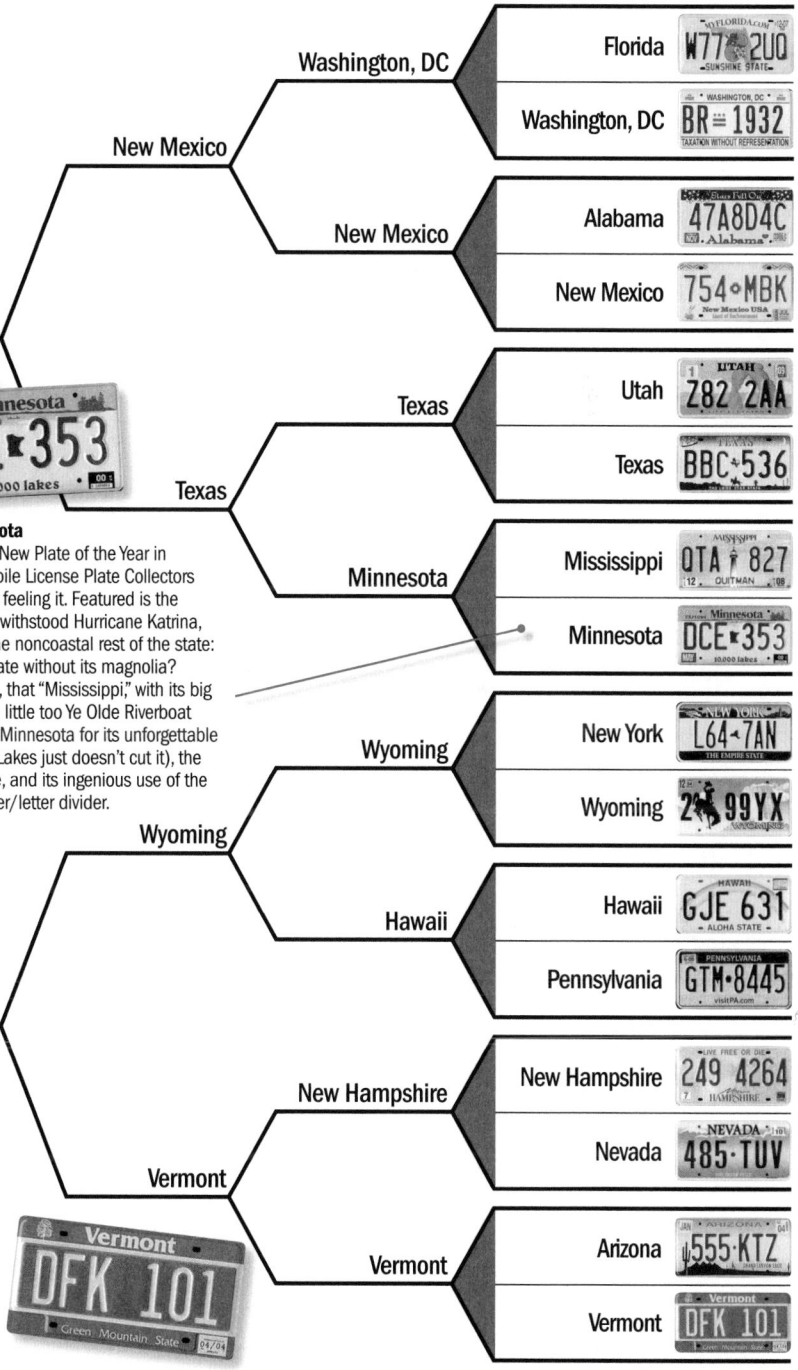


**New Mexico vs. Vermont**
Vermont's tag is as understated and verdant as the state is, but New Mexico triumphs in the end with its vivid yellow background (I was sad when Wisconsin ditched its cheese-colored tags), its quirky "New Mexico USA" designation (so as not to confuse it with New Mexico, Mexico?), and killer "Enchantment" slogan (compare that to the Keystone State's lamentable "Visitpa.com"), the sacred "Zia" sun symbol in the center, and subtle but evocative graphic treatments.

*Thanks to David Nicholson's invaluable website (www.15q.net) for license plate information.*

# State Birds

**By Scott Mowbray**

Scott Mowbray is a Brooklyn-based magazine editor. He has been editor of *Popular Science*, Health.com, *Joe*, and *Eating Well* magazine.

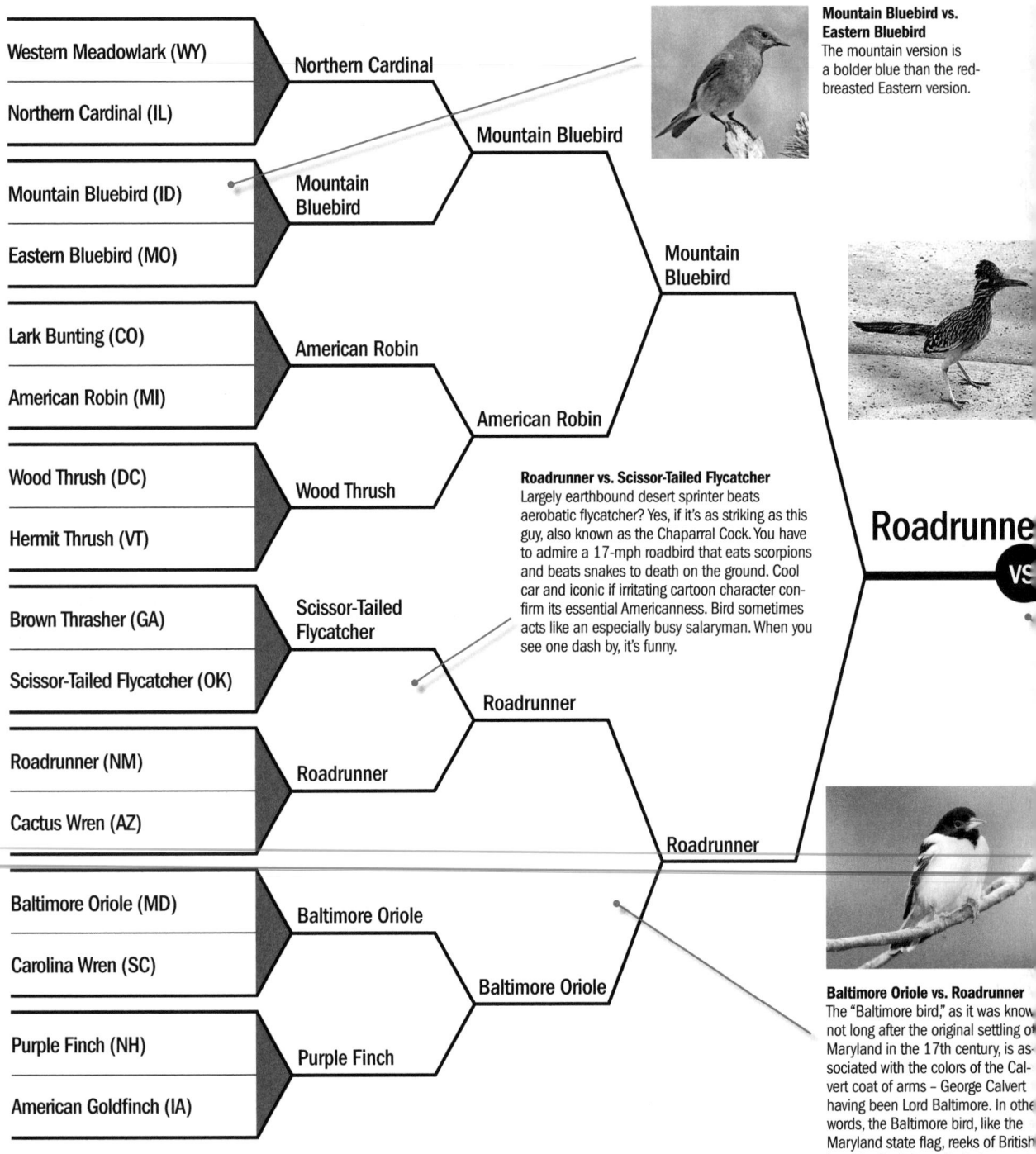


**Mountain Bluebird vs. Eastern Bluebird**
The mountain version is a bolder blue than the red-breasted Eastern version.

**Roadrunner vs. Scissor-Tailed Flycatcher**
Largely earthbound desert sprinter beats aerobatic flycatcher? Yes, if it's as striking as this guy, also known as the Chaparral Cock. You have to admire a 17-mph roadbird that eats scorpions and beats snakes to death on the ground. Cool car and iconic if irritating cartoon character confirm its essential Americanness. Bird sometimes acts like an especially busy salaryman. When you see one dash by, it's funny.

**Baltimore Oriole vs. Roadrunner**
The "Baltimore bird," as it was know not long after the original settling o Maryland in the 17th century, is associated with the colors of the Calvert coat of arms – George Calvert having been Lord Baltimore. In othe words, the Baltimore bird, like the Maryland state flag, reeks of British heraldry. That doesn't win here.

THE 1920S SAW THE FIRST WAVE OF STATE-BIRD NAMINGS, but laggards included New York, which waited more than 40 years to pick the Bluebird. Seven states claimed the Cardinal between 1928 and 1950. Five picked the Mockingbird. All this me-too bird-boosting means we don't have 32 different state birds to fill this bracket, even though more than 800 species hang here, according to John James Audubon. (No one wanted the Lesser Prairie Chicken?) The first state to pick the bird – e.g., Texas grabbing the Mockingbird three months before Florida in 1927 – gets the honors here.

THE WINNER

**Brown Pelican (LA)**

**Ruffed Grouse vs. Ring-Necked Pheasant**
Extra points for having an edible state bird. Ring-necked pheasant is a more handsome dinner companion but I'm not going to argue with John James Audubon, who said this grouse was better eating than "every other land-bird which we have in the United States, except the Wild Turkey, when in good condition."

**Common Loon vs. Mockingbird**
Sure, Mockingbird is a fantastic mimic, but the call of the loon may be the most haunting bird sound in the world.

**Northern Flicker, a.k.a. Yellowhammer vs. Blue Hen Chicken**
Blue Hen's fierce cockfighting rep was associated with the warrior spirit of Delaware's Revolutionary War soldiers. Yellowhammer, meanwhile, brings Civil War memories: Alabama Confederate fighters wore duds that reminded some of the 'hammer. But the North beat the South – even if we're talking different wars here, so the Blue Hen wins.

**Brown Pelican vs. Roadrunner**
The Bald Eagle has national-symbol mojo, but at the state level I like the Brown Pelican, a magnificent, charming utility animal that can skim the sea in an easy glide employing "ground effect" or fly in conga-line formation up the coast. These are very social birds. And they stand for the power of American law: DDT and related pesticides so decimated pelican populations that by 1970 they were on the brink. Chemical bans produced an amazing bounce-back, and in 1985 the BP was pulled from the endangered list in parts of the East, and in the West in 2008. Welcome back, champ.

- Brown Pelican
  - Brown Pelican
    - Brown Pelican
      - Rhode Island Red (RI)
      - Brown Pelican (LA)
    - Ruffed Grouse
      - Ruffed Grouse (PA)
      - Ring-Necked Pheasant (SD)
  - Common Loon
    - Common Loon
      - Mockingbird (TX)
      - Common Loon (MN)
    - Blue Hen Chicken
      - Blue Hen Chicken (DE)
      - Northern Flicker, a.k.a. Yellowhammer (AL)
- Willow Ptarmigan
  - Willow Ptarmigan
    - California Valley Quail
      - California Gull (UT)
      - California Valley Quail (CA)
    - Willow Ptarmigan
      - Willow Ptarmigan (AL)
      - Nene (HI)
  - Black-Capped Chickadee
    - Black-Capped Chickadee
      - Yellow Breast, a.k.a. Bananaquit (U.S. Virgin Islands)
      - Black-Capped Chickadee (ME)
    - Totot
      - Marianas Rose Crown Fruit Dave, a.k.a. Totot (Guam)
      - Stripe-Headed Tanager (Puerto Rico)

# Pseudonyms

**By Stanley Bing**

Stanley Bing is the pen name of a writer whose true identity is none of your business. You coul find it anyway with Internet search engines that have taken the mystery out of everything. Bir adopted the name long ago to keep his corporate masters off his back, but it has failed miserab

Francis Ethel Gumm
a.k.a. Judy Garland

Jacob Julius Garfinkle
a.k.a. John Garfield

Judy Garland

William Sydney Porter
a.k.a. O. Henry

Theodore Geisel
a.k.a. Dr. Seuss

Dr. Seuss

Dr. Seuss

Dino Crocetti
a.k.a. Dean Martin

Joey Levitch
a.k.a. Jerry Lewis

Dean Martin

Eileen Regina Edwards
a.k.a. Shania Twain

Samuel Langhorne Clemens
a.k.a. Mark Twain

Mark Twain

Mark Twain

Mark Twain

Marshall Mathers
a.k.a. Eminem

Robert Van Winkle
a.k.a. Vanilla Ice

Eminem

Norma Jean Baker
a.k.a. Marilyn Monroe

Brian Hugh Warner
a.k.a. Marilyn Manson

Marilyn Monroe

Marilyn Monroe

Marilyn Monroe

Marion Morrison
a.k.a. John Wayne

Leonard Franklin Slye
a.k.a. Roy Rogers

John Wayne

Ralph Lifschitz
a.k.a. Ralph Lauren

Chloe Ardelia Wooford
a.k.a. Toni Morrison

Toni Morrison

John Wayne

THE WINNER

**Samuel Langhorne Clemens**
a.k.a. Mark Twain

VS

**Bob Dylan vs. Mark Twain**
Two titans face off, each one with a pseudonym arrived at creatively. But the title must go to Mr. Clemens, simply because he has no peer in American letters. Mr. Zimmerman, on the other hand, must contend with the notion that if Leonard Cohen had decided to be Lex Christian, the boxes might have stacked up otherwise.

**Marilyn Monroe vs. John Wayne**
While Mr. Morrison's body of work stands taller in many ways than Norma Jean's, Marilyn Monroe's persona is far more resonant than the Duke's. Her image is continuously cloned, down to the current iterations of Madonna, Gwen Stefani, and Christina Aguilera; even now, new Marilyns are in gestation. Her pseudonym itself is a unique and iconic presence in our collective unconscious.

THE USE OF PEN NAMES AND STAGE NAMES by writers, actors, and other obfuscators is as ancient as the human desire to morph into whatever is necessary. Some wish to appear less of whatever momentarily outré race, religion, or ethnic persuasion they might be. Some have simply been saddled with monikers that are useless in their chosen profession. Whatever the rationale, the pseudonym forever changes the fate of the individual who takes it on. The most influential men in history began as Emmanuel and Gautama, and Calcutta's poor were soothed by a sweet lady named Agnes Gonxha Bojaxhiu.

**Mel Brooks vs. McG**
Who is more powerful? The mature pseudonym who has produced his greatest work or the younger sensibility coming up the ramp? Mr. Nichol's music videos for Korn and Sugar Ray were groundbreaking re-thinkings of the genre, which he followed with his brilliant big-screen version of *Charlie's Angels*. But he can't yet equal Mr. Kaminsky's legacy on universal subjects like race, Hitler, religious intolerance, and flatulence.

Mel Brooks

Twain

Bob Dylan

**Bob Dylan vs. Woody Allen**
As Myron Cohen might have pointed out, what we have here are two elderly gentlemen of the Jewish persuasion – ultra-productive *alter kockers* – who have eradicated their roots to one extent or another. But it is Mr. Zimmerman's pseudonym – if not his work – that has been more effective at the job of mythmaking, for which it was intended.

Lemony Snicket

**Lemony Snicket vs. JT Leroy**
Handler's creation has a certain reality as an author of creepy children's tales. But Mr. Leroy achieved a virtually unprecedented level of nonexistence with a fabricated biography that invalidated much of "his" oeuvre. Moreover, Leroy was two people – one who wrote the material and another who impersonated the author in public. Snicket's win is assured because a pseudonym cannot be utilized to create a pseudo-person.

- Bob Dylan
  - Mel Brooks
    - Mel Brooks
      - David Daniel Kaminsky a.k.a. Danny Kaye
      - Melvin Kaminsky a.k.a. Mel Brooks
    - McG
      - Joseph Nichol a.k.a. McG
      - Lawrence Tureaud a.k.a. Mr. T
  - Bob Dylan
    - Bob Dylan
      - Robert Zimmerman a.k.a. Bob Dylan
      - Milton Supman a.k.a. Soupy Sales
    - Perez Hilton
      - Mario Armando Lavandeira, Jr. a.k.a. Perez Hilton
      - Bruce Bibby a.k.a. Ted Casablanca
- Woody Allen
  - Woody Allen
    - Natalie Wood
      - Maria Rosario Pilar Martinez Molina de les Esperades Santa Ana Romanguera y de la Najosa Rasten a.k.a. Charo
      - Natasha Nikoleavna Zacharenko-Gurdin a.k.a. Natalie Wood
    - Woody Allen
      - Allen Stewart Konigsberg a.k.a. Woody Allen
      - Michael Igor Peschkowsky a.k.a. Mike Nichols
  - Lemony Snicket
    - Wavy Gravy
      - Hugh Romney a.k.a. Wavy Gravy
      - Jamal Woolard a.k.a. Gravy
    - Lemony Snicket
      - Daniel Handler a.k.a. Lemony Snicket
      - Laura Alpert-Savannah Knoop a.k.a. JT Leroy

# Iconic Photographs

**By James Danziger**

James Danziger operates Danziger Projects in New York City. He was picture editor of the *London Sunday Times Magazine* and director of Magnum Photos.

*Coney Island*
by Weegee (1940)

*Twins*
by Diane Arbus (1967)

Arbus

*Omaha Beach, 1944*
by Robert Capa

*VJ Day*
by Alfred Eisenstadt (1945)

Capa

Arbus

*Penny Picture Display*
by Walker Evans (1936)

*Trolley Car*
by Robert Frank (1955)

Frank

Frank

Arbus

*Flatiron Building*
by Edward Steichen (1905)

*Dunes, Oceano*
by Edward Weston (1936)

Steichen

*Abraham Lincoln*
by Mathew Brady (1860)

*The Horse in Motion*
by Eadweard Muybridge (1878)

Brady

Avedon

*Tomoko in Her Bath, Minimata*
by W. Eugene Smith (1971)

*Dovima with Elephants*
by Richard Avedon (1955)

Avedon

Avedon

**Capa vs. Eisenstadt**
Two indelible World War I images, one of war, one of peace, from transplanted European photographers who made their way to America to find fame. Capa's picture was taken as bullets flew, Eisenstadt's as confetti streamed down. Victory goes to the photographer who risked his life, hands down.

Avedon

VS

*Raising the Flag on Iwo Jima*
by Joe Rosenthal (1945)

*Earthrise*
by William Anders of *Apollo* 8 (1968)

Rosenthal

*The Vanishing Race*
by Edward Curtis (1904)

*Steerage*
by Alfred Stieglitz (1907)

Stieglitz

Rosenthal

**Adams vs. Avedon**
The uber-landscape against the uber-fashion photograph from two of the most controlled artists in American photography. Both pictures, while carefully set up on large-format cameras, could have only been taken the split second they were taken. Both are perfect in every way. But such is the spirituality in Adams's image that it even trumps a beautiful woman and an elephant.

LET'S START BY SAYING AMERICAN PHOTOGRAPHY SO DOMINATES THE MEDIUM as to make other countries' contributions a footnote. So we're really choosing the most iconic photograph of all time. And what are we looking for? A visceral image, one that is embedded in our cultural subconscious, one taken with the greatest skill by an artist whose entire body of work is capped by one transcendent image that is totally unreplicable. One that you can close your eyes to and it will come floating into the space between your mind and your eyelids, with something between a shiver and a sigh of pleasure.

THE WINNER

**Moonrise, Hernandez**
Ansel Adams (1941)

- Adams
  - Adams
    - Adams
      - *Moonrise, Hernandez* by Ansel Adams (1941)
      - *First Flight (Wright Brothers)* by Unknown (1903)
    - Edgerton
      - *Stapelia (Flower)* by Imogen Cunningham (1928)
      - *Milk Drop* by Harold Edgerton (1957)
  - Abbott
    - Orkin
      - *Italian Family* by Paul Strand (1953)
      - *American Girl in Italy* by Ruth Orkin (1951)
    - Abbott
      - *New York at Night* by Berenice Abbott (1934)
      - *Drive-In* by Winston O. Link (1956)
- Lange
  - Lange
    - Hine
      - *Odalisque* by E. J. Bellocq (1912)
      - *Powerfitter* by Lewis Hine (1920)
    - Lange
      - *Martha Graham* by Barbara Morgan (1940)
      - *Migrant Mother* by Dorothea Lange (1936)
  - Leibovitz
    - Leibovitz
      - *John and Yoko* by Annie Leibovitz (1980)
      - *Igor Stravinsky* by Arnold Newman (1946)
    - Stock
      - *Marilyn Monroe* by Philllipe Halsman (1952)
      - *James Dean in Times Square* by Dennis Stock (1955)

**Link vs. Abbott**
Two of the greatest nighttime photographs ever taken, each a technical tour de force. The Abbott is filled with the romance and promise of the big city, the Link with the romance of small-town America and wonder at man's ingenuity. Link is schmaltzier, which means Abbott wins.

**Lange vs. Leibovitz**
Head to head go two female heavyweight contenders. Leibovitz's photograph is not just about a famous couple but is the high-point of her sneakily conceptual imagery – pulling a theatrical gesture out of her famous subjects. Lange's Great Depression image combining photojournalism and great portraiture has come to symbolize man's dignity in the face of hardship. Lange by a whisker, if only because she came first.

# Ridiculous Celebrity Auctions

**By Leila Dunbar**

Leila (Lee) Dunbar, who headed Sotheby's collectibles department for nine years and has been an appraiser for PBS's *Antiques Road Show* since its inception, runs her own consulting and appraisal business.

Tiger Stadium dugout urinal, $900, Schneider Industries (2007)

Can of bug spray used by Yankee pitcher Joba Chamberlain in 2007 playoffs, $673, MLB Auctions (2007)

**Joba's bug spray**

Arizona Diamondbacks Luis Gonzalez's chewed gum, $10,000, nocontraction.com (2002)

Ty Cobb's full dentures, $8,000, Sotheby's (1999)

**Cobb's dentures**

**Cobb's dentures**

Babe Ruth's letter to his mistress, $86,250, Sotheby's & SCP Auctions (2004)

Thurman Munson's Yankee shower sandals, $1,100, Hunt Auctions (2008)

**Ruth's letter**

**Ruth's letter**

LeBron James's high school, game-used "King James" mouthpiece, $1,445.95, Leland's (2008)

David Ortiz's Red Sox jersey buried in construction of new Yankee Stadium, $175,000, Jimmy Fund (2008)

**Ortiz's jersey**

Jarful of Elvis Presley's dyed black hair, $115,000, Mastro (2002)

Britney Spears's hair from her head-shaving, unsold, eBay (2007)

**Elvis's hair**

**Elvis's hair**

Elvis's clay molars and front teeth molds, $1,1018.66, Leland's (2003)

John Wayne's blond toupee, $1,920, Julien's (2006)

**Elvis's molds**

**Ruth's letter**

**Elvis's hair**

William Shatner's kidney stone, $25,000, Julien's for Habitat for Humanity (2006)

Marilyn Monroe's bottle of prescription nose drops, $2,520, Julien's (2006)

**Shatner's kidney stone**

"Brangelina's" first baby sonogram, $3,800, eBay (2006)

Suri Cruise's bronzed "first poop," $10,000, eBay for Kristin Brooks Hope Center (2006)

**Suri's "first poop"**

**Suri's first poop**

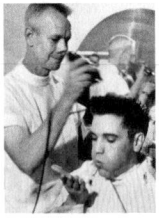

THE WINNER

**Jarful of Elvis Presley's dyed black hair**

$115,000, Mastro (2002)

VS

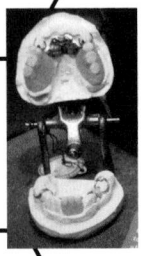

**Cobb's dentures vs. Ruth's letter**
"The Georgia Peach's" choppers probably gnawed into a few ballplayers' arms and ankles but off the field he never got around like the Babe. From this letter to his mistress it's obvious that the Babe scored with more than home runs. He wrote: "The club is watching so the only way I will be able to see you all night is for you to stop in at the Aldine Hotel and I can see you. Babe. P.S. Don't call."

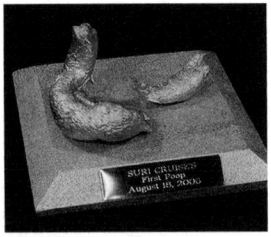


**Shatner's kidney stone vs Suri's "first poop"**
With no greater meaning attached to Shatner's stone beyond hurting like hell leaving him, Suri's re-imagined first artistic output wins, pants down. Sculptor Daniel Edwards said that it's "partially a statement on modern media that 'celebrity poop' ha more entertainment value than health, famine or other critical issues facing society and governments today." But sometimes a poop is just a poop.

IT SEEMS NORMAL FOR DEVOTED FANS to pay enormous sums for a game-used Babe Ruth bat, a sweat-stained Elvis jumpsuit, or Marilyn Monroe's halter dress from *The Seven Year Itch.* Far more mysterious is the impulse to acquire the underwear, toenails, or prescription medicine vials of the stars, as if a relationship with Britney Spears can be forged by bidding on her laundry lint. Celebrities beware: Unless you have a charity in mind, lock your medicine cabinets, burn your correspondence, and sweep up your own hair clippings – or everything's for sale.

**Elvis's hair vs. Holly's glasses**
n this battle of survival tales, the King's weird one wins. When Elvis's barber, Homer Gilleland, dyed the star's blond hair black, he cut the locks into towels and stored them in plastic bread bags. Before dying, Gilleland gave this hunka hunka hair (one of many bagged hunkas) to a friend, who put it up for auction. Confidence is high that these are authentic Elvis snippings even without a DNA test.

# Holly's glasses

**Maf photos vs. Holly's glasses**
Why would someone pay $225,000 for six snaps of Marilyn's French poodle? Easy: the dog, a gift from Frank Sinatra, was named for one of his Cosa Nostra pals. But for historical value, Holly's horn-rimmed glasses win; thought to be destroyed in the '59 crash, they were discovered, scarred, in a sheriff's office in 1994. On the day the music died, his glasses survived. Rave on.

**Madonna's personal gym barbells vs. Elvis's gold exercise bike**
Madge has spent countless hours honing her bodacious bod, using weights, dance, yoga, and the occasional wayward ballplayer. But Elvis – he of the grilled peanut butter and banana sandwich – working out? Of course he would have a gold-plated exercycle. But odds are that, like most ordinary Americans, Elvis used the bike as a hanger for his gold lamé jumpsuits.

**Cher's roach pillow vs. Dean's doorknobs**
While it would be nice to touch something that Dean twisted and left his epithelium on, the greater weirdness rests in the deliciously narcissistic decorative pillow from Cher's Malibu beach house that answers, finally, the burning question of her mortality.

- Holly's glasses
  - Holly's glasses
    - Holly's glasses
      - Michael Jackson's white bullet-proof Kevlar vest, $1,400, Guernsey's (2007)
      - Buddy Holly's glasses from fatal 1959 plane crash, $80,000, Civic Lubbock (1998)
    - Monroe's insurance notice
      - Marilyn Monroe's black lace strapless padded brassiere, $5,700, Julien's (2007)
      - Marilyn Monroe's notice of insurance policy cancellation, sent three months after her death, $1,020, Julien's (2007)
  - Dean's registration
    - Hepburn's driftwood
      - Katharine Hepburn's handmade hair rollers (made by Hepburn's hands), $3,300, Sotheby's (2004)
      - Katharine Hepburn's driftwood and rock collection, $1,800, Sotheby's (2004)
    - Dean's registration
      - Roadside reflector from James Dean's fatal car crash site, $1,105, Heritage (2006)
      - James Dean's signed registration form for Salinas race that he was killed driving to, $23,900, Heritage (2008)
  - Maf photos
    - Maf photos
      - Six Polaroid photos of Marilyn Monroe's dog, Maf, $225,000, Christie's (1999)
      - Jacqueline Kennedy Onassis's "JKO" monogrammed Tiffany tape measure, $48,875, Sotheby's (1996)
    - Gable bracelet
      - Clark Gable's 14K gold medical I.D. bracelet, with blood type, unsold, Guernsey's (2008)
      - Walther PPK .380 pistol, a gift from Elvis Presley to Jack Lord, $28,800, Julien's (2007)
  - Elvis's bike
    - Elvis's bike
      - Madonna's personal gym barbells, $2,200, Julien's (2001)
      - Elvis's gold Barkleigh exercise bike, $12,000, Guernsey's (2008)
    - Cher's roach pillow
      - Antique doorknobs from James Dean's Manhattan apartment, $1,912, Heritage (2006)
      - Cher's pillow: asking what will survive nuclear war. "Cockroaches and Cher," $7,800, Julien's and Sotheby's (2008)

# Board Games

## By Stefan Fatsis

Stefan Fatsis is the author of *Word Freak: Heartbreak, Triumph, Genius, and Obsession in the World of Competitive Scrabble Players,* so you know where this bracket is heading. He writes about a game contested on a board of a different kind in his latest book, *A Few Seconds of Panic: A 5-foot-8, 170-pound, 43-year-old Sportswriter Plays in the NI*

AMERICAN STUDIES REGIONAL

- Acquire (1962) vs. The Mansion of Happiness (1843) → Acquire
- Careers (1955) vs. Trivial Pursuit (1981) → Trivial Pursuit
- The Landlord's Game (1904) vs. Monopoly (1935) → Monopoly
- The Checkered Game of Life (1860) vs. The Game of Life (1960) → Checkered Game of Life

COMBAT REGIONAL

- Stratego (1947) vs. Battleship (1967) → Battleship
- Strat-O-Matic Baseball (1961) vs. Win, Place & Show (1966) → Strat-O-Matic
- Diplomacy (1959) vs. Rise and Decline of the Third Reich (1974) → Third Reich
- Risk (1959) vs. Cosmic Encounter (1977) → Risk

Acquire → Trivial Pursuit

Trivial Pursuit → Monopoly

Monopoly → Monopoly

Battleship → Strat-O-Matic

Strat-O-Matic → Strat-O-Matic

Third Reich → Risk

Risk → Risk

Monopoly → Monopoly

Strat-O-Matic → Strat-O-Matic

Monopoly vs. Strat-O-Matic

**Acquire vs. Mansion of Happiness**
Track America's moral decline! The Mansion of Happiness rewarded Puritan virtues, the Checkered Game of Life worldly achievement (it included a "Suicide" space), The Landlord's Game monopolistic wealth. The goal of Acquire – created by game-design legend Sid Sackson – is simple: corporate conquest. Naked greed trumps good deeds. Acquire moves on.

**Strat-O-Matic vs. Monopoly**
Before the pestilence of fantasy sports, there was the purity of Strat-O-Matic: stat cards, dice, a long season. Monopoly struggled to get this far. A controversial history (it was a rip-off of The Landlord's Game), a shameless parade of "special" editions (Scooby-Doo, Red Sox, M&Ms, etc.), and a paucity of required skill sully its reputation. But it's hard to argue with more than 200 million sets sold.

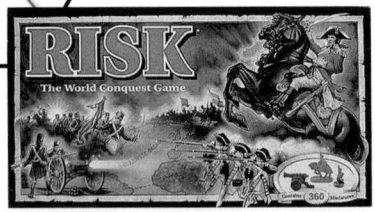


**Third Reich vs. Risk**
Like its first-round opponent – Henry Kissinger's favorite game – the epic World War II simulation Third Reich is beloved by serious board gamers who favor complex themes over ease of play. (A quick game of Downtown: Air War Over Hanoi, 1965–1972, anyone?) Risk is pooh-poohed for its reliance on dice and luck. A valid complaint, but the power of Irkutsk cannot be denied.

IN MY MID-30S, I BECAME OBSESSED with a board game. I believe that game belongs on Mount Rushmore with the ancient classics chess, backgammon, and Go. Others think it's something to play only when hopelessly bored. But play we all do. The first American board game – Traveller's Tour Through the United States – was published in 1822. Ever since, games have helped us endure our childhoods, stretch (and atrophy) our brains, and define our culture. Oh, and behave like idiots. I'm looking at you, Twister.

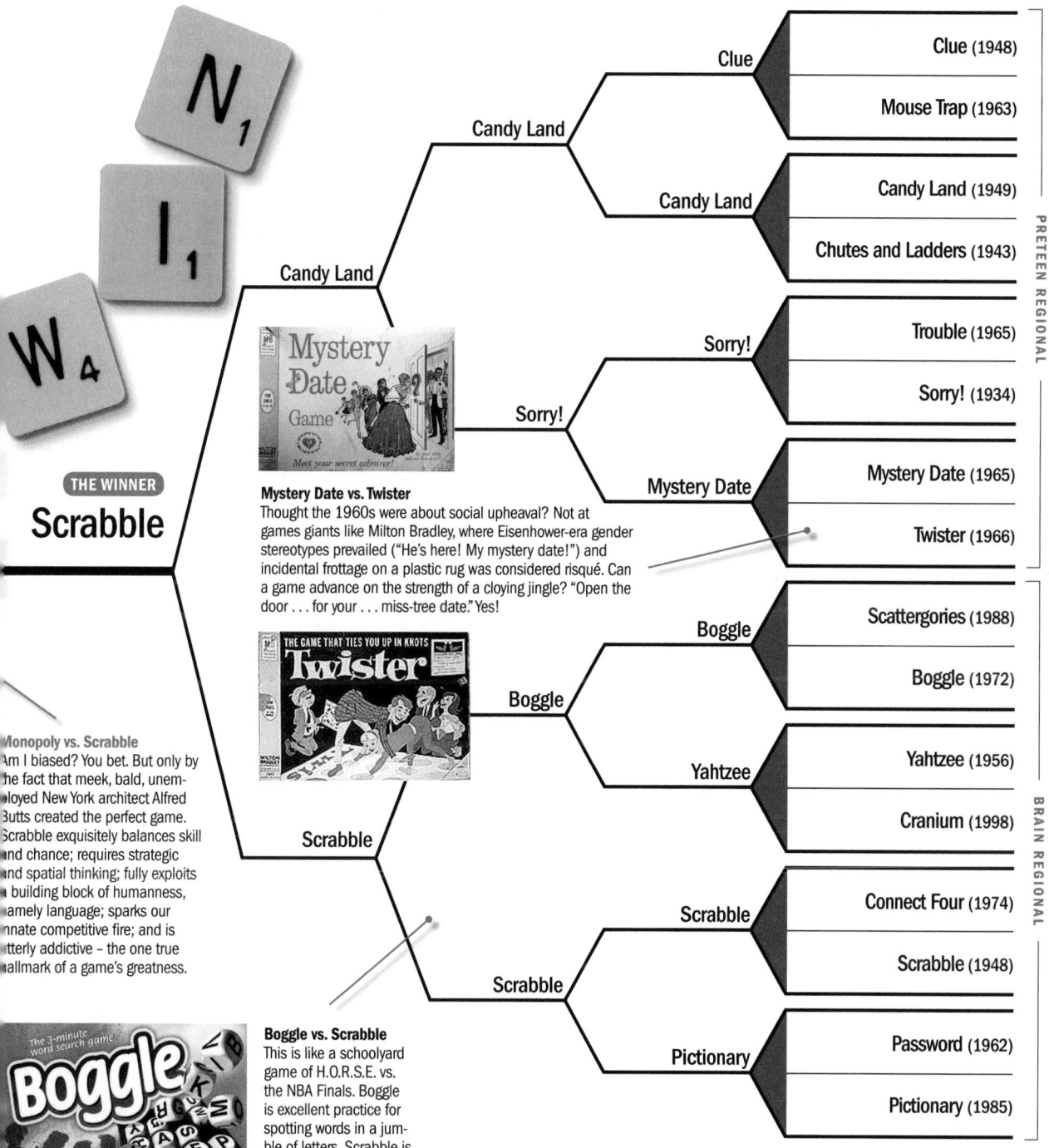


**Mystery Date vs. Twister**
Thought the 1960s were about social upheaval? Not at games giants like Milton Bradley, where Eisenhower-era gender stereotypes prevailed ("He's here! My mystery date!") and incidental frottage on a plastic rug was considered risqué. Can a game advance on the strength of a cloying jingle? "Open the door . . . for your . . . miss-tree date." Yes!

**Monopoly vs. Scrabble**
Am I biased? You bet. But only by the fact that meek, bald, unemployed New York architect Alfred Butts created the perfect game. Scrabble exquisitely balances skill and chance; requires strategic and spatial thinking; fully exploits a building block of humanness, namely language; sparks our innate competitive fire; and is utterly addictive – the one true hallmark of a game's greatness.

**Boggle vs. Scrabble**
This is like a schoolyard game of H.O.R.S.E. vs. the NBA Finals. Boggle is excellent practice for spotting words in a jumble of letters. Scrabble is the artful deployment of that talent.

# Magic Tricks

**By Joshua Jay**

Joshua Jay has performed and lectured all over the world, and won the coveted World Magic Seminar in 1998. He is the author of *MAGIC: The Complete Course* and has no desire to catch a bullet in his teeth, onstage or otherwise.

**Pulling a rabbit from a top hat:** no list would be complete without this venerable but iconic trick

**Sawing Through a Woman** by P.T. Selbit

**Sawing a Woman**

**Pulling a coin from a participant's ear,** as popularized by weird uncles worldwide

**Miser's Dream:** an unlimited production of coins as performed by Jean Eugene Robert-Houdin, T. Nelson Downs, and others

**Miser's Dream**

**Sawing a Woman**

**Cups and Balls,** perhaps the oldest and most frequently performed trick

**Linking Rings,** a rite of passage in magic; nearly every great magician has a version

**Cups and Balls**

**Cups and Balls**

**Changing a one-dollar bill** into a hundred-dollar bill by Vladimir Vladimirov and Mike Kozlowski

**Four Coins That Gather Invisibly** by Yank Hoe and Al Schneider

**Four Coins**

**Bullet Catch,** catching or withstanding fired ammunition, as performed by Coullew, Chung Ling Soo, and Penn and Teller

**Blooming Fruit or Flowers,** as performed by Jean Eugene Robert-Houdin, Bautier De Kolta, and others.

**Bullet Catch**

**Bullet Catch**

**Bird Productions,** as performed by Chen Kai, Channing Pollock, Lance Burton, and others.

**Vanishing Bird Cage** by Bautier De Kolta

**Bird Productions**

**Sawing a Woman**

**Sawing a Woman**

**Bullet Catch**

**Cremation Illusion,** by Charles McDonald, in which the magician or an assistant is cremated onstage, and later revealed alive and unharmed

**The Disembodied Head,** as first described in Reginald Scot's early text on conjuring

**Disembodied Head**

**The Magician Changes** into someone else and reappears at the back of the theater

**Spirits Come Alive in an Enclosed Cabinet** by the Davenport Brothers

**Spirits Come Alive**

**Spirits Come Alive**

**Bullet Catch**

**Rabbit from a Hat vs. Sawing a Woman**
Pulling a rabbit from a top hat is hard to beat at a child's birthday party. It's also a powerful metaphor for the creation of life. But Sawing Through a Woman is an even more powerful metaphor for the danger of death. When P.T. Selbit debuted this feat, audiences actually feared for the life of the girl in the box. They couldn't look – but they couldn't look away.

**Sawing a Woman vs. Cups and Balls**
The Cups and Balls has everything: misdirection, suspense, surprise, audience interaction, potential for humor, and a rich history. But Sawing a Woman has an element of danger that, when it was first created, seemed real. It has become the most recognized magic trick in the world.

THE WINNER

**Bullet Catch**

VS

**Bullet Catch vs. Human Levitation**
We've all dreamed of flying, so Human Levitation fascinates us. But the Bullet Catch scares us. It's a magic feat with both perceived and real danger. More than 12 people have died performing the stunt, beginning with the French magician Coulew, who was beaten with his own gun by an irate assistant, to Chung Ling Soo in London in 1918. Penn and Teller perform it with two guns. The Bullet Catch wins because it's as topical and scary today as when it debuted more than 300 years ago.

TOM ROBBINS SAID IT BEST: "Using words to describe magic is like using a screwdriver to cut roast beef." Ranking magic isn't any easier. But we can all agree about what makes magic great: the illusion of impossibility. Anything impossible is considered: telepathy, telekinesis, and unexplainable escapes are all fair game. Tricks that are topical rank high, but timeless tricks rank higher. Believable tricks are preferred, and above all else, we are in search of memorable, meaningful magic.

**Spoon Bending vs. Second Sight**
Magic tricks require a willing suspension of disbelief. But these two tricks look so plausible that they are accepted as genuine by audiences worldwide. When a blindfolded mentalist is able to discern the owner of a watch only by feeling it, or when he is able to call out details on someone's driver's license without looking, people attribute real psychic abilities to the performer (it's not the case, sorry). Spoon Bending wins here, precisely because it is so believable. Although the metal bends less than an inch, it appears to do so by the mind.

# Human Levitation

- **Human Levitation**
  - **Human Levitation**
    - **Mysterious Escapes**
      - **Mysterious Escapes** in which no explanation seems possible: as performed by Houdini, Doug Henning, David Copperfield, and others.
      - **Substitution Trunk,** popularized by Houdini, in which he and his wife would transpose through a locked chest
    - **Human Levitation**
      - **Human Levitation,** an ancient trick that still astounds, by practitioners like Servais Le Roy, David Copperfield, and David Blaine
      - **The Water Torture Cell** by Houdini, in which the magician, inverted and shackled in a clear tank of water, magically escapes
  - **Spoon Bending**
    - **Spoon Bending**
      - **Spoon Bending,** as performed by Uri Geller and others
      - **Second Sight Acts,** in which a blindfolded mentalist "sees" objects and thoughts
    - **Pepper's Ghost**
      - **Pepper's Ghost,** an uncanny illusion of a see-through apparition (think holographic) by Henry Dircks and John Pepper
      - **Black Art Magic,** in which people and objects levitate, vanish, and change with no cover
- **Vanishing the Statue of Liberty**
  - **Light and Heavy Chest**
    - **Light and Heavy Chest**
      - **Indian Rope Trick,** wherein a rope becomes rigid in midair and a boy is able to climb it and ultimately vanish
      - **Light and Heavy Chest** by Jean Eugene Robert-Houdin
    - **Red cards from black cards**
      - **Turning a Card Inside Out** by Roy Walton
      - **Magically separating red cards from black cards** by Paul Curry and John Scarne
  - **Vanishing the Statue of Liberty**
    - **Ultra-Mental Deck**
      - **Rising Card** by Abram Colorni, wherein a playing card mysteriously rises from the deck
      - **Turning an Invisible Card Visible** by Judson Brown, Joe Berg, Dai Vernon, and Eddie Fields
    - **Vanishing the Statue of Liberty**
      - **Vanishing the Statue of Liberty** by David Copperfield and Andre Kole
      - **The Turk:** a thinking, chess-playing machine by Baron Wolfgang von Kempelen

**Indian Rope Trick vs. Light and Heavy Chest**
The Indian Rope Trick is the only trick here that cannot be performed. It is mythic, fabricated, and romantically discussed as if it were real. A fakir throws a rope into the air and it is suspended, erect. A boy then climbs the rope and disappears at the top. But Robert-Houdin's Light and Heavy Chest wins this round, if only because his trick can be and has been performed.

**Light and Heavy Chest vs. Vanishing the Statue of Liberty**
Napoleon III called Robert-Houdin to Algeria in 1856 to use his magic to quash a rebellion by a superstitious tribe called the Marabout. In a theater in Algiers, Houdin showed the Marabout how he could easily lift a small chest off the ground, then "take away" an opponent's strength; when the strongest Marabout tried to lift the small chest, it was impossible. Rebellion over.
A century later, David Copperfield vanished one of the most famous landmarks in the world. Performed but once, in 1983, it is still among the most talked-about tricks ever.

# Roller Coasters

**By Scott Rutherford**

Scott Rutherford is senior editor/writer for the trade publication *Amusement Today* and author of *The American Roller Coaster.*

WOODEN REGIONAL

**Shivering Timbers**
Michigan's Adventure, MI (1998)

**Thunderhead**
Dollywood, TN (2004)

**Thunderhead**

**Phoenix**
Knoebels, PA (1985)

**Jack Rabbit**
Kennywood, PA (1921)

**Phoenix**

**Thunderhead**

**The Voyage**
Holiday World, IN (2006)

**Viper**
Six Flags Great America, IL (1995)

**The Voyage**

**El Toro**
Six Flags Great Adventure, NJ (2006)

**Lightning Racer**
Hersheypark, PA (2000)

**El Toro**

**The Voyage**

**Thunderhead**

**Boulder Dash**
Lake Compounce, CT (2000)

**Screamin' Eagle**
Six Flags St. Louis, MO (1978)

**Screamin' Eagle**

**Hades**
Mt. Olympus Theme Park, WI (2005)

**Ravine Flyer II**
Waldameer Park, PA (2008)

**Ravine Flyer II**

**Ravine Flyer II**

**Thunderbolt**
Kennywood, PA (1968)

**Cyclone**
Coney Island, NY (1927)

**Cyclone**

**Comet**
The Great Escape, NY (1994)

**Giant Dipper**
Santa Cruz Beach Boardwalk, CA (1924)

**Giant Dipper**

**Cyclone**

**Cyclone**

**El Toro vs. The Voyage**
Both of these stalwart powerhouses opened in 2006 yet are very different rides. El Toro is the first wooden coaster in the U.S. to sport a prefabricated track rendered so precise that it performs like a steel coaster. In contrast, The Voyage's traditional construction methods exhaust riders with a record-breaking collection of steep hills, 90-degree banks, triple-dipping underground tunnels, and enough turbulent airtime for three separate coasters.

**Ravine Flyer II vs. Cyclone**
The RFII is an impressive recreation of the original 1923 model built on the same bluff overlooking Lake Erie. The RFII is a worthy contender but it must bow to the raw, primal energy of the venerable Coney Island Cyclone. A striking, three-layered seaside twister that operates in much the same fashion as it has for the last 82 summers, this ferocious NYC historical landmark grabs riders and refuses to let go. Not for the timid, this one.

THE WINNER

**Thunderhea**
Dollywood, TN (2006)

VS

THE CAROUSEL MAY BE THE SOUL OF AN AMUSEMENT PARK, but the roller coaster is its iconic, adrenaline-filled heart. Inspired by 17th-century Russian ice slides, it took American ingenuity in 1884 at New York's Coney Island to refine the concept. More than 2,000 were built in the Roaring '20s, but only a handful from that first Golden Age survived the wave of destruction that began during the Great Depression. Today's coaster renaissance commenced in 1972 and shows no signs of faltering. The sky is quite literally the limit.

**Batman vs. Mind Bender**
While these two loopers share the same German designer (Werner Stengel), they offer vastly dissimilar experiences. Swooping in as the world's first inverted coaster, Batman rocks riders into floorless ski lift-style vehicles and rockets them through five rapid-fire inversions. But its senior Southern cousin excels due to its inspired concealment in a forested ravine, unexpected moments of ejector airtime, and a mere lap bar to restrain passengers. Even at 30 years old, Mind Bender still riddles the Dark Knight.

# Superman

- Superman
  - Superman
    - Superman
      - Superman Ride of Steel — Six Flags New England (2000)
      - Space Mountain — Walt Disney World, FL (1975)
    - Mind Bender
      - Mind Bender — Six Flags over Georgia, GA (1978)
      - Batman the Ride — Six Flags Great America, IL (1992)
  - Goliath
    - Goliath
      - Goliath — Six Flags over Georgia, GA (2006)
      - Maverick — Cedar Point, OH (1978)
    - Magnum XL-2000
      - Big Bad Wolf — Busch Gardens Europe, VA (1984)
      - Magnum XL-2000 — Cedar Point, OH (1989),
- Millennium Force
  - Millennium Force
    - Apollo's Chariot
      - Shock Wave — Six Flags over Texas, TX (1978)
      - Apollo's Chariot — Busch Gardens Europe, VA (1999)
    - Millennium Force
      - Millennium Force — Cedar Point, OH (2000)
      - Whizzer — Six Flags Great America, IL (1976)
  - Steel Force
    - Volcano
      - Dueling Dragons — Islands of Adventure, FL (1999)
      - Volcano Kings — Dominion, VA (1998)
    - Steel Force
      - Steel Force — Dorney Park, PA (1997)
      - Top Thrill Dragster — Cedar Point, OH (2003)

STEEL REGIONAL

**Superman vs. Millennium Force**
Like most everything at Cedar Point, Millennium Force is all about gargantuan dimensions. The imposing 300-foot first drop takes one's breath away, but after that it's all speed and little else. Superman flies circles around its larger cousin by virtue of an imaginative layout laced with a euphoric collection of floating speed hills, dark subterranean tunnels, and other surprises that continue to rake in the accolades.

**Superman vs. Thunderhead**
Superman is a stellar ride, and perhaps the best steel coaster operating today. But the purist in me prefers Dollywood's all-wood Thunderhead. Nestled within a narrow valley high in the Smoky Mountains, this rambunctious thriller embodies the absolute pinnacle of creativity and expert engineering. After plunging through the treetops into a deep ravine, Thunderhead's articulated trains defy gravity as they scream through a knot of convoluted transitions with a grace unparalleled. Thunderhead is outrageous, unbeatable fun.

# SAT Success Strategies

**By Laura Wilson**

Laura Wilson is CEO and founder of the WilsonDailyPrep, an online SAT/ACT program, and WilsonPrep, a test prep company. She is the author of two books, *English in English* and *Write the 25-Minute SAT Essay Right.*

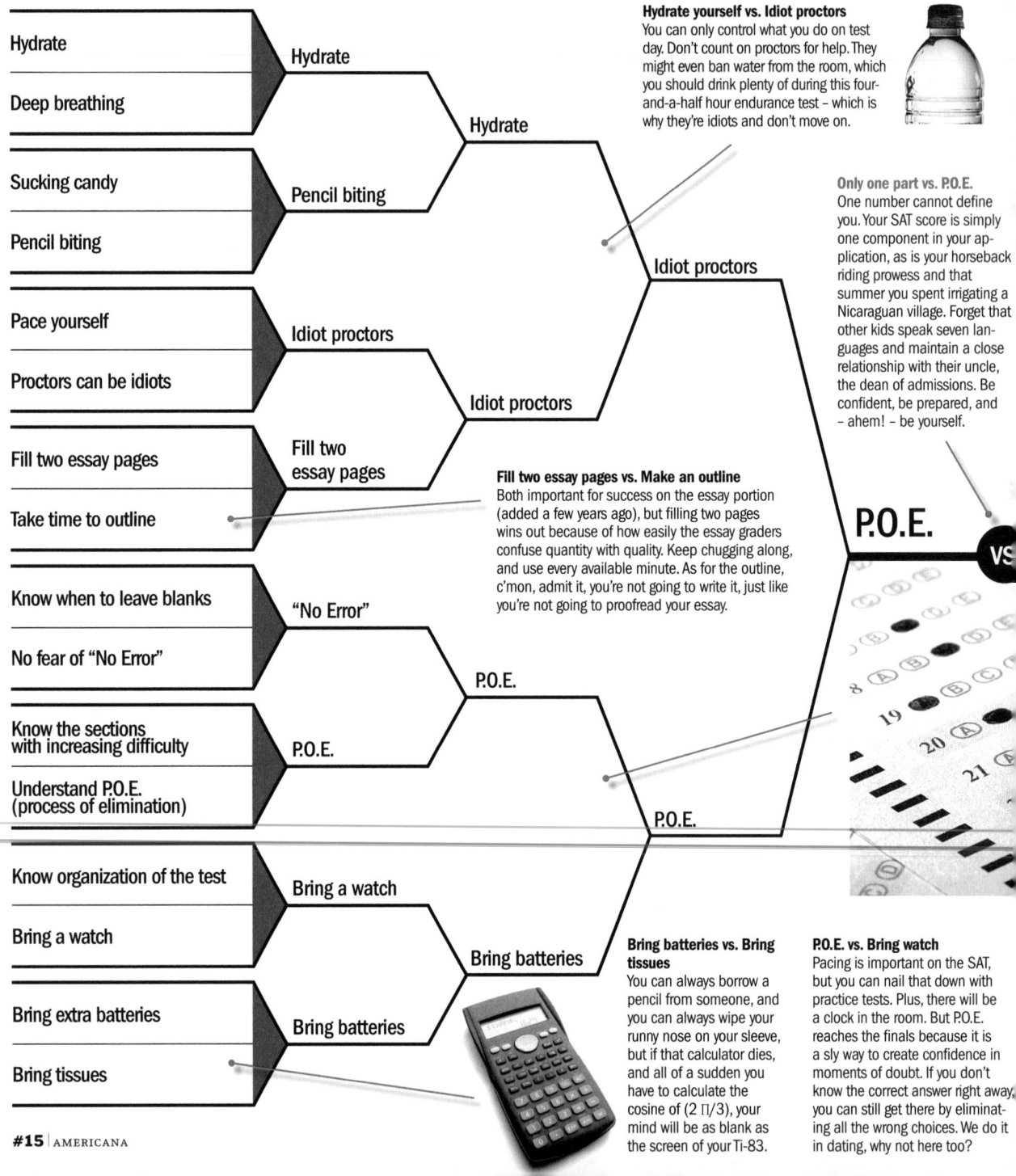

REMEMBER THOSE HALCYON (repugnant, purgative, quotidian?) days of studying for your SAT? Our aim here is not to espouse practice (that's a given) but to rank 32 test-taking strategies that you might not have considered. They are a mixture of logistical tips, ways to feel confident, and below-the-surface eccentricities on the test itself. All of them have the same goal: to put the next generation of prodigious (precocious, perspicacious) neophytes into schools where they will feel challenged and proud of their accomplishments.

**Don't share scores vs. Bring ID**
Photo identification is the Mac Daddy of all things to bring to the test. If you forget the ID, you have to call mom, mom has to get back in the car and rush to the site, and inevitably someone gets blamed, and everyone stresses. Not a good frame of mind for taking the test. It's all about being relaxed and In the Zone.

THE WINNER

# It's only one part of the application process

- Only one part
  - Bring ID
    - Don't share scores
      - 200 points for signing your name
      - Don't share scores with friends
    - Bring ID
      - Bring layers of clothing
      - Bring ID
  - Only one part
    - No pen on essay
      - No pen on essay
      - Never leave a grid-in blank
    - Only one part
      - Offered 7 times per year
      - It's only one part of the application process
- Wallpaper bathroom
  - Wallpaper bathroom
    - Wallpaper bathroom
      - Wallpaper the bathroom with vocabulary
      - Read *New York Times* Op-eds regularly before bed
    - One right answer
      - Pre-drive the route to the site
      - There is one right answer per question
  - Good night sleep
    - Good night sleep
      - Listen to "pump-up" music before exam
      - Get a good night of sleep
    - Bite-size pieces
      - This is a reasoning test, not an academic test
      - Break answers down to bite-size pieces

**Wallpaper bathroom vs. Read *NYT* Op-Eds**
Op-Eds not only hone critical reasoning skills, but also provide great topics for your essay. But index-carding your bathroom wall is more essential. Staring at the words exculpate, expurgate, expunge, and excise during "office hours" leading up to the test will lock in their definitions for the big day.

**Good night sleep vs. Bite-size pieces**
If any long question is remotely confusing, take it piece by piece until you're comfortable with it. "Bite-size" is also a reminder to bring a brain-food snack (granola is great!). That said, nothing improves your cognitive processes better than a good night of sleep. Lack of sleep makes you grumpy, and grumps don't do very well on tasks that require full concentration.

# Screen Cowboys

**By Neil Amdur**

Neil Amdur has spent a lifetime covering tournaments of all kinds – from tennis to the Olympics – as a reporter and then as sports editor of the *New York Times* for 12 years. His knowledge of cowboys extends from childhood to manhood.

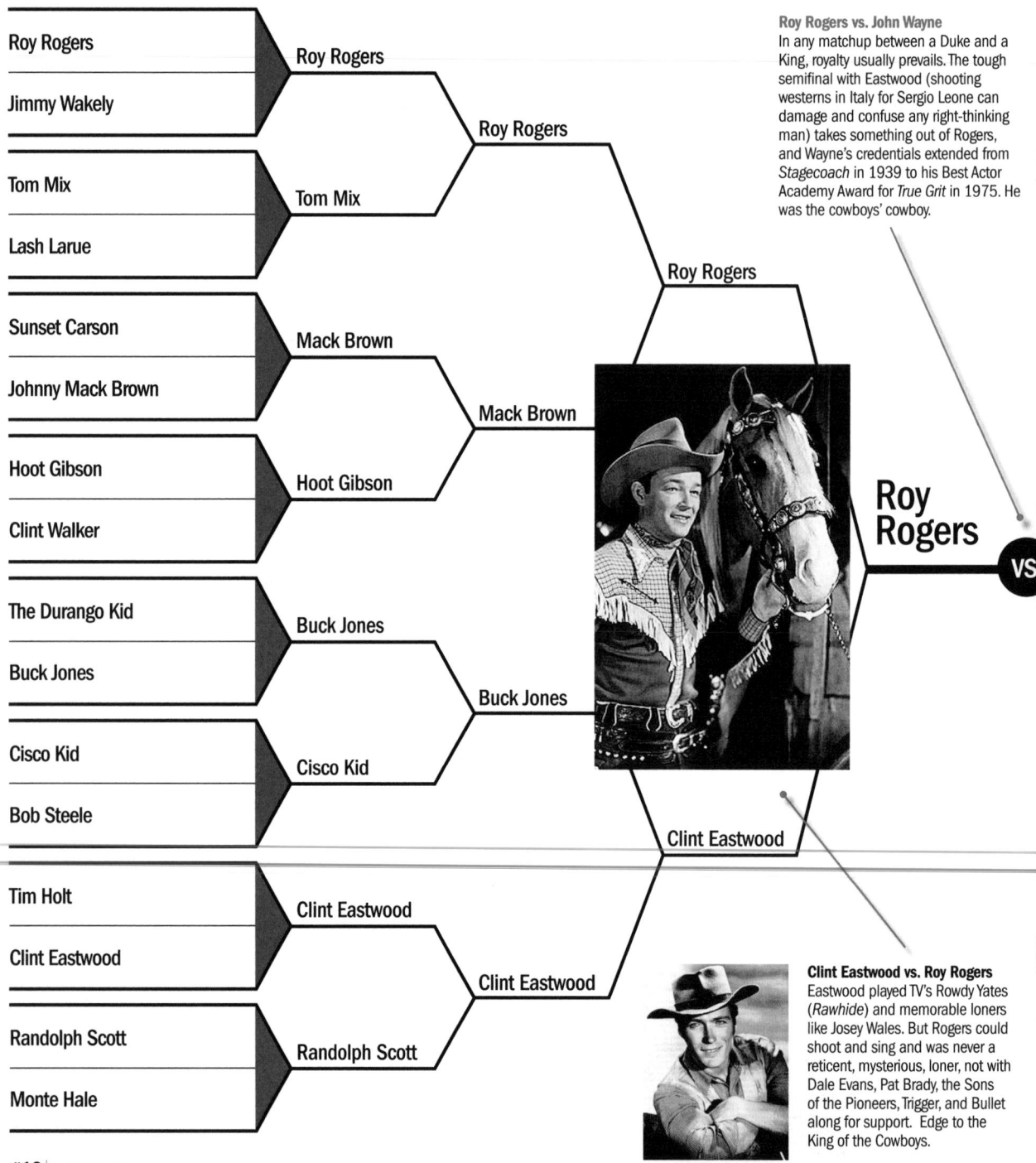


**Roy Rogers vs. John Wayne**
In any matchup between a Duke and a King, royalty usually prevails. The tough semifinal with Eastwood (shooting westerns in Italy for Sergio Leone can damage and confuse any right-thinking man) takes something out of Rogers, and Wayne's credentials extended from *Stagecoach* in 1939 to his Best Actor Academy Award for *True Grit* in 1975. He was the cowboys' cowboy.

**Clint Eastwood vs. Roy Rogers**
Eastwood played TV's Rowdy Yates (*Rawhide*) and memorable loners like Josey Wales. But Rogers could shoot and sing and was never a reticent, mysterious, loner, not with Dale Evans, Pat Brady, the Sons of the Pioneers, Trigger, and Bullet along for support. Edge to the King of the Cowboys.

IN THE AMERICAN PSYCHE, cowboys were our heroes, transported from the range to movie theaters and TV screens with personalities we could only envision in our dreams. They each brought their own identity, with slick costumes, exotic horses, elaborate disguises, finely crafted hardware, diverse sidekicks, and even the ability to deliver a song amid the madness. And all in the name of law and order.

**John Wayne vs. James Arness**
It doesn't get any grittier than this. Arness's Marshal Matt Dillon controlled one town – down-and-dirty Dodge City – for 20 television seasons. But the Duke conquered big-screen venues and bad guys from Red River to Fort Apache. Plus (spoiler alert), he was the man who shot Liberty Valance.

**Long Ranger vs. Hopalong Cassidy**
The Lone Ranger had Tonto, Silver, a mask, silver bullets, and a noble mission. But Hopalong Cassidy traveled with Topper and a collection of funky sidekicks (Andy Clyde, Al St. John, Edgar Buchanan), and had silver hair and gifted hands.

THE WINNER
**John Wayne**

- John Wayne
  - John Wayne
    - John Wayne
      - John Wayne
      - Rex Allen
    - Tex Ritter
      - Alan (Rocky) Lane
      - Tex Ritter
  - James Arness
    - James Arness
      - Guy Madison
      - James Arness
    - Lee Van Cleef
      - Chuck Connors
      - Lee Van Cleef
- Gene Autry
  - Hopalong Cassidy
    - Hopalong Cassidy
      - Hopalong Cassidy
      - Ken Maynard
    - Lone Ranger
      - The Lone Ranger
      - Crash Corrigan
  - Gene Autry
    - Joel McCrea
      - Joel McCrea
      - Richard Boone
    - Gene Autry
      - Hoss Cartwright
      - Gene Autry

# A New National Anthem

**By Richard Sandomir**

Richard Sandomir, the co-editor of this book, was instructed in eighth-grade music class to always mouth the words so that no one would hear his voice.

ALL-AMERICAN REGIONAL

"America" (from *West Side Story*) vs. "America" (Simon and Garfunkel) → "America" (S&G)

"American Pie" (Don McLean) vs. "American Tune" (Paul Simon) → "American Pie"

"Born in the USA" (Bruce Springsteen) vs. "Back in the USA" (Chuck Berry) → "Back in the USA"

"America the Beautiful" (Ray Charles) vs. "God Bless the USA" (Lee Greenwood) → "America the Beautiful"

"God Bless America" (Kate Smith and others) vs. "We're an American Band" (Grand Funk Railroad) → "God Bless America"

"America" (My Country 'Tis of Thee) vs. "U.S. Blues" (Grateful Dead) → "America"

"America" (Neil Diamond) vs. "Living in America" (James Brown) → "Living in America"

"R.O.C.K. In the U.S.A." (John Mellencamp) vs. "American Dream" (Neil Young) → "American Dream"

"American Pie" vs. "America the Beautiful" → "American Pie"

"Back in the USA" vs. "America the Beautiful" → "America the Beautiful"

"God Bless America" vs. "Living in America" → "God Bless America"

"America the Beautiful" vs. "God Bless America" → "America the Beautiful"

**"American Pie" vs. "America the Beautiful"**
"American Pie" is a rock lament, not traditional anthemic material, yet Garth Brooks proved its galvanizing power during President Obama's pre-Inaugural concert at the Lincoln Memorial. Still, "America the Beautiful" has patriotism and optimism, God and military sacrifice and cities, mountains and farms – and poetry too ("amber waves of grain" rolls off the tongue nicely).

**"America the Beautiful" vs. "God Bless America"**
"God Bless America" is Irving Berlin's patriotic grabber, a short, declarative, musical thrust ("Stand beside her and guide her") that ends with a needlework saying ("My home sweet home"). "America the Beautiful" is, well, more beautiful, more expansive, more emotional, more religious – and more satisfying. And I'll take Ray Charles's signature version over the ubiquitous Kate Smith recording, which is beginning to test my patience.

**"God Bless America" vs. "We're An American Band"**
OK, nobody's going to approve Grand Funk Railroad's story about a rock band and their groupies. But it is catchy. "God Bless America" is Irving Berlin's earnest flag-waving song that long ago should have replaced "The Star-Spangled Banner." It is easy to sing and can make you cry. And when Frank Sinatra sang it in 1943, it approached high art.

**"America" vs. "Living in America"**
Separate Diamond's emotional "America" from its egregious source, *The Jazz Singer,* and you've got a moving immigrant's song ("Far/We've been traveling far/Without a home") that's been crowd-tested effectively in arenas and stadiums. But "Living in America" offers a chance for a funk anthem that is just as hopeful ("You might not be looking for the promised land, but you might find it anyway") and gives us a chance to sing "Smokestack, fatback/Many miles of railroad track." We feel good!

"America the Beautiful" VS

SHOW OF HANDS: how many of you think "The Star Spangled Banner" must go? Polls show that most American adults don't know the words, why it was written, or why it is sung to the melody of a British drinking song. It's a tough tune to carry, with a one-and-a-half octave range and two "o'er's" just in the one verse (of four) that we sing. Here we begin the search for a song: one not mired in bellicose imagery observed from a 19th-century fort, one that prompts a mass singalong, and one that even Roseanne can sing.

**Blowin' in the Wind" vs. "Yankee Doodle"**
Yankee Doodle" is a short, jolly earwig that fails the sense test: if Yankee Doodle is Uncle Sam's nephew (an august station in life), how can he justify going to London just to ride the ponies? Would you want Whitney Houston singing that to 75,000 fans? Dylan's song, a serious part of the American folk/protest songbook, has three advantages: it is philosophical, angry, and easy to sing.

**America the Beautiful" vs. This Land"**
Guthrie's astonishing song – a folk classic and a political response to God Bless America" – is an ode to the nation he "roamed and rambled" on foot and by train. Yes, Brother Ray gives you chills, but Woody's song crisply evokes America's coast-to-coast natural beauties and also finds him "wonderin'" about whether "this land's still made for you and me" when you and me are on relief.

THE WINNER

## "This Land Is Your Land"
(Woody Guthrie)

**"Stars and Stripes Forever" vs. "We Shall Overcome"**
Sousa's good-times masterpiece has lyrics, but they're rarely sung. Still, you can hum along and march to the beat of the brass and piccolos, can't you? But "We Shall Overcome" has already proved its musical mettle as the anthem of the civil rights movement, a gospel classic that assures believers that we are neither alone nor afraid – and isn't that worth singing about?

- "This Land Is Your Land"
  - "Blowin' in the Wind"
    - "Blowin' in the Wind"
      - "Blowin' in the Wind" (Bob Dylan)
      - "You're a Grand Old Flag" (various)
    - "Yankee Doodle"
      - "I'm a Yankee Doodle Dandy" (James Cagney)
      - "Battle Hymn of the Republic" (various)
  - "This Land Is Your Land"
    - "This Land Is Your Land"
      - "This Land Is Your Land" (Woody Guthrie)
      - "I've Been Everywhere" (Johnny Cash)
    - "Georgia on My Mind"
      - "Georgia on My Mind" (Willie Nelson, Ray Charles)
      - "City of New Orleans" (Arlo Guthrie)
- "We Shall Overcome"
  - "Stars and Stripes"
    - "Stars and Stripes"
      - "Stars and Stripes Forever" (John Philip Sousa)
      - "Fanfare for the Common Man" (Aaron Copland)
    - "The Rising"
      - "If I Had a Hammer" (Peter, Paul and Mary)
      - "The Rising" (Bruce Springsteen)
  - "We Shall Overcome"
    - "Halls of Montezuma"
      - "Halls of Montezuma" (various)
      - "The Army Goes Rolling Along" (1956 version of "Caisson Song")
    - "We Shall Overcome"
      - "We Shall Overcome" (Pete Seeger and others)
      - "Graceland" (Paul Simon)

AMERICANA REGIONAL

# HISTORY & POLITICS

**Vestiges of the 20th Century** *by Kurt Andersen* 18
**Conservative Texts** *by Mary Matalin* 19
**First Ladies** *by Gail Collins* 20
**Panic Attacks** *by Jack Hitt* 21
**Memorable Speech Lines** *by Jeff Shesol* 22
**Innovators** *by Harold Evans* 23
**Supreme Court Decisions** *by Adam Liptak* 24
**Presidential Pardons** *by P.S. Ruckman, Jr.* 25
**Military Heroes** *by Richard Goldstein* 26
**Enduring One-Liners** *by Jan Van Meter* 27
**Financial Villains** *by Joe Nocera* 28
**Political Rivalries** *by Adam Clymer* 29
**Presidential Speeches** *by Curt Smith* 30
**Influential Radicals and Extremists** *by David Oshinsky* 31
**Biographies** *by James McGrath Morris* 32

# Vestiges of the 20th Century

**By Kurt Andersen**

Kurt Andersen does a lot, but his obituary written near the end of the 21st century migh mention that he co-founded *Spy*, edited *New York*, hosted "Studio 360," and, beginning with *Turn of the Century* and *Heyday*, wrote many critically acclaimed bestselling novel

the inevitable triumph of socialism

serious new architecture = modernist architecture

modernist architecture

gray-haired women

World's Fairs

gray hair

modernist architecture

delayed gratification and patience

printed magazines and newspapers

patience

patience

record albums

the end of Christian fundamentalism

albums

patience

the civil rights struggle

thinness

thinness

worry-free promiscuity

clear distinction between high and low culture

high-low distinction

thinness

Hydrox cookies

non-telegenic presidents

non-telegenic presidents

cigarette-smoking

gigantic TV audiences

cigarettes

cigarettes

thinness

patience

**patience vs. America #1**
Once upon a time – before FedEx, before ATMs, before email, before Google, before DVRs, before serial get-rich quick bubbles in tech stocks and houses, before *American Idol* – people expected to have to wait a while to get what they wanted, to have a little patience. Yet until it's possible to download knowledge and emotion and enlightenment itself directly into our brains, patience will continue to be required.

**cigarettes vs. thinness**
As we all know, quitting cigarettes tends to mean gaining weight, and so when these two wound up in a one-on-one faceoff without any manipulation on my part (I swear), I felt that providence was at work.

THE WINNER

**delayed gratification and patience**

VS

DURING MOST OF THE 20TH CENTURY, these 32 beliefs, artifacts, habits, paradigms, and phenomena were all givens, defining features of modern life, and seemingly permanent. Yet as the century ended and this new one proceeds, we've discovered that they are, um, not. In each round the winner is the one that will take longer to peter out entirely. In the long run, and with uncanny metaphysical aptness, it turned out to be patience that triumphs.

America #1

- medical mystery
  - radio
    - feminism
      - serious new art = abstract art
      - the feminist struggle
    - radio
      - broadcast commercial radio
      - Freudianism and psychoanalysis
  - medical mystery
    - medical mystery
      - medical mystery (e.g., fetal gender, DNA flaws)
      - photographic film
    - network greatness
      - network TV greatness
      - evolution as a settled fact
- America #1
  - America #1
    - America #1
      - global American hegemony
      - letters
    - pubic hair
      - objectivity
      - pubic hair
  - capitalism
    - fossil fuels
      - fossil fuels
      - serious new orchestral music = anxious music
    - capitalism
      - the inevitable triumph of capitalism
      - printed books

**global capitalist triumph vs. fossil fuels**
Our per capita use of petroleum and coal should start declining relatively soon. Capitalism, however, despite its regular crises, will continue to look triumphant for decades more – until that moment at which the Chinese and American economies have become so intertwined and hybridized, and global corporations so large, that the old capitalism-vs.-socialism question finally becomes moot.

**capitalism vs. America #1**
Back at the end of the last century, there was no difference between the triumph of capitalism and American global hegemony. History had ended and they were locked in. But the Great Unraveling of 2008 and 2009 seems to be queering the former, and together with other factors – the rise of China and Islamist radicalism, and the arrogant, imprudent laziness of Americans – is taking care of the latter as well.

**anxious music vs. fossil fuels**
For most of the 20th century – from Schoenberg through John Cage, Elliott Carter, Karlheinz Stockhausen, and beyond – new orchestral music was required to be dissonant and/or disconcerting. But even as serious new music starts to get pretty and likable again, we're still listening to it on devices powered by not-so-clean, coal-generated electricity.

# Conservative Texts

**By Mary Matalin**

Mary Matalin, former assistant to President George W. Bush and counselor to Vice President Dick Cheney, is a conservative TV and radio commentator and publisher of Threshold, a conservative book imprint.

*Democracy and Leadership*
by Irving Babbitt (1924)

*The Content of Our Character*
by Shelby Steele (1990)

*Is Life Worth Living*
by W. H. Mallock (1879)

*Modern Times*
by Paul Johnson (1984)

*The Art of War*
by Sun Tzu (6th century BC)

*Orthodoxy*
by G.K. Chesterton (1908)

*Vamps and Tramps*
by Camille Paglia (1994)

*Gone with the Wind*
by Margaret Mitchell (1936)

*The Portable Conservative Reader*
by Russell Kirk (1982)

*The Road to Serfdom*
by Friedrich Hayek (1944)

*Democracy in America*
by Alexis de Tocqueville (1835)

*Reflections on the Revolution of France*
by Edmund Burke (1790)

*Conservatism: Dream and Reality*
by Robert Nisbet (1986)

*Age and Guile Beat Youth, Innocence, and a Bad Haircut*
by P. J. O'Rourke (1995)

*The Conservative Mind*
by Russell Kirk (1953)

*God and Man at Yale*
by William F. Buckley (1951)

*Democracy and Leadership*

*Is Life Worth Living*

*Art of War*

*Vamps and Tramps*

*Road to Serfdom*

*Reflections on the Revolution*

*Conservatism: Dream and Reality*

*Conservative Mind*

*Democracy and Leadership*

*Art of War*

*Reflections on the Revolution*

*Conservative Mind*

*Art of War*

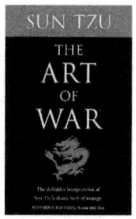


*Art of War*

VS

*Reflections on the Revolution*

***God and Man at Yale* vs. *The Conservative Mind***
George Will called Buckley's first book – where the young author attacked Yale for foisting liberal views on unwitting undergrads – "a lover's quarrel with his alma mater." More a career launch for Buckley than a classic conservative text, it cannot compete against the 20th-century Big Daddy, Russell Kirk. *The Conservative Mind* revived the ideas of Edmund Burke, gave shape to conservative thinking after FDR, and established Kirk, along with Burke and Irving Babbit, as the conservative sine qua non.

CONSERVATISM IS COMMONLY, AND OFTEN MALICIOUSLY, MISCHARACTERIZED as an ideology and its adherents as ideologues. Unlike modern liberalism (not to be confused with classical liberalism), conservatism is not a product of some abstract philosophical tract or Utopian theory. From Edmund Burke (the father of political conservatism) to contemporary champions, conservative conviction comes from the accumulated experience of individuals and nations over time. Choosing the best conservative text (which is as difficult as choosing a favorite Beatles song) demands that you savor the variety of offerings, appreciating their shared common origin: individual freedom.

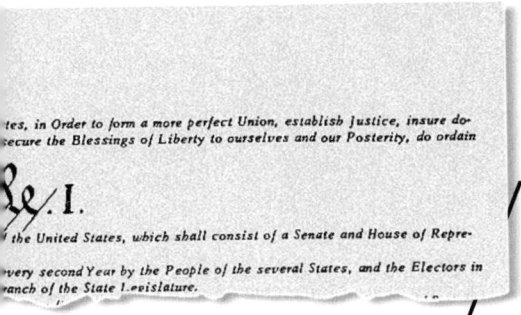


THE WINNER

**United States Constitution**

by the Founding Fathers (1788)

- **Atlas Shrugged**
  - **Capitalism and Freedom**
    - *Capitalism and Freedom* by Milton Friedman (1962)
    - *Basic Economics* by Thomas Sowell (2004)
  - **Wealth and Poverty**
    - *Wealth and Poverty* by George Gilder (1981)
    - *The Machiavellians* by James Burnham (1987)
- **U.S. Constitution**
  - **Atlas Shrugged**
    - **Liberal Fascism**
      - *Radical Son* by David Horowicz (1997)
      - *Liberal Fascism* by Jonah Goldberg (2007)
    - **Atlas Shrugged**
      - *1984* by George Orwell (1949)
      - *Atlas Shrugged* by Ayn Rand (1957)
  - **U.S. Constitution**
    - **U.S. Constitution**
      - United States Constitution by the Founding Fathers (1788)
      - *The Reagan Diaries* by Ronald Reagan (2007)
    - **John Adams**
      - *John Adams* by David McCullough (2001)
      - *Recovering the Past: A Historian's Memoir* by Forrest McDonald (2004)
  - **Federalist Papers**
    - **Federalist Papers**
      - The Federalist Papers by Alexander Hamilton, James Madison, and John Jay (1788)
      - *Common Sense* by Thomas Paine (1776)
    - **Definition of Culture**
      - *Notes Toward the Definition of Culture* by T.S. Eliot (1948)
      - *Essays of E.B. White* by E.B. White (1977)

***Capitalism and Freedom* vs. *Atlas Shrugged***
Milton Friedman provided the most accessible understanding of the moral basis of capitalism. But Ayn Rand brilliantly gave us the John Lennon of capitalism, John Galt – a fictional hero who still speaks to young people in every generation. I don't see her novel's influence ending soon. Bonus points to Rand for her personal and intellectual impact on a rising Alan Greenspan.

***Art of War* vs. Constitution**
No text captures the essence of conservatism better than the Constitution. The Founders' creation was the result of their experiences in the original 13 colonies and their acute understanding of human nature. It is the purest expression of guidance for balancing the tension between the individual's freedom and the authority required in a civil society. *The Art of War* resolves that tension in favor of authority. Conservatives, via the Constitution, prefer erring on the side of freedom, believing at the cellular level that "freedom is not free" or automatic. To preserve and advance it, we can't presume that all men seek freedom for the masses over power for themselves. In the words of Burke, "All that is necessary for the triumph of evil is that good men do nothing."

**Federalist Papers vs. Constitution**
The Federalist Papers are the outtakes of the Founders' great drama, lodged within the text of the Constitution. By definition they must stand down.

# First Ladies

**By Gail Collins**

Gail Collins is an op-ed columnist for the *New York Times* and the author of *America's Women: 400 Years of Dolls, Drudges, Helpmates and Heroines.*

Dolley Madison
Bess Truman

Rosalynn Carter
Ida McKinley

Sarah Polk
Julia Tyler

Jackie Kennedy
Margaret Taylor

Abigail Adams
Louisa Adams

Grace Coolidge
Mary Todd Lincoln

Lady Bird Johnson
Jane Pierce

Martha Washington
Mamie Eisenhower

Dolley Madison

Rosalynn Carter

Sarah Polk

Jackie Kennedy

Abigail Adams

Grace Coolidge

Lady Bird Johnson

Martha Washington

Dolley Madison

Jackie Kennedy

Abigail Adams

Lady Bird Johnson

Dolley Madison

Abigail Adams

**Dolley Madison vs. Jackie Kennedy**
Both were known for their social graces, but Dolley did it all first – and without electricity or Oleg Cassini.

**Abigail Adams vs. Louisa Adams**
In this pairing of women married to irritable, one-term presidents, who happened to be father (John) and son (John Quincy), Abigail wins for her great pre-Declaration of Independence letter to John in 1776 urging him to "remember the ladies and be more generous and favorable to them than your ancestors."

## Dolley Madison VS

**Dolley Madison vs. Abigail Adams**
Dolley and Abigail both got through British invasions with courage and grace, but Dolley wins for saving the White House furniture during the War of 1812.

THIS COMPETITION IS BIG ENOUGH to include virtually every First Lady who survived her White House tenure, from Martha Washington to Laura Bush. Preference goes to actually using the position to do something useful for the country – like Lady Bird Johnson's beautification campaign – and to setting a good example, enduring hardship, engaging the interest of the public in a positive way, and putting up with difficult, even philandering men. We'll give Michelle Obama a little more time before we push her into the playoffs.

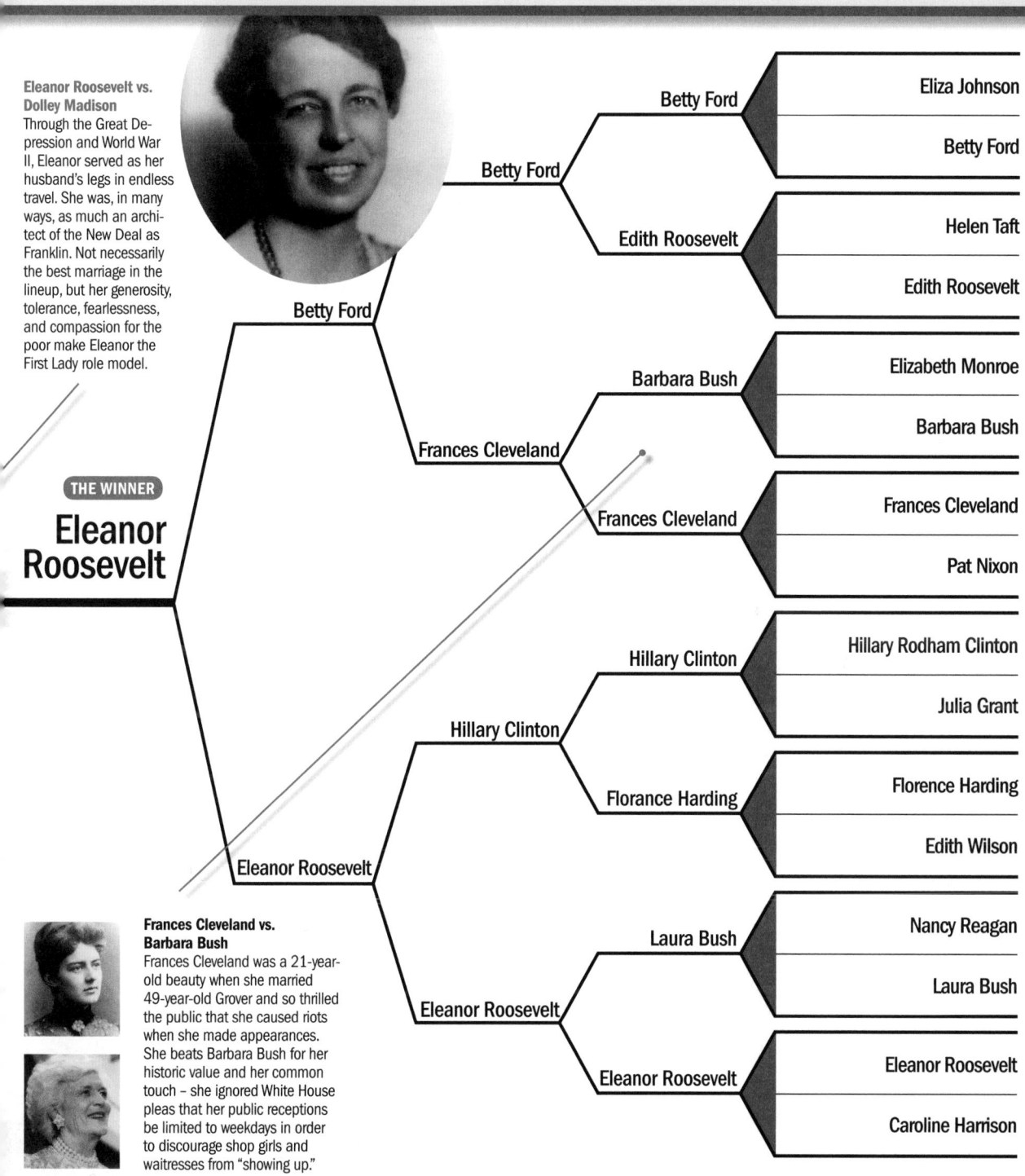

# Panic Attacks

**By Jack Hitt**

Jack Hitt is a contributing writer for the *New York Times Magazine* and *Harper's*.

**Journalistic Hoax** (1835, new moon telescopes, says *NY Sun*, reveal miniature zebras and men with "bat-like wings")

Razor blades in Halloween apples, 1959

**Gold Rush** (1848, gold)

Elvis's Pelvis (1956, proof that pop music is too heterosexual)

Madonna kisses Britney (2003, proof that pop music is too homosexual)

**Freaks with Too Much Freedom** (1830, Rutting Mormons, heading West)

**Electoral Mob** (1876, phony vote in states such as Florida elects Rutherford B. Hayes)

*Sopranos* ending (2007)

**Righteous mob** (1775, Boston Tea Party)

Who Killed JR?

**Economic Frenzy** (1797, English banks collapse)

Sharon Stone's .5-second-long upskirt flash in *Basic Instinct*

**Bears** (1776, in the woods, clawing your face)

Gerbilling. As if.

**Mass Hysteria** (1944, Mad Gasser of Mattoon, Indiana – 29 victims suffer nausea from "phantom anesthetist")

Any Wal-Mart Opening

**Journalistic Hoax** (1936, *Reefer Madness* says pot leads teens to homicidal mayhem and suicide)

**Gold Rush** (2000, Nigerian letter)

**Freaks with Too Much Freedom** (1965, Rutting hippies, heading West)

**Electoral Mob** (2000, phony Florida "riot" stops recount and elects George Bush)

**Righteous Mob** (2008, Wall Street protests, esp. that guy with the sign, "Jump, you fuckers.")

**Economic Frenzy** (1837, speculative bubble)

**Bears** (1975, in the suburbs, clawing your trash)

**Mass Hysteria** (1954, Seattle Windshield Pitting Epidemic – no, really: exactly what it says, 3000 cars "affected.")

**Journalistic Hoax** (1938, *War of the Worlds* broadcast, prompting anti-Martian vigilantism)

**Freaks with Too Much Freedom** (1995, Rutting senior citizens in RVs, heading West)

**Economic Frenzy** (1857, railroad failures)

**Bears** (2008, on Wall Street, clawing your 401K)

**Journalistic Hoax** (2003, *Oprah*, "rainbow parties" causing trembling parents to type those words into Google)

**Economic Frenzy** (1893, run on gold)

THE WINNER

## Economic Frenzy

(a lot of them: 1907, run on banks; 1918, hyper-inflation; 1929, banking collapse; 1953, post-war recession;1973, stagflation; 1982, energy-price spike; 1991, sales collapse; 2001, dot-com bubble bursts)

VS

FROM THE VERY FOUNDING OF THE COUNTRY, when pioneers swore they saw vaporous demons cavorting in New World swamps, to last week's food scare, Americans love a good panic. We can freak out about anything – fingernail clippers at the airport, the latest fatigue syndrome, a Dixie Chicks song. If something barely real can't be found, we're preternaturally gifted at spotting a flying saucer or conjuring some Satanic ritual abuse to explain it.

**Economic Frenzy vs. Lurking Menace**
2008–2009: Subprime mortgages, housing bubble, hedge fund losses, Madoff swindle, credit default swaps, Fannie/Freddie/Lehman/Bear Sterns/AIG, TARP, executive compensation, toxic assets; all erupt leading to planetary financial meltdown. Economic frenzy wins!

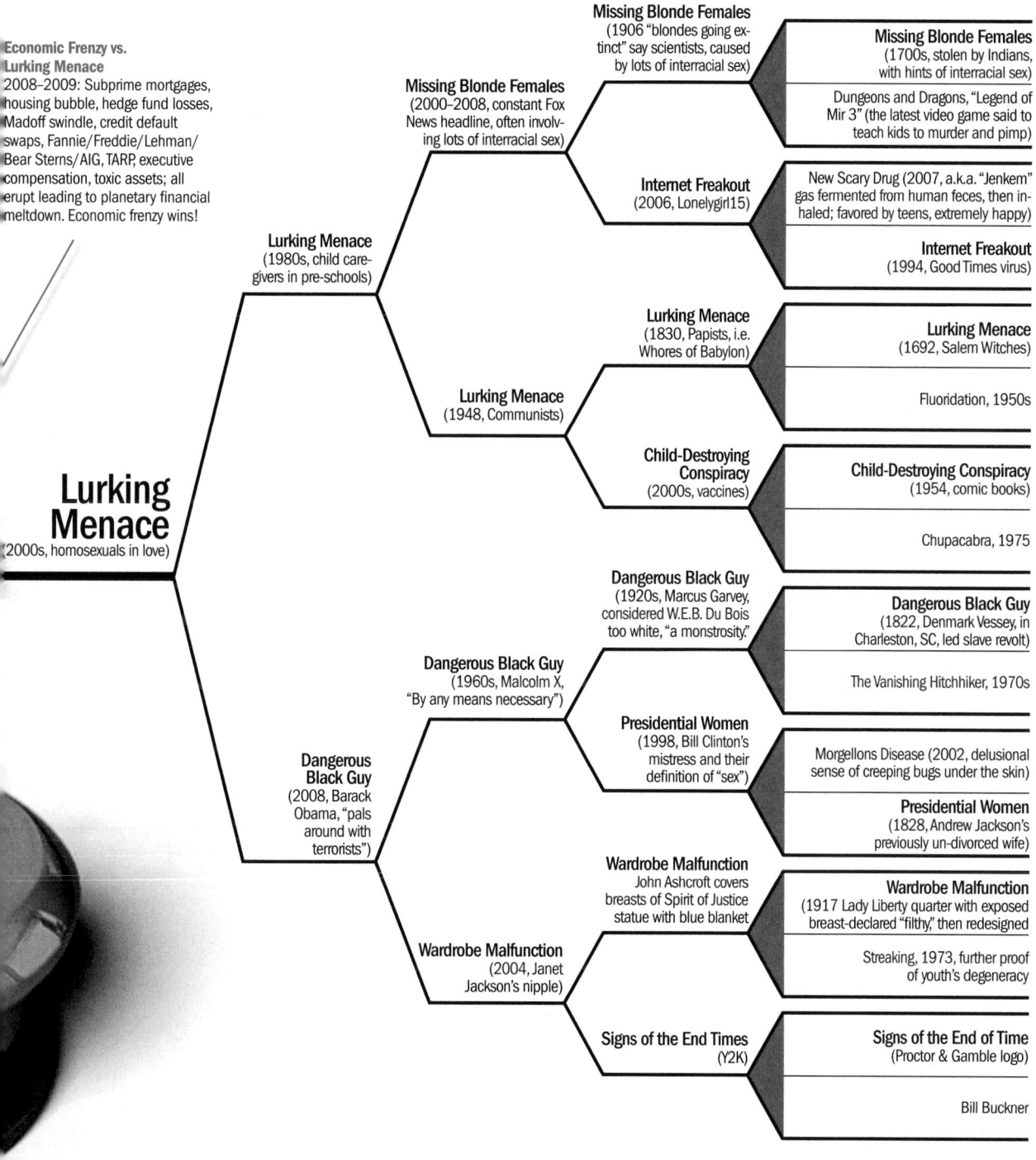

# Memorable Speech Lines

**By Jeff Shesol**

Jeff Shesol, a former speechwriter for President Bill Clinton, is disappointed that none of his own best lines made the opening round. Shesol is the author of *Mutual Contempt: Lyndon Johnson, Robert Kennedy and the Feud That Defined a Decade.*

"I want a kinder and gentler nation" – **George H. W. Bush, 1988**

"Either you are with us or you are with the terrorists" – **George W. Bush, 2001**

"with the terrorists"

**George H. W. Bush vs. George W. Bush**
Father vs. son, "mano-a-mano," as 43 once said to 41. Two very different notions of America. Poppy Bush offered a new brand of politics, but his bare-knuckled campaign for president showed that his heart was never really in it. George W., by contrast, was deadly serious about his intentions, and his words sent a chill wind across post-9/11 America.

"with the terrorists"

"Those who hate you" – **Richard Nixon, 1974**

"You like me – right now, you really like me!" – **Sally Field, 1985**

"Those who hate you"

"We have nothing to fear"

"It is not the critic who counts . . . the credit belongs to the man who is actually in the arena" – **Teddy Roosevelt, 1910**

"We must not confuse dissent with disloyalty" – **Edward R. Murrow, 1954**

"confuse dissent"

"We have nothing to fear"

"We have nothing to fear but fear itself" – **Franklin Delano Roosevelt, 1933**

"Our long national nightmare is over" – **Gerald Ford, 1974**

"We have nothing to fear"

**Nixon vs. Field**
Two exquisite moments of self-revelation: Considering that it was his hatred of others that brought him down, Nixon's farewell to the White House staff is either a political deathbed confession or an extraordinary bit of irony. Field, after winning her second Oscar, for *Places in the Heart,* simply showed the insecurity within all of us. Heartfelt and often misquoted.

"Give me liberty or give me death!" – **Patrick Henry, 1775**

"Extremism in the defense of liberty is no vice" – **Barry Goldwater, 1964**

"Give me liberty"

"new birth of freedom"

"With malice toward none; with charity for all" – **Abraham Lincoln, 1865**

"This nation, under God, shall have a new birth of freedom" – **Lincoln, 1863**

"new birth of freedom"

"new birth of freedom"

THE WINNER

"This nation, under God, shall have a new birth of freedom" – Abraham Lincoln, 1863

VS

"The world must be made safe for democracy" – **Woodrow Wilson, 1917**

"Peace, commerce, and honest friendship with all nations; entangling alliances with none" – **Thomas Jefferson, 1801**

"safe for democracy"

"military-industrial complex"

"We must guard against . . . unwarranted influence . . . by the military-industrial complex" – **Dwight D. Eisenhower, 1961**

"Battle is the most magnificent competition in which a human being can indulge" – **Gen. George Patton, 1943**

"military-industrial complex"

**Wilson vs. Eisenhower**
Wilsonian idealism never dies; it just fades away, only to be resurrected by successive generations. Ike shared Wilson's mission, if not his missionary zeal. In his farewell address, the old soldier warned against the "economic, political, even spiritual" costs of militarization without end.

A SOUND BITE IS LIKE A SMOKE RING – a neat trick, but gone in an instant. A truly great line transcends its time and place, and does more than simply endure. The very best lines change the way people think or act. Most of the first-round entries here are from political speeches, the majority from presidents (because they weigh in on vital issues and people pay close attention). But a few civilian speeches make the cut because they have the same effect: they redefine your reality, burrow into your brain, and get you talking.

**Lincoln vs. King**
Delivered a century apart, these speeches address the unfinished business of American history. In Lincoln's case, the ideals of the Declaration of Independence; in King's the promise of the Emancipation Proclamation. But Lincoln, in the end, can't be surpassed. After all, he didn't just save the Union, he reconceived it, as his words proclaim.

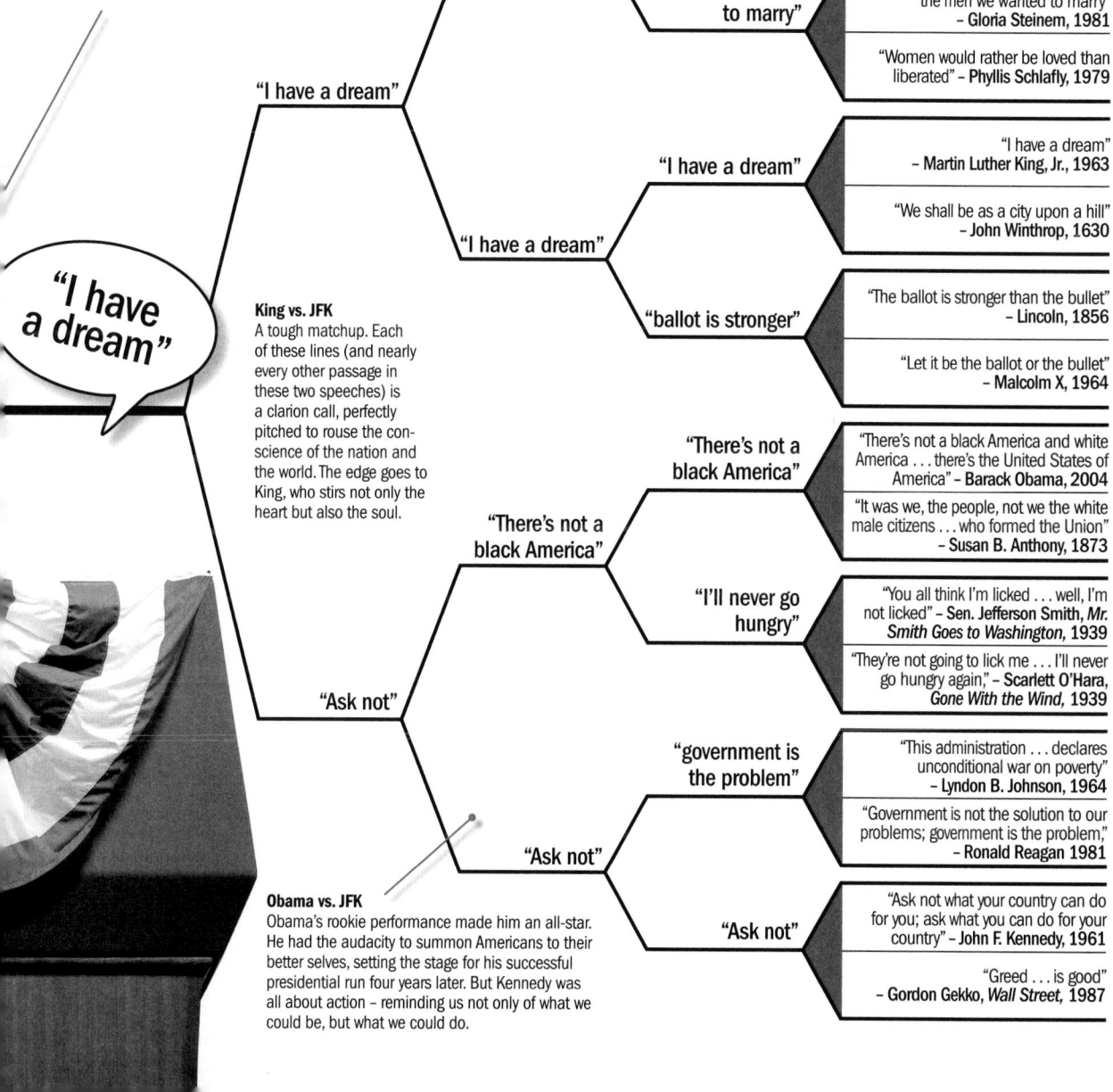


**King vs. JFK**
A tough matchup. Each of these lines (and nearly every other passage in these two speeches) is a clarion call, perfectly pitched to rouse the conscience of the nation and the world. The edge goes to King, who stirs not only the heart but also the soul.

**Obama vs. JFK**
Obama's rookie performance made him an all-star. He had the audacity to summon Americans to their better selves, setting the stage for his successful presidential run four years later. But Kennedy was all about action – reminding us not only of what we could be, but what we could do.

# Innovators

**By Harold Evans**

Harold Evans is author of *They Made America: From the Steam Engine to the Search Engine: Two Centuries of Innovators*. Now an American citizen, he was knighted for his services to journalism as editor of *The Sunday Times* and *Times of London*.

**Orville and Wilbur Wright**
(fathers of flight)

**Robert Fulton**
(made steamboats pay)

**Wright Brothers**

**Leo Hendrik Baekeland**
(his formula became plastic)

**Charles Goodyear**
(solved mystery of vulcanized rubber)

**Goodyear**

**Wright Brothers**

**Herbert Boyer and Robert Swanson**
(Genentech, created biotech)

**Edwin Drake**
(discovered oil in Pennsylvania)

**Boyer and Swanson**

**Boyer and Swanson**

**Ted Turner**
(CNN, 24-hour electronic news cycle)

**Walt Disney**
(built an empire around a mouse)

**Ted Turner**

**Boyer and Swanson**

**Raymond Damadian**
(MRI scanner)

**Ida Rosenthal**
(created the Maidenform bra business)

**Damadian**

**Levi Strauss**
(durable clothes for the working man)

**Isaac Singer**
(sewing machines, first multinational)

**Singer**

**Damadian**

**Larry Page and Sergey Brin**
(the Google omnivore)

**Elisha Otis**
(a safe elevator)

**Page and Brin**

**Thomas Edison**
(made science serve innovation)

**Sam Colt**
(exquisite firearms, celebrity marketing)

**Edison**

**Edison**

**Edison**

**Boyer and Swanson**

**THE WINNER**

**Herbert Boyer and Robert Swanson**
(Genentech, created biotech)

VS

**Leo Baekeland vs. Charles Goodyear**
Baekeland gave us the first man-made plastic. Some think we'd have been better off without out it but look around at its multiple uses and the example of what chemistry could do. But you could not get through a day without Goodyear's vulcanized rubber. Tires, trainers, floor tiles, tennis and golf balls, life jackets – and condoms – are obvious; insulating seals and gaskets and the rubber in electronic instruments are unseen but just as vital.

**Walt Disney vs. Ted Turner**
Walt Disney created a worldwide entertainment empire that has brought joy to millions and still does. Ted Turner beat all naysayers – who've since copied him – to bring us CNN television news when we want it. Turner advances because at the end of a Disney show we need to leave fantasy and return to the real world.

**Damadian vs. Rosenthal**
Damadian built the first MRI machine, revealing what lay beneath the skin. Today his stand-up MRI machine spares patients the claustrophobia of being treated like a cigar, and also reveals the effects of weight-bearing, unlike the common lie-down MRI. His Fonar company in Long Island also innovated a mobile MRI scanner. But it takes more than brilliance to beat Edison, who not only invented the incandescent bulb but also the first power station and inspirations that led to recorded music and the movies.

**Edison vs. Page and Brin**
The Google boys are not used to defeat at the hands of superior technological prowess. But Edison, holder of the most U.S. patents, also invented invention at his New Jersey labs, the forerunner of all specialized R&D departments. No him, no them.

WE LIVE IN A WORLD CREATED BY INNOVATORS. Invention and scientific discovery may be the start, but innovators do more. They take a brain wave and bring it to the bustle of the marketplace – the hard part, Thomas Edison said – so all may benefit. American innovators gave us the steamboat and air travel, personal computers and the uplift brassiere, MRI scanners and stereo FM, and container shipping, which initiated globalization. To win among these 32 great innovators of the last 200 years, your innovation must go on and on and on.

# Kildall

**Kildall vs. Armstrong**
Gary Kildall wins for his sheer original genius in devising an operating system for the personal computer that would enable any software to run on, well, any hardware. He wrote code like Mozart wrote concertos (and like Mozart, died young, at 52). With Tom Rolander he also created the CD-ROM. Though Microsoft marketed Kildall's innovations, the leap he made trumps even Armstrong.

**Boyer and Swanson vs. Kildall**
A perverse choice over Edison, Jobs, or Page and Brin? Not really. Boyer and Swanson put up $500 apiece in 1976 to explore whether bacteria could be tricked into making a human protein. Boyer's scientific genius in genetic engineering and Swanson's business acumen led to Genentech – and the biotech industry. They opened a new chapter in the fight against human disease and we are still reading it.

**Farnsworth vs. Armstrong**
Philo T. Farnsworth invented television (though others tried to claim the credit), the most democratizing piece of technology in the last half of the 20th century. But he's edged out by Armstrong, whose original discoveries and innovations in the transmission of sound – think AM and FM radio and the foundation of your cell phone – resonate every time we hear a clear sound over the air.

- Kildall
  - Kildall
    - Kildall
      - **Thomas Watson, Jr.** (IBM, the model corporation,)
      - **Gary Kildall** (the father of PC software)
    - McLean
      - **Georges Doriot** (venture capital pioneer)
      - **Malcom Mclean** (innovator of the shipping container)
  - Giannini
    - Insull
      - **Samuel Insull** (brought cheap electricity into all homes)
      - **Samuel F. B. Morse** (invented telegraph, speedy communication)
    - Giannini
      - **Cyrus McCormick** (mechanical reaper, easy credit system)
      - **A. P. Giannini** (first banker for the masses, founder, Bank of America)
- Armstrong
  - Farnsworth
    - Gates
      - **George Eastman** (Kodak, "You press the button. We do the rest.")
      - **Bill Gates** (Microsoft, a computer on every desk)
    - Farnsworth
      - **Philo T. Farnsworth** (electronic television)
      - **Joan Ganz Cooney.** (*Sesame Street,* adult TV for kids)
  - Armstrong
    - Armstrong
      - **Edwin Armstrong** (father of modern radio, and every other clear transmitted sound)
      - **Steve Jobs** (Apple, beautiful user-friendly gadgets that fill our unknown needs)
    - Ford
      - **Juan Trippe** (PanAm, brought world into jet age)
      - **Henry Ford** (maker of "The People's Car," assembly line pioneer)

# Supreme Court Decisions

**By Adam Liptak**

Adam Liptak covers the Supreme Court for the *New York Times*.

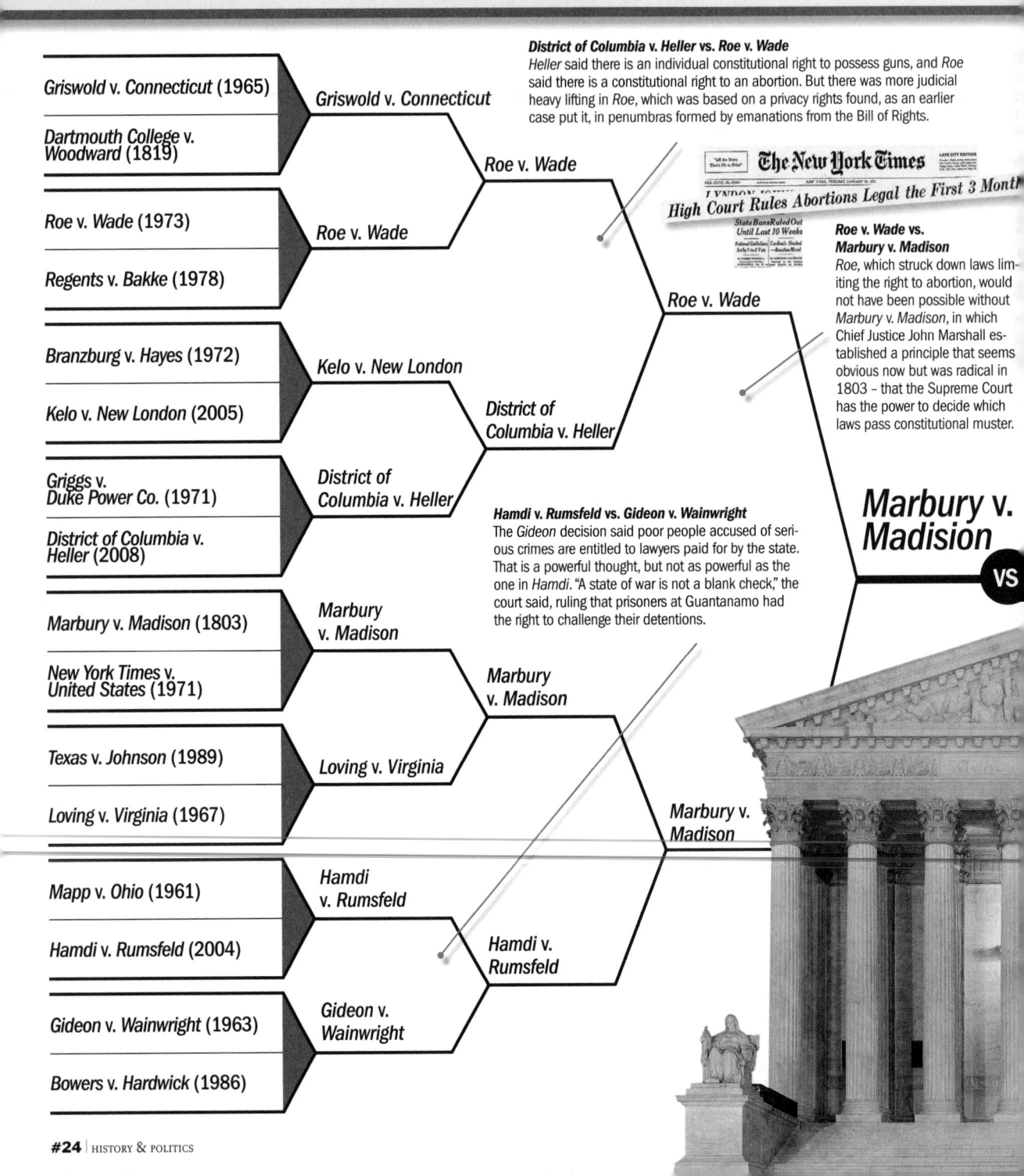

SOME OF THE MOST FAMOUS Supreme Court cases are ones in which the Court got it preposterously wrong, like *Dred Scott,* which said black people could be property but not citizens, or *Korematsu*, which upheld the internment of 120,000 Americans of Japanese descent in detention camps during World War II. Those cases don't get into this bracket. But unpopularity does not disqualify cases if their reasoning has lasting force or if the rulings themselves altered the social structure. It's all about impact.

***Brown* v. *Board* vs. *Marbury* v. *Madison***
The Supreme Court's unanimous decision in *Brown*, which said that segregating students by race in public schools was constitutionally intolerable, remains the Court's undisputed triumph. Some quarrel with its reasoning and with the studies on which it relied. No one doubts its moral power.

**THE WINNER**

***Brown* v. *Board of Ed.***
(1954)

***Baker* v. *Carr* vs. *Bush* v. *Gore***
*Baker v. Carr*, which Chief Justice Earl Warren called "the most vital decision" of his tenure, helped establish the principle of "one person, one vote." *Bush v. Gore* established the principle of "five justices, one election" and then cautioned that the decision was "limited to the present circumstances" – a ticket good for one ride only.

- *Brown v. Board of Ed.*
  - *Brown v. Board of Ed.*
    - *Brown v. Board of Ed.*
      - *Furman v. Georgia* (1972)
      - *Brown v. Board of Ed.* (1954)
    - *Grutter v. Bollinger*
      - *Wickard v. Filburn* (1942)
      - *Grutter v. Bollinger* (2003)
  - *Baker v. Carr*
    - *Baker v. Carr*
      - *Baker v. Carr* (1962)
      - *Bush v. Gore* (2000)
    - *Buckley v. Valeo*
      - *Buckley v. Valeo* (1976)
      - *United States v. Carolene Products* (1938)
- *Youngstown v. Sawyer*
  - *Miranda v. Arizona*
    - *Lawrence v. Texas*
      - *Branzburg v. Hayes* (1972)
      - *Lawrence v. Texas* (2003)
    - *Miranda v. Arizona*
      - *Miranda v. Arizona* (1966)
      - *Brandenburg v. Ohio* (1969)
  - *Youngstown v. Sawyer*
    - *Youngstown v. Sawyer*
      - *McCulloch v. Maryland* (1819)
      - *Youngstown Sheet & Tube Co. v. Sawyer* (1952)
    - *New York Times v. Sullivan*
      - *McConnell v. Federal Election Commission* (2003)
      - *New York Times v. Sullivan* (1964)

# Presidential Pardons

**By P.S. Ruckman, Jr.**

P.S. Ruckman, Jr. is the editor of the Pardon Power blog. His research on pardons appears in several social science journals and he is the author of the forthcoming book *Pardon Me, Mr. President: Adventures in Crime, Politics and Mercy.*

PROFESSIONAL & WHITE-COLLAR CRIMINAL REGIONAL

**Jean LaFitte and the Baratarian Pirates** (1815) Helped Andy Jackson in the Battle of New Orleans

**George Steinbrenner** (1989) Made illegal campaign contributions to Nixon, struggled with accepting his guilt

**Henry Starr** (1903) Robbed many banks; started on horses, moved up to automobiles

**Gerald Chapman** (1925) "Super Bandit" became a folk hero. Commutation cleared way for his execution

**Charles W. Morse** (1912) Wall Street tycoon who was responsible for financial panic of 1907

**Marc Rich** (2001) Fugitive millionaire whose former wife was a major donor to president and Mrs. Clinton

**William H. Harlan** (1911, 1913) Nephew of a Supreme Court justice guilty of peonage

**Angelo De Carlo** (1972) Methodical gangland executioner who claimed his pardon was secured by Frank Sinatra

HIGH POLITICS REGIONAL

**Richard Nixon** (1974) After his resignation, he was pardoned for crimes he "may have" committed

**George W. Parr** (1946) Stuffed ballot box 13 to ensure Senate victory for Lyndon Johnson

**Iran Contra** (1992) Secretary of Defense and five others pardoned on Christmas Eve for their "patriotism"

**Whiskey Ringers** (1876, 1877) Avery and McDonald were President Grant's friends and key players in fraud scheme

**Jimmy Hoffa** (1971) Teamsters president whose conditional commutation probably violated the Bill of Rights

**Eugene Debs** (1921) Fiery socialist called a "traitor" by Woodrow Wilson, but pardoned by Harding for Christmas

**Thomas Callender** (1801) Newspaperman funded by Thomas Jefferson to chew on John Adams

**Justus Erik Bollman** (1807) Rejected Jefferson's blank pardon on stand during Aaron Burr conspiracy trial

George Steinbrenner

Gerald Chapman

Charles W. Morse

William H. Harlan

Richard Nixon

Iran Contra

Jimmy Hoffa

Justus Erik Bollman

Gerald Chapman

Charles W. Morse

Richard Nixon

Jimmy Hoffa

Charles W. Morse

Richard Nixon

**Steinbrenner vs. Chapman**
Chapman got a 25-year sentence for robbery, escaped, and then murdered a Connecticut policeman. President Coolidge commuted his 25-year federal sentence to time served so the state could execute him. Chapman tried to reject the unrequested act of "mercy," but the courts forced it on him. Some would say that Steinbrenner's crime wasn't that harsh and that his contributions were loose change compared to Chapman's bank scores!

**Morse vs. Rich**
The Rich pardon by President Clinton was hardly unique. He was wealthy, a fugitive, and a campaign donor. But when lobbying on Morse's behalf failed, he drank a concoction to simulate a fatal condition, prompting a "death bed pardon." He then recovered and outlived Taft, the president who pardoned him. It was later discovered that Taft's attorney general was given piles of cash to support the pardon.

**Charles W. Morse**

VS

**Nixon vs. Morse**
Nixon will always be *the* pardon for many, especially journalists with deadlines. But the pardon raised no constitutional issues, subsequent investigations uncovered nothing shady, and even critics came to praise President Ford's decision as necessary to heal a Watergate-fatigued country. Morse generated just as many headlines, and there is no positive angle to his pardon.

THE POWER TO GRANT PARDONS is probably the most imperial power that a president wields. It is shrouded in secrecy, virtually without limit, and suspiciously arbitrary in an age when so much of the justice system is meticulously regulated by statutes and the requirements of the due process clause. Every generation of Americans has experienced its seemingly "unforgettable" pardon(s), but the most notable have involved notorious crimes and criminals., celebrities, constitutional questions, and political hijinks.

THE WINNER

**FALN**
(1999)
Unrepentant Puerto Rican terrorists who planted 120 bombs causing property damage, deaths, and injury

**FALN vs. Morse**
In an age of anxiety about victims' rights and heightened concern about terrorism, the deputy attorney general recommended clemency for FALN terrorists over the objections of a world of law enforcement officials and without reference to the opinions of the victims of the group's violent acts. Morse was bizarre, but President Clinton's FALN pardons were flabbergasting.

**Lincoln Conspirators vs. Schick**
Schick's case was ugly. But the military tribunal recommended mercy for Lincoln conspirator Mary Surratt. President Andrew Johnson (who reviewed and approved sentences) said he was not informed of the ruling. The judge advocate general said Johnson was informed. Against all expectations, Surratt was hanged. Additional late-term pardons for the conspirators suggest that Johnson may not have lied.

- FALN
  - Quartet of Terror
    - Quartet of Terror
      - **Quartet of Terror** (1979) Puerto Rican Nationalists filled House of Representatives with bullets. Hit 5 congressmen
      - **Oscar Collazo** (1952, 1979) Attempted to assassinate Harry Truman and never bothered to apologize for it
    - Lupo the Wolf
      - **Lupo the Wolf** (1921) Leader of the "Black Hand" and CEO of the "Murder Stable" in New York City
      - **Robert Stroud** (1920) Hollywood double murderer turned lovable "Birdman," but prison officials say he "hated people."
  - FALN
    - FALN
      - **FALN** (1999) Unrepentant Puerto Rican terrorists who planted 120 bombs causing property damage, deaths, and injury
      - **Capt. William Van Schaick** (1912) Steered 1,000-plus women and children to fiery death in East River
    - Thomas M.C. Bram
      - **Thomas M.C. Bram** (1919) Twice convicted for a triple ax murder but successful in business
      - **Alexander Holmes** (1842) Sailor overly skilled/enthusiastic at tossing passengers into sea during a storm
- Lincoln Conspirators
  - Lincoln Conspirators
    - Lincoln Conspirators
      - **Lincoln Conspirators** (1869) Mudd, Spangler, and Arnold perhaps pardoned because Mary Surratt was hanged
      - **Gen. Fitz John Porter** (1882) Blamed for Union defeat at Bull Run, his case divided political elites for 20 years
    - Nazi U-Boaters
      - **Nazi U-Boaters** Dasch, Burger, et.al. successfully landed on the East Coast with money, weaponry, and plans to terrorize
      - **Lt. Henry Flipper** (1999) First African American graduate of West Point, who was dead at the time of his pardon
  - Sgt. Maurice Schick
    - Sgt. Maurice Schick
      - **Adm. Bowman H. McCalla** (1900) Hero and drinker who had a thing for abusing imprisoned sailors
      - **Sgt. Maurice Schick** (1960, 1977) Sexually assaulted and suffocated an 8-year-old
    - Sgt. John A. Mason
      - **Sgt. John A. Mason** (1883) Attempted to kill Charles Guiteau, who had assassinated President Garfield
      - **Lt. Leon Gilbert** (1950) Got the death penalty for refusing to obey order to fall back during Korean War

FOUR-STAR BLOOD AND VIOLENCE REGIONAL

MILITARY MERCY REGIONAL

# Military Heroes

**By Richard Goldstein**

Richard Goldstein is the author of *America at D-Day* and *Desperate Hours: The Epic Rescue of the Andrea Doria.*

REVOLUTIONARY WAR REGIONAL

**George Washington** Commander-in-chief of Continental Army; shunned monarchial trappings as president

**Henry Knox** Chief artillery officer of Washington's army, first secretary of state

**Washington**

**John Paul Jones** Naval commander, refused to surrender: "I have not yet begun to fight"

**Nathan Hale** Continental Army officer, hanged by British: "I regret that I have but one life to lose for my country."

**Jones**

**Washington**

**George Rogers Clark** Forced British to cede Northwest Territory

**Nathanael Greene** Quartermaster at Valley Forge

**Greene**

**Greene**

**Francis Marion** Father of guerilla warfare in South, nicknamed "The Swamp Fox"

**Hugh Mercer** Physician and commander who, unhorsed in battle, fought with saber unto death

**Marion**

**Washington vs. Knox**
Knox oversaw the American artillery units in the Revolutionary War, played a role in erecting the winter forts at Valley Forge, and became the first Secretary of War. But as the commander of the Continental Army and the first commander-in-chief as president, Washington is pre-eminent.

CIVIL WAR REGIONAL

**Ulysses S. Grant** Lincoln's most effective general in besting Robert E. Lee

**Joshua Lawrence Chamberlain** Received Medal of Honor for gallantry at Gettysburg

**Grant**

**Grant**

**Stonewall Jackson** Confederate general who got sobriquet while leading rebels at first Battle of Bull Run

**Robert Gould Shaw** Abolitionist, commanded all-black 54th Massachusetts Volunteer Infantry

**Shaw**

**Grant**

**Robert E. Lee** Confederate commander, known for tactical brilliance against superior Union manpower

**Philip Kearny** Fearless horseman and leader of Union forces in Peninsula campaign

**Lee**

**Lee**

**P.G.T. Beauregard** Confederate commander in upset victory at first Battle of Bull Run

**Philip H. Sheridan** Leader of Union cavalry in major victories in Shenandoah Valley

**Sheridan**

**Grant vs. Lee**
In Grant, Lincoln finally got a general who would vigorously take the war to the Confederacy. Commanding forces inferior to the Union in manpower, Lee won major battles. Grant fought for the survival of America while Lee fought for states' rights and slavery. Grant was on the right side of history.

THE WINNER

**George Washington**

Commander-in-chief of Continental Army; shunned monarchial trappings as president

VS

**Washington vs. Doss**
It's the Father of Our Country vs. a humble soldier whose bravery, while forsaking the act of killing, represented the best in America's citizen soldiers. Two exceedingly worthy men, but Washington stands supreme.

MEDAL OF HONOR RECIPIENTS invariably reject the tag of "heroes," saying that the real American heroes never come home from the wars they fought. Still, battlefield heroes acted "above and beyond the call of duty," giving their lives without regard to their own safety to protect their comrades. Men who refuted the common wisdom that they would not fight because of their race or forefathers are also heroes. So are those who have led in battle but never forgot the welfare of their soldiers and sailors.

**Doss**

**Buckles vs. Doss**
Buckles drove an Army ambulance in France during World War I; he never served in combat. But he came to represent a generation of embattled Americans as the last surviving doughboy. Doss, an unarmed medic, saved dozens of soldiers under heavy fire in the battle for Okinawa in World War II and received the Medal of Honor.

**Eisenhower vs. MacArthur**
Eisenhower's ability to work with the British as Supreme Allied Commander and his command of the D-Day invasion contrasts with MacArthur's self-glorification in the Pacific campaign. As president, Eisenhower was ahead of his times in warning against the military-industrial complex. Ike gets the nod.

- Buckles
  - Buckles
    - York
      - **Alvin York** Denied conscientious objector status, received Medal of Honor for killing 20-plus Germans
      - **John J. Pershing** Commander of American Expeditionary Force
    - Buckles
      - **Hobey Baker** Amateur hockey star led fighter squadron in France, killed in training crash
      - **Frank Buckles** Ambulance driver in France who became the last surviving doughboy
  - Rickenbacker
    - Whittlesey
      - **The Unknown Soldier** Interred at Arlington in 1921, first of Unknowns representing nation's dead
      - **Charles W. Whittlesey** Won Medal of Honor for leading cut-off unit in Meuse-Argonne campaign
    - Rickenbacker
      - **Eddie Rickenbacker** Fighter pilot who shot down record 26 German planes
      - **Billy Mitchell** Commander of American air combat units in France, father of Army Air Forces
- Doss
  - Doss
    - Doss
      - **Jimmy Doolittle** Led storied air raid on Japan in 1942, thrilling stateside after Pearl Harbor
      - **Desmond Doss** Seventh-day Adventist refused to carry weapon but, as medic, saved dozens at Okinawa
    - Davis
      - **Daniel Inouye** Lost arm fighting with famed Japanese-American unit in Italy; belated Medal of Honor recipient
      - **Benjamin O. Davis, Jr.** Commander of Tuskegee Airmen, broke racial barriers with brilliant combat record
  - Eisenhower
    - Eisenhower
      - **Dwight D. Eisenhower** As general, oversaw D-Day invasion; as president, warned of military-industrial complex
      - **Vernon Baker** Heroics in Italy earned him Medal of Honor
    - MacArthur
      - **The Sullivan Brothers** Five sailors who died together in sinking of light cruiser *Juneau* in the Pacific
      - **Douglas MacArthur** Vowed "I shall return" after Philippines defeat; then returned and recaptured it

WORLD WAR I REGIONAL

WORLD WAR II REGIONAL

# Enduring One-Liners

**By Jan Van Meter**

Jan Van Meter has had many jobs, four careers, but only one retirement, which gave him the time to research and write *Tippecanoe and Tyler Too: Famous Slogans and Catchphrases in American History.*

**"Wait 'til next year"** 1941 *Brooklyn Eagle* headline to comfort Dodgers fans after World Series loss to Yankees

**"I'd rather be right than be president"** Perennially unsuccessful candidate Henry Clay's 1839 statement was not sour grapes

**"Lafayette, we are here"** Col. Charles Stanton, at Lafayette's rave in Paris in 1917

**"Remember the *Maine*"** Hearst's *New York Journal* headline promoting Spanish-American War in 1898

**"Three yards and a cloud of dust"** Ohio State football coach Woody Hayes's 1957 defense of offensive philosophy

**"Mr. Gorbachev, tear down this wall"** Ronald Reagan's forceful words at Berlin Wall in 1987, hastened Cold War's end

**"These are the times that try men's souls"** Thomas Paine's words in darkest days of 1776

**"Frankly my dear, I don't give a damn"** Rhett Butler's patience with Scarlett finally ran out

**"We stand at Armageddon and we battle for the Lord"** Teddy Roosevelt's last stand in unsuccessful bid for presidency

**"Nice guys finish last"** Dodgers manager Leo Durocher's success formula in 1947

**"Duck and cover"** Civil defense's answer to the nuclear threat in 1951

**"Damn the torpedoes, full speed ahead"** Union Admiral David Farragut at Mobile Bay in 1864

**"The only thing we have to fear is fear itself"** Franklin Delano Roosevelt's reassurance at 1933 Inaugural

**"Float like a butterfly, sting like a bee"** Cassius Clay's plan to beat Sonny Liston for heavyweight title in 1964

**"I only regret that I have but one life to lose for my country"** Nathan Hale's reported last words on the gallows, in 1776

**"Make the world safe for democracy"** President Woodrow Wilson's argument for U.S. entry into World War I

"Wait 'til next year"

"Lafayette"

"Tear down this wall"

"These are the times"

"Nice guys"

"Damn the torpedoes"

"fear itself"

"one life to lose"

"Wait 'til next year"

"These are the times"

"Nice guys"

"fear itself"

"These are the times"

"fear itself"

**"Wait 'til next year" vs. "I'd rather be right than be president"**
Clay's words and deeds should have been longer remembered as illustrative of his role as one of America's greatest statesmen. More durable is the endless and patient optimism of Brooklyn Dodger fans that captures the eternal and often-unrewarded spirit of loyal fans everywhere – and reflects an important cultural value.

**"These are the times" vs. "I have a dream"**
Both summon memories of the nation's greatest struggles: Paine's for victory over the world's greatest military power and Dr. King's for victory in the last battle of the Civil War – over racism. King's indelible words resound beyond the battles over segregation and typify American optimism in the face of intractable wrongs.

**"These are the times" vs. "Fear itself"**
In a contest between masters of oratory, FDR's words are lasting but Tom Paine's eloquent and poetic speech, read to all Revolutionary troops in their darkest hours, is a call to action and perseverance. Paine's words were central to the greatest of American achievements – independence.

**"Nice guys" vs. "Fear itself"**
Durocher's sentiment about "nice guys," the type of personality he certainly was not, quickly moved beyond baseball to symbolize our deep-seated convictions about the cost of success. But FDR's words of comfort – a palliative to citizens who had legitimate reasons to fear -- continue to reassure us as the country faces yet another crisis.

**"These are the times"**

VS

THAT SLOGANS AND CATCHPHRASES are part of the American character was recognized nearly a century ago, long after they had begun to accumulate. Whether they have sprung to life in battles, speeches, boxing rings, campaigns, or films, they capture historical moments, national ideals, and pervasive attitudes. Still others endure for trivial reasons. But the best survive because what they were meant to convey continues to be important to the nation.

**"No taxation" vs. "Say it ain't so, Joe"**
The pre-Revolutionary War "no taxation" slogan is deeply embedded in our culture since no one likes paying taxes. The newsboy's plea to Shoeless Joe Jackson survives since it catches the feeling of betrayed ideals common to our lives. "Joe" wins because every time someone named Joe disappoints us, the phrase is trotted out once more.

THE WINNER

## "I have a dream"

r. Martin Luther King, Jr.'s words at 1963 March on Washington

- "I have a dream"
  - "Say it ain't so"
    - "No taxation"
      - **"No taxation without representation"** Henry Otis's pre-Independence exhortation in 1773
      - **"Give 'em hell, Harry"** Campaign cry during Harry S. Truman's come-from-behind victory in 1948 presidential election
    - "Say it ain't so"
      - **"Ich bin ein Berliner"** President John F. Kennedy at the Berlin Wall in 1963
      - **"Say it ain't so, Joe"** Young fan to Shoeless Joe Jackson about 1919 World Series fix scandal
  - "I have a dream"
    - "Give me liberty"
      - **"Give me liberty or give me death"** From Patrick Henry's greatest speech, in 1775
      - **"I shall return"** Forced to leave besieged troops in 1942, Gen. Douglas MacArthur kept his promise
    - "I have a dream"
      - **"Yes, Virginia, there is a Santa Claus"** *New York Sun*'s response to Virginia O'Hanlon's 1897 question
      - **"I have a dream"** Dr. Martin Luther King, Jr.'s words at 1963 March on Washington
- "Speak softly"
  - "A house divided"
    - "Hit 'em where they ain't"
      - **"Hit 'em where they ain't"** Major leaguer Wee Willie Keeler's hitting secret
      - **"Go West, young man"** *New York Tribune* editor Horace Greeley's success tip in 1850s
    - "A house divided"
      - **"Tippecanoe and Tyler too"** Rhyming slogan helped elect William Henry Harrison president in 1840; he lasted a month
      - **"A house divided against itself cannot stand"** Words from1858 that brought Abraham Lincoln national renown
  - "Speak softly"
    - "Speak softly"
      - **"Speak softly and carry a big stick"** Teddy Roosevelt's favorite proverb, first noticed in 1901
      - **"Prosperity is just around the corner"** Herbert Hoover didn't really say this in 1930, but the Great Depression went on
    - "Don't fire"
      - **"Don't fire 'til you see the whites of their eyes"** American troop strategy in 1775 on Breed's Hill shocked British
      - **"Remember the Alamo"** Battle cry as Sam Houston's men attacked Santa Ana's army in 1836

# Financial Villains

**By Joe Nocera**

Joe Nocera, the "Talking Business" columnist for the *New York Times,* is the author of *Good Guys and Bad Guys: Behind the Scenes with the Saints and Scoundrels of American Business (and Everything in Between)* and *A Piece of the Action: How the Middle Class Joined the Money Class.*

**Robert Vesco**
accused swindler, long-time fugitive

**Martha Stewart**
home doyenne convicted of lying to feds on stock sale

**Walter Forbes**
Cendant chairman

**Barry Minkow**
ZZZZ Best con man

**Richard Scrushy**
HealthSouth CEO

**William McGuire**
United Health CEO, options backdater

**Conrad Black**
Hollinger International CEO

**Crazy Eddie Antar**
Crazy Eddie fugitive

**Kenneth Lay**
Enron CEO

**John Thain**
chief executive of Merrill Lynch

**Charles Mitchell**
president, First National City Bank

**Charles Ponzi**
inventor of eponymous scheme

**Charles Keating**
Lincoln Savings & Loan

**Mark Whitacre**
Archer Daniels Midland

**Bernard Cornfeld**
Investors Overseas Services, stock promotion

**Ivan Boesky**
convicted of insider trading

Vesco | Minkow | Scrushy | Antar | Lay | Ponzi | Keating | Boesky

Vesco | Scrushy | Ponzi | Boesky

Vesco | Ponzi

PONZI GOES TO JAIL; RIVAL OPERATORS ARE ALSO TAKEN

Four Officers of Old Colony Foreign Exchange Company Held on Larceny Charge.

CROWD STORMS OFFICES

Forty Additional Counts Placed Against "the Wizard," Who Fears for Life.

Vesco role detailed

NEW YORK (AP) — A government witness testified Thursday that bears after fugitive Robert Vesco made a secret $200,000 cash contribution to President Nixon's re-election campaign, then-Atty. Gen. John N. Mitchell set up a "very productive" meeting between Vesco's lawyer and the head of the Securities and Exchange Commission.

Vesco aide Harry Sears testified in United States

**Vesco vs. Ponzi**
After bilking investors out of $200 million in the early 1970s, Vesco spent the rest of his life on the lam, dying in Cuba in 2008. He was a small-timer compared to the great Charles Ponzi, who created a frenzy in Boston in the 1920s with his promises of 50 percent returns – and an even bigger frenzy when his scheme collapsed and his hapless investors lost everything.

THE WINNER

**Charles Ponzi**
inventor of eponymous scheme

VS

Officials: $50B lost in fraud

Securities industry leader Bernard Madoff charged

By Matt Krantz
USA TODAY

Federal authorities have charged a Wall Street veteran with running a Ponzi scheme that prosecutors allege lost a staggering $50 billion.

Bernard Madoff, founder of Bernard L. Madoff Investment Securities, 70, was charged on Thursday by the Manhattan U.S. Attorney's office and the Securities and Exchange Commission with securities fraud. The charge comes a day after the complaint says Madoff told some high-level employees that

**Madoff vs. Ponzi**
For decades Madoff took money from sophisticated investors worldwide, promising sure and steady returns. So sure and steady, in fact, that they turned out to be fictitious. He confessed in 2008 that as much as $50 billion (later, $65 billion) may have gone up in smoke, making him the greatest fraudster of all time. Yet what did he call his scheme when he 'fessed up? A Ponzi scheme. Game, set, match, Ponzi.

YOU CAN'T HAVE CAPITALISM WITHOUT CROOKS, or at least without the occasional harmless villainy. Okay, maybe it's not so harmless, not when investors are led astray, when people are snookered out of their savings, and when traders try to hide multi-billion dollar losses from their unsuspecting bosses, the eventual discovery of which can bring down even the mightiest of giant institutions. But the world would be a far less colorful place without financial schemers trying to put one over on us.

**Nicholas vs. Milken**
Yes, we know: Milken is still portrayed as the biggest scoundrel of the 1980s, but the crimes he was convicted of were small potatoes – and his subsequent efforts to cure prostate cancer have given him a redemptive glow. Nicholas was indicted in 2008 for backdating options and allegedly used cocaine, spiked clients' drinks with Ecstasy, and built a secret sex den under his house (allegations he denies). Add sex to money and you advance.


Broadcom executive is charged with fraud

E. Scott Reckard and Kim Christensen
Los Angeles Times

LOS ANGELES — A federal grand jury has indicted Henry T. Nicholas III on fraud charges, according to documents unsealed Thursday that also accuse the Orange County billionaire of supplying customers with prostitutes and drugs and slipping Ecstasy into the drinks of unwitting tech-

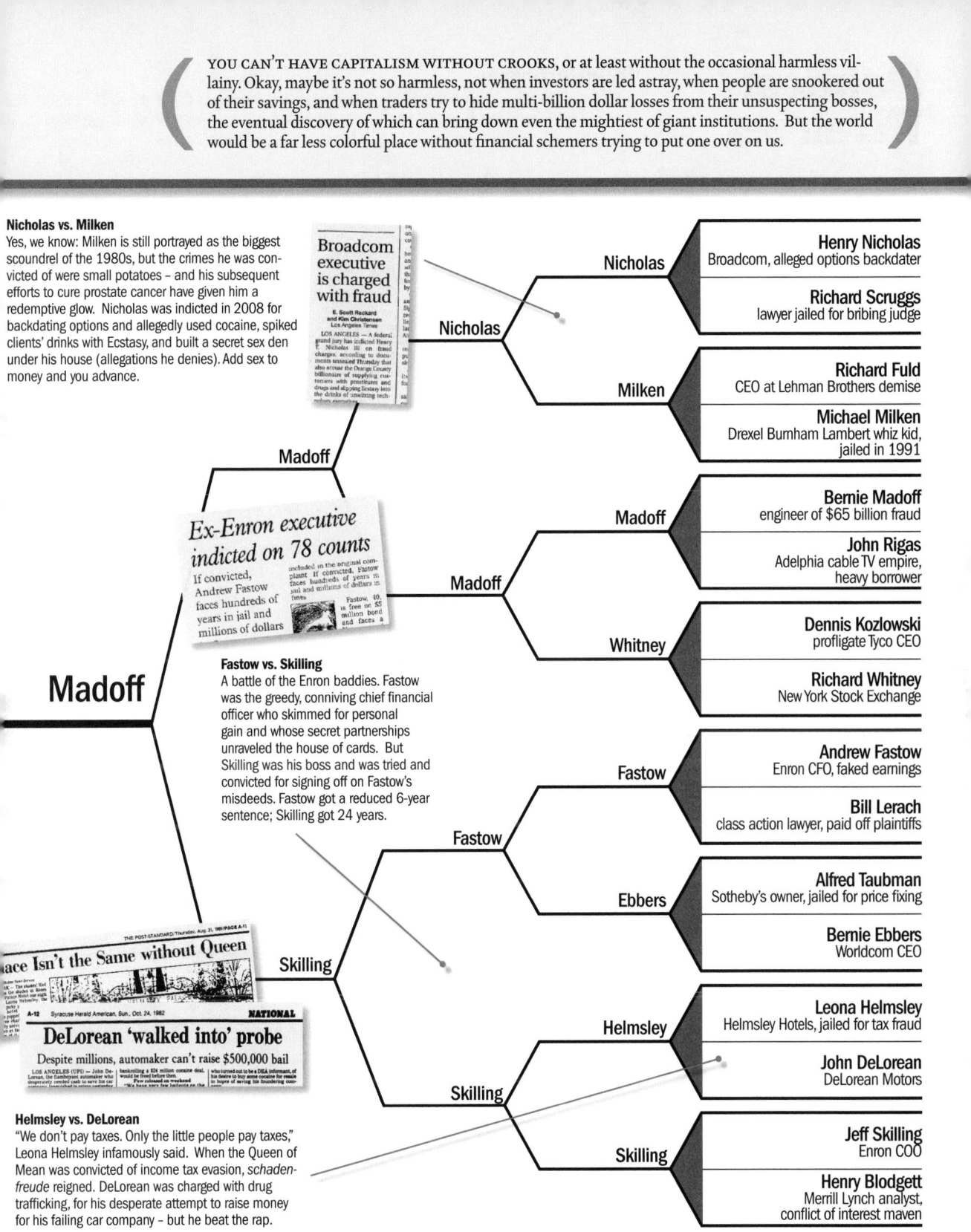


Ex-Enron executive indicted on 78 counts

If convicted, Andrew Fastow faces hundreds of years in jail and millions of dollars

included in the original complaint. If convicted, Fastow faces hundreds of years in jail and millions of dollars in fines.

Fastow, 40, is free on $5 million bond and faces a

**Fastow vs. Skilling**
A battle of the Enron baddies. Fastow was the greedy, conniving chief financial officer who skimmed for personal gain and whose secret partnerships unraveled the house of cards. But Skilling was his boss and was tried and convicted for signing off on Fastow's misdeeds. Fastow got a reduced 6-year sentence; Skilling got 24 years.

THE POST-STANDARD/Thursday, Aug. 31, 1961/PAGE A-11

ace Isn't the Same without Queen

A-12 Syracuse Herald American, Sun., Oct. 24, 1982 NATIONAL

DeLorean 'walked into' probe

Despite millions, automaker can't raise $500,000 bail

LOS ANGELES (UPI) — John DeLorean, the flamboyant automaker who desperately needed cash to save his car company, [illegible] bankrolling a $24 million cocaine deal, would be freed before then.

He was released on weekend.

"We have very few bailouts on the [illegible] who turned out to be a DEA informant, of his desire to buy some cocaine for resale in hopes of saving his floundering company.

**Helmsley vs. DeLorean**
"We don't pay taxes. Only the little people pay taxes," Leona Helmsley infamously said. When the Queen of Mean was convicted of income tax evasion, *schadenfreude* reigned. DeLorean was charged with drug trafficking, for his desperate attempt to raise money for his failing car company – but he beat the rap.

# Political Rivalries

**By Adam Clymer**

Adam Clymer is the former chief Washington correspondent of the *New York Times*, author of *Edward M. Kennedy: A Biography* (1999) and *Drawing the Line at the Big Ditch: The Panama Canal Treaties and the Rise of the Right* (2008; and in the opinion of George W. Bush and Dick Cheney, "major league."

Woodrow Wilson vs. Henry Cabot Lodge

Franklin D. Roosevelt vs. Alfred E. Smith

William McKinley vs. William Jennings Bryan

George W. Bush vs. John McCain

Thomas Jefferson vs. John Adams

Grover Cleveland vs. Benjamin Harrison

Dwight Eisenhower vs. Joseph McCarthy

Condoleezza Rice vs. Dick Cheney

Barry Goldwater vs. Nelson Rockefeller

James Michael Curley vs. John F. (Honey Fitz) Fitzgerald

Alexander Hamilton vs. Aaron Burr

Frank Lautenberg vs. Robert Torricelli

Lyndon B. Johnson vs. Robert F. Kennedy

William M. (Boss) Tweed vs. Samuel Tilden

Theodore Roosevelt vs. William Howard Taft

Ronald Reagan vs. Gerald Ford

Wilson vs. Lodge

McKinley vs. Bryan

Jefferson vs. Adams

Eisenhower vs. McCarthy

Goldwater vs. Rockefeller

Hamilton vs. Burr

LBJ vs. RFK

Roosevelt vs. Taft

Wilson vs. Lodge

Jefferson vs. Adams

Hamilton vs. Burr

LBJ vs. RFK

Wilson vs. Lodge

LBJ vs. RFK

**Wilson-Lodge vs. Jackson-Clay**
In the final round, the long-simmering feud between Senator Lodge and President Wilson killed Americans joining the League of Nations. Their hatred made compromise impossible and shaped the nation's isolationist role in the world for two decisive decades, creating a more consequential rivalry than disputes over banks, tariffs, and roads.

THE WINNER

## Woodrow Wilson vs. Henry Cabot Lodge

VS

**Hamilton-Burr vs. LBJ-RFK**
Both rivalries were marked by years of mounting distrust. Burr killed Hamilton in a duel, a device not available to Johnson and Kennedy, whose ultimate dispute was over the raging Vietnam War while they fought over the presidency. Burr and Hamilton were past their heights of power when they dueled.

THE BEST POLITICAL RIVALRIES involve more than personal competition for office. They have far-reaching consequences. They are contests for power: in government, like President Truman vs. General MacArthur; in a political movement, like William F. Buckley's crusade against Robert Welch and his John Birch Society, or best of all, over the future of the nation, like Henry Clay vs. Andrew Jackson. Antipathy approaching hatred, adds luster; see Alexander Hamilton and Aaron Burr. Great rivalries last for years.

**Kennedy-Nixon vs. Buckley-Welch**
Like many famous rivalries, the Kennedy-Nixon feud was more intense on the loser's side, and Nixon carried it on long after Kennedy's death. When Buckley read Welch out of the conservative movement, he assured conservatism a durable respectability untroubled by nut conspiracy theories that could have doomed its electoral prospects.

# Jackson vs. Clay

**Jackson-Clay vs. Truman-MacArthur**
MacArthur challenged Truman's insistence on civilian control of the military, and lost quickly. Years of mutual loathing between Senator Clay and President Jackson had their roots in presidential ambition. It peaked over Clay's speeches denouncing Jackson's antagonism to banks, internal improvements, and tariffs protecting new industries. Jackson prevailed, a historic president defeating the Congress' greatest.

- Jackson vs. Clay
  - Truman vs. MacArthur
    - Truman vs. MacArthur
      - Truman vs. MacArthur
        - Harry Truman vs. Douglas MacArthur
        - Thomas E. Dewey vs. Robert A. Taft
      - Norris vs. Cannon
        - George Norris vs. Joseph Cannon
        - Mario Cuomo vs. Ed Koch
    - Buckley vs. Welch
      - Kennedy vs. Nixon
        - John F. Kennedy vs. Richard Nixon
        - Sam Rayburn vs. Howard (Judge) Smith
      - Buckley vs. Welch
        - William F. Buckley, Jr. vs. Robert Welch
        - Thomas Jefferson vs. Alexander Hamilton
  - Jackson vs. Clay
    - Lincoln vs. Douglas
      - Carter vs. Kennedy
        - Jimmy Carter vs. Ted Kennedy
        - Rudolph Giuliani vs. David Dinkins
      - Lincoln vs. Douglas
        - Abraham Lincoln vs. Stephen Douglas
        - Daniel Webster vs. John C. Calhoun
    - Jackson vs. Clay
      - Obama vs. Clinton
        - Charles Sumner vs. Preston Brooks
        - Barack Obama vs. Hillary Clinton
      - Jackson vs. Clay
        - Bill Clinton vs. Newt Gingrich
        - Andrew Jackson vs. Henry Clay

**Obama-Clinton vs. Sumner-Brooks**
Obama vs. Clinton made up for its brevity and relative civility with the significance of a contest between potential firsts – the first African American or female president. That mattered more than the bloodier and one-sided caning Representative Brooks gave the abolitionist Senator Sumner to punish his anti-slavery speech in 1856.

# Presidential Speeches

**By Curt Smith**

Curt Smith wrote more speeches than anyone for President George H. W. Bush. A member of the prestigious Judson Welliver Society of former presidential speechwriters, he teaches presidential rhetoric and public speaking at the University of Rochester.

LEFT-WING REGIONAL

- George Washington, First Inaugural *(1789)*
- Abraham Lincoln, First Inaugural *(1861)*
- George Washington, Farewell Address *(1796)*
- Thomas Jefferson, First Inaugural *(1801)*
- Abraham Lincoln, Gettysburg Address *(1863)*
- Theodore Roosevelt, "Man with the Muck-rake" *(1906)*
- Abraham Lincoln, Second Inaugural *(1865)*
- Woodrow Wilson, World War I Message *(1917)*
- Franklin D. Roosevelt, Acceptance Speech *(1936)*
- Harry Truman, "Truman Doctrine" *(1947)*
- Franklin D. Roosevelt, World War II Message *(1941)*
- Dwight Eisenhower, Farewell Address *(1961)*
- Franklin D. Roosevelt, "Arsenal of Democracy" *(1940)*
- John F. Kennedy, Cuban Missile Crisis *(1962)*
- Franklin Roosevelt, "Four Freedoms" *(1941)*
- John F. Kennedy, Inaugural Address *(1961)*

Lincoln, First Inaugural

Jefferson, First Inaugural

Lincoln, Gettysburg

Lincoln, Second Inaugural

FDR, Acceptance

FDR, WWII

FDR, "Arsenal"

JFK, Inaugural

Lincoln, First Inaugural

Lincoln, Second Inaugural

FDR, WWII

JFK, Inaugural

Lincoln, Second Inaugural

JFK, Inaugural

**Washington, Farewell vs. Jefferson, First Inaugural**
All presidents crave abiding, enduring language. Washington urged that we spurn "permanent alliances," but Jefferson topped him with his fervent argument to uphold "this government, the world's best hope" and his plea for unity: "We are all Republicans, we are all Federalists."

**Lincoln, Gettysburg vs. Lincoln, Second Inaugural**
Winston Churchill equated English with ammunition. And in this Abe vs. Abe matchup, the Great Emancipator gave Churchill a few lessons. His "government of the people, by the people, for the people" vies with, yet cannot prevail over, the more soaring, spartan prose he used at Gettysburg of "with malice toward none, with charity for all . . . let us strive . . . to bind up the Nation's wounds."

THE WINNER

## Abraham Lincoln, Second Inaugural *(1865)*

VS

**FDR, WWII vs. JFK, Inaugural**
Two Rembrandts of rhetoric at work, delivering lines as memorable as any in presidential oratory. FDR called Japan's attack on Pearl Harbor a "date which will live in infamy," but Kennedy countered brilliantly with, "Ask not what your country can do for you" and "the torch has been passed to a new generation of Americans."

THE MOST SUCCESSFUL PRESIDENTS have employed what Teddy Roosevelt labeled the "bully pulpit": the office's power to persuade. Their best speeches are remembered for social impact, political consequence, and/or rhetorical artistry, which create a form of oral history. Some of the speeches contain only two of the criteria, while others, like Abraham Lincoln's Second Inaugural and Franklin Delano Roosevelt's First Inaugural, contain all three. Memorable pre-presidential speeches such as Lincoln's 1858 "house divided speech" and Barack Obama's 2008 tour de force on race, did not qualify.

**incoln, Second Inaugural vs. DR, First Inaugural**
DR hated vacant "weasel ords" (a term coined by his ousin Teddy), so he must ave admired the clarity of ncoln's simple, frequently eligious address, which soars ith its summons to peace nd healing 41 days before ncoln's violent death. With is, the presidency's most plifting poetry ever, Lincoln efeats FDR's inspirational iagnosis that "the only thing e have to fear is fear itself."

# FDR, First Inaugural

- FDR, First Inaugural
  - FDR, First Inaugural
    - FDR, First Inaugural
      - Franklin Roosevelt, First Inaugural *(1933)*
      - John F. Kennedy, "Ich Bin Ein Berliner" *(1963)*
    - Nixon, "Silent Majority"
      - Lyndon Johnson, Post-JFK Assassination Speech *(1963)*
      - Richard Nixon, "Silent Majority" Speech *(1969)*
  - Nixon, Farewell
    - Nixon, Leningrad
      - Richard Nixon, Leningrad Address on Soviet TV *(1972)*
      - Ronald Reagan, "Evil Empire" Speech *(1983)*
    - Nixon, Farewell
      - Richard Nixon, White House Farewell *(1974)*
      - Gerald Ford, Swearing-in Speech *(1974)*
- Reagan, *Challenger*
  - Reagan, *Challenger*
    - Reagan, *Challenger*
      - Ronald Reagan, *Challenger* Explosion *(1986)*
      - George H. W. Bush, Pearl Harbor *(1991)*
    - Reagan, D-Day
      - Lyndon Johnson, Voting Rights Act *(1965)*
      - Ronald Reagan, D-Day Speech *(1984)*
  - Reagan, Brandenburg
    - Reagan, Brandenburg
      - Ronald Reagan, Brandenburg Gate *(1987)*
      - Bill Clinton, Martin Luther King, Jr., Speech *(1993)*
    - Obama, Inaugural
      - George W. Bush, National Cathedral *(2001)*
      - Barack Obama, Inaugural Address *(2009)*

RIGHT-WING REGIONAL

**Reagan, *Challenger* vs. Reagan, Brandenburg**
When seven astronauts died, the Great Communicator was at his best, saying they "slipped the surly bonds of earth" to "touch the face of God," brilliant imagery (borrowed from a sonnet by World War II aviator John Gillespie Magee, Jr.) that offered solace. In Berlin, he blared, "Mr. Gorbachev, tear down this wall." In 1989, the German people did.

**Bush, National Cathedral vs. Obama, Inaugural**
Bush was rarely as eloquent as in this post-9/11 sermon. But Obama's Inaugural was historic; the first African American president. His centrist message, artfully written and delivered, touted a new foreign policy, traditional values, the United States' remembered past, and a lyric plea for justice. "We are ready," he said, "to lead once more."

# Influential Radicals and Extremists

**By David Oshinsky**

David Oshinsky holds the Jack S. Blanton Chair in History at the Univer of Texas and is a distinguished scholar-in-residence at New York Univers His latest book, *Polio: An American Story,* won the Pulitzer Prize for Histo

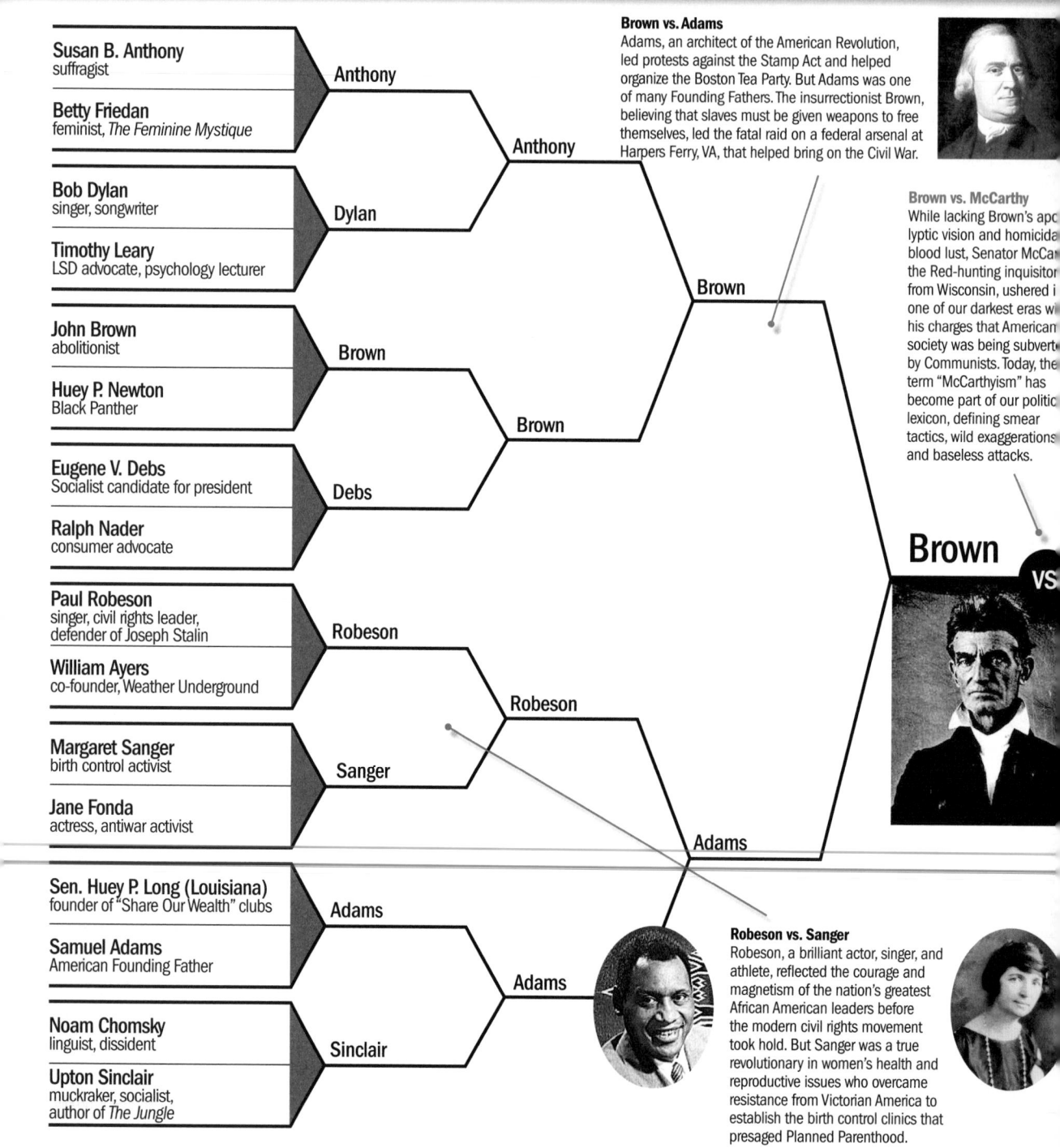


**Brown vs. Adams**
Adams, an architect of the American Revolution, led protests against the Stamp Act and helped organize the Boston Tea Party. But Adams was one of many Founding Fathers. The insurrectionist Brown, believing that slaves must be given weapons to free themselves, led the fatal raid on a federal arsenal at Harpers Ferry, VA, that helped bring on the Civil War.

**Brown vs. McCarthy**
While lacking Brown's apo lyptic vision and homicida blood lust, Senator McCa the Red-hunting inquisitor from Wisconsin, ushered i one of our darkest eras w his charges that American society was being subvert by Communists. Today, the term "McCarthyism" has become part of our politic lexicon, defining smear tactics, wild exaggerations and baseless attacks.

**Robeson vs. Sanger**
Robeson, a brilliant actor, singer, and athlete, reflected the courage and magnetism of the nation's greatest African American leaders before the modern civil rights movement took hold. But Sanger was a true revolutionary in women's health and reproductive issues who overcame resistance from Victorian America to establish the birth control clinics that presaged Planned Parenthood.

HISTORIANS HAVE TRIED WITH LIMITED SUCCESS to measure the influence of individuals who wrote books, pushed theories, or led movements that society considered radical or extremist. What is clear, though, is that radicals and extremists of the Right and Left have altered our history by raising fundamental questions about the tyranny of government, the expansion of human rights, the limits of national security, and the role of violent and nonviolent protest in a free society. All should be judged on their continuing impact on society.

**Jarvis vs. Schlafly**
Jarvis authored California's Proposition 13, the revolutionary but ultimately limited 1978 initiative that began a national tax revolt and cleared Ronald Reagan's path to the White House. But Schlafly enjoyed a longer, more varied career on the political fringes, beginning with A *Choice, Not an Echo,* her rousing defense of Goldwater Republicanism in 1964, and continuing with her strident opposition to modern feminism and the Equal Rights Amendment, which she helped to defeat.

THE WINNER

**Sen. Joseph R. McCarthy**
red-baiter

**Falwell vs. Hearst**
The father of yellow journalism, Hearst floated some wild but widely believed conspiracy theories related to the British Empire and international banking. But televangelist Falwell, the founder of the Moral Majority, brought millions of conservative Christians into the electoral process, forever changing the face of American politics. "The idea that religion and politics don't mix," said Falwell, "was invented by the devil to keep Christians from running their own country."

McCarthy
- McCarthy
  - Calhoun
    - **John C. Calhoun** — South Carolina senator, advocate of slavery and states' rights
    - **Timothy McVeigh** — Oklahoma City bomber
  - McCarthy
    - **Sen. Joseph R. McCarthy** — red-baiter
    - **Madison Grant** — eugenicist
- Schlafly
  - Forrest
    - **Benedict Arnold** — Revolutionary War general, defector to British Army
    - **Nathan Bedford Forrest** — Confederate general, Ku Klux Klan co-founder
  - Schlafly
    - **Howard Jarvis** — anti-property tax activist
    - **Phyllis Schlafly** — anti-feminism activist

Buckley
- Falwell
  - Hearst
    - **William Randolph Hearst** — publisher, model for *Citizen Kane*
    - **Robert Welch** — co-founder, John Birch Society
  - Falwell
    - **Rev. Jerry Falwell** — founder, Moral Majority
    - **Charlton Heston** — actor, civil rights activist, president National Rifle Association
- Buckley
  - Limbaugh
    - **Rush Limbaugh** — conservative radio talk show host
    - **Ayn Rand** — author of *Atlas Shrugged* and *The Fountainhead*
  - Buckley
    - **Henry Clay Frick** — industrialist, strikebreaker
    - **William F. Buckley, Jr.** — author, founder *National Review,* leader of conservative movement, novelist

# Biographies

**By James McGrath Morris**

James McGrath Morris, author of *Joseph Pulitzer: A Life in Politics, Print, and Power* and *The Rose Man of Sing Sing*, is also the editor of the monthly newsletter *The Biographer's Craft*.

*No Ordinary Time: Franklin and Eleanor Roosevelt: The Home Front in World War II* by Doris Kearns Goodwin (1994)

*Three Who Made a Revolution* by Bertram Wolfe (1948)

**No Ordinary Time**

*Admiral of the Ocean Sea: A Life of Christopher Columbus* by Samuel Eliot Morison (1942)

*American Caesar: Douglas MacArthur 1880–1964* by William Manchester (1978)

**Admiral of the Ocean Sea**

**No Ordinary Time**

*The Five of Hearts: An Intimate Portrait of Henry Adams and His Friends, 1880–1918* by Patricia O'Toole (1990)

*Mr. Clemens and Mark Twain: A Biography* by Justin Kaplan (1966)

**The Five of Hearts**

*Titan: The Life of John D. Rockefeller, Sr.* by Ron Chernow (1998)

*Morgan: American Financier* by Jean Strouse (1999)

**Morgan**

**Morgan**

**Morgan**

*A Bright Shining Lie: John Paul Vann and America in Vietnam* by Neil Sheehan (1989)

*Bearing the Cross: Martin Luther King, Jr., and the Southern Christian Leadership Conference* by David J. Garrow (1986)

**Bearing the Cross**

*John Osborne: The Many Lives of the Angry Young Man* by John Heilpern (2007)

*Norman Thomas, the Last Idealist* by W.A. Swanberg (1976)

**Norman Thomas**

**Bearing the Cross**

**Morgan**

**VS**

**Paul Robeson**

*Abraham Lincoln: The Prairie Years* by Carl Sandburg (1927)

*Paul Robeson* by Martin B. Duberman (1988)

**Paul Robeson**

*Eugene V. Debs: Citizen and Socialist* by Nick Salvatore (1982)

*Max Perkins, Editor of Genius* by A. Scott Berg (1978)

**Max Perkins**

**Paul Robeson**

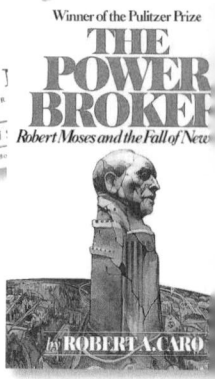

***A Bright Shining Lie* vs. *Bearing the Cross***

The cruelty of fickle first-round pairing is most evident in this matchup between two profound biographies published in the 1980s about men and events of the 1960s. Garrow's *Bearing the Cross* gets the edge here because it tackles a more famous man in Rev. King – and adds immeasurably to our understanding of the political and private pressures he faced.

***Morgan* vs. *The Power Broker***

Strouse's scrupulously researched *Morgan* may be the better biography of the two, but the best doesn't always win. Caro's *Power Broker* not only exposed the hidden story of Robert Moses, New York's political Wizard of Oz, but also left no breathing room for another biographer to even consider trying it again. In fact, Moses might have been a footnote in history had it not been for Caro. It is Caro's book, not Moses's work, that gives the man immortality.

THE FAMOUS HAVE AN EDGE HERE. Few readers will invest $34.95 for *The Life of Lenart Elckerlijc,* who sent his kids to college, mowed his lawn on Saturdays, and bowled 300 five years before dying. Still, in biography it's the telling that counts. A great biographer scores points by weaving a great narrative. "Just the facts, ma'am" works only for the LAPD. Virginia Woolf, while writing a life of Roger Fry, asked, "How can one make a life out of six cardboard boxes full of tailors' bills, love letters and old picture postcards?" The biographers here know the answer.

**THE WINNER**

## *The Power Broker: Robert Moses and the Fall of New York*

by Robert Caro (1974)

- *The Most Famous Man*
  - *The Most Famous Man*
    - *The Most Famous Man*
      - *Being Bernard Berenson* by Meryle Secrest (1980)
      - *The Most Famous Man in America* by Debbie Applegate (2007)
    - *Clara Bow*
      - *Clara Bow: Runnin' Wild* by David Stenn (1988)
      - *Woody Guthrie: A Life* by Joe Klein (1999)
  - *Henry James*
    - *Henry James*
      - *Henry James, five volumes* by Leon Edel (1953-1972)
      - *The Skeptic: A Life of H.L. Mencken* by Terry Teachout (2002)
    - *Young Man Luther*
      - *Young Man Luther: A Study in Psychoanalysis and History* by Erik H. Erikson (1958)
      - *Jung: A Biography* by Deirdre Bair (2004)
- *Power Broker*
  - *Power Broker*
    - *Power Broker*
      - *The Power Broker: Robert Moses and the Fall of New York* by Robert Caro (1974)
      - *Walter Lippmann and the American Century* by Ronald Steele (1980)
    - *When Pride Still Mattered*
      - *When Pride Still Mattered* by David Maraniss (1999)
      - *Ben Hogan: An American Life* by James Dodson (2004)
  - *Rise of Theodore Roosevelt*
    - *Truman*
      - *Luckiest Man: The Life and Death of Lou Gehrig* by Jonathan Elg (2005)
      - *Truman* by David McCullough (1992)
    - *Rise of Theodore Roosevelt*
      - *The Rise of Theodore Roosevelt* by Edmund Morris (1979)
      - *Edith Wharton: A Biography* by R.W.B. Lewis (1975)

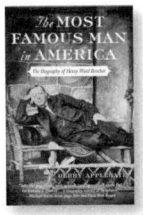


***The Most Famous Man in America* vs. *Henry James***
Applegate's profile of Rev. Henry Ward Beecher accomplishes, with aplomb, one of the essential tasks of biography: bring to life a once-famous person who has slipped our collective memory. While Edel's five volumes on Henry James's life is much admired for its definitive ambition and persistence, when it comes down to it, reforming a nation makes for better reading than the tale of someone who spends the day at a desk with a pen.

***Rise of Theodore Roosevelt* vs. *The Power Broker***
Morris's *Theodore Roosevelt* loses, not so much for any failures but against an indomitable foe. Still, there are flaws in Morris. Though an epic of a biography, as the pages turn over, readers could justifiably wonder if Morris has not confused his note cards with his manuscript.

# PEOPLE

**Astronauts** *by Jeffrey Kluger* **33**
**Supermodels** *by Crystal Renn and Marjorie Ingall* **34**
**Celebrity Mugshots** *by Willie Geist* **35**
**Mary** *by Mary C. Curtis* **36**
**Bald Guys** *by Richard Sandomir* **37**
**Geniuses** *by Peter Richmond* **38**
**Celebrity Baby Names** *by Linda Rosenkrantz and Pamela Redmond Satran* **39**
**Untimely Deaths** *by Mark Reiter* **40**
**David** *by David Fisher* **41**
**Celebrity Memoirs** *by Charles Leerhsen* **42**
**Lousy Husbands** *by Kari Boyer* **43**
**William et. al.** *by William/Bill Geist* **44**
**Disappearing Acts** *by Franz Lidz* **45**
**Richard vs. Dick** *by Richard Sandomir* **46**
**American Pinups** *by Gregory Curtis* **47**
**Pundits** *by Franklin Foer* **48**
**Great Brother Acts** *by Mark Reiter* **49**
**Tom vs. Thomas** *by Tom Chiarella* **50**
**Immigrants** *by Tony Quinn* **51**

# Astronauts

**By Jeffrey Kluger**

Jeffrey Kluger is the science editor of *Time* magazine and the author of numerous books, including *Apollo 13*, which served as the basis of the 1995 movie.

**Alan Shepard**
*first American in space; moonwalker*

**Al Bean**
*Moonwalker,* Apollo 12

**Deke Slayton**
*One of the original Seven*

**Buzz Aldrin**
Apollo 11; *second man on the moon*

**Scott Carpenter**
*One of the original Seven*

**Guion Bluford**
*First African American astronaut*

**Wally Schirra**
*Original Seven; flew three times*

**Ed Mitchell**
*Moonwalker,* Apollo 14

**Gordon Cooper**
*Original Seven; flew twice*

**Dick Gordon**
*Orbited moon,* Apollo 12

**John Glenn**
*First American to orbit Earth*

**Jim McDivitt**
*Commander of first spacewalk mission*

**Gus Grissom**
*Original Seven*

**Tom Stafford**
*orbited moon,* Apollo 10

**Jim Lovell**
*Commander,* Apollo 13; *flew four times*

**Story Musgrave**
*Six shuttle missions*

Alan Shepard

Buzz Aldrin

Guion Bluford

Wally Schirra

Gordon Cooper

John Glenn

Gus Grissom

Jim Lovell

Buzz Aldrin

Wally Schirra

John Glenn

Jim Lovell

Buzz Aldrin

Jim Lovell

**Lovell vs. Young**
When the final chapter on space history is written, the scholars will point to three truly great missions: *Apollo 8* (the first lunar orbit); *Apollo 11* (the first lunar landing); and *Apollo 13*, one of the greatest life-and-death tales ever told. Lovell flew aboard two of them. As navigator on *Apollo 8* he made sure the crew threaded the necessary trajectory needles to get to the moon and back alive. As commander of *Apollo 13*, his easy calm and pure skill as a rudder and stick man set him apart. And all of this was after his work as co-pilot on *Gemini 7* – with its historic rendezvous with *Gemini 6* – and his command of *Gemini 12*. Remember the criteria: history, danger, and thrills. Lovell takes the medal round.

THE WINNER

**Jim Lovell**

VS

**Grissom vs. Stafford**
Rough sledding for Stafford. His complex Gemini missions and his Apollo lunar orbit don't trump Grissom's popgun suborbital in a Mercury capsule and three-orbit Gemini jaunt. Why? Watch *The Right Stuff*. Grissom had that Original Seven cred.

**Glenn vs. Lovell**
You have to love Glenn. His three orbits in 1962 and return to space in 1998 – when he was 77 – were as sweet as a story gets. But in the space biz, pure piloting beats public relations, and Lovell, with four total missions and two to the moon, was a genius behind the wheel.

AN UNFAIR BRACKET, SINCE THERE SHOULD BE JUST TWO SEEDS: people with the moxie to go into space and all of the rest of us. But we're starting with 32 slots and once you send out the invitations to the tournament, how do you compare guys who flew to the moon twice with a man who flew aboard a temperamental ship like the space shuttle half a dozen times and survived all six trips? What about the first man to walk in space versus the first woman to break into the hard-drinking, fast-driving, crotch-grabbing boys' club? The winner should be the astronaut who makes history, survives danger – and thrills us down to our last nerve ending.

**Armstrong vs. Collins**
A lot of talent in Round 1 means tough pairings. Collins could have made it deep into the competition, but for the bad luck of winding up against crewmate Armstrong. A moonwalker trumps the guy they left behind to mind the store in lunar orbit.

**John Young**

**Young vs. Scott**
Mano a mano between two giants. Scott flew three times, nearly buying the farm on *Gemini 8* and flying his LEM through lunar mountains on *Apollo 15*. But Young's longevity (including two shuttle trips) gives him the edge.

**Armstrong vs. Young**
The first man on the moon doesn't make it out of the second round? No, sir. Six missions beats two, and two lunar trips beat one. Armstrong's a hero. Young was an institution.

- John Young
  - Neil Armstrong
    - **Neil Armstrong** — *First man on moon,* Apollo 11
    - **Mike Collins** — *Orbited moon,* Apollo 11
  - John Young
    - **John Young** — *Moonwalker, flew six times in three ships*
    - **Pete Conrad** — *Moonwalker,* Apollo 12; *Skylab astro*
- Ed White
  - Ed White
    - **Ed White** — *First American to walk in space*
    - **Bob Crippen** — *Flew first shuttle*
  - Sally Ride
    - **Fred Haise** — *Survived* Apollo 13
    - **Sally Ride** — *First American woman in space*
- Dave Scott
  - Dave Scott
    - **Dave Scott** — *Moonwalker,* Apollo 15; *flew three times*
    - **Eugene Cernan** — *Last man on moon,* Apollo 17
  - Frank Borman
    - **Frank Borman** — *Commander,* Apollo 8 *lunar orbit*
    - **Harrison Schmitt** — *First geologist on moon,* Apollo 17
- Ken Mattingly
  - Jack Swigert
    - **Bill Anders** — *LEM pilot,* Apollo 8
    - **Jack Swigert** — *Survived* Apollo 13
  - Ken Mattingly
    - **Ken Mattingly** — *Lunar orbit,* Apollo 16; *flew shuttle*
    - **Eileen Collins** — *First female shuttle pilot*

# Supermodels

**By Crystal Renn and Marjorie Ingall**

Crystal Renn, the leading plus-size model in America, has written with Marjorie Ingall the memoir, *Hungry: A Woman's Story of Appetite, Ambition, and the Embrace of Curves.*

Angela Lindvall
Erin Wasson
Erin

Frankie Rayder
Missy Rayder
Missy

Missy

Dorian Leigh
Suzy Parker
Dorian

Carmen Dell'Orefice
Anita Colby
Carmen

Carmen

Carmen

Carol Alt
Kim Alexis
Carol

Gia Carangi
Cindy Crawford
Gia

Gia

Gia

Cheryl Tiegs
Christie Brinkley
Christie

Beverly Johnson
Lauren Hutton
Lauren

Lauren

Gia

Gia

VS.

**Dorian vs. Carmen**
Dorian was the face of Revlon's Fire & Ice in the '50s and was supposedly the inspiration for Audrey Hepburn's character in *Funny Face.* Carmen started modeling in 1945, a year before Dorian, has been shot by everyone from Irving Penn to Cecil Beaton, and was a muse of Salvador Dali. For working steadily for over 60 years while looking better every year, Carmen wins.

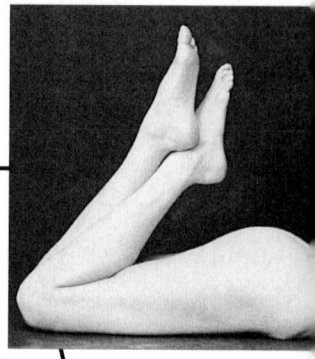

**Gia vs. Crawford**
Bad luck for the iconic Cindy, who early in her career was called "baby Gia," to bump up against her similarly strong-browed brunette predecessor.

**Tiegs vs. Brinkley**
What we talk about when we talk about the classic American supermodel. Brinkley gets the edge for surviving the tabloids and Chuck Norris.

**Gia vs. Lauren**
Clash of the tough-girl titans: Gap-toothed motorcyle-riding girl from the Florida swamps vs. super-lipped bisexual from Philadelphia. Lauren's amazing, but Gia's more unconventional look takes it.

**Gia vs. Christy**
Ask any insider: Turlington is the best ever. A total professional for 25 years, she's the embodiment of clean living (a devotee of yoga and Ayurveda, an anti-smoking activist, a devoted mom) and she'll stop working when she decides, not when the industry says so. Against all that, the hard-living, heroin-addicted Gia (subject of Stephen Fried's bio, *Thing of Beauty,* and played by Angelina Jolie in the movie) never had a chance. Gee, this bracket turned into an unintentional moral lesson. Sorry.

THE STEREOTYPICAL AMERICAN MODEL is a toothy sun-baked hair-tossing blonde. But we're actually a diverse lot: different races, ethnicities, body types, vibes. In the first round of this battle for foxy supremacy, we paired like with like: sisters Missy & Frankie and Dorian & Suzy; tragic contemporaries Margaux & Tina; obsessive-fan-faves Phoebe & Dovima; Victoria's Secret va-va-voomsters Jill & Tyra. We also pitted stars of the same era against each other (we're catty that way). Actresses who put their mugs on fashion mags were not invited.

**Hemingway vs. Chow**
Margaux was Ernest's granddaughter. In the 1970s she won the first million-dollar cosmetics contract. In 1996, the day before the anniversary of her grandfather's suicide, she OD'd on phenobarbital and was found dead at age 41. Tina Chow was a fashion and art-world icon in the late '70s and early '80s who married restaurateur Michael Chow. She died of AIDS in 1992 at age 41. For her piercing eyes and intense gaze, Margaux wins.

THE WINNER
**Christy Turlington**

- Christy Turlington
  - Christy
    - Christy
      - Christy
        - Christy Turlington
        - Veronica Webb
      - Hilary
        - Hilary Rhoda
        - Joy Bryant
    - Dovima
      - Dovima
        - Phoebe Cates
        - Dovima
      - Maggie
        - Maggie Rizer
        - Josie Moran
  - Amber
    - Niki
      - Tyra
        - Jill Goodacre
        - Tyra Banks
      - Niki
        - Bridget Hall
        - Niki Taylor
    - Amber
      - Amber
        - Amber Valetta
        - Carolyn Murphy
      - Margaux
        - Margaux Hemingway
        - Tina Chow

**Cates vs. Dovima**
Phoebe was the idol of early '80s *Seventeen* magazine readers; Dovima (her name was derived from the first syllables of her given name: Dorothy Virginia Margaret) was a '50s superstar best known for an iconic Avedon portrait posing in black Dior with circus elephants (see bracket #10). Yes, Phoebe is remembered as red-bikini spank-the-monkey bait in *Fast Times at Ridgemont High* (see #90), but not by us.

# Celebrity Mugshots

**By Willie Geist**

Willie Geist is the co-host of MSNBC's *Morning Joe* and the host of *Zeitgeist*, a satirical video blog on MSNBC.com. There are no known mugshots of him, but he is wanted in several states across the Southwest. He has vowed never to be taken alive.

Nick Nolte

Wynona Judd

Rip Torn

Kid Rock

Mike Tyson
face tattoo version

Jane Fonda
1970 classic

Paul Reubens
a.k.a. "Pee Wee Herman"

Rush Limbaugh

Paris Hilton

Larry Craig

O.J. Simpson
1994

Jim Traficant

Andre The Giant

Dawn Wells
Mary Ann from
*Gilligan's Island*

Hugh Grant

Heather Locklear

Nick Nolte

Rip Torn

Mike Tyson

Paul Reubens

Larry Craig

O.J. Simpson

Andre The Giant

Hugh Grant

Nick Nolte

Mike Tyson

O.J. Simpson

Hugh Grant

Nick Nolte

**Paris Hilton vs. Larry Craig**
Paris Hilton violated the spirit of the celebrity mugshot by doing her hair and makeup before turning herself in. Not cool. But Larry Craig's shot is a perfect portrait of dissonance: the conservative United States senator in the plain blue suit who knows his exotic private life, or at least the one in the airport men's room, is about to become public.

**James Brown vs. Nick Nolte**
Nolte's angry shot, the very image of human dissipation, screams: *Celebrities, don't let this happen to you.* Nolte's insurmountable challenge here is a hair-to-hair battle with Brown. Nolte's locks look held in place with carpenter's glue but Brown's coiffure is only a slightly electrified version of his stage do. Brown didn't feel good as the camera snapped, but Whoa!, he looks fantastic.

**Nick Nolte**

VS

Hugh Grant

**O.J. Simpson vs. Hugh Grant**
O.J.'s almost banal mugshot is the shocking and enduring symbol of an ugly moment in American history. But Hugh Grant's famous shoulder-shrug booking photo says, "Yes, I just cheated on Elizabeth Hurley with a hooker named Divine. Can we get this over with?" Human frailty – and post-humiliation self-deprecation – beats human evil in this one.

CELEBRITIES EXIST IN A SCRIPTED, AIR-BRUSHED PARALLEL UNIVERSE where every image of them is controlled. The beauty of their mugshots is the absolute loss of control. They can't summon Annie Leibovitz for their shoots or demand a second take. Instead, they're at the mercy of fluorescent lights, cinderblock backdrops, and the officer working the night shift at the Santa Monica Police Department. A classic mugshot is the inartful result of bad photography, the absence of hairstylists, and a great backstory.

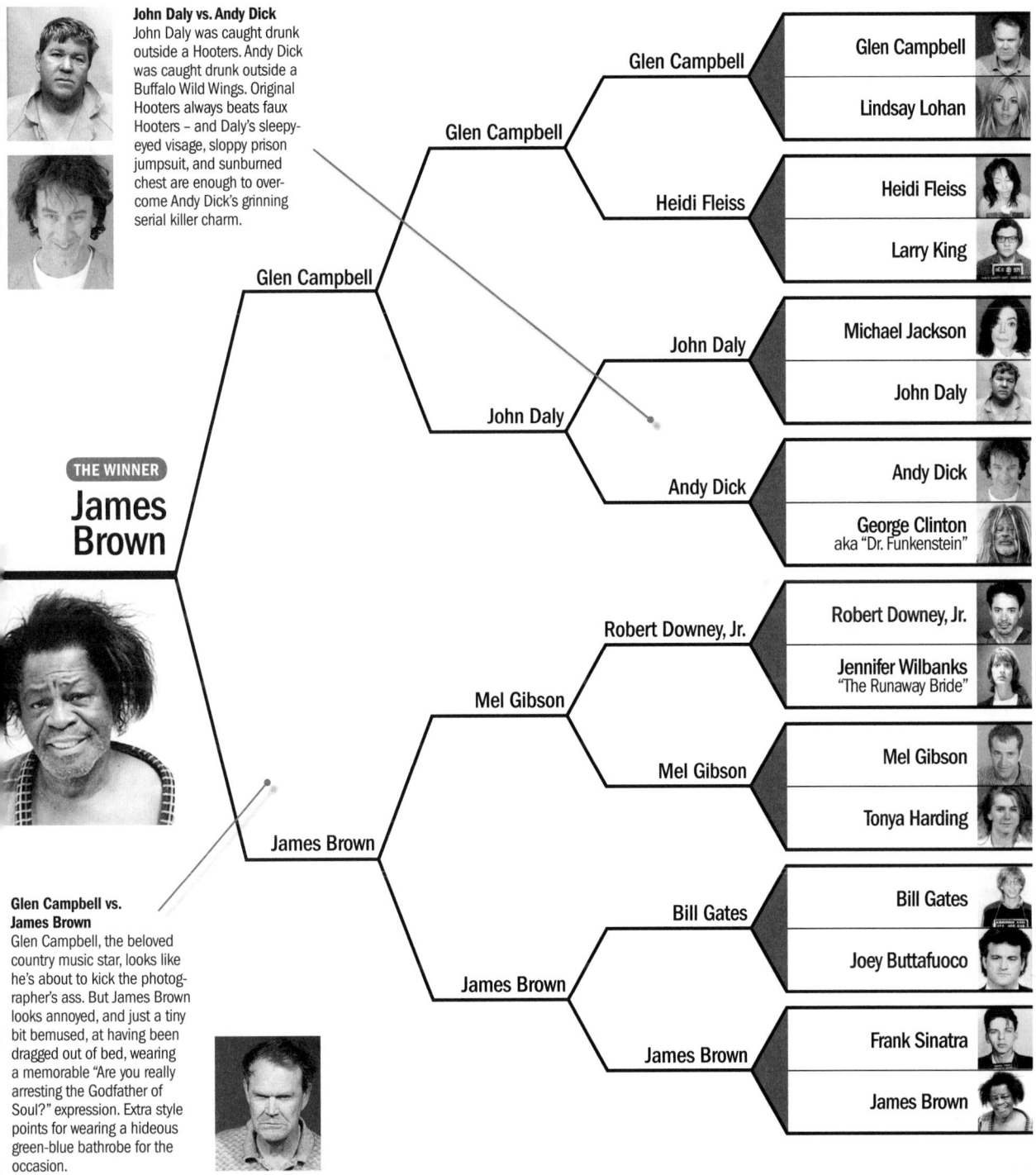

# Mary

**By Mary C. Curtis**

Mary C. Curtis, a writer and editor based in Charlotte, N.C., was named after her grandmother Mary Cecelia. As a Catholic schoolgirl in Baltimore, she was convinced that every fourth girl at St. Pius V Elementary School was named Mary.

**Mary-Kate Olsen**
actress/twin/business mogul

**Mary Tyler Moore**
sitcom megastar

**Tyler Moore**

**Mary Pickford**
silent movie superstar, "America's Sweetheart"

**Mary Astor**
actress, *The Maltese Falcon*

**Pickford**

**Tyler Moore**

**Mary Baker Eddy**
founder, Christian Science movement

**Mother Mary Lange**
founder of Oblate Sisters of Providence

**Baker Eddy**

**Eddy**

**Tyler Moore**

**Mary Carillo**
tennis player and broadcaster

**Mary Kay Letourneau**
had affair with underage student, went to jail, married him

**Letourneau**

**Martin vs. Retton**
Peter Pan vs. the pixie. Retton's face launched a thousand Wheaties boxes after she won the all-around gymnastics title at the 1984 Los Angeles Summer Olympics. The boycotting Soviets gave her a leg up on the uneven bars. Besides flying into living rooms as TV's "Pan" for the ages, Martin created Nellie Forbush and Maria von Trapp onstage and wrung every entendre out of Cole Porter's "My Heart Belongs to Daddy." And was Larry Hagman's mom.

**Mary Martin**
stage and screen star, Broadway's Peter Pan

**Mary J. Blige**
"Queen of Hip-Hop Soul"

**Martin**

**Martin**

**Mary Ann Mobley**
Miss America, 1959

**Mary Cassatt**
Impressionist painter

**Cassatt**

**Martin**

THE WINNER

## Mary Tyler Moore

VS

**Mary Lou Retton**
gold-medal Olympic gymnast

**Mary T. Meagher**
gold-medal Olympic swimmer

**Retton**

**Retton**

**Mary Beth Hurt**
stage and screen actress

**Mary-Louise Parker**
Tony and Emmy-winning actress

**Parker**

**Bethune vs. Tyler Moore**
One is a civil rights icon, the other an actress. One hands the gift of learning to children in a statue in Washington's Lincoln Park; the other tosses her tam in a bronze Minneapolis memorial. Still, television art reflected an evolution in American life as Moore morphed from Laura, dutiful and sexy wife of Rob Petrie, sitcom stand-ins for Jack and Jackie Kennedy, to Mary Richards, the single career woman. And she really did turn the world on with her smile.

"PLAIN AS ANY NAME CAN BE," George M. Cohan called Mary, even as the all-American entertainer was moved to immortalize the ordinary name in song. "When her name is Mary, there is no falseness there," Cohan wrote. The name is deceptively simple, so simple many people think it needs accompaniment, which explains Mary Lou, Mary Jane, and Mary Ann. Mary is an ocean of classic calm in a sea of churning Britneys and Lindsays. Deeds noble and notorious have hidden behind its mask of sweetness. A "grand old name," indeed.

**Wilson vs. Wells**
Two Motown pioneers. Wells was "the first lady" of Detroit's history-making label, admired by the Beatles, who became tourmates. Just try to get "My Guy" out of your head. Wilson was part of a group, but what a group. This original Supreme – a real-life Dreamgirl – advances for her ability to sing, sway, and survive, while keeping peace with Diana Ross.

**Lincoln vs. Bethune**
Abraham Lincoln himself might have trouble picking the winner. His wife had her problems, but she was also the victim of bad PR. During the Civil War, she visited wounded soldiers and raised money to aid impoverished blacks. Bethune, the child of former slaves, founded a school that became a university and counseled Eleanor and Franklin Roosevelt. Bethune stood on her own – with a cane she carried for "swank."

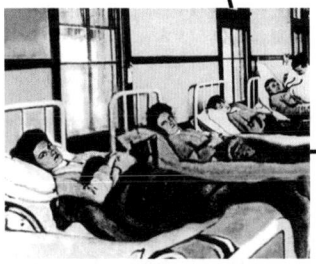

**Typhoid Mary vs. Mother Jones**
Both were born in Ireland, carried durable nicknames, and achieved fame in America. The similarity ends there: Mallon, a healthy carrier, infected dozens and killed three but refused to stop working as a cook while Jones, the labor movement's "Miners' Angel," organized the families of strikers, and children working in mills. Indifference to spreading disease and having your name forever associated with it, trumps inspiring a magazine.

- **Bethune**
  - **Lincoln**
    - **Lincoln**
      - **Lincoln**
        - **Mary Todd Lincoln** – wife of Abraham Lincoln
        - **Mary Decker** – star-crossed distance runner
      - **Steenburgen**
        - **Mary Elizabeth Mastrantonio** – actress, *The Color of Money*
        - **Mary Steenburgen** – Oscar-winning actress, married to Ted Danson
    - **Wilson**
      - **Wilson**
        - **Mary Travers** – folk singer, last name in Peter, Paul and Mary
        - **Mary Wilson** – original member of the Supremes
      - **Wells**
        - **Mary Wells** – Motown star, sang "My Guy"
        - **Mary Chapin-Carpenter** – folk and country singer
  - **Bethune**
    - **Bethune**
      - **Bethune**
        - **Mary McLeod Bethune** – educator, civil rights activist
        - **Mary McCarthy** – critic and author, *The Group*
      - **Matalin**
        - **Mary Matalin** – Republican political strategist
        - **Mary Landrieu** – Democratic senator from Louisiana
    - **Typhoid Mary**
      - **Typhoid Mary**
        - **Typhoid Mary Mallon** – cook, disease carrier
        - **Mary Harris (Mother) Jones** – labor and community organizer
      - **Mary Kay Ash**
        - **Mary Kay Ash** – cosmetics mogul
        - **Mary Young Pickersgill** – sewed "The Star Spangled Banner"

# Bald Guys

**By Richard Sandomir**

Richard Sandomir wrote a memoir of his long-faded hairline, *Bald Like Me: The Hair-Raising Adventures of Baldman*. He was stimulated to shave his Larry Fine-like fringe of unkempt hair by Charles Barkley, who told him, "Brother, what you got ain't working for you." Barkley's intervention exempts him from this competition.

FRINGE REGIONAL

Joe Garagiola
Rudy Giuliani
John Glenn
Ron Howard
Larry David
Charles Kuralt
Dick Cheney
John Adams
Gerald Ford
Ray Nitschke
Dwight Eisenhower
Adlai Stevenson
Terry Bradshaw
Dr. Phil McGraw
Homer Simpson
Hulk Hogan

Garagiola
Glenn
David
Adams
Nitschke
Eisenhower
Bradshaw
Simpson

Glenn
David
Eisenhower
Simpson

Glenn
Simpson

**David vs. Kuralt**
David is one of America's most articulate bald advocates, always eager to snarl at those who deny bald men their due (he's especially strong on the right to sympathy sex). He sought hate-crime status in *Curb Your Enthusiasm* when two teenaged girls to whom he denied Halloween candy, spray-painted "Bald Asshole" on his front door. If Kuralt ever raised his voice to protect his brethren, he did it in a whisper lost to the tumbleweeds out on the road.

**Jordan vs. Glenn**
Both men soared, Glenn into outer space (at age 40 and again at 77) and Jordan above the rim. Orbiting the earth is more impressive than leaping over Patrick Ewing, and what could have been more macho than being a star astronaut in the '60s? But Jordan flew under his own power, not with the help of rocket boosters. And while Glenn's bald head has all the right structural stuff, Jordan's shaved bean embodies the sleek aerodynamics needed for flight.

**Eisenhower vs. Simpson**
Eisenhower led us to victory on D-Day, a feat that should have clinched his victory over a fat, stupid toon. But there's something about Homer – that elliptical head, those squiggly hairs framing his meager fringe, and that singular level of buffoonery at home and at the nuclear plant – that elevates him above an easy-but-bland choice like Ike. And Homer worked naked.

Glenn VS.

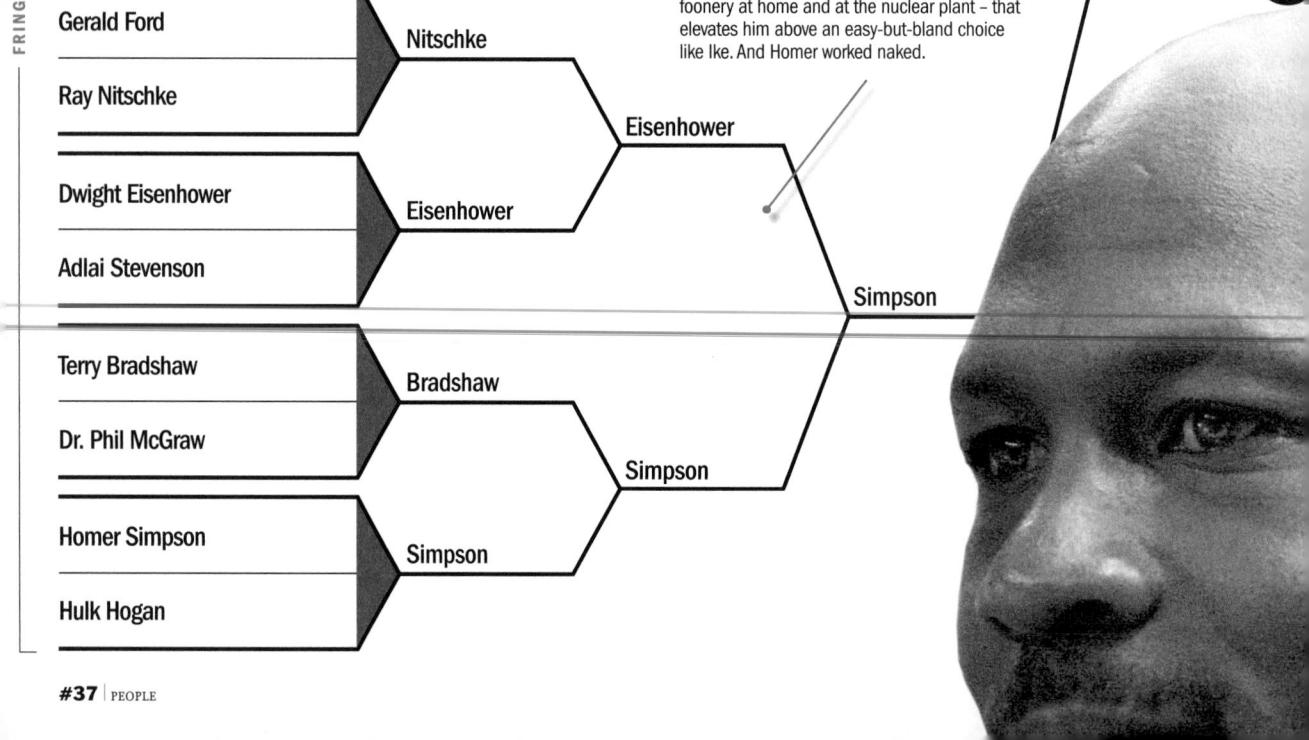

WHO IS THE TRUE BALDIE: the one whose hair loss is genetically programmed or the one who shears all the hair from his head? The debate will continue unabated as long as men lose their hair or see a benefit in shaving it all off. In this celebration of both species of homo baldus, we derived spiritual guidance from the words of the fringe-haired dyspeptic, Larry David, who said: "Anyone can be confident with a full head of hair. But a confident bald man – there's your diamond in the rough."

**Jordan vs. Brynner**
Jordan shaved his balding head early in his NBA career, which enhanced the imagery of his aerodynamics and also led other players and millions around the world to "Be Like Mike." He wasn't the first famous man to go smooth (Louis Gossett, Jr. was prominent among the early adopters), but he is the most influential. Brynner's look probably led Savalas to reach for the razor and shaving cream, but not many others.

**Mr. Clean vs. Brynner**
No one established the image of the smooth-headed foreign exotic with more élan than Brynner. He was smart, imperious, and manly as a Siamese king, a gunfighter, or an Egyptian pharaoh. Procter & Gamble's grime-fighting Mr. Clean is an enduring marketing vision of macho purity a half-century since his creation, but Brynner proved the commercial impact of regularly shaving one's head down to his Mongolian skin.

THE WINNER
**Michael Jordan**

- Jordan
  - Jordan
    - Jordan
      - Michael Jordan
      - Bruce Willis
    - Hayes
      - Isaac Hayes
      - Mark Messier
  - Jackson
    - Agassi
      - Andre Agassi
      - George Foreman
    - Jackson
      - Marvin Hagler
      - Samuel L. Jackson
- Brynner
  - Savalas
    - Savalas
      - Michael Chiklis
      - Telly Savalas
    - Shakur
      - Tupac Shakur
      - Montel Williams
  - Brynner
    - Mr. Clean
      - Mr. Clean
      - Curly Howard
    - Brynner
      - Yul Brynner
      - Stone Cold Steve Austin

SHAVED-HEAD REGIONAL

# Geniuses

**By Peter Richmond**

Author and journalist Peter Richmond has interviewed hundreds of famous people, including a few geniu But he's always found that the guy sitting next to at him at the bar in a Ruby Tuesday's just off the intersta next to the Marriott Courtyard is more interesting. Then, he's no genius. For which he is eternally grateful.

Linus Pauling
Bill Veeck
Pauling

Steve Jobs
Emily Dickinson
Dickinson

Pauling

Noam Chomsky
R. Crumb
Chomsky

George Gershwin
B. F. Skinner
Gershwin

Chomsky

Richard Feynman
David Foster Wallace
Feynman

Frank Lloyd Wright
George Washington Carver
Carver

Feynman

Thomas Edison
Stanley Kubrick
Edison

Theodor Geisel (Dr. Seuss)
Louis Armstrong
Armstrong

Edison

**Pauling vs. Edison**
It's hard to eliminate a man considered by some to be the intellectual equal of Newton, Galileo, and Einstein, and who won two Nobels, and whose brainy anti-nuke activism may have helped keep modern civilization from going up in a mushroom cloud. On the other hand, the industrialized world that Linus Pauling wanted to preserve was more or less invented by Thomas Alva. Nod to Edison for getting music onto vinyl, more or less.

Pauling

Edison

VS

**Carver vs. Feynman:**
Yes, the agricultural pioneer was without peer; anyone who could make explosives out of peanuts certainly deserved *Time* magazine's laurel: the "Black Leonardo." But Nobel-winning, Manhattan-Project alumnus physicist Feynman not only occupied a cerebral realm inaccessible to most of us, he had a certifiable sense of humor. Feynman gets the nod here if only for the YouTube video of him playing bongos.

**Dr. Seuss vs. Armstrong**
In a battle of two American originals, it's hard to bet against a poet/author/illustrator whose sui generis cartoon creations have not only lulled a trillion whiny kids to sleep but enlightened their parents as well. But without the cornet/trumpet man, America might have never moved beyond Lutheran church music. Satchmo wins by a couple of grace notes.

IN PICTURES, THEIR HAIR IS NEVER QUITE RIGHT and they have a weird look in their eyes. But they fascinate us in a way that the rich, beautiful, and otherwise famous cannot. After all: any of us might get rich or famous; none of us will ever be geniuses. But what, exactly, makes them geniuses? I.Q.? Historical impact? Wisdom? Talent? Self-promotional ability? I defer to Supreme Court Justice Potter Stewart's definition of obscenity in trying to define genius: "I know it when I see it." Or hear it. Or read it. Or witness it. Or, in the end, feel it in my gut.

**Fischer vs. Franklin**
Alas, quantifiable intelligence only goes so far. The chess grandmaster was smarter than Einstein, Stanford-Binet wise. But Bobby's impact on the world (a clear genius criterion) diminished exponentially the longer he stuck around. Whereas Ben (who was lucky not to have a lost a whole lot of IQ points himself in that kite-in-a-lightning-storm-stunt) grew better with age. Franklin, the American Conscience with the good hair, in a romp.

THE WINNER

## Thomas Jefferson

**Jefferson vs. Edison**
The Wizard of Menlo Park invented a lot of great stuff, but eventually someone would have come up with most of it. But could anyone except Jefferson have written the most eloquent manifesto in all of history? And inspired the Bill of Rights? We could have lived comfortably without light bulbs – but not without Jeffersonian Democracy. The winner: the writer, scientist, musician, politician, farmer, and architect who was infinitely curious about everything. And that's genius.

- Franklin
  - Fischer
    - Fischer
      - Dr. Benjamin Spock
      - Bobby Fischer
    - Ford
      - W.E.B. Du Bois
      - Henry Ford
  - Franklin
    - Dylan
      - Craig Ventner
      - Bob Dylan
    - Franklin
      - Ben Franklin
      - Trey Anastasio
- Jefferson
  - Clemens
    - Groucho
      - Philo T. Farnswroth
      - Groucho Marx
    - Clemens
      - Samuel Clemens
      - Howard Hughes
  - Jefferson
    - Oppenheimer
      - Robert Oppenheimer
      - Ayn Rand
    - Jefferson
      - Thomas Jefferson
      - James Buchanan Eads

# Celebrity Baby Names

**By Linda Rosenkrantz and Pamela Redmond Satran**

Linda Rosenkrantz and Pamela Redmond Satran's shared obsession with names has led to a website, nameberry.com, and 10 bestselling books on the subject, including *Beyond Jennifer and Jason* and *The Baby Name Bible.*

**Shiloh** (Angelina Jolie and Brad Pitt) vs. **Suri** (Katie Holmes and Tom Cruise) → **Suri**

**Croix** (Cedric the Entertainer) vs. **Cruz** (Victoria "Posh Spice" & David Beckham) → **Cruz**

**Suri** vs. **Cruz** → **Cruz**

**Levi** (Matthew McConnaughey) vs. **Denim** (Toni Braxton) → **Denim**

**Sailor** (Christie Brinkley) vs. **Navy** (Nivea) → **Navy**

**Denim** vs. **Navy** → **Navy**

**Bronx** (Ashlee Simpson and Pete Wentz) vs. **Moxie CrimeFighter** (Penn Jillette) → **Moxie**

**Gable** (Kevin Nealon) vs. **Harlow** (Nicole Richie and Joel Madden) → **Harlow**

**Moxie** vs. **Harlow** → **Moxie**

**Happy** (Macy Gray) vs. **Lucky** (Cedric the Entertainer) → **Lucky**

**Karma** (Ludacris) vs. **Cash** (Annabeth Gish) → **Karma**

**Lucky** vs. **Karma** → **Karma**

**Cruz** vs. **Navy** → **Navy**

**Moxie** vs. **Karma** → **Moxie**

**Navy** vs. **Moxie** → **Moxie**

**Shiloh vs. Suri**
In Brangelina vs. TomKat, Shiloh gets a shared family credit for having five equally unusually named sibs, but Suri takes it for being the name with the most meanings, including "pickpocket" in Japanese and "pointy nose" in an Indian dialect.

**THE WINNER**

**Moxie CrimeFight** (Penn Jillette)

VS

**Moxie vs. Banjo**
Moxie CrimeFighter Jillette, daughter of Penn, wins the prize for both product placement cred – Moxie originated as a carbonated soft drink in 1876 (see bracket #148) – and best paternal explanation of Mad Middle Name: "When she's pulled over for speeding, Moxie can say, 'But officer, we're on the same side. My middle name is CrimeFighter.'" And also for, you know, sheer baby-naming moxie.

THE COMPETITION AMONG CELEBS for most original (a.k.a. weirdest) baby name is as fierce as the Tour de France, with contenders constantly looking over their shoulders to make sure no other parent gets to their name first. Extra points for an equally outré middle name, equally iconoclastic sibling names, staying unique but creating a trend, and engendering a tsunami of outraged publicity

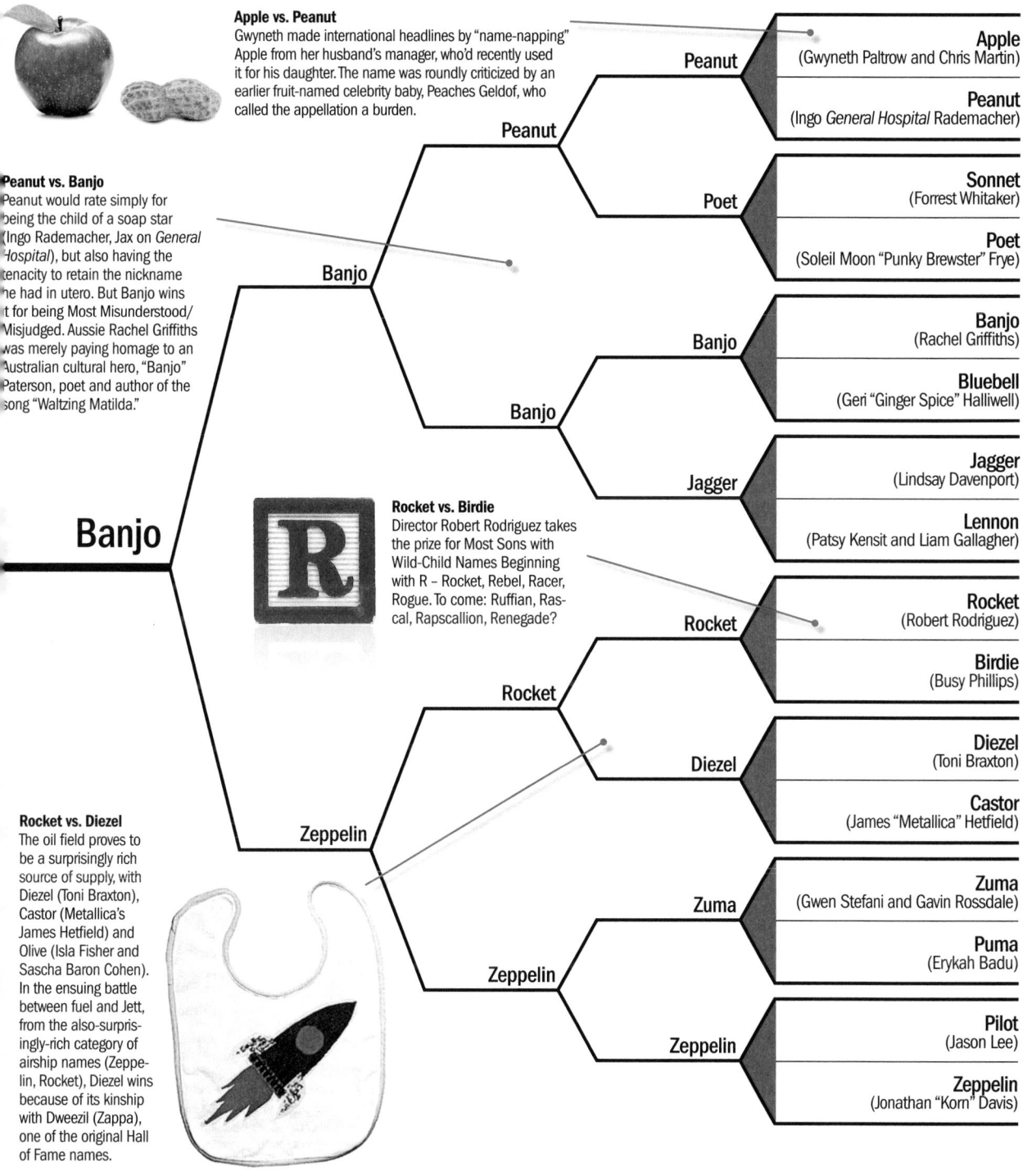

# Untimely Deaths

**By Mark Reiter**

Mark Reiter, co-editor of this book, is getting used to the fact that no one lives forever.

**Buddy Holly**
singer/songwriter, 22
d. 2/3/59 plane crash

**Ronnie Van Zandt**
singer, 29
d. 10/20/77, plane crash

**Duane Allman**
guitar hero, 24
d. 10/29/71, motorcycle accident

**Jimi Hendrix,**
guitar hero, 27
d. 9/18/70, asphyxiation

**John Belushi,**
actor, 33
d. 3/5/82, drug abuse

**Elvis Presley,**
singer, 42
d. 8/16/77, drug abuse

**Michael Kelly**
journalist, 46
d. 4/3/03, Iraq war

**David Blum**
journalist, 39
d. 4/9/03, Iraq war

**Sam Cooke**
singer, 33
d. 12/11/64, gunshot

**Selena**
singer, 24
d. 3/31/95, gunshot

**Thurman Munson**
baseball player, 32
d. 8/2/79, plane crash

**Lou Gehrig**
baseball player, 37
d. 6./2/41, "Lou Gehrig's disease"

**Payne Stewart**
golfer, 42
d. 10/25/99, plane crash

**Tony Lema**
golfer, 32
d. 7/24/66, plane crash

**Brian Piccolo**
football player, 26
d. 6/16/70, cancer

**Ernie Davis**
football player, 22
d. 5/18/63, leukemia

Buddy Holly

Jimi Hendrix

Elvis Presley

Michael Kelly

Sam Cooke

Lou Gehrig

Tony Lema

Ernie Davis

Buddy Holly

Elvis Presley

Lou Gehrig

Tony Lema

Buddy Holly

Lou Gehrig

**Holly vs. Hendrix**
It is scary to imagine where Jimi Hendrix would have taken rock music if he had stuck around (like imagining Mozart composing into his 40's). But there were hints in his last recordings that he was meandering, not hitting a new stride. He also loses points for self-destructive behavior, whereas Holly was an irresistible songwriter whose accidental death inspired a song about "the day the music died."

**Kelly vs. Presley**
Kelly was an editorial prodigy who by age 33 had edited two major magazines and written a wartime classic *(Martyr's Day)*. But even a mighty pen cannot compete against the King.

**Cooke vs. Gehrig**
Cooke had the sweetest pipes ever and could rock the house (hear *Live at the Harlem Square Club*). But how great was Gehrig? In Babe Ruth's 60-home-run season (1927), Gehrig batted cleanup and was the league MVP. ALS, his lethal disease, now bears his name.

**Stewart vs. Lema**
Although Stewart perished four months after winning his second U.S. Open, he was an aging athlete at 42. Lema, at 29, was in his prime. Competing against the likes of Palmer, Nicklaus, and Player, Champagne Tony won 12 times in four seasons, including the '64 British Open. Macabre factor: Lema's plane crashed on a golf course.

**Lou Gehrig**

VS

**Gehrig vs. Redding**
Gehrig's records have all been broken, but Otis Redding's recordings are indestructible. Not only did he establish a level of vocal expression that all other singers aim for, but once he put his stamp on a song (e.g., "Try a Little Tenderness") it's hard to hear it any other way. Plus, he wrote the greatest soul song ever (see bracket #82).

WHILE NO DEATH IS TIMELY (unless you're 109 years old and pass in your sleep with a smile on your face), inevitably some passings are more tragic than others. You lose points for self-destructive behavior or taking your own life. You gain points for going in car accidents, plane crashes, or senseless shootings. No war heroes or assassination victims allowed either (so don't expect Abe Lincoln to be squaring off against MLK, JFK, RFK, or Harvey Milk in the final). This is a contest of interrupted potential and the magnitude of What If.

**Brown vs. Henson**
Jazz fans sigh or weep thinking of all the notes Brownie left unplayed when his car crashed on the Pennsylvania Turnpike. Henson, the oldest competitor here, reached hundreds of millions around the world with the Muppets – and has his own bracket (#3) – but had even bigger plans before dying of a "cold."

**Kulwicki vs. Earnhardt**
Kulwicki died young and only six months after winning his first NASCAR season championship, but raced long enough to invent the Polish Victory Lap (i.e., backward). Earnhardt's seven championships suggest a full career, but he wasn't coasting when he crashed at Daytona – and no individual's death has left a bigger hole in his sport.

THE WINNER

# Otis Redding

- Otis Redding
  - Jim Henson
    - Jim Henson
      - Tupac Shakur
        - **Tupac Shakur** – rap artist, 25 – d. 9/13/96, gunshot
        - **Notorious B.I.G.** – rap artist, 24 – d. 3/9/97, gunshot
      - Jim Henson
        - **John F. Kennedy, Jr.** – publisher, lawyer, 38 – d. 7/16/99, plane crash
        - **Jim Henson** – Muppet master, 53 – d. 5/15/90, pneumonia
    - Clifford Brown
      - Clifford Brown
        - **Clifford Brown** – jazz trumpeter, 25 – d. 6/26/56, car crash
        - **William Kappell** – pianist, 33 – d. 10/30/53, plane crash
      - Carole Lombard
        - **Carole Lombard** – actress, 33 – d. 1/16/42, plane crash
        - **Marilyn Monroe** – actress, 36 – d. 8/5/62, drug overdose
  - Otis Redding
    - Otis Redding
      - James Dean
        - **Kurt Cobain** – musician, 27 – d. 4/5/94, suicide
        - **James Dean** – actor, 24 – d. 9/30/55, car crash
      - Otis Redding
        - **Otis Redding** – singer, 26 – d. 12/10/67, plane crash
        - **Marvin Gaye** – singer, 44 – d. 4/1/84, gunshot
    - Hank Williams
      - Dale Earnhardt
        - **Dale Earnhardt** – NASCAR champion, 49 – d. 2/18/01, car crash
        - **Alan Kulwicki** – NASCAR champion, 29 – d. 4/1/93, plane crash
      - Hank Williams
        - **Hank Williams** – singer/songwriter, 29 – d. 1/1/53, car crash
        - **Patsy Cline** – singer, 30 – d. 3/5/63, plane crash

# David

**By David Fisher**

David Fisher has written or collaborated on 15 *New York Times* bestsellers. He lives happily in the Bronx, New York, with a beautiful wife, two sons, a dog, and a cat – none of whom is named David.

**David Wells**
rotund Yankees lefthander

**David Cone**
Yankees and Mets righthander

**David Wright**
Mets third baseman

**David Ortiz**
Red Sox slugger called "Big Papi"

**David Copperfield**
magician and illusionist

**David Blaine**
magician known for endurance stunts

**David E. Kelley**
TV writer, *Boston Legal, Ally McBeal*

**David Mamet**
corrosive playwright, trickster film-maker

**David Gergen**
pundit/White House official

**David Broder**
*Washington Post* columnist

**David Halberstam**
best and brightest journalist on war, sports

**David Foster Wallace**
tour de force writer

**David Axelrod**
President Obama strategist

**David Plouffe**
Obama campaign manager

**David Caruso**
actor, *CSI: Miami, NYPD Blue*

**David Hasselhoff**
actor, *Bay Watch*, sort-of singer

Wells

Ortiz

Copperfield

Kelley

Gergen

F. Wallace

Axelrod

Caruso

Ortiz

Kelley

Gergen

Axelrod

Ortiz

Axelrod

**Cone vs. Wells**
Two great major league pitchers who ended their careers with nearly identical winning percentages and pitched perfect games for the Yankees. While Cone would probably be a better-behaved party guest, Wells, the beer-bellied battler and Babe Ruth worshipper, showed that in the postseason he is the choice to make one crucial start.

**Ortiz vs. Kelley**
Two of the nation's leading hit-makers; Kelley's plot pitches have led to some of our best TV series while Ortiz's clutch hitting has led the Boston Red Sox to their first two World Series championships since 1918. History tells us that creating a hit TV show is merely impossible, while winning two World Series in Boston is a miracle. Miracles top impossible.

THE WINNER

**David Axelrod**

VS

**Axelrod vs. Plouffe**
The Team of Davids led Barack Obama to the presidency with Alexrod as the head of strategy and Plouffe as the campaign manager. But the far more public Axelrod, a frequent talking head on Obama's behalf, advances because he's worked since 2002 with the first black president, most notably on his famous anti-Iraq War speech and on the winning "Change We Can Believe In" campaign strategy.

DAVID MEANS "BELOVED," an auspicious start for any name. Michelangelo's marble nude, *David,* beckons people from thousands of miles away. The statue's impressive namesake, the biblical King David, was a leading statesman, writer, musician, and soldier who vanquished the heavily-favored Goliath in history's greatest upset. In doing so he established the name as one with such potent simplicity that only the most loving parents bestowed it on their fortunate sons. Some of those sons turned into great guys. Some didn't.

**rockett vs. Axelrod**
rockett's mythical place in storybooks and merican history is certain. But Axelrod turned a ate senator from Illinois with a Muslim name to America's first African American president. e changed the way political campaigns will be onducted, and with Plouffe, kept internal battles uiet, created the most tech-savvy campaign ver, and raised $750 million to defeat Hillary linton and then John McCain. And he never eeded a coonskin cap.

**Letterman vs. Barry**
Letterman has been a source of intelligent laughter for more than two decades, creating a unique late-night structure while his rival Leno pursued an easier, lower common-denominator path to higher ratings. While Barry is the best thing to happen to humor since someone first saw the possibilities in a banana peel and a staircase, Letterman wins for carrying on the legacy of Johnny Carson with longevity and sagacity.

# Celebrity Memoirs

**By Charles Leerhsen**

Charles Leerhsen is a former assistant managing editor at *People* magazine and the survivor of five celebrity ghostwriting projects. He is also the author of *Crazy Good: The True Story of Dan Patch, the Most Famous Horse in America.*

*Elsie the Cow*
by Elsie the Cow

*The Autobiography of Dan Patch*
by Dan Patch

**Elsie the Cow**

*Losing It: And Gaining My Life Back One Pound at a Time*
by Valerie Bertinelli

*Life with My Sister Madonna*
by Christopher Ciccone

**Christopher Ciccone**

**Christopher Ciccone**

*Love, Lucy*
by Lucille Ball

*A Book*
by Desi Arnaz

**Desi Arnaz**

**George Takei**

*Get a Life!*
by William Shatner

*To the Stars: The Autobiography of George Takei,, Star Trek's Mr. Sulu*
by George Takei

**George Takei**

*Safe at Home: Confessions of a Baseball Fanatic*
by Alyssa Milano

*By All Means Keep on Moving*
by Marilu Henner

**Marilu Henner**

**Marilu Henner**

*Just When I Thought I'd Dropped My Last Egg and Other Calamities*
by Kathie Lee Gifford

*Labor of Love: The Story of One Man's Extraordinary Pregnancy*
by Thomas Beatie

**Kathie Lee Gifford**

*I Lived to Tell It All*
by George Jones

*You Have to Stand for Something Or You'll Fall for Anything*
by Star Jones

**George Jones**

**George Jones**

*I Should Be Dead by Now*
by Dennis Rodman

*I May Be Wrong But I Doubt It*
by Charles Barkley

**Charles Barkley**

**Dan Patch vs. Elsie the Cow**
These quite early examples of the genre are notable for being first-person accounts ostensibly penned, or maybe dictated, by farm animals. Elsie loses points for being Borden's corporate symbol and anathema to the dairy-detesting queen of the genre, Marilu Henner. But the cow's musings have a poignancy lacking in the great horse's scattershot reminiscences which were compiled by a pioneering PR hack.

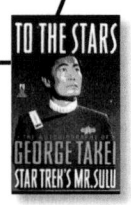


**George Takei vs. Marilu Henner**
Takei is a master of upholstery, stuffing his autobiography with arbitrary specifics and unnecessary descriptions of everyday events, and identifying people by their title every time he mentions them, sometimes several times on the same page. But he ineptly leaves out information about his *Star Trek* audition that leaves the reader baffled. Henner pads, too, but her filler – musings about on-set sex and the evils of mozzarella – is often just as tasty as Takei's best stuff.

THE WINNER

***By All Means Keep on Moving***
by Marilu Henner

VS

**George Jones vs. Charles Barkley**
Although Barkley has a DUI arrest and admits to excessive gambling, he is not defined by his addictions like "No Show" Jones. Both men admitted they had forgotten, or never read, all or part of their autobiographies. But Jones wins because he tones down the braggadocio and tells better stories, such as the time he sidled up to singer Porter Wagoner at a urinal and grabbed Wagoner's penis as a way of saying, "Listen, you, stay away from my gal."

REVIEWING *TRUMP: SURVIVING AT THE TOP,* which I cowrote with Donald Trump and considered my magnum opus until I learned a little Latin, smarty-pants author Michael Lewis called it a "sloppy job of façade-repair." Lewis thought he was insulting The Donald in the *New York Times* when in fact he was defining what a celebrity memoir should be: something not too fastidious and not too fair. I mean, who wants a celebrity with a flawless façade and impeccable judgment about what he puts down for posterity? Dish beats decorum every time.

**Wilt Chamberlain vs. Marilu Henner**
Chamberlain's claim that he shtupped 20,000 women is really all he's got. After two autobiographies (the better one came 18 years earlier) he seems sour and spent. Henner's banal blathering adds up to one gloriously unfiltered puff: she confesses to being "cross addicted to dairy and roast beef," reveals affairs with Tony Danza and Judd Hirsch, and admits to an (unconsummated) thing for Danny DeVito because he was charming, funny, and "already down there."

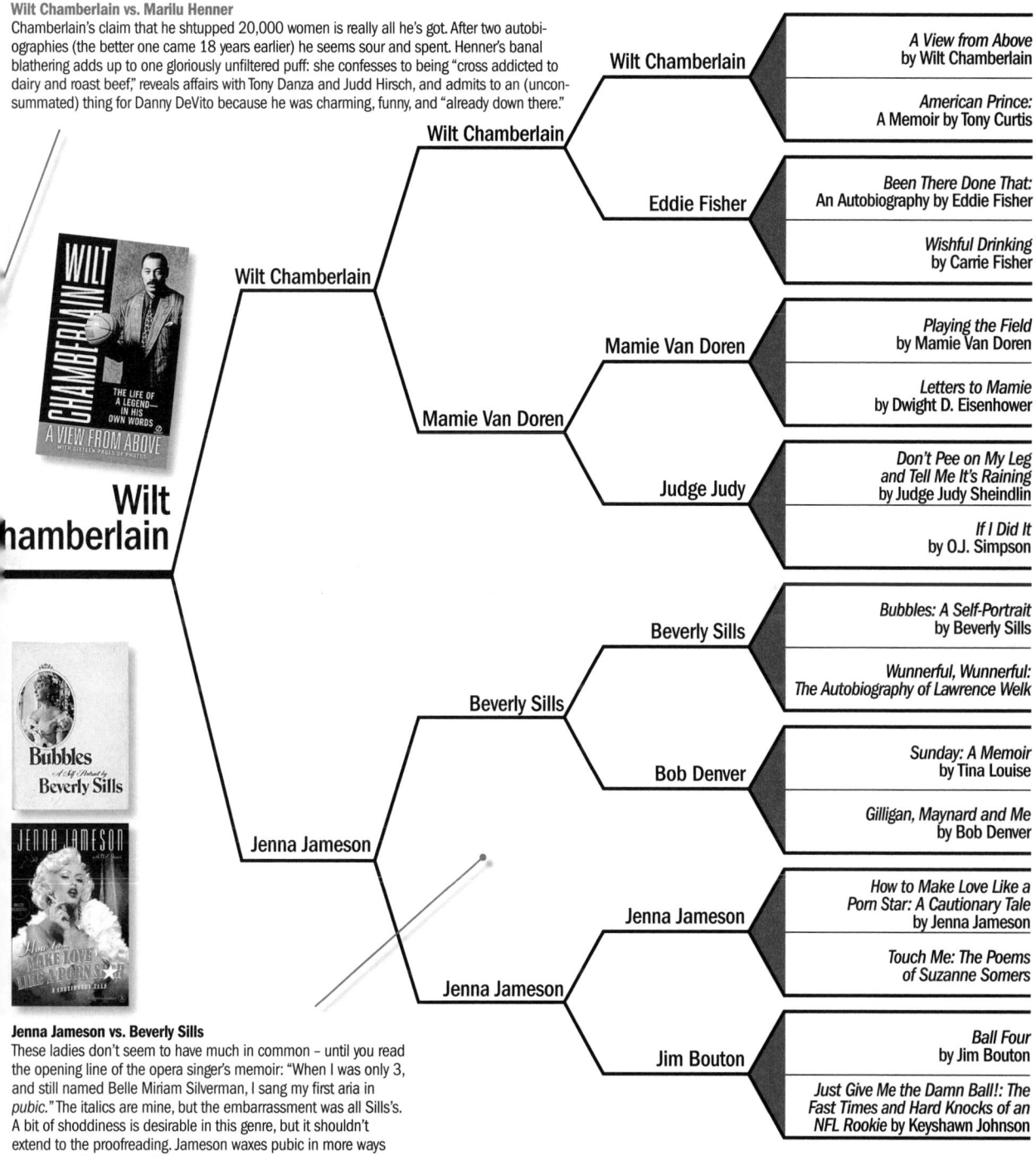


**Jenna Jameson vs. Beverly Sills**
These ladies don't seem to have much in common – until you read the opening line of the opera singer's memoir: "When I was only 3, and still named Belle Miriam Silverman, I sang my first aria in *pubic.*" The italics are mine, but the embarrassment was all Sills's. A bit of shoddiness is desirable in this genre, but it shouldn't extend to the proofreading. Jameson waxes pubic in more ways than one with a straightforwardness that keeps you riveted.

# Lousy Husbands

**By Kari Boyer**

Kari Boyer, a veteran food reporter and editor, would never put her husband Peter on this list. Not yet.

**Robert Blake**
*Baretta* star at scene of crime, does no time

**Ike Turner**
He swings, Tina sings

**Tony Soprano**
"Father knows best" if Father is a killer mob boss who owns a strip joint

**Norman Mailer**
Misogynist writer somehow convinces six women to marry him, stabbing one

**J.R. Ewing**
From *Dallas* with malice

**Jack Welch**
Married GE honcho does magazine interview – and interviewer, too

**Brad Pitt**
Dumps Jen, inflicts the age of Brangelina on us all

**Spencer Tracy**
Does "right" thing by wife and faith; shuns divorce for 25-year fling with Hepburn

**Warren G. Harding**
Republican Romeo's infidelity costs GOP $50k

**John F. Kennedy**
Had White House liaison with Marlene Dietrich, his father's ex-lover

**Rudy Giuliani**
Announced marriage breakup in a press conference

**Newt Gingrich**
Married his high school teacher, dumped her after cancer

**Bill Clinton**
"I did not have sex with that woman, Miss Lewinsky"

**Jesse Jackson**
Ministered to Clinton while fathering a love child

**John Edwards**
Presidential candidate cheats on cancer-stricken wife

**Antonio Villaraigosa**
LA mayor cheats on cancer-stricken wife

Robert Blake

Norman Mailer

J.R. Ewing

Brad Pitt

Warren G. Harding

Rudy Giuliani

Bill Clinton

John Edwards

Robert Blake

Brad Pitt

Warren G. Harding

John Edwards

Robert Blake

John Edwards

**Warren G. Harding vs. John F. Kennedy**
Kennedy was an incorrigible rake, but he was quiet about it. Harding is unique as the only adulterous president whose infidelity prompted extortion payments by his party. The 1920 GOP paid $50,000 to Harding's miffed lover (and wife of a close friend). He was also accused by yet another woman of fathering her child while in the White House. Bonus points for cuckolding his wife, who was the brains behind his business and political success – and for inspiring the concise, if ungenerous, epitaph from e.e. cummings: "The only man, woman, or child who wrote a simple declarative sentence with seven grammatical errors is dead."

John Edwards

VS

**Bill Clinton vs. John Edwards**
Bill Clinton humiliated wife Hillary, lied to the country, and shamed the office of the presidency for an adolescent-level fling with a White House intern. Presidential candidate John Edwards milked wife Elizabeth's advanced cancer for political gain while dallying with his videographer, Rielle Hunter. Both lied about it until the evidence overwhelmed. Elizabeth's cancer and Rielle's daughter trump Clinton's cigar-and-intern escapade.

WHAT MAKES A BAD HUSBAND? Violence and emotional cruelty, certainly. Humiliation cuts deep, too. That's why so many politicians make world-class lousy husbands. Because American politics insists on the image of domestic perfection, a betrayed political wife is triply humiliated: first in the adoring spouse phase, then with the revelation of the betrayal, and finally during the stand-by-your-fallen-man press conference. Maybe some of them still have faith in their lout. But on the evidence here (including two fictional TV heels who are so vivid they serve as role models for others in the bracket), they shouldn't.

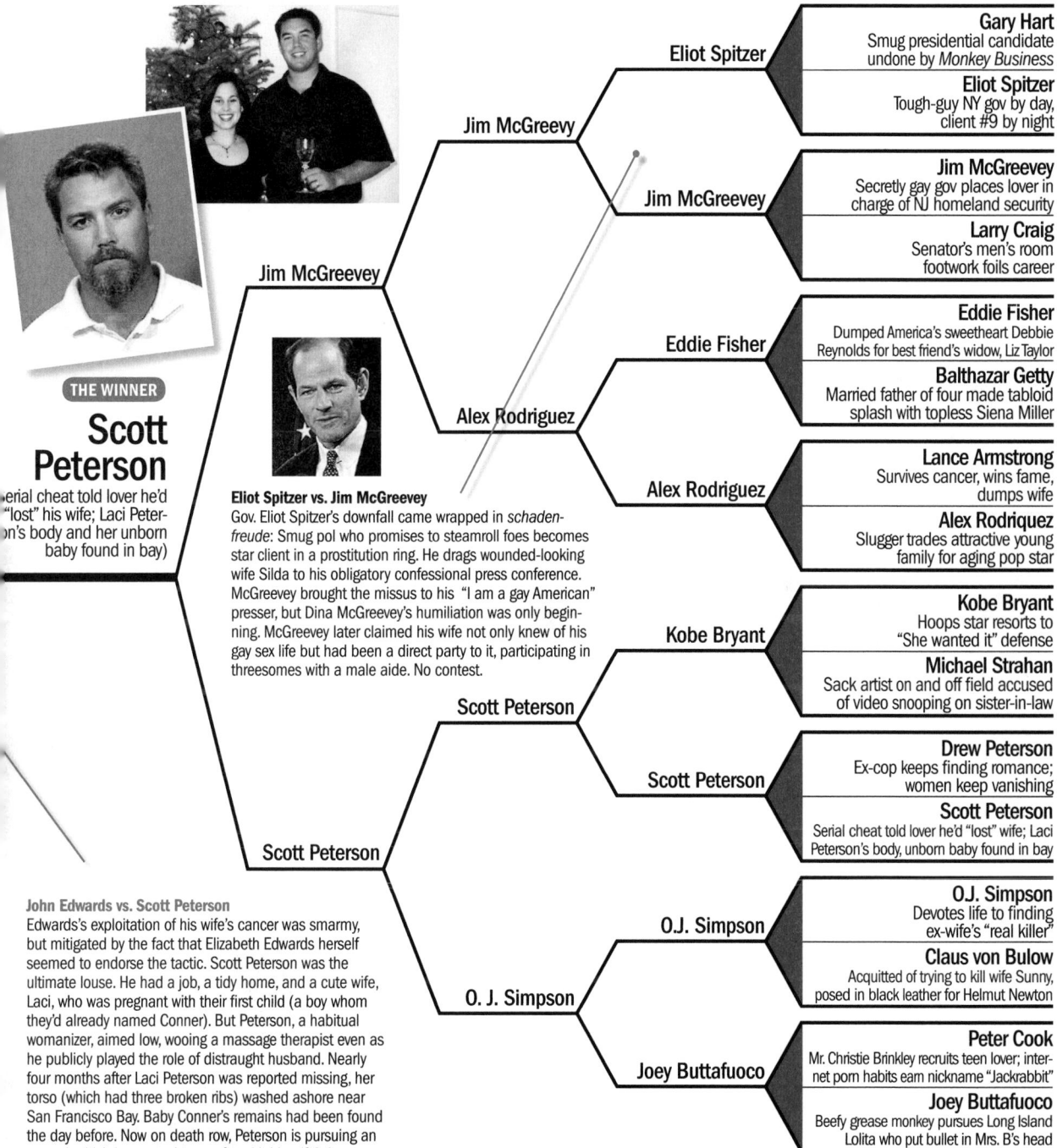


**Eliot Spitzer vs. Jim McGreevey**
Gov. Eliot Spitzer's downfall came wrapped in *schadenfreude*: Smug pol who promises to steamroll foes becomes star client in a prostitution ring. He drags wounded-looking wife Silda to his obligatory confessional press conference. McGreevey brought the missus to his "I am a gay American" presser, but Dina McGreevey's humiliation was only beginning. McGreevey later claimed his wife not only knew of his gay sex life but had been a direct party to it, participating in threesomes with a male aide. No contest.

**John Edwards vs. Scott Peterson**
Edwards's exploitation of his wife's cancer was smarmy, but mitigated by the fact that Elizabeth Edwards herself seemed to endorse the tactic. Scott Peterson was the ultimate louse. He had a job, a tidy home, and a cute wife, Laci, who was pregnant with their first child (a boy whom they'd already named Conner). But Peterson, a habitual womanizer, aimed low, wooing a massage therapist even as he publicly played the role of distraught husband. Nearly four months after Laci Peterson was reported missing, her torso (which had three broken ribs) washed ashore near San Francisco Bay. Baby Conner's remains had been found the day before. Now on death row, Peterson is pursuing an appeal, which he wanted to pay for with his wife's insurance money. A California court told him no.

# William et. al.

**By William/Bill Geist**

Bill Geist is an Emmy Award-winning correspondent for CBS News and a *New York Times* bestselling author.

**William F. Buckley, Jr.**
Founder, *National Review,* seminal conservative commentator

**Billy (White Shoes) Johnson**
Stylish wide receiver, kick returner, Houston Oilers

**William Howard Taft**
27th president and 10th Chief Justice of the Supreme Court

**Mr. Bill**
Accident-prone *Saturday Night Live* Play-Doh character

**Bill Gates**
Co-founder, Microsoft, one of the richest men in the world

**William Least Heat Moon**
Author, *Blue Highways*

**Bill Russell**
Center, Boston Celtics, winner of 11 NBA championships

**William Faulkner**
Southern writer, author of *As I Lay Dying*

**Bill O'Reilly**
Fox News Channel host, enemy of Keith Olbermann

**Billy Jack**
Cultish "half-breed" film character created by Tom Laughlin

**Billie Jean King**
Winner of 12 tennis singles Grand Slams; feminist

**William Shatner**
Space-traveling Capt. Kirk of *Star Trek,* Denny Crane of *Boston Legal,* Priceline negotiator

**Bill Clinton**
42nd president of the United States

**William Boyd**
Played cowboy hero Hopalong Cassidy

**Buffalo Bill Cody**
Medal of Honor-winning soldier, Western showman

**Billy Joe (Boondocks) Royal**
Country singer, known for "Down in the Boondocks"

Buckley

Mr. Bill

Gates

Faulkner

Billy Jack

Shatner

Clinton

Buffalo Bill

Mr. Bill

Gates

Shatner

Clinton

Gates

Shatner

**William F. Buckley, Jr. vs. Billy (White Shoes) Johnson**
This remarkable contest of contrasting styles saw Buckley, the polysyllabic conservative, put the brakes on showboating kickoff and punt returner Johnson, the father of modern end-zone celebrations. Buckley employed maximum erudition to overcome the former Houston Oiler's famed jelly-legged "funky chicken" dance.

**Clinton vs. Shatner**
Shatner isn't blessed with the enormously talented 42nd president's natural gifts. But Shatner always gives 110% and will play any position – from Captain Kirk to T.J. Hooker; from *Rescue 911* host to Priceline pitchman to Denny Crane, who at least admits that he has "mad penis." Clinton complained that the cheerleaders hired by Shatner at a local gentlemen's club distracted him.

THE WINNER

## William Shatner

Space-traveling Capt. Kirk *Star Trek*, eccentric Denny Crane of *Boston Legal*, Priceline negotiator

VS

I'VE BEEN A WILLIAM/BILL FOR AS LONG AS I CAN REMEMBER. I never liked Wilma or Wilhelmina, which is why I "stayed put" when the transgender thing hit. I was named for my uncle Bill and my son is Willie (a permutation of William that gets a dispensation here even if said Willies were not born as William). I wish more babies were named William/Bill instead of Baron or D'Brickashaw, but I'm elated by excesses such as the double Billing of William Carlos Williams and Billy Dee Williams. My favorite team: the Buffalo Bills.

**Cyrus vs. Sherman**
Billy Ray Cyrus, the Cinderella of this tournament, wasn't supposed to get this far. But after knocking off William Penn and President McKinley, the underestimated Cyrus, who fathered both "Achy Breaky Heart" and Hannah Montana, lasted as long as a mediocre singer could before "Scorched Earth" Sherman set fire to his mullet.

**Sherman vs. Perry**
It was payback time for the 382-pound Fridge. Born and raised in South Carolina – the first state to secede from the Union – Perry sacked Sherman, who pretty much burned the Bear's home state to the ground in 1865. Sherman's Confederate rivals had never seen anything like his army, but the general had never seen anything like the Refrigerator.

**Perry vs. Shatner**
Perry dazzled as a running back and defensive lineman, even scoring a touchdown in Super Bowl XX. But the relentless Shatner wore down The Fridge with his remarkable endurance, much as he has done to audiences over the past half-century in a metastasizing career without end.

- **Perry**
  - **Sherman**
    - **Cyrus**
      - **Cyrus**
        - **Billy Ray Cyrus** — Country singer, "Achy Breaky Heart"
        - **William Penn** — British-born founder-namesake of Pennsylvania
      - **McKinley**
        - **William McKinley** — 25th president, assassinated in first year of his second term
        - **Billy Bob Thornton** — Star of *Sling Blade,* ex-husband of Angelina Jolie
    - **Sherman**
      - **Sherman**
        - **Gen. William Tecumseh Sherman** — Union general who burned down Atlanta
        - **Willie Mays** — Baseball's "Say Hey Kid" hit 660 home runs
      - **Nelson**
        - **Wild Bill Hickok** — Old West scout, soldier, gunfighter, lawman
        - **Willie Nelson** — Country singer, wrote "Crazy," sang "Georgia on My Mind"
  - **Perry**
    - **Murray**
      - **Murray**
        - **Bill (Bojangles) Robinson** — Dancer, actor, inspiration for the song "Mr. Bojangles"
        - **Bill Murray** — Comic, actor in *Ghostbusters, Groundhog Day, Lost in Translation*
      - **Harrison**
        - **Billy the Kid** — Outlaw, killer, gunned down by Sheriff Pat Garrett
        - **William Henry Harrison** — 9th president, died of pneumonia after 32 days in office
    - **Perry**
      - **Graham**
        - **Billy Graham** — Crusading evangelist, friend of presidents
        - **William Hung** — Off-key *American Idol* "singer" and early YouTube star
      - **Perry**
        - **William (The Refrigerator) Perry** — Enormous Chicago Bear defensive tackle, and occasional fullback
        - **William Carlos Williams** — Modernist poet (and practicing MD), wrote "The Red Wheelbarrow"

# Disappearing Acts

**By Franz Lidz**

Franz Lidz is the author of *Unstrung Heroes, Ghosty Men,* and *Fairway to Hell.* He lives quietly on Barmy Farm with 2 Great Pyrenees, 2 cats, 13 chickens, 8 guinea fowl, and 1 wife.

**Homer and Langley Collyer**
Harlem hermits

**Marlon Brando**
actor-turned-Tahitian-atoll

**Collyer Brothers**

**Emily Dickinson**
poet

**Phil Spector**
record producer, gun enthusiast

**Emily Dickinson**

**Collyer Brothers**

**Henry David Thoreau**
civil disobeyer

**B. Traven**
author, *The Treasure of the Sierra Madre*

**B. Traven**

**B. Traven**

**Ted Kaczynski**
Unabomber

**Sly Stone**
founder, Sly & The Family Stone

**Ted Kaczynski**

**Collyer Brothers**

**Bill Watterson**
creator, Calvin and Hobbes

**Bobby Fischer**
20th-century chess grandmaster

**Bobby Fischer**

**Bobby Fischer**

**Djuna Barnes**
author, *Nightwood*

**Brian Wilson**
Beach Boys singer

**Brian Wilson**

**Paul Morphy**

**Harper Lee**
author, *To Kill a Mockingbird*

**Howard Hughes**
germophobic plutocrat

**Harper Lee**

**Paul Morphy**

**Sandy Koufax**
Hall of Fame pitcher

**Paul Morphy**
19th-century chess grandmaster

**Paul Morphy**

**B. Traven vs. Henry Thoreau**
Thoreau's two years of living in Emerson's cabin at Walden Pond are trumped by Traven's slipperiness. Nobody is quite sure where he was from, what he looked like, or whether he was really Hal Croves, Otto Feige, Goetz Ohly, Anton Räderscheidt, or Ret Marut, who wrote, "I shall always and at all times prefer to be pissed on by dogs than reveal who I am."

**Paul Morphy vs. Bobby Fischer**
In the intensely cerebral world of tournament chess, Morphy set the bar too high. After abandoning the game at 21, he retreated to his New Orleans madhouse, where he arranged women's shoes in a semicircle and died Marat-like in his bathtub at 47. Fischer quit as the world champion at 32 and turned electro-shock jock, a wanderer from Pasadena to Iceland, ultimately going nowhere.

**Howard Hughes vs. Harper Lee**
The billionaire Hughes's idea of human interaction was to watch his toenails grow. So the game goes to Lee, who created Boo Radley in her own image. For most of her only novel, the character silently observes the goings-on from afar and resists attempts to be drawn out. Eventually, he emerges, does one spectacular thing, then recoils from public gaze.

THE WINNER

**Homer and Langle Collyer**
Harlem hermits

VS

A LIFE OF SOLITUDE AND CONTEMPLATION WAS ONCE A VIRTUE. Nowadays, it's suspect. No longer just figures of mystery and fascination, recluses have devolved into a kind of sub-people to be pitied for their failure to appreciate the worth of TiVo, electric mascara, and Berry Chai Tazo Tea Infusions. The more famous the recluse or the longer the self-imposed exile, the more these disappearing acts' decisions to disappear and enjoy their privacy – basically to say no to human contact, no to everything – invites speculation about their psychological shortcomings. Sometimes fairly, often not.

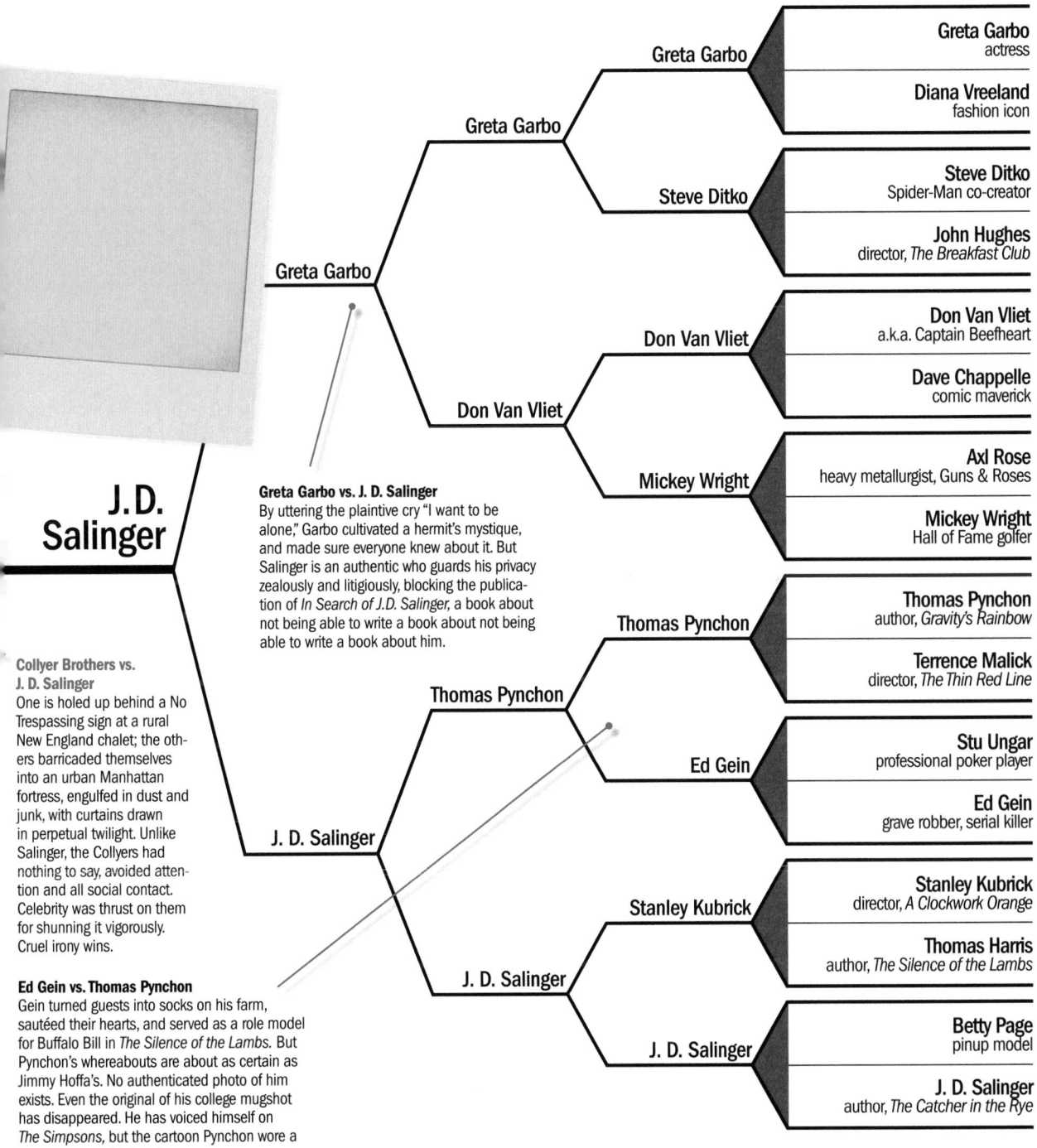


**Greta Garbo vs. J. D. Salinger**
By uttering the plaintive cry "I want to be alone," Garbo cultivated a hermit's mystique, and made sure everyone knew about it. But Salinger is an authentic who guards his privacy zealously and litigiously, blocking the publication of *In Search of J.D. Salinger*, a book about not being able to write a book about not being able to write a book about him.

**Collyer Brothers vs. J. D. Salinger**
One is holed up behind a No Trespassing sign at a rural New England chalet; the others barricaded themselves into an urban Manhattan fortress, engulfed in dust and junk, with curtains drawn in perpetual twilight. Unlike Salinger, the Collyers had nothing to say, avoided attention and all social contact. Celebrity was thrust on them for shunning it vigorously. Cruel irony wins.

**Ed Gein vs. Thomas Pynchon**
Gein turned guests into socks on his farm, sautéed their hearts, and served as a role model for Buffalo Bill in *The Silence of the Lambs*. But Pynchon's whereabouts are about as certain as Jimmy Hoffa's. No authenticated photo of him exists. Even the original of his college mugshot has disappeared. He has voiced himself on *The Simpsons*, but the cartoon Pynchon wore a paper bag over his head.

# Richard vs. Dick

**By Richard Sandomir**

Richard Sandomir, the co-editor of this book, was born a Richard and rarely answers to anything but his full name, Rich or Richie. Only older men call him Dick, to which he will respond reluctantly.

RICHARD REGIONAL

**Nixon**
37th president, unindicted co-conspirator in Watergate scandal

**Gere**
Hunk married a pretty woman

**Avedon**
Fashion photographer, portraitist

**Holbrooke**
Peripatetic diplomat, socialite, peace junkie

**Dreyfuss**
Brash actor who played a Dick – Cheney

**Daley (the Elder)**
Tough-guy Chicago mayor for 21 years, spawned a successor

**Petty**
"The King" of NASCAR won seven championships

**Byrd**
Polar explorer, aviator, Navy admiral

**Rodgers**
Oh, what a beautiful lyricist, etcetera, etcetera

**Little**
Good golly, Mr. Penniman!

**Speck**
Mass murderer with hormone-enlarged breasts.

**Feynman**
Helped develop atom bomb, played bongos.

**Clarke**
Counter-terrorism czar who said Bush ignored terrorism before 9/11

**Pryor**
Brilliant, fiery, game-changing comic raised in a brothel

**Roundtree**
One word: Shaft!

**Sears**
Mail-order genius's name came before Roebuck's

Nixon | Holbrooke | Daley | Petty | Rodgers | Feynman | Pryor | Sears

Nixon | Petty | Feynman | Pryor

Nixon | Pryor

**Gere vs. Nixon**
Nixon's toxic brew of physical awkwardness, paranoia, and mendacity overwhelms the suave, handsome actor, who only rose to officer and gentleman. No one can ignore the significance of on-screen romancing of Julia Roberts and Diane Lane, but Tricky Dick did that China thing. Tricky Dick sweeps into the second round with Gere in his arms.

**Little Richard vs. Richard Rodgers**
It's tempting to reward Little Richard's sexualized outrageousness, but it's difficult to place "A-Wop-bop-a-loo-lop-a-lop-bam-boo" and "Good golly, Miss Molly, sure like to ball" against Rodgers's *South Pacific, The King and I,* and *Oklahoma.* Little's music could send you into a tizzy, but Rodgers could make you swoon.

THE WINNER

**Richard Nixon**

VS

**Nixon vs. Pryor**
I kid you not: Nixon's Checkers and resignation speeches are funnier than "That Nigger's Crazy." His "Republican cloth coat" and "my mother was a saint" routines were both pathetic and hysterical. Nixon's inadvertent wit – he didn't play blue in public – put an oratorical cherry on his amazing and tragic political oeuvre.

**Feynman vs. Pryor**
Feynman was a physicist for the people – he divined what caused the space shuttle *Challenger* to blow up and played bongos – and was awfully funny for an A-bomb guy. But Pryor was a storyteller and linguist whose otherworldly use of the language, not just his glorious deployment of profanity, illustrated the possibilities of humor, not just black humor.

IN THIS BATTLE OF RICHARDS AND DICKS, we omit Ricks, Dickies, and Rickys as too much clutter, and foreign greats like Richard III, Dick Francis, or Richard the Lionheart, who aren't eligible. Despite Richard's enormous etymological edge (Old German for "powerful leader") over Dick (a genitalian. lunkheaded variant of Richard that flatters no one), both regions display an astonishing breadth of talent in politics, culture, sports, and science. And in any gathering of Dicks, a little Trickle must fall.

**Cavett vs. Button**
Cavett's version of the late-night talk show was about erudition and Groucho, but Button won Winter Olympic figure skating gold in 1948 and 1952, performed the first double axel and toe loop in competition, and then became TV's most influential and acerbic figure skating commentator.

**Nixon vs. Cheney**
This creepy smackdown of megalomaniacs comes down largely to this: Nixon was the president and Cheney only thought he was. Cheney scores for staying in office when reluctant Congress doesn't even try to impeach him and his sidekick. Plus, doctors located Cheney's tiny heart in order to implant a defibrillator; there was no evidence of Nixon's.

- **Cheney**
  - **Tracy**
    - **Button**
      - **Cavett**
        - **Cavett** — Erudite talk show host couldn't beat Carson
        - **Sargent/York** — The two Darrins of *Bewitched*
      - **Button**
        - **Fosbury** — Back-first flop revolutionized high-jumping
        - **Button** — Figure skating and broadcasting innovator with a Harvard Law degree
    - **Tracy**
      - **Tracy**
        - **Wolf** — The *Law & Order* mogul
        - **Tracy** — Cartoon enforcer of law and order with neat watch
      - **Schaap**
        - **Williams** — Hall of Fame manager, only Yankee skipper never to manage a game
        - **Schaap** — Writer-editor who dubbed New York "Fun City"
  - **Cheney**
    - **Cheney**
      - **Van Dyke**
        - **Van Dyke** — Comic actor who tripped over, then sidestepped, an ottoman
        - **Vitale** — Hoops (and Hooters) voice
      - **Cheney**
        - **Butkus** — Snot-kicking, bone-rattling Chicago Bears linebacker
        - **Cheney** — Quail-hunting v.p.; a danger to friends and Constitution
    - **Clark**
      - **Clark**
        - **Clark** — World's oldest teenager, *American Bandstand*
        - **Weber** — Popular bowling legend fathered unpopular bowling legend
      - **Gregory**
        - **Gregory** — Pioneering black standup comic and diet guru
        - **Trickle** — NASCAR racer smoked while driving; should have stayed a Richard

DICK REGIONAL

# American Pinups

**By Gregory Curtis**

Gregory Curtis is the former editor of *Texas Monthly*. Until he wrote *Disarmed: The Story of the Venus de Milo*, he had never, ever, not even once, noticed a pinup.

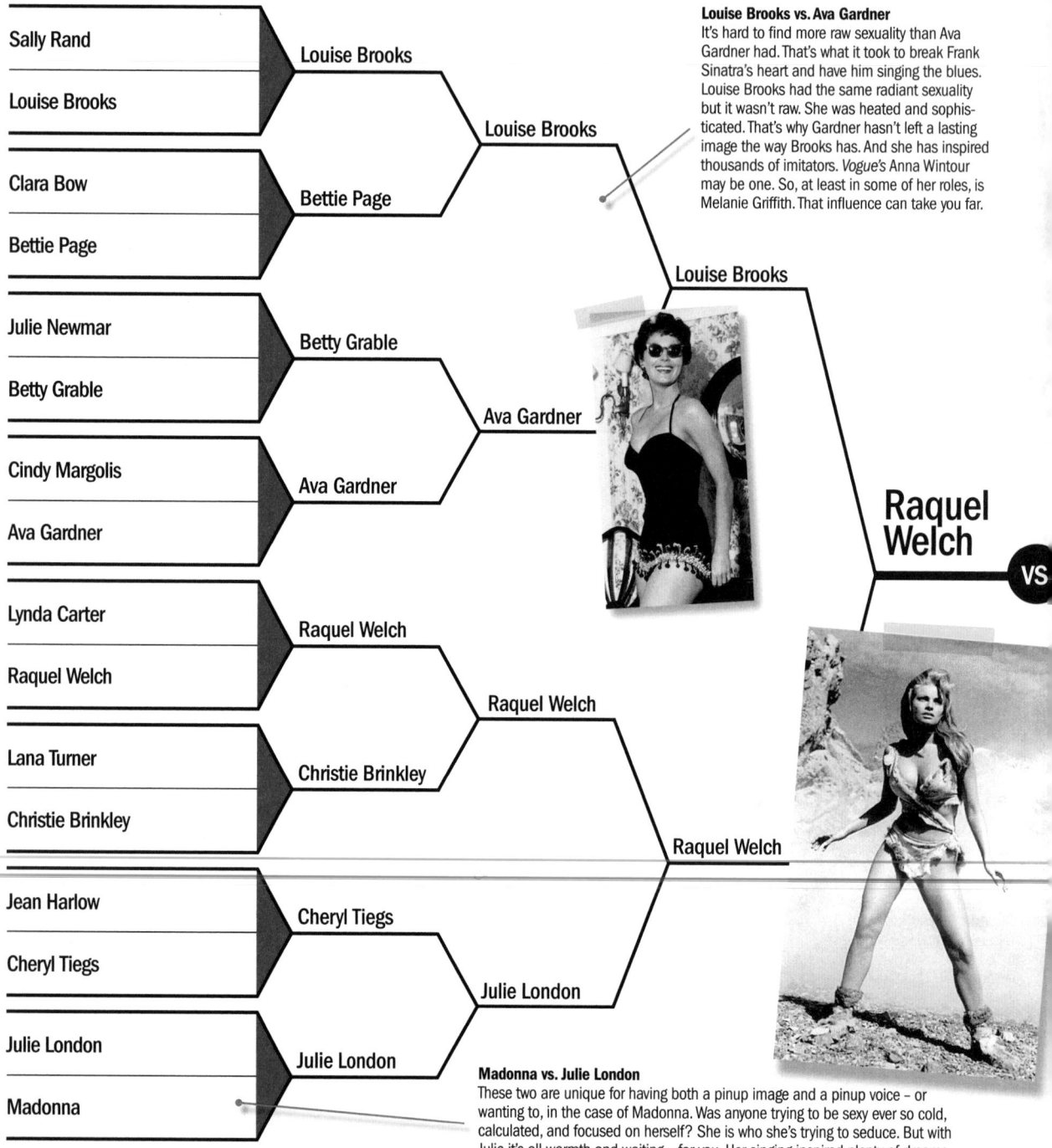


**Louise Brooks vs. Ava Gardner**
It's hard to find more raw sexuality than Ava Gardner had. That's what it took to break Frank Sinatra's heart and have him singing the blues. Louise Brooks had the same radiant sexuality but it wasn't raw. She was heated and sophisticated. That's why Gardner hasn't left a lasting image the way Brooks has. And she has inspired thousands of imitators. *Vogue's* Anna Wintour may be one. So, at least in some of her roles, is Melanie Griffith. That influence can take you far.

**Madonna vs. Julie London**
These two are unique for having both a pinup image and a pinup voice – or wanting to, in the case of Madonna. Was anyone trying to be sexy ever so cold, calculated, and focused on herself? She is who she's trying to seduce. But with Julie it's all warmth and waiting – for you. Her singing inspired plenty of dreams. Her album covers inspired even more.

PINUPS COME IN TWO VARIETIES. She can be the girl next door, turned into a goddess but still nice, e.g., Cheryl Tiegs, Christie Brinkley, Farrah Fawcett, even Bettie Page in bondage smiling sweetly. Or she can be Miss Va Va Voom, an extreme physical specimen that seems other-worldly, e.g., Jane Russell, Marilyn Monroe, Jayne Mansfield. A pinup of the first style is a nice girl. Miss Va Va Voom is beyond being a nice girl (or a bad girl) and so becomes soulless. A nice bust doesn't make up for that.

**Annette Funicello vs. Marilyn Monroe**
This is entirely generational. Marilyn – I'm happy to let JFK have her. But if you grew up watching the *Mickey Mouse Club*, you noticed Annette, if you know what I mean, and I think you do. She could still get under your skin even during her silly movie career.

THE WINNER

## Rita Hayworth

**Farrah Fawcett vs. Rita Hayworth**
This is a brown swimsuit vs. a satin and lace negligee; sand on the beach vs. white, satin sheets; a mop of wild hair vs. soft and radiant curls; the scent of wind and salt vs. a delicate and expensive perfume that seems to waft by as you look at her picture. All that outdoorsy stuff is nice, but after a while you're going to want to come inside.

**Raquel Welch vs. Rita Hayworth**
Is it coincidence that these are the two plot-pivotal pinups hanging on Andy Dufresne's prison cell wall in *The Shawshank Redemption?* Raquel gets this far because she has a very great body and a very great face and because she looks primal and iconic just standing there, whether in a bikini, lingerie, or some ersatz caveman getup. Just stay right like that, you think. You don't want her to move and you probably don't even want to get too close. Rita . . . well, with Rita you do want to.

**Heidi Van Horne vs. Jayne Mansfield**
Heidi is one of several models trying to forge a career by using hair styles, makeup, and costumes that attempt to recreate the pinup look of the '40s and '50s, often inspired by Bettie Page. But what you see is a re-creation, sort of, not something genuine. There are problems with Jayne (see intro) but she was smack in the middle of her time. I once slightly knew a man who had married her before she was famous. He had a kindly, but rather shell-shocked air.

- Farrah Fawcett
  - Annette Funicello
    - Annette Funicello
      - Vargas Girl
      - Annette Funicello
    - Marilyn Monroe
      - Marilyn Monroe
      - Gloria Swanson
  - Farrah Fawcett
    - Farrah Fawcett
      - Farrah Fawcett
      - Lauren Hutton
    - Veronica Lake
      - Veronica Lake
      - Kathy Ireland
- Rita Hayworth
  - Rita Hayworth
    - Rita Hayworth
      - Barbie Benton
      - Rita Hayworth
    - Jane Russell
      - Lauren Hutton
      - Jane Russell
  - Jayne Mansfield
    - Mae West
      - Gypsy Rose Lee
      - Mae West
    - Jayne Mansfield
      - Heidi Van Horne
      - Jayne Mansfield

# Pundits

**By Franklin Foer**

Franklin Foer is a pundit who lives among pundits in Washington, DC. He is editor of the *New Republic* and author of *How Soccer Explains the World: An Unlikely Theory of Globalization.*

**Tucker Carlson**
MSNBC correspondent, former CNN host

**George F. Will**
*Washington Post, Newsweek* columnist

**Will**

**Arianna Huffington**
Syndicated columnist, founder, *Huffington Post*

**Tina Brown**
Editor, *Vanity Fair, The New Yorker,* creator, *The Daily Beast*

**Huffington**

**Will**

**Walter Lippmann**
Author, presidential advisor, syndicated columnist

**Chris Matthews**
Extremely loud MSNBC host

**Lippmann**

**Lippmann**

**David Gergen**
Former aide to Democratic and Republican presidents

**Robert Reich**
Ex-secretary of labor, college professor

**Gergen**

**Ann Coulter**
Self-styled polemicist; anti-liberal books include *Slander* and *Treason*

**Mary Matalin**
Editor of conservative book imprint, former aide to Vice President Cheney

**Coulter**

**Coulter**

**James Carville**
Political strategist behind Bill Clinton, Matalin's husband

**Paul Begala**
Former Carville partner and co-host, CNN's *Crossfire*

**Carville**

**Fred Barnes**
Executive editor, *The Weekly Standard*

**Mort Kondracke**
Columnist and co-host, with Barnes, of Fox News Channel's *The Beltway Boys*

**Barnes**

**McLaughlin**

**Pat Buchanan**
Former Nixon speechwriter, presidential candidate, columnist, MSNBC commentator

**John McLaughlin**
Host, *The McLaughlin Group*

**McLaughlin**

**Letters**

**OPINIO**

**OP-ED**

**Lippmann**

**Lippmann**

**Coulter**

**Lippmann**

**VS**

**McLaughlin vs. Coulter**
McLaughlin invented the TV screamfest and provided fodder for *Saturday Night Live.* Coulter understood how a buffoonish pundit could make millions, using outrageous claims about liberalism to ascend the bestseller lists. Marketing ludicrous ideas with such consistency takes true pundit genius. If you can't appreciate her greatness, she'll accuse you of treason, pedophilia, or a crime against humanity.

**Buckley vs. Lippmann**
Lippmann started out with greater intellectual chops, writing lasting works of political philosophy. But over his career, he acquired increasingly more blowhard tendencies. Buckley launched the American conservative movement – a footprint on political life that no pundit can match. Although he shifted his attention to writing forgettable spy novels, Buckley maintained a charming public persona that even his detractors could love.

IN THE GOLDEN AGE OF PUNDITS – before bloggers, YouTube, and the slow demise of newspapers eroded their influence – creatures discoursed from television thrones and bejeweled columns with sage authority, even if their wisdom was only gleaned earlier that day over lunch at The Palm. Some were blowhards, some were more entrepreneur than commentator, but some were genuine intellectuals and great reporters. The best destroyed old strands of conventional wisdom in the course of creating new ones. The others, well, they shouted.

**Irving Kristol vs. Bill Kristol**
The Oedipal neo-con match is pretty even. Daddy founded a journal *(The Public Interest)* and so did his son *(The Weekly Standard)*. The father propagated the theory of the "new class"; the son championed the Iraq War. But only Bill has been a Fox News All-Star.

THE WINNER

**William F. Buckley, Jr.**
Conservative giant, editor-publisher, *The National Review*

**Kinsley vs. Buckley**
Two of the greatest wits to emerge from American opinion journalism – and perhaps the greatest magazine editors of their eras. Buckley founded *National Review* and hosted "Firing Line." Kinsley founded Slate. On TV, they could argue one another to a draw. But Buckley never looked like he was trying.

**Dowd vs. Krugman**
She has bon mots, pop cultural references galore, and a hatred for all things Clinton. He preaches neo-Keynsian economics and thunders against defenders of plutocracy. She's funny, writes in Latin, and has a Pulitzer. But he's got a Nobel Prize.

- Kinsley
  - Bill Kristol
    - Irving Kristol
      - **Irving Kristol** – Godfather of neoconservatism, father of William
      - **Peggy Noonan** – Ex-Reagan speechwriter, *Wall Street Journal* columnist
    - Bill Kristol
      - **Bill Kristol** – Fox News Channel commentator, columnist; once dubbed "Dan Quayle's brain"
      - **Michelle Malkin** – Columnist, defended WWII Japanese internment in U.S. camps
  - Kinsley
    - Kinsley
      - **Joe Klein** – *Time* columnist, author of *Primary Colors*
      - **Michael Kinsley** – Columnist, former editor, *The New Republic*
    - Friedman
      - **William Safire** – Former *New York Times* op-ed columnist and Nixon speechwriter
      - **Thomas Friedman** – *Times* columnist, three Pulitzers
- Buckley
  - Hitchens
    - Hitchens
      - **Christopher Hitchens** – Columnist, literary critic, author of *God Is Not Great*
      - **Norman Podhoretz** – Former editor-in-chief, *Commentary*
    - Rich
      - **Frank Rich** – *Times* columnist
      - **Bob Herbert** – *Times* columnist
  - Buckley
    - Krugman
      - **Paul Krugman** – *Times* columnist, Princeton economist, Nobel Prize winner
      - **Maureen Dowd** – *Times* columnist, one Pulitzer
    - Buckley
      - **William F. Buckley, Jr.** – Conservative giant, editor-publisher, *The National Review*
      - **Sean Hannity** – Host, Fox News

OP-ED THU
EDITORIAL
OPINION

# Great Brother Acts

**By Mark Reiter**

Mark Reiter, the co-editor of this book, has one brother but they live 6,000 miles apart, which makes it tough to get their act together.

**Neville**
Aaron, Art, Charles, Cyril (R&B)

**Farrelly**
Bobby and Peter (filmmakers, *Dumb and Dumber*)

**Kennedy**
John, Robert, Edward (politics)

**Louvin**
Charlie and Ira (country music)

**Smothers**
Dick and Tommy (comedy)

**Gallo**
Ernest and Julio (wine)

**Everly**
Don and Phil (pop music)

**Rockefeller**
Nelson, David, John D. III (public service)

**Smith**
Andrew and William (cough drops)

**Wright**
Orville and Wilbur (aviation)

**Allman**
Duane and Gregg (rock music)

**Hanson**
Isaac, Taylor, Zac (pop music)

**Isley**
Kelly, Rudy, Ronnie, Vernon (soul music)

**Parker**
George, Charles, Edward (board games, Monopoly)

**Baldwin**
Alec, Daniel, Stephen, William (acting)

**Bush**
George W. and Jeb (politics)

Farrelly | Kennedy | Smothers | Everly | Wright | Allman | Parker | Baldwin

Kennedy | Smothers | Wright | Parker

Kennedy | Wright

**Smothers vs. Everly**
Where the Everlys blended voices into magical harmonies, the Smothers were polar opposites. Buttoned-up Dick was the foil while knucklehead Tommy pulled in the yuks, crying, "Mom always liked you best!" Rudely cancelled in 1969, their *Comedy Hour* is one of TV's most underrated shows (and spawned Pat Paulsen's bid for president). The act has worked for over 50 years, so they move on.

THE WINNER

## Wright Brothers, Orville and Wilbur

VS

**Marx vs. Wright**
A tough choice between the Marxs' fanciful flights of mayhem and mirth and the Wrights' daring liftoff from Earth in 1903. Although the Wrights never coined immortal musings like Groucho's "I don't want to belong to any club that will accept me as a member," they did invent the controls that let pilots actually steer an airplane. Without that innovation, planes would be as out of control as the Marx Brothers in *Duck Soup* and *A Night at the Opera*. We can't have that.

**Bush vs. Baldwin**
Most of the Baldwin brothers have mercifully disappeared from film and TV screens – and the best of the bunch, Alec, has rebuilt his image as a deft comedian. But they were never great as a team. Only time will tell if W's victory in the decisive 2000 Florida recount while brother Jeb was governor is passing strange or the greatest brother act in U.S. history.

TO BE A GREAT BROTHER ACT you have to operate as a team, creating a sum greater than the parts. It's not enough to be in the same line of work, like the brothers McEnroe in tennis or the DiMaggios in baseball. You have to complement and enhance each other, and one sib cannot overshadow the others so greatly that it sunders the act itself (which is why the Jacksons don't get past the second round). After that, the main criterion here is achievement and impact.

**Coen vs. Ringling**
While the Ringling Brothers refashioned the small-town circus into the "greatest show on earth," largely by switching to trains for transport, it could be argued that the Coen brothers, in films like *Fargo*, *The Big Lebowski*, and their Oscar-winner *No Country for Old Men*, have turned the entire world into a freak show. And they're not finished.

**Gershwin vs. Manning**
The Mannings were the winning quarterbacks in consecutive Super Bowls in 2007 and 2008. But the Gershwins – with music by George, words by Ira, including *Porgy and Bess* and "Someone to Watch Over Me" – remain music's most successful brother act.

- **Marx**
  - Gershwin
    - Coen
      - Ringling
        - **Jones** – Thad, Hank, Elvin (jazz)
        - **Ringling** – Albert, August, Otto, Alfred T., Charles, John, Henry (circus)
      - Coen
        - **Howard** – Moe, Curly, Shemp (The Three Stooges)
        - **Coen** – Joel and Ethan (film-makers, *Fargo*)
    - Gershwin
      - Manning
        - **Kaczynski** – Ted and David (Unabomber and his captor)
        - **Manning** – Peyton and Eli (football)
      - Gershwin
        - **Gershwin** – George and Ira (songwriting)
        - **Dean** – Dizzy and Daffy (baseball)
  - Marx
    - Marx
      - Jackson
        - **Jackson** – Jackie, Jermaine, Marlon, Michael, Randy, Tito (music)
        - **Bridges** – Beau and Jeff (actors)
      - Marx
        - **Osmond** – Alan, Donny, Jay, Jimmy, Merrill, Wayne (music)
        - **Marx** – Groucho, Harpo, Chico, and Zeppo (comedy)
    - Warner
      - Warner
        - **Warner** – Albert, Harry, Jack, Sam, (movie studio moguls)
        - **Jonas** – Joe, Kevin, Nick (pop music)
      - Wachowski
        - **Adderley** – Cannonball and Nate (jazz)
        - **Wachowski** – Andy and Larry (film-makers, *The Matrix*)

# Tom vs. Thomas

**By Tom Chiarella**

Tom Chiarella is fiction editor and writer-at-large for *Esquire* magazine. He is a visiting professor at DePauw University in Greencastle, Indiana. Author of three books, his next is *The Proposition.* No one calls him Thomas.

**Tom Sawyer**
literary archetype

**Tom, the Cat**
partner of Jerry

**Tom Brady**
supercool quarterback

**Tom Watson**
golfer

**Tom Glavine**
Hall of Fame caliber pitcher

**Tom Seaver**
Hall of Fame pitcher

**Tom Petty**
rock star

**Tom Cruise**
movie star

**Tom Brokaw**
anchorman

**Tom Ford**
fashion designer

**Tom Wolfe**
well-dressed writer

**Tom Waits**
poet-musician

**Tommy Lee**
musician, home-video star

**Tommy Lee Jones**
A-list actor

**Tom Hanks**
A-list actor

**Tommy Tune**
very tall dancer

Sawyer

Brady

Seaver

Cruise

Brokaw

Waits

Lee Jones

Hanks

Sawyer

Seaver

Waits

Lee Jones

Sawyer

Waits

**Waits vs. Sawyer**
Gravel-voiced lothario Tom Waits upends the schoolboy fave Sawyer, mostly because it's even odds that the clever boy Sawyer grew up to be another of Waits's cigarette-smoking, bourbon-scarfing barflies. When you start out owing your life to Twain and end up in debt to Waits, the latter wins.

**Cruise vs. Seaver**
For sheer fame, Cruise has the edge, but what has he done with the name? Seaver takes this one because his nickname "Tom Terrific" did more for the name than the increasingly weird Cruise has in his many cinematic passes at immortality.

**Tom Waits**

VS

**Lee vs. Jones**
You can argue that Motley Crüe drummer Tommy Lee did more for the name with one widely circulated honeymoon video than Tommy Lee Jones did with a lifetime of growling roles, like his Oscar turn in *The Fugitive*. But I don't buy it. Jones wins because he's aged like fine leather, hides his Harvard education well, and single-handedly improved the status of anything with "little sprinkles on top."

GENERALLY SPEAKING, you'd want to have a beer with a Tom and have your taxes done by a guy named Thomas. As for Tommy, well, take my word for it: never lend money to a guy named Tommy. Tom is affable, Thomas self-serious, and Tommy flirts with edgy. Hence, two regionals here, one for Tom and the occasional Tommy, the other for Thomas. Only first names were invited, thus avoiding some tasty first-round match-ups (Clarence Thomas vs. Helen Thomas) and brand names like Tommy Gun and that nourishing semi-final lock, Thomas' English Muffins.

**Paine vs. Friedman**
After defeating Thomas Frank, who identified the head-slapping insight that conservatives vote values over their economic self-interest in *What's the Matter with Kansas?*, Paine (who wrote a pamphlet) rolls over to the master phrasemaker of the 21st-century punditocracy. Friedman, after all, is a thrice-Pulitzerized journalist who, upon identifying globalization, sold us millions of copies of *The World Is Flat*.

THE WINNER

# Thomas Jefferson

**Waits vs. Jefferson**
Good tunes can only take you so far, so Waits's unlikely journey to the final ends in a walk for a polymath Founding Father who wrote our Constitution, built an architectural masterpiece at Monticello, became our third president, and died at age 83 on the Fourth of July. As JFK said on greeting 49 Nobel laureates to the White House, "This is the most extraordinary collection of talent and of human knowledge that has ever been gathered together at the White House – with the possible exception of when Thomas Jefferson dined alone."

**Hearns vs. Pynchon**
If "a screaming comes across the sky," it's probably one of the Hit Man's hydraulic left jabs, which makes Pynchon see *Gravity's Rainbow* fo' real.

- Jefferson
  - Friedman
    - Paine
      - Thomas Frank, common-sense author
      - Thomas Paine, author, *Common Sense*
    - Friedman
      - Thomas Friedman, op-ed phrasemaker
      - Thomas Stearns Eliot, poet (T.S.)
  - Jefferson
    - Jefferson
      - Thomas Jefferson, founding father
      - Thomas McGuane, author, *92 in the Shade*
    - Benton
      - Thomas Kinkade, "artist"
      - Thomas Hart Benton, artist
- Edison
  - Edison
    - Edison
      - Thomas Edison, inventor
      - Thomas Nast, 19th c. cartoonist
    - Wolff
      - Thomas Wolff, author, *You Can't Go Home Again*
      - Thomas Jane, B-list actor
  - Hearns
    - Harris
      - Thomas Harris, author, *Silence of the Lambs*
      - Thomas Hampson, opera baritone
    - Hearns
      - Thomas "Hitman" Hearns, boxer
      - Thomas Pynchon, novelist, academic darling

# Immigrants

**By Tony Quinn**

Tony Quinn is the former editor of *Irish Connections* magazine and sports editor of *Home and Away* newspaper. He came to the U.S. from Newry in Ireland in 1993 and lives in Brooklyn.

**Albert Einstein**
physicist, Germany

**Farouk El-Baz**
NASA scientist, Egypt

**St. Patrick's Day**
holiday, Ireland

**Cinco de Mayo**
holiday, Mexico

**Henry Kissinger**
diplomatic strategist, Germany

**Madeline Albright**
diplomat, Czech Republic

**Deepak Chopra**
mind and body guru, India

**St. Frances Xavier Cabrini**
patron saint of immigrants, Italy

**Bob Hope**
entertainer, England

**Al Jolson**
entertainer, Lithuania

**Arnold Schwarzenegger**
bodybuilder, politician, Austria

**Charles Atlas**
bodybuilder, Italy

**Marcus Garvey**
activist, Jamaica

**Emma Goldman**
activist, Russia

**Oscar de la Renta**
fashion designer, Dominican Republic

**Liz Claiborne**
fashion designer, Belgium

Einstein

St. Patrick's Day

Kissinger

Cabrini

Hope

Schwarzenegger

Garvey

Claiborne

Einstein

Kissinger

Schwarzenegger

Garvey

Kissinger

Schwarzenegger

**Kissinger vs. Murdoch**
The Australian-born, global media mogul against the German-born former secretary of state. Murdoch wields a lot of influence, but will never carry as many titles – political scientist, bureaucrat, diplomat, Nobel Peace Prize winner, and to some, war criminal – as Kissinger. Murdoch shapes what we watch and read. Kissinger shaped the global landscape of who we like and who likes us.

**Atlas vs. Schwarzenegger**
Is this really any competition? While Charles Atlas remains a bodybuilding icon, Schwarzenegger conquered the U.S. first as a bodybuilder and then, with iron will, as an actor and action hero. Then he married into the Kennedy clan. Then he ran for governor of California as a Republican – and won. Atlas wilts. The Governator advances.

THE WINNER

**Henry Kissinger**
diplomatic strategist

VS

A BRONZE PLAQUE OUTSIDE THE CHELSEA HOTEL in New York City reads: "To America, my new found land: The man that hates you hates the human race." Though the author of these words, the Irish writer Brendan Behan, never actually became a U.S. citizen, his words express the hope of every immigrant: to discover a love for a country that is not your own. America draws people from every corner of the world. Driven by ambition, curiosity, dreams of safety or freedom, we are a nation of immigrants. Here, some of the most influential.

**Carnegie vs. Murdoch**
The Scottish-born industrialist and businessman is often regarded as the second richest person in history. But he made his lasting mark as a philanthropist, giving most of his money away to fund schools and libraries. If there's a large, beautiful, imposing library in your home town, chances are Carnegie paid for it. Murdoch's News Corp is one of the world's largest media conglomerates and shows no signs of slowing down.

**Kudzu vs. Boll Weevil**
While the cotton-eating boll weevil is the only agricultural pest to have its own monument (in Enterprise, Alabama, where it reminds citizens not to depend solely on cotton), kudzu the climbing vine costs the U.S. half a billion dollars annually to control. Called mile-a-minute vine, foot-a-night vine, and the vine that ate the South, kudzu creeps into the next round.

**Houdini vs. Brin**
The ultimate escape artist, Houdini was a mesmerizing, confounding star, until a punch in the stomach killed him. Brin's brainchild Google has become the way to illuminate (almost) any subject. For answering our questions daily, Brin advances.

- **Rupert Murdoch**
  - Murdoch
    - Murdoch
      - Navratilova
        - **Martina Navratilova** — tennis player, Czech Republic
        - **Hakeem Olajuwon** — basketball player, Nigeria
      - Murdoch
        - **Andrew Carnegie** — businessman, Scotland
        - **Rupert Murdoch** — media mogul, Australia
    - Audubon
      - Lee
        - **Elia Kazan** — director, Turkey
        - **Ang Lee** — director, Taiwan
      - Audubon
        - **John Muir** — naturalist, Scotland
        - **John J. Audubon** — ornithologist, Haiti
  - Kudzu
    - Kudzu
      - Wiesel
        - **Elie Wiesel** — author, Romania
        - **Frank McCourt** — author, Ireland
      - Kudzu
        - **Boll Weevil** — agricultural menace, Mexico
        - **Kudzu** — vegetative pest, Japan
    - Brin
      - Houdini
        - **Mikhail Baryshnikov** — ballet dancer, Latvia
        - **Harry Houdini** — escape artist, Hungary
      - Brin
        - **Sergey Brin** — Co-founder of Google, Russia
        - **Jerry Yang** — Co-founder of Yahoo, Taiwan

Aldo

# SPORTS


**Olympic Athletes** *by David Maraniss* 52
**NFL Team Logos** *by D.W. Pine* 53
**Dallas Cowboys** *by Jeff Pearlman* 54
**Jewish Baseball Players** *by Daniel Okrent* 55
**All-Time Fantasy Sports Performances** *by Matt Pitzer* 56
**21st-Century Sports Books** *by Will Leitch* 57
**Ringless Athletes** *by Dick Friedman* 58
**Donald Ross Courses** *by Bob Carney* 59
**American Hockey Players** *by Nick Paumgarten* 60
**Steroid-Era Moments** *by Shaun Assael* 61
**Sports Clichés** *by Steve Rushin* 62
**Instant Replays** *by Alan Schwarz* 63
**Sexually Inadequate Nicknames** *by Hart Seely* 64
**Baseball Moments** *by John Thorn* 65
**Absurd College Nicknames** *by Richard Sandomir and Pete Thamel* 66
**Toughest Golf Holes** *by Chris Millard* 67
**Dubious Sports Achievements** *by Richard Hoffer* 68
**From Athlete to Actor** *by Mark Reiter* 69
**Sportscasters** *by Richard Deitsch* 70
**SEC Athletes** *by Steve Eubanks* 71
**Pound-for-Pound Fighters** *by Steve Farhood* 72
**Field Goals and PATs** *by Stefan Fatsis* 73
**Golf Books** *by John Garrity* 74
**New York Athletes** *by George Vecsey* 75
**Boston Athletes** *by Dan Shaughnessy* 76
**Sportswriters** *by Glenn Stout* 77
**Advertising Icons** *by Bryan Curtis* 78
**Greatest Sports Year** *by Mike Vaccaro* 79

# Olympic Athletes

**By David Maraniss**

David Maraniss, an associate editor of the *Washington Post,* won a 1993 Pulitzer Prize for his articles on Bill Clinton. His books include *When Pride Still Mattered* and *Rome 1960.*

**Carl Lewis**
sprinter and long jumper

**Tommie Smith**
sprinter

**Bob Beamon**
sprinter

**Edwin Moses**
hurdler

**Jackie Joyner-Kersee**
heptathlete

**Mary Lou Retton**
gymnast

**Greg Louganis**
diver

**Pat McCormick**
diver

**Jim Thorpe**
decathlete and pentathlete

**Avery Brundage**
decathlete, Olympic executive

**Michael Johnson**
sprinter

**Jesse Owens**
sprinter, long jumper

**Cassius Clay**
boxer

**Sugar Ray Leonard**
boxer

**Dick Button**
figure skater

**Wilma Rudolph**
sprinter

Carl Lewis

Edwin Moses

Jackie Joyner-Kersee

Pat McCormick

Jim Thorpe

Jesse Owens

Cassius Clay

Wilma Rudolph

Carl Lewis

Jackie Joyner-Kersee

Jesse Owens

Wilma Rudolph

Carl Lewis

Jesse Owens

**Jesse Owens vs. Carl Lewis**
Lewis won 10 medals, 9 of them gold, in a brilliant Olympic career that spanned 1984 to 1996. He ran faster and jumped farther than Owens. But Owens was the first to win the same 4 golds (3 sprints, one a relay, and the long jump) in the 1936 Berlin Games, the triumph of a black man long before integration was widely accepted in sports.

**Jim Thorpe vs. Avery Brundage**
Thorpe won the 1912 pentathlon and decathlon golds, defeating Brundage among others, but was stripped of the medals for being paid to play baseball. Thorpe's efforts to have the medals reinstated were opposed by Brundage, the despotic ruler of the United States and International Olympic Committees. Fortunately, Brundage lived to see Thorpe's amateur status restored but died before the medals were returned to Thorpe's family.

THE WINNER

**Jesse Owens**
sprinter, long jumper

VS

**Wilma Rudolph vs.Cassius Clay**
The 1960 light heavyweight gold medalist, who would become Muhammad Ali, was not yet "The Greatest" – at least not when it came to facing Wilma, the shining star of the U.S. track team who overcame childhood polio and won three golds that year in Rome. With Clay at age 18 more impressed by the 20-year-old Wilma than he would later be by Sonny Liston, Wilma races to the next heat.

THE BEAUTY OF THE OLYMPICS is that the world takes the same stage at the same time, performing a passion play of nations, races, ideologies, sports, talents, and aspirations unmatched in any other venue in the world. The greatest Olympians, including scores of Americans, cannot be fairly judged against each other over nearly 100 years because of the evolution in training techniques, field conditions, and equipment. Surely, Michael Phelps was better prepared in 2008 in Beijing than Johnny Weissmuller was 84 years earlier in Paris. So gut instinct and lasting social significance produced the gold medalists here.

**Jesse Owens vs. Michael Phelps**
Despite Phelps's 14 gold medals, world records, and dominance of the pool in 2004 and 2008, Owens, the brilliant African American athlete from Ohio State, not only beat his peers but stuck it in the shocked faces of Hitler and the Nazis. There have been other significant moments when history and sports converged, including Tommie Smith's black power salute as the 200 meter winner in 1968, but nothing can match Owens's performance – not even Phelps's eight golds in Beijing.

# Michael Phelps

**1960 basketball team vs. 1992 Dream Team**
How could Michael, Magic, and Larry – that phenomenal collection of glittering professionals playing to guarantee gold – lose to a bunch of college kids? It's easy when the real amateurs, the ones without apparel sponsors or accommodations in luxury hotels, are led by the greatest backcourt in history, Oscar Robertson and Jerry West, and coached by Pete Newell.

**Bonnie Blair vs. Eric Heiden**
Two immortal Midwestern speedskaters, each with 5 gold medals. Taking all his medals at age 21 at Lake Placid in 1980, Heiden was more versatile, sweeping all five races from 500 meters to 10,000 meters. But Blair wins for an amazing perseverance, gaining her golds at 2 distances in 3 different Olympic Games as she aged from 23 to 31.

- Michael Phelps
  - Mark Spitz
    - Mark Spitz
      - Mark Spitz – swimmer
      - Andrea Mead-Lawrence – skier
    - 1960 Dream Team
      - 1960 Dream Team – basketball
      - 1992 Dream Team – basketball
  - Michael Phelps
    - Michael Phelps
      - Michael Phelps – swimmer
      - 2000 women's soccer team
    - Al Oerter
      - Joan Benoit – marathoner
      - Al Oerter – discus
- Bonnie Blair
  - Bonnie Blair
    - Bonnie Blair
      - Bonnie Blair – speed skater
      - Peggy Fleming – figure skater
    - 1980 Miracle
      - 1960 Miracle on Ice – hockey
      - 1980 Miracle on Ice – hockey
  - Eric Heiden
    - Rafer Johnson
      - Rafer Johnson – decathlete
      - Bruce Jenner – decathlete
    - Eric Heiden
      - Eric Heiden – speed skater
      - Dorothy Hamill – figure skater

# NFL Team Logos

## By D.W. Pine

D.W. Pine, the designer of this book, is the deputy art director of *Time* magazine, a former sportswriter for the *Atlanta Journal-Constitution* and a lifelong Steelers fan. He's currently crying into his Terrible Towel for picking the Browns.

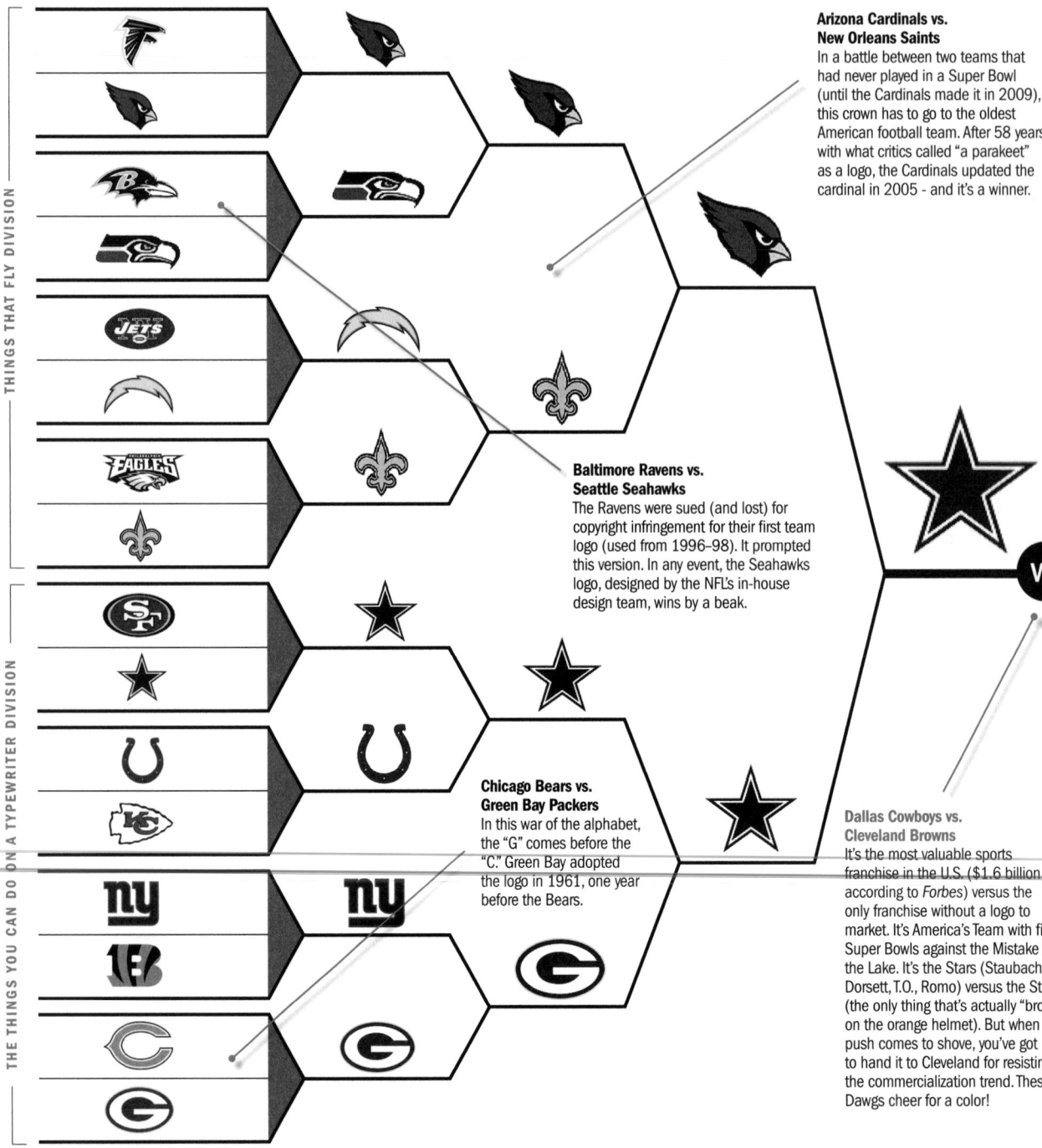


**Arizona Cardinals vs. New Orleans Saints**
In a battle between two teams that had never played in a Super Bowl (until the Cardinals made it in 2009), this crown has to go to the oldest American football team. After 58 years with what critics called "a parakeet" as a logo, the Cardinals updated the cardinal in 2005 - and it's a winner.

**Baltimore Ravens vs. Seattle Seahawks**
The Ravens were sued (and lost) for copyright infringement for their first team logo (used from 1996–98). It prompted this version. In any event, the Seahawks logo, designed by the NFL's in-house design team, wins by a beak.

**Chicago Bears vs. Green Bay Packers**
In this war of the alphabet, the "G" comes before the "C." Green Bay adopted the logo in 1961, one year before the Bears.

**Dallas Cowboys vs. Cleveland Browns**
It's the most valuable sports franchise in the U.S. ($1.6 billion according to *Forbes*) versus the only franchise without a logo to market. It's America's Team with five Super Bowls against the Mistake by the Lake. It's the Stars (Staubach, Dorsett, T.O., Romo) versus the Stripe (the only thing that's actually "brown" on the orange helmet). But when push comes to shove, you've got to hand it to Cleveland for resisting the commercialization trend. These Dawgs cheer for a color!

WE SPEND NEARLY HALF A YEAR passionately pleading (praying) for our favorite NFL team to win a game — any game! But in the end, we're not cheering for the players (who are hidden behind helmets), we're rooting for the actual helmets. A color. A symbol. A design. Players come and go, but it's the logos that keep us coming back year after year.

**Denver Broncos vs. Miami Dolphins**
The Broncos went nearly 30 years featuring a bronco jumping through a capital "D." But those "Orange Crush" years didn't produce one championship. In 1997 they redesigned to their current logo and won their first Super Bowl the same season. All that said, it's hard to beat up on a smiling dolphin. Fins win!

THE WINNER

**Oakland Raiders vs. Tampa Bay Buccaneers**
Aaarrgghh! This sword fight goes to the most feared NFL logo of all. Black. Silver. Swords. A Patch. A Shield. That beats a tattered flag any given Sunday (except Super Bowl XXXVII that is). However, it is slightly better than "Bucco Bruce," the effeminate orange pirate that winked at you the team used when they went 0-26 their first two seasons in the 1970s.

**Cleveland Browns vs. Pittsburgh Steelers**
Even though I'm partial to the black and gold and the fact that the Steelers are the only team with its logo on only one side of the helmet, the curtain falls on the Steelers' run.

THE ANIMALS DIVISION

THE PEOPLE DIVISION

# Dallas Cowboys

**By Jeff Pearlman**

Jeff Pearlman is the author of the *New York Times* bestseller *Boys Will Be Boys: The Glory Days and Party Nights of the Dallas Cowboys Dynasty.*

**Emmitt Smith**
running back

**Billy Joe DuPree**
tight end

**Smith**

**Bob Hayes**
wide receiver

**Danny White**
quarterback

**Hayes**

**Smith**

**Don Meredith**
quarterback

**Daryl Johnston**
fullback

**Meredith**

**Larry Allen**
guard

**Drew Pearson**
wide receiver

**Allen**

**Allen**

**Smith**

**Smith vs. Staubach**
Sure, it's hard to pick against the league's all-time leading rusher. But while Smith put up marvelous statistics, more than one teammate considered the University of Florida product to be a tad selfish. Such a charge was never leveled against Staubach, who would have donated his kidney for a victory.

**Staubach vs. White**
Staubach, Staubach, Staubach – enough already. Though offense garnered most of the attention in the 1970s and '80s, it was White – the ferocious defensive tackle from Delaware – who dictated the tone of the oft-ferocious Dallas defense. Usually double- and triple-teamed, White was a nine-time Pro Bowler who retired with 111 sacks and a legacy of unrivaled dominance.

**Roger Staubach**

**VS**

**Troy Aikman**
quarterback

**Don Perkins**
fullback

**Aikman**

**Roger Staubach**
quarterback

**Jay Novacek**
tight end

**Staubach**

**Staubach**

**Staubach**

**Michael Irvin**
wide receiver

**Tony Hill**
wide receiver

**Irvin**

**Rayfield Wright**
tackle

**Tony Dorsett**
running back

**Wright**

**Irvin**

**Staubach vs. Aikman**
The two greatest quarterbacks in franchise history duke it out spiral to spiral – and Staubach wins in a blowout. Though Aikman boasts one of the great arms of his generation, he lacks both Staubach's leadership skills and ability to improvise on the run. Down by five, two minutes left, no time-outs – there was nobody better than Roger the Dodger.

IN THE LONG HISTORY OF THE NATIONAL FOOTBALL LEAGUE, no team has elicited both the love and hate of the average fan more than the Dallas Cowboys. They're amazing and arrogant, cocky and charismatic, boastful and blessed. The Cowboys are blonde, long-legged cheerleaders. They're Tom Landry's fedora, Jimmy Johnson's sideways grin, Jerry Jones's prideful strut, and the hole atop Texas Stadium. Yet most of all, they're the dazzling assortment of Pro Bowlers and Hall of Famers who, over 39 seasons, have not only dominated the league but often revolutionized it.

THE WINNER

**Randy White**
defensive tackle

- White
  - Howley
    - Howley
      - Chuck Howley, linebacker
      - Everson Walls, cornerback
    - Woodson
      - Darren Woodson, strong safety
      - Harvey Martin, defensive end
  - White
    - White
      - Randy White, defensive tackle
      - Bill Bates, safety/special teams ace
    - Lilly
      - Cliff Harris, free safety
      - Bob Lilly, defensive tackle
- Haley
  - Waters
    - Waters
      - Mel Renfro, cornerback
      - Charlie Waters, strong safety
    - Jones
      - Deion Sanders, cornerback
      - Ed (Too Tall) Jones, defensive end
  - Haley
    - Haley
      - Charles Haley, defensive end
      - Dave Edwards, linebacker
    - Jordan
      - Cornell Green, cornerback/safety
      - Lee Roy Jordan, linebacker

**Deion Sanders vs. Ed (Too Tall) Jones**
The greatest athlete on this chart, Deion Sanders brought bushels of pizzazz and spunk to the Dallas locker room in 1995. Yet while Sanders won a Super Bowl with the Cowboys, he was a divisive presence who refused to lift weights or risk injury by, oh, tackling people. Jones, on the other hand, was a tireless workhorse who anchored the Dallas defensive line for 16 seasons.

**Waters vs. Haley**
Charlie Waters played in five Super Bowls, winning two of them. Charles Haley played in five Super Bowls, winning all five of them. Although stories of Haley's bizarre locker room behavior poison the well, the defensive end arrived from San Francisco after the 1991 season and single-handedly transformed the Cowboys' defense from average to dominant.

# Jewish Baseball Players

**By Daniel Okrent**

Daniel Okrent's books include the baseball classic *Nine Innings*, as well as *Great Fortune: The Epic of Rockefeller Center*, a finalist for the 2004 Pulitzer Prize in history. He was also the first public editor of the *New York Times*.

Al Rosen
Sydney Cohen
Brad Ausmus
Harry Danning
Ron Blomberg
David Newhan
Shawn Green
Ken Holtzman
Moe Berg
Buddy Myer
Lipman Pike
Morrie Arnovich
Saul Rogovin
Sandy Koufax
Larry Sherry
Norm Sherry

Rosen
Ausmus
Blomberg
Green
Berg
Pike
Koufax
Larry Sherry

Rosen
Green
Berg
Koufax

Rosen
Koufax

**Ausmus vs. Danning**
Danning could hit, but Ausmus's accomplishment was far greater: he was catching the day that Al Clark was the home plate umpire and Shawn Green came to bat – the first known incident of three Jews at home plate at the same time.

**Rosen vs. Green**
The 1953 American League MVP advances.

**Blomberg vs. Green**
Because he could run, throw, field, hit for average, and hit for power, Green called himself "the first five-tool Jew." Blomberg, the first man ever to appear as a DH, clearly was a one-tool Jew.

**Berg vs. Pike**
Princeton graduate Berg was a World War II spy and a celebrated linguist. It was said he could speak 12 languages, but couldn't hit in any of them. Still, he was reportedly a lot of fun on road trips.

**Pike vs. Arnovich**
Pike had a truly unappealing name, but he was baseball's ur-Jew, making his debut in centerfield for the St. Louis Brown Stockings in 1876.

**Rogovin vs. Koufax**
Rogovin had 17 complete games, a .611 winning percentage, and a 2.48 ERA with the White Sox in '52 – for Koufax, a lousy year.

**Greenberg vs. Koufax**
Hank might have been able to hit Sandy's fastball. But his curve? Never.

THE WINNER
**Sandy Koufax**

VS

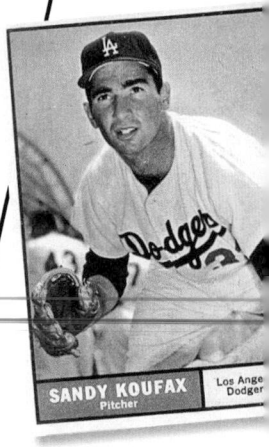

ONCE THERE WERE BALLPLAYERS WITH NAMES LIKE "Sydney Cohen" and "Moe Berg." Those days are gone, but the Jewish ballplayer remains. Only now, he's named "Ryan," or "Shawn," or "Kevin." In this tournament of 32 great, good, decent, or barely adequate Major League Jews (it's not as if there were thousands to choose from), face-offs are won by the better player – except when I don't like the outcome. That's when I turn to Diamond Semitology, allowing either "Hebraic pride" or "yiddishe irony" to trump on-field evidence. Take your base, Mose Solomon; doff your cap, Adam Greenberg.

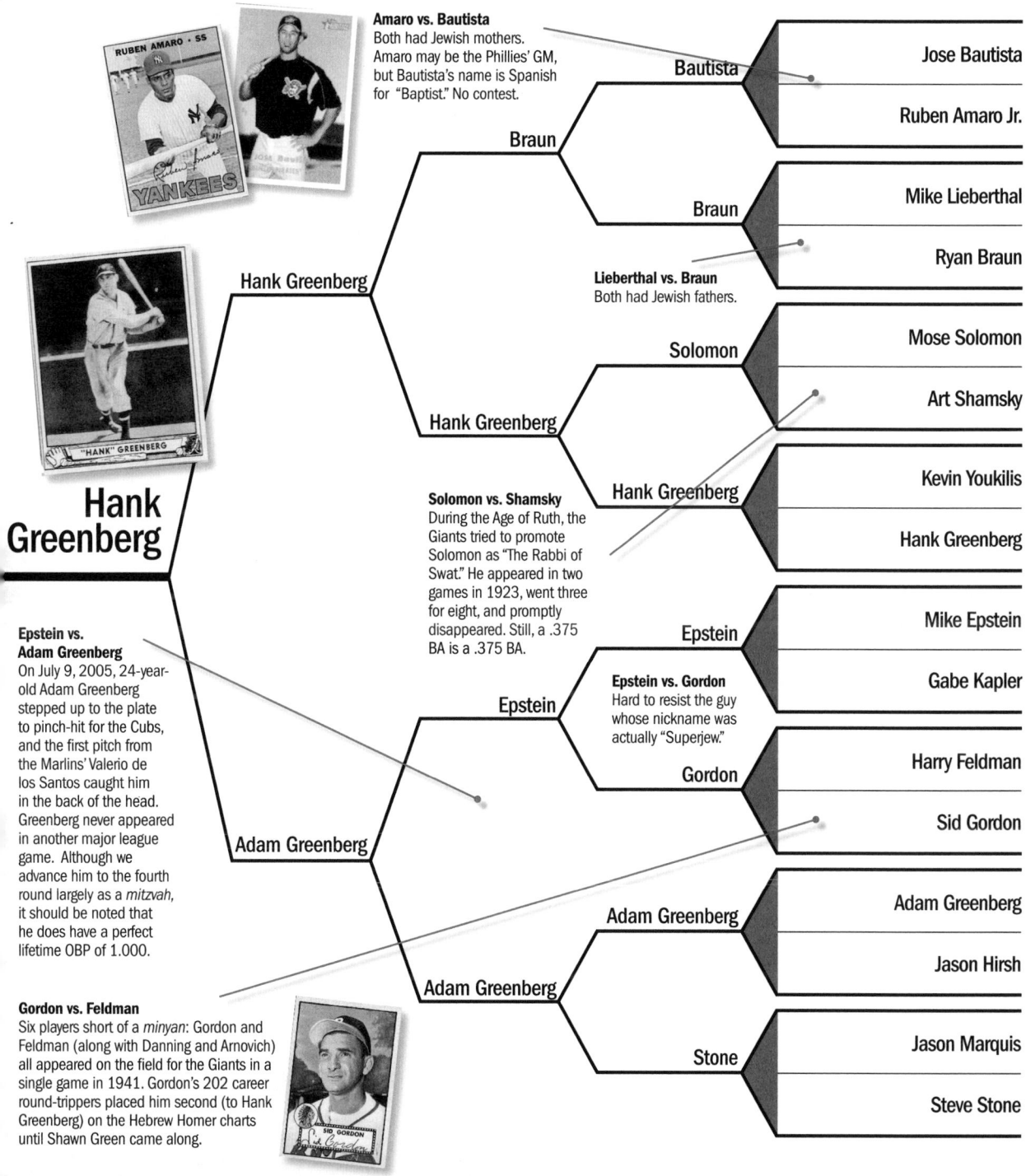


**Amaro vs. Bautista**
Both had Jewish mothers. Amaro may be the Phillies' GM, but Bautista's name is Spanish for "Baptist." No contest.

**Lieberthal vs. Braun**
Both had Jewish fathers.

**Solomon vs. Shamsky**
During the Age of Ruth, the Giants tried to promote Solomon as "The Rabbi of Swat." He appeared in two games in 1923, went three for eight, and promptly disappeared. Still, a .375 BA is a .375 BA.

**Epstein vs. Gordon**
Hard to resist the guy whose nickname was actually "Superjew."

**Epstein vs. Adam Greenberg**
On July 9, 2005, 24-year-old Adam Greenberg stepped up to the plate to pinch-hit for the Cubs, and the first pitch from the Marlins' Valerio de los Santos caught him in the back of the head. Greenberg never appeared in another major league game. Although we advance him to the fourth round largely as a *mitzvah*, it should be noted that he does have a perfect lifetime OBP of 1.000.

**Gordon vs. Feldman**
Six players short of a *minyan*: Gordon and Feldman (along with Danning and Arnovich) all appeared on the field for the Giants in a single game in 1941. Gordon's 202 career round-trippers placed him second (to Hank Greenberg) on the Hebrew Homer charts until Shawn Green came along.

# All-Time Fantasy Sports Performances

**By Matt Pitzer**

Matt Pitzer writes about fantasy football for *USA Today*. Previously, he covered fantasy sports for the *Sporting News*. He occasionally leaves his basement.

BASEBALL REGIONAL

**Nate Colbert,** San Diego Padres vs. Atlanta Braves, Aug. 1, 1972 (doubleheader), 7-9, 7 runs scored, 5 HR, 13 RBI, 0 SB

**Joe Adcock,** Milwaukee Braves vs. Brooklyn Dodgers, July 31, 1954, 5-5, 5 runs scored, 4 HR, 7 RBI, 0 SB

Colbert

**Mark Whiten,** St. Louis Cardinals vs. Cincinnati Reds, Sept. 7, 1993, 4-5, 4 runs scored, 4 HR, 12 RBI, 0 SB

**Kenny Lofton,** Cleveland Indians vs. Baltimore Orioles, Sept. 3, 2000, 4-7, 4 runs scored, 1 HR, 1 RBI, 5 SB

Whiten

Colbert

**Whiten vs. Lofton**
This is the classic matchup of speed vs. power featuring Lofton's single-game record of five steals vs. Whiten's best-ever combination of home runs and RBIs. Stolen bases directly affect only one category while each home run counts for a hit, a run scored, and at least one RBI. Great thievery lacks the impact of a bundle of homers.

**Jim Bottomley,** St. Louis Cardinals vs. Brooklyn Robins, Sept. 16, 1924, 6-6, 3 runs scored, 2 HR, 12 RBI, 0 SB

**Heinie Zimmerman,** Chicago Cubs vs. Boston Rustlers, June 11, 1911, 4-4, 4 runs scored, 2 HR, 9 RBI, 1 SB

Bottomley

**Shawn Green,** Los Angeles Dodgers vs. Milwaukee Brewers, May 23, 2002, 6-6, 6 runs scored, 4 HR, 7 RBI, 0 SB

**Nomar Garciaparra,** Boston Red Sox vs. Seattle Mariners, May 10, 1999, 3-4, 3 runs scored, 2 HR, 10 RBI, 0 SB, 2 grand slams

Green

Green

Colbert

**Colbert vs. Blanda**
How to value a great performance? Just consider how much better a player could have done. While Colbert's numbers are jaw-dropping, he accumulated his stats in a doubleheader and could have had two Whiten-like games. Blanda might have lost one scoring chance to an interception, but a more extraordinary individual performance is difficult to fathom.

**Kerry Wood,** Chicago Cubs vs. Houston Astros, May 6, 1998, 9 IP, 1 H, 0 ER, 0 BB, 20 Ks, W

**Jon Lester,** Boston Red Sox vs. Kansas City Royals, May 19, 2008, 9 IP, 0 H, 0 ER, 2 BB, 9 Ks, W

Wood

**Tom Cheney,** Washington Senators vs. Baltimore Orioles, Sept. 12, 1962, 16 IP, 10 H, 1 ER, 4 BB, 21 Ks, W

**Chris Short,** Philadelphia Phillies vs. New York Mets, Oct. 2, 1965, 15 IP, 9 H, 0 ER, 3 BB, 18 Ks, no decision

Cheney

Wood

**Wood vs. Koufax**
How many strikeouts is one hit worth? That is the only slender difference between the two games; remember, in fantasy, there is no extra credit for a perfect game. One hit barely affects Wood's base-runners' allowed average, while his six extra strikeouts might be what you would expect from another whole start.

Wood

Nate Colbert

VS

**Nolan Ryan,** California Angels vs. Detroit Tigers, July 15, 1973, 9 IP, 0 H, 0 ER, 4 BB, 17 Ks, W

**Harvey Haddix,** Pittsburgh Pirates vs. Milwaukee Braves, May 26, 1959, 12.2 IP, 1 H, 1 R, 0 ER, 1 BB, 8 Ks

Ryan

**Sandy Koufax,** Los Angeles Dodgers vs. Chicago Cubs, September 9, 1965, 9 IP, 0 H, 0 ER, 0 BB, 14 Ks, W. Perfect game.

**Gaylord Perry,** San Francisco Giants vs. Cincinnati Reds, Sept. 1, 1967, 16 IP, 10 H, 0 ER, 3 BB, 12 Ks, no decision

Koufax

Koufax

7 PATs

7 TDs

IN DETERMINING THE BEST FANTASY PERFORMANCE, one must acknowledge that (a) fantasy is barely 20 years old and (b) football players have one-tenth fewer chances for single-game achievements than everyday baseball players (and half as many as most starting pitchers). So, as this bracket goes back and forth in time, we use modern fantasy's valuation tools to compare the feats of running backs, receivers, and quarterbacks against each other, and then, a slugger and quarterback's most astonishing days. If fantasy had existed in 1924, fans with Jim Bottomley would have drooled over his 12 RBIs in a single game.

**Blanda vs. Cannon**
Oh, if only Billy Cannon could kick like Blanda, his Oilers' teammate. Blanda's extra points are the equivalent of an additional touchdown, giving him 49 points to Cannon's 30, an unbeatable advantage – even if Cannon set a single-game AFL record for yards gained from scrimmage, which are more valuable in fantasy than a quarterback's passing yardage.

**Cannon vs. Sayers**
Sayers's spectacular game, featuring astonishing moves executed on a muddy field, is regarded as an NFL classic. But its fantasy value is less significant. In fantasy, a punt return is usually credited to the team, not the individual, so Cannon matches Sayers on individual scores and beats him significantly on yards from scrimmage.

THE WINNER

## George Blanda

- Blanda
  - Blanda
    - Blanda
      - **QB Sid Luckman,** Chicago Bears vs. NY Giants, Nov. 14, 1943, 21-32, 433 yards, 7 TDs, 1 INT
      - **QB George Blanda,** Houston Oilers vs. NY Titans, Nov. 19, 1961, 20-32, 418 yards, 7 TDs, 1 INT, 7 PATs
    - Van Brocklin
      - **QB Norm Van Brocklin,** Los Angeles Rams vs. NY Yankees, Sept. 28, 1951, 27-41, 554 yards, 5 TDs, 1 rushing TD, 2 INTs
      - **WR Stephone Paige,** Kansas City Chiefs vs. San Diego Chargers, Dec. 22, 1985, 309 receiving yards, 2 TDs
  - Rice
    - Rice
      - **WR Jerry Rice,** San Francisco 49ers vs. Atlanta Falcons, Oct. 14, 1990, 225 receiving yards, 5 receiving TDs
      - **WR Elroy Hirsch,** Los Angeles Rams vs. NY Yankees, Sept. 28, 1951, 173 receiving yards, 4 TDs
    - Winslow
      - **TE Kellen Winslow,** San Diego Chargers vs. Oakland Raiders, Nov. 22, 1981, 144 receiving yards, 5 TDs
      - **K Rob Bironas,** Tennessee Titans vs. Houston Texans, Oct. 21, 2007, 8 field goals, 2 PATs
- Cannon
  - Cannon
    - Cannon
      - **RB Billy Cannon,** Houston Oilers vs. NY Titans, Dec. 10, 1961, 216 rushing yards, 114 receiving yards, 3 rushing TDs, 2 receiving TDs
      - **RB Corey Dillon,** Oct. 23, 2000, Cincinnati Bengals vs. Denver Broncos, 278 yards, 1 TD
    - Sayers
      - **RB Dub Jones,** Cleveland Browns vs. Chicago Bears, Nov. 25, 1951, 115 rushing yards, 5 rushing TDs, 1 receiving TD
      - **RB Gale Sayers,** Chicago Bears vs. San Francisco 49ers, Dec. 12, 1965, 113 rushing yards, 89 receiving yards, 6 total TDs
  - Gilchrist
    - Gilchrist
      - **RB Clinton Portis,** Denver Broncos vs. Kansas City Chiefs, Dec. 7, 2003, 218 rushing yards, 5 TDs
      - **RB Cookie Gilchrist,** Buffalo Bills vs. NY Jets, Dec. 8, 1963, 243 rushing yards, 5 TDs
    - Peterson
      - **RB Adrian Peterson,** Nov. 4, 2007, Minnesota Vikings vs. Chicago Bears, 296 rushing yards, 3 TDs
      - **RB Paul Hornung,** Green Bay Packers vs. Baltimore Colts, Oct. 8, 1961, 111 rushing yards, 3 rushing TDs, 1 receiving TD, 6 PATs, 1 field goal

FOOTBALL REGIONAL

# 418 yards

Sources: Retrosheet.org; Pro-Football-Reference.com; NFL.com

# 21st-Century Sports Books

**By Will Leitch**

Will Leitch is a contributing editor at *New York* magazine, a columnist for *Sporting News*, and the founder of Deadspin.com. He has written three books, *Life As A Loser* (2003), *Catch* (2005), and *God Save The Fan* (2008). He grew up in rural Mattoon, IL.

*Moneyball*
by Michael Lewis

*The Punch*
by John Feinstein

*My Losing Season*
by Pat Conroy

*Spalding's World Tour*
by Mark Lamster

*Triumph*
by Jeremy Schaap

*The Soul of Baseball*
by Joe Posnanski

*Boys Will Be Boys*
by Jeff Pearlman

*The Real All-Americans*
by Sally Jenkins

*Seabiscuit*
by Laura Hillenbrand

*Men with Balls*
by Drew Magary

*The Miracle of St. Anthony*
by Adrian Wojnarowski

*Fantasyland*
by Sam Walker

*To Hate Like This Is to Be Happy Forever*
by Will Blythe

*Pistol*
by Mark Kriegel

*Joe DiMaggio: The Hero's Life*
by Richard Ben Cramer

*The Crowd Sounds Happy*
by Nicholas Dawidoff

*Moneyball*

*My Losing Season*

*The Soul of Baseball*

*Boys Will Be Boys*

*Seabiscuit*

*Fantasyland*

*To Hate Like This*

*Joe DiMaggio*

*Moneyball*

*Boys Will Be Boys*

*Seabiscuit*

*Joe DiMaggio*

***Triumph* vs. *Soul of Baseball***
Schaap's Jesse Owens biography cannot hold off the devastating one-two punch of Posnanski and Buck O'Neil, natural storytellers and indestructible forces of hilarity and affirmation. This book will make you want to give up your life and just travel the country watching baseball . . . if you didn't want to do that already.

***Moneyball* vs. *Joe DiMaggio***
As dogged a reporter as Cramer is, you can't shake the feeling, reading this masterwork, that you might need to take a shower afterwards. You might have known Joe DiMaggio was a bit of a jerk. You might not have heard of Voros McCracken before. The unveiling of what's behind the curtain wins.

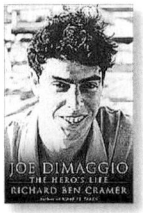


**THE WINNER**

***Moneyball***
by Michael Lewis

VS

***Moneyball* vs. *The Bronx Is Burning***
Mahler's book sheds light on a rich baseball/political/sociological past, but *Moneyball* brings us something new, opens the world up, and makes us look at a game we love in an entirely different way. I'll never quite be convinced a walk's as good as a hit, but *Moneyball* turned a nation of athlete wannabes into a national of aspiring general managers.

***Seabiscuit* vs. *Fantasyland***
On one hand, the heartwarming story of an underdog, a fable that makes us believe in the proverbial miracle. On the other, 12 pasty middle-aged men sit around a conference room table, eating Cheetos and screaming out names like "Yuniesky Betancourt!" Is horse racing more a national pastime than fantasy sports? *Seabiscuit* by a nose because horses at least get a little bit of sun.

I PREFER BOOKS THAT EMPHASIZE the silliness and fun of sports rather than the mythos inherent in much sportswriting. Anytime you see a list of the top sports books, you're lucky to see so much as one or two books from the last 25 years. This is a shame, particularly when you consider how dramatically sportswriting has changed in the last decade. Not all of these can stand with Bernard Malamud, but they're closer than you think. Oh, and a third of the authors in this bracket also write blogs.

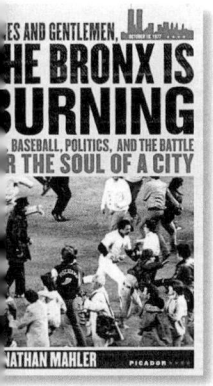


## The Bronx Is Burning

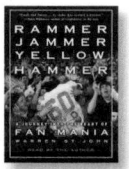

***Rammer Jammer* vs. *Three Nights in August***
I hope Buzz isn't mad at me here, but as compelling as the strange, obsessive brain of Tony LaRussa might be to this diehard Cardinals fan, it can't compare to the glorious lunatics who turn their lives (and everybody else's) upside down just to watch a bunch of enormous teenagers run into each other at high speeds.

***Sunday Money* vs. *:07 Seconds***
If that Steve Nash-led Phoenix Suns team had ever won a title, more people would appreciate McCallum's achievement, a chronicle of the most fascinating team in recent NBA history. Of course, the Suns were fast, but not NASCAR fast, and their fans don't hang around McGregor shirtless on top of RVs.

- *Bronx Is Burning*
  - *Bronx Is Burning*
    - *The Bronx Is Burning* by Jonathan Mahler
    - *You Cannot Be Serious* by John McEnroe with James Kaplan
  - *Word Freak*
    - *Game of Shadows* by Mark Fainaru-Wada and Lance Williams
    - *Word Freak* by Stefan Fatsis
- *How Soccer Explains . . .*
  - *Sandy Koufax*
    - *Sandy Koufax: A Lefty's Legacy* by Jane Leavy
    - *Big Game, Small World* by Alexander Wolff
  - *How Soccer Explains . . .*
    - *How Soccer Explains the World* by Frankin Foer
    - *Opening Day* by Jonathan Eig
- *Sunday Money*
  - *Sunday Money*
    - *Sunday Money* by Jeff MacGregor
    - *The Rivalry* by John Taylor
  - *Rammer Jammer*
    - *Rammer Jammer Yellow Hammer* by Warren St. John
    - *Three Nights in August* by Buzz Bissinger
- *:07 Seconds or Less*
  - *Clemente*
    - *Clemente* by David Maraniss
    - *The Teammates* by David Halberstam
  - *:07 Seconds or Less*
    - *Playing the Enemy* by John Carlin
    - *:07 Seconds or Less* by Jack McCallum

# Ringless Athletes

**By Dick Friedman**

A longtime editor at *Sports Illustrated,* Dick Friedman grew up in the Boston area and in his mind has won 27 rings: 17 with the Celtics, three with the Patriots, two each with the Bruins and Red Sox, and three with the Mad Dogs street hockey team.

Y.A. Tittle
Dominique Wilkins
Tittle

Barry Sanders
Willie McCovey
McCovey

Alan Page
Ken Griffey, Jr.
Griffey

Karl Malone
Bob Lanier
Malone

Jim Kelly
Alydar
Kelly

Ernie Banks
Don Mattingly
Banks

Dick Butkus
Dan Marino
Marino

Mike Piazza
Charles Barkley
Barkley

Tittle
Tittle

Malone
Malone

Kelly
Banks

Barkley
Barkley

Tittle
Barkley

Tittle VS

**Sanders vs. McCovey**
Willie Mac advances for two reasons: First, if his screaming line drive to Bobby Richardson to end the '62 World Series had been 18 inches to the left or right, he doesn't even make the bracket. But that out means that he's in. Second, he represents a supremely talented generation of mid-century San Francisco Giants (Juan Marichal, Gaylord Perry, Bobby Bonds) who just couldn't get over the hump. (Teammate Willie Mays got his Giants ring in New York in 1954.)

**Malone vs. Griffey**
In a distinguished 19-year NBA career, Malone made it to three Finals, two with the Utah Jazz against Michael Jordan's unstoppable Chicago Bulls. (It was Malone from whom Air poked away the ball in '98, the play that led to Jordan's clinching bucket.) However, the crowning indignity came when Malone, at age 40, joined the three-time defending champion Los Angeles Lakers for the express purpose of getting a ring – whereupon L.A. and the Mailman were dispatched by the Detroit Pistons in the NBA Finals.

**Barkley vs. Tittle**
Sir Charles's most valiant near-miss came in the 1993 NBA Finals with the Phoenix Suns, when (as the league's MVP) he put up a 42-point masterpiece a triple-overtime win, only to be pipped in Game 6 by the clinching shot of the Bulls' John Paxson. But he is pipped again here by Tittle. From 1961 through '63, Y and his New York Giants passed the NFL silly, and annually made it to the outdoor, cold-weather championship game, losing twi to the Lombardi Packers and th to the Chicago Bears on a brutal day at Wrigley Field unsuited fo passing. Today these games mi have been in a dome, and Tittle might have gotten that ring.

**Banks vs. Kelly**
Star-crossed players, but in different ways. Hall of Famer Banks had the misfortune (though Mr. Cub wouldn't see it that way) to play all his 2,528 big-league games as a Cub, and not one of those contests took place in the postseason. Kelly and his Buffalo Bills made the Super Bowl four straight years, losing a heartbreaker to the Giants, then suffering three blowouts. The tantalization factor gives the quarterback the nod.

THE MONKEY ON THE BACK: That's usually the phrase employed to describe the plight of the great athlete who can't win a championship. Sometimes ringlessness arises from being stuck on the wrong franchise. Sometimes the superstar has the bad fortune to play in an era dominated by an opposing supernova (Bill Russell, Michael Jordan, Tiger Woods, Affirmed). And let's face it, sometimes he or she chokes. Our scale is subjective, but we give a lot of special consideration for multiple misses, with bonuses for multiple consecutive misses – and a wild card for gut-wrenching, rip-your-heart-out failure.

**Tittle vs. Baylor**
At least in this bracket, Elg is a champ! And what a swellagant, elegant heartbreak kid he is! Seven times his Lakers (Minneapolis and L.A.) lost to Bill Russell's Boston Celtics in the NBA Finals, three of the defeats in seven games, once after Elg had singed the Celts for 62 points. Add another seven-game Finals loss to the New York Knicks. To top it off: As a collegian, Baylor made the NCAA finals with Seattle, only to lose to Kentucky. Can't we at least give this man an honorary ring?

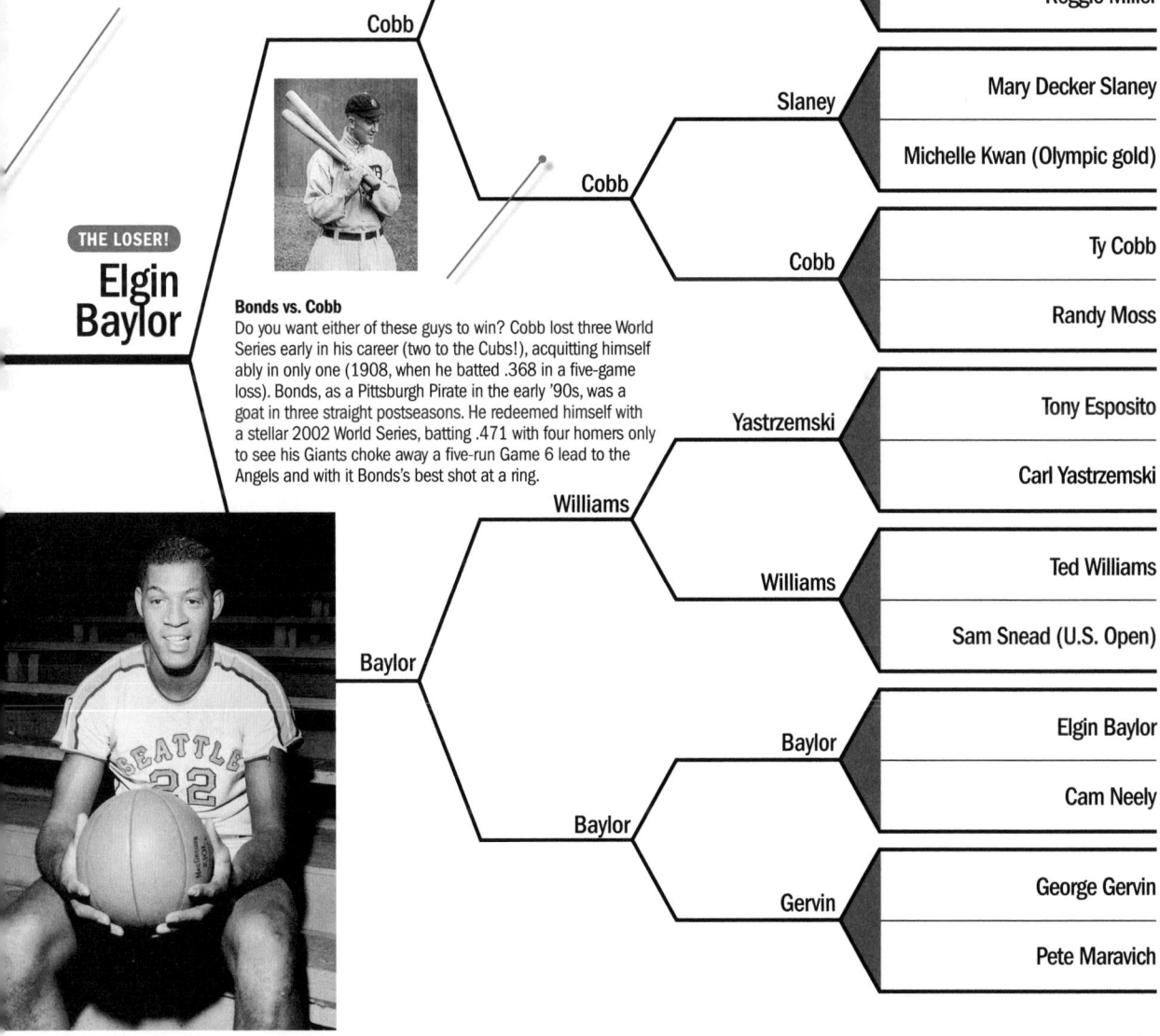


**Bonds vs. Cobb**
Do you want either of these guys to win? Cobb lost three World Series early in his career (two to the Cubs!), acquitting himself ably in only one (1908, when he batted .368 in a five-game loss). Bonds, as a Pittsburgh Pirate in the early '90s, was a goat in three straight postseasons. He redeemed himself with a stellar 2002 World Series, batting .471 with four homers only to see his Giants choke away a five-run Game 6 lead to the Angels and with it Bonds's best shot at a ring.

# Donald Ross Courses

## By Bob Carney

Bob Carney, creative director at *Golf Digest,* oversees the magazine's course ranking. His home course, Brooklawn, is by Tillie, not Ross, but he's okay with that. Special thanks to caddy Ron Whitten.

**Oakland Hills CC (South)**
Bloomfield Hills, MI (1917)

**Barton Hills CC**
Ann Arbor, MI (1920)

**Monroe GC**
Pittsfield, NY (1923)

**Plainfield CC**
Plainfield, NJ (1921)

**Oyster Harbors GC**
Ostervillle, MA (1927)

**Seminole GC**
North Palm Beach, FL (1929)

**Scioto GC**
Columbus, OH (1916)

**Rhode Island CC**
West Barrington, RI (1912)

**Inverness Club**
Toledo, OH (1920)

**Interlachen CC**
Edina, MN (1921)

**Franklin Hills CC**
Franklin, MI (1930)

**French Lick Springs Resort**
French Lick, IN (1922)

**Orchards GC**
S. Hadley, MA (1922)

**Salem CC**
Peabody, MA (1925)

**East Lake CC**
Atlanta, GA (1914)

**Linville GC**
Linville, NC (1928)

Oakland Hills

Plainfield

Seminole

Scioto

Inverness

French Lick

Salem

Linville

Oakland Hillls

Seminole

Inverness

Linville

Seminole

Inverness

**Barton Hills vs. Oakland Hills**
A Michigan matchup, a state where Ross did some of hi best work (Detroit GC, Franklin Hills, several Detroit publ courses). Barton Hills represents all of the great "membe courses" that Ross created. Faced with the masterpiece Oakland Hills 40 miles away, it falls (unlike what happer in the New York pairing where noble Oak Hill, de-Rossed bit by new Fazio holes, falls to the purer Buffalo CC).

**Seminole vs. Oakland Hills**
The Ben Hogan matchup. Seminole, the club Ben Hogan chose to join, meets Oakland Hills, the monster he named – and tamed – to win the 1951 Open. While Oakland Hills inspires awe, Seminole is a place to love. (And yes, I'm counting the locker room!)

**Seminole vs. Inverness**
While Holston Hills, a pure Ross jewel in the relatively barren golf state of Tennessee, is worn down by hefty Pinehurst in the other semi, Seminole's brilliant routing and beautiful greens helps it edge Inverness, site of five major championships, the famous Hinkle Tree, and some re-working that has left Ross aficionados glum.

**Inverness vs. Interlachen**
Two sites of thrilling majors past: Interlachen, where Bob Jones won the third leg of his Grand Slam in 1930, and Inverness, where Bob Tway holed a bunker shot on the 72nd hole to snatch the 1987 PGA Championship from Greg Norman. Both are too short for today's (male) pros, but Inverness is sturdier.

**Pinehurst vs. Seminole**
Ross said he preferred to lay out a course on level land. Though he liked Seminole "very much," Pinehurst No. 2 is where he chose to live (after emigrating from Scotland in 1899) until his death in 1948, and its length, strength, and amazing greens prevail. "Select your putting green locations, if possible, to give desirable undulating surfaces. Nature does this sort of thing best." It does if you have Donald Ross and North Carolina's sandy terrain to improve upon it. It's good to be No. 2.

OF GOLF'S "CULT" ARCHITECTS, from Tillinghast to Raynor to Dye, Donald Ross is the most prolific, credited in name or legitimate design with over 500 courses in the U.S. The first question about a Ross course is, "How Ross is it?" The second: "Who restored it?" These 32, though tweaked and toughened over the years, are "all Ross." Mostly. Which means they have skillful routing and greens that aren't all pushed-up, crowned surfaces resembling the top of a bowler hat (though many are). Choosing the greatest is like choosing the finest Frank Lloyd Wright home, if Wright had done subdivisions.

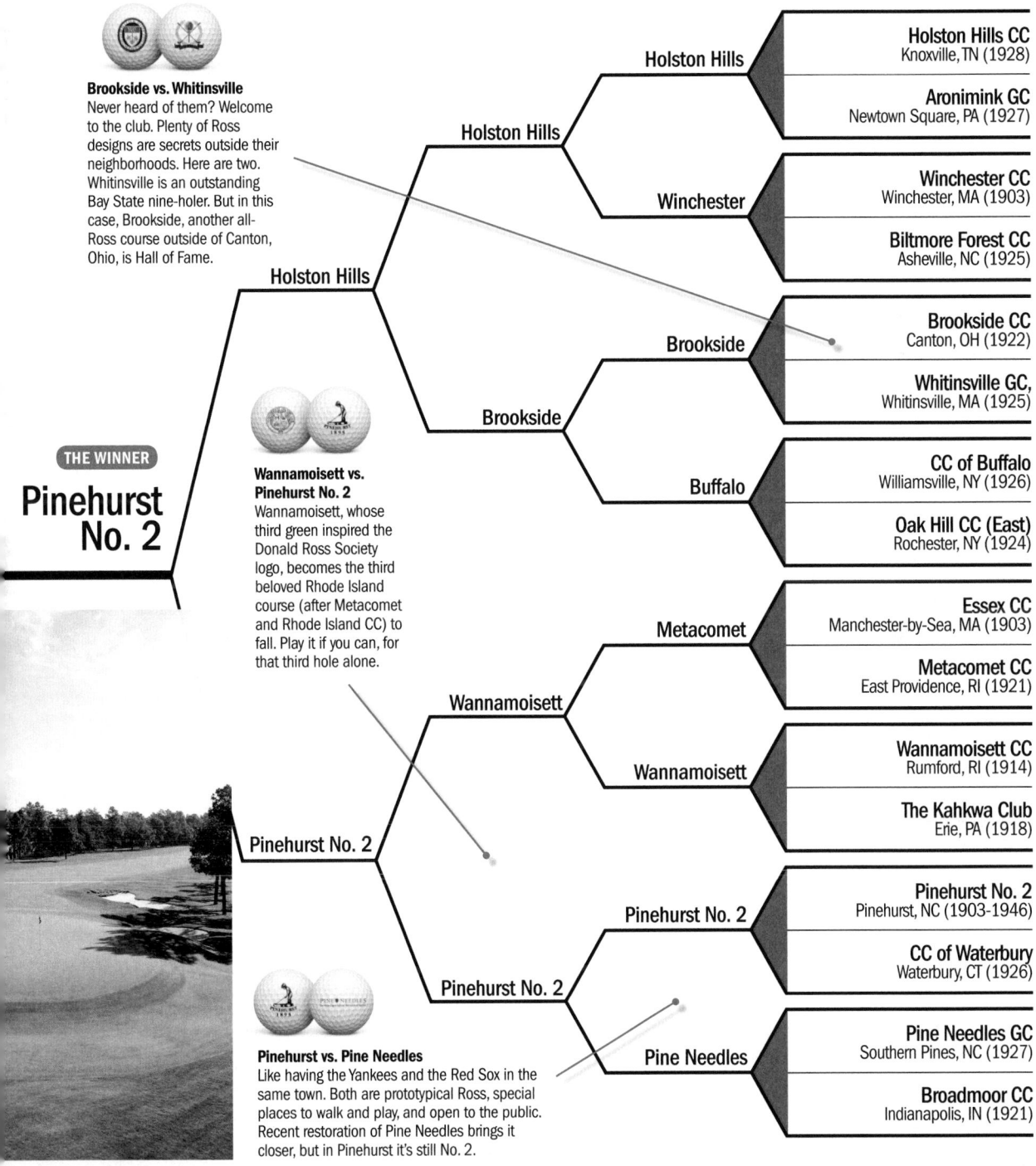

# American Hockey Players

**By Nick Paumgarten**

Nick Paumgarten is a staff writer at *The New Yorker,* and an American-born beer-league mucker.

## SCORERS REGIONAL

**Pat LaFontaine**
Scored more in juniors than Mario Lemieux

**Doug Weight**
Speedy passer

**Keith Tkachuk**
Big boy, big ego, soft hands

**Joe Mullen**
Son of Hell's Kitchen, '80s scoring machine

**Tony Amonte**
Speedy shooter, greatest American mullet

**Jeremy Roenick**
Big heart, big mouth, iron jaw

**Bobby Carpenter**
*SI* cover boy in '81; iconic Boston-accent name

**Mike Modano**
Tops in goals and points; the face of the Stars

## GOALIES, OLDIES, GOONS & GIRLS REGIONAL

**Mike Richter**
Cup-winning Rangers netminder

**Tom Barrasso**
Cup-winning Penguins netminder

**Frank Brimsek a.k.a. "Mr. Zero"**
Bruin backstop; 1939 Rookie of the Year

**Hobey Baker**
American pioneer; hockey's Heisman

**The Granatos**
Tony (retired Ranger/King) and Cammi (Olympic captain)

**The Hanson Brothers**
The "Slap Shot" goons

**Paul Holmgren**
Post-Dave Schultz Flyers brawler and a scorer, too

**Chris "Knuckles" Nilan**
Holds NHL record for most penalty minutes per game

Pat LaFontaine

Joe Mullen

Jeremy Roenick

Mike Modano

Mike Richter

Hobey Baker

Granatos

Chris Nilan

Pat LaFontaine

Mike Modano

Mike Richter

Granatos

**Pat Lafontaine vs. Mike Modano**
Pat Lafontaine was the most talented and prolific U.S. player, a wizard with the puck, but concussions cut short his career. Modano, with longevity and a Cup on his bench, takes this semifinal round in triple OT.

**Hobey Baker vs. Frank Brimsek**
Long before Bobby Orr or the "Miracle on Ice," there was Brimsek and Baker, the two great old-timers of American hockey. Brimsek, a stand-up goalie from the Bruins, was called Mr. Zero. But Baker was the first great American player, a prep and college star after whom the trophy for the best college player is named. Baker died in a post-World War I plane crash, and inspired the character Amory Blaine in F. Scott Fitzgerald's *This Side of Paradise.* His iconic status as a gentleman athlete gives him the mojo to steal a round or two against bigger, younger players in better equipment.

**The Hansons vs. The Granatos**
The Hanson Brothers, the brawling naifs from *Slap Shot,* may be fictional, but the Minnesota minor-leaguers who played them (two of the three are actually brothers, named Carlson) are real, so they qualify on a technicality. Unfortunately, they face the Granatos, Tony and Cammi. Tony, a fine player back in the day, would be no match for them, but sister Cammi is the greatest American woman player, doing more lately than even NHL Commissioner Gary Bettman to change hockey's face.

**Mike Modano vs. Jeremy Roenick**
Jeremy Roenick, who played on the same prep-school team with Tony Amonte (I pity the freshmen in that dorm), once remarked that the two best American players were Mike Modano and himself. Not so fast, J.R. You're not even in the top three forwards (see Pat LaFontaine and Joey Mullen).

Modano

VS

ALTHOUGH AMERICAN HOCKEY TEAMS have won big international competitions (Olympics, World Cup, World Juniors) and various regions qualify as hockey hotbeds, puck has always been a marginal sport – one of the few areas where we let Canadians feel superior. We've bred many very good players, but few great ones, much less a Great One – which is why ranking American players, though a staple of rec-league locker rooms, has hardly been a high priority on sports talk radio. We correct that here.

**Mike Modano vs. Chris Chelios**
Modano, as of 2008 the all-time scoring leader among Americans in the NHL, was silky smooth in his prime, so fast that his jersey flapped behind him in the wind. Though diminished by age and ill-considered investments, he's still a majestic centerman. But after taking LaFontaine, he's no match for the physical play and peerless conditioning of Chelios, who, at 47, is still a rock, and a cuss to play against. Forget the Hall of Fame; Chelios deserves a place on Mount Rushmore.

THE WINNER

## Chris Chelios

iseled Hab/Hawk/Wing; still going strong at 47

**Jim Craig vs. Neal Broten**
Yes, to single out members of the "Miracle on Ice" Olympic team of 1980 is a sacrilege. But single out we must, because the victory over the Soviets was, as every schoolgirl knows, the single most important geopolitical event of the last 200 years. Most reflective of that team's spirit is goalie Jim Craig, who famously draped the American flag around his neck and sought out his widowed dad in the stands. He stones all comers, including teammate Broten, Minnesota's Larry Bird.

**Brian Leetch vs. Chris Chelios**
Leetch won two Norris trophies, as best NHL defenseman, and helped lead the New York Rangers to their first Stanley Cup in 54 years. With his risky, rushing style, he conjured visions of Bobby Orr, but not vividly enough to knock out Chris Chelios, a Chicagoan who won the Norris and the Cup three times each. He once forgot the Cup on a Malibu beach. It's hard enough to win the thing, but to leave it behind takes game.

Jim Craig
- Neal Broten
  - Neal Broten
    - **Neal Broten** – Minnesota legend; longtime pro; fought Gretzky
    - **Mark Johnson** – Most talented 1980 Olympian
  - Ken Morrow
    - **Ken Morrow** – Longtime Islander defenseman with an excellent beard
    - **Mike Ramsey** – Longtime Sabres defenseman; nickname "Rammer"
- Jim Craig
  - Dave Christian
    - **Dave Christian** – Hockey-dynasty scion; prolific NHL career
    - **Mark Pavelich** – One of Herb Brooks's "Smurfs" on '82-'83 Rangers
  - Jim Craig
    - **Jim Craig** – Gold-medal goalie; short-time pro
    - **Mike Eruzione** – The Captain, scored a big one against the Russkies

MIRACLE MEN REGIONAL

Chris Chelios
- Chris Chelios
  - Chris Chelios
    - **Chris Chelios** – Chiseled Hab/Hawk/Wing; still going strong at 47
    - **Taffy Abel** – Depression-era stalwart for Rangers and Blackhawks
  - Phil Housley
    - **Phil Housley** – Small, slick, peripatetic; second in points to Modano
    - **Derian Hatcher** – Big fella with a mean streak and a world-class twitch
- Brian Leetch
  - Rod Langway
    - **Rod Langway** – Classy '80s-era Washington Capital; best mustache
    - **Mark Howe** – Son of Gordie; longtime Flyer
  - Brian Leetch
    - **Gary Suter** – 1986 rookie of the year
    - **Brian Leetch** – Puck-rushing Ranger; 1994 Stanley Cup MVP

BLUELINERS REGIONAL

# Steroid-Era Moments

**By Shaun Assael**

Shaun Assael, a senior writer for *ESPN the Magazine*, is the author of three books, among them *Steroid Nation*, which had the ridiculously long subtitle: *Juiced Home Run Totals, Anti-aging Miracles, and a Hercules in Every High School: The Secret History of America's True Drug Addiction.*

IRS agent Jeff Novitzky sparks government probe of steroids in sport with raid on BALCO laboratory

Jose Canseco becomes best-selling author by spilling names of fellow steroid users

**Novitzky**

Chinese-made human growth hormone floods U.S.

Rogue chemist Patrick Arnold creates THG, a.k.a. "The Clear," a designer super-steroid, exclusively for BALCO

**THG**

Marion Jones goes to jail in '08 for lying about her drug use in 2000 Olympics, gives back five medals

Tim Montgomery, Jones's ex-beau and formerly the world's fastest man, banned for steroid use, jailed for selling heroin

**Jones**

BALCO founder Victor Conte becomes face of steroid era. Does jail time. Gets out vowing to clean up sport

Barry Bonds trainer, Greg Anderson, does over a year in jail for refusing to testify about what he gave Bonds from BALCO

**Conte**

Bonds breaks Hammering Hank's homerun record

Mark McGwire breaks down in front of Congress

**Bonds**

Roger Clemens insists he never took steroids or HGH

Ex-Clemens trainer Brian McNamee produces "smoking gauze"

**Clemens**

Bud Selig gets raked over the congressional coals for ignoring MLB's drug problem

Baseball revenues go from $1.3 billion in 1995 to $6.2 billion in 2007

**$6.2b**

Ex-Senator George Mitchell paid an estimated $40 million to write 409-page baseball steroids report

I earn a lot less to write *Steroid Nation*

**Mitchell**

**Novitzky**

**Conte**

**Bonds**

**$6.2b**

**Bonds**

**Bonds**

**VS**

**HGH vs. THG**
Chinese chemists are artists at making synthetic human growth hormone, which looks so much like what we produce naturally that testers can't catch it. But HGH can't compete with the more powerful and toxic THG, which Patrick Arnold chemically modified from testosterone to create a super-powerful muscle-builder that kept going and going and going.

**Novitzky vs. THG**
Jeff Novitzky, the Eliot Ness of the steroids era, created an industry of aggressive investigations that placed the United States Anti-Doping Agency on the map and led to a raft of headline indictments, notably the perjury case against Bonds. With the backing of the White House, Mr. Clean outlasted "The Clear."

**Jones vs. Montgomery**
After serving a six-month federal term for lying to the feds, Jones went on *Oprah* but couldn't admit to doing anything wrong, insisting she had no clue what she got from BALCO. Montgomery played it straighter on HBO: "I knew. I'm not going to lie. I knew." Trouble was, he did the interview from federal prison while serving an 8½-year sentence for check-kiting and heroin-dealing. Edge: Jones.

**Bonds vs. Clemens**
Clemens put himself in a box by telling Congress – and Mike Wallace – that he never took performance enhancers. Bonds just told a grand jury he didn't know what was in his BALCO "supplements" and then kept on hitting home runs. Those who might be able to contradict Bonds – namely Anderson and Conte – have chosen not to do so.

THE STEROID ERA WILL BE RECALLED AS A QUAINT TIME when the sports world cared little about the bizarre physical transformations unfolding before its eyes. Front-office execs saw nothing strange about cartoon-sized biceps, back acne, and strangely expanding heads. Fans ignored the reasons behind amazing home run and Olympic records. In this juiced-up game of cat and mouse between the alleged cheaters and those trying to catch them, players advance by winning the most, or losing the least.

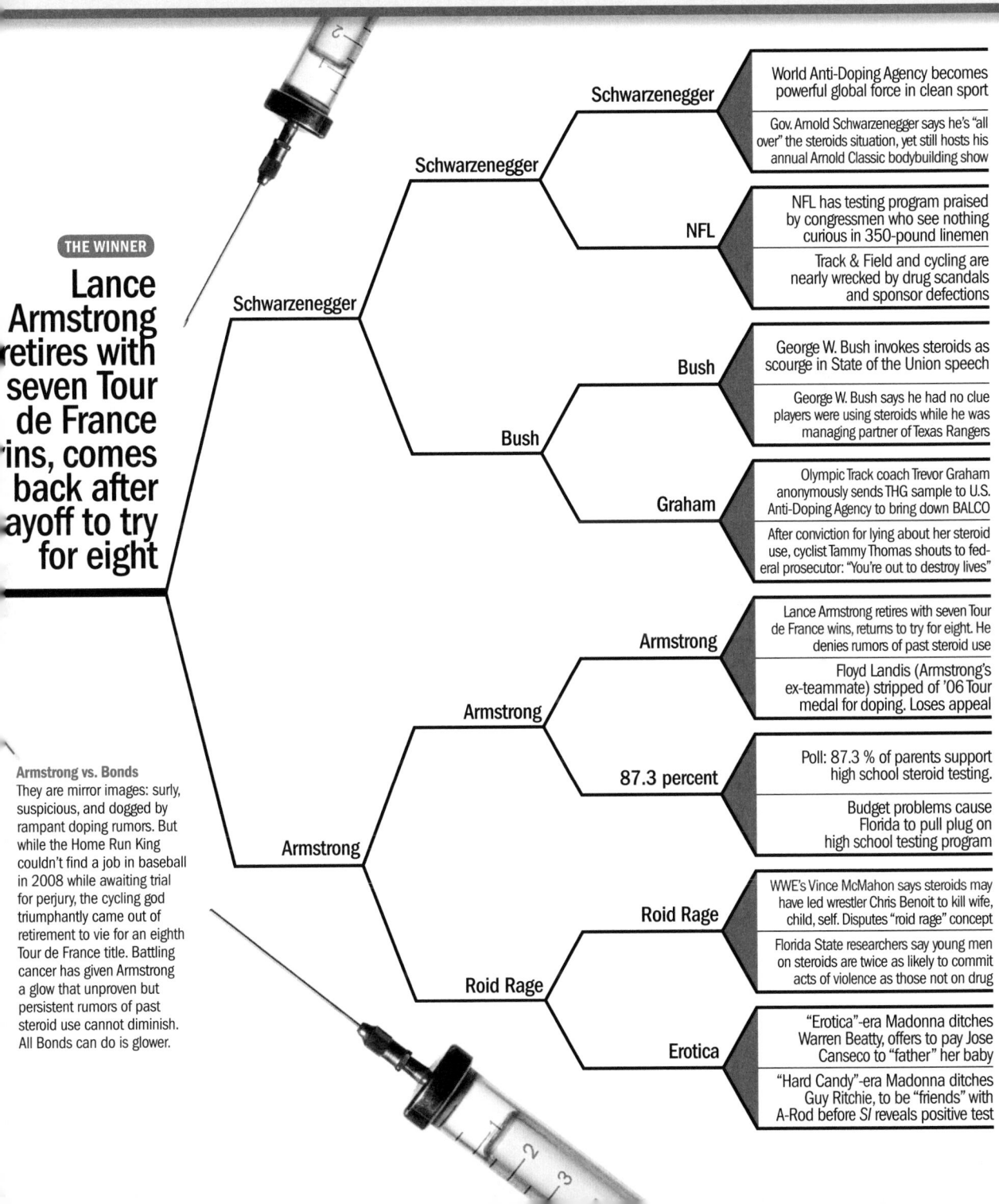


**Armstrong vs. Bonds**
They are mirror images: surly, suspicious, and dogged by rampant doping rumors. But while the Home Run King couldn't find a job in baseball in 2008 while awaiting trial for perjury, the cycling god triumphantly came out of retirement to vie for an eighth Tour de France title. Battling cancer has given Armstrong a glow that unproven but persistent rumors of past steroid use cannot diminish. All Bonds can do is glower.

# Sports Clichés

**By Steve Rushin**

Steve Rushin is the author of the nonfiction books *Road Swing* and *The Caddie Was a Reindeer* and a forthcoming novel, *The Pint Man*. He has been a columnist for *Sports Illustrated* and an essayist for *Time*.

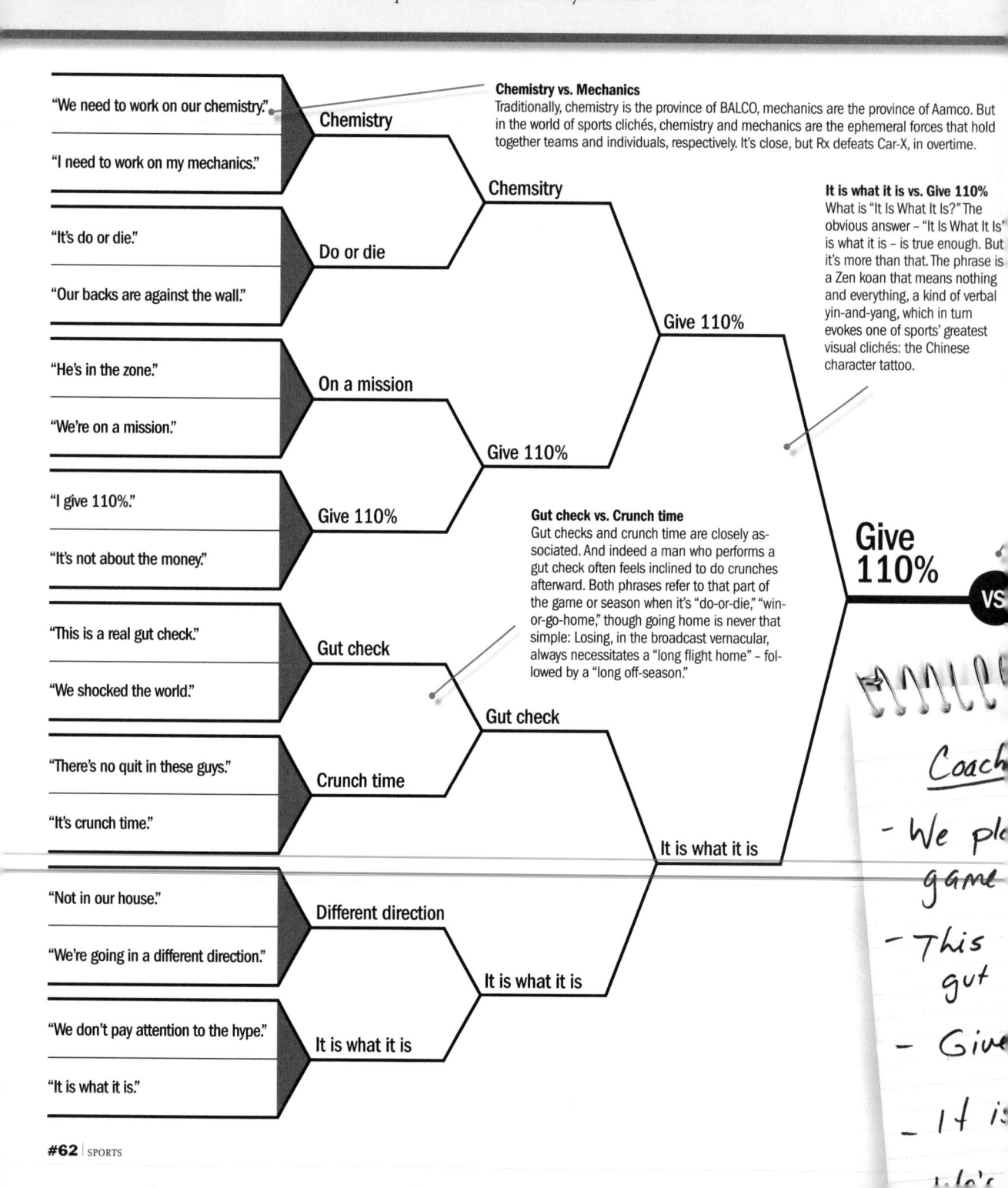


**Chemistry vs. Mechanics**
Traditionally, chemistry is the province of BALCO, mechanics are the province of Aamco. But in the world of sports clichés, chemistry and mechanics are the ephemeral forces that hold together teams and individuals, respectively. It's close, but Rx defeats Car-X, in overtime.

**It is what it is vs. Give 110%**
What is "It Is What It Is?" The obvious answer – "It Is What It Is" is what it is – is true enough. But it's more than that. The phrase is a Zen koan that means nothing and everything, a kind of verbal yin-and-yang, which in turn evokes one of sports' greatest visual clichés: the Chinese character tattoo.

**Gut check vs. Crunch time**
Gut checks and crunch time are closely associated. And indeed a man who performs a gut check often feels inclined to do crunches afterward. Both phrases refer to that part of the game or season when it's "do-or-die," "win-or-go-home," though going home is never that simple: Losing, in the broadcast vernacular, always necessitates a "long flight home" – followed by a "long off-season."

THE FRENCH HAVE MORE NAMES FOR BOREDOM THAN CHEESES, among them ennui and malaise and plat ("flat"), from which we get such touchstones of tedium as "platitude" and North Platte, Nebraska. But no word conveys existential weariness quite like cliché, and no cliché deadens the soul quite like a sports cliché, in which all fired coaches "step down" and all winning teams "step up." But you know that. The sports cliché, to use a cliché, needs no introduction.

**Gave 110% vs. One game at a time**
Athletes traditionally give 110%, unless they're calculating the tip on a restaurant check, in which case 5% is more typical. Whereas all games – except bingo and some speed-chess exhibitions – are played one at a time. And so the favorite phrase of *Bull Durham*'s Crash Davis (this bracket's patron saint) shocks the world. It's going to Disneyland. Nobody gave it a chance.

THE WINNER

**"We play 'em one game at a time."**

- One game at a time
  - Threw him under the bus
    - Nobody gave us a chance
      - "The kid's got tremendous upside."
      - "Nobody gave us a chance."
    - Threw him under the bus
      - "We have to stay within ourselves."
      - "They threw him under the bus."
  - One game at a time
    - All credit to my Lord
      - "All credit goes to my Lord and Savior."
      - "All credit goes to my Offensive Line."
    - One game at a time
      - "We play 'em one game at a time."
      - "The guys have to dig deep."
- More time with my family
  - Family to feed
    - Family to feed
      - "I have a family to feed."
      - "We sent them a message today."
    - Left it all on the field
      - "We left it all on the field."
      - "He has ice water in his veins."
  - More time with my family
    - Step up
      - "This was a wake-up call."
      - "Someone needs to step up."
    - More time with my family
      - "Let's take it to the next level."
      - "I want to spend more time with my family."

**Lord and Savior vs. Offensive Line**
Running backs and quarterbacks have been known, in consecutive sound bytes, to give all credit to the Almighty and all credit to their offensive lines. In that way, sports really are a microcosm of America – there's another cliché – in which overextended lines of credit lead to depression.

**Family to feed vs. More time with my family**
"I've got a family to feed" was given new life by Latrell Sprewell, who said it plaintively while drawing a $14.6 million salary. But this cliché owes less to Sprewell than to Orwell, who wrote: "The great enemy of clear language is insincerity." Ask any athlete or coach who retires to spend more time with his "family" (i.e., "golf clubs").

# Instant Replays

**By Alan Schwarz**

Alan Schwarz is a sports reporter for the *New York Times* and the author of *The Numbers Game: Baseball's Lifelong Fascination with Statistics.* Like most of the *Times* staff, he sits within earshot of this book's co-editor, Richard Sandomir.

- Vinko Bogataj's "Agony of Defeat" ski-jump fall (1970)
- Joe Namath raises finger after Super Bowl III (1969)
- **Vinko's crash**
- Brandi Chastain's bra-baring penalty shot (1999)
- Ozzie Smith barehands bad-hop grounder (1978)
- **Ozzie Smith**
- **Vinko's crash**
- Steve Young scrambles through the Vikings (1988)
- Nebraska's Fumblerooskie in 1984 Orange Bowl
- **Young's scramble**
- **Young's scramble**
- Lou Gehrig's "Luckiest Man" speech (1939)
- Doug Flutie's Hail Mary to Gerald Phelan (1984)
- **Flutie's Hail Mary**
- **Vinko's crash**
- Dr. J dunks from foul line in ABA contest (1976)
- Don Beebe chases down Leon Lett (1993)
- **Dr. J's dunk**
- **Carlton Fisk**
- Secretariat wins Belmont by 31 lengths (1973)
- Carlton Fisk's home run in the 1975 World Series
- **Carlton Fisk**
- **Carlton Fisk**
- Willie Mays's back-to-the-plate catch in World Series (1954)
- Willis Reed peels himself off the Garden floor (1970)
- **Willie Mays**
- **Willie Mays**
- Joe Montana to Dwight Clark – "The Catch" (1982)
- Rodney McCray crashes through outfield wall (1991)
- **Rodney McCray**

**Young's scramble vs. Flutie's Hail Mary**
Flutie's Hail Mary pass to Gerald Phelan was shocking, but it was also relatively lucky. Young's TD heroic scramble through almost the entire Vikings team has been called by replay expert Steve Sabol "the greatest run in the history of the game."

**"The Play" vs. Carlton Fisk**
Fisk's frantic "Stay fair! Stay fair!" dance captures how major leaguers can be just like Little Leaguers, and helped popularize the reaction shot. But five laterals (one of them totally blind), 144 Stanford Band members, and one smushed trombone player in a highlight universally known as "The Play" still defies belief with every replay.

**Vinko's crash vs. Young's scramble**
Bogataj was from Slovenia, sure, but generations of Americans have grown up with his fall and crash on the slopes and it permanently defines (via Jim McKay's voice on *Wide World of Sports*) the agony of defeat.

**Dr. J's dunk vs. Don Beebe/Leon Lett**
Before ESPN and YouTube, kids would salivate over the chance to see Dr. J pull his legendary dunk. He loses, though, because Beebe knocking the ball from the celebrating Lett still elicits cries of "Idiot!" from all of us who dreamed of scoring a Super Bowl touchdown.

**Carlton Fisk**

**VS**

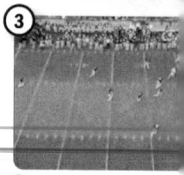

SPORTS REPLAYS AREN'T JUST ABOUT GREAT MOMENTS – they have to be visually arresting, with rarely-seen moves or compelling audio that you want to experience over and over again. (Alan Ameche's TD in the 1958 Ice Bowl is a flashpoint in sports history, but the footage is actually quite dull.) If you were stranded on a desert island (with a DVD player), these catches, scrambles, and legendary maneuvers (some of them bloopers) would justify our fascination with sports, even if you only watched them with a volleyball named Wilson.

**Miracles vs. Cal & Stanford**
Al Michaels's "Do you believe in miracles?" call makes this the only clip to rise so high solely on its audio (the video isn't particularly special). But it's a tough draw versus the astonishing no-time-left kickoff return by the University of California Golden Bears, through the entire Stanford band, to win "The Game." Comic lunacy wins.

**Ali-Foreman vs. Jordan's jumper**
Watching Ali outsmart and then pummel Foreman is one of the great sports lessons of all time. But seeing Jordan sink this series-winning running jumper, leap in the air, pump his fist, and leave Craig Ehlo eating hardwood encapsulates the greatest hoops hero ever.

THE WINNER

## "The Play": Cal return team runs through Stanford band (1982)

- "The Play"
  - Hockey miracle
    - Hockey miracle
      - "Do you believe in miracles?" U.S. Hockey gold (1980)
      - 46-year-old Nolan Ryan beats up Robin Ventura (1993)
    - Laettner's turnaround
      - "Playoffs???" Jim Mora clarifies the obvious (2001)
      - Christian Laettner's turnaround jumper beats KU (1992)
  - "The Play"
    - "The Play"
      - "The Play": Cal return team runs through Stanford band (1982)
      - Jackie Robinson steals home; Yogi goes nuts (1955)
    - Boise State
      - Derek Jeter flips to catcher Jorge Posada who tags out nonsliding Jeremy Giambi (2001)
      - Boise State's Statue of Liberty play wins 2007 Fiesta Bowl
- Jordan's jumper
  - Ali-Foreman
    - Ali-Foreman
      - Muhammad Ali rope-a-dopes George Foreman (1974)
      - Randall Cunningham scrambles, throws 95-yd TD (1990)
    - "Music City Miracle"
      - Gary Matthews, Jr., scales the Arlington wall (2006)
      - "Music City Miracle": Wycheck to Dyson to TD (2000)
  - Jordan's jumper
    - Darryl Dawkins
      - Darryl Dawkins shatters the backboard – twice (1979)
      - Dicky Maegle tackled by player off sideline (1954)
    - Jordan's jumper
      - Michael Jordan jumper beats the Cavaliers (1989)
      - Michael Phelps lunge wins seventh gold by .01 (2008)

8

13

14

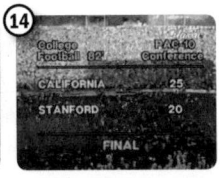

# Sexually Inadequate Nicknames

**By Hart Seely**

Hart Seely, author of *Mrs. Goose Goes to Washington: Nursery Rhymes for the Political Barnyard,* ruminates daily about the New York Yankees on his website, *It Is High, It Is Far, It Is Caught.*

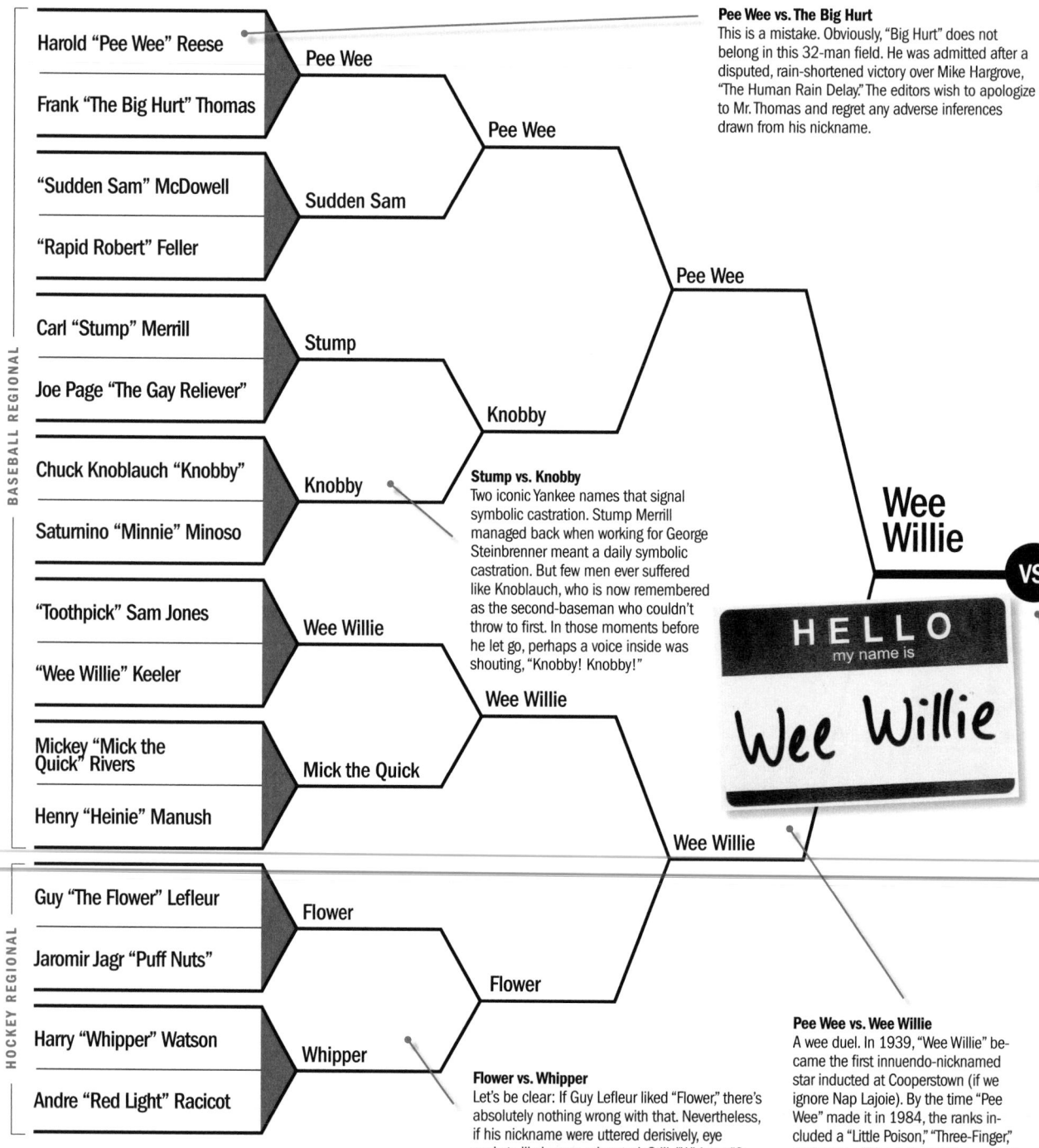


**Pee Wee vs. The Big Hurt**
This is a mistake. Obviously, "Big Hurt" does not belong in this 32-man field. He was admitted after a disputed, rain-shortened victory over Mike Hargrove, "The Human Rain Delay." The editors wish to apologize to Mr. Thomas and regret any adverse inferences drawn from his nickname.

**Stump vs. Knobby**
Two iconic Yankee names that signal symbolic castration. Stump Merrill managed back when working for George Steinbrenner meant a daily symbolic castration. But few men ever suffered like Knoblauch, who is now remembered as the second-baseman who couldn't throw to first. In those moments before he let go, perhaps a voice inside was shouting, "Knobby! Knobby!"

**Flower vs. Whipper**
Let's be clear: If Guy Lefleur liked "Flower," there's absolutely nothing wrong with that. Nevertheless, if his nickname were uttered derisively, eye sockets likely were relocated. Still, "Whipper"? Can you imagine how Mrs. Watson felt?

**Pee Wee vs. Wee Willie**
A wee duel. In 1939, "Wee Willie" became the first innuendo-nicknamed star inducted at Cooperstown (if we ignore Nap Lajoie). By the time "Pee Wee" made it in 1984, the ranks included a "Little Poison," "Three-Finger," and even a "Biscuit Pants." For coming first, "Wee Willie" advances.

FROM BASEBALL'S VLADIMIR GUERRERO ("Vlad the Impaler") to hockey's Georges Vezina ("The Chicoutimi Cucumber"), our great male athletes traditionally receive great phallic nicknames. Unfortunately, though, a few stars suffer nicknames on the field of play that imply mediocrity on the field of love. With each shout of his name, he hears a taunt of inadequacy, impotence, unhealthiness, or poor technique. Here, we honor those who overcame nicknames that would have sent lesser men to the bench.

**The Rash vs. The Worm**
A clash of humiliation titans. Bruce Bowen earned "The Rash" by his skintight defense. Dennis Rodman became "The Worm" due to his wriggle while playing pinball. Imagine their plight. "He's tall and handsome. Trust me, you'll love 'The Rash'!" Or, "Folks call him 'The Worm.' To me, though, he's just Wormy." "The Worm" won five NBA championships. For that, he advances.

HELLO
my name is
The Worm

THE WINNER
**Dennis "The Worm" Rodman**

**Wee Willie vs. Dennis "The Worm" Rodman**
"Wee Willie" was, indeed, wee – 5'7" and 140 pounds. Let's face it. If "Wee Willie" were 6'5" and 240, folks would wonder what was so wee? But no one could humiliate "The Worm." Dennis Rodman dated porn stars, gay men, Madonna, and even Carmen Electra, whom he married for 10 days. For that, "The Worm" wriggles to the top.

**All Day vs. Two-Minute**
Years ago, most men would proudly be called "All Day." Then came certain TV ads warning of "erections that last more than four hours." They have unleashed a primal fear of being told by a smirking ER attendant that your next nickname will be "Chopping Block." Still, you can't play a Barry Manilow song in two minutes. You can't boil an egg. You can't do – well – a lot of things.

- Worm
  - Worm
    - The Worm
      - Nate "Tiny" Archibald
      - Dennis "The Worm" Rodman
    - The Rash
      - Bruce Bowen "The Rash"
      - Eric "Sleepy" Floyd
  - Ickey
    - Lights Out
      - "Lights Out" James Toney
      - Roberto "Hands of Stone" Duran
    - Ickey
      - William "Hickey" Hickok
      - Elbert "Ickey" Woods
- Two-Minute
  - Two-Minute
    - Two-Minute
      - Adrian "All Day" Peterson
      - "Two-Minute" Tommy Kramer
    - Greasy
      - Elroy "Crazy Legs" Hirsch
      - Earl "Greasy" Neale
  - Mr. Outside
    - The Molester
      - Lester "The Molester" Hayes
      - Jerome Kearse "The Freak"
    - Mr. Outside
      - Glen Davis "Mr. Outside"
      - Doc Blanchard "Mr. Inside"

BASKETBALL REGIONAL
BOXING
FOOTBALL REGIONAL

# Baseball Moments

**By John Thorn**

John Thorn has written and edited many baseball books over the past 35 years, including *Total Baseball, Baseball's 10 Greatest Games,* and *Treasures of the Baseball Hall of Fame.*

**Lou Gehrig** says farewell, Yankee Stadium, 1939

**Harvey Haddix,** 12-inning perfecto but loses in 13, 1959

**Gehrig farewell**

**Ted Williams** hits .406 with final day 6-for-8, 1941

**Jackie Robinson** takes the field, April 15, 1947

**Robinson**

**Robinson**

Ball rolls through **Bill Buckner's** legs, Series Game 6, 1986

**Fred Merkle's** base-running boner costs Giants pennant, 1908

**Merkle boner**

**Merkle**

**Roger Maris** hits 61st homer, topping Ruth, 1961

**Mark McGwire** hits 62nd homer, topping Maris, 1998

**Maris's 61st homer**

**Robinson**

**Bobby Thomson's** "shot heard 'round the world," Game 3, NL playoff, 1951

**National League** founded, 1876

**Thomson "shot"**

**Thomson**

**Hitless Wonder White Sox** upset Cubs in WS, 1906

**Kirk Gibson** hits HR to win Game 1 of World Series, 1988

**White Sox upset**

**Thomson**

**Cal Ripken** tops Gehrig with 2131 straight games, 1995

**Mark Whiten** hits 4 homers, drives in 12 runs, 1993

**Whiten slugging**

**Larsen**

**Don Larsen** perfect game, World Series, Game 5, 1956

**Nolan Ryan** notches 7th no-hitter, 1991

**Larsen perfecto**

THE WINNER

## Jackie Robinson

takes the field, April 15, 1947

VS.

**Robinson vs. Bosox 2004**
Jackie was The First, and he remains The Greatest. The Red Sox had reached the summit before (though not since 1918) and they would do so again. The story of Robinson's heroism, resilience, and tenacity forms a cornerstone of both the game and the nation.

**Thomson vs. Larsen**
If the Hall of Fame inducted players for single-game accomplishments, these guys would be the first picks. Larsen is the only man to throw a perfect game in the World Series, but his team still had to play the next game. Thomson's blast capped a frenzied Giants' comeback against Brooklyn and turned the 1951 NL pennant race upside down.

SINCE, AS CASEY STENGEL MIGHT OBSERVE, most of our readers are above ground at the present time, most of these moments occurred after World War II. A moment is ideally a single play, or a game, or even an extended feat, that is epitomized in a single contest. Even a jaw-dropping accomplishment like Pedro Martinez's ERA of 1.74 in 2000, when the American League average was 5.07, does not reduce to a moment, any more than does Ichiro Suzuki's record of 262 hits in 2004. A great moment ought to be memorable or unique, preferably both.

**Seitz vs. Bosox 2004**
Peter Seitz's 1975 ruling ushered in free agency, which has transformed the game so that despite the owners' wailing and rending of (flannel?) garments, everyone makes more money than they used to. But Boston's championship, and the way it transpired – with seven straight postseason victories at the very brink of elimination – is a tale for the ages.

**Okrent vs. Ruth**
Oddly, both these contestants may be termed fantasy baseball. Ruth was a myth-making machine, and his greatest creation had him waving his finger at the Cubs' pitcher, or their dugout, or center field, at Wrigley. The invention of fantasy baseball by Okrent's Rotisserie lunchmates (Eisenberg, Waggoner, et al.) has proved to be more important and influential.

**Aaron's 715 vs. DiMaggio's 56**
Henry Aaron topped, under cruel hardship, the greatest career record in the game, held by its most beloved hero. But he was destined to be surpassed, and probably surpassed again. No one has come close to DiMaggio's streak of hitting in 56 consecutive games, and mathematicians say no one will.

**Bosox 2004**

- **Seitz**
  - **Okrent**
    - **Clemens**
      - **Roger Clemens** fans 20, decade after having done so, 1996
      - **Willie Mays** makes "The Catch," Game 1 of World Series, 1954
    - **Okrent**
      - **Dan Okrent et al.** create Rotisserie baseball, 1980
      - **Babe Ruth** called shot, Game 5 of World Series, 1932
  - **Seitz**
    - **Seitz ruling**
      - **Fred Toney and Hippo Vaughn,** double no-hit game, 1917
      - **Arbitrator Peter Seitz** rules for free agency, 1975
    - **Vander Meer duo**
      - **Johnny Vander Meer** second straight no-hitter, 1938
      - **Jack Morris** 1-0 win in 10 innings, Game 7 of World Series, 1991
- **Bosox 2004**
  - **DiMaggio's 56**
    - **Aaron's 715**
      - **Bill James** Abstract published commercially, 1982
      - **Hank Aaron** hits 715th homer to top Ruth, 1974
    - **DiMaggio's 56**
      - **Carlton Fisk** home run takes Red Sox to Series finale, 1975
      - **Joe DiMaggio** hits in 56th straight game, 1941
  - **Bosox 2004**
    - **Mazeroski homer**
      - **Brooklyn Atlantics** snap Cincinnati Reds' 70-win streak, 1870
      - **Bill Mazeroski** home run in Game 7 wins World Series, 1960
    - **Bosox end curse**
      - **Red Sox** win ALCS in 0-3 comeback, Series in sweep, 2004
      - **Pete Rose** gets hit No. 4,192, topping Cobb, 1985

# Absurd College Nicknames

**By Richard Sandomir and Pete Thamel**

Richard Sandomir attended Queens College, where he watched, but did not play for, the Knights. He dropped gym class before he could fail it. Pete Thamel is the college sports re porter for the *New York Times* and a proud Syracuse graduate who eats only one fruit: ora

**Battling Bishops**
Ohio Wesleyan University

**Fighting Saints**
John Carroll University

**Gentlemen and Ladies**
Centenary College

**Vandals**
University of Idaho

**Polar Bears**
Ohio Northern University

**Banana Slugs**
University of California-Santa Cruz

**Tarzans and Janes**
University of Puerto Rico-Mayaguez

**Pygmies**
New Mexico Institute of Mining and Technology

**Gorloks**
Webster University

**Eutetic**
St. Louis College of Pharmacy

**Fighting Artichokes**
Scottsdale Community College

**Boll Weevils and Cotton Blossoms**
University of Arkansas-Monticello

**Hustlin' Owls**
Oregon Institute of Technology

**Hustlin' Quakers**
Earlham College

**Anteaters**
University of California-Irvine

**Zips**
University of Akron

Fighting Saints

Vandals

Banana Slugs

Tarzans & Janes

Gorloks

Artichokes

Quakers

Zips

Vandals

Banana Slugs

Gorloks

Zips

Banana Slugs

Zips

Banana Slugs

VS

**Polar Bears vs. Banana Slugs**
Global warming hasn't sent the polar bears with great low-post moves to Ada, Ohio, yet their ferocity suits collegiate nicknaming needs. At least the slow-moving mollusk called the banana slug is indigenous to Santa Cruz and honestly, can you forget its name or its song ("You know you twist so good/You know you slime so fine")?

**Banana Slugs vs. Zips**
The Banana Slugs became chic when John Travolta wore one of the team's T-shirts in *Pulp Fiction,* which led to a failed campaign for state mollusk-hood. The silly yet exotic slugs face blue-collar opposition from the Zips, named for the zipper on hometown B.F. Goodrich's rubber overshoes. But the Slugs win because the Zips' mascot is not an anthropomorphized zipper, but, inexplicably, a kangaroo.

**Fighting Artichokes vs. Gorloks**
Conferring a combative personality on a weird vegetable took cojones – and a campus political smackdown – but credit Webster's mythmakers for creating a make-believe critter that is part cheetah, part buffalo (for the horns) and part St. Bernard, and naming it for local streets. Such an animal, if real, would truly whip a Nittany Lion.

OF ALL OF COLLEGE SPORTS' WONDERFUL RITUALS – the bands, the chants, the tailgating – none is more absurd than team nicknames. Gators, Seminoles, Tigers, Trojans, Hoyas, Longhorns, Badgers, Wildcats, Eagles, and Fighting Irish (more believable in Hell's Kitchen than South Bend) dominate major college programs. But small, lesser-known schools that do not play in major conferences have inane monikers that are at least as inappropriate for sensate humans. So, go Eutetic, kill those Hustlin' Owls!

THE WINNER

**Nads**
Rhode Island School of Design

**Dustdevils vs. Kangaroos**
Only a few weather systems, like hurricanes or tornadoes, are suitable inspirations for college teams. A Dustdevil's namesake is a mini-tornado that might strike the Laredo campus, not the Dustbuster or Dirt Devil vacuum cleaners that would have given opposing teams' fans free reign to declare that the Dustdevils suck. Putting a Kangaroo in Texas is flat-out lazy lexicography.

**Nads vs. Banana Slugs**
The Slugs have made their case, which lacks the élan of the Nads, who don't play many sports, but sport a name that is short for gonads. A nad is technically a coenzyme, but at the Providence art school the teams are named for testicles. It takes gonads to win, not a slug's antennae, plus an audacious mascot, Scrotie, a man dressed as full genitalia. Go Nads!

- Dustdevils
  - Dustdevils
    - Nanooks
      - **Nanooks** – University of Alaska Fairbanks
      - **Fighting Scots** – College of Wooster
    - Dustdevils
      - **Dustdevils** – Texas A&M International University
      - **Nor'Easters** – University of New England
  - Kangaroos
    - Kangaroos
      - **Kangaroos** – Austin College
      - **Rock Llamas** – Bard College at Simon's Rock
    - Judges
      - **Judges** – Brandeis University
      - **Bridges** – Brooklyn College
- Nads
  - Poets
    - Poets
      - **Profs** – Rowan University
      - **Poets** – Whittier College
    - Sagehens
      - **Fightin' Blue Hens** – University of Delaware
      - **Sagehens** – Pomona College
  - Nads
    - Gusties
      - **Golden Gusties** – Gustavus Adolphus College
      - **Threshers** – Bethel College
    - Nads
      - **Nads** – Rhode Island School of Design
      - **Great Danes** – University at Albany

# Toughest Golf Holes

**By Chris Millard**

Chris Millard is the author of *Golf's 100 Toughest Holes* and co-author with Jack Nicklaus of *Nicklaus By Design*. He thinks all holes are tough.

13th at Medinah CC
No.3 Course, Par 3

5th at Pine Valley
Par 3

15th at Bethpage
Black Course, Par 4

18th at Whistling Straits
Straits Course, Par 4

5th at Colonial CC
Par 4

18th at Doral Golf Resort & Spa
Blue Course, Par 4

12th at Augusta National GC
Par 3

17th at TPC at Sawgrass
Par 3

18th at Koolau GC
Par 4

18th at Quail Hollow Club
Par 4

18th at Southern Hills CC
Par 4

18th at TPC at Sawgrass
Par 4

12th at Peachtree GC
Par 4

10th at Augusta National GC
Par 4

9th at Pebble Beach GL
Par 4

18th at Bay Hill Club and Lodge
Par 4

5th at Pine Valley

18th at Whistling Straits

18th at Doral

17th at TPC Sawgrass

18th at Quail Hollow

18th at TPC Sawgrass

12th at Peachtree

9th at Pebble Beach

5th at Pine Valley

17th at TPC Sawgrass

18th at Quail Hollow

9th at Pebble Beach

5th at Pine Valley

9th at Pebble

**5th at Pine Valley vs. 17th at Sawgrass**
Not only is the tee shot harder into Pine Valley's legendary par-3 (driver for many vs. a short iron at Sawgrass), but assuming you miss the green on both (fair assumption), the 5th offers no easy recovery whereas Sawgrass gives you a friendly drop zone.

**18th at Quail Hollow vs. 18th at TPC Sawgrass**
Of these two lethal home holes, Quail Hollow wins for registering more double bogeys than any other non-major layout on the PGA Tour. In his 1997 redesign, Tom Fazio lengthened the hole and brought the creek dominating the entire left side more clearly into play. Consider David Toms who wobbled to a win with a snowman here in the 2003 Wachovia Championship.

THE WINNER

## 5th at Pine Valley

Par 3

VS

**18th at Merion vs. 5th at Pine Valley**
Merion's 18th offers the burde of yardage (it's a 505-yard pa 4), camber (all bounces lead to trouble on the left), and a narrow neck leading to a gree that runs quickly and harshly away from the player. It will re-enter the debate on Grand Sla difficulty when it hosts the 20 U.S. Open. But Pine Valley's 5t described by Herbert Warren Wind as "an anthology of hazards," wins because it plays straight uphill at an imposing 232 yards from the back tee and offers virtually no bailout. The nerve-wracking tee shot d mands of most players a drive or hybrid. The volcano-like gree is a fast, dynamic surface whe even three putts are applaude by members and caddies. Medals should be awarded for achieving par, Medals of Freedom for a birdie.

AMERICANS ARE ATTRACTED TO DIFFICULTY. How else to explain the audacity of moon launches, Microsoft Vista, or so many hackers playing the back tees? George Thomas, who designed the courses at Bel-Air, Riviera, and Los Angeles, said that difficulty contributes to the essence of the game. "Place the golf course on a level plane; have no traps of any kind; let the fairway be flat, the green unprotected and without rolls; let there be no rough . . . and the green itself absolutely level; and what would be the result? A thing . . . on which there is no thrill of accomplishment worthwhile."

**13th at Stanwich vs. 11th at CC of Charleston**
Stanwich is the Northeast's best-kept secret. Its diabolical William F. Gordon-designed par-3 debuted nationally at the 2002 U.S. Mid-Am. With the pin anywhere from 200 to 215 yards, and trees, bunkers, and water to negotiate, the 13th got into contestants' heads and never departed. Charleston's 187-yard par-3, even softened in the last decade, still feels like a penalty box. Says one member, "At some small events three-fourths of the field wouldn't even post a score on the 11th out of embarrassment."

**15th at The Bayonet Course vs. 18th at Merion**
There's tough and then there's Army Tough. The Bayonet at the old Fort Ord in Seaside, California, was designed in 1953 by a crusty left-handed Major General named Bob McClure. The par-4 428-yard 15th is the toughest hole on a course that routinely decimates Tour and U.S. Open hopefuls. In 2000's first stage of Q-School here 12-over made it to the second stage.

**1st at Oakmont vs. 16th at Cypress**
Hard to believe that anyone would actually do it, but the par-3 16th at Cypress Point does offer a tiny but short bailout for those who would rather assure bogey than flirt with the Pacific Ocean. The opener at Oakmont, a course designed to be the hardest in the world, offers no such comfort.

**16th at Cypress vs. 18th at Butler National**
The Beauty vs. The Beast. In the 17 years that Butler National hosted the Western Open (1974-1990) the Tour never used the back tees on No. 18. Said Hale Irwin, "If we played this course all the way back, some guys wouldn't finish." Still, coming up with a nice shot at Cypress' 16th is like coming up with a clever line when you meet Penelope Cruz. Dream on.

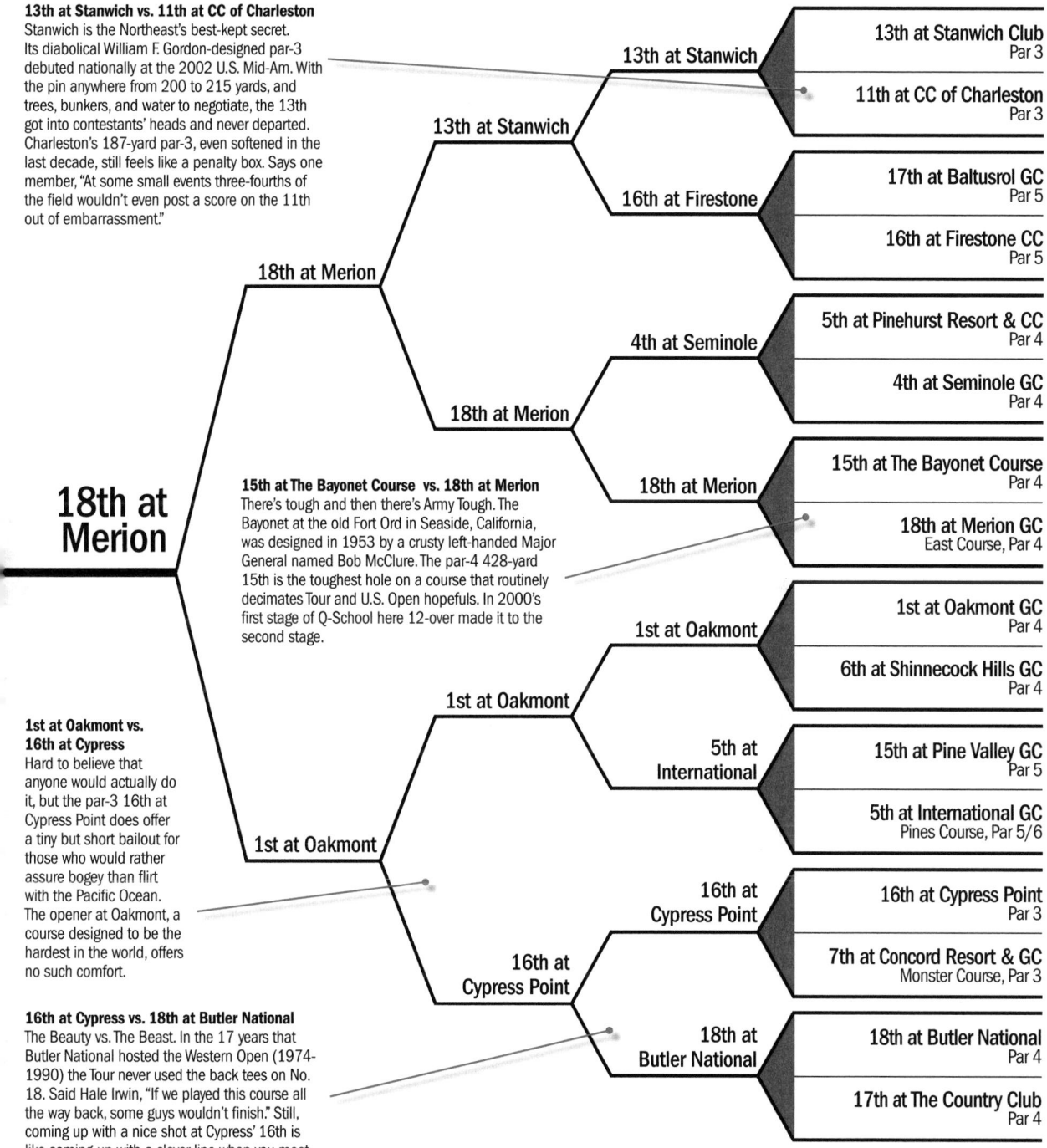

# Dubious Sports Achievements

**By Richard Hoffer**

Richard Hoffer, a long-time writer for *Sports Illustrated,* is the author of *A Savage Business,* which the magazine once included in its list of the 100 best sports books ever. As dubious as it gets.

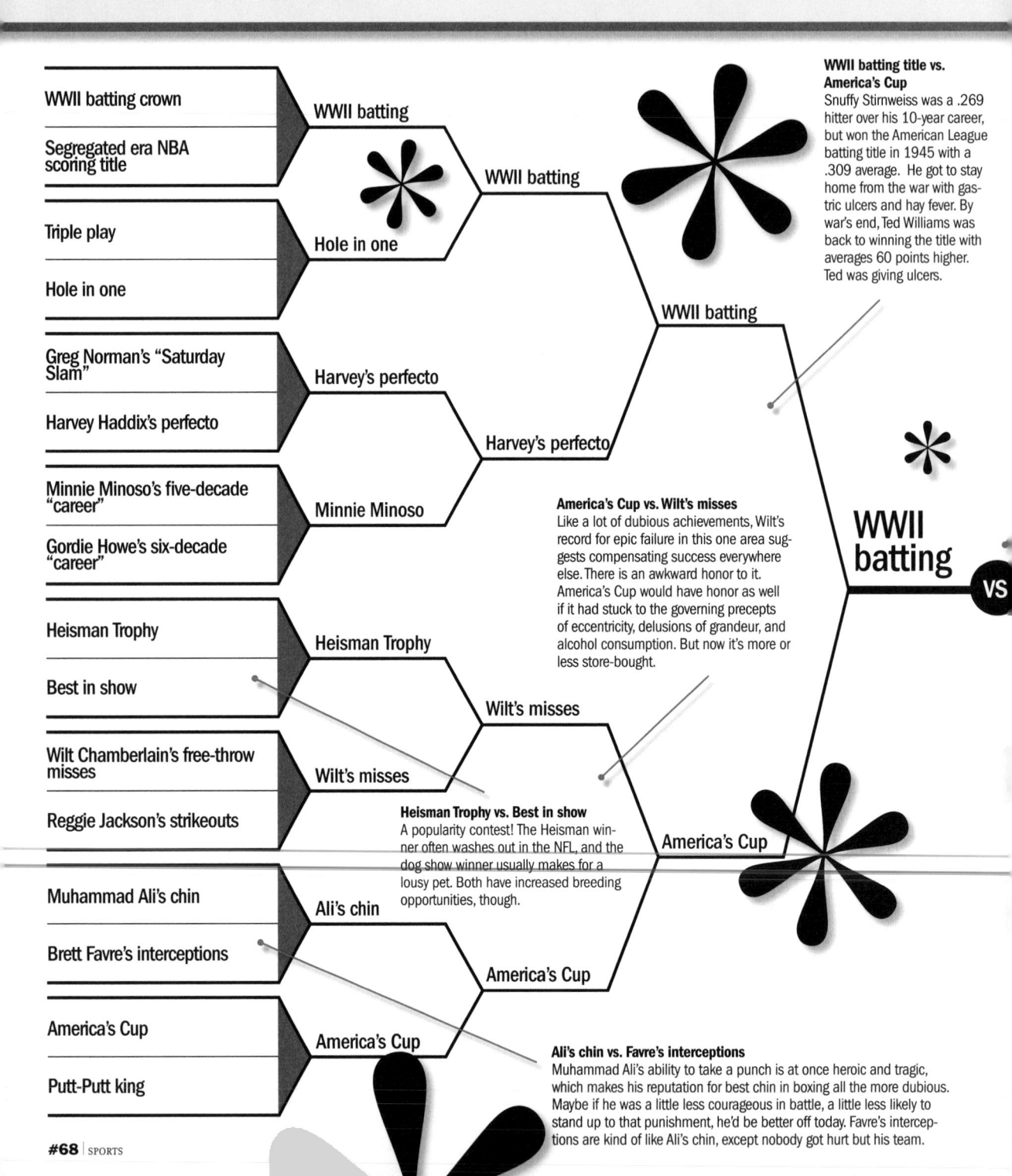

WE HAVE CAST A WIDE NET, mingling the merely embarrassing with the hopelessly irrelevant, the outright freakish with the downright felonious, the innocently unintended with the cynically pursued. Not every dubious achievement deserves shame. Mostly they're just a matter of somebody being in the wrong place at the wrong time, accepting a distinction neither sought nor earned. To qualify, a dubious sports achievement should demand explanations, asterisks, and at the very least, a sheepish shrug of the shoulders. In any case, nothing to be proud of here.

**Steroid era vs. WWII batting**
At least Snuffy competed honestly. But every slugger from the steroid era will be dogged by suspicion that he didn't. If they don't quite get an asterisk, they have a perpetual taint and premature hair loss. Do you have any idea how many home runs Joe Bauman could have hit at Roswell if he had had access to BALCO?

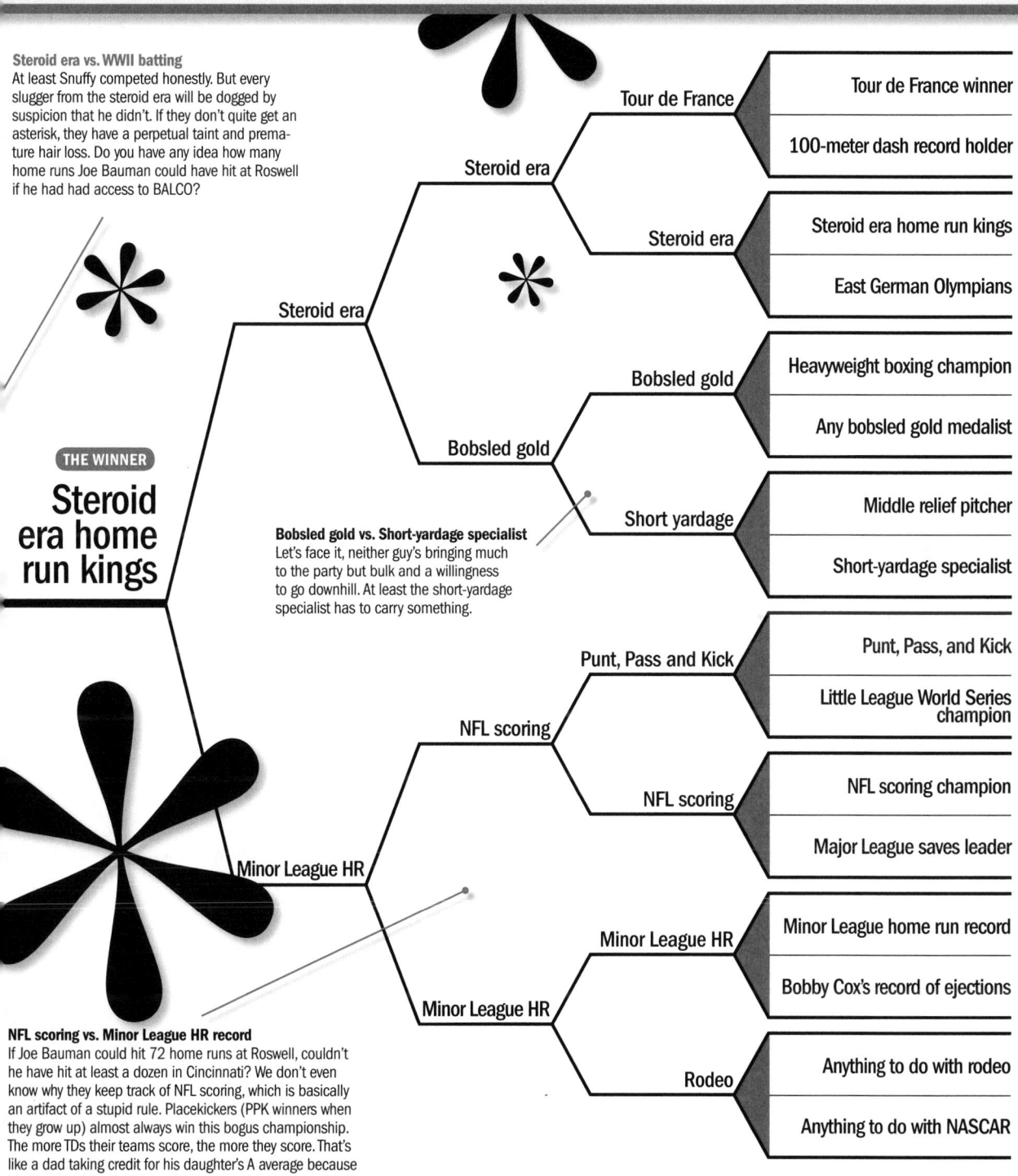


**Bobsled gold vs. Short-yardage specialist**
Let's face it, neither guy's bringing much to the party but bulk and a willingness to go downhill. At least the short-yardage specialist has to carry something.

**NFL scoring vs. Minor League HR record**
If Joe Bauman could hit 72 home runs at Roswell, couldn't he have hit at least a dozen in Cincinnati? We don't even know why they keep track of NFL scoring, which is basically an artifact of a stupid rule. Placekickers (PPK winners when they grow up) almost always win this bogus championship. The more TDs their teams score, the more they score. That's like a dad taking credit for his daughter's A average because he drives her to school.

# From Athlete to Actor

**By Mark Reiter**

Mark Reiter, co-editor of this book, has never acted and he's not much of an athlete either.

**Merlin Olsen**
From LA Rams to *Little House on the Prairie, Father Murphy* (TV)

**John Matuszak**
From Oakland Raiders to *North Dallas Forty*

**Olsen**

**Bruce Jenner**
From '76 decathlon gold to *Can't Stop the Music*

**Cathy Rigby**
From gymnastics to *Peter Pan*

**Rigby**

**Olsen**

**Carl Weathers**
From pro football to Apollo Creed in *Rocky*

**Shaquille O'Neill**
NBA giant, moonlights in *Blue Chips, Kazaam*

**Weathers**

**Karras**

**Alex Karras**
From Detroit Lions to *Blazing Saddles, Webster* (TV)

**Dick Butkus**
From NFL bruiser to *Blue Thunder* (TV)

**Karras**

**Karras**

**Bernie Casey**
From SF '49ers to *Never Say Never Again*

**Mark Harmon**
From UCLA QB to *St. Elsewhere, NCIS* (TV)

**Harmon**

**Alex English**
From NBA scoring machine to *Fish That Saved Pittsburgh*

**Kareem Abdul Jabbar**
From NBA all-timer to *Airplane!*

**Abdul-Jabbar**

**Harmon**

**Dean Cain**
From Princeton football star to *Superman* (TV)

**Randall "Tex" Cobb**
From heavyweight contender to *Raising Arizona*

**Cobb**

**Schwarzenegger**

**Arnold Schwarzenegger**
Ultimate bodybuilder to action hero, *The Terminator*

**Chuck Connors**
From pro baseball and basketball to *The Rifleman*

**Schwarzenegger**

**Karras vs. Olsen**
Why do grizzly defensive linemen become pussycats when they hit the screen? After a glorious career as part of the Rams' Fearsome Foursome, Olsen went from playing a gentle giant on *Little House on the Prairie* to a saintly *Father Murphy*. Karras, an all-pro for 15 seasons in Detroit, went from Mongo in *Blazing Saddles* (a role that existed primarily for the sound gag, "Mongo! Santamaria!") to a deft comedian in *Webster*. Holiness is nice, but comedy is hard. Karras wins.

**Harmon vs. Abdul-Jabbar**
Two UCLA Bruins face off. Harmon has put together such a charming, long-running success as a TV actor – from *St. Elsewhere* to *NCIS* – that many fans forget he was UCLA's starting quarterback for two seasons in the early '70s. That double success is more than enough to stuff Kareem, whose greatness on the basketball court towers over his work on a film set.

THE WINNER

**Arnold Schwarzenegg**
Ultimate bodybuilder to ac hero, *The Terminator*

VS

**Reynolds vs. Schwarzenegge**
At some point in their careers both Burt and Arnold were th biggest-grossing stars in Hollywood. But Schwarzenegger also the greatest bodybuilder ever, whereas Reynolds' time in the Florida State backfield was cut short by injury. Being number one in both chosen fields is so difficult, only the Terminator has done it.

IF YOU'RE AN ATHLETE WHO REALLY WANTS TO ACT, it helps to be a great athlete, but it's not essential. On the evidence, it's more important that you bulk up – which explains why so many large and tall people take on show biz. It also helps to be a man. In this tournament of athletes who made the switch from sports to acting, only one woman gets an invite. Advancement is a function of how well you performed as both athlete and actor, with bonus points for playing a role rather than yourself. Dominance in both, while rare, takes the prize.

# Reynolds

- **Reynolds** — **Burt Reynolds**, From Florida State running back to '70s movie stardom
- **Reynolds** — **O. J. Simpson**, From USC and NFL greatness to *The Naked Gun, The Towering Inferno*
- **Uecker** — **Bob Uecker**, From baseball and TV booth to *Mr. Belvedere* (TV), *Major League*
- **Uecker** — **Ray Allen**, NBA sharpshooter, moonlights with *Harvard Man, He Got Game*
- **Fred Dryer** — **Fred Williamson**, From NFL secondary to film secondary, *That Man Bolt*
- **Fred Dryer** — **Fred Dryer**, From LA Rams pass rusher to *Hunter* (TV)
- **Jim Brown** — **Jim Brown**, From NFL greatness to *Rio Conchos, The Dirty Dozen*
- **Jim Brown** — **Howie Long**, From Oakland Raiders to *Firestorm, Broken Arrow*
- **Marinaro** — **Bubba Smith**, From NFL greatness to *Police Academy* series
- **Marinaro** — **Ed Marinaro**, From NCAA rushing title at Cornell to *Hill Street Blues*
- **Bradshaw** — **Joe Namath**, From Broadway Joe in NFL to *C.C. and Company*
- **Bradshaw** — **Terry Bradshaw**, From 4 Super Bowl rings to *Failure to Launch*
- **Crabbe** — **Brian Bosworth**, From Oklahoma linebacker to action figure in *Stone Cold*
- **Crabbe** — **Buster Crabbe**, From 1932 Olympic swimming gold to *Flash Gordon*
- **Weismuller** — **Johnny Weismuller**, From five 1924–28 Olympic swimming golds to *Tarzan*
- **Weismuller** — **Rick Fox**, From NBA to *He Got Game, Oz, Ugly Betty* (TV)

**Reynolds** → **Reynolds** → **Reynolds**

**Reynolds** → **Reynolds** → **Brown**

**Reynolds** → **Brown** → **Bradshaw**

**Reynolds** → **Weismuller** → **Weismuller**

**Marinaro vs. Bradshaw**
After winning the NCAA rushing title at Cornell and some journeyman running back work for the Minnesota Vikings, Marinaro broke though with his role as a cop in *Hill Street Blues*. He had it all: good looks, acting chops, and a profile that didn't say big jock. But he faded. Bradshaw has a comic persona that jumps out of the screen, most deftly in his fish-tending scene in *Failure to Launch*. A small film career, but a big impression.

**Weismuller vs. Crabbe**
An all-wet matchup of 1920–30s swim gods. Crabbe knew his limitations: "Some say my acting rose to the level of incompetence and then leveled off." But Weismuller understood why his athlete-to-actor move succeeded, saying, "How can a guy climb trees, say 'Me, Tarzan, you, Jane,' and make a million? The public forgives my acting because they know I was an athlete. They know I wasn't make-believe."

# Sportscasters

**By Richard Deitsch**

Richard Deitsch is a sports media writer and special projects editor for *Sports Illustrated*, and writes the Media Circus column for SI.com.

POSTHUMOUS VOICES

**Red Barber,** vivid, lyrical Southern radio voice of Reds, Dodgers, and Yankees

**Don Dunphy,** exciting boxing specialist who called over 2,000 bouts

**Jack Buck,** gravelly, distinctive voice of St. Louis Cardinals and CBS Radio

**Harry Caray,** radio voice of Cardinals, White Sox, Cubs, renowned later for singing "Take Me Out to the Ballgame"

**Mel Allen,** Yankees' radio-TV voice who spoke of "Ballantine Blasts" and "How about that?" moments

**Lindsey Nelson,** original Mets voice, also called college football game introducing instant replay

**Howard Cosell** (ABC), controversial, brilliant, verbose boxing commentator and MNF lightning rod

**Marty Glickman,** long-time New York voice of Knicks and football Giants

**Chick Hearn,** the phrasemaking radio voice of Lakers

**Graham McNamee,** called baseball on radio as early as 1923

**Curt Gowdy** (NBC, ABC), versatile do-anything announcer

**Al McGuire** (NBC, CBS), Marquette coach turned loopy college basketball analyst

**Chris Schenkel** (ABC), mild-mannered all-purpose announcer who even did bowling

**Bob Prince,** Pirates announcer with vivid phrases, a.k.a. "The Gunner"

**Bill Stern,** multi-sport radio voice, known for storytelling and embellishments

**Jim McKay,** (ABC, CBS, NBC), Olympic host who chronicled the thrill of victory and the agony of defeat

Red Barber

Jack Buck

Mel Allen

Howard Cosell

Chick Hearn

Curt Gowdy

Chris Schenkel

Jim McKay

Red Barber

Howard Cosell

Curt Gowdy

Jim McKay

Red Barber

Jim McKay

**Jack Buck vs. Harry Caray**
Buck and Caray shared the same St. Louis Cardinals radio booth in 1954 before Caray was fire and left St. Louis for Chicago in 1970. Both were Midwest institutions: Buck the witty baseball classicist; Caray the outsized, increasingly beery, beloved warbler of Wrigley Field. The less-oster tatious Buck advances, not for baseball, but for his distinguished work as CBS Radio's NFL voic

**Red Barber vs. Howard Cosell**
Cosell was the most outspoken sportscaster of his time, an idiosyncratic trailblazer and world-clas egotist who spoke of everything from racism and antitrust law to *Monday Night Football* and the pu niness of his detractors. But Barbe with a literate style flavored by his Southern cadences and argot, established nearly all the ground rule for calling baseball on radio – and for keeping one's objectivity.

**Chick Hearn vs. Curt Gowdy**
Hearn is, by most reckonings, the greatest basketball announcer ever, having coined the seminal hoop terms "baby hook," "charity stripe," and "no-look pass." But Gowdy's multi-sport versatility made "The Cowboy" the go-to big game voice of a generation: he broadcast 16 World Series, nine Super Bowls, eight Olympics, 12 Rose Bowls, and 24 NCAA Final Fours, and was the first sportscaster to win a Peabody Award.

THE WINNER

## Jim McKay

(ABC, CBS, NBC) Olympic host who chronicled the thrill of victory and the agony of defeat

VS

COMPETENCE, EGO, HONESTY, intellect, showmanship, storytelling, and voice are commonplace traits with every great sportscaster. But most of all it is the underlying professionalism and an instinctive sense of what to say – and what not to say – that defines this small community.

# Vin Scully

**Vin Scully vs. Jim McKay**
Scully is cool jazz on a summer night, a Barber acolyte who became baseball's greatest voice. McKay was the pioneering host of ABC's *Wide World of Sports*, but more important, the network's premier guide to the Olympic funhouse: equal parts historian, traffic cop, geopolitical expert, and journalist. His words in delivering the solemn news that 11 Israelis had been killed by terrorists at the 1972 Munich Summer Games – "They're all gone." – is the signature sports broadcasting moment of the 20th century.

**James Brown vs. Pat Summerall**
An ego-free broadcaster in a sea of self-promoting booyahs, Brown's style (and his ability to let partners shine) was in evidence as he anchored Fox's football pre-game show to a decade of dominance, then moved on to host CBS's rival program. But Summerall's masterful minimalism is more influential, a tonic to some of the bloviating maximalism that is now commonplace.

- Vin Scully
  - Vin Scully
    - **Vin Scully,** lyrical voice of Dodgers since 1950 and student of Barber's; also NBC's lead baseball announcer
    - **Jim Nantz** (CBS), NFL announcer; golf anchor; top college basketball play-by-play
  - John Madden
    - **John Madden** (CBS, Fox, ABC, NBC), former Raiders coach turned top NFL analyst, with sound effects
    - **Keith Jackson** (ABC), voice of college football known for Southern vernacular
  - Marv Albert
    - **Marv Albert** (NBC, TNT), NBA announcer with signature "Yes!" call.
    - **Harry Kalas,** mellifluous baritone for Phillies and NFL Films
  - Al Michaels
    - **Al Michaels** (ABC, NBC), voice of *Monday* and *Sunday Night Football.* Greatest call: "Do you believe in miracles?"
    - **Verne Lundquist** (CBS), college football and golf; "In your life!"
- Bob Costas
  - Dick Enberg
    - **Dick Enberg** (NBC, CBS, ESPN), emotional big-game football, basketball, golf, tennis announcers. "Oh, my!"
    - **Mike Emrick** (CBS, Fox, ABC, NBC, Versus), no national hockey announcer is better
  - Bob Costas
    - **Bob Costas** (NBC, HBO), sophisticated host of Olympics and multi-sport voice
    - **Jack Whitaker** (ABC, CBS), elegant reporter and essayist
  - Pat Summerall
    - **Pat Summerall** (CBS, Fox), former place-kicker who made rare move from player to play-by-play announcer
    - **James Brown** (CBS, Fox), versatile studio host, college and pro football announcer
  - Ernie Harwell
    - **Mary Carillo** (NBC, CBS, ESPN, USA, HBO), tennis commentator, Olympic reporter and host, documentarian
    - **Ernie Harwell,** genteel Southern baseball voice, most notably Tigers

# SEC Athletes

**By Steve Eubanks**

Steve Eubanks is a contributing columnist for FoxSports.com and author of too many books. He lives in Peachtree City, Georgia, with his family and more animals than city ordinances allow.

**Peyton Manning**
football, Tennessee, 1994–97

**Steve Spurrier**
football, Florida, 1963–66

**Pat Riley**
basketball, Kentucky, 1964–67

**Jack "Hacksaw" Reynolds**
Tennessee, 1967–69

**Fran Tarkenton**
football, Georgia, 1957–60

**Hines Ward**
football, Georgia, 1994–97

**Tim Tebow**
football, Florida, 2006–

**Herschel Walker**
football, Georgia, 1980–83

**Bo Jackson**
football, Auburn, 1982–85

**John Hannah**
football, Alabama, 1970–72

**Jerry Pate**
golf, Alabama, 1972–75

**Abby Wambach**
soccer, Florida, 1999–2001

**Danny Wuerffel**
football, Florida, 1993–1996

**Shaquille O'Neal**
basketball, LSU, 1989–91

**CoCo Miller**
women's basketball, Georgia, 1997–2000

**Joe Namath**
football, Alabama, 1962–64

Peyton Manning

Pat Riley

Fran Tarkenton

Tim Tebow

Bo Jackson

Jerry Pate

Shaquille O'Neal

Joe Namath

Peyton Manning

Tim Tebow

Bo Jackson

Joe Namath

Tim Tebow

Bo Jackson

**Peyton Manning vs. Steve Spurrier**
Spurrier has a Heisman but is there anybody left who thinks 1997 Heisman winner Charles Woodson was a better college football player than Peyton Manning?

**Peyton Manning vs. Tim Tebow**
As pure passers go, Manning was the best that stepped onto a field. But Tebow won the Heisman as a sophomore, should have won it again as a junior, and picked up two national championship rings before his senior year. Close call, but Tebow can run and pass – and carry an entire team on his shoulder padsdots.

**Shaquille O'Neal vs. Joe Namath**
Shaq might have shattered backboards at LSU, but only time has erased the memories of Namath's brilliance at QB for the Crimson Tide (and his then-outrageous $427,000 contract to go to the fledgling AFL). Truly, he was the first college athlete since Red Grange with star power before he turned pro.

**Bo Jackson**

VS

**Jerry Pate vs. Bo Jackson**
Not a fair fight with the man who inspired the phrase "Bo Knows." But Pate's closer than you think. Cary Middlecoff won more majors and Doug Sanders had more wins, but no SEC golfer had a college career like Pate. As a senior, he won the NCAA, the U.S. Amateur, and was low amateur at the U.S. Open. Then he won the U.S. Open at Atlanta Athletic Club with a miraculous 5-iron into the 72nd as a 22-year-old PGA Tour rookie.

THE SOUTHEASTERN CONFERENCE is the best in college sports, with powerhouse teams in so many sports from Florida, Alabama, Tennessee, Kentucky, Auburn, LSU, Georgia, and more. If you want to argue the point, here's who didn't make the list: Cornelius Bennett, Garrison Hearst, Cris Collinsworth, Frank Thomas, Robert Horry, Shaun Alexander, Joaquim Noah, Cadillac Williams, DeLisa Milton-Jones, David Toms, and Champ Bailey, among others. Good doesn't cut it here; you have to be legendary. Bonus points for later success in the pros, but it's the college performance that counts here.

THE WINNER

## "Pistol" Pete Maravich

**Bo Jackson vs. Pete Maravich**
In a conference known for football, a Heisman trophy winner and unreal two-sport athlete like Bo Jackson should be a lock, right? Not so fast. LSU's skinny, sad-eyed basketball savant with the droopy locks averaged an NCAA record 44.2 points per game over three seasons – and that's before the three-point line came along. Maravich invented ShowTime. His YouTube clips still dazzle two decades after his death. No doubt, Pistol Pete is the best the SEC has ever produced.

**Gwen Torrence vs. Emmitt Smith**
Three Olympic gold medals and three world championships beats a school touchdown record and a *Dancing with the Stars* crown any day. Torrence would have won at least six golds had East German Katrin Krabbe been disqualified after testing positive for steroids.

**Charles Barkley vs. Rowdy Gaines**
Two of Auburn's greatest Hall of Fame legends, but Barkley's rebounds don't come close to Rowdy's three Olympic gold medals and eleven world records.

- Pete Maravich
  - Gwen Torrence
    - Eli Manning
      - Kevin Butler — football, Georgia, 1981–84
      - Pete Maravich — basketball, LSU, 1968–70
    - Emmitt Smith
      - Frank Sinkwich — football, Georgia, 1940–42
      - Pete Maravich — football, Auburn, 1969–72
  - Rowdy Gaines
    - Bart Starr
      - Bart Starr — football, Alabama, 1953–55
      - Dominique Wilkins — basketball, Georgia, 1979–81
    - Rowdy Gaines
      - Frank Shorter — track, Florida, 1966–69
      - Rowdy Gaines — swimming, Auburn, 1978–81
- Rowdy Gaines
  - Charles Barkley
    - Charles Barkley
      - Ken Stabler — football, Alabama, 1965–67
      - Charles Barkley — basketball, Auburn, 1981–83
    - Archie Manning
      - Archie Manning — football, Ole Miss, 1968–70
      - Jack Youngblood — football, Florida 1967–70

SOUTHEASTERN SEC CONFERENCE

# Pound-for-Pound Fighters

**By Steve Farhood**

Steve Farhood is a former editor-in-chief of *The Ring* and *KO* magazines, and is now an on-air analyst for Showtime.

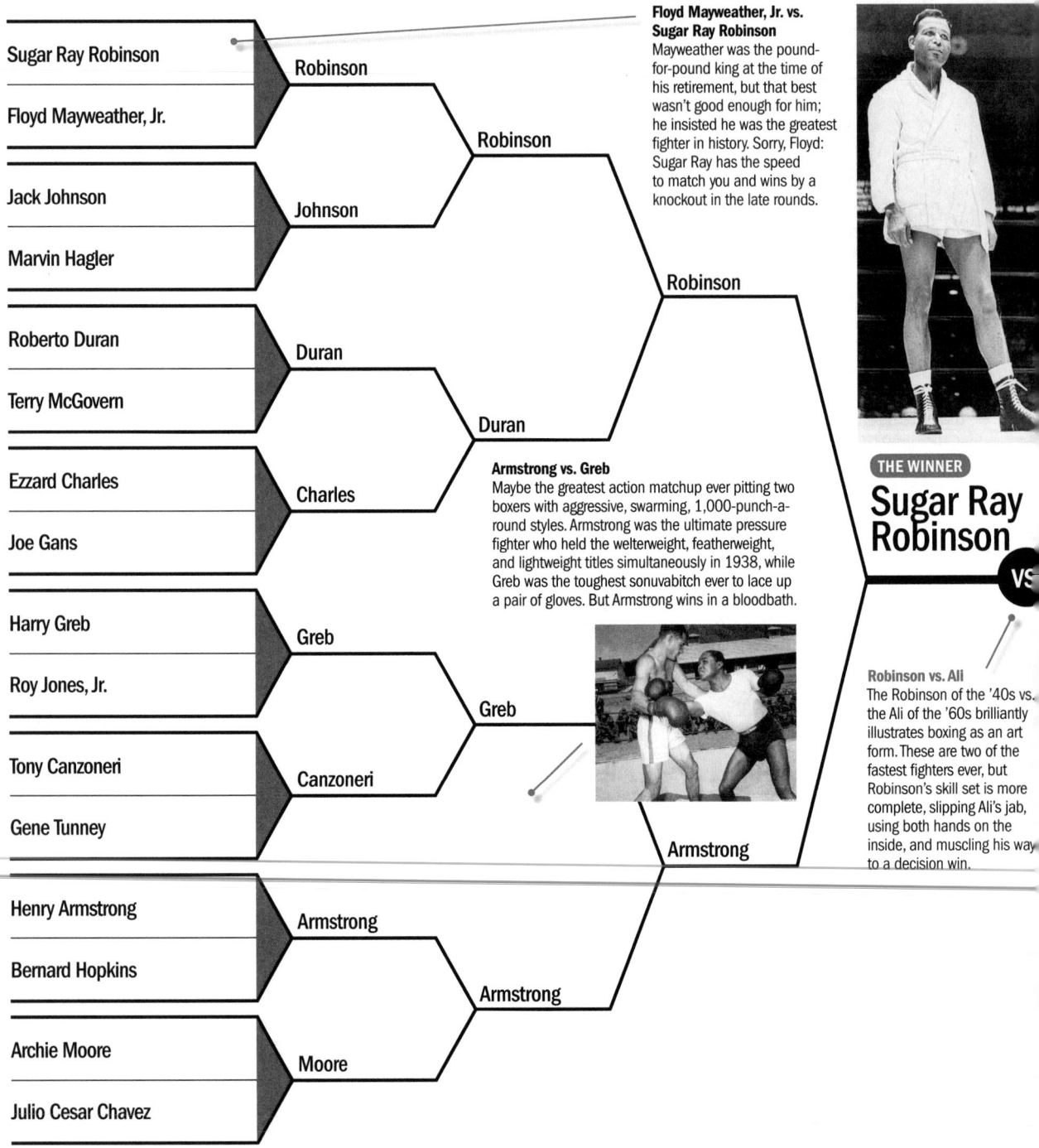


**Floyd Mayweather, Jr. vs. Sugar Ray Robinson**
Mayweather was the pound-for-pound king at the time of his retirement, but that best wasn't good enough for him; he insisted he was the greatest fighter in history. Sorry, Floyd: Sugar Ray has the speed to match you and wins by a knockout in the late rounds.

**Armstrong vs. Greb**
Maybe the greatest action matchup ever pitting two boxers with aggressive, swarming, 1,000-punch-a-round styles. Armstrong was the ultimate pressure fighter who held the welterweight, featherweight, and lightweight titles simultaneously in 1938, while Greb was the toughest sonuvabitch ever to lace up a pair of gloves. But Armstrong wins in a bloodbath.

**Robinson vs. Ali**
The Robinson of the '40s vs. the Ali of the '60s brilliantly illustrates boxing as an art form. These are two of the fastest fighters ever, but Robinson's skill set is more complete, slipping Ali's jab, using both hands on the inside, and muscling his way to a decision win.

THE PROLIFERATION OF BOXING WORLD TITLES, with its alphabet soup's worth of sanctioning body confusion, has cluttered the sport, demeaned the value of championship belts, and elevated the importance of a best pound-for-pound fighter. The pound-for-pound standard lets us judge fighters from different eras through their accomplishments, skill, artistry, longevity, and quality of opposition. It breaks my heart to exclude greats who fought in America, like Emile Griffith, Bob Foster, Ruben Olivares, Ike Williams, and Sandy Saddler; and picking a winner was like going 12 rounds with my eventual champ.

**Leonard vs. Ali**
Leonard is the best fighter I've covered in my 30 years at ringside, but Ali is still "The Greatest." Leonard clearly can't outfinesse Ali. Leonard looks to brawl, but his aggressiveness works against him; he repeatedly walks into Ali's punching range and gets tagged by counter right hands. Ali wins by unanimous decision.

**Ali vs. Louis**
Ali and Louis are the two greatest heavyweights in history, and it's a long drop to number three. Louis's one edge, his punching power, is neutralized by Ali's fast feet and reliable chin. Ali jabs with persistence and precision, steals a couple of rounds with flurries, and recovers quickly from a knockdown to win by unanimous decision.

**Ali**

- Ali
  - Leonard
    - Leonard
      - Benny Leonard
      - Rocky Marciano
    - Walker
      - Mickey Walker
      - Pernell Whitaker
  - Ali
    - Ali
      - Muhammad Ali
      - Jimmy Wilde
    - Leonard
      - Sugar Ray Leonard
      - Sam Langford
- Louis
  - Pep
    - Pep
      - Willie Pep
      - Jimmy McLarnin
    - Ross
      - Barney Ross
      - Jack Dempsey
  - Louis
    - Louis
      - Joe Louis
      - Eder Jofre
    - Ketchel
      - Stanley Ketchel
      - Carlos Monzon

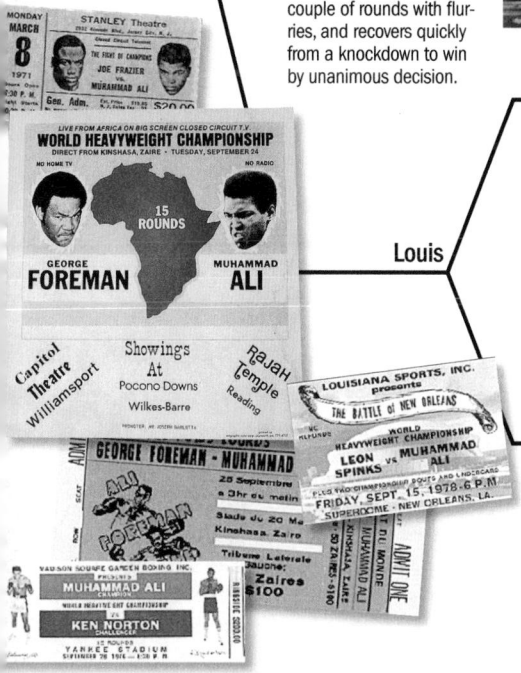

# Field Goals and PATs

**By Stefan Fatsis**

Stefan Fatsis is the author of *A Few Seconds of Panic: A 5-foot-8, 170-pound, 43-year-old Sportswriter Plays in the NFL* and talks about sports on NPR's *All Things Considered.* He insists he can still make a 40-yard field goal. Or at least a 35.

**NFL PRE-1990 REGIONAL**

**George "The Fossil" Blanda,** 48, kicks 41-yard FG in career finale, 1976

**Lou "The Toe" Groza** 16-yard FG wins championship, 1950

**Groza**

**Jim O'Brien** 32-yard FG wins Super Bowl V for Colts, 1971

**Tom Dempsey** 63-yard FG sets record, 1970

**Dempsey**

**Dempsey**

"Snowplow Game": Furloughed convict shovels spot for game-winning **John Smith** 33-yard FG, 1982

"Greatest Game": **Steve Myhra** 20-yard FG sends championship to OT, 1958

**Myhra**

**Myhra**

Longest barefoot FG: **Tony Franklin,** 59 yards, 1979

**Rich Karlis** barefoot 33-yard OT FG wins "The Drive" game, 1987

**Karlis**

**Dempsey**

**Norwood wide right vs. Dempsey**
The epitomes of kicking failure and success. Norwood's narrow miss for Buffalo was Shakespearean in its tragedy. Dempsey's make (for the New Orleans Saints to defeat Detroit, 19–17) reminds us of the resilience of man – he was born without toes on his right foot – and the glorious arc of a well-struck ball.

**ELLIS ISLAND REGIONAL**

**Garo Yepremian** 37-yard FG ends longest NFL game, 1971

**Rolf Benirschke** 29-yard FG ends 41-38 NFL classic, 1982

**Yepremian, longest game**

**Yepremian vs. Benirschke**
For ending an 82:40 marathon – and for his bald head and scrunched-down Wallace Shawn frame – Cyprus-born Yepremian advances. But his type, central to the apotheosis of the immigrant European kicker stereotype, hasn't. Today's kicker is bigger, stronger, more accurate, and more American. Save for one Canadian, every NFL placekicker in 2008 grew up in the U.S.

**Jan Stenerud** passes George Blanda on NFL career FG list, 1983

"Garo's Gaffe": **Garo Yepremian** tries to pass blocked FG in Super Bowl, 1973

**Yepremian, gaffe**

**Yepremian, gaffe**

**Gogolak**

Soccer-style pioneer **Pete Gogolak** makes 57-yard FG in pro debut, 1964

**Morten Andersen** point after breaks NFL scoring record, 2006

**Gogolak**

**Gogolak**

**Ola Kimrin** non-record 65-yard FG in NFL preseason game, 2002

Longest NFL FG attempt: **Sebastian Janikowski,** 76 yards, 2008

**Kimrin**

**Gogolak vs. Dempsey**
After fleeing Hungary with his family in 1956, Gogolak drew stares in high school, college, and the old AFL when he approached the ball from the side instead of in a straight line. He changed kicking, and football, forever. But he loses here to the greatest toe kick of all time.

**THE WINNER**

## Tom Dempsey's 63-yard FG sets record

VS

HATE THAT FOOTBALL GAMES are contested by brave and magnificent athletes but often decided by guys in clean uniforms and size-8 cleats? Get over it. From football's primordial 19th-century origins, no body part has been more important than the foot. Memorable kicks come from impossible distances, under unfathomable pressure, and, it seems, under the goofiest circumstances. Here's one kick that didn't make the cut: a 28-yarder that saved the Denver Broncos 30 minutes of meetings during training camp in 2006. The kicker? Me.

**Johannson, 69 yards vs. Gramatica, 65 yards.**
No one has matched Johansson's bomb for tiny Abilene Christian. But like the 67- and 68-yarders in this regional, it got a boost from the steroid of field-goal kicking: a two-inch-high block, since banned. Gramatica made his 65-yarder the old-fashioned way, without the aid of a tee. Still, four yards is four yards.

**Vinatieri "tuck rule" vs. Vinatieri's Super Bowl winner**
Vinatieri is the greatest clutch kicker ever – and lucky to have had the chances. His last-second 45-yarder for New England in a blizzard – after New England retained a controversial lost fumble – to send the game into overtime was remarkable. His last-second 48-yarder two weeks later to give the Patriots their first Super Bowl title was a kicker's fairy tale.

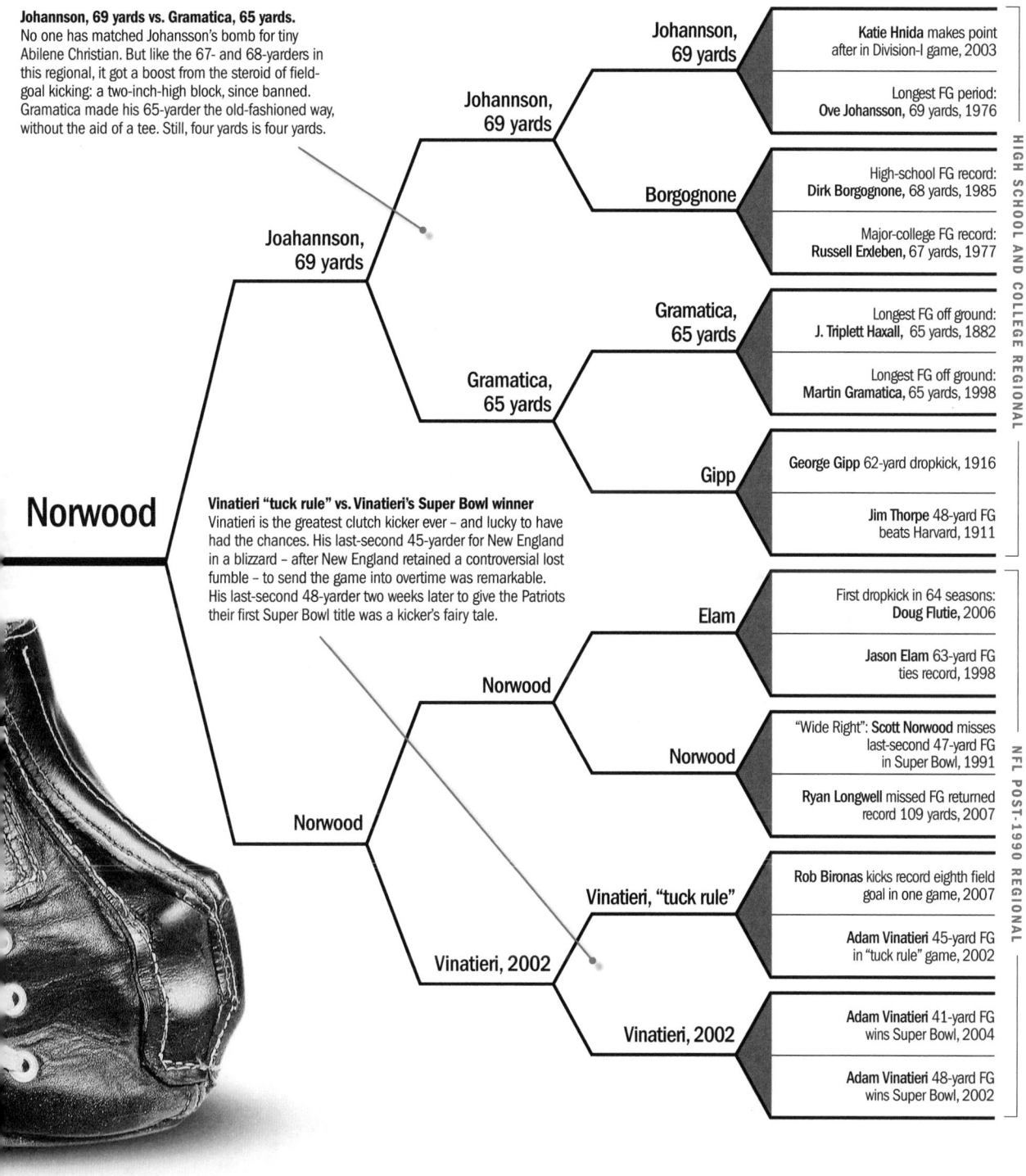

# Golf Books

## By John Garrity

John Garrity, a longtime *Sports Illustrated* writer, has contributed numerous books to the golf underbracket, including *Tiger 2.0, Ancestral Links,* and *America's Worst Golf Courses* – and one that belongs here, *Tour Tempo,* co-authored with John Novosel.

*Missing Links*
by Rick Reilly (1996)

*Golf in the Kingdom*
by Michael Murphy (1972)

*Golf in the Kingdom*

*The Golf Omnibus*
by P. G. Wodehouse (1980)

*A Nasty Bit of Rough*
by David Feherty (2002)

*The Golf Omnibus*

***Nasty Bit of Rough* vs. *Golf Omnibus***
Save your nativist rants for Lou Dobbs. Wodehouse, though born in England, became an American citizen and lived for decades in New York. Irish Feherty, not to be outdone, is a naturalized Texan.

*Golf in the Kingdom*

*Fore!*
by Charles E. Van Loan (1918)

*Train*
by Pete Dexter (2003)

*Fore!*

***Fore!* vs. *Train***
The Woodrow Wilson–era collection of country-club tales knocks off a rare *golf noir* novel by the masterly Pete Dexter.

*Dead Solid Perfect*

*Golf in the Kingdom*

*Fast Greens*
by Turk Pipkin (1996)

*Dead Solid Perfect*
by Dan Jenkins (1974)

*Dead Solid Perfect*

***Dead Solid Perfect* vs. *Golf in the Kingdom***
Metaphysical classic by Esalen co-founder needs three overtimes to beat 72-hole romp by *Semi-Tough* author. The difference: a strong bench led by the 1,100-member Shivas Irons Society.

*Hogan*
by Curt Sampson (1996)

*The U.S. Open: Golf's Ultimate Challenge*
by Robert Sommers (1987)

*Hogan*

*The Golf Course*
by Geoffrey Cornish and Ronald Whitten (1981)

*Golf's Golden Grind*
by Al Barkow (1974)

*Golf's Golden Grind*

*Hogan*

***Hogan* vs. *Story of American Golf***
Sampson's compelling biography makes the pertinent point that watching your father commit suicide with a handgun can stunt your emotional growth.

*Hogan*

*Down the Fairway*
by Robert T. Jones, Jr. and O.B. Keeler (1927)

*Tommy's Honor*
by Kevin Cook (2007)

*Down the Fairway*

*Story of American Golf*

*The Greatest Game Ever Played*
by Mark Frost (2002)

*The Story of American Golf*
by Herbert Warren Wind (1978)

*Story of American Golf*

***Golf in the Kingdom* vs. *Out of the Bunker***
If golf is a cosmic mystery, then Murphy's is the book for the ages. The Shivas Iron logo, after all, is the infinity symbol. But if you'd sell your soul to break 100, Lardner is your man. "Golf has been a puzzle to players for hundreds of years," he writes in his foreword. "It has now finally been straightened out."

*Golf in the Kingdom* VS

GOLF WRITERS TURN OUT DISTINGUISHED PROSE, George Plimpton said, because their attempts to play the game lead to "the state of contained melancholy that so often produces first-rate writing." In other words, golf writing flows from the same fountain of remorse, paranoia, and wounded self-esteem that makes comedians funny and tech tycoons rich. That said, the best golf writing shows no correlation between handicap and literary merit. Some golf writers actually play the game well, which is to be expected. If frustration were the magic ingredient, we'd have 26 million Hemingways.

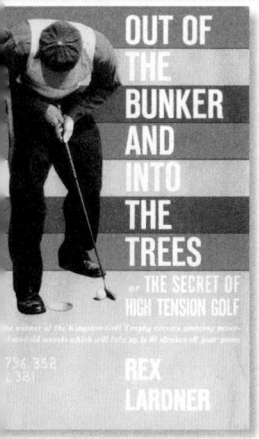


THE WINNER

**Out of the Bunker and Into the Trees**
by Rex Lardner (1960)

***Who's Your Caddy?* vs. *Dogged Victims***
Battle of big swinging dicks (each with two books here) goes to the veteran Jenkins, a role model for so many writers, on the strength of his backlist, especially his Goat Hills memoir, *The Glory Game*.

***Dogged Victims* vs. *Out of the Bunker***
How good is Lardner's long-out-of-print parody? Even Jenkins might bow down to a winning sentence such as, "The putter is a club designed to hit the ball partway to the hole."

***Five Lessons* vs. *A Round of Golf***
Armour's course-management tome is a great read. And let's be honest, Hogan lecturing on "pronation" and "supination" is more anal than analytical.

***Out of the Bunker* vs. *Little Red Book***
Subtitled "The Secret of High Tension Golf," Lardner's parody is the *Spinal Tap* of golf books. Humor always triumphs in golf, even against one of the most earnest, sincere, well-written golf instructionals of all time.

- *Out of the Bunker*
  - *Dogged Victims*
    - *Dogged Victims*
      - ***The Dogged Victims of Inexorable Fate*** by Dan Jenkins (1970)
      - ***Pro: Frank Beard on the Golf Tour*** with Dick Schaap (1970)
    - *Who's Your Caddy?*
      - ***Bud, Sweat, and Tees*** by Alan Shipnuck (2001)
      - ***Who's Your Caddy?*** by Rick Reilly (2003)
  - *The Bogey Man*
    - *The Bogey Man*
      - ***The Bogey Man*** by George Plimpton (1968)
      - ***The Confidential Guide to Golf Courses*** by Tom Doak (1996)
    - *To the Linksland*
      - ***To the Linksland*** by Michael Bamberger (1992)
      - ***Golf Dreams*** by John Updike (1996)
  - *A Round of Golf*
    - *Five Lessons*
      - ***Five Lessons*** by Ben Hogan (1957)
      - ***Dave Pelz's Short Game Bible*** by Dave Pelz (1999)
    - *A Round of Golf*
      - ***A Round of Golf with Tommy Armour*** by Tommy Armour (1959)
      - ***Golf My Way*** by Jack Nicklaus (1974)
  - *Out of the Bunker*
    - *Out of the Bunker*
      - ***Bobby Jones on Golf*** by Robert Tyre Jones (1966)
      - ***Out of the Bunker and Into the Trees*** by Rex Lardner (1960)
    - *Little Red Book*
      - ***Harvey Penick's Little Red Book*** by Harvey Penick with Bud Shrake (1992)
      - ***The Golf Swing*** by David Leadbetter (2001)

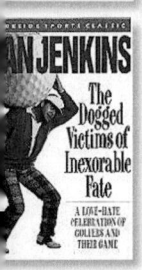

# New York Athletes

**By George Vecsey**

George Vecsey has been in journalism since the late 1950s, covering high schools for *Newsday* and later the World Cup of soccer, his favorite event, for the *New York Times*. He moved away from New York for a few years and found himself critically homesick.

**Whitey Ford,** crafty Yankees lefthander won 236 games

**Secretariat** (horse), won 1973 Triple Crown at Belmost by 31 lengths

**Mickey Mantle,** Yankee succeeded Joe DiMaggio in centerfielder, hit 536 home runs

**Frank Gifford** (Giants), halfback led Giants to three NFL title games

**Babe Ruth** (Yankees), hit 113 home runs in first two seasons at Yankee Stadium and 60 in 1927

**Sugar Ray Robinson** (boxer), won first of six world titles at Madison Square Garden, fought in New York City 38 times

**Julius Erving** (Nets), acrobatic ABA forward who turned the vertical game into an art form

**Mark Messier** (Rangers), legendary center whose scoring and personality led Rangers to Stanley Cup

**Willie Mays** (Giants), home run-hitting centerfielder who brought joy and basket catches to Polo Grounds

**Derek Jeter** (Yankees), shortstop and captain, helped guide Yankees to four World Series rings in five years

**Sandy Koufax** (Dodgers), Brooklyn-born left-hander whose wildness in Brooklyn was tempered in L.A.

**Grete Waitz** (runner), Norwegian won the New York City Marathon nine times

**Joe DiMaggio** (Yankees), graceful Joltin' Joe had only slightly more home runs (361) than he had strikeouts (369)

**Carol Blazejowski,** high-scoring women's basketball pioneer, president of NY Liberty

**Christy Mathewson** (Giants), peerless pitcher, won all but one of his 373 games for New York team

**John McEnroe** (tennis), Queens-born brat won four U.S. Open singles

Secretariat

Mantle

Mantle

Ruth

Ruth

Ruth

Erving

Mays

Mays

Waitz

McEnroe

DiMaggio

McEnroe

McEnroe

**Mantle vs. Secretariat**
I can just hear Mantle's earthy incredulity about being matched against a horse, comparing his stamina and his anatomy to Big Red. Secretariat won the 1973 Belmont by 31 lengths but Mantle could also run – and hit homers off the old Yankee Stadium façade. In this battle of naturals, the Mick wins.

**Mark Messier vs. Julius Erving**
Messier willed the Rangers to win the Stanley Cup in the Garden, ending a 54-year famine, but Doctor J lit up his sport with slam-dunking acrobatics before Michael Jordan was even invented. In this duel of powerful but very different types of charismatics, I put aerodynamics over inspiration and went with my Long Island homey.

**McEnroe vs. Mays**
Johnny Mac knocks off two immortal center fielders who captivated New York, first the cool Joe D, then the infectious Say Hey Kid. In his own miserable fashion, McEnroe had as much style and touch as any athlete who played this town. Under a full moon, he could start a riot in his home borough of Queens by picking on some hapless official. Plus, he has never lost his Queens chewing-gum accent.

THE WINNER

## Babe Ruth

(Yankees) hit 113 home runs in first two seasons at Yankee Stadium and 60 in 1927

VS

WE NEW YORKERS BELIEVE WE ARE THE CENTER OF THE UNIVERSE and that everything comes to us, including superstar athletes. (We don't believe it; it's true.) I give style points to New York natives, New York residents, New York accents, New York noses, and New York attitude – athletes who could handle the fickle crowds, shrug off the media jokers, and in general, got it and thrived. I know, I know, I left off your favorite athlete. Stop hocking me! It's the Big City. It's got tough brackets, too.

**Jackie Robinson vs. Babe Ruth**
Jackie was a revolutionary and changed baseball through the force of his skill and personality. But Ruth reinvented his sport more than any athlete I know. He wore goofy hats and winked at the world and was a great pitcher before he was a great slugger. Baltimore guy who came over from Boston and made the Yankees build a stadium worthy of him. Gave panache to the city that endures to this day. Nobody's forgotten him. Still the champion. The Babe.

# Jackie Robinson

**Namath vs. Robinson**
Broadway Joe thrilled New York by guaranteeing a Super Bowl victory, and the Jets haven't won one since. But Jackie changed the world as the first black major leaguer of the 20th century. I still get chills when I see films of Jackie taking an extra base and sliding in hard. Jackie did it with my team, the Brooklyn Dodgers. Plus, he left us Rachel, one of the great people of our city, and a foundation in his name.

- **Namath**
  - **Namath**
    - **Stengel**
      - **Casey Stengel,** shrewd, eccentric, managed Yankees to seven World Series championships
      - **Gene Sarazen** (golfer), born in Harrison, NY, won seven majors, including two in-state
    - **Namath**
      - **Willis Reed** (Knicks), sweet-shooting center who inspired team to first NBA title in 1970
      - **Joe Namath** (Jets), stylish media superstar, first NFL quarterback to pass for 4,000 yards in a season
  - **Gehrig**
    - **Gehrig**
      - **Lou Gehrig** (Yankees), local boy, Columbia graduate, the "Iron Horse" hit 493 home runs
      - **Martin Brodeur** (Devils), one of NHL's greatest goalies
    - **Jackson**
      - **Reggie Jackson** (Yankees), "straw that stirs the drink" hit homers on three consecutive at-bats in '77 Series
      - **Althea Gibson** (tennis), first African American player to win Wimbledon and the United States singles titles
- **Robinson**
  - **Frazier**
    - **Taylor**
      - **Lawrence Taylor** (Giants), ferocious, disruptive outside linebacker, altered game forever
      - **Bill Bradley** (Knicks), former Rhodes scholar and small forward who started on both NBA title teams
    - **Frazier**
      - **Walt Frazier** (Knicks), stylist "Clyde" with smooth backcourt élan and very fast hands
      - **Mike Bossy** (Islanders), high-scoring forward, cornerstone of four Stanley Cup championships
  - **Robinson**
    - **Seaver**
      - **Tom Seaver** (Mets), hard-throwing right-hander who won 25 games for Mets' 1969 World Series miracle
      - **Pele** (Cosmos), Brazilian at end of career brought charm and skills to New York
    - **Robinson**
      - **Jackie Robinson** (Dodgers), broke color barrier in 1947, brought fierce, aggressive style to team
      - **Sarah Hughes** (figure skater), born in Great Neck, won the 2002 Winter Olympic ladies' gold medal

# Boston Athletes

**By Dan Shaughnessy**

Dan Shaughnessy, a sports columnist for the *Boston Globe,* was born in Groton and lives in Newton, Massachusetts. He has written 11 books, including *The Curse of the Bambino* and *Senior Year: A Father, a Son, and High School Baseball.*

**Bill Russell (Celtics)**
center and defensive genius

**Jimmie Foxx (Red Sox)**
50 home runs, 175 RBIs in 1938

Russell

**Doug Flutie (Boston College)**
overachieving, pint-sized QB

**Pedro Martinez (Red Sox)**
three Cy Young Awards

Flutie

Russell

**Carl Yastrzemski (Red Sox)**
left fielder and last man to win Triple Crown

**Milt Schmidt (Bruins)**
center and deft playmaker

Yastrzemski

Yastrzemski

Russell

**Ray Bourque (Bruins)**
defenseman, best of his generation

**Jim Rice (Red Sox)**
power-hitting Red Sox left fielder

Bourque

**Brady vs. Cousy**
Cousy re-invented playmaking and was the face of the NBA for more than a decade, the de facto "Mr. Basketball." Yet he loses to a sixth round draft pick who didn't start a game in his first season with the Patriots. But Brady carved out his place on the Mount Rushmore of Boston sports with three Super Bowl rings and two Super Bowl MVPs – and then he threw a record 50 touchdown passes in the near-perfect 2007 season.

**Tom Brady (Patriots)**
preternaturally great QB

**Dave Cowens (Celtics)**
tenacious, undersized center

Brady

Brady

**Roger Clemens (Red Sox)**
flame-thrower, first 20Ks in 9-inning game

**Bill Rodgers**
four Boston Marathon wins

Clemens

Brady

THE WINNER

**Bill Russell**

V.

**Bob Cousy (Celtics)**
seminal playmaking guard

**Phil Esposito (Bruins)**
immovable center, 76 goals in 1970–71

Cousy

Cousy

**Cy Young (Americans, Rustlers)**
won 196 of 511 games for precursors to Red Sox and Braves

**John Bucyk (Bruins)**
545 goals in 21 Beantown seasons

Young

**Russell vs. Williams**
Williams had better numbers and played the most important sport of his time, but Russell is the greatest winner in American professional sports: 11 championships in 13 seasons, including two as player-coach. He was the first black head coach in American sports. He never lost a seventh game. And he wins here. Again.

IN A CITY BLESSED WITH FOUR PROFESSIONAL TEAMS, multiple colleges and individual greats in road-running and boxing, the best in Boston are judged by heart, championships, and the love of the fans. It's not always about stats, which is why Tony Conigliaro and Harry Agganis, whose baseball careers (and lives) were far too short, make this roster over another Red Sox player, Dwight Evans, with better numbers and longer service. It didn't take the Red Sox' and Patriots' recent titles to pack this bracket – only one 21st century player, Patriots quarterback Tom Brady, is here, for his early, astonishing accomplishments.

**Hannah vs. Fisk**
Fisk is famous for his World Series midnight homer in 1975, yet his excellence as a catcher was overshadowed by Johnny Bench's greatness. But at Hannah's retirement, he was considered the greatest offensive linemen ever.

**Williams vs. Orr**
Orr won more championships (2–0) and rivals Gretzky as the greatest hockey player ever – all on bad knees. But Williams was Boston sports' biggest newsmaker in the 20th century and, with 521 homers and a .343 lifetime BA, the game's greatest left-handed hitter. He played over parts of four decades, served his country in two wars, homered in his last at-bat, and has his very own tunnel in Boston. The Kid stays in the bracket.

**Bird vs. Ruth**
Preposterous that Bird beats the Bambino? Not exactly. Though Ruth won three World Series in his six seasons in Boston (mostly as a pitcher), he didn't become the Rabelaisian Bambino until he was sold off to New York. Bird did all of his work for the Celtics, winning three rings and reviving Red Auerbach's moribund Celtics franchise.

- **Williams**
  - **Orr**
    - **Orr**
      - **Orr**
        - **Bobby Orr (Bruins)** – redefined defenseman role with a strong offense
        - **Tony Conigliaro (Red Sox)** – 1965 HR champ, cut short by beanball
      - **Hannah**
        - **John Hannah (Patriots)** – left guard, 9-time Pro Bowler
        - **Carlton Fisk (Red Sox)** – slugging catcher, Game Six hero in 1975
    - **Marciano**
      - **Marciano**
        - **Rocky Marciano** – undefeated heavyweight champion
        - **Paul Pierce (Celtics)** – small forward, 2008 NBA Finals MVP
      - **Havlicek**
        - **John Havlicek (Celtics)** – sixth man extraordinaire, team's all-time scorer
        - **Adam Vinatieri (Patriots)** – pressure-loving place-kicker
  - **Williams**
    - **Bird**
      - **Bird**
        - **Larry Bird (Celtics)** – clutch forward with uncanny anticipation, revived franchise
        - **Andre Tippett (Patriots)** – linebacker with 100 career sacks
      - **Ruth**
        - **Babe Ruth (Red Sox)** – pitcher-slugger with 89 wins and 49 home runs before Yankees
        - **Harry Agganis (Red Sox)** – B.U. football star turned first basemen, died young
    - **Williams**
      - **Shore**
        - **Eddie Shore (Bruins)** – ultra-tough defenseman
        - **Kevin McHale (Celtics)** – power forward with great low-post moves
      - **Williams**
        - **Marvin Hagler** – great middleweight boxer
        - **Ted Williams (Red Sox)** – last of the .400 hitters

# Sportswriters

**By Glenn Stout**

Glenn Stout has been series editor of *The Best American Sports Writing* series since its inception in 1991. Since he probably reads more sportswriting than anyone else on the planet, he is eternally grateful that so much of it is good, and occasionally great.

**Frank Deford**
*Sports Illustrated* mainstay

**Mary Garber**
pioneering female journalist

**Deford**

**Roger Kahn**
author of *The Boys of Summer*

**Herbert Warren Wind**
golf writer for *The New Yorker* and *Sports Illustrated*

**Wind**

**Deford**

**Henry Chadwick**
one of America's first sportswriters

**Tim Murnane**
*Boston Globe* baseball writer

**Murnane**

**Runyon**

**John Kieran**
*NY Times* columnist

**Damon Runyon**
baseball and boxing, then short stories

**Runyon**

**Deford**

**W.C. Heinz**
newspaper columnist, magazine writer, novelist

**George Plimpton**
participatory journalist, *Paper Lion*

**Heinz**

**Heinz**

**Dan Jenkins**
author, *Semi-Tough*

**Grantland Rice**
celebrated writer of 1920s

**Jenkins**

**Heinz**

**John Drebinger**
covered baseball at *NY Times* for 41 years

**Dick Young**
writer-columnist, *Daily News*

**Young**

**Murray**

**Frank Graham**
writer-columnist, *NY Sun*

**Jim Murray**
Pulitzerized columnist for *LA Times*

**Murray**

**Deford vs. Heinz**
Frank Deford once wrote that being considered the world's best sportswriter was like being "the world's tallest midget," and since joining *Sports Illustrated* in 1962, he has cast the shadow to prove it. But on a list of the best columnists, feature writers, and profilers, Bill Heinz is the only writer near the top of all three categories. Add to that his novel on boxing, *The Professional,* and his co-authorship of *M*A*S*H,* and even Deford doesn't quite measure up.

**Rice vs. Jenkins**
"Outlined against a blue-gray October sky," Grantland Rice wrote, giving us famine, pestilence, destruction and death, a.k.a. the Notre Dame backfield of Stuhldreher, Miller, Crowley, and Layden of the 1920s. In *Semi-Tough,* Dan Jenkins gave us Billy Clyde Puckett, "the humminest sumbitch that ever carried a football." The inspirational heroism that Rice invested athletes with was rarely as funny or rambunctious as Puckett – or Jenkins.

**Murray vs. Young**
Of the Indy 500, the lyrical Jim Murray wrote, "Gentlemen, start your coffins." Murray was half-blind but wrote columns so clear-eyed and sure that even today the ink seems barely dry. Dick Young, who prefigured today's beat writers with his opinionated insider's reporting, ended his career half-blind as well – with rage, as his "Young Ideas" failed to keep pace.

THE WINNER

**W.C. Heinz**

VS

SPORTSWRITERS TODAY stand in the shadow of these 32 giants, nearly all of them writers of yesteryear. Some were pioneers, some were innovators, and some are and were first-rate stylists who never recognized the limitations of the genre. They all loved writing more than they loved sports, and combined curiosity, first-rate reporting, research, a good grasp of the fundamentals of the language, and, oh, a little music, an attentive ear, some empathy, and intelligence.

**Halberstam vs. Lardner**
David Halberstam won a Pulitzer for telling the truth about the Vietnam War but turned to sports to write classics like *Summer of '49* and *The Teammates*. Lardner never won a Pulitzer but covered the "World Serious" for papers in Chicago, St. Louis, and Boston before penning the epistolary novel *You Know Me, Al*, and becoming teammates with legendary American literary humorists like Mark Twain and James Thurber.

**Heinz vs. Smith**
Heinz and Smith, the first sportswriter to win a Pulitzer, were colleagues and close friends. Although each man made writing seem effortless, neither found it easy. Red Smith described it this way: "All you do is sit down at the typewriter and open a vein." But even though Smith's name is on the highest honor the Associated Press Sports Writers can bestow, Heinz wins with articles like "Death of a Racehorse" and "The Brownsville Bum." Even Smith thought his pal Bill was the best.

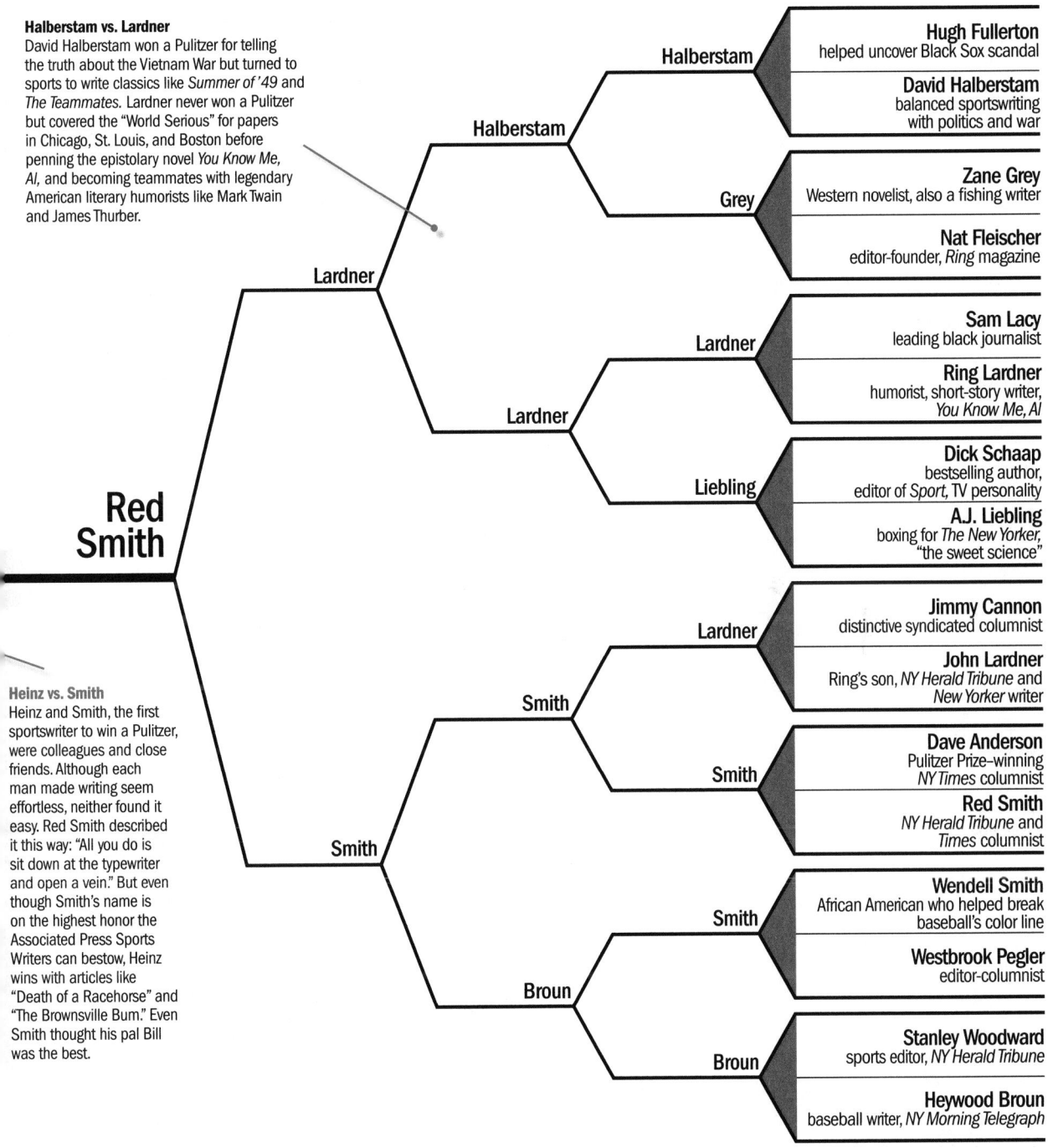

# Advertising Icons

**By Bryan Curtis**

Bryan Curtis was a columnist at *Play: The New York Times Sports Magazine,* for its (too) short, (ludicrously) happy life. He is now a senior editor at *The Daily Beast.*

**Michael Jordan**
Nike

**Joe DiMaggio**
Mr. Coffee

**Jordan**

**Bob Uecker**
Miller Lite

**Bo Jackson**
Nike

**Bo**

**Jordan**

**Football-Playing Clydesdales**
Budweiser

**Terry Tate, office linebacker**
Reebok

**Tate**

**Mean Joe Greene**
(Coke)

**"Nothin' But Net" Larry Bird**
McDonald's

**Bird**

**Bird**

**Jordan**

**Lil Penny**
Nike

**Mars Blackmon**
Nike

**Blackmon**

**Mickey Mantle**
Maypo

**Pete Rose**
Aqua Velva

**Mantle**

**Blackmon**

**Jordan**

**Richard Petty**
Goody's Headache Powder

**John Madden**
Tough Actin' Tinactin

**Petty**

**Rafael Palmeiro**
Viagra

**Keith Hernandez**
Just for Men

**Hernandez**

**Hernandez**

**Jordan vs. Bird**
Jordan brings a years-long series of Nike commercials. Bird brings an ad for McDonald's, in which he tried to humanize Jordan. It's a tough call: the iconic face of Nike or the nice guy shooting hoops for Big Mac? In the end, as it usually did on the court, Jordan's ruthlessness triumphs over friendship.

**Jordan vs. Barkley**
Classic contrast of styles: Jor was a TV chameleon, capable peddling anything (underwea hot dogs) and assuming nea any persona asked of him by director. Barkley, even when h was doing battle with Godzill retained a certain immutable Barkleyness. Thus, while Jorda may have moved more shoes Barkley won our hearts and minds. He wins in a squeake

**Jordan** VS

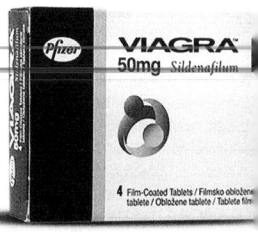


**Hernandez vs. Palmeiro**
Athletes are often asked to impart manliness to a product men don't want to want. Hernandez pitches Just for Men hair dye – the idea being that by blackening the gray, even a washed-up ex-athlete could "keep his edge." Palmeiro took $500,000 to pitch Viagra but denied using the performance-enhancing drug himself – though not quite as emphatically as he denied using steroids in front of Congress.

AS FORMER BALTIMORE ORIOLE BOOG POWELL ONCE PUT IT, "You make one Miller Lite commercial, it's like then everyone forgets you played ball for 20 years." Indeed, sports advertising has taken jocks known for their jump shots and made them into catchphrase dispensers ("Tastes great!" "I'm going to Disney World!"). But not all athlete-pitchmen are created equally. Some slip into their product as comfortably as Hanes briefs, while others look positively mortified. Only a jock who truly embodies his product can make it to the top.

THE WINNER

**"I am not a role model" —Charles Barkley**
Nike

**Barkley vs. Agassi**
Matchup of two jocks trading off their images as rebels. Barkley was a teller of hard truths and, occasionally, a bar brawler. Nike mixed these strands into Barkley's famous ad, in which he argued, convincingly, that children shouldn't look up to him. Agassi's rebellions were more stylistic – long hair and '90s fashion at Wimbledon – and meshed with Canon's "Rebel" camera. Barkley's message still resonates; Andre's clothes look absurd.

**Barkley**
- **Leon**
  - **Woods impostors**
    - People who say they are going to Disney World — Disney World
    - People who claim to be Tiger Woods — Nike
  - **Leon**
    - Nolan Ryan — Advil
    - Leon — Budweiser
- **Barkley**
  - **Montana**
    - O.J. Simpson — Hertz
    - Joe Montana — Hanes
  - **Barkley**
    - Hulk Hogan — Right Guard
    - "I am not a role model" Charles Barkley — Nike

**Agassi**
- **Agassi**
  - **Agassi**
    - Andre Agassi — Canon
    - Dr. J — Dr Pepper
  - **Namath**
    - Mia Hamm — Gatorade
    - Joe Namath — Noxzema
- **Maddux/Glavine**
  - **Maddux/Glavine**
    - Greg Maddux and Tom Glavine — Nike
    - Dan and Dave — Reebok
  - **Landry**
    - Tom Landry — Quality Inn
    - Phil Rizzuto — The Money Store

**Maddux and Glavine vs. Landry**
Sports fans always get a thrill out of watching hardened jocks play against type. Maddux and Glavine were soft-spoken Atlanta Braves pitchers convinced that "chicks dig the longball" and embarked on an un-Bondsian bodybuilding regimen. Landry's Quality Inn commercial, in which the deadpan ex-Cowboys coach popped out of a suitcase, was the only time anyone remembered him cracking a smile. The pitchers were funnier.

# Greatest Sports Year

**By Mike Vaccaro**

Mike Vaccaro, sports columnist for the *New York Post,* is author of *Emperors and Idiots,* a narrative history of the Yankees-Red Sox rivalry, plus another book whose title gives this bracket away.

## 2001

**1941**
(DiMaggio's 56-game hitting streak; Williams's .406, Whirlaway Triple Crown)

**1961**
(Maris's 61 HRs; Vince Lombardi's first NFL title)

**2001**
(Bonds shatters HR mark, Yanks-Diamondbacks classic World Series)

**1968** (Gibson 1.12 era; McClain's 31 wins; Beamon's long jump record)

**1973** (Knicks win NBA title; Bill Walton 21–22 in NCAA Final; Secretariat's Triple Crown)

**1955**
(Brooklyn Dodgers win World Series; Fleck upsets Hogan at Open)

**1967** ("Impossible Dream" Red Sox; Dallas-Green Bay "Ice Bowl"; Lew Alcindor wins first NCAA title)

**1989** (Earthquake World Series; Pete Rose banished; Michigan NCAA basketball title)

**2008** (Giants stun Patriots in Super Bowl; Kansas wins NCAA in OT; Tiger wins U.S. Open, Phelps wins 8 golds)

**1991** (Duke stuns UNLV in NCAA final; Seles wins 3 tennis majors; Giants beat Bills in Super Bowl)

**1947** (Jackie Robinson breaks color barrier; Lavagetto's pinch hit; Gionfriddo's World Series catch)

**1979**
(Magic beats Bird in NCAA title game; Alabama's Bear Bryant wins last title)

**1927**
(Babe Ruth hits 60 HRs; Dempsey-Tunney "Long Count")

**1908**
(Cubs win last World Series; Merkle's Boner costs Giants)

**1972** (Spitz's 7 Olympic gold medals; Dolphins' unbeaten season; Lakers win 33 in row)

**1986**
(Ball skitters through Buckner's legs; Nicklaus wins Masters at 46)

1941 | 1968 | 1973 | 1967 | 2008 | 1947 | 1927 | 1986

1941 | 1967 | 1947 | 1986

1941 | 1986

**1941 vs. 1969**
While the nation inched closer to war on two fronts, people sought solace in one of the most incomparable sporting years ever. Whirlaway, the most beloved thoroughbred racehorse of his day, won the Triple Crown. Joe Louis rallied to defeat lightweight champion Billy Conn before a mesmerized national audience. And Ted Williams hit .406 and Joe DiMaggio hit safely in 56 straight games, setting one of baseball's most sacred – and unapproachable – records.

THE WINNER

**1941**
(DiMaggio hitting streak, Williams .406, Whirlaway)

VS

**1968 vs. 2001**
Both years were significant not only for absorbing sporting tales but for their juxtaposition against raging events of the times. But 1968 – when Denny McLain and Bob Gibson dominated batters, Bob Beamon obliterated the long jump record at the Mexico City Olympics, and Vince Lombardi won his final NFL Championship – offers a deeper narrative than 2001, with what many believe to be the best World Series ever, played a month after the 9/11 attacks.

**1986 vs. 1947**
By itself, Jackie Robinson's impact on the face of American sports qualifies 1947 as a great year. A brilliant World Series followed. But in 1986, not only was there a baseball miracle (the Mets won the Series, thanks to a ball trickling through Bill Buckner's legs), but also two dynasties (the Boston Celtics and Montreal Canadians) won titles and Jack Nicklaus, at age 46, won his sixth Masters and 18th professional golf major.

## '86

A GREAT SPORTS SEASON MUST ADVANCE with an almost unabated sense of drama, suspense, accomplishment, and excellence. It is helpful if great athletes perform great feats within those 12 months, but what is necessary is that the games that serve as yard markers for the 52-week grind are memorable, if not actually magical. Mostly, a great sports year makes you shake your head in wonder that so many different athletes from so many diverse sports could all leave their footprints so indelibly on that calendar year.

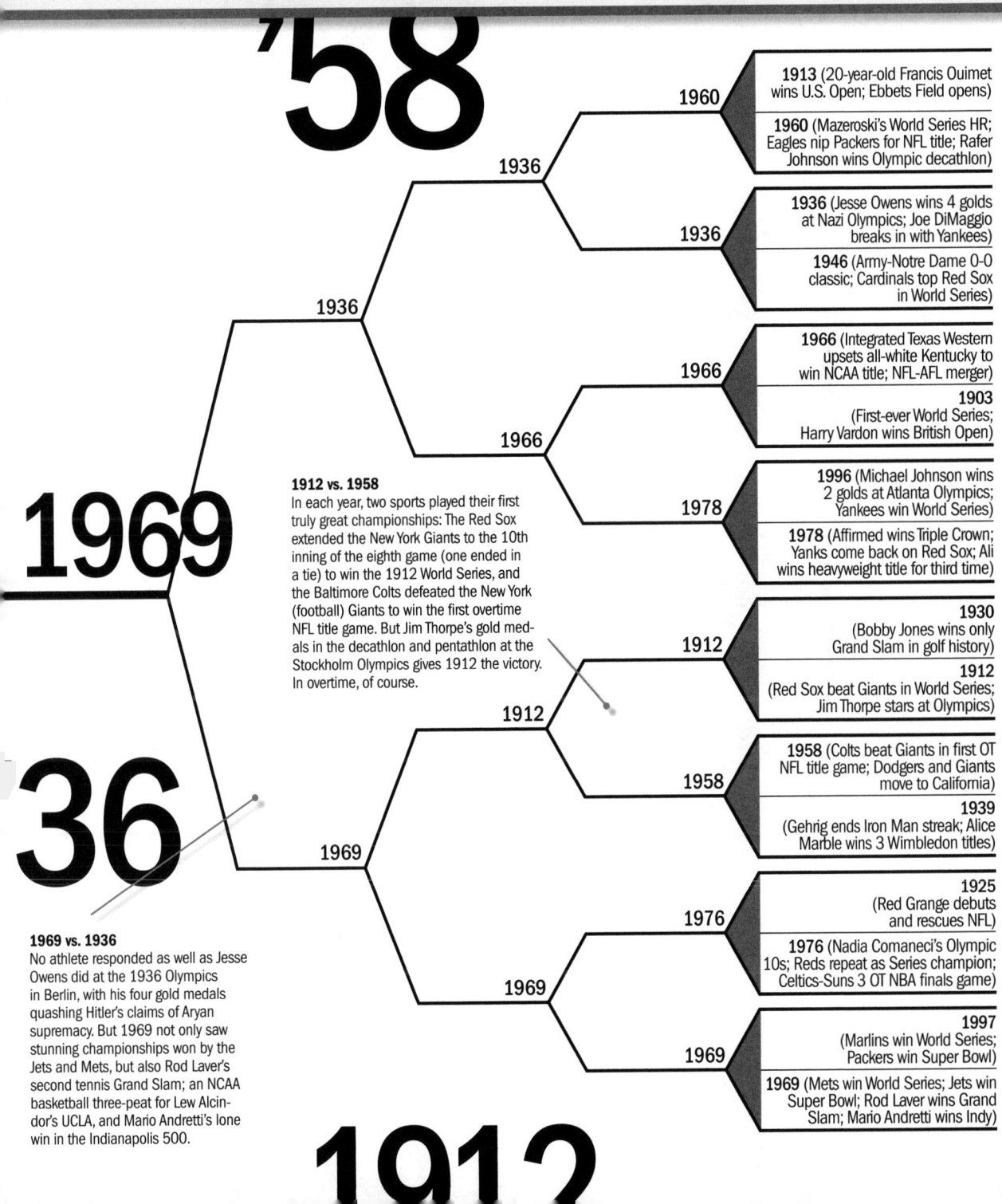


**1912 vs. 1958**
In each year, two sports played their first truly great championships: The Red Sox extended the New York Giants to the 10th inning of the eighth game (one ended in a tie) to win the 1912 World Series, and the Baltimore Colts defeated the New York (football) Giants to win the first overtime NFL title game. But Jim Thorpe's gold medals in the decathlon and pentathlon at the Stockholm Olympics gives 1912 the victory. In overtime, of course.

**1969 vs. 1936**
No athlete responded as well as Jesse Owens did at the 1936 Olympics in Berlin, with his four gold medals quashing Hitler's claims of Aryan supremacy. But 1969 not only saw stunning championships won by the Jets and Mets, but also Rod Laver's second tennis Grand Slam; an NCAA basketball three-peat for Lew Alcindor's UCLA, and Mario Andretti's lone win in the Indianapolis 500.

# POP CULTURE


**Movie Gunfights** *by Stephen Hunter* 80
**YouTube Videos** *by Virginia Heffernan* 81
**Soul Songs** *by John Leland* 82
**Paul Newman Roles** *by Mark Reiter* 83
**Sitcom Dads** *by Steven Reddicliffe* 84
**Sitcom Moms** *by Richard Sandomir* 85
**Talk-Show Graveyard** *by Bill Carter* 86
**Children's Books** *by Jon Scieszka* 87
**Cinematic Interrogatories** *by John Steinbreder* 88
**Comic Strips** *by R.C. Harvey* 89
**High School Movies** *by Rick Staehling* 90
**Stunt Scenes** *by Kevin Conley* 91
**Impressionists** *by Richard Sandomir* 92
**Literary Heroes** *by B.R. Myers* 93
**Comedy Routines** *by Bill Scheft* 94
**Worst Movies by Great Directors** *by A.O. Scott* 95
**George Carlin Hunks** *by Kelly Carlin-McCall* 96
**Cop Movies** *by Lorenzo Carcaterra* 97
**Reality TV Stars** *by Bob Boden* 98
**Fictional Lawyers** *by Thane Rosenbaum* 99
**Good Imus vs. Evil Imus** *by Richard Sandomir* 100
**Steve Earle Songs** *by Mark Reiter* 101
**Most American Superhero** *by Peter Coogan* 102
**Gangster Films** *by Lorenzo Carcaterra* 103
**Disney Animated Films** *by Richard Corliss* 104
***Honeymooners*** *by Peter Crescenti* 105
**You Call This Acting?** *By Will Reiter* 106
**Talk Radio Hosts** *by David Hinckley* 107
**Child Actors** *by Griffin Miller* 108
**Detroit Celluloid** *by Kevin Conley* 109
**Girl Singers** *by Tom Moon* 110
**Cathartic Movie Deaths** *by David Edelstein* 111
**Game-Show Hosts** *by Mark Leblang* 112
**Grateful Dead Songs** *by John Steinbreder* 113
**Romance Novels** *by Isabel Swift* 114
**TV Catchphrases** *by Robert J. Thompson* 115
**Jazz Solos** *by Nick Trautwein* 116
**Romantic Comedies** *by David Denby* 117
**Cats and Dogs** *by Lon Tweeten* 118
**Clint Eastwood Films** *by Manohla Dargis* 119
**Comedy Teams** *by Robert Wuhl* 120
**Comic Book Superpowers** *by Peter Coogan* 121

# Movie Gunfights

**By Stephen Hunter**

Stephen Hunter has written books called *American Gunfight, The Master Sniper,* and *Point of Impact* (which became the movie *Shooter*). He won a Pulitzer Prize for film criticism in 2003.

***The Big Sleep*** *(1946)*
Bogie chills out Lash Canino's fury with a fistful of .45s

***The Untouchables*** *(1987)*
A shootout shout-out to Sergei Eisenstein's *Potemkin*

***The Big Sleep***

***Butch Cassidy and the Sundance Kid*** *(1969):* Butch and the Kid draw down on a passle o' Meskins

***Will Penny*** *(1968)*
Chuck "Mr. NRA" Heston leverages Donald Pleasance to Baptist hell

***Butch Cassidy***

***The Big Sleep***

***Tombstone*** *(1993)*
Memo to young actors: always play Doc if given the chance

***The Wild Bunch*** *(1969)*
The all-time, big-daddy shoot 'em up, -out, -around and –through

***The Wild Bunch***

***The Wild Bunch***

***Terminator*** *(1984)*
Arnold comes back, as he said he would; exterminates police station

***Key Largo*** *(1946)*
Bogie cleans out Eddie Robinson's four-man gang on Hemingway's boat

***Terminator***

***The Man Who Shot Liberty Valance*** *(1962)* Pappy Ford probes meaning of gunfight in myth and reality

***Taxi Driver*** *(1976)*
Scorsese gun fever dream follows last of the Mohawks to brothel fireworks

***Taxi Driver***

***Dirty Harry*** *(1971)*
Eastwood makes .44 magnum S&W's all-time bestseller

***L.A. Confidential*** *(1997)*
Pearce and Crowe take out crooked coppers

***Dirty Harry***

***Dirty Harry***

***Open Range*** *(2003)*
A kind of whole unified field theory of gunfights

***Bonnie & Clyde*** *(1967)*
Fun couple shoots way out of Joplin motel and across three states

***Bonnie & Clyde***

***Bullitt*** *(1968)*
Ultra-cool McQueen in probably most ultra-real shootout ever

***My Darling Clementine*** *(1946)*
Ford's OK Corral take, muzzle flashes in the dust

***Bullitt***

***Bullitt***

***Bullitt***

***The Wild Bunch***

**THE WINNER**

***The Wild Bunch*** *(1969)*

**VS**

***The Wild Bunch* vs. *Bullitt***
In *Bullitt,* Steve McQueen stalks Pat Renella across the face of the 'Frisco airport, but the finale comes down, as most gunfights in real life do, to two men in a compass of about six feet, where speed, determination, and oh yes, a head start, determine the outcome. McQueen commands his Colt Diamondback superbly, making you believe that he is so cool he remembers to aim and follow-through, track the fallen adversary to the ground to assure he's dead, and only then restore his weapon to holster.

***The Wild Bunch* vs. *The Lady from Shanghai***
What else could it be? *The Wild Bunch* changed all that came after and remains mesmerizing to this day. It's a violent whirligig of gun moves, maximum destruction to flesh, insane courage, nihilism, great reloading technique, as well as a fine endorsement of tripod-mounted automatic weapons in squad-size or larger engagements. It has always represented something in the male subconscious that few other filmmakers have gotten: the reptile-brain urge to destroy, and in destroying be destroyed. It's always called "anti-violence," but it's actually pro-violence in the way its rhythms urge you to confront your own impulses. Maybe that's a good thing. Maybe not.

AMERICAN MOVIES INVENTED MEN WITH GUNS, but it sometimes seems movies are more about guns with men. Directors love lethal contests and the toys that make them lethal. The criterion here isn't realism (though some fights are realistic) or stylization (some are stylized unto abstraction), or even cool guns (though Thompsons are very cool). Originality of movement counts. No war movies, no executions, and no CGI. Just good old American gunwork, where speed and guts count as much as firepower and social authority.

**Heat vs. The Lady from Shanghai**
*The Lady from Shanghai* shows what happens when you ask a rogue genius to find a new way to shoot the gunfight's generic conventions. Orson Welles clearly doesn't give a damn about guns or anything else that preoccupied his peers. He just wants to make it look so new it's almost abstract, with the dazzling cutting, the twisted mirrors, the shattering glass. There's no reason at all why some live and others die, except that Orson wanted it that way.

**The Killers vs. Heat**
What the gunfight was, what it became. In this noir extension of the Hemingway story, insurance ace O'Brien and Pittsburgh cop Sam Levene lay a trap for the two tough man-killers we saw take out the Swede (a debuting Burt Lancaster). The takedown is short, violent, incredibly satisfying; more points for the fact that the future *Dragnet* tune plays throughout. *Heat,* by contrast, represents the gigantic-ism that would influence the post-*Wild Bunch* gunfight; it's an assault-weapon festival with way-cool guns, actors who stay in character, coherent action, plot integration, and advancement. And great breaking glass.

**Them! vs. The Lady from Shanghai**
*Them!*? Afraid so. James Arness is trapped behind fallen timbers and tunnel debris with four giant ants coming in from all sides. He's clearly worked with the Thompson, and his size (he's a big guy!) helps him manipulate, combat reload, stay cool, find and destroy targets fast. It's a little virtuoso gunhandling from the man who would become, the next year, Matt Dillon, U.S. Marshal. The only thing that would make it better would be if the ants were commies.

- **The Lady from Shanghai**
  - **Heat**
    - **Heat**
      - **The Killers**
        - ***Dillinger*** *(1973):* Warren Oates and Richard Dreyfuss machinegun their way out of Little Bohemia
        - ***The Killers*** *(1946)* Good guys O'Brien and Leven whack bad guys Conrad and MacGraw
      - **Heat**
        - ***Heat*** *(1995):* Maximum cast (DeNiro, Pacino), maximum firepower, the ne plus ultra bank heist
        - ***Silverado*** *(1985)* Costner makes himself a star with double-trouble fast draw
    - **White Heat**
      - **White Heat**
        - ***Shane*** *(1953)* Idealized Alan Ladd in idealized myth of a fight
        - ***White Heat*** *(1949)* Cagney's charisma at the top of the world, Ma
      - **Magnificent Seven**
        - ***The Magnificent Seven*** *(1960)* Last fight, McQueen still deals in lead, friend
        - ***Gunfight at OK Corral*** *(1957)* Pokey Lancaster classic shows old studio way
  - **Matewan**
    - **Madigan**
      - ***Robocop*** *(1987)* Mechanico-human shoots straight, often and loudly
      - ***Madigan*** *(1968):* Feisty Richard Widmark goes to two Dick Specials to face psycho hotel shooter
    - **Matewan**
      - ***Matewan*** *(1987)* Labor vs. Company thugs, set in old West . . . Virginia
      - ***McCabe and Mrs. Miller*** *(1971)* Quirky Beatty, stoked on keefe, fights big RR guns
  - **The Lady from Shanghai**
    - **The Lady from Shanghai**
      - ***Them!*** *(1954)* Matt Dillon with Tommygun vs. Giant ants
      - ***The Lady from Shanghai*** *(1947)* Welles throws down all-time campy-arty funhouse shindig
    - **High Noon**
      - ***High Noon*** *(1952)* Does not forsake liberal vaues as Coop faces McCarthite shootists
      - ***True Grit*** *(1969)* The Duke, hell-bent for leather, goes mano-a-quatro-mano

# YouTube Videos

**By Virginia Heffernan**

Virginia Heffernan is "The Medium" columnist at the *New York Times Magazine* and is the co-author, with Mike Albo, of the comic novel *The Underminer.*

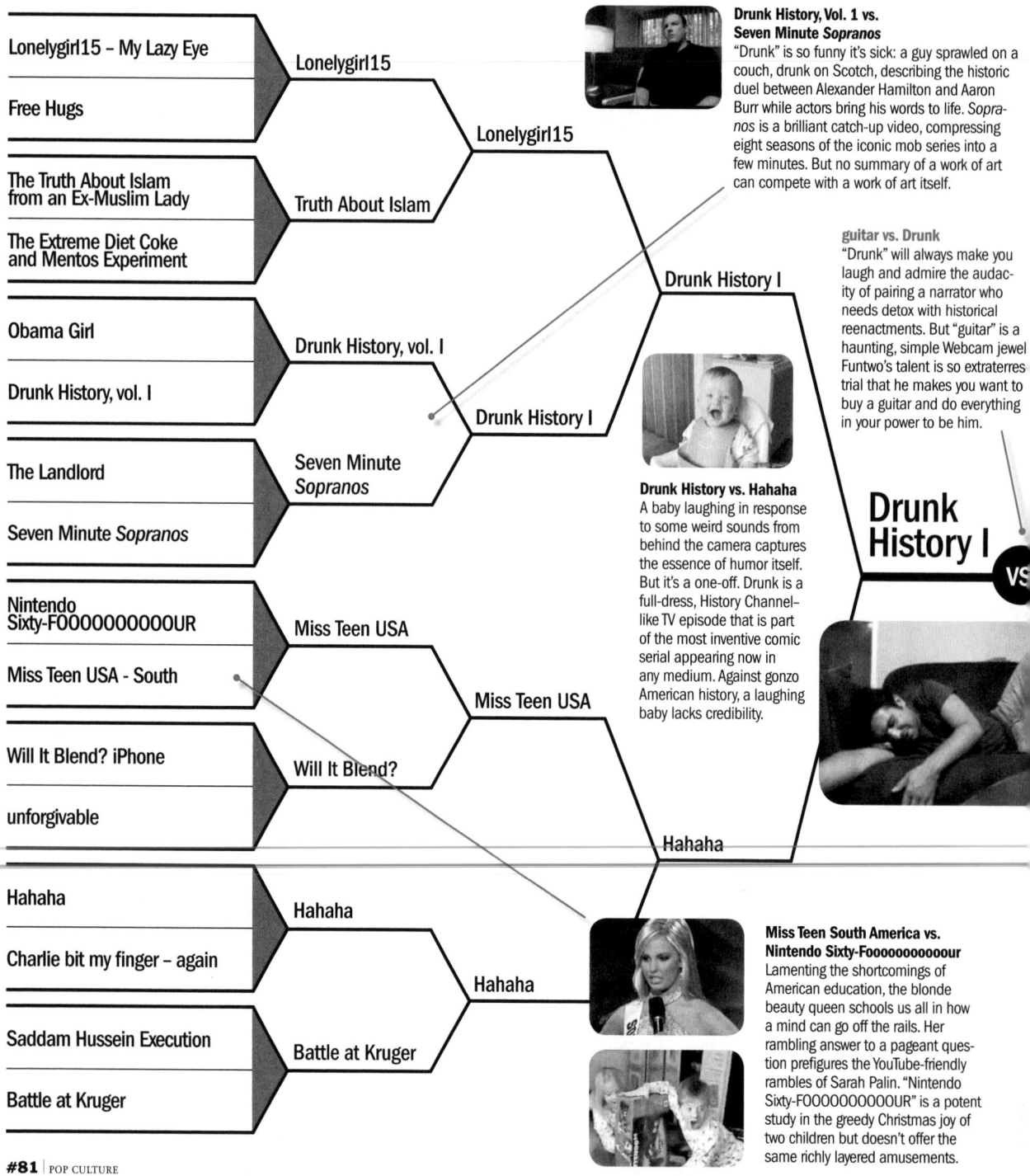

YOUTUBE IS FAMOUS FOR JUNK, but amid the garbage, what's gold glitters. That focus on eccentric or beautiful faces (Chris Crocker from "Leave Britney Alone") jostles against others using vérité and stagey mise-en-scène techniques that are entirely their own (the reverse-surveillance "Don't Tase Me, Bro"). Videos using visceral surprise ("George Bush Shoe Attack") bump into those built on juxtaposition ("Real Estate Downfall," which inserts subtitles on the economic crisis into a 2004 movie about Hitler). There's no sense comparing the genres, which is like equating bobby-pins with constitutional law.

**geriatric1927 vs. Chocolate Rain**
Peter Oakley, an English pensioner, was an early adopter of YouTube in 2005; he promised to gripe and grumble but delivered a personal story of being a widower, a blues fanatic, and a retired Army radar technician. But Tay Zonday, with his unmistakable voice and uncanny songwriting, offered a commentary on race that is both on-the-nose and utterly idiosyncratic.

THE WINNER

## guitar: Funtwo's version of Canon Rock

**guitar vs. Vote Different**
The pro-Obama Vote Different is a brilliant amateur political ad – a take-off on Apple's dystopian "1984" commercial. But even its brilliant video craftsmanship cannot capture the shy/outrageous electric guitar virtuosity of "funtwo," a young Korean wearing a T-shirt and a face-obscuring cap playing a rock version of Pachelbel's "Canon."

- Chocolate Rain
  - Real Estate Downfall
    - Real Estate Downfall
      - The Real Estate Downfall
      - Urban Ninja
    - Bus Uncle
      - Brokeback to the Future
      - Bus Uncle (with English subtitles)
  - Chocolate Rain
    - Chocolate Rain
      - geriatric1927's – first try
      - Chocolate Rain
    - Leave Britney Alone
      - Sneezing Panda
      - Leave Britney Alone
- guitar
  - guitar
    - guitar
      - Ronaldhino: Touch of Gold
      - guitar: Funtwo's version of Canon Rock
    - Don't Tase Me, Bro
      - Don't Tase Me, Bro
      - George Bush shoe attack
  - Vote Different
    - Vote Different
      - Vote Different
      - Antidisestablishmentarianism
    - Blasphemy Challenge
      - Evolution of Dance
      - The Blasphemy Challenge

# Soul Songs

**By John Leland**

John Leland is a reporter at the *New York Times* and author of *Why Kerouac Matters: The Lessons of 'On the Road' (They're Not What You Think)* and *Hip: The History.* He can't carry a tune in a bucket.

Ray Charles
"I've Got a Woman"

Sam & Dave
"Soul Man"

"I've Got a Woman"

James Carr
"The Dark End of the Street"

Al Green
"Love and Happiness"

"Love and Happiness"

"I've Got a Woman"

Sam Cooke
"Bring It On Home to Me"

Soul Stirrers
"By and By"

"Bring It to Me"

"Bring It to Me"

Persuaders
"Thin Line Between Love & Hate"

Impressions
"It's All Right"

"It's All Right"

"I've Got a Woman"

Irma Thomas
"It's Raining"

Carla Thomas
"B-A-B-Y"

"It's Raining"

"Respect"

Etta James
"Tell Mama"

Aretha Franklin
"Respect"

"Respect"

"Respect"

Donny Hathaway
"The Ghetto"

D'Angelo
"Brown Sugar"

"The Ghetto"

"In the Midnight Hour"

O. V. Wright
"A Nickel and a Nail"

Wilson Pickett
"In the Midnight Hour"

"In the Midnight Hour"

**"Bring It on Home to Me" vs. "By and By"**
Gospel purists prefer Cooke's Soul Stirrers records to his pop hits, and some prefer the original group, before he replaced the volcanic R.H. Harris. But "Bring It On Home to Me" melds sanctified emoting with swell make-out music, plus the sexiest word in the soul canon: home.

**"Respect" vs. "When a Man Loves a Woman"**
Throughout the '60s Atlantic Records owned soul music, creating a template heard on both of these records: deep Southern grooves, percussive horns and a mighty voice raised in the church, unpolished for pop consumption. Aretha takes it for intricacy of composition.

THE WINNER

**Aretha Franklin**
"Respect"

VS

AMERICAN MUSIC IS ABOUT SYNTHESIS, and the soul music that emerged out of Holiness churches and hellified nightclubs in the early 1950s drew on two mighty mother-lodes: the unrelenting fury of gospel and the profane backbeat of rhythm and blues. It became a scandal to some church folks and the elevating soundtrack of the civil rights movement, a liturgy for a nation that knew both pain and the promised land.

**"Respect" vs. "Cold Sweat"**
Otis Redding wrote "Respect," but Aretha made it an anthem of an odd sort: She's giving her man all her money, and all she asks is a little of the sweet stuff. The slinky opening guitar is all the invitation she needs. What we want, baby she's got it. In heaps.

# "Cold Sweat"

**"Cold Sweat" vs. "When a Man Loves a Woman"**
Brown ran the tightest and hardest working bands in show business, able to start and stop at the speed of grunt. Every instrument was a drum, including James's voice. "Cold Sweat" looks forward to his greasy funk. Alas, poor Percy, without him the world would be a less populous place.

**"Bridge Over Troubled Water" vs. "Tell It Like It Is"**
A second-round blowout, but don't sell Paul and Art short. Until Simon joins on the last verse, "Bridge Over Troubled Water" is pristine gospel soul, as healing as the funkier stuff. A hymn to holy friendship.

- "Cold Sweat"
  - "Sweet Soul"
    - "Sweet Soul Music"
      - **Arthur Conley** "Sweet Soul Music"
      - **William DeVaughn** "Be Thankful for What You Got"
    - "Walk on By"
      - **Willie Nelson** "Night Life"
      - **Isaac Hayes,** "Walk on By"
  - "Cold Sweat"
    - "Cold Sweat"
      - **James Brown** "Cold Sweat"
      - **Luther Ingram** "(If Loving You Is Wrong) I Don't Want to Be Right"
    - "Bridge Over"
      - **Aaron Neville** "Tell It Like It Is"
      - **Simon and Garfunkel** "Bridge Over Troubled Water"
- "When a Man Loves a Woman"
  - "Loving You"
    - "Loving You"
      - **Otis Redding** *"I've Been Loving You Too Long (To Stop Now)"*
      - **Bobby "Blue" Bland** "Ain't No Love in the Heart of the City"
    - "Soulful Strut"
      - **King Curtis** "Memphis Soul Stew"
      - **Young Holt Unlimited** "Soulful Strut"
  - "When a Man Loves a Woman"
    - "Take You There"
      - **Staple Singers** "I'll Take You There"
      - **Ann Peebles** "I'm Gonna Tear Your Playhouse Down"
    - "When a Man Loves a Woman"
      - **Percy Sledge** "When a Man Loves a Woman"
      - **Solomon Burke** "Everybody Needs Somebody to Love"

# Paul Newman Roles

**By Mark Reiter**

Mark Reiter, co-editor of this book, deals with any dilemma by asking himself, "What would Paul Newman do?"

**Judge Roy Bean**
*The Life and Times of Judge Roy Bean* (1972)

**Frank Galvin**
*The Verdict* (1982)

*The Verdict*

**Gov. Earl Long**
*Blaze* (1989)

**Rocky**
*Somebody Up There Likes Me* (1956)

*Blaze*

*The Verdict*

**Fast Eddie Felson**
*The Color of Money* (1986)

**Jim Kane**
*Pocket Money* (1972)

*The Color of Money*

**Fast Eddie Felson**
*The Hustler* (1961)

**Ari Ben Canaan**
*Exodus* (1960)

*The Hustler*

*The Color of Money*

**Lew Harper**
*Harper* (1966)

**Lew Harper**
*The Drowning Pool* (1975)

*Harper*

**Murphy**
*Fort Apache, The Bronx* (1981)

**Luke**
*Cool Hand Luke* (1967)

*Cool Hand Luke*

*Cool Hand Luke*

**Henry Gondorff**
*The Sting* (1973)

**Butch**
*Butch Cassidy and the Sundance Kid* (1969)

*The Sting*

**Walter Bridge**
*Mr. and Mrs. Bridge* (1990)

**Frank Capua**
*Winning* (1969)

*Mr. and Mrs. Bridge*

*The Sting*

***The Sting* vs. *The Verdict***
Newman was said to rank his down-and-out lawyer Frank Galvin as his favorite performance. It's hard to argue with him, but it's painful to watch him taking punches to the psyche for so much of *The Verdict*. Much more pleasant to watch is his swaggering con-man-on-the-lam, Henry Gondorff, in *The Sting* (a movie so delicious, the first time I saw it I stayed in my seat for a second viewing). A tip of the nose to his poker face-off with Robert Shaw, where Newman goes to the edge of hamminess, but stays kosher.

***The Hustler* vs. *The Color of Money***
How'd this happen? Fast Eddie 1961 meets Fast Eddie 25 years later in a more brutal matchup than, say, Newman's two Harper roles. As the young arrogant pool shark Newman is note-perfect. But in the Scorsese update, he gets a few more showy scenes with Tom Cruise – and it's hard to top the confusion and misery on Newman's face after he gets hustled by a knucklehead played by Forest Whitaker. Plus, it earned him an Oscar.

*The Sting*

VS

PAUL NEWMAN WORKED LONG ENOUGH IN FILMS, from 1954 to 2006, that it's tempting to pigeonhole his career into convenient chronological phases, from newcomer through smoldering rogue to artisanal actor – and grade each on a curve. But the only criterion here is how good was the role and the performance? Could you forget the blue eyes and the legendary persona and only see the character he's playing? When Paul Newman disappears completely and yet invests the character with his charisma and wit, that's what wins here.

***The Sting* vs. *Absence of Malice***
A perverse choice for the actor who created Hud, Luke, Brick, and Butch? I don't think so. In *Absence of Malice,* Newman's Michael Gallagher is an average man forced, by perfidy and folly all around him, to do unto others as they have done unto him. No gunplay, no fighting, no dark suspense, just Newman's brainpower and guile at play. At every step, you never think this is the guy on the salad bottle. In the final scene, where everyone gets their comeuppance, Wilford Brimley's U.S. Attorney turns to Newman's Gallagher and asks, "Are you that smart?" He is, he was, and it doesn't get better than that.

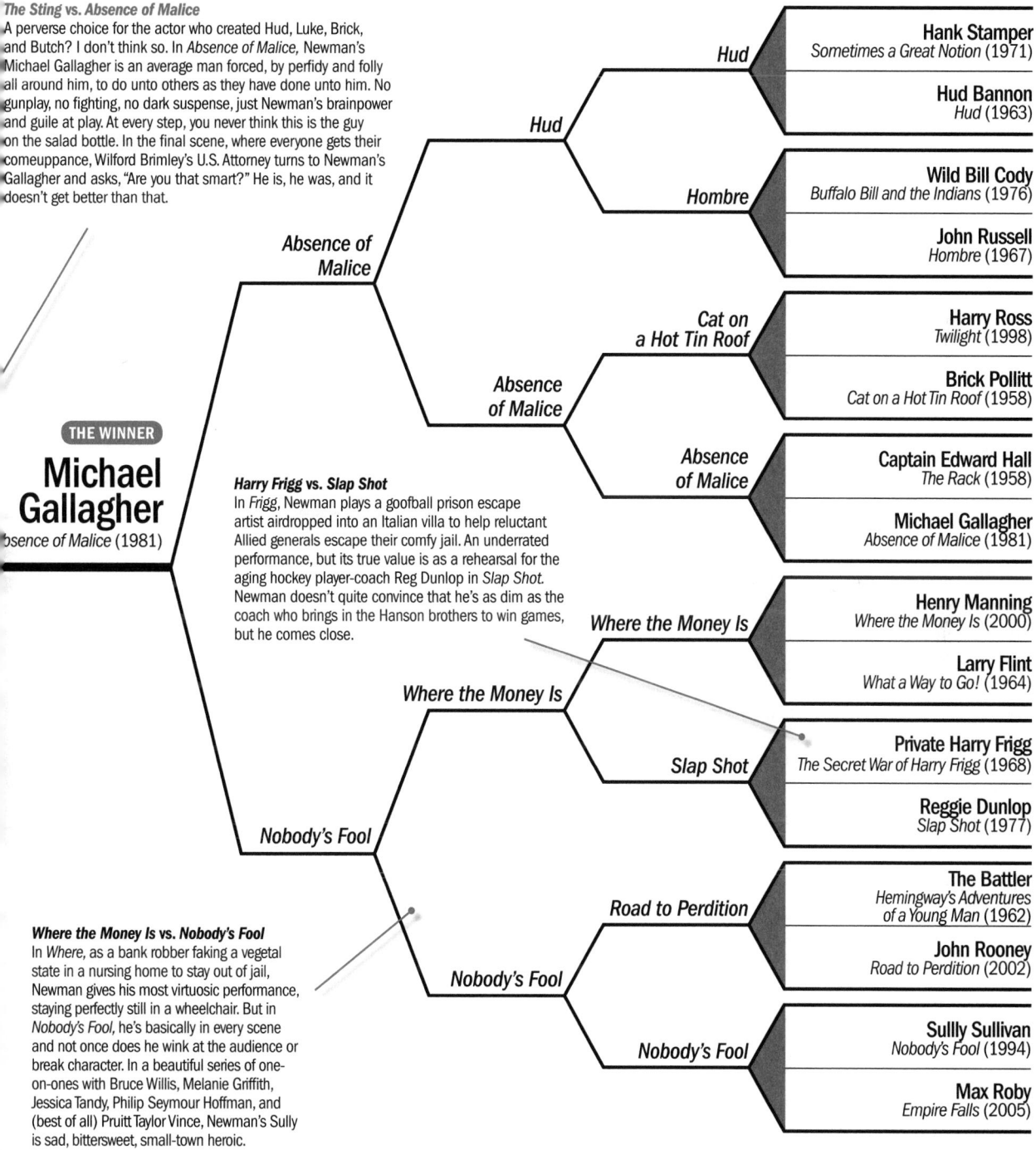


***Harry Frigg* vs. *Slap Shot***
In *Frigg,* Newman plays a goofball prison escape artist airdropped into an Italian villa to help reluctant Allied generals escape their comfy jail. An underrated performance, but its true value is as a rehearsal for the aging hockey player-coach Reg Dunlop in *Slap Shot.* Newman doesn't quite convince that he's as dim as the coach who brings in the Hanson brothers to win games, but he comes close.

***Where the Money Is* vs. *Nobody's Fool***
In *Where,* as a bank robber faking a vegetal state in a nursing home to stay out of jail, Newman gives his most virtuosic performance, staying perfectly still in a wheelchair. But in *Nobody's Fool,* he's basically in every scene and not once does he wink at the audience or break character. In a beautiful series of one-on-ones with Bruce Willis, Melanie Griffith, Jessica Tandy, Philip Seymour Hoffman, and (best of all) Pruitt Taylor Vince, Newman's Sully is sad, bittersweet, small-town heroic.

# Sitcom Dads

**By Steven Reddicliffe**

Steven Reddicliffe, a media editor at the *New York Times,* has been a suburban dad for 18 years (his children contributed to the Danny Tanner entry here). He has always tried to be more Cleaver than Cheever.

**Bernie McCullough**
*The Bernie Mac Show*

**Bentley Gregg**
*Bachelor Father*

**Howard Cunningham**
*Happy Days*

**Steven Keaton**
*Family Ties*

**Red Forman**
*That '70s Show*

**Al Bundy**
*Married . . . With Children*

**Ricky Ricardo**
*I Love Lucy*

**Fred Sanford**
*Sanford and Son*

**Jed Clampett**
*Beverly Hillbillies*

**Tony Micelli**
*Who's the Boss?*

**Danny Williams**
*Make Room for Daddy*

**Ward Cleaver**
*Leave It to Beaver*

**James Evans, Sr.**
*Good Times*

**Ozzie Nelson**
*Ozzie and Harriet*

**Carl Winslow**
*Family Matters*

**Jim Anderson**
*Father Knows Best*

Bernie McCullough

Steven Keaton

Red Forman

Fred Sanford

Jed Clampett

Ward Cleaver

James Evans, Sr.

Jim Anderson

Bernie McCullough

Red Forman

Ward Cleaver

Jim Anderson

Bernie McCullough

Ward Cleaver

**Howard Cunningham vs. Steven Keaton**
Two TV parents best described as obligatory, but with genuine decency. Howard had only to deal with the easily likable Richie, Potsie, and Fonzie, the least delinquent JD ever. Liberal Steven had son Alex P., a conservative careerist who carried a briefcase to school and a brief for William F. Buckley, Jr. As a baby Alex had a Nixon rattle. Once said, "People who have money don't need people." Case closed.

**Bernie McCullough vs. Red Forman**
Gruff, tough-talking dads. Red was master of the bitter barb; Bernie could bluster with the best. But wouldn't you rather hang in the den with the guy who also regularly showed a softer side? Bernie was a supremely entertaining embodiment of TV's custodial dad tradition, uncles who include Bentley Gregg of *Bachelor Father* and Bill Davis of *Family Affair.* Unlike them, Bernie had a sweet soul soundtrack, smoked cigars, and paid absolutely no attention to the fourth wall.

**THE WINNER**

## Ward Cleaver

*Leave It to Beaver*

VS

DAD'S A DOOFUS – that's the long-lived misconception when it comes to television. Although there may be the occasional dips and dorks, situation comedy dads are usually sane and sensitive fellows, wry guys who can impart useful life lessons between mowing the lawn and conducting goldfish funerals. There are exceptions, sure (Frank Costanza's discourse on the brassiere somehow leaps to mind), but mellow understanding prevails. As the '60s soul group The Winstons once put it, "I think I'll color this man love."

**Cliff Huxtable vs. Ward Cleaver**
No one ever should have been worried about the Beaver. Ward was the unshakable foundation for the admirable TV dad – affectionate, patient, good-humored, capable of making a mistake and of deftly repairing one. Also dried the dishes. Cliff played a genuinely funny, contemporary riff on Ward (he cooked, wife was a lawyer), but there can be no rancor or raised voices in this battle; wouldn't be fatherly. As both Cliff and Ward would tell their children, there is only one champion, and sometimes the good guy who gets there first wins the prize.

**Herman Munster vs. Dan Conner**
Physically imposing dads, one built in a laboratory, the other built with cholesterol. Herman, a genuine sweetheart, is challenged only by his vampire father-in-law; Dan's challenge comes from the most formidable wife in sitcom history. But winning the dad trophy often comes down to the better bowler, and based on bendability alone, that man would be Dan.

**Danny Tanner vs. Steve Douglas**
This one's strictly a numbers game. Tanner: kids D.J., Stephanie, and Michelle, a dog named Comet, Joey, Jesse, Jesse's wife Becky, and their twins Alex and Nicky. Douglas: three biological sons, one adopted son, triplet grandkids, a dog named Tramp, a wife late in the game, Bub, and Uncle Charley. That's a fuller house.

**Cliff Huxtable**

- Cliff Huxtable
  - Andy Taylor
    - Andy Taylor
      - Andy Taylor – *The Andy Griffith Show*
      - Jack Arnold – *The Wonder Years*
    - Dan Conner
      - Herman Munster – *The Munsters*
      - Dan Conner – *Roseanne*
  - Cliff Huxtable
    - Cliff Huxtable
      - Cliff Huxtable – *The Cosby Show*
      - Alex Stone – *The Donna Reed Show*
    - Hal Wilkerson
      - George Bluth, Sr. – *Arrested Development*
      - Hal Wilkerson – *Malcolm in the Middle*
- Steve Douglas
  - Julius Rock
    - Julius Rock
      - Julius Rock – *Everybody Hates Chris*
      - Ray Barone – *Everybody Loves Raymond*
    - Frank Costanza
      - Tim Taylor – *Home Improvement*
      - Frank Costanza – *Seinfeld*
  - Steve Douglas
    - Danny Tanner
      - Danny Tanner – *Full House*
      - Nick Russo – *Blossom*
    - Steve Douglas
      - Steve Douglas – *My Three Sons*
      - Mike Brady – *The Brady Bunch*

# Sitcom Moms

**By Richard Sandomir**

Richard Sandomir's mother is most like Edith Bunker in her consummate decency, innocence, and depth of caring. But she loved watching *Maude*.

**CLASSIC MOMS I REGIONAL**

- June Cleaver — *Leave It to Beaver*
- Samantha Stevens — *Bewitched*
- Margaret Anderson — *Father Knows Best*
- Edith Bunker — *All in the Family*

**ALMOST MOMS REGIONAL**

- Aunt Bee — *The Andy Griffith Show*
- Fran Fine — *The Nanny*
- Doris Ziffel — *Green Acres*
- Edna Garrett — *The Facts of Life*

**MOMMY DEAREST REGIONAL**

- Marie Barone — *Everybody Loves Raymond*
- Estelle Costanza — *Seinfeld*
- Sylvia Buchman — *Mad About You*
- Lois Wilkerson — *Malcolm in the Middle*

**WORKING MOMS I REGIONAL**

- Julia Baker — *Julia*
- Clair Huxtable — *The Cosby Show*
- Shirley Partridge — *The Partridge Family*
- Maude Findlay — *Maude*

June Cleaver | Edith Bunker | Aunt Bee | Doris Ziffel | Marie Barone | Lois Wilkerson | Clair Huxtable | Shirley Partridge

Edith Bunker | Aunt Bee | Marie Barone | Clair Huxtable

Edith Bunker | Clair Huxtable

**June Cleaver vs. Samantha Stevens**
Without magic or a family of witches and warlocks, June became the archetypal TV mother of her era – she was nurturing, suspicious of creeps like Eddie Haskell, and a homemaker who kept a perfect house while wearing a dress and a lovely strand of pearls. And no matter how often she said, "Beaver," she never cracked up.

**Clair Huxtable vs. Roseanne**
Both redefined sitcom motherhood for the working-class and professional divisions. But while Roseanne gave voice to viewers living paycheck to paycheck (forget the ridiculous lottery-winning story arc in the final season), Clair's (and Cliff's) life showed that wealthy blacks on TV didn't have to be stereotypes like the Jeffersons and could presage the appearance of a family resembling theirs in the White House.

**Aunt Bee vs. Doris Ziffel**
Doris deserves plenty of praise for helping to raise Arnold, a very special pig, as her own, into young maturity. But Bee raised Opie, her grand-nephew, into a fine teenager, baked cherry pies, cooked fried chicken, and made dreadful pickles. The results speak for themselves: Opie is a great director and Arnold, long-digested bacon.

**Marie Barone vs. Clair Huxtable**
Marie is the quintessential nihilist of sitcom mothers, a calculating, lasagna-baking monster who never lost control of her family; her sons, Raymond and Robert, are her emotionally crippled victims. But Clair, a regal lawyer in a loving marriage where her husband is not a moronic boob, offered a new vision of the sitcom working mother.

**THE WINNER**

## Clair Huxtable

*The Cosby Show*

VS

THESE MOTHERS (sorry, Peg Bundy, Donna Stone, Sophia Petrillo) demonstrated wide and varied abilities to provide the glue to their families, with food (Marie Barone), magic (Samantha Stevens), wise-cracking tough-love (Roseanne Conner), husband-exasperating antics (Lucy Ricardo), perky sexuality (Laura Petrie), or in case of a doofus mate, steady practicality (Marge Simpson). Some, like June, Edith, and Laura, you'd really want for your mother; others, like Marie, Maude, or Estelle, you'd need lifelong therapy.

**Marge Simpson vs. Roseanne**
It's not easy being married to Homer (think of how often he's been naked in public), but Roseanne wasn't very nice, insulted her kids, didn't keep house very well, dressed without style, and argued loudly with Dan. Blue-collar life had been depicted on TV before (nobody was poorer than Alice Kramden), but never as a comedic primal scream.

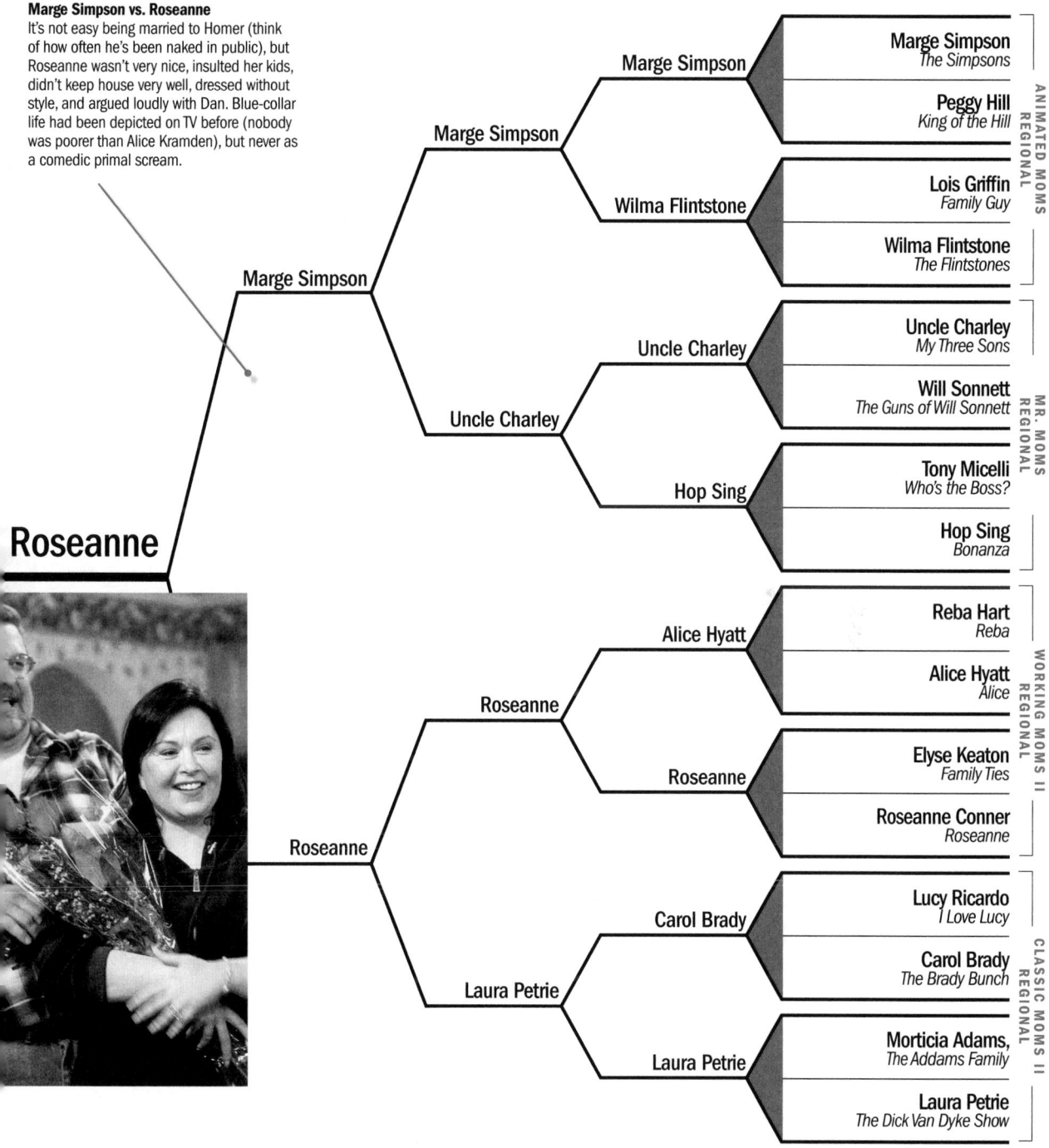

# Talk-Show Graveyard

**By Bill Carter**

Bill Carter has covered the television industry for the *New York Times* for 20 years. He is the author of three books about the business: *Monday Night Mayhem* (with Marc Gunther), *The Late Shift*, and *Desperate Networks*.

Megan Mullally
Queen Latifah
Mullally

Dr. Laura Schlessinger
Marsha Warfield
Dr. Laura

Dr. Laura

Roseanne Barr
John Salley
Salley

Whoopi Goldberg
Dennis Miller
Miller

Salley

Dr. Laura

Howie Mandel
Byron Allen
Allen

Caroline Rhea
Jesse Ventura
Ventura

Ventura

Joan Rivers
Greg Behrendt
Rivers

Zack Galifianakis
Keenan Ivory Wayans
Wayans

Rivers

Rivers

**Rivers vs. Dr. Laura**
Joan Rivers's career-sabotaging decision to launch a late-night show behind Johnny Carson's back – and her increasingly shrill comic delivery – installed her as a favorite to win this tournament. But gay-baiting and hypocritical Dr. Laura generated more cringe-worthy moments and alienated viewers and advertisers in droves.

**Allen vs. Ventura**
A matchup out of wrestling central casting: Allen, a real-life babyface and a sycophantically-pleasant personality, had no chance against an all-time heel like Ventura, a.k.a. "The Body." MSNBC wanted the former World Wrestling Entertainment star-turned-Minnesota governor to host a nightly talk slugfest, but all he could manage was a low-rated Saturday night show that died meekly after less than three months.

THE WINNER

**Dr. Laura Schlessinger**

VS

**Chase vs. Dr. Laura Schlessinger**
Chase's talk show was late-night's most memorable flop. Dr. Laura was the most hated daytime talk show ever. Chase was stale and uninspired but at least had fun with his fiasco in a Doritos commercial and *The Larry Sanders Show*. But Dr. Laura, unable to moderate her intolerant radio style for TV, reached an ignominious nadir interviewing a staff member passing herself off as various guests. For most egregious failure, small-minded beats old hat.

MOST OF TELEVISION IS ABOUT FAILURE. Usually, it's not a disgrace: shows are mounted, viewers give them a look (or not) and reject them. But when talk shows flop, there is a special humiliation – a direct rejection of the "person behind the desk," as Johnny Carson called the host. Simple failures fade. But the colossal ones are memorable debacles that recall both the great expectations with which the shows started and questions about why you'd give a show to these people.

**Wilton-North vs. Tom Green**
The *Wilton-North Report* stood out for its sheer obscurity and the unparalleled idiocy of the Fox network's choosing it to replace a temporary late-night host named Arsenio Hall. Unable to match such superior incompetence, Green's obnoxious show with its outrageous stunts was a minor MTV hit that was curtailed by his bout with cancer.

**cEnroe vs. Pat Sajak**
cEnroe rode his renowned nnis-world reputation for an ntamed mouth to a CNBC ot, but his vocal serves cked pace; he wasn't bratty amusing enough to get a se from viewers. But Sajak, ardly scintillating on *Wheel of ortune*, generated more sleep-alkers than viewers – and osolutely no vowels – with his l-consuming blandness.

- **Chase**
  - Sajak
    - Sajak
      - Sajak
        - Pat Sajak
        - Wayne Brady
      - Thicke
        - Lauren Hutton
        - Alan Thicke
    - McEnroe
      - McEnroe
        - John McEnroe
        - Ron Reagan
      - *Wilton-North*
        - *Wilton-North Report*
        - Tom Green
  - Chase
    - Magic
      - Magic
        - Magic Johnson
        - Chuck Woolery
      - Pauley
        - McLean Stevenson
        - Jane Pauley
    - Chase
      - Brandmeier
        - Jonathon Brandmeier
        - Gayle King
      - Chase
        - Wayne Brady
        - Chevy Chase

# Children's Books

**By Jon Scieszka**

Jon Scieszka, author of *The True Story of the 3 Little Pigs!* and *The Stinky Cheese Man,* was appointed the nation's first National Ambassador for Young People's Literature by the Librarian of Congress.

DR. SEUSS REGIONAL

*Green Eggs and Ham* — *Green Eggs*

*Oh, the Places You'll Go!*

*One Fish Two Fish Red Fish Blue Fish* — *One Fish*

*How the Grinch Stole Christmas*

*The Cat in the Hat* — *Cat in Hat*

*Horton Hears A Who*

*Hop On Pop* — *If I Ran the Circus*

*If I Ran the Circus*

*Green Eggs*

*Cat in Hat*

*Green Eggs*

*Cat in Hat*

***Green Eggs* vs. *Cat in Hat***
Two Dr. Seuss heavyweights going toe to toe – both hugely popular, perfectly rhymed, and deliciously surreal. But *Eggs* stays truer to the surreal while all the cleaning up and worrying about mother in *Cat* is a downer ending. And *Eggs's* final Joycean affirmation, "I do so like green eggs and ham! Thank you! Thank you, Sam-I-Am," wins it. Yes it says yes it does Yes.

*Green Eggs*

*Charlotte's Web* by E.B. White — *The Giver*

*The Giver* by Lois Lowry

*Tales of a Fourth Grade Nothing* by Judy Blume — *Fourth Grade Nothing*

*Bridge to Terabithia* by Katherine Paterson

*The Giver*

*The Giver*

***The Giver* vs. *Fourth Grade Nothing***
*Nothing* nearly beats the heavier and more thematically complex *Giver* because of Judy Blume's ability to bring real topics to children's books, where a narrator could hate a younger brother, and a character could worry about divorce, sex, or religion. But *The Giver* wins with a beautifully crafted, mind-boggling reveal in mid-story and an ending that won't let go of you.

*The Adventures of Huckleberry Finn* by Mark Twain — *Hatchet*

*Hatchet* by Gary Paulsen

*The Catcher in the Rye* by J.D. Salinger — *Wrinkle*

*Wrinkle In Time* by Madeleine L'Engle

*Hatchet*

JUDGING THE AWESOME RANGE OF CHILDREN'S LITERATURE – from beginning picture books and easy readers to young adult novels – is like comparing green eggs to talking dogs. It's a mind-bending mission, but bending kids' minds by giving them reasons to be a reader is what great children's literature is all about. The best books combine popularity, repeat-readability, kid-friendliness, longevity, and literary merit. Only Dr. Seuss got a regional of his own, because his books are a force and region all their own.

***Green Eggs* vs. *Go, Dog. Go!***
Eggs possesses undeniable narrative power with Seuss's unmatched illustrative imagination. But Eastman's *Go, Dog. Go!* offers zen purity in describing the now ("The blue dog is in. The red dog is out."), a pleasingly complex multi-strand story, and a glorious climax of a dog party atop a tree. But most important, *Go, Dog. Go!* is the book I loved as a kid. And that is what kids' books are all about – the book you loved most.

**THE WINNER**

***Go, Dog. Go!***
By P. D. Eastman

***Goodnight Moon* vs. *Polar Express***
The toughest first-round matchup: with its rich, realistically detailed illustrations of the fantastic and its message of believing, Van Allsburg's *Polar Express* could have crushed almost any other opponent. But the read-aloud cadence and the go-to-sleep power of *Goodnight Moon* is just too good, too strong. Goodnight, *Polar Express*.

***Captain Underpants* vs. *The Stupids Die***
*Underpants,* and the sequels it spawned, are the sort of funny, smart-alecky, easy-to-read, generously illustrated books that have inspired millions of boys to actually pick up a book. But the understated wit of the *Stupids'* text and simple line drawings are original genius, as is that title.

- *Go, Dog. Go!*
  - *Goodnight Moon*
    - *Wild Things*
      - *Where the Wild Things Are* by Maurice Sendak
      - *Sylvester and the Magic Pebble* by William Steig
    - *Goodnight Moon*
      - *Goodnight Moon* by Margaret Wise Brown
      - *The Polar Express* by Chris Van Allsburg
  - *Go, Dog. Go!*
    - *Go, Dog. Go!*
      - *The Very Hungry Caterpillar* by Eric Carle
      - *Go, Dog. Go!* by P.D. Eastman
    - *Pigeon*
      - *No, David!* by David Shannon
      - *Don't Let the Pigeon Drive the Bus!* by Mo Willems
- *Frog and Toad*
  - *Frog and Toad*
    - *Frog and Toad*
      - *A Series of Unfortunate Events* by Lemony Snicket
      - *Frog and Toad* readers by Arnold Lobel
    - *Bone*
      - *Bone* by Jeff Smith
      - *The Way Things Work* by David Macaulay
  - *The Stupids Die*
    - *Pat the Bunny*
      - *Pat the Bunny* by Dorothy Kunhardt
      - *Where the Sidewalk Ends* by Shel Silverstein
    - *The Stupids Die*
      - *Captain Underpants* by Dav Pilkey
      - *The Stupids Die* by James Marshall

# Cinematic Interrogatories

**By John Steinbreder**

John Steinbreder has written eight books, none about films. He's still asking himself why that is.

"You know how to whistle, don't you Steve?"
*(To Have and Have Not)*

"Oh, I'm sorry, did I break your concentration?"
*(Pulp Fiction)*

"How to whistle"

"You speaking to me?"
*(Shane)*

"You talkin' to me?"
*(Taxi Driver)*

"You talkin' to me"

"Talkin' to me"

"You take drugs, Danny?"
*(Caddyshack)*

"You know what happens to nosy fellows?"
*(Chinatown)*

"Nosy fellows"

"How can I lose?"
*(The Hustler)*

"What have I done to deserve such generosity?"
*(The Godfather)*

"What have I done"

"What have I done"

"Why did you have to come to Casablanca?"
*(Casablanca)*

"Why do men chase women?"
*(Moonstruck)*

"Casablanca"

"Joey, do you like movies about gladiators?"
*(Airplane!)*

"Hey . . . Dad? You want to have a catch?"
*(Field of Dreams)*

"Hey, Dad"

"Hey, Dad"

"Talkin' to me"

"Talkin' to me"

"Talkin' to me" VS

"Who are those guys"

"Who are those guys"

"Say, didn't you used to be big?"
*(Sunset Boulevard)*

"You want the moon?"
*(It's A Wonderful Life)*

"Used to be big"

"Badges?"
*(The Treasure of the Sierra Madre)*

"Who are those guys?"
*(Butch Cassidy and the Sundance Kid)*

"Who are those guys"

**Talkin' to me vs. Speaking to me**
In the same way that "No" is a great conversation-stopper, these two questions are great fight-starters. But De Niro repeated his in front of a mirror, indelibly singeing the phrase into our heads – and later into stand-up acts and 1970s Springsteen concerts. And he did it all sporting a mean Mohawk, while all Alan Ladd had was lifts.

**Hey, Dad? vs. Who are those guys?**
Men are mesmerized by the magic of *Field of Dreams* and inevitably begin sobbing when Kevin Costner meets his supernatural father. It's a sappy line, and real men do not go to movies to cry. We would much rather ride with Butch and Sundance than dab at our eyes with a hankie.

**Talkin' to me vs. Feel lucky**
Although De Niro's question is piercing, memorable, and has entered the national argot, must of the credit belongs to his playful interpretive phrasings. Eastwood's interrogative actually contains two questions, the first sarcastic, the second expressing a nation's rage against thugs and thieves. It's memorable, yes, but unlike the *Taxi Driver* line, it's also morally clear and unambiguous.

**Used to be big vs. Who are those guys?**
Sundance's question about the dauntless posse chasing him and Butch is funny but rhetorical. We don't care about the answer. What's special about William Holden's question to Gloria Swanson's aging film star is her even more memorable response: "I'm still big. It's the pictures that got smaller."

A GREAT MOVIE FEATURES AT LEAST ONE GREAT QUESTION. It could be the interrogative itself that shines. Or it's the answer that makes the query stand out. Still other questions stick in the mind because of constant repetition, as if recited by a Greek chorus (e.g., "Who are those guys?"). But the questions that go far here are the ones that define the individual asking them. For example, where would De Niro and Eastwood be as actor-icons if they never uttered a sharp interrogative early in their careers? Good question.

THE WINNER

"You've got to ask yourself one question: 'Do I feel lucky?' Well, do ya, punk?"

- "Come up and see me"
  - "Come up and see me"
    - "Come up and see me"
      - "Why don't you come up sometime and see me?" *(She Done Him Wrong)*
      - "Is that a gun in your pocket, or are you just happy to see me?" *(She Done Him Wrong)*
    - "Where shall I go"
      - "Where shall I go? What shall I do?" *(Gone With The Wind)*
      - "Are you a good witch or a bad witch?" *(The Wizard of Oz)*
  - "Mrs. Robinson"
    - "Masked man"
      - "Who was that masked man?" *(The Legend of the Lone Ranger)*
      - "Why would a guy want to marry a guy?" *(Some Like It Hot)*
    - "Mrs. Robinson"
      - "Have you ever done it in an elevator?" *(Fatal Attraction)*
      - "Mrs. Robinson, you're trying to seduce me. Aren't you?" *(The Graduate)*
- "Feel lucky"
  - "Dates"
    - "Dates"
      - "Do you mind if we dance with your dates?" *(Animal House)*
      - "Is it safe?" *(Marathon Man)*
    - "Mind if I smoke"
      - "Snakes. Why'd it have to be snakes?" *(Raiders of the Lost Ark)*
      - "Mind if I smoke while you're eating?" *(Deep Throat)*
  - "Feel lucky"
    - "Feel lucky"
      - "You've got to ask yourself one question: 'Do I feel lucky?' Well, do ya, punk?" *(Dirty Harry)*
      - "Is it true how they say that you people are . . . gifted?" *(Blazing Saddles)*
    - "Why a duck"
      - "Why a duck?" *(The Cocoanuts)*
      - "Who's on first?" *(The Naughty Nineties)*

**Come up and see me vs. Where shall I go**
Not much of a contest here, as brassy Mae West, mistress of innuendo and entendre, stomps a sniveling Scarlett O'Hara. Rhett Butler didn't give a damn, and neither does Mae.

**Come up and see me vs. Mrs. Robinson**
A matchup of scenes where two "older women" are in seduction mode. Mae West hits on a much younger Cary Grant in one film while Anne Bancroft intimidates a confused Dustin Hoffman in the other. West earns bonus points – and wins – for boldness because (a) she delivered her saucy and much-quoted line in tamer times (1933); and (b) she wrote her own material.

**You people are . . . gifted vs. Feel lucky**
Madeline Kahn quickly answers her own question when she and the Rock Ridge sheriff hook up in her "dwessing room." But Eastwood's interrogative, cruel and twisted and in many ways gratuitous if you believe his Dirty Harry was never at risk in the scene, initiated a tradition of catchy one-liners for the star. It made him number one, with a bullet.

# Comic Strips

**By R.C. Harvey**

R.C. Harvey, one-time cartoonist and all-time comics chronicler, has authored nearly a dozen books about the arts and artisans of cartooning, all of which are described at his website, RCHarvey.com.

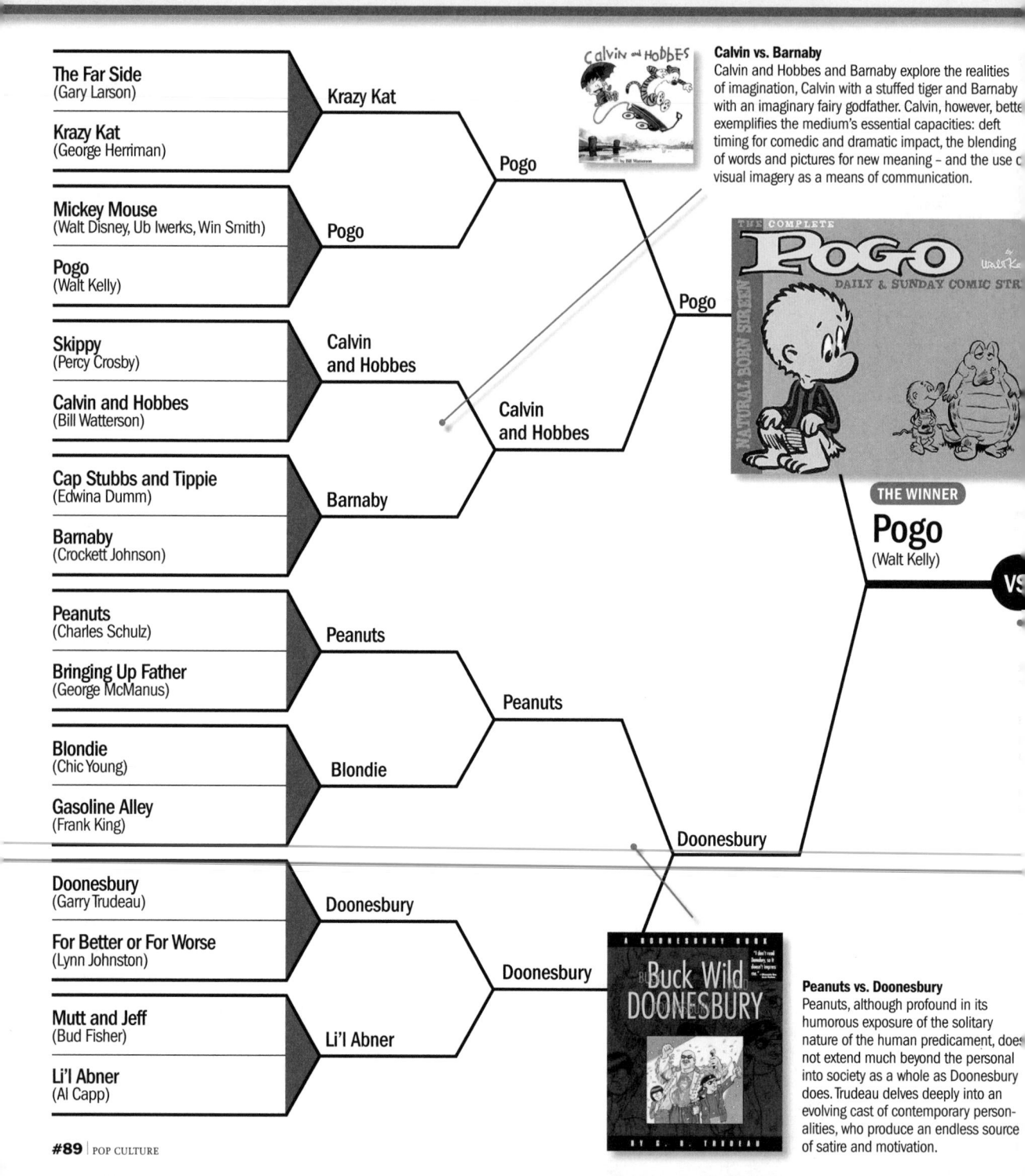

THE BEST COMIC STRIPS over the past century blend the verbal and the visual to create a meaning that neither words nor pictures alone can achieve. Some of the of the masterworks are pace-setters (Mutt and Jeff, Wash Tubbs, The Far Side, Peanuts) or superb examples of the realistic illustration (Tarzan, Flash Gordon). Others are inimitable exploitations of the medium's capacities (Krazy Kat, Popeye, Calvin and Hobbes, Alley Oop) while still more are brilliantly satirical (Li'l Abner, Doonesbury, Pogo).

**9 Chickweed Lane vs. The Gumps**
Both are narratives that explore human relationships. The Gumps, a pioneering storytelling strip that used day-to-day suspense to sustain continuity, was highly melodramatic. Chickweed advances because it is realistic, intensely personal, and socially pertinent, dealing compassionately and humorously with premarital sex and homosexuality.

# Terry and the Pirates

**Terry and the Pirates vs. Pogo**
Both Terry and Pogo exemplified better than any other strip the medium's potential for blending words and pictures to a narrative purpose. But by transforming its animal cast into caricatures of political miscreants, Pogo created high art without sacrificing humor. Kelly's comedic chorus is so unified, so mutually dependent for satiric meaning, that it crystallized forever the essence of cartoon art.

**Zits vs. Terry and the Pirates**
Zits plumbs the potential of the art form, using imagery symbolically. But Terry and the Pirates redefined the adventure strip with its use of the realistic chiaroscuro, realistic visual detail, and characterization that lent exotic incidents a palpable authenticity.

- Zits
  - Zits
    - Zits
      - Zits (Jerry Schott and Jim Borgman)
      - Little Orphan Annie (Harold Gray)
    - 9 Chickweed Lane
      - 9 Chickweed Lane (Brook McEldowney)
      - The Gumps (Sidney Smith)
  - Wash Tubbs
    - Popeye
      - Popeye the Sailor Man (Elzie Crisler Segar)
      - Joe Palooka (Ham Fisher)
    - Wash Tubbs
      - Alley Oop (V.T. Hamlin)
      - Wash Tubbs (Roy Crane)
- Terry and the Pirates
  - Flash Gordon
    - Flash Gordon
      - Prince Valiant (Hal Foster)
      - Flash Gordon (Alex Raymond)
    - Brenda Starr
      - Brenda Starr (Dale Messick)
      - Dennis the Menace (Hank Ketchum)
  - Terry and the Pirates
    - Dick Tracy
      - Tarzan (Hal Foster and others)
      - Dick Tracy (Chester Gould)
    - Terry and the Pirates
      - Terry and the Pirates (Milton Caniff)
      - Little Nemo in Slumberland (Winsor McCay)

# High School Movies

**By Rick Staehling**

Rick Staehling is the Canadian Broadcasting Corporation's film critic in British Columbia. His first published article, "The Truth About Teen Movies," appeared in *Rolling Stone* 40 years ago this year.

*Rebel Without a Cause* (1955)
*Love Finds Andy Hardy* (1938)
*High School Confidential* (1958)
*The Outsiders* (1983)
*Bye Bye Birdie* (1963)
*Grease* (1978)
*Rock 'n' Roll High School* (1979)
*High School Musical 3: Senior Year* (2008)
*Fast Times at Ridgemont High* (1982)
*Clueless* (1995)
*Superbad* (2007)
*American Pie* (1999)
*American Graffiti* (1973)
*Dazed and Confused* (1993)
*The Virgin Suicides* (1999)
*Ghost World* (2001)

*Rebel*
*Outsiders*
*Grease*
*Rock 'n' Roll High*
*Fast Times*
*Superbad*
*Dazed*
*Ghost World*

*Rebel*
*Grease*
*Fast Times*
*Dazed*

*Rebel*
*Fast Times*

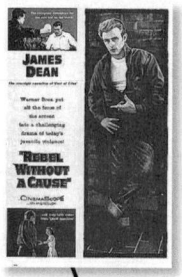


***Rebel* vs. *Grease***
Two views of the '50s with *Rebel* the winner. The bullet points are all here: knife fight and hot-rod chicken-run; planetarium and red jacket; the doomed, tender triangle of James Dean, Natalie Wood, and Sal Mineo. The big stuff too: dated yet eerily timeless, *Rebel* – like *Bigger Than Life*, director Nicholas Ray's other luxe mid-century melodrama – reveals new truths with the passage of time.

***Rock 'n' Roll High School* vs. *High School Musical 3: Senior Year***
High marks to Disney for an energetic musical, more teen-pleasing and genuine than the ironic, hipster-filled (Paul Bartel, Mary Woronov, Darby Crash) "parody" from Roger Corman sweat-shoppers Alan Arkush and Joe Dante. But music (12 songs from The Ramones, including the original title tune) still matters. *Rock 'n' Roll* rules.

THE WINNER

## *Fast Times at Ridgemon High* (1982)

***Fast Times* vs. *Dazed***
Rather than flip a coin to settle this contentious bracket battle we defer to the grown-ups, namely Ray Walston: history teacher, sarcastic disciplinarian and Platt Amendment expert. Both films are loaded with stars-to-be and uncanny re-creations of period and place. But only *Fast Times* has Walston's Mr. Hand.

HIGH SCHOOL MOVIES, like first loves, summer songs, and out-of-business liquor stores, are potent reminders of our youth. They are also generational signifiers, as anyone who has witnessed unseemly arguments over the relative merits of *American Graffiti* and *Dazed and Confused* can attest. But unless you're like Matthew McConaughey's 22-year-old drivers' license bureau worker in *Dazed,* you eventually move on. Which is what we've done here: looking at 70 years of this enduring genre and making the calls based on merit, not personal memories.

***erris Bueller's Day Off* vs. *Risky Business***
ughes and Cruise. The director and actor who defined this genre's olden decade, examine the upper-class Chicago teen. In both films chool is skipped, show-stopping tunes lip-synched, and an absentee ad's sports car totaled, suggesting that with privilege comes peer and arental pressure. Hooker-free *Bueller* takes a close one.

***ast Times* vs. *Rushmore***
*ast Times* isn't perfect. The omic timing is sketchy. Some f the music stinks. But it's m-packed with eager-to-lease talent (Sean Penn, ennifer Jason Leigh, Phoebe ates, Judge Reinhold, Forest hitaker, Eric Stolz, Anthony dwards) and written with enre-transcending savvy y a 22-year-old Cameron rowe. It has it all. Sex, drugs, ull teachers, dead-end jobs. ost wallets, wrecked cars. bortion. Racism. The Platt mendment. It is exhilarating, ainfully funny, and simply ainful. Just like high school.

**Rushmore**

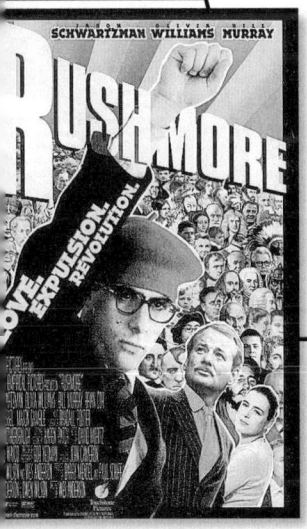


***Napoleon Dynamite* vs. *Elephant***
Sundance and Cannes. Artless and artful. A new century dawns and the school halls of Indiefilm, USA, are filled with *Dynamite's* time-warped losers and *Elephant's* Columbine-like losses. Both films are formally cool and emotionally earnest but here, at least, tragedy trumps comedy.

- **Rushmore**
  - **Elephant**
    - **Napoleon Dynamite**
      - *Napoleon Dynamite* (2004)
      - *Welcome to the Dollhouse* (1995)
    - **Rushmore**
      - *Rushmore* (1998)
      - *Dead Poets Society* (1989)
  - **Breakfast Club**
    - **Heathers**
      - **Elephant**
        - *Elephant* (2003)
        - *Boyz n the Hood* (1991)
      - **Heathers**
        - *Heathers* (1988)
        - *Mean Girls* (2004)
    - **Breakfast Club**
      - **Carrie**
        - *Carrie* (1976)
        - *Lucas* (1986)
      - **Breakfast Club**
        - *The Breakfast Club* (1985)
        - *Pretty in Pink* (1986)
      - **Ferris Bueller**
        - *Ferris Bueller's Day Off* (1986)
        - *Risky Business* (1983)
    - **Back to the Future**
      - *Back to the Future* (1985)
      - *Peggy Sue Got Married* (1986)

***Heathers* vs. *Mean Girls***
With the much cheerier *Clueless* ousted, the battle of the high school bitches tilts between *Heathers* (blunt, nasty) and *Mean Girls* (smart but toothless). One is a ragged quickie from the New World exploitation factory, the other a smoothly successful brand extension of *Saturday Night Live.* See you at the drive-in.

***The Breakfast Club* vs. *Rushmore***
An uncomfortable pairing of two films that nail the self-absorption of adolescence in all its heartbreaking and insufferable glory. *Rushmore,* the screwball story of a prep-school outcast too eager to grow up, is a movie about being a kid for adults. *Club,* with its stage-play structure and group-therapy student stereotypes, acts old but is strictly teen bait. *Rushmore* advances.

# Stunt Scenes
## (or Greatest Gags)

**By Kevin Conley**

Kevin Conley has written two books, the latest being *The Full Burn: On the Set, At the Bar, Behind the Wheel, and Over the Edge with Hollywood Stuntmen,* duri the course of which his interview subjects were kind enough to set him on fire.

- *The Keystone Kops* (body of work)
- Buster Keaton's sight gag with the two-ton house falling around him in *Steamboat Bill, Jr.*

**Steamboat Bill, Jr.**

- Pearl White and Polly Burson's stuntwork in *Perils of Pauline*
- Harold Lloyd dangling from a clock in *Safety Last*

**Safety Last**

**Steamboat Bill, Jr.**

- Yakima Cannutt's stagecoach gag in *Stagecoach*
- Errol Flynn's stunt double in *The Adventures of Robin Hood*

**Stagecoach**

- Chuck Roberson doubling John Wayne in *True Grit*
- Jeannie Epper doubles lead in *The Adventures of Wonder Woman*

**The Adventures of Wonder Woman**

**Stagecoach**

**Stagecoach**

- The chariot race in *Ben-Hur*
- Ronnie Rondell's high fall in *Kings of the Sun*

**Ben-Hur**

- The gunfight in *How the West Was Won*
- Flyboy aerial stunts in *The Skywayman*

**The Skywayman**

**Ben-Hur**

**Ben-Hur**

***How the West Was Won* vs. *The Skywayman***

Two gags gone epically wrong. During a gunfight on a train in *West,* stuntman Bob Morgan was hiding behind logs on a boxcar when the chain holding them broke and the loose tree trunks crushed his legs. In *Skywayman,* the flyboy Lt. Ormer Locklear failed to pull his plane out of a death spiral filmed at night and crashed to earth.

**THE WINNER**

**Stagecoac**

**VS**

- High fall out of car and over waterfall in *Romancing the Stone*
- The tank work in *The Poseidon Adventure*

**Romancing the Stone**

- The 232-foot fall from a helicopter in *Hooper*
- Terry Leonard re-creates the *Stagecoach* gag for *Raiders of the Lost Ark*

**Raiders of the Lost Ark**

**Raiders of the Lost Ark**

***Stagecoach* vs. *xXx***

Both finalists offered terrifying stunts with no trick photography, but Rigby made the mistake of making it all look easy. In *Stagecoach,* Canutt made the gag look both dangerous and out of control. Credited with inventing stunt coordination, he performed three famous gags in *Stagecoach* in one scene: he jumped from a horse onto the yoke of a stagecoach, then fell between the horses, slid under the stagecoach, then climbed back on, and up the other side. But he pulled it off with style – providing an adrenaline surge for viewers long after the sound of the hoof beats faded away.

HOLLYWOOD STUNTMEN refer to their feats as gags, a leftover from Keystone Kop days. A chase scene is a car gag; getting engulfed in flame is a fire gag; sliding beneath and between a stagecoach team moving at 35 miles an hour is a horse gag. Fame isn't a primary motivation for such derring-do. Stuntmen are contractually anonymous, and, what's worse, their greatest achievements often wind up in box-office losers. Determining the greatest stunts is left to stuntmen themselves, who know exactly what goes into their rough brand of movie magic. This tourney distills their shoptalk on the set.

***Matrix Reloaded* vs. *The Bourne Supremacy***
The *Bourne* sequence is more exciting. But Debbie Evans, the greatest stuntwoman and one of the best drivers, takes this for her extended race, against traffic, on a motorcycle at up to 90 miles an hour. Her achievements were overlooked because viewers assumed that her impossible feats were CGI. Emphatically untrue: during the shoot, she was hit by a car and nearly broke her ankle but still nailed the maneuvers on every take through weeks of shooting.

***xXx***

***The French Connection* vs. *The Bourne Supremacy***
This battle between two car chases pits one sequence whose value lay more in the acting (Gene Hackman as Popeye Doyle, slamming his fist against the dashboard) against another where behind-the-scenes technical innovations (by the GoStunts crew, which specializes in a dizzying array of high-speed camera cars) changed forever the way chases would be filmed. *Bourne* wins, in a slam-bang finish.

***The Dukes of Hazzard* vs. *xXx***
*Dukes* meets a just demise. Tim Rigby's extreme gag in *xXx* – he climbs out of the back of a Corvette as it flies off a bridge, then base-jumps 700 feet to safety down a California ravine – is a brass-balls classic hidden in a cursed movie (another stuntman died on the second take of a stunt in Prague). And it's all real, not CGI.

***300* vs. *The Dukes of Hazzard***
What appears to be a face-off between two genres – TV vs. computer-generated imagery or CGI – is actually a battle of money and contracts: the steady paychecks from the residuals that stuntmen get for the rebroadcast of old TV gags, against the uncompensated use of talent in a CGI-fest (one stuntman in a motion-capture suit can reappear on film as a combat horde of *300*). *300* may be the more satisfying entertainment, but *Dukes*, an atrocious show with often half-ass stunts, paid full weight – and wins.

- *Matrix Reloaded*
  - *Matrix Reloaded*
    - Debbie Evans's motorcycle chase, against traffic, in *Matrix Reloaded*
    - Zoe Bell's high-speed chase, hooked to car's hood, in *Grindhouse*
  - *The Italian Job*
    - The 18-wheeler skiing on two wheels in *Live Free or Die Hard*
    - The Mini-Cooper chase in *The Italian Job* (2003 version)
- *The Bourne Supremacy*
  - *The French Connection*
    - Steve McQueen's car chase in *Bullitt*
    - The car chase in *The French Connection*
  - *The Bourne Supremacy*
    - The car chases in *Ronin*
    - The Moscow car chase in *The Bourne Supremacy*
- *xXx*
  - *300*
    - The fight scenes in *300*
    - The ocean rescue in *The Perfect Storm*
  - *The Dukes of Hazzard*
    - Incessant car jumps of *The Dukes of Hazzard* (TV version, 1979-85)
    - Weekly shootouts and bar fights in *Gunsmoke* (TV, 1955-75)
  - *xXx*
    - Tim Rigby base-jumps out of flying Corvette in *xXx*
    - *Beastmaster*
  - *Fists of Fury*
    - The bare-knuckle fighting in *Fight Club*
    - Bruce Lee's karate sequences in *Fists of Fury*

# Impressionists

**By Richard Sandomir**

Richard Sandomir, the co-editor of this book, scares people with his Truman Capote impression.

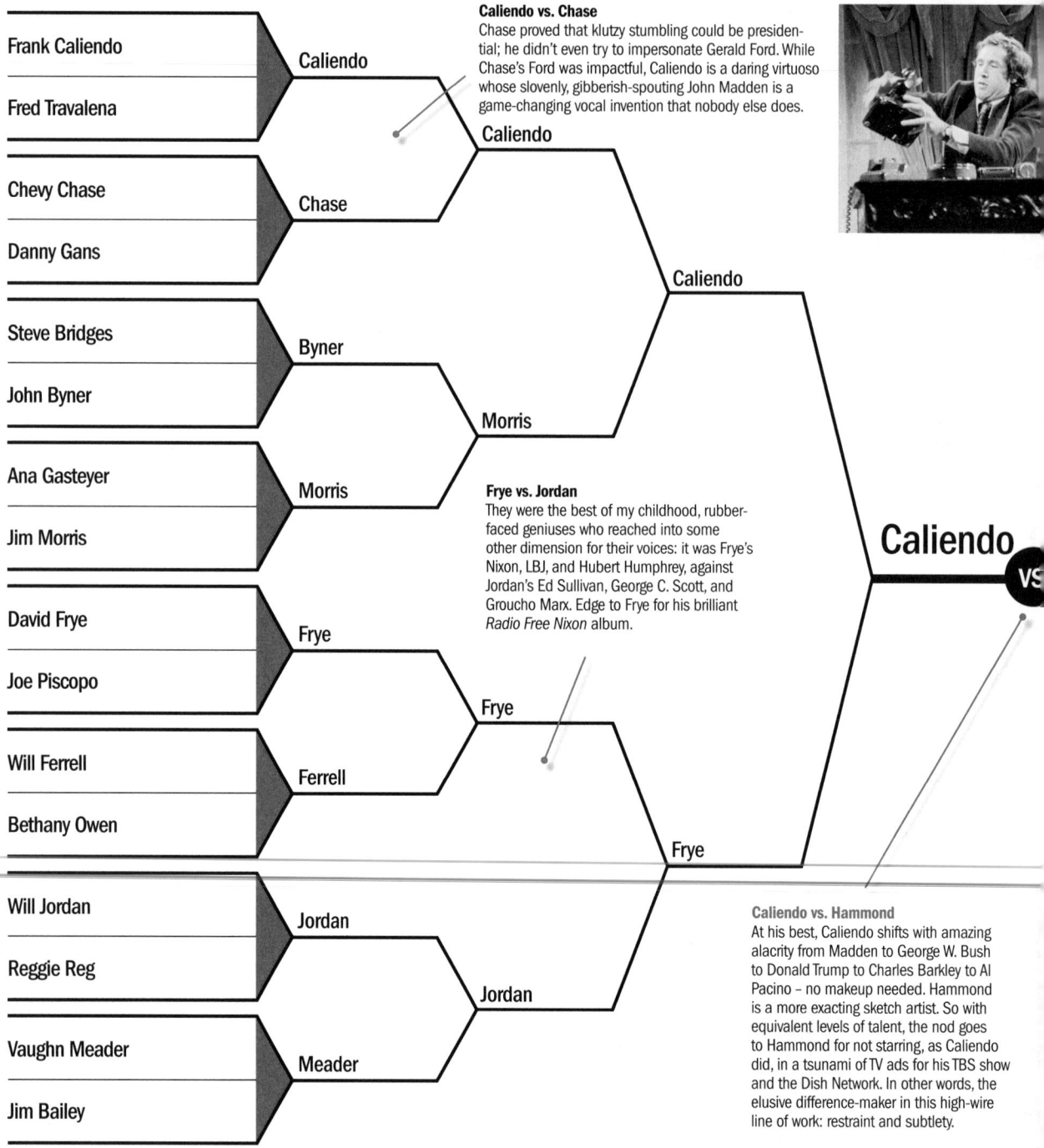


**Caliendo vs. Chase**
Chase proved that klutzy stumbling could be presidential; he didn't even try to impersonate Gerald Ford. While Chase's Ford was impactful, Caliendo is a daring virtuoso whose slovenly, gibberish-spouting John Madden is a game-changing vocal invention that nobody else does.

**Frye vs. Jordan**
They were the best of my childhood, rubber-faced geniuses who reached into some other dimension for their voices: it was Frye's Nixon, LBJ, and Hubert Humphrey, against Jordan's Ed Sullivan, George C. Scott, and Groucho Marx. Edge to Frye for his brilliant *Radio Free Nixon* album.

**Caliendo vs. Hammond**
At his best, Caliendo shifts with amazing alacrity from Madden to George W. Bush to Donald Trump to Charles Barkley to Al Pacino – no makeup needed. Hammond is a more exacting sketch artist. So with equivalent levels of talent, the nod goes to Hammond for not starring, as Caliendo did, in a tsunami of TV ads for his TBS show and the Dish Network. In other words, the elusive difference-maker in this high-wire line of work: restraint and subtlety.

I'VE BEEN DOING IMPRESSIONS SINCE I WAS A KID, starting with Frank Fontaine's Crazy Guggenheim from *The Jackie Gleason Show* and building to Ed Sullivan (my version of John Byner's) and Richard Nixon (a knockoff of David Frye's). I'm fascinated by the triggers that mimics find to capture a voice, such as Frank Caliendo developing his Charles Barkley around the Round Mound of Rebound's pronunciation of "terrible." Everyone here is talented but the edge goes to verbal skill coupled with great material, which a great mimic like Rich Little (a Canadian, thus not invited) has never had.

**Michaels vs. Fey**
If versatility were mimicry's sole measure, then Michaels would win. But Fey's Sarah Palin defined the zeitgeist of a misbegotten vice-presidential campaign and exposed how unprepared the governor of Alaska would have been behind a 72-year-old president.

THE WINNER

# Darrell Hammond

**Carvey vs. Hammond**
Carvey brought a genteel savagery to George H.W. Bush ("On track . . . stay the course . . . a thousand points of light") and Ross Perot, but he's more a comic actor than full-time mimic. Hammond brought President Clinton, Al Gore, Dick Cheney, John McCain, Al Sharpton, Ted Koppel, and Sean Connery into vivid second lives.

- Carvey
  - Carvey
    - Carvey
      - Dana Carvey
      - Mike McRae
    - Gorshin
      - Eddie Murphy
      - Frank Gorshin
  - Fey
    - Fey
      - Tina Fey
      - Marilyn Michaels
    - Spacey
      - Kevin Spacey
      - Dan Aykroyd
- Hammond
  - Hammond
    - Hammond
      - Darrell Hammond
      - Robin Williams
    - Kirby
      - George Kirby
      - Roy Firestone
  - Hartman
    - Hartman
      - Phil Hartman
      - Billy Crystal
    - Magnotti
      - Rob Magnotti
      - Joe Alaskey

# Literary Heroes

**By B.R. Myers**

B.R. Myers is a contributing editor of *The Atlantic* and the author of *A Reader's Manifesto.*

**Tom Sawyer** *(The Adventures of Tom Sawyer)* vs. **Huck Finn** *(Adventures of Huckleberry Finn)* → **Huck**

**Jo March** *(Little Women)* vs. **Fern** *(Charlotte's Web)* → **Fern**

**Philip Marlowe** *(The Big Sleep)* vs. **Sam Spade** *(The Maltese Falcon)* → **Marlowe**

**Jay Gatsby** *(The Great Gatsby)* vs. **Binx Bollings** *(The Moviegoer)* → **Gatsby**

**Robert E. Lee Prewitt** *(From Here to Eternity)* vs. **Sergeant Croft** *(The Naked and the Dead)* → **Prewitt**

**Ignatius J. Reilly** *(Confederacy of Dunces)* vs. **Garp** *(The World According to Garp)* → **Reilly**

**Carol Milford** *(Main Street)* vs. **Hester Prynne** *(The Scarlet Letter)* → **Carol**

**Tom Joad** *(The Grapes of Wrath)* vs. **Per Hansa** *(Giants in the Earth)* → **Joad**

**Huck** vs. **Fern** → **Huck**

**Marlowe** vs. **Gatsby** → **Marlowe**

**Prewitt** vs. **Reilly** → **Prewitt**

**Carol** vs. **Joad** → **Joad**

**Huck** vs. **Marlowe** → **Huck**

**Prewitt** vs. **Joad** → **Prewitt**

**Huck** vs. **Prewitt** → **THE WINNER**

**Robert E. Lee Prewitt** *(From Here to Eternity)*

**Fern vs. Jo March**
"Hero" was originally Greek for "protector," which is to say that this tomboy grudge match goes to Miss Arable. Wrestling a man with an axe, arguing boldly for animal rights, saving a life – and all this quite literally before breakfast. As a spider might put it, that's some girl.

**Marlowe vs. Gatsby**
Gatsby's charisma and glamour so captivate us that the details of his sordid past never quite sink in. Chandler's sardonic gumshoe would have seen through him right away. It's too bad Marlowe doesn't get to investigate the West Egg shooting: he would have riffed memorably on the trappings of the bootlegger's wealth. Starting with those shirts.

**Tom Joad vs. Per Hansa**
Whenever they's beating on a guy, Tom'll be there. He'll also be in the next round. Per's the man you'd want on your own farm, and his Nordic taciturnity makes a nice change. (Our fictional heroes tend to go on a bit.) But stealing land from fellow settlers? Tom would have died first.

WOULD WE BE AS INTERESTED IN OUR LITERARY HEROES if they were real people? Take all those existential Everymen with their midlife crises and ridiculous names: we wouldn't cross the road to say hello, let alone emulate them. Literary purists may be outraged, but it's time to separate the protagonists from the heroes – using the latter word in its popular sense. Entrants hail from fiction of established literary standard or fame, but now they're on their own. To advance you need heroic qualities, with points subtracted for things like murder and rudeness.

**Prewitt vs. McMurphy**
Alas, a second-rate film has supplanted Jones's first-rate novel from our consciousness, so that Americans now think of Prewitt, the soldier who refuses to box, as a minor figure, if they recognize the name at all. And yet the bugler's brave defense of his private code of ethics is one of the most stirring tales in modern fiction. "That's my right as a man," he says. "To not be kicked around." Spoken like a true hero.

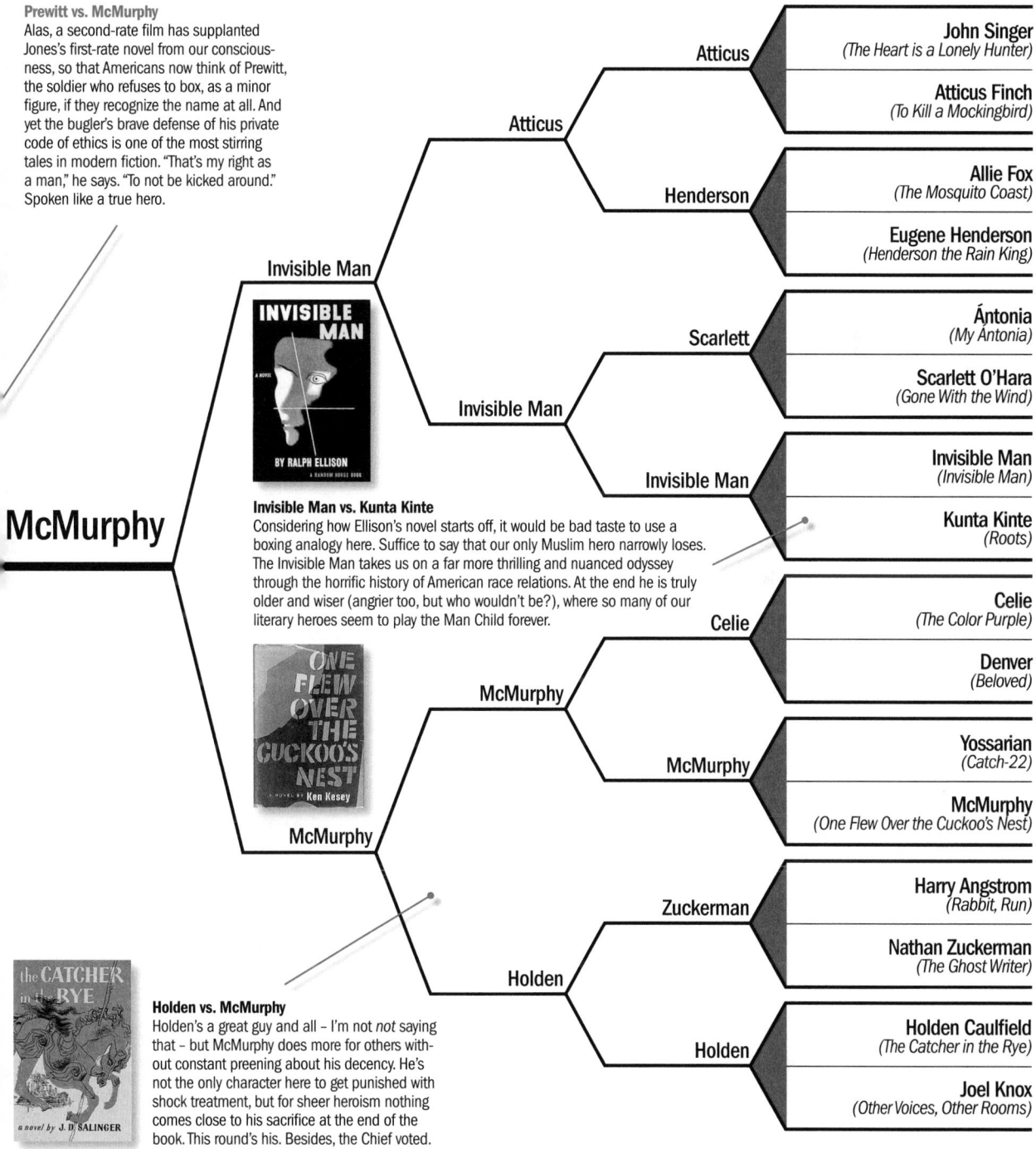


**Invisible Man vs. Kunta Kinte**
Considering how Ellison's novel starts off, it would be bad taste to use a boxing analogy here. Suffice to say that our only Muslim hero narrowly loses. The Invisible Man takes us on a far more thrilling and nuanced odyssey through the horrific history of American race relations. At the end he is truly older and wiser (angrier too, but who wouldn't be?), where so many of our literary heroes seem to play the Man Child forever.

**Holden vs. McMurphy**
Holden's a great guy and all – I'm not *not* saying that – but McMurphy does more for others without constant preening about his decency. He's not the only character here to get punished with shock treatment, but for sheer heroism nothing comes close to his sacrifice at the end of the book. This round's his. Besides, the Chief voted.

# Comedy Routines

**By Bill Scheft**

Bill Scheft, a longtime writer for David Letterman, is the author of three novels, including *Everything Hurts*. Once a house MC at Catch a Rising Star in New York, he is not bitter about the less talented acts who wound up with bigger careers. Don't even go there.

POST-1980 REGIONAL

**Rob Bartlett**
"Pope at Yankee Stadium"

**Jeff Foxworthy**
"You Might Be a Redneck"

**Larry David**
"The Masturbator"

**Sam Kinison**
"World Hunger"

**Roseanne**
"Domestic Goddess"

**Jerry Seinfeld**
"That's Incredible/Bob Hughes"

**Bill Hicks**
"Smoking"

**Ray Romano**
"Twins"

**Chris Rock**
"Niggas vs. Black People"

**Larry Miller**
"Five Levels of Drinking"

**Richard Jeni**
"Jaws 2"

**Ron White**
"Drunk in Public"

**Bill Maher**
"New Rules"

**Lewis Black**
"Speaking before the President"

**Jackie Mason**
"Jews vs. Gentiles"

**Tim Allen**
"Men Are Pigs"

Foxworthy
Kinison
Roseanne
Hicks
Rock
Jeni
Black
Mason

Foxworthy
Hicks
Rock
Black

Foxworthy
Rock

THE WINNER

**Jeff Foxworthy,**
"You Might Be a Redneck"

VS

**Rock vs. Jeni**
If not for the regionals separating the generations, Rock, the student, might have out-schooled Pryor, the teacher. When I first saw Chris, he was a jeri-curled 18-year-old spouting, "I just came back from Johannesburg . . . or was it Boston?" Ten years later, this black-on-black tour de force was the harvest of that riotous self-examination.

THERE ARE TWO TYPES OF JOKES: The first makes you say, "Why didn't I think of that?" The second makes you say, "In a million years, I couldn't come up with that." Welcome to 32 people writing nothing but the second type. I know, I know. Many are missing but I limited the field to first-hand knowledge of self-contained bits by comics, which meant no line guys, non-sequitarians, or topical monologists. Regrets to, among others, Mitch Hedberg, Dave Atell, Steven Wright, Mort Sahl, Robin, Jon, Johnny, Joan. And um, Dave, I'll have my desk cleared out Monday.

# Richard Pryor

**Pryor vs. Bruce**
Pryor glides by Rodney with relentless physicality and relevance, hops over Newhart, and outlasts Bruce at the buzzer by staying on stage using the same words Lenny got jailed for.

**Foxworthy vs. Pryor**
Upset? Only to those who overlook craft and appeal. Myth-expanding and cracker-barrel hip ("The primary color of your car is bondo . . ." or "You refer to the fifth grade as 'my senior year.'"), the former IBM worker built a cottage-industrial complex on this sturdiest of mainframes. The accessibility of this material and the guy delivering it are undeniable. So we won't.

**Carlin vs. Bruce**
Carlin was the Jackie Robinson of the language barrier but he doesn't cross the line without the fieldwork done by Bruce, whose routine is the Rosetta Stone of modern stand-up. "Palladium" finds a hack comic bombing in the biggest room; it is a set-piece comet hurtling with all of Lenny's gifts of mimicry, satire, and hypocrisy-hunting.

**Newhart vs. Allen**
If possible, "Submarine Commander" is better than Newhart's telephone pieces, if for no other reason than that it contains the world's greatest segue, "Looking back on the mutiny . . ."

- Pryor
  - Pryor
    - Pryor
      - Richard Pryor — "Black and White Lifestyles"
      - Tim Thomerson — "Stagecoach"
    - Dangerfield
      - Robert Klein — "FM DJ"
      - Rodney Dangerfield — "No Respect"
  - Newhart
    - Newhart
      - Bob Newhart — "Submarine Commander"
      - Woody Allen — "The Moose"
    - Cosby
      - Bill Cosby — "My Brother, Russell"
      - Betty Walker — "Hello, Ceil"
- Bruce
  - Carlin
    - Carlin
      - George Carlin — "Seven Words"
      - Mal Z. Lawrence — "Catskills Clientele"
    - Winters
      - Jonathan Winters — "Flying Saucer"
      - Steve Martin — "Excuse Me"
  - Bruce
    - Brooks
      - Albert Brooks — "Rewriting National Anthem"
      - Totie Fields — "Buying a Dress"
    - Bruce
      - Lenny Bruce — "Palladium"
      - Bill Dana — "The Astronaut"

PRE-1980 REGIONAL

# Worst Movies by Great Directors

**By A.O. Scott**
A.O. Scott is a film critic at the *New York Times.*

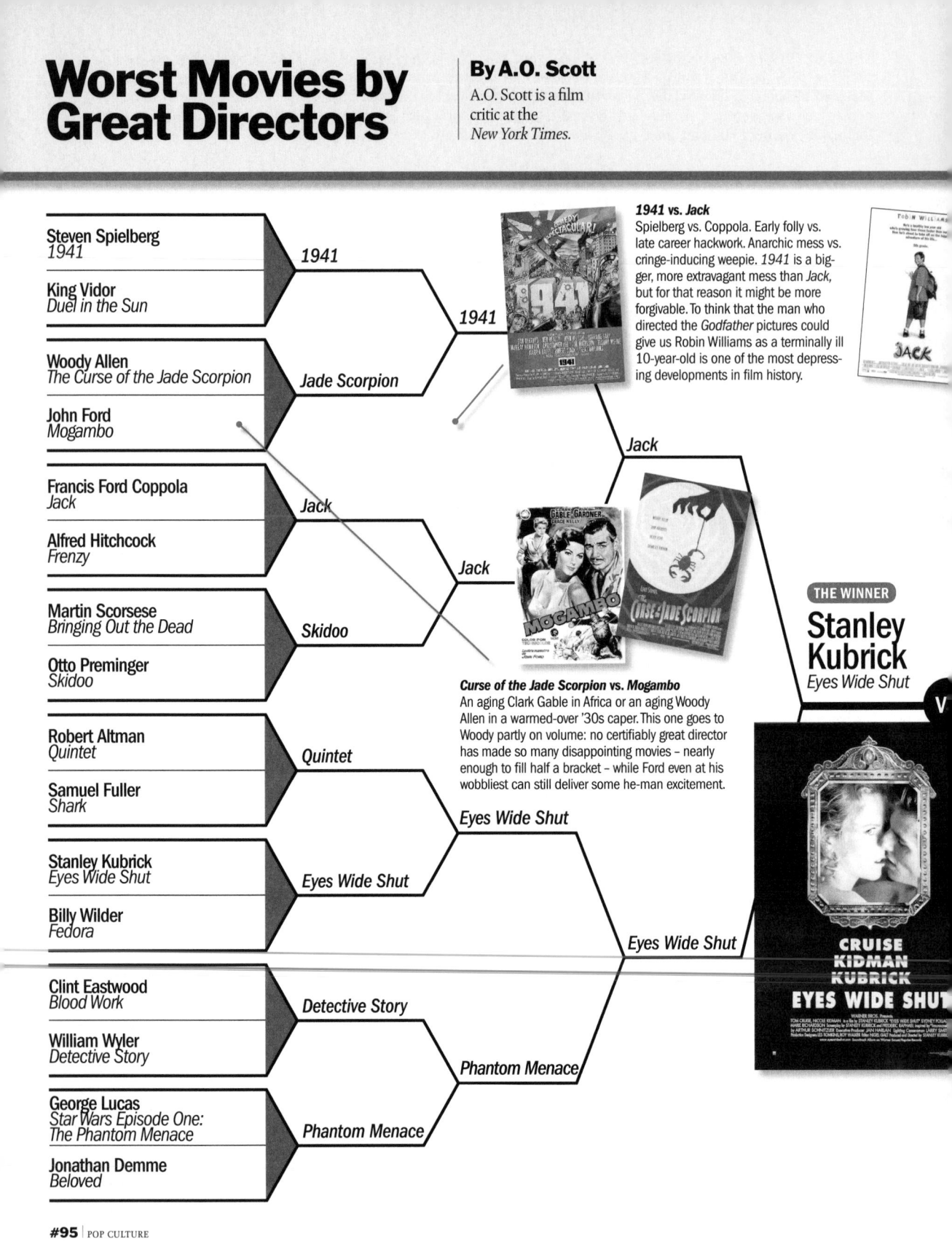


***1941* vs. *Jack***
Spielberg vs. Coppola. Early folly vs. late career hackwork. Anarchic mess vs. cringe-inducing weepie. *1941* is a bigger, more extravagant mess than *Jack*, but for that reason it might be more forgivable. To think that the man who directed the *Godfather* pictures could give us Robin Williams as a terminally ill 10-year-old is one of the most depressing developments in film history.

***Curse of the Jade Scorpion* vs. *Mogambo***
An aging Clark Gable in Africa or an aging Woody Allen in a warmed-over '30s caper. This one goes to Woody partly on volume: no certifiably great director has made so many disappointing movies – nearly enough to fill half a bracket – while Ford even at his wobbliest can still deliver some he-man excitement.

NOBODY SETS OUT TO MAKE A BAD MOVIE, and an old adage holds that a stinker is just as hard to produce as a masterpiece. But amid the heap of bombs, turkeys, and dogs that Hollywood has churned out, a special place is reserved for the failures of artists who should have known better. A Qualitative Inversion Formula™ is applied to the pictures below, whereby what is rewarded is not just the raw awfulness of a given movie, but also the gap between its putrescence and the awesomeness of its director's grandest accomplishments.

***Eyes Wide Shut* vs. *Alexander***
Stone will tell you that his movie should have been a masterpiece. Kubrick's passionate devotees insist that his last film really is one. And to be truly the worst, as opposed to merely bad, a film must have at least a kernel of greatness in it. Not even Stone's most hallucinatory sequences in Persia or India can match the preposterous solemnity of that masked ball orgy out on Long Island.

***Sandpiper* vs. *Time to Love***
Preminger, his era's prestige director, might have been able to improve upon Sirk's labored direction (of an epic romance about a handsome, decent Nazi soldier, played by John Gavin), but he was saving his worst for Richard Burton and Elizabeth Taylor, who were saving their worst (which is saying something) for him. Liz and Dick beat the nice Nazi by a nose.

***Alexander* vs. *Samson***
The ancient world, rendered in color and on a wide screen, accounts for some of the most dreadful movies ever. *Samson*, an overripe, late-period DeMille extravaganza, with Victor Mature and Hedy Lamarr, was a big hit, and retains a certain maniacal charm. But in spite of an inert lead performance by Colin Farrell, *Alexander* advances on a sheer craziness embodied by Angelina Jolie as the emperor's snake-fetishizing, Slavic-accented mama.

- **Alexander**
  - *Sandpiper*
    - *Let's Make Love*
      - *King of Kings*
        - **Sidney Lumet** *The Wiz*
        - **Nicholas Ray** *King of Kings*
      - *Let's Make Love*
        - **Spike Lee** *Sucker-Free City*
        - **George Cukor** *Let's Make Love*
    - *Sandpiper*
      - *Sandpiper*
        - **Gus Van Sant** *Finding Forrester*
        - **Vincente Minnelli** *The Sandpiper*
      - *Time to Love*
        - **Steven Soderbergh** *Full Frontal*
        - **Douglas Sirk** *A Time to Love and a Time to Die*
  - *Samson*
    - *Samson*
      - *Samson*
        - **Roman Polanski** *Bitter Moon*
        - **Cecil B. DeMille** *Samson and Delilah*
      - *The Ladykillers*
        - **Joel and Ethan Coen** *The Ladykillers*
        - **Paul Schrader** *The Walker*
    - *Alexander*
      - *Dune*
        - **David Lynch** *Dune*
        - **Raoul Walsh** *The Naked and the Dead*
      - *Alexander*
        - **Sam Peckinpah** *The Osterman Weekend*
        - **Oliver Stone** *Alexander*

# George Carlin Hunks

**By Kelly Carlin-McCall**

Kelly Carlin-McCall writes for *Fresh Yarn* and the *Huffington Post*. Oh, and she is George's daughter.

**Seven Words You Can't Say on Television:** "Shitpissfuckcuntcocksuckermotherfuckerandtits" *Class Clown, 1972*

**The Prayer:** "Our father who art in heaven . . ." *Carlin on Campus, 1984*

**Baseball and Football:** "Baseball is pastoral; football is technological." *Carlin on Campus, 1984*

**Childhood Clichés:** "Well, It just didn't get up and walk away, did it?" *Occupation: Foole, 1973*

**Free-Floating Hostility:** "Bad hair day? Put on a hat and go to work." *Back in Town, 1996*

**Euphemisms:** "Gourmet means, 'We're going to charge you more.'" *Doin' It Again, 1990*

**Airline Announcements:** "Get on the plane? Let Evel Knievel get on the plane." *Jammin in NY, 1992*

**People I Can Do Without:** "A cross-eyed nun with a bullwhip and a bottle of gin." *What Am I Doing in NJ?, 1988*

**Having to Fart in Public:** "A fart that could end a marriage." *Back in Town, 1996*

**Hair Poem:** "Fred Astaire got no hair, nor does a chair, nor a chocolate éclair." *FM & AM, 1971*

**Little Things We Share:** "Didja ever notice how all day Wednesday you think it's Thursday?" *Jammin in NY, 1992*

**Losing Things:** "First thing when you get to heaven, they give back everything you lost." *Playin' with Your Head, 1986*

**Modern Man:** "I know the upside of downsizing and the downside of upgrading." *Life Is Worth Losing, 2006*

**Why We Don't Need the Ten Commandments:** "The first three, pure bullshit." *Complaints and Grievances, 2001*

**Advertising Lullaby:** "Free admission, free delivery, free estimates, free parking." *You Are All Diseased, 1999*

**Let's Make a Deal:** "Monty, Monty! . . . Door number one-three-two-wait!" *FM & AM, 1971*

Seven words

Baseball and football

Euphemisms

Airline announcements

Farting in public

Little things we share

Modern man

Advertising lullaby

Seven words

Euphemisms

Farting in public

Modern man

Seven words

Seven words

Modern man

**Seven words vs. Rockets and penises**
Carlin became famous for the seven dirty words, and they changed American culture by being spoken in the U.S. Supreme Court in *FCC vs. Pacifica*. But "Rockets and Penises" is masterful. You are watching an artist at full command of his tools – language, performance, and most of all, truth.

**Farting in public vs. Little things we share**
File both hunks under Universal Comedy – a category Carlin invented. "Little Things We Share" asked the question, "D'ja ever notice how awful your face looks in a mirror in a restroom that has fluorescent lights? Every cut, scrape, scratch, scar, scab, bruise, boil, bump, pimple, zit, wart, welt, and abscess you've had since birth, all seem to come back at the same time." But fart jokes tested his love of metaphor: "A fart that could strip the varnish off a foot locker."

**Modern man vs. Advertising lullaby**
Dad was always writing things down to use in routines later. Both of these hunks reveal his discipline and commitment to his craft, and his skill for turning everyday language into poetry. "Modern Man" wins because it is 3:33 of nonstop insight throwing our words back at us. "I'm an alpha male on beta blockers . . . I have a love child who sends me hate mail." Comics are in awe of this hunk.

**Seven words**

**VS**

UNTIL HIS DEATH AT 71 IN 2008, comedian George Carlin enjoyed a legendary performing career. But he also had a prolific "recording" career, from LPs to CDs to the DVDs of his 14 HBO specials. That's where his routines, which he called "hunks," are gathered for posterity as 10:51 or 6:54 of genius. The 32 hunks here cover five decades of biting social criticism, wordplay, and insight about small moments of human interaction. His body aged (whose doesn't?), but his body of work will not.

THE WINNER

## Rockets and Penises in the Persian Gulf

"The Persian Gulf was othin' more than a prick-waving dick fight."
*Jammin in NY, 1992*

- **Rockets and penises**
  - **A place for my stuff**
    - **A place for my stuff**
      - **A Place for My Stuff:** "Their stuff is shit, your shit is stuff." *A Place for My Stuff, 1980*
      - **Icebox Man:** "Could be meat. Could be cake. Looks like Meatcake!" *Carlin at Carnegie, 1982*
    - **Hippie Dippie Weatherman**
      - **Al Sleet, Hippie Dippie Weatherman:** "Tonight's forecast, dark." *FM & AM, 1971*
      - **Indian Sergeant:** "Tall guys over by the trees. Fat guys down behind the rocks." *Take-Offs and Put-Ons, 1966*
  - **Rockets and penises**
    - **Rockets and penises**
      - **Muhammad Ali:** "If you won't kill 'em, we won't let you beat 'em up." *Class Clown, 1972*
      - **Rockets and Penises in the Persian Gulf:** "Nothin' more than a prick-waving dick fight." *Jammin in NY, 1992*
    - **Dogs and cats**
      - **Cars:** "Have you noticed that anybody driving slower than you is an idiot?" *Carlin on Campus, 1984*
      - **Dogs and Cats:** "Fuckin' Meow!" *Carlin at Carnegie, 1982*
- **The planet is fine**
  - **Religion is bullshit**
    - **Death and dying**
      - **Squeamish:** "One time Michael Davy passed an entire cheese sandwich through his nose." *Class Clown, 1972*
      - **Death and Dying:** "Now, first of all, there is no up there." *It's All Bad for Ya, 2008*
    - **Religion is bullshit**
      - **Religion Is Bullshit:** "But he loves you, and he needs money!" *Life Is Worth Losing, 2005*
      - **Abortion:** "How come when it's us, it's an abortion, and when it's a chicken, it's an omelet?" *Back in Town, 1996*
  - **The planet is fine**
    - **The planet is fine**
      - **The Planet Is Fine:** "The planet will shake us off like a bad case of fleas." *Jammin in NY, 1992*
      - **Fuck the Children:** "All you hear is help the children. You know what I say – fuck the children." *You Are All Diseased, 2004*
    - **Keeping people alert**
      - **Keeping People Alert:** "Didja ever try backing out of a drive-through bank?" *What Am I Doing in New Jersey?, 1988*
      - **I Wonder:** "I wonder why there is no blue food?" *HBO in Phoenix, 1978*

**Death and dying vs. Religion is bullshit**
Carlin takes on the big subjects. "Religion Is Bullshit" is breathtaking, employing crisp logic to assess our silly acceptance of "the man up in the sky with a beard," and how he will send us to hell for eternity, "but he loves us, and he needs money." "Death and Dying" is poignant because it's from his last HBO show shot three months before he died. He harangues us for relying on our dead parents to "watch over us" while they are "up there." Sorry, Dad. Guilty as charged.

**Fuck the children vs. The planet is fine**
Two hunks that made us squirm in our seats. In "The Planet is Fine" he lets us humans have it with, "Pack your bags, folks, we're going away." In "Fuck the Children," he questions why our love of our children is so sacrosanct. Prickly stuff, but we laugh. Planet wins here because he even manages to piss off environmentalists.

# Cop Movies

**By Lorenzo Carcaterra**

Lorenzo Carcaterra is the author of *Sleepers* and *Apaches*, as well as a writer for *Law & Order*.

*The French Connection* (1971)
*The Taking of Pelham One Two Three* (1974)
→ *The French Connection*

*The Seven-Ups* (1973)
*To Live and Die in L.A.* (1985)
→ *The Seven-Ups*

*Se7en* (1995)
*The Silence of the Lambs* (1991)
→ *The Silence of the Lambs*

*Manhunter* (1986)
*The Boston Strangler* (1968)
→ *Manhunter*

*The Racket* (1951)
*Heat* (1995)
→ *Heat*

*Bullitt* (1968)
*Dirty Harry* (1971)
→ *Bullitt*

*Lethal Weapon* (1987)
*Die Hard* (1988)
→ *Die Hard*

*48 Hrs.* (1982)
*Madigan* (1968)
→ *48 Hours*

***The French Connection* vs. *The Seven-Ups***
Roy Scheider plays the same cop in both. Other than that, it's all *The French Connection*.

→ *The French Connection*

***Se7en* vs. *The Silence of the Lambs***
Closest game in bunch – Brad Pitt, Morgan Freeman, and an ending that chills. Jodie Foster, Anthony Hopkins, and two great final scenes – one sends shivers; one forces an uncomfortable smile. *The Silence of the Lambs* brings it.

→ *The Silence of the Lambs*

→ *The French Connection*

***Bullitt* vs. *Die Hard***
Bruce Willis is cool, very cool. But Steve McQueen invented cool.

→ *Bullitt*

→ *Die Hard*

→ *Bullitt*

THE WINNER

## *The French Connection*

VS

***The French Connection* vs. *In the Heat of the Night***
Hackman and Schneider are blood-brother NYPD partners. Steiger and Poitier are reluctant Deep South partners. Great dialogue in both with the manic drive that's needed to make a movie cop seem real. But *The French Connection*, filmed docudrama style by William Friedkin, bodyslams the audience into the day-to-day struggles of two savvy street cops who won't quit. Both movies stand the test of time as portraits of their era. *The French Connection* wins on points.

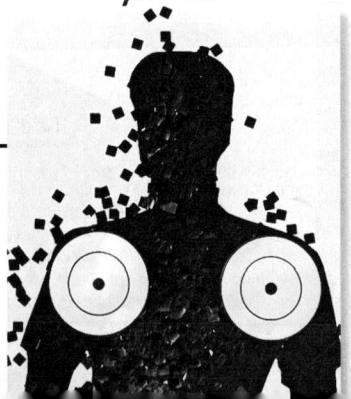

YOU MAY NOT WANT POPEYE DOYLE to date your daughter, but these are the movie cops you want knocking on your door in time of need. The rules were simple: The officer with the badge must propel the action, the more realistic the better. No joke movies, no private eyes. Our cops had to be members of a bureau or department, called to action by a crime, not by a hire. So, sit back, pour yourself a glass of Chianti, pick your feet if you're near Poughkeepsie, and make your day with our top cops.

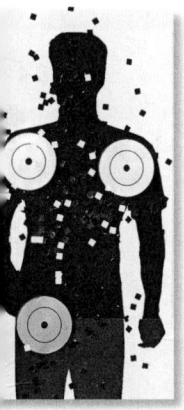

# n the Heat f the Night

***Prince of the City* vs. *The Naked City***
The most corrupt guys in town against honest detectives working a case the hard way. *Prince* is too good – also the movie that launched Jerry Orbach to *Law & Order.*

***L.A. Confidential* vs. *Prince of the City***
They might think they're corrupt in L.A. But you haven't seen dirty until you brush against the Prince and his team.

***Sea of Love* vs. *Serpico***
Pacino against Pacino. Older Al chases serial killer; sleeps with Ellen Barkin. Young Al is hounded by corrupt department; has a sheepdog. Young Al breaks your heart – *Serpico* wins.

***G-Men* vs. *The Untouchables***
Kevin Costner and crew face off against Al Capone (De Niro). Cagney makes the FBI his own. Cagney alone is no match for Kevin's team – led by Andy Garcia and Sean Connery.

***Training Day* vs. *Black Rain***
Pick your corrupt cop – Michael Douglas or Denzel Washington. Denzel is just too mean to lose.

***In the Heat of the Night* vs. *In the Line of Fire***
Clint is always good. But hard to beat Rod Steiger working with Mr. Tibbs himself, Sidney Poitier.

***Detective Story* vs. *Across 110th Street***
Both old school. Kirk Douglas vs. Anthony Quinn. But Douglas is all-cop in this one and tough to beat – *Detective Story* takes it.

***Walking Tall* vs. *Across 110th Street***
Joe Don Baker's got his slab of wood. That might work in his town. Over on 110th Street, they bury you in wood. Anthony Quinn packs a gun with lots of bullets. *Across 110th Street* wins.

***Serpico* vs. *In the Heat of the Night***
Great Pacino performance. Oscar winner for Steiger and top-tier Poitier. One makes you cry; the other makes you cheer. Both are high-wire dramas: *Serpico* had to dodge a division; *In the Heat of the Night* had to crack a case and beat back racial hatred. Tip of the patrol cap to *In the Heat of the Night.*

- *Serpico*
  - *Prince of the City*
    - *L.A. Confidential*
      - *Internal Affairs* (1990)
      - *L.A. Confidential* (1997)
    - *Prince of the City*
      - *Prince of the City* (1981)
      - *The Naked City* (1948)
  - *Serpico*
    - *Serpico*
      - *Sea of Love* (1989)
      - *Serpico* (1973)
    - *Training Day*
      - *Training Day* (2001)
      - *Black Rain* (1989)
- *In the Heat of the Night*
  - *In the Heat of the Night*
    - *The Untouchables*
      - *G-Men* (1935)
      - *The Untouchables* (1987)
    - *In the Heat of the Night*
      - *In the Heat of the Night* (1967)
      - *In the Line of Fire* (1993)
  - *Detective Story*
    - *Detective Story*
      - *The Onion Field* (1979)
      - *Detective Story* (1951)
    - *Across 110th Street*
      - *Across 110th Street* (1972)
      - *Walking Tall* (1973)

# Reality TV Stars

**By Bob Boden**

Bob Boden is senior vice president, Programming, Production and Development, for Fox Reality Channel, the only all-reality, all-the-time cable and satellite network and co-creator of the game show *GREED.*

**The Loud family**
*An American Family*

**The Roloff family**
*Little People, Big World*

**Evan Marriott**
*Joe Millionaire*

**Matt Kennedy Gould**
*The Joe Schmo Show*

**Rick Rockwell & Darva Conger**
*Who Wants to Marry a Multi-Millionaire?*

**Trista Rehn & Ryan Sutter**
*The Bachelor, The Bachelorette*

**Paris Hilton & Nicole Richie**
*The Simple Life, My New BFF*

**Mike (Boogie) Malin & Dr. Will Kirby**
*Big Brother*

**Richard Hatch**
*Survivor, Survivor All-Stars*

**Rob & Amber**
*Survivor, The Amazing Race All-Stars*

**Kelly Clarkson**
*American Idol*

**Sanjaya Malakar**
*American Idol*

**Allen Funt**
*Candid Camera*

**Ashton Kutcher**
*Punk'd*

**Flavor Flav**
*The Surreal Life, Strange Love, Flavor of Love*

**New York**
*Flavor of Love, I Love New York*

Loud family

Evan Marriott

Trista & Ryan

Paris & Nicole

Richard Hatch

Kelly Clarkson

Allen Funt

Flavor Flav

Evan Marriott

Paris & Nicole

Richard Hatch

Flavor Flav

Paris & Nicole

Flavor Flav

**Evan Marriott vs. The Loud Family**
Cameras documented a real family in live-action crisis: Mom and Dad were separating and so Lance was coming out as TV's first openly gay character. Groundbreaking? Sure. But that was before the reality genre had a name; thirty years later, 30 million more people saw Marriott pur potential brides by posing as a millionaire bachelor – and spawned a wave of other hoaxes.

**Trista & Ryan vs. Rick & Darva**
The Trista-Ryan union proved that true love (and profit) can emerge from a husband-selection format that had advanced eons from its more innocent *Dating Game* roots. But a storybook reality ending eluded Darva and Rick: she annulled her marriage after a separate bedrooms honeymoon upon learning that Rick (1) probably wasn't a multi-millionaire, (2) had a different name, and (3) had a pending restraining order against him.

**Richard Hatch vs. Flavor Flav**
Hatch, the naked reality pioneer, used superior strategy to take the first *Survivor* million but ended up in jail for refusing to pay taxes on his winnings. Rapper Flav, cast as a Romeo (with a gold dental grille), delivered delicious, audacious, controversial parodies of *The Bachelor* when he filled a mansion with trashy ladies vying for his love.

**Paris & Nicole**

VS

**Flavor Flav vs. Paris & Nicol**
No matter how far and deftly Flav twisted the world of D-level celebreality, he couldn't match the influence of the tw rich and luscious ladies, the founding mothers of the gen The breakup of the real-life best friends during *The Surre Life* made headlines and, in the true nature of reality success, spawned a hit MTV sho during which Paris searched for a new BFF.

WITH ITS OVERT APPEALS TO greed, self-image, sex, upward mobility, bitchiness, adventure, and competitiveness, reality television has created a generation of characters unimagined by scriptwriters: real people living in communal houses, vying for jobs, singing in talent shows, nabbing bail-jumpers. They are dysfunctional civilians and celebrities, survivors and bachelors, real and phony millionaires, and people with and without talent – the most successful ones impose (or inflict) their personalities on America.

**Paris & Nicole vs. Omarosa**
Omarosa, reality TV's first queen bitch, began as a liar and backstabber to get an edge on Donald Trump in *The Apprentice*, then challenged Janice Dickinson in the *Surreal Life* house and Piers Morgan on *Celebrity Apprentice*. Paris and Nicole are brilliant news manipulators, but Omarosa's bad girl archetype lives on in other shows and in references to other characters' evil-doing as "pulling an Omarosa."

THE WINNER

**Omarosa**
*The Apprentice, The Surreal Life, Celebrity Apprentice*

- Donald Trump
  - Donald Trump
    - Donald Trump
      - **Duane (Dog) Chapman** — *Dog the Bounty Hunter*
      - **Donald Trump** — *The Apprentice*
    - Heidi & Spencer
      - **Heidi Montag & Spencer Pratt** — *The Hills*
      - **Tila Tequila** — *A Shot at Love*
  - Danny Bonaduce
    - Johnny Knoxville
      - **Johnny Knoxville** — *Jackass*
      - **Puck** — *The Real World*
    - Danny Bonaduce
      - **Danny Bonaduce** — *Celebrity Boxing, Breaking Bonaduce*
      - **Paula Abdul** — *American Idol, Hey Paula!*
- Omarosa
  - Omarosa
    - Janice Dickinson
      - **Adrianne Curry** — *America's Next Top Model, My Fair Brady*
      - **Janice Dickinson** — *America's Next Top Model, The Janice Dickinson Modeling Agency*
    - Omarosa
      - **Omarosa** — *The Apprentice, The Surreal Life, Celebrity Apprentice*
      - **Kathy Griffin** — *My Life on the D-List*
  - Tim Gunn
    - Blurred criminals
      - **Blurred cheaters** — *Cheaters*
      - **Blurred criminals** — *Cops*
    - Tim Gunn
      - **Queer Eye guys** — *Queer Eye for the Straight Guy*
      - **Tim Gunn** — *Project Runway, Tim Gunn's Guide to Style*

# Fictional Lawyers

**By Thane Rosenbaum**

Thane Rosenbaum is the John Whelan Distinguished Lecturer in Law at Fordham Law School, where he teaches courses in law and literature and also directs the Forum on Law, Culture & Society

**Atticus Finch,** *To Kill a Mockingbird* — **Vincent Gambini** *My Cousin Vinny*

**Lawrence Preston** *The Defenders* — **Benjamin Matlock** *Matlock*

**Arthur Kirkland** *. . . And Justice For All* — **Bartleby** *Bartleby, the Scrivener*

**Edward (Eddie) Dodd** *True Believer* — **Sandy Stern** *Presumed Innocent*

**Amanda Bonner** *Adam's Rib* — **Joe Miller** *Philadelphia*

**Billy Flynn** *Chicago* — **Boris Max** *Native Son*

**Prof. Charles W. Kingsfield, Jr.** *The Paper Chase* — **Judge Amy Gray** *Judging Amy*

**Jack McCoy** *Law & Order* — **Forrest Bedford** *I'll Fly Away*

Atticus Finch

Lawrence Preston

Arthur Kirkland

Sandy Stern

Joe Miller

Billy Flynn

Prof. Kingsfield

Jack McCoy

Atticus Finch

Sandy Stern

Joe Miller

Jack McCoy

Atticus Finch

Jack McCoy

**Arthur Kirkland vs. Bartleby**
Yes, Bartleby is a copyist, but his long-suffering occupation entitles him to honorary lawyer status. Both barristers are disillusioned by the legal system, and both are famous for lawyer quotations: "You're out of order!" shouts Al Pacino-as-Kirkland, and "I prefer not to," says Bartleby. Kirkland wins when Bartleby can't muster the energy to mount a defense.

**Atticus Finch vs. Jack McCoy**
McCoy, who defeated his Southern sibling, Forrest Bedford, in the first round, now meets his role model, Atticus Finch. Both lawyers are highly principled and modest, with a deep sense of moral clarity and awareness that the law doesn't always produce the right outcome. But in a battle of legal legends, Finch doesn't flinch.

THE WINNER

## Atticus Finch

*To Kill a Mockingbird*

VS

**Atticus Finch vs. Perry Mason**
Finch and Mason are responsible for more law school applications than all other influences combined. And both lawyers have largely defined America's image of the quick-thinking trial attorney. Mason never loses, but Finch is the lawyer, and father, of our dreams.

AMERICANS LOVE LAWYER JOKES and seemingly hate lawyers, yet, paradoxically, the drama of fictional lawyers has become America's favorite pastime and guilty pleasure. The lawyers of our imagination, the ones who can't be retained but are still loved and loathed, have craftily argued, adjudicated, and plotted their way through novels, television dramas, and feature films, animating our culture with Lawyer Madness and a deep longing to see that justice is done – even if it exists only in art.

**Alan Shore vs. Daniel Kaffee**
Kaffee doesn't worry whether his adversary can handle the truth since Shore is rarely bothered by such mundanely ethical and moral dilemmas. In this battle of former brat packers-turned-attorneys, the lieutenant's strong sense of honor is clearly outmatched by Shore's street smarts and occasional sleaze.

- **Perry Mason**
  - Alan Shore
    - Alan Shore
      - Alan Shore — *The Practice* and *Boston Legal*
      - Aaron Levinsky — *Nuts*
    - Daniel Kaffee
      - Kathryn Murphy — *The Accused*
      - Lt. Daniel Kaffee — *A Few Good Men*
  - Paul Biegler
    - Paul Biegler
      - Paul Biegler — *Anatomy of a Murder*
      - Jake Brigance — *A Time to Kill*
    - Rita Harrison Williams
      - Rita Harrison Williams — *I Am Sam*
      - John Shaunessy — *Kramer vs. Kramer*
  - Perry Mason
    - Frank Galvin
      - Ann Talbot
        - Ann Kelsey — *L.A. Law*
        - Ann Talbot — *Music Box*
      - Frank Galvin
        - Frank Galvin — *The Verdict*
        - Michael Clayton — *Michael Clayton*
    - Perry Mason
      - Henry Drummond
        - Henry Drummond — *Inherit the Wind*
        - Pudd'nhead Wilson — *Pudd'nhead Wilson*
      - Perry Mason
        - Elle Woods — *Legally Blonde*
        - Perry Mason — *Perry Mason*

**Frank Galvin vs. Perry Mason**
In their opening rounds Galvin dispatches another lawyer-burnout, Michael Clayton, while Mason reminds the perky Elle Woods that quoting Aristotle is not enough against a man who has yet to lose a case. Galvin surmounts alcoholism and mixes law with religion, but he can't match Mason's TV longevity or sober presentation of the brilliant defense attorney.

# Good Imus vs. Evil Imus

**By Richard Sandomir**

Richard Sandomir has interviewed Imus thrice. The first time, Imus confiscated his notebook. The second time, he took away his notebook and tape recorder. The third time, he showed off a recent surgical scar; a week later, he called Sandomir a "bald-headed pedophile" on the air.

**WEASELS I REGIONAL**

- Calls CBS's Lesley Stahl a "gutless, lying weasel"
- Calls Yasir Arafat a "rodent-looking weasel"
- **Stahl**
- Calls Al Gore a "transparent weasel"
- Calls Bill Clinton a "pot-smoking weasel"
- **Clinton/weasel**
- **Clinton/weasel**

**SAINT REGIONAL**

- Opens Imus Ranch for kids with cancer
- Marries Deirdre Coleman, 24 years his junior, becomes vegan, humps healthy cleaning products
- **Imus Ranch**
- Raises millions for Center for the Intrepid, for soldiers wounded in Iraq War
- Introduces ground-breaking comedian Dick Gregory to a new generation of listeners
- **Center for the Intrepid**
- **Center for the Intrepid**

**VENDETTAS REGIONAL**

- Scorns *Wall Street Journal* reporter for misreporting probe into ranch finances
- Targets Texas Rep. Joe Barton for stalling autism legislation
- **Joe Barton**
- Calls ranch doctor an "absolutely disgraceful piece of shit" for his treatment of 16-year-old girl; doctor sues
- Vows to eat dead dog's penis if Howard Stern got better ratings
- **Dead dog's penis**
- **Joe Barton**

**TESTIMONIALS REGIONAL**

- Tony Kornheiser: "How can he do five minutes on the size of his penis and then interview Bill Bradley?"
- *Newsday*'s Les Payne: "He is all coil, terrible eyes and scales."
- **"terrible eyes and scales"**
- CBS's Jim Nantz pays homage to cattle-auction-watching Imus by saying "just one more cow" during AFC championship
- Relentless critic Philip Nobile: "I don't know why people think he's H.L. Mencken when he's George Wallace."
- **"just one more cow"**
- **"just one more cow"**

**Opens Imus Ranch for Kids vs. Marrying Deirdre**
Deirdre is the most influential person in Imus's life, but the impact of sick kids working on his New Mexico cattle ranch counterbalances nearly every rotten thing he's ever said or done, except perhaps for ending each Teddy Kennedy sketch with the sounds of screeching tires and a drowning, gurgling woman.

**Clinton/weasel vs. Center for the Intrepid**
The charitable impulse competes with his anti-social side for control of a questionable soul. He has raised money for SIDS research, world hunger, and his ranch for kids with cancer. Then came the ex-Marine's patriotic surge: raising millions of dollars for a state-of-the-art rehabilitation center for wounded Iraqi vets. It just doesn't get any better than that.

**"Just one more cow" vs. "terrible eyes and scales"**
How best to demonstrate Imus's power to get the media elite to willingly suck up to him? Ask Jim Nantz to work "just one more cow" into his play-by-play. Nantz did it organically and brilliantly ("Genius!" crowed Imus), as if he were following an Imus-led game of "Simon Says." Calling Imus a snake? Exactly what he wants.

**Center for the Intrepid**

**VS**

THERE ARE TWO ERAS IN DON IMUS'S RADIO HISTORY. In the first, he was a shock-jock, known for telephoning unsuspecting women to ask, "Are you naked?" In the second, the misanthropic Imus is no more mature (calling Venus Williams "Penis" is not a sign of wisdom) but he has turned his show into a salon for politicians, journalists, and singers seeking his approval, and a forum for his charitable causes. He still goads guests to say something that "ruins their life" – which he nearly did to himself.

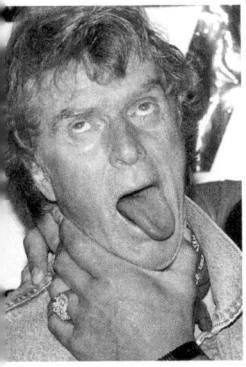

THE WINNER

## "nappy-headed ho's"

**"Nappy-headed ho's" vs. Clinton infidelities**
The president is fair game, even in front of his wife and a roomful of spectators. But not elite women college basketball players – not with racial epithets, irrespective of his intent or defense that he insults everyone. This might not have been the worst thing he (or his crew) has ever said, but he unleashed it at the wrong target, at the wrong time. It doesn't get any worse than that.

**Center for the Intrepid vs. "nappy-headed ho's"**
Imus's passionate advocacy for the center is a career highlight, and while he was a burning cattle prod for funding, he was not the only one involved. But Imus's Rutgers screed was a short and solo rant, nearly a Satanic verse, one that will be noted by the third paragraph of his obituaries. The evil that men do lives after them but will Imus's good be interred with his bones?

- Clinton infidelities
  - Recovering alcoholic
    - Fired by WNBC
      - Fired for cocaine abuse by WNBC Radio
      - Suffers collapsed lung, broken bones, when thrown by horse
    - Recovering alcoholic
      - Recovering alcoholic
      - Breaks legs in mining accident
  - Clinton infidelities
    - D'Amato
      - Lures Sen. Alfonse D'Amato into Japanese accent to mock O.J. Simpson judge Ito
      - Orders 1,200 hamburgers to go from McDonald's
    - Clinton infidelities
      - Returns to radio and TV eight months after being fired for Rutgers women's basketball team insults, with two black sidekicks
      - Jokes about Clinton's infidelities at Radio and Television Correspondents dinner with irate Bill and Hillary on dais
- "nappy-headed ho's"
  - "juiceless gerbil"
    - "sniveling weasel"
      - Calls Al Franken a "sniveling weasel"
      - Says Sen. Joe Lieberman has "great weasel potential"
    - "juiceless gerbil"
      - Calls Nantz a "butt-kissing suck-up, a cowardly, gutless weasel": amends to "juiceless gerbil"
      - Calls enemy Nobile a "spineless, gutless, pathetic little weasel"
  - "nappy-headed ho's"
    - "nappy-headed ho's"
      - Calls Judge Harold Rothwax "scuzwax" for not releasing Deirdre from jury duty
      - Calls Rutgers women's basketball team "nappy-headed ho's," gets fired by CBS Radio and MSNBC
    - "cleaning lady"
      - Describes Clinton as "fat pantload"
      - Calls PBS's Gwen Ifill "cleaning lady"

SELF-INFLICTED SUFFERNG REGIONAL

DUBIOUS EVENTS REGIONAL

WEASELS II REGIONAL

INSULTS REGIONAL

# Steve Earle Songs

**By Mark Reiter**

Mark Reiter, co-editor of this book, regrets all the other Earle songs he couldn't invite to this tournament.

"More Than I Can Do"
*(I Feel Alright, 1996)*

"Lonelier Than This"
*(Transcendental Blues, 2000)*

"More Than I Can Do"

"Telephone Road"
*(El Corazon, 1997)*

"Copperhead Road"
*(Copperhead Road, 1988)*

"Copperhead Road"

"City of Immigrants"
*(Washington Square Serenade, 2007)*

"The Galway Girl"
*(Transcendental Blues, 2000)*

"City of Immigrants"

"Tennessee Blues"
*(Washington Square Serenade, 2007)*

"Guitar Town"
*(Guitar Town, 1986)*

"Guitar Town"

"The Week of Living Dangerously"
*(Exit 0, 1987)*

"Here I Am"
*(El Corazon, 1997)*

"The Week of Living Dangerously"

"Poison Lovers"
*(El Corazon, 1997)*

"Days Aren't Long Enough"
*(Washington Square Serenade, 2007)*

"Poison Lovers"

"Over Yonder"
*(Transcendental Blues, 2000)*

"Ellis Unit One"
*(Sidetracks, 2002)*

"Over Yonder"

"Hard-Core Troubador"
*(I Feel Alright, 1996)*

"Pilgrim"
*(The Mountain, 1999)*

"Hard-Core Troubadour"

"More Than I Can Do"

"Guitar Town"

"The Week of Living Dangerously"

"Hard-Core Troubadour"

**"Copperhead Road" vs. "More Than I Can Do"**
For launching Earle's comeback on 1996's *I Feel Alright*, "More Than I Can Do" scores enough points to beat one of his classic Nashville renegade anthems.

**"The Week of Living Dangerously" vs. "Hard-Core Troubador"**
"Week of Living Dangerously" is a complete screenplay in 4:26 that should have been snapped up by a movie studio. But the self-referring "Troubador," with Earle channeling the Van Morrison of "Brown-Eyed Girl" vintage, actually shows up in the stock car spoof, *Talladega Nights*.

"Guitar Town"

VS

**"Guitar Town" vs. "Jerusalem"**
"Guitar Town" with its snappy lyrics ("I got a two-pack habit and a motel tan") may be one of country's great sing-alongs, but when's the last time you were moved by a song – more like a prayer – about the Middle East crisis? That's "Jerusalem." A perfect pop protest tune with the usual Earle components – acoustic guitars, drums, harmonica – and a message that mixes despair and optimism ("But I believe there'll come a day when the lion and the lamb /Will lie down in peace together in Jerusalem"). The State Department should play this song once a week – for inspiration.

AS A SINGER-SONGWRITER, Steve Earle is Bruce Springsteen with a twang (but without the stadium-sized fan base). There's the guitar-driven hooks, the sharp lyric commentary, the high-pop taste. But Earle adds a willingness to expose every personal nerve ending. His backstory of addiction, jail time, and seven marriages is well known. But while artists like Billy Joel and Stevie Wonder are fading creatively, Earle, now past 50, keeps getting better. Had we a Final Four of Living American Songwriters, he'd be in there with Dylan, Simon, and Gill (as in Vince).

**"Valentine's Day" vs. "Sometimes She Forgets"**
Two sides of the same coin about lapses in memory and love. "Valentine's Day" wins for its simple melodic beauty and the embedded irony of being infinitely superior to any Hallmark card.

THE WINNER

**"Jerusalem"**
*(Jerusalem, 2004)*

**"John Walker's Blues" vs. "Fort Worth Blues"**
"Fort Worth Blues," a mournful but gorgeous travelogue about being homesick, loses to Earle's ballsiest song – in which he assumes the persona of John Walker Lindh, the 20-year-old from California who was captured fighting for the Taliban in Afghanistan and is now serving 20 years in an Indiana prison. Over a haunting Arabic chorus, Earle makes you understand what happened to "just an American boy."

**"I Remember You" vs. "You're Still Standing There"**
No one writes better boy-girl duets than Earle, and this matchup features two of his best – with Emmylou Harris and Lucinda Williams helping out. Emmylou by a whisker.

- "Valentine's Day"
  - "Valentine's Day"
    - "Valentine's Day" (*I Feel Alright, 1996*)
    - "Sometimes She Forgets" (*Train a Comin', 1995*)
  - "I Don't Want to Lose You Yet"
    - "When I Fall" (*Transcendental Blues, 2000*)
    - "I Don't Want to Lose You Yet" (*Transcendental Blues, 2000*)
- "Transcendental Blues"
  - "Transcendental Blues"
    - "Transcendental Blues" (*Transcendental Blues, 2000*)
    - "Fearless Heart" (*Guitar Town, 1996*)
  - "John Walker's Blues"
    - "John Walker's Blues" (*Jerusalem, 2002*)
    - "Fort Worth Blues" (*El Corazon, 1997*)
- "Jerusalem"
  - "Devil's Right Hand"
    - "I Feel Alright" (*I Feel Alright, 1996*)
    - "The Devil's Right Hand" (*Copperhead Road, 1988*)
  - "Jerusalem"
    - "Down Here Below" (*Washington Square Serenade, 2007*)
    - "Jerusalem" (*Jerusalem, 2004*)
- "I Remember You"
  - "I Remember You"
    - "Mystery Train Part II" (*Train a Comin', 1995*)
    - "I Remember You" (*Jerusalem, 2004*)
  - "You're Still Standing There"
    - "When the People Find Out" (*The Hard Way, 1990*)
    - "You're Still Standing There" (*I Feel Alright, 1996*)

# Most American Superhero

**By Peter Coogan**

Dr. Peter Coogan, director of the Institute for Comics Studies and author of *Superhero: Secret Origin of a Genre,* has achieved his childhood dream of getting paid to read comic
His daughter fights for truth, justice, and her own way as the superheroine Flashgirl.

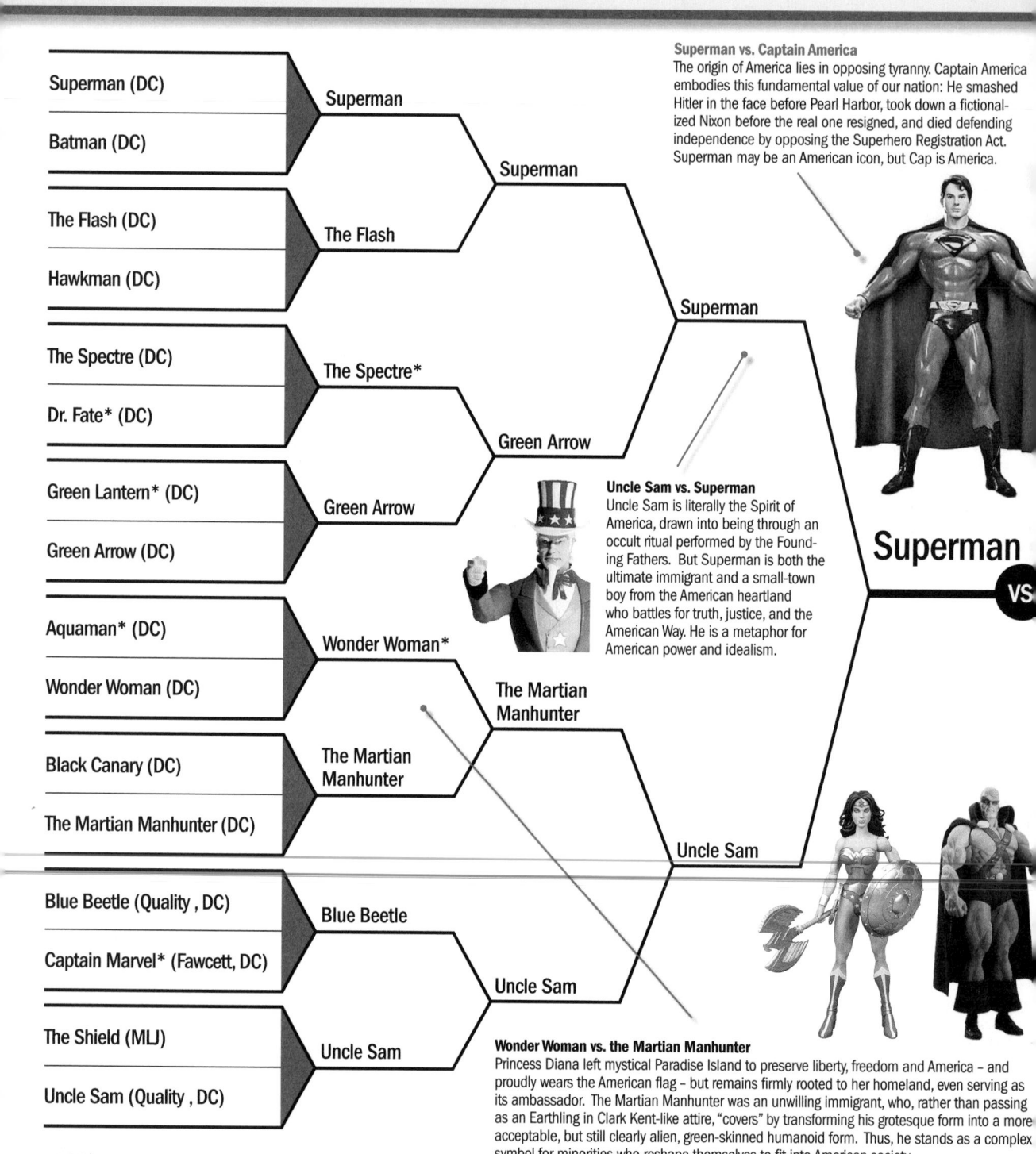


**Superman vs. Captain America**
The origin of America lies in opposing tyranny. Captain America embodies this fundamental value of our nation: He smashed Hitler in the face before Pearl Harbor, took down a fictionalized Nixon before the real one resigned, and died defending independence by opposing the Superhero Registration Act. Superman may be an American icon, but Cap is America.

**Uncle Sam vs. Superman**
Uncle Sam is literally the Spirit of America, drawn into being through an occult ritual performed by the Founding Fathers. But Superman is both the ultimate immigrant and a small-town boy from the American heartland who battles for truth, justice, and the American Way. He is a metaphor for American power and idealism.

**Wonder Woman vs. the Martian Manhunter**
Princess Diana left mystical Paradise Island to preserve liberty, freedom and America – and proudly wears the American flag – but remains firmly rooted to her homeland, even serving as its ambassador. The Martian Manhunter was an unwilling immigrant, who, rather than passing as an Earthling in Clark Kent-like attire, "covers" by transforming his grotesque form into a more acceptable, but still clearly alien, green-skinned humanoid form. Thus, he stands as a complex symbol for minorities who reshape themselves to fit into American society.

WE TEND TO RANK SUPERHEROES BY THEIR POWER, but what makes them quintessentially American? Superheroes are vivid metaphors for the balance between power and responsibility, and the tension of the public and private self. But they also embody American mythology and the American creed. But most American? Is it Superman, the ultimate immigrant? Batman, the self-made man? Iron Man, the technological expression of the military-industrial complex? Green Arrow, the rebel-in-chief? The X-Men, the embodiment of every sort of diversity?

THE WINNER

## Captain America

- Captain America
  - The Old Soldier
    - Plastic Man
      - Plastic Man (Quality, DC)
      - The Question (Charlton, DC)
    - The Old Soldier
      - Spawn* (Image)
      - The Old Soldier (Astro City)
  - Captain America
    - Human Torch
      - The Sub-Mariner* (Marvel)
      - The Human Torch (Marvel)
    - Captain America
      - Captain America (Marvel)
      - Fantastic Four (Marvel)
- The X-Men
  - Spider-Man
    - The Hulk*
      - The Hulk (Marvel)
      - Thor* (Marvel)
    - Spider-Man
      - Spider-Man (Marvel)
      - Dr. Strange* (Marvel)
  - The X-Men
    - The X-Men
      - Iron Man (Marvel)
      - The X-Men (Marvel)
    - Luke Cage
      - Daredevil (Marvel)
      - Luke Cage (Marvel)

**The Sub-Mariner vs. the Human Torch**
The Sub-Mariner's American father makes him an American, but his kingship of Atlantis without the consent of Congress poses a serious question of loyalty. By comparison, when Dr. Phineas Horton built the Human Torch – an android who bursts into flame and flies – he used 100% American-made parts.

**Spider-Man vs. the X-Men**
Spider-Man represents American success mythology – both the Horatio Alger "pluck and luck" of the 19th century and the media manipulation of the 20th. But the X-Men, in all their racial, ethnic, gender, religious, and genetic variety are the pre-eminent superhero metaphors for American diversity and multiculturalism.

*Indicates an allegiance to or acceptance of a title of nobility from a foreign or alien power.

# Gangster Films

**By Lorenzo Carcaterra**

Lorenzo Carcaterra, a novelist and screenwriter, is the author of *Sleepers* and *Gangster*.

*Scarface* (1932)

*Scarface* (1983)

Pacino in a cult classic and Paul Muni in a timeless one. Pacino takes it.

*Scarface*

*White Heat* (1949)

*Charley Varrick* (1973)

*White Heat*

A coked-out Pacino vs. an insane Cagney. Not even close – Cagney by a mile.

*White Heat*

*Key Largo* (1948)

*The Petrified Forest* (1936)

If you're going to be held hostage – Edward G. Robinson takes the prize. Plus, you still get your Bogart fix.

*Key Largo*

*The Big Heat* (1953)

*Point Blank* (1967)

*The Big Heat*

Even the great Lee Marvin couldn't take on Edward G. Robinson.

*Key Largo*

*High Sierra* (1941)

*Angels With Dirty Faces* (1938)

*Angels With Dirty Faces*

Cagney against Cagney. Both tough guys with tender hearts. But nobody, and I mean nobody, tops Rocky Sullivan – *Angels* takes the prize.

*Angels With Dirty Faces*

*Little Caesar* (1931)

*Public Enemy* (1931)

*Public Enemy*

*Pulp Fiction* (1994)

*Reservoir Dogs* (1992)

*Pulp Fiction*

Tarantino vs. Scorsese. Tough call, very tough – but we'll ride with Scorsese's crew.

*Mean Streets*

*Mean Streets* (1973)

*Carlito's Way* (1993)

*Mean Streets*

Insane Cagney going gun-to-gun against an equally insane Edward G. Robinson. Cagney has insane down by a large margin. On to the final four for Cody.

*White Heat*

Cagney and the Dead End Kids bring an end to De Niro, Harvey, and the other Little Italy tough guys.

*Angels With Dirty Faces*

Two great movies. Cagney, Bogart, Pat O'Brien, Ann Sheridan, and the Dead End Kids mix street gangster with romance and warmth topped by an ending that will bring tears. But you want pure gangster – Cagney can't be touched as Cody Jarrett. No one comes close. *White Heat* moves to the finals.

**THE WINNER**

***White Heat***

VS

***White Heat* vs. *Goodfellas***

Both have it all – great actors, great directors, terrific scripts. But *White Heat* has Cagney giving the single greatest gangster performance of his career and that's saying quite a bit. No one can ever top Cody Jarrett in intensity and insanity. He would have taken on the De Niro crew by himself and still have come out on top of the world – one way or another. It's a close match, but *White Heat* wins it.

IT'S NOT EASY CHOOSING THE BEST GANGSTER FILM – even when we slide *The Godfather* and *The Godfather II* into a category of their own. I chose only pure gangster movies, ruling out comedies (*Analyze This* would have been a contender) and any movie where the gangster does not propel the action (this eliminated *The Untouchables; Heat* with Pacino and DeNiro, not with Burt Reynolds; and *On The Waterfront*). To qualify, the films had to be all gangster all the time and the less we saw of men with badges the better.

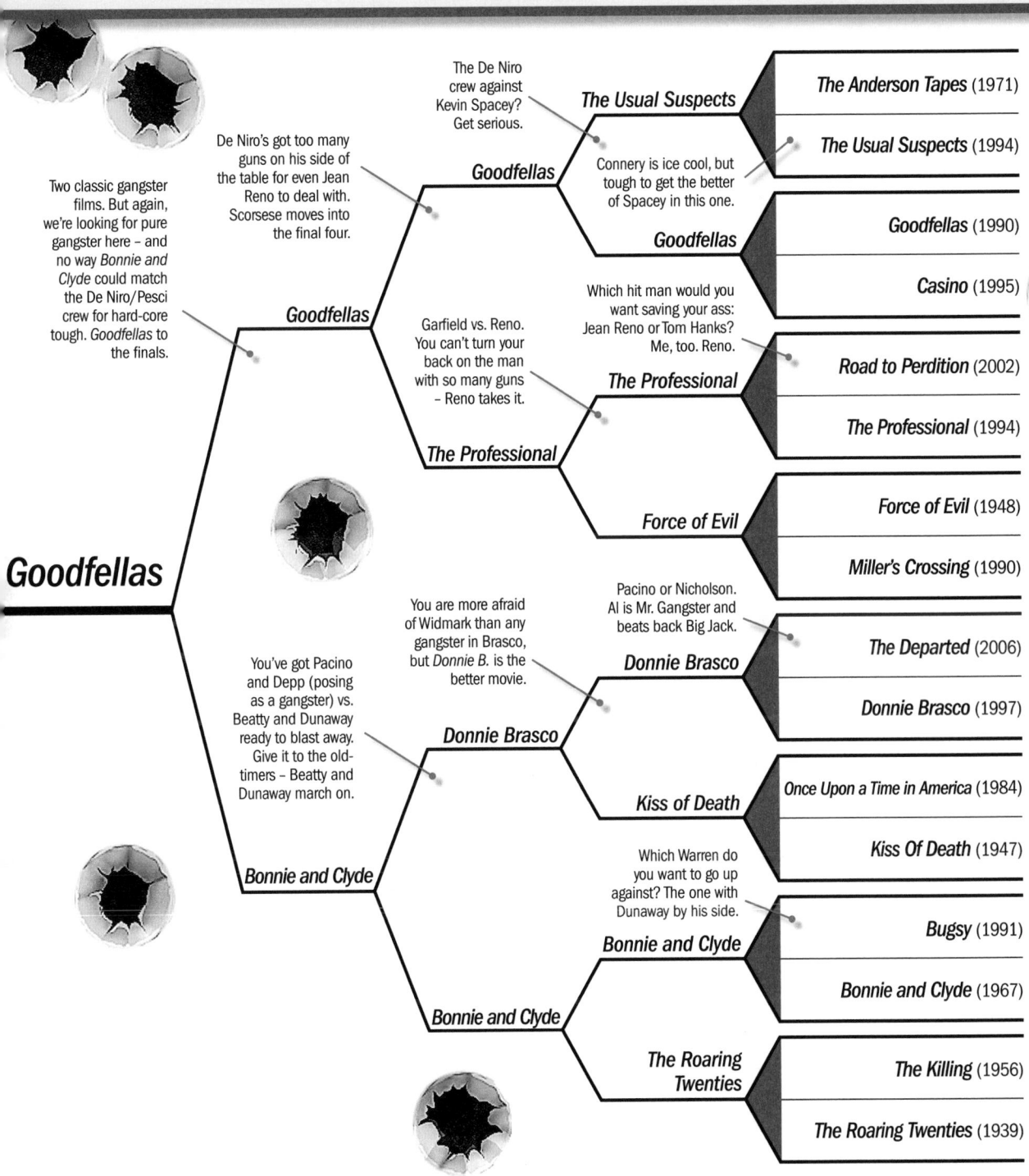

# Disney Animated Films

**By Richard Corliss**

Richard Corliss, a *Time* movie critic, has watched Disney films all his life, but he's really a Warner Bros. cartoon man.

*Lady and the Tramp* (1955)
*Bolt* (2008)
→ *Lady and the Tramp*

*101 Dalmatians* (1961)
*Oliver & Company* (1988)
→ *Oliver & Company*

→ *Lady and the Tramp*

*Steamboat Willie* (1928)
*Beauty and the Beast* (1991)
→ *Beauty and the Beast*

*Bambi* (1942)
*The Rescuers* (1977)
→ *Bambi*

→ *Bambi*

→ *Bambi*

*The Three Little Pigs* (1933)
*Alice in Wonderland* (1951)
→ *Three Little Pigs*

*The Jungle Book* (1967)
*The Lion King* (1994)
→ *The Lion King*

→ *The Lion King*

→ *The Lion King*

*Snow White and the Seven Dwarfs* (1937)
*Pocahontas* (1995)
→ *Snow White*

*The Band Concert* (1935)
*Fantasia* (1940)
→ *Fantasia*

→ *Snow White*

***Lady and the Tramp* vs. *Bolt***
It's dogs-eat-dog, as the '50s spaniel and mutt take a bite out of a superhero white shepherd, then go on to defeat Oliver the cat. Survival of the cutest.

***The Lion King* vs. *The Jungle Book***
When Disney goes to Africa, a man-cub has no chance against the king of beasts. Simba KO's Mowgli in this rumble in the jungle.

***The Lion King* vs. *Pinocchio***
And a little wooden child shall lead them. The rich visual style and still-hummable tunes lent charm to this morality tale on the perils of telling lies and playing hooky.

## *The Lion King* VS

***Bambi* vs. *The Lion King***
Nobody tops Disney in coming-of-age-after-the-violent-death-of-a-parent stories. The Tim Rice-Elton John score helps the lion lie down on the deer.

THE VERY FIRST MOVIES SEEN BY GENERATIONS OF KIDS, Disney animated features had pretty songs and cute animals. But in their plumbing of toddler fears – abandonment, humiliation, instant orphandom – these were also primal horror films that could literally scare the poo out of wee ones. A genre more or less created by one man, the Disney cartoon factory has enthralled and troubled audiences for 80-plus years. In this tournament, Walt's early shorts duke it out with some of the most widely seen feature films ever made. No Pixar movies, though; those wizards from the Bay Area would be ringers.

***Dumbo* vs. *The Little Mermaid***
Two parables of prejudice set a big-eared elephant against a fish out of water. The winner is the first masterpiece of Disney's Renaissance era.

THE WINNER
***Pinocchio***
(1940)

- *The Little Mermaid*
  - *Dumbo*
    - *Chicken Little*
      - *The Wise Little Hen* (1934)
      - *Chicken Little* (2005)
    - *Dumbo*
      - *Dumbo* (1940)
      - *Cinderella* (1951)
  - *The Little Mermaid*
    - *The Old Mill*
      - *The Old Mill* (1937)
      - *The Hunchback of Notre Dame* (1996)
    - *The Little Mermaid*
      - *Lonesome Ghosts* (1937)
      - *The Little Mermaid* (1989)
- *Pinocchio*
  - *Pinocchio*
    - *Pinocchio*
      - *Pinocchio* (1940)
      - *Mulan* (1998)
    - *Skeleton Dance*
      - *Skeleton Dance* (1929)
      - *The Adventures of Ichabod and Mr. Toad* (1949)
  - *Aladdin*
    - *Three Caballeros*
      - *The Three Caballeros* (1946)
      - *Sleeping Beauty* (1959)
    - *Aladdin*
      - *Peter Pan* (1953)
      - *Aladdin* (1992)

# The Honeymooners Lexicon

**By Peter Crescenti**

Peter Crescenti is co-founder of *The Honeymooners* fan club, RALPH (Roy Association for the Longevity and Preservation of the Honeymooners), an has authored/co-authored five books about the series.

"The applicant is a bum"

"I'm going bowling, but I'm not going bowling"

"The applicant is a bum"

"If he keeps this up he's going to be a buried treasure"

"I liked it better with a sock in it"

"If he keeps this up"

"If he keeps this up"

"Bang, zoom!"

"Eureka! My garbage can is full"

"Bang, zoom!"

"Baby, you're the greatest!"

"Zip Zip, it's zipping the modern way"

"Baby, you're the greatest!"

"Baby, you're the greatest!"

**"Bang, zoom!" vs. "Baby, you're the greatest"**
These signature lines define the two sides, both of them enormous, of Ralph Kramden. The former is his all-purpose expression of anger and frustration, but it is Ralph's one term of endearment that reveals the repentant big mouth who ultimately realizes he hit the jackpot when he married Alice.

"Baby, you're the greatest!"

"You're one of nature's noblemen"

"Can it core a apple?"

"Can it core a apple?"

"Can it core a apple?"

"Official space helmet on, Captain Video"

"Hello, ball"

"Hello ball"

**"Official space helmet on, Captain Video" vs. "Hello, ball"**
Two seminal lines, brilliantly delivered, from Norton. One, done solo, illustrates his childlike devotion to watching TV's earliest sci-fi series. But Norton's two words of beginner's golf advice to Ralph forever reshaped how many of us react to being told to "address the ball."

"Can it core a apple?"

"Can it core a apple?"

THE WINNER

"Can it core a apple?"

VS

"And by the way, you are a bum!"

"Hello Bunny, this is ol' Buttercup"

"And by the way"

"How can anyone so round be so square?"

"If that's the Good Humor man, get me a popsicle"

"Get me a popsicle"

"And by the way"

MORE THAN 50 YEARS since the classic 39 episodes of *The Honeymooners* had their first TV run, they represent a perfect storm of once-in-a-lifetime cast chemistry, extraordinary comic talent, and first-class writing. In a dingy tenement in postwar Brooklyn, Ralph Kramden and Ed Norton strive, in hysterical and poignant ways, for the American Dream that they and their wives can never achieve. Kramden and Norton defined an exquisite black-and-white minimalism and set the standard for buddy sitcoms.

**"BLABBERMOUTH" vs "Can it core a apple?"**
"Can it core a apple?" comes from the scene where Ralph and Norton try to sell a multi-purpose kitchen gadget on live TV. This great extended scene blended superb writing with Gleason and Carney's instinctive ad-libbing skills, and anticipated the cheesy absurdity of low-budget, household product infomercials ever since. While it didn't generate huge laughs at its filming, its staying power makes it the King of the Castle of *Honeymooners* lines.

# "BLABBER-MOUTH!!!"

- "Homina, homina, homina"
  - "Boomph!"
    - "P.S. 31, Oyster Bay"
      - "P.S. 31, Oyster Bay"
      - "Lulu!"
    - "Boomph!"
      - "You wanna wiggle? Wiggle over to the stove and get my supper."
      - "Boomph!"
  - "Homina homina homina"
    - "The cat'll get it"
      - "Leave it there, the cat'll get it"
      - "This is my friend Harvey"
    - "Homina homina homina"
      - "Homina homina homina . . ."
      - "What's that, your lunchbox?"
- BLABBERMOUTH!!!
  - "BLABBERMOUTH!!!"
    - "BLABBERMOUTH!!!"
      - "YOU are a BLABBERMOUTH!!!"
      - "I can't even put my arms around you"
    - "Swanee River?"
      - "Maybe we oughta say something about spear fishing"
      - "Who is the composer of 'Swanee River'?"
  - "king of my castle!"
    - "My wife's taking a bath"
      - "Your salary couldn't drip out"
      - "My wife's taking a bath in the sink"
    - "king of my castle!"
      - "I am the king of my castle!"
      - "Rx!"

**"Boomph" vs. "Homina"**
Never has a comedy team milked so many laughs from the word that Norton utters to try to unlock the handcuffs that link him to Kramden between their train berths. But Ralph's occasional blabbering of "homina, homina, homina" unmasks him in his most desperate moments. Haven't we all had "homina, homina, homina" moments of our own?

**"YOU are a BLABBERMOUTH" vs. "homina"**
Ralph is never madder than when his acerbic mother-in-law spills the beans about a hit Broadway mystery he plans to see. The punchline is that much sweeter because we see Ralph building toward his Mt. Vesuvius moment as Alice's mother pelts him with praise for Alice's old beaus and brushes off the Broadway show's virtues.

# You Call This Acting?

**By Will Reiter**

Will Reiter, a former editorial staffer at *OK!* magazine, could easily play himself in the movie version.

**Julia Roberts,** *Notting Hill* (American movie star marries a nobody)

**Bill Murray,** *Caddyshack* (anarchic golf-addicted comedian plays anarchic golf addict)

**Murray**

**Tina Fey,** *30 Rock* (producer of comedy show on hit show which she created and produces)

**Tracy Morgan,** *30 Rock* (funny performer on hit sketch show playing funny sketch show performer)

**Fey**

**Fey**

**Clint Eastwood,** *White Hunter, Black Heart* (macho film director making a movie in Africa, starring and directed by Clint Eastwood)

**George Burns and Gracie Allen,** *The Burns and Allen Show* (husband/wife comedy team playing husband and wife)

**Burns and Allen**

**Burns and Allen**

**Woody Allen,** *Annie Hall* (Jewish man dates young beautiful woman)

**Larry David,** *Curb Your Enthusiasm* (rich Jewish curmudgeon named Larry David gets into trouble)

**Allen**

**Sylvester Stallone,** *Rocky* (out-of-luck blue-collar scrapper hits it big)

**Henry Fonda,** *On Golden Pond* (prickly geezer has troubled relationship with daughter, played by Jane Fonda)

**Stallone**

**Stallone**

**Mickey Rourke,** *The Wrestler* (addicted down-on-his-luck performer makes comeback)

**Jack Black,** *School of Rock* (funny rocker slob, good with kids)

**Rourke**

**Danny DeVito,** *Batman Returns* (penguin-shaped man plays a penguin)

**Charlie Sheen,** *Two and a Half Men* (alcoholic man-whore with less talented brother)

**Sheen**

**Eminem,** *8 Mile* (out-of-luck rapper from Detroit hits it big)

**Marlon Brando,** *The Freshman* (the Godfather replays the Godfather)

**Eminem**

**Eminem**

**Burns and Allen vs. Tina Fey**
Tina's great as Liz Lemon, comedy show producer, but Burns and Allen broke through our TV screens and into our homes without leaving their home or changing their names. Burns often broke the "fourth wall" by talking to the camera, commenting on plot lines and what other characters were doing. George and Gracie even cast their real-life kids Sandy and Ronny as, well, their kids Sandy and Ronny. In his finest meta-move, Burns would actually turn on his TV to see what the other characters were doing while he was off camera.

**Woody Allen vs. Larry David**
It must be hard for New York Jews to play anything but New York Jews. But these two funny men don't even pretend they're trying on a role. David seemingly has the edge here for keeping his name, wealth, and *Seinfeld* résumé intact on *Curb Your Enthusiasm,* but Woody wins because (a) he's played himself in more than 30 films, and (b) real Jews don't move to Los Angeles.

**Sylvester Stallone vs. Mickey Rourke**
Two fighters, one looking to get back on top and the other just getting there. Stallone wins for writing the part that launched a career – not to mention five sequels – and coming out looking a hell of a lot better than Mickey does today.

**Burns and Allen**

**Stallone**

**Stallone**

**Stallone**

**VS**

**Stallone vs. Malkovich**
Close to the Stallone bone as Rocky may be, to beat Malkovich here he shudda called his movie *Sly*. In *Being John Malkovich,* Malkovich not only gets to play himself, but everyone else gets to play in his brain for 15 minutes too. Ironically, as an actor, Malkovich has never been better. The line between acting and being doesn't get thinner

ACTORS DREAM OF FINDING ROLES THAT THEY WERE "BORN TO PLAY." But how hard can it be to play a part where you're basically playing yourself? Was that Rocky we were rooting for in *Rocky,* or Sylvester Stallone? Were we watching a dancer in *Top Hat,* or Fred Astaire? In this bracket we aim to measure the thin line between what a star does on screen and who he or she really is. The thinner the line, the better – at least here.

**Will Smith vs. Kid 'n Play**
Both can rap and dance, '90s style. Both kept their name on screen. And both end up with the girl. But Smith shed the Fresh Prince persona and went on to bigger roles that expanded his acting chops, while Kid 'n Play never gave up on playing themselves. But Sydney, she's got a house! With a rec room!

**Astaire vs. Malkovich**
Frankly, you don't want to see Fred Astaire in any movie where he's not playing Fred Astaire, whatever name the screenwriters gave him. And though his acting might not have been a stretch, the dancing required Herculean rehearsal and execution. For that alone – he was playing himself but working really hard! – he loses to Malkovich.

THE WINNER

**John Malkovich**
*Being John Malkovich*

- Astaire
  - Astaire
    - **Fred Astaire,** *Top Hat* (professional dancer dancing in elegant clothes)
    - **Billy Crystal,** *Mr. Saturday Night* (great NY stand-up plays slightly less successful NY stand-up)
  - Beyonce
    - **Diana Ross,** *Lady Sings the Blues* (singer plays jazz singer Billie Holiday)
    - **Beyonce Knowles,** *Dreamgirls* (singer plays singer based on Diana Ross)
- Kid 'n Play
  - Kid 'n Play
    - **Will Smith,** *The Fresh Prince of Bel-Air* (Philadelphia rapper named Will Smith moves to California)
    - **Kid 'n Play,** *House Party* (wannabe rappers who dance well together)
  - Sinatra
    - **Elvis Presley,** *Viva Las Vegas* (The King takes Vegas)
    - **Frank Sinatra,** *Ocean's 11* (leader of the Rat Pack takes Vegas)
- Malkovich
  - Malkovich
    - **Jerry Stiller,** *The Heartbreak Kid* (Ben Stiller's dad plays Ben Stiller's dad)
    - **John Malkovich,** *Being John Malkovich* (plays himself as movie star with open portal into his psyche)
  - Cera
    - **Adrian Grenier,** *Entourage* (good-looking, maybe-talented young actor from Queens)
    - **Michael Cera,** *Arrested Development* (most awkward kid in the world)
- Arnaz
  - Arnaz
    - **Desi Arnaz,** *I Love Lucy* (Cuban band leader married to funny redhead)
    - **Roseanne Barr,** *Roseanne* (overstuffed domestic goddess with a loud mouth)
  - Nicholson
    - **Jack Nicholson,** *Something's Gotta Give* (rich old guy, never married, shtups younger women)
    - **Warren Beatty,** *Shampoo* (1960s playboy shtups anything that moves)

# Talk Radio Hosts

**By David Hinckley**

David Hinckley was first drawn to talk radio when he heard the late Joe Pyne tell a caller to "go gargle with razor blades." The image still intrigues him. He has spent the last 28 years as an editor and writer with the *New York Daily News,* covering, among other things, radio.

**Click & Clack**
NPR's jovial "Car Talk" duet

**Luis Jimenez**
El Bad Boy of Hispanic radio

**Opie and Anthony**
Morning team known for getting fired

**Larry Josephson**
Pioneer of irreverent mornings

**Imus**
Shock jock who grew up, sort of

**Steve Dahl**
Pushing the morning envelope for Chicago

**Mancow**
Conservative talk guy trying to shed shock-jock past

**Star**
Hip-hop meets Ayn Rand

**Joe Pyne**
Prototype of "you're not just wrong, you're stupid" talk

**Long John Nebel**
Late-night talk institution

**Tokyo Rose**
American woman who sold Japan on radio to World War II GIs

**Bob & Ray**
Radio's drollest satirists

**Jean Shepherd**
Radio's best storyteller, ever

**Larry King**
Larry being Larry

**Barry Gray**
Pioneering progressive talk host

**Father Coughlin**
Fiery priest of 1930s radio – populist, isolationist, anti-Semitic

Jimenez
Josephson
Imus
Star
Nebel
Bob & Ray
Shepherd
Coughlin

Jimenez
Imus
Bob & Ray
Shepherd

Imus
Bob & Ray

THE WINNER

**Bob & Ray**

VS

**Jimenez vs. Josephson**
Luis Jimenez reached Howard Stern-like levels of success in New York with the same recipe: laughs and explicit sex talk. But Jimenez did it on Hispanic radio, where he's important enough to advance even though Larry Josephson years earlier was among the first to serve full-scale comedy and grownup talk for breakfast.

**Imus vs. Jimenez**
Don Imus has taken unflattering adjectives like "cranky" and "self-absorbed" and blended them right into an entertainment persona that has evolved from fast-talking top-40 jock to morning comedian to a serious commentator with an A-list roster of political and media guests. That chameleon-like adaptability puts him through this round.

**Limbaugh vs. Bob & Ray**
Both Rush and Bob & Ray dissect what's unfolding around them with world-class flair. But where Rush fires grenades, both serious and witty, Bob and Ray lobbed water balloons. They found the absurd and made it absurder, which meant more laughs for longer. It meant even their soaking-wet victims laughed. And it means they win.

TALK ON THE RADIO, like music, has always had a magnetic power, making the listener part of the American conversation. In recent years talk's dominant voice, or at least its loudest, has been conservative politics. But whatever ideological nudges it has given the country, talk radio remains primarily an entertainment medium, touching everything from sports to spanakopita. A host who can't make a show lively and fun doesn't get into the conversation at all.

**Limbaugh vs. Stern**
Limbaugh and Stern reshaped old styles of talk radio – politics and comedy – into new, more aggressive forms, spawning cults of more than 10 million listeners plus hundreds of imitators who think it's as easy as it sounds. Limbaugh wins here because, unlike Stern who now creates radio theater via satellite, he is a pure talk host, holding listeners for three hours with words.

**Mike and the Mad Dog vs. Gamblings**
Mike Francesa and Chris Russo were red-meat sports radio, stirring up Yankees arguments for 19 years, then splitting acrimoniously. The Gamblings – John B. (1925–1959), John A. (1959–1991), and John R. (since 1991) – have been called bland, which should be fatal. But they've lasted 83 years, suggesting that some listeners enjoy "welcoming" and "civil" at 7 a.m.

- **Limbaugh**
  - Limbaugh
    - Limbaugh
      - **Rush Limbaugh** – Defining voice of modern conservative talk
      - **Bob Grant** – Pioneer of modern conservative talk
    - Savage
      - **Barry Farber** – Major early conservative talk host
      - **Michael Savage** – Fiery conservative prophet of doom
  - Hannity
    - Fass
      - **Bob Fass** – Free-form lefty talk pioneer, with humor
      - **Alex Bennett** – Early progressive talker
    - Hannity
      - **Laura Ingraham** – Proving guys don't have all the right-wing fun
      - **Sean Hannity** – Crown Prince of conservative talk
- **Stern**
  - Stern
    - Stern
      - **Howard Stern** – Dramatist who turned morning radio into mainlining caffeine
      - **Art Bell** – Late-night god of the paranormal
    - Schlessinger
      - **Bruce Williams** – Sensible money and life advice
      - **Dr. Laura Schlessinger** – The drill instructor of radio shrinks
  - Gambling
    - Gambling
      - **John Gambling** – Three generations of morning radio for the family
      - **Mike and the Mad Dog** – Definitive NY sports-talk team
    - McBride
      - **Mary Margaret McBride** – Soft-spoken destroyer of gender and racial barriers
      - **Dr. Joy Browne** – Your level-headed shrink friend

# Child Actors

**By Griffin Miller**

Griffin Miller is theater editor for the Davler Media publications "*City" Guide, Promenade,* and *NY Metro Parents.* Her inner child is the best (but unsung) kid actor ever.

**Lukas Haas**
Breakout role as Amish boy who witnesses a whacking in *Witness*

**Haley Joel Osment**
*Forrest Gump, A.I.,* spotted dead people in *The Sixth Sense*

Haley Joel Osment

**Shirley Temple**
Depression-era Hollywood superstar and winner of a special Oscar

**Tatum O'Neal**
Oscar-winner for role as con-artist moppet in *Paper Moon*

Shirley Temple

**Jackie Coogan**
Discovered by Charlie Chaplin, who starred with him in *The Kid*

**Paul Petersen**
Sitcom son Jeff Stone on *The Donna Reed Show* from 1958–1966

Jackie Coogan

**Mickey Rooney**
Hollywood star defined by two roles: Mickey McGuire; Andy Hardy, the all-American teen

**Macaulay Culkin**
Resourceful boy who thwarts buffoon robbers in *Home Alone*

Mickey Rooney

**Jerry Mathers**
"The Beav" on *Leave It to Beaver*

**Ron Howard**
Opie on *The Andy Griffith Show*

Ron Howard

**Jodie Foster**
Coppertone commercial at age three, adolescent hooker in *Taxi Driver*

**Helen Hunt**
Many TV roles in 1970s, Murray Slaughter's daughter on *The Mary Tyler Moore Show*

Jodie Foster

**Jaleel White**
Embodied the ultimate nerd, Steve Urkel, on *Family Matters*

**Mary-Kate & Ashley Olsen**
Tag-team portrayal of little Michelle on *Full House* starting at the age of nine months

Jaleel White

**Natalie Wood**
Remembered fondly as the sweet-faced Santa skeptic in *Miracle on 34th Street*

**Drew Barrymore**
Scene-stealer in *E.T.,* youngest host of *Saturday Night Live*

Natalie Wood

Shirley Temple

Mickey Rooney

Ron Howard

Natalie Wood

Shirley Temple

Ron Howard

**Shirley Temple vs. Ron Howard.**
The most naturally gifted child actors ever. Shirley had her ringlets and tap duets with Buddy Ebsen and Bill Robinson; Howard's Opie, even at his youngest, held his own in one-on-one scenes with Barney Fife. While both acted as if they'd been in the business for twenty years, Howard was a supporting actor (absorbing lessons that made him an Oscar-winning director) whereas Temple was a tiny leading lady.

**Jackie Coogan vs. Paul Petersen**
The earnest Petersen was a kibble on the buffet of child actors. Coogan was an early mini-giant. But they are forever entwined: Petersen started a foundation in 1990 to help child actors deal with their post-celebrity lives but Coogan was the object lesson for Petersen's cause. The future Uncle Fester was a victim of his parents' insatiable greed, squandering his millions. The 1939 Coogan Act protected a portion of underage actors' earnings.

**Shirley Temple vs. Patty Duke**
If they had switched eras, who knows what Patty's impact would have been? But her time was the early '60s and she won the adoration of teenyboppers. Shirley's time was, fortuitously, the Great Depression, where her otherworldly talent and incandescent smile made her a beacon of hope for an entire country. FDR said it best when he declared: "As long as our country has Shirley Temple, we will be all right." *The Good Ship Lollipop* sailed into the winner's circle.

THE WINNER

**Shirley Temple**

VS

FROM SILENT FILMS TO THE DISNEY CHANNEL, America's adorable, precocious, gifted, spunky, and bratty child actors have been known as much for their professional success as for their psychological meltdowns that often doomed their adult careers. But their happy/sad quotient cannot erase the charm they exuded when they were at their peak cuteness, demonstrating their preternatural talents. Since it would take another bracket to fit in the *Cosby* kids, the *Eight is Enoughers,* and the *Brady Bunches*, they were eliminated from consideration.

**Judy Garland vs. Patty Duke**
Aside from the cult cachet of *The Wizard of Oz,* Garland's child-actress status is negligible. One could say the same of Duke's thin résumé outside of *The Miracle Worker.* But when you compare their seminal performances, Duke's blind, deaf, and mute Helen Keller knocks Judy's rainbow-chasing Dorothy Gale right out of her ruby slippers.

**Danny Bonaduce vs. Frankie Muniz**
After David Cassidy's teen sex appeal, Bonaduce was the major reason to tune in to *The Partridge Family:* what would that scamp Danny do next? Muniz was smart (Mensa fodder) and the odd kid out in a lunatic clan, arbiter of family sanity. Danny's IQ was more felicitously deployed for chaos in a family of goody-two-shoes stiffs.

# Patty Duke

- **Patty Duke**
  - **Judy Garland**
    - **Judy Garland**
      - **Judy Garland** — '30s musical darling whose crowning moment came on a trip to Oz in 1939
      - **Margaret O'Brien** — '40s musical darling who shared screen with Garland in *Meet Me in St. Louis*
    - **Britney Spears**
      - **Annette Funicello** — Original *Mickey Mouse Club* break-out hottie
      - **Britney Spears** — Revamped *Mickey Mouse Club* break-out hottie
  - **Patty Duke**
    - **Patty Duke**
      - **Patty Duke** — Oscar for Helen Keller *(The Miracle Worker)*; youngest actor with TV series bearing name
      - **George (Spanky McFarland)** — *Our Gang*'s Spanky, undisputed leader of rascally pack
    - **Dakota Fanning**
      - **Kirsten Dunst** — Fashion model at three; bloodthirsty vampire by 12 *(Interview with the Vampire)*
      - **Dakota Fanning** — Heartbreaker in *I Am Sam; War of the Worlds*
- **Billy Mumy**
  - **Danny Bonaduce**
    - **Danny Bonaduce**
      - **Danny Bonaduce** — Über-sassy *Partridge Family* troublemaker
      - **Gary Coleman** — Undersized Arnold "whatchootalkinaboutwillis" Jackson on *Diff'rent Strokes*
    - **Frankie Muniz**
      - **Fred Savage** — Central character and youngest sibling Kevin Arnold in *The Wonder Years*
      - **Frankie Muniz** — Title role in off-kilter sitcom *Malcolm in the Middle*
  - **Billy Mumy**
    - **Jackie Cooper**
      - **Melissa Gilbert** — *Little House on the Prairie's* Laura, a.k.a. "Half-Pint"
      - **Jackie Cooper** — First Oscar-nominated child *(Skippy)*; early *Our Gang* member
    - **Billy Mumy**
      - **Ricky Schroder** — Nine-year-old Golden Globe winner for his film debut in 1979 remake of *The Champ*
      - **Billy Mumy** — Scariest kid ever on *The Twilight Zone* and smart Will Robinson on *Lost in Space*

# Detroit Celluloid

**By Kevin Conley**

Kevin Conley grew up on Detroit's East Side and pretty much hasn't been scared since.

*The Island* / *RoboCop* → *RoboCop*

*8 Mile* / *Four Brothers* → *8 Mile*

*Blue Collar* / *Over the Bridge* → *Blue Collar*

*Beverly Hills Cop* / *Zebrahead* → *Beverly Hills Cop*

*Roger & Me* / *Detroit: Ruin of a City* → *Roger & Me*

*Madonna: Truth or Dare* / *High Tech Soul: The Creation of Techno Music* → *Madonna*

*Narc* / *T-Men* → *Narc*

*The Evil Dead* / *Transformers* → *The Evil Dead*

*RoboCop* / *8 Mile* → *8 Mile*

*Blue Collar* / *Beverly Hills Cop* → *Beverly Hills Cop*

*Roger & Me* / *Madonna* → *Roger & Me*

*Narc* / *The Evil Dead* → *Narc*

*8 Mile* / *Beverly Hills Cop* → *8 Mile*

*Roger & Me* / *Narc* → *Roger & Me*

*8 Mile* / *Roger & Me* → *8 Mile* VS

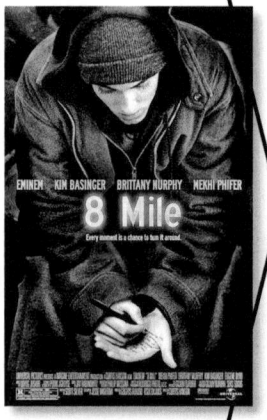


***8 Mile* vs. *Gran Torino***
*8 Mile*, for all its rap battles and racial bantering, follows a predictable trajectory to the film's final victory. *Gran Torino*, which also betrays strong influences (especially Eastwood's earlier work in *Dirty Harry* and *Unforgiven*), is the more surprising and unpredictable film. This drag race is a close call – Detroit wins, either way – but *Gran Torino*, named for a bitching '70s muscle car, burns a little more rubber and takes the checkers here.

***8 Mile* vs. *Roger & Me***
In 2002, "Lose Yourself" went #1 and won an Academy Award for Eminem, a.k.a. Marshall Mathers. But to Detroiters *8 Mile* was more famous for all its insider shout-outs and recognizable hangouts. The hip-hop auto-bio-pic shows Rabbit (Mathers) and his homeboys hanging out in the Michigan Theatre, a onetime art-deco movie palace-turned-parking lot, and later sets a quickie sex scene during a break on the factory floor. Detroiters, who kind of like it greasy, laughed in recognition. No film is better than *Roger & Me* at depicting the despondency and economic hangover caused by the flight of the auto industry; it's Michael Moore's best and angriest film. But *8 Mile* is angrier, funnier, with much better music and wins in a slaughter.

HOLLYWOOD LOVES A GRITTY "Down and Out in Motor City" story, but it balks at actually filming there. Nearly half the films here were shot in safer locations. This is a shame, and to Detroiters, a betrayal. The D of today is the Mickey Rourke of locations: one look and you see all the decades of drugs, riot, late nights, bare knuckles. Though old photos of postwar Warsaw, with its bombed-out buildings and meadows of rubble, make native Detroiters feel homesick, the Motor City remains ready for its closeup.

***Gran Torino* vs. *Virgin Suicides***
*Gran Torino* ends with the title car driving beside the bright blue waters of Lake St. Clair, along Lakeshore, in Grosse Pointe Shores. It could be headed toward the private school attended by the Lisbon sisters, the suicides in Sofia Coppola's directorial debut. But Coppola copped out, transplanting the pitch-perfect suburban adolescents of the Eugenides novel to Toronto. The result is a dreamy, homogenous, hormonal tone poem that can't stand up to the challenge of Eastwood's foul-mouthed elegy for the working man. *Gran Torino* in a walkover.

***True Romance* vs. *Detroit 9000***
A Quentin Tarantino faceoff: the writer-director offered the first taste of his sado-weisenheimer style with his screenplay for *True Romance.* Five years later, after the success of *Pulp Fiction,* he arranged the re-release of *Detroit 9000,* a key 1973 Blaxploitation pic. In a squeaker, the ironic remake beats the cultural touchstone.

***52 Pick-Up* vs. *Dreamgirls***
Both of these movies should have been filmed in Detroit. *52 Pickup* takes a juicy Elmore Leonard story and transposes it to an antiseptic L.A. *Dreamgirls* takes a Motown origin myth – how Berry Gordy created the top soul group of the '60s, the Supremes, by demoting its most soulful voice to a backup singer – and profanes it by setting it in a generic midwestern city. *52 Pickup,* which at least retained Leonard's dialogue, wins this duel of disappointments.

THE WINNER

## *Gran Torino*

***Out of Sight* vs. *Shadows of Motown***
*Out of Sight* is the best Elmore Leonard movie set in his adopted hometown. The city looks both rough and romantic, with a hotel love scene between George Clooney and Jennifer Lopez in Detroit's wishfully named Renaissance Center. The documentary *Standing in the Shadows* tells the story of Motown's studio musicians – largely anonymous during the label's heyday, then abruptly abandoned when Gordy moved production to LA. As in life, star power trounces the backup band.

- *Gran Torino*
  - *True Romance*
    - *True Romance*
    - *Assault on Precinct 13*
  - *Detroit 9000*
    - *Action Jackson*
    - *Detroit 9000*
  - *Virgin Suicides*
    - *Virgin Suicides*
    - *Hoffa*
  - *Gran Torino*
    - *Grosse Pointe Blank*
    - *Gran Torino*
- *Out of Sight*
  - *52 Pick-Up*
    - *52 Pick-Up*
    - *Dreamgirls*
  - *Out of Sight*
    - *Out of Sight*
    - *Scarecrow*
  - *Shadows*
    - *The Upside of Anger*
    - *Standing in the Shadows of Motown*
  - *The Betsy*
    - *The Betsy*
    - *Nevermore*

# Girl Singers

**By Tom Moon**

Tom Moon, a former music critic at the *Philadelphia Inquirer*, is a regular contributor to NPR's *All Things Considered* and the author of the bestselling *1000 Recordings to Hear Before You Die*.

R&B/BLUES/GOSPEL REGIONAL

Aretha Franklin
Sister Rosetta Tharpe
Franklin

Bessie Smith
Whitney Houston
Smith

Franklin

Tina Turner
Mariah Carey
Turner

Mary J. Blige
Etta James
James

Turner

Franklin

ROCK/COUNTRY REGIONAL

Janis Joplin
Emmylou Harris
Joplin

Rickie Lee Jones
Shania Twain
Jones

Joplin

Linda Ronstadt
Dolly Parton
Parton

Patsy Cline
Patti Smith
Cline

Cline

Joplin

**Aretha Franklin vs. Sister Rosetta**
The firebrand of the 1940s gospel-blues (and the first great female guitarist) loses narrowly to the supreme siren of the 1960s. Franklin grew up singing gospel – during her string of hits in the early '70s, she recorded the live gospel gem "Amazing Grace," which features a huge choir led by her father, the Rev. C.L. Franklin.

**Patsy Cline vs. Janis Joplin**
Patsy or Janis. Sugar or spice? A showdown between two talents with tragedy-shortened careers – Cline's the most vulnerable, angelic voice ever to sing country, and Joplin's the most intense belter ever to front a rock band. Joplin represents the bigger leap forward, however: after her, rock singing changed forever.

THE WINNER

**Aretha Franklin**

VS

**Billie Holiday vs. Aretha Franklin**
With Aretha, it's never just about commanding pipes or ballet-dancer phrasing. Aretha Franklin believes what she sings. Whether she's tearing out a weary blues ("Trouble in Mind") or an operatic aria ("Nessun Dorma" from Puccini's *Turandot*), it's her talent for communicating conviction that earns her ultimate respect.

SINCE THE DAWN OF RECORDED SOUND, the girl singer has exerted extraordinary pull on the American imagination – as a beacon of virtue/piety (Marian Anderson) or a corruptor of men (Bessie Smith), a take-no-bullshit realist (Aretha Franklin) or a weaver of dreams (Patsy Cline), a witness to love's anguish (Billie Holiday) or a witness to the cruelties of society (Nina Simone). To divine the fairest behind the microphone, we start with four basic styles – opera, jazz, rock/country, blues/R&B (including gospel). Advancement is determined by influence on the art of singing. Those who cast the longest shadow stay in the game.

**Ella Fitzgerald vs. Sarah Vaughan**
There are two types of people in the world – Ella people and Sarah people, a musical polarity as sharp and vivid as liberal vs. conservative. Sarah's the more adventurous singer, but Ella prevails here on the strength of her blithely bouyant, peerless scat-singing, which everyone since (including Sarah) emulated.

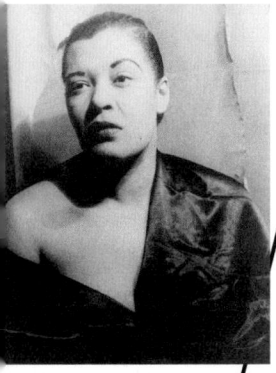

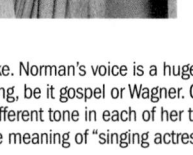


JAZZ REGIONAL

OPERA REGIONAL

**Nina Simone vs. Shirley Horn**
A faceoff between two adept jazz singers who accompanied themselves on piano. Classically trained Simone advances mainly because, in addition to her deep-mahogany voice, she gave the world such trenchant songs as "To Be Young, Gifted and Black."

**Billie Holiday vs. Maria Callas**
Both Callas and Holiday kept singing after their vocal luster diminished. But Billie, especially in her Verve years, did more with her devastated cords, much more.

**Maria Callas vs. Jessye Norman**
A choice no opera lover wants to make. Norman's voice is a huge, seamless, radiant instrument that seems to thrive in any setting, be it gospel or Wagner. Callas's voice was not as organic – she projected a distinctly different tone in each of her three registers – but her dramatic interpretations redefined the meaning of "singing actress."

# Cathartic Movie Deaths

**By David Edelstein**

David Edelstein is the film critic for *New York* magazine, NPR's *Fresh Air*, and CBS *Sunday Morning*.

*Once Upon a Time in the West*
Bronson outguns Fonda

*Shane*
Ladd outguns Palance

*High Noon*
Coop takes out bad guy holding Grace Kelly

*The Silence of the Lambs*
Jodie Foster blows away serial killer

*Terminator 2*
Arnold gives bad Terminator a molten bath

*Star Wars*
Death Star explodes

*Halloween*
Jamie Lee Curtis and Donald Pleasance finish off Michael – for now

*The French Connection*
Gene Hackman shoots assassin

*The Adventures of Robin Hood*
Flynn skewers Rathbone

*Kill Bill, Vol. 1*
Uma Thurman bisects Lucy Liu's skull

*Casablanca*
Bogie shoots Conrad Veidt

*Double Indemnity*
MacMurray kills Stanwyck in a clinch

*Taxi Driver*
De Niro to Keitel: Suck on this!

*Straw Dogs*
Hoffman springs the man-trap on Scottish creep

*Marathon Man*
Olivier impales himself in Central Park

*Fatal Attraction*
Anne Archer nails Glenn Close in the tub

*Once Upon a Time in the West*

*The Silence of the Lambs*

*Terminator 2*

*The French Connection*

*Robin Hood*

*Casablanca*

*Taxi Driver*

*Fatal Attraction*

*Once Upon a Time in the West*

*The French Conection*

*Casablanca*

*Fatal Attraction*

***Once Upon a Time* vs. *The French Connection***
The finale of cinema's jangliest car chase is orgasmic but not orgasmic and lyrical, as in Sergio Leone's lovingly drawn-out showdown, his camera circling (to Ennio Morricone's voluptuous score) as duelists Fonda and Bronson assume their classic positions. The end comes so fast that we're as stunned as Fonda as he reels into the camera and sinks to his knees.

***Casablanca* vs. *Fatal Attraction***
*Casablanca* has the greatest applause-getting twist ("Round up the usual suspects") but it pales beside Glenn Close in that bathtub as our misogynistic bloodlust builds to a frenzy: "KILL THE BITCH!!!!!!!"

*Once Upon a Time in the West*

***Jaws* vs. *Once Upon a Time in the West***
A tough call, but for sheer cathartic bliss, it's sushi all around.

*Once Upon a Time in the West*

VS

FEW THINGS IN MOVIES give as much pleasure as the moment the villain gets it – gets it so it hurts, so the audience screams as one as in a giant cinematic orgasmatron. Alas, I've had to disqualify many fine old films because the bad guy gets arrested. Bummer. To make this list there must be no shades of gray, no twinge of sympathy for the devil. To paraphrase Shakespeare: "Nothing becomes these monsters' lives like the leaving of them."

***The Manchurian Candidate* vs. *Jaws***
What a joy it is to see *Manchurian*'s monster Mom, so smug in triumph, get shot full of lead. But to see the Great White moving in on Roy Scheider as John Williams's music plugs into our heartbeats while bullet after bullet does nothing to slow the charge and then . . . "Smile you son of a bitch!" BLAM!

***The Big Sleep* vs. *Carrie***
It's a joyous moment in *The Big Sleep* when Bogie forces the bad guy into his own ambush, but for anti-matriarchal audacity (with sacrilege to boot!), Piper Laurie's lingering kitchen-implement crucifixion has no peers.

**THE WINNER**

***Jaws***
Roy Scheider blows up man-eating shark

- *Jaws*
  - *Jaws*
    - *Dirty Harry*
      - ***Dirty Harry*** — Eastwood has one bullet left for psycho-killer
      - ***Die Hard*** — Bruce Willis drops Alan Rickman
    - *Jaws*
      - ***Alien*** — Sigourney Weaver blasts alien into space
      - ***Jaws*** — Roy Scheider blows up man-eating shark
  - *Manchurian*
    - *Manchurian*
      - ***The Manchurian Candidate*** — Laurence Harvey blasts Angela Lansbury and stepdad
      - ***Death Proof (Grindhouse)*** — Karate babes pummel Kurt Russell
    - *The Fury*
      - ***Platoon*** — Charlie Sheen goes righteous on Tom Berenger
      - ***The Fury*** — Amy Irving vaporizes John Cassavettes
- *Carrie*
  - *Carrie*
    - *Carrie*
      - ***Carrie*** — Sissy Spacek telepathically nails Piper Laurie
      - ***The Wizard of Oz*** — Judy Garland melts Wicked Witch with $H_2O$
    - *Blue Velvet*
      - ***Blue Velvet*** — Kyle MacLachlan surprises Dennis Hopper
      - ***Midnight Express*** — Brad Davis spikes Turkish jailer
  - *The Big Sleep*
    - *One False Move*
      - ***One False Move*** — Bill Paxton takes out very mean killers
      - ***A History of Violence*** — "Gee Richie," Viggo shoots brother William Hurt
    - *The Big Sleep*
      - ***The Big Sleep*** — Bad guy's own men riddle him with bullets
      - ***North by Northwest*** — Martin Landau takes one in the back on Rushmore

# Game-Show Hosts

**By Steve Leblang**

Steve Leblang, a senior research executive for FOX's cable networks, frequently roamed NBC's Rockefeller Center (the 1970s home of *Jackpot* and *To Tell the Truth*) and the corner of West 58th Street and 7th Avenue in New York City (home to the *$20,000 Pyramid* and *The Big Showdown*).

**Bill Cullen**
*The Price Is Right* and *Blockbusters*

**Howie Mandel**
*Deal or No Deal*

**Richard Dawson**
*Family Feud*

**Geoff Edwards**
*Jackpot!* and *The New Treasure Hunt*

**Wink Martindale**
*Gambit* and *Tic-Tac-Dough*

**Marc Summers**
*Double Dare*

**Jack Narz**
*Beat the Clock* and *Concentration*

**John Charles Daly**
*What's My Line?*

**Monty Hall**
*Let's Make a Deal*

**Hal March**
*The $64,000 Question*

**Bert Convy**
*Tattletales*

**Art James**
*Who, What or Where Game*

**Alex Trebek**
*Jeopardy!* and *High Rollers*

**Drew Carey**
*The Price Is Right* and *Whose Line Is It Anyway*

**Gene Rayburn**
*The Match Game*

**Chuck Woolery**
*Love Connection* and *Wheel of Fortune*

Bill Cullen

Richard Dawson

Wink Martindale

John Charles Daly

Monty Hall

Bert Convy

Alex Trebek

Gene Rayburn

Bill Cullen

Wink Martindale

Monty Hall

Alex Trebek

Alex Trebek

Bill Cullen

**Alex Trebek vs. Monty Hall**
Hall used trickery and mystery to make viewers of *Let's Make a Deal's* human circus care whether a man dressed as a giant rutabaga would win a Chevelle by correctly pricing a box of Creamettes macaroni. *Deal* was vaudeville but *Jeopardy!* is intellect – and Trebek's cool, professorial approach over 25 years has made the smartest game show a grade or two smarter.

THE WINNER

**Bill Cullen,**
*The Price Is Right* and *Blockbusters*

VS

**Bill Cullen vs. Tom Kennedy**
Kennedy was brainy and warm but Cullen was all that and more. No host was more versatile than the crew-cut Cullen, who made civilian contestants feel at home, gave celebrity guests the spotlight they needed, and was a coveted panelist on other game shows. Groucho Marx, who hosted *You Bet Your Life,* more as a comedy showcase than a real game show, once called Cullen "the second wittiest man in the business" – a comic genius's confirmation of Cullen's status.

FOR NEARLY SIXTY YEARS Americans have come on down, spun the wheel, beat the clock, named that tune, and become queen for a day, nearly always guided by suave, attractive purveyors of wealth, fantasy, and good luck. To contestants and viewers, the best game-show hosts are entertainers who inform and somehow make us feel they're our friend. They keep us returning to solve that rebus on *Concentration*, to guess what Monty Hall has in his jacket pocket, and to give the answer in the form of a question.

**Regis Philbin vs. Bud Collyer**
Collyer, the radio voice of *Superman,* presided over his shows like a low-key pastor but with a steely sense of order. But Philbin's wild exuberance and genuine fascination with contestants on the savvily produced *Millionaire* single-handedly saved ABC's prime-time schedule, at least for a while.

**Betty White vs. Bob Barker**
White, a gifted comic actress who married into game shows (she wed Allen Ludden during *Password*'s first run in the '60s), is the only woman to win the Emmy for outstanding host for the very short-lived *Just Men!* But for more than a half-century, Barker made thousands of contestants giddy and content – even when they priced that washing machine too high – with a common man's gentility and an absence of snarkiness.

**Bob Eubanks vs Pat Sajak**
Sajak is the Iron Man of active game-show hosts, a steady hand at the giant wheel for 28 years. But Eubanks possessed a unique ability to maintain decorum – if not a straight face – during four decades of newly married couples' innuendo and double entendres in the service of awarding a "special super-deluxe grand prize chosen just for you!"

**Tom Kennedy**

- **Dick Clark**
  - **Regis Philbin**
    - **Regis Philbin** – *Who Wants to Be a Millionaire* and *Million Dollar Password*
    - **Bud Collyer** – *To Tell the Truth* and *Beat the Clock*
  - **Dick Clark**
    - **Dick Clark** – various *Pyramids*
    - **Peter Marshall** – *Hollywood Squares*
- **Bob Barker**
  - **Betty White**
    - **Jack Barry** – *Twenty-One* and *Joker's Wild*
    - **Betty White** – *Just Men!*
  - **Bob Barker**
    - **Bob Barker** – *The Price Is Right* and *Truth or Consequences*
    - **Meredith Vieira** – *Who Wants to Be a Millionaire*
- **Tom Kennedy**
  - **Allen Ludden**
    - **Peter Tomarken**
      - **Garry Moore** – *I've Got a Secret* and *To Tell the Truth*
      - **Peter Tomarken** – *Press Your Luck*
    - **Allen Ludden**
      - **Allen Ludden** – several versions of *Password*
      - **Dennis James** – various shows
  - **Tom Kennedy**
    - **Bob Eubanks**
      - **Bob Eubanks** – *The Newlywed Game*
      - **Pat Sajak** – *Wheel of Fortune*
    - **Tom Kennedy**
      - **Tom Kennedy** – *You Don't Say* and *Name That Tune*
      - **Jim Lange** – *The Dating Game*

# Grateful Dead Songs

**By John Steinbreder**

John Steinbreder, who writes for *Golf Digest* and *Forbes Life*, has more than fifty Dead shows under his belt, the last in 1992. His daughter often borrows from his collection of *Dick's Picks*, and does not necessarily agree with his winner here.

"Stella Blue"
*(Wake of the Flood, 1973)*

"Scarlet Begonias"
*(Grateful Dead from the Mars Hotel, 1974)*

"Stella Blue"

"Dark Star"
*(Live Dead, 1969)*

"Black-Throated Wind"
*(Ace, 1972)*

"Dark Star"

"Dark Star"

"Uncle John's Band"
*(Workingman's Dead, 1970)*

"Unbroken Chain"
*(Grateful Dead from the Mars Hotel, 1974)*

"Uncle John's Band"

"St. Stephen"

"St. Stephen"
*(Live Dead, 1969)*

"Cassidy"
*(Ace, 1972)*

"St. Stephen"

"China Cat Sunflower"
*(Europe '72, 1972)*

"Bird Song"
*(Garcia, 1972)*

"China Cat"

"Eyes of the World"

"Eyes of the World"
*(Wake of the Flood, 1973)*

"Brown-Eyed Women"
*(Europe '72, 1972)*

"Eyes of the World"

"Box of Rain"

"Casey Jones"
*(Workingman's Dead, 1970)*

"Candyman"
*(American Beauty, 1970)*

"Casey Jones"

"Box of Rain"

"Box of Rain"
*(American Beauty, 1970)*

"Ripple"
*(American Beauty, 1970)*

"Box of Rain"

**"Dark Star" vs. "St. Stephen"**
Irrevocably connected as part of the otherworldly *Live Dead* album and frequent components of the same concert medleys, these songs share both sound and aura, to say nothing of quality. "Dark Star" consistently lets the band stretch itself, but "St. Stephen" almost advances on irony: Garcia's 1995 memorial service was held at Marin County's St. Stephen's Episcopal Church.

**"Box of Rain" vs. "Eyes of the World"**
"Eyes of the World" is the Buddhist-inspired highlight of *Wake of the Flood*, especially for Garcia's jaunty guitar and a nice bass solo by Phil Lesh at the end. But Lesh's songwriting on "Box of Rain," honoring his dying father, wins in a walk for being the Dead's final encore in Chicago in 1995. Garcia would die a month later.

**"Candyman" vs. "Casey Jones"**
In a battle between songs that appeared on different Dead albums in 1970, the cocaine-sniffing train engineer edges out the fellow offering drugs and sex to "all those pretty women." But only because "Casey Jones" provided a band with its first "hit."

THE WINNER

**"Dark Star"**
*(Live Dead, 1969)*

VS

**"Dark Star" vs. "Truckin'"**
"Truckin'," a mini-history of the band, has been recognized by the Library of Congress as a "national treasure," and contains the classic summation: "What a long, strange trip it's been." But "Dark Star" is quintessential Dead. The band stopped playing it publicly in 1974, creating a mystique that forced needy Deadheads to count the dates since its last performance. It returned to their live set in the late 1980s but was never the same. The 23-minute "moment" captured on 1969's *Live Dead* stands tall 40 years on

THE GRATEFUL DEAD ARE CELEBRATED for their improvisatory live performances, often six hours long, and their staying power (returned by their devoted fan base of Deadheads), but not nearly enough for their songwriting. Jerry Garcia, Bob Weir, and Phil Lesh composed most of the music, while Robert Hunter and John Perry Barlow handled the words. The tunes vary in style, mood, and inspiration – and the winner, it can safely be said, could only have been written by the Dead.

**"Friend of the Devil" vs. "Sugar Magnolia"**
Musical siblings from the same classic album. A close call for Bob Weir's "Sugar Magnolia" because who wouldn't rather be "rolling in the rushes" with the lovely lady than hanging out with the devil.

**"Tennessee Jed" vs. "Cumberland Blues"**
"Tennessee Jed" followed "Cumberland Blues" the first time it was performed in concert, at the University of Minnesota in 1971, and it plays second fiddle here too. "Cumberland Blues," a heartfelt tribute to coal mining, shows the Dead blending rock, bluegrass, and country. Jerry's banjo solo is back-porch picking at its best.

- "Truckin'"
  - "Sugar Magnolia"
    - "Sugar Magnolia"
      - "Friend of the Devil" — "Friend of the Devil" (*American Beauty, 1970*); Wharf Rat (*Skull & Roses, 1971*)
      - "Sugar Magnolia" — "Sugar Magnolia" (*American Beauty, 1970*); "Sugaree" (*Garcia, 1972*)
    - "Bertha"
      - "Jack Straw" — "Jack Straw" (*Europe '72, 1972*); "Ramble On Rose" (*Europe '72, 1972*)
      - "Bertha" — "Bertha" (*Skull & Roses, 1971*); "Comes A Time" (*Hundred Year Hall, 1995*)
  - "Truckin'"
    - "Cumberland Blues"
      - "Tennessee Jed" — "Tennessee Jed" (*Europe '72, 1972*); "Mississippi Half-Step Uptown Toodleloo" (*Wake of the Flood, 1973*)
      - "Cumberland Blues" — "Cumberland Blues" (*Workingman's Dead, 1970*); "U.S. Blues" (*Grateful Dead from the Mars Hotel, 1974*)
    - "Truckin'"
      - "Ship of Fools" — "Ship of Fools" (*Grateful Dead from the Mars Hotel, 1974*); "Brokedown Palace" (*American Beauty, 1970*)
      - "Truckin'" — "Playing in the Band" (*Skull & Roses, 1971*); "Truckin'" (*American Beauty, 1970*)

# Romance Novels

**By Isabel Swift**

Isabel Swift, a former editor at Harlequin, has been a spokesperson for the romance genre and has developed and launched romance lines for Pocket Books and Silhouette Books.

**ROMANTIC COMEDIES**

*Anyone But You* by Jennifer Crusie (1996)

*Nobody's Baby But Mine* by Susan Elizabeth Phillips (1998)

**Phillips**

**TIME TRAVEL**

*A Knight in Shining Armour* by Jude Deveraux (1989)

*Outlander* by Diana Gabaldon (1991+)

**Gabaldon**

**Gabaldon**

**MULTI-CULTURAL**

*No Compromise* by Rochelle Alers (2002+)

*Irresitible Force* by Brenda Jackson (2008)

**Jackson**

**AMERICANA**

*Little Women-Good Wives* by Louisa May Alcott (1868-1869)

*The Shop on Blossom Street* by Debbie Macomber (2004)

**Alcott**

**Alcott**

**Alcott**

**HISTORICAL REGENCY**

*Whitney My Love* by Judith McNaught (1985)

*The Gift* by Julie Garwood (1991)

**McNaught**

**POTBOILER**

*The Flame and the Flower* by Kathleen Woodiwiss (1972)

*Sweet, Savage Lover* by Rosemary Rogers (1974)

**Woodiwiss**

**Woodiwiss**

**Wister**

**HISTORICAL WESTERN**

*The Virginian* by Owen Wister (1902)

*Riders of the Purple Sage* by Zane Grey (1912)

**Wister**

**CATEGORY ROMANCE**

*Lightning That Lingers* by Sharon & Tom Curtis (1983)

*Long Tall Texans* by Diana Palmer (1988+)

**Palmer**

**Wister**

**Alcott vs. Wister**
Going for genre impact over reading pleasure, Wister's defining Western overcomes opposition with an iconic laconic cowboy hero and the Code of the West; but in the realm of romance, relationships, and readability, abolitionist and feminist Louisa May Alcott's story of Marmie, her four girls, and their lives and loves, is an often reread treasure and the clear winner.

**Alcott**

**VS**

**McNaught vs. Woodiwiss**
It's true McNaught launched the sexy *Regency*, but the ship would not have sailed without the queen of the sweeping, sexy, swashbuckling saga. Picking one favorite Woodiwiss title is a thankless task, but *The Flame and the Flower* is a good place to start.

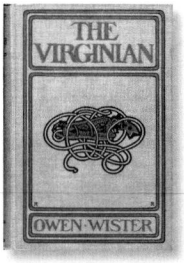


**Wister vs. Grey**
It's a mistake to think that guys are clueless about romance. There are an enlightened few. Not just Wister and Grey. But Hammett in *The Thin Man* and Sparks in a raft of bestsellers that began with *The Notebook*! The most impressive are the love stories set in the mythical West, and the best of breed is Wister's.

THE BOOKS HERE MAY STRETCH the Romance Writers of America's definition of romance fiction: "A central love story and an emotionally satisfying and optimistic ending." Some have vampires in the mix, others are sweeping historicals, still others are set in the Wild West. But they all deliver satisfaction, touching readers' hearts, offering an uplifting reading experience, and reinforcing the belief in the transformative power of love.

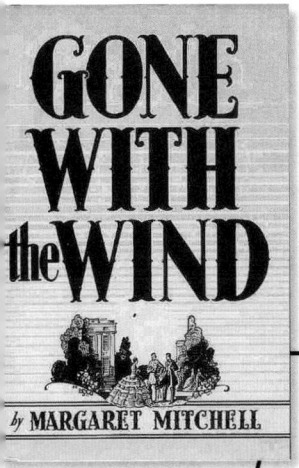


THE WINNER

**Gone With the Wind**
by Margaret Mitchell (1936)

**Howard vs. Roberts**
While top contender Linda Howard beat out tough competition, Nora Roberts is golden. She's received every award for excellence in the romance field and has countless #1 bestsellers. Whether writing romantic suspense, paranormal, futuristic, category, historical, or contemporary romances, her characters come alive and find their way into readers' hearts.

**Alcott vs. Mitchell**
OK, it's an open question whether "Tomorrow I'll think of some way to get him back. After all, tomorrow is another day" delivers the requisite HEA (Happy Ever After) ending. But Mitchell's lone effort at the novel form is vivid, sweeping, quintessentially American. It won the Pulitzer Prize in 1937 and spawned one of the most beloved films ever. It never ages, rewards repeat readings, and burrows its way into the imaginations of girls and women – and guys too.

- Roberts
  - Howard
    - Ward
      - *Fantasy Lover* by Sherrilyn Kenyon (2002+) — VAMPIRE
      - *Dark Lover* by J.R. Ward (2005+) — VAMPIRE
    - Howard
      - *Dream Man* by Linda Howard (1995) — ROMANTIC SUSPENSE
      - *Out of Control* by Suzanne Brockman (2002) — ROMANTIC SUSPENSE
  - Roberts
    - Roberts
      - *Morning Glory* by LaVyrle Spencer (1989) — CONTEMPORARY
      - *Born in Fire* by Nora Roberts (1994+) — CONTEMPORARY
    - Sparks
      - *The Thin Man* by Dashiell Hammett (1934) — MARRIED
      - *The Notebook* by Nicholas Sparks (1996) — MARRIED
- Mitchell
  - Meyer
    - Meyer
      - *Princess in Love* by Meg Cabot (2002) — YOUNG ADULT
      - *Twilight* by Stephanie Meyer (2005+) — YOUNG ADULT
    - Marshall
      - *Christy* by Catherine Marshall (1967) — INSPIRATIONAL
      - *Redeeming Love* by Francine Rivers (1991) — INSPIRATIONAL
  - Mitchell
    - Lindsey
      - *Sweet Starfire* by Jayne Castle a.k.a. Jayne Ann Krentz (1986) — FUTURISTIC
      - *Warrior's Women* by Johanna Lindsey (1990) — FUTURISTIC
    - Mitchell
      - *Gone With the Wind* by Margaret Mitchell (1936) — HISTORICAL
      - *Flowers from the Storm* by Laura Kinsale (1992) — HISTORICAL

# TV Catchphrases

**By Robert J. Thompson**

Robert Thompson is director of the Bleier Center for Television and Popular Culture at Syracuse University, where he is also a Trustee professor. He has written or edited six books about American television.

"Yabba, dabba, doo"
*The Flintstones*

"Yadda, yadda, yadda"
*Seinfeld*

"Yabba, dabba, doo"

"Beam me up, Scotty"
*Star Trek*

"Just the facts, ma'am."
*Dragnet*

"Just the facts, ma'am"

"Yabba, dabba, doo"

**"Beam me up, Scotty" vs. "Just the facts, ma'am"**
Neither of these phrases was ever uttered in either show, though there were countless variations. Sgt. Joe Friday's polite, deadpan exhortation to quit blathering and get to the point still has many practical applications in everyday life. Not so much Captain Kirk's request to be teleported from point A to point B.

"Sock it to me"
*Laugh-In*

"The Devil made me do it"
*The Flip Wilson Show*

"Sock it to me"

"Live from New York"
*Saturday Night Live*

"Here's Johnny"
*The Tonight Show*

"Live from New York"

"Sock it to me"

"Sock it to me"

**"Yabba, dabba, doo" vs. "Sock it to me"**
Fred Flintstone's pithy ode to joy is tough to beat for sheer emotion and clever use of rhyme and alliteration. Although "Sock it to me" wasn't original – it'd been used already by Mark Twain and Aretha Franklin – it's the only contender that helped get a candidate (the often humorless Richard Nixon) into the White House.

"Say, kids, what time is it?"
*Howdy Doody*

"Won't you be my neighbor?"
*Mister Rogers' Neighborhood*

"Say, kids, what time is it?"

"Your mission, should you decide to accept it . . ."
*Mission: Impossible*

"Sorry about that, Chief"
*Get Smart*

"Sorry about that, Chief"

"Say, kids, what time is it?"

"Is that your final answer?"
*Who Wants to Be a Millionaire*

"The tribe has spoken"
*Survivor*

"Is that your final answer?"

"Dy-no-mite!"
*Good Times*

"Whachootalkin'about?"
*Diff'rent Strokes*

"Whachoo-talkin' about?"

"Whachoo-talkin' about?"

"Whachoo-talkin' about?"

THE WINNER

**"Whachoo talkin' about?"**
*Diff'rent Strokes*

VS

THE HALCYON DAYS FOR TELEVISION CATCHPHRASES started in the mid-1950s and ended in the late 1970s. Weekly repetition on sitcoms, dramas, game shows, news programs, and cartoons seared these phrases into the American vernacular and they are still as easily accessed from our memory banks as the names of our closest relatives. But by the mid-1980s, the form came to be associated with high cheesiness – something to be mocked, albeit with affection. With a few notable exceptions (like *Seinfeld,* a mother lode of single-episode, zeitgeist-defining phrases), the catchphrase, like the jingle, was in bad decline.

# "And that's the way it is"

**"D'oh" vs "And that's the way it is"**
Cronkite's six-word sign-off delivered during the headiest days of CBS News was a bold and mind-bogglingly exaggerated declaration of certainty in very uncertain times. But Cronkite was known as "the most trusted man in America," while Homer, with his frequent epiphanies regarding his own stupidity, was only America's favorite nebbish.

**Whachootalkin'about" vs. And that's the way it is"**
Arnold Jackson's sentence-is-word is catchphrase art at its most pure: cheesy, original, repeated in every episode. In the end, it's a battle between two epistemological paradigms: Cronkite reports knowledge as fact; Arnold responds to knowledge with suspicion, incredulity, and even a sense of betrayal. Merily, Arnold is a modern man.

**"D'oh!" vs. "Cowabunga"**
"Cowabunga" should take this round if for no other reason than it served as a principal catchphrase on no fewer than three TV series – *The Howdy Doody Show, Teenage Mutant Ninja Turtles,* and *The Simpsons.* But for sheer poetic economy nothing beats the three-letters-and-apostrophe of Homer Simpson's emphatic "D'oh."

- "D'oh"
  - "Smile, you're on Candid Camera"
    - "Smile, you're on Candid Camera"
      - "Come on down!" *The Price Is Right*
      - "Smile, you're on Candid Camera" *Candid Camera*
    - "One of these days, Alice..."
      - "One of these days, Alice . . . to the moon" *The Honeymooners*
      - "Stifle yourself" *All in the Family*
  - "D'oh"
    - "D'oh"
      - "D'oh" *The Simpsons*
      - "Aaaaaay" *Happy Days*
    - "Cowabunga"
      - "Kawabonga/Cowabunga" (various)
      - "We've got a really big show" *The Ed Sullivan Show*
- "And that's the way it is"
  - "Book 'im, Danno"
    - "Book 'im, Danno"
      - "Who loves ya, baby?" *Kojak*
      - "Book 'im, Danno" *Hawaii Five-O*
    - "Sharon!!!!"
      - "Let's be careful out there" *Hill Street Blues*
      - "Sharon!!!!" *The Osbournes*
  - "And that's the way it is"
    - "Say good night, Gracie"
      - "Say good night, Gracie" *The George Burns and Gracie Allen Show*
      - "Good night, John-Boy" *The Waltons*
    - "And that's the way it is"
      - "Good night and good luck" Edward R. Murrow on CBS News
      - "And that's the way it is" *The Evening News with Walter Cronkite*

# Jazz Solos

**By Nick Trautwein**

Nick Trautwein is an editor and saxophonist in New York City. His last gig was Friday night, at a dive on Avenue B. The piano player won.

**Sydney Bechet** *"Blue Horizon"* vs. **Lester Young** *"Back to the Land"* → **Lester Young**

**Louis Armstrong** *"West End Blues"* vs. **Ella Fitzgerald** *"How High the Moon"* → **Louis Armstrong**

**Lester Young** vs. **Louis Armstrong** → **Louis Armstrong**

**Papa Jo Jones** *"Mr. Hi-Hat"* vs. **Coleman Hawkins** *"Body and Soul"* → **Coleman Hawkins**

**Art Tatum** *"Willow Weep for Me"* vs. **Wynton Kelly** *"Freddie Freeloader"* → **Art Tatum**

**John Coltrane** *"Crescent"* vs. **Cannonball Adderley** *"Soon"* → **John Coltrane**

**Art Tatum** vs. **John Coltrane** → **John Coltrane**

**Wes Montgomery** *"D-Natural Blues"* vs. **John Scofield** *"Teo"* → **Wes Montgomery**

**Coleman Hawkins** vs. **Wes Montgomery** → **Coleman Hawkins**

**Louis Armstrong** vs. **Coleman Hawkins** → **Louis Armstrong**

**Joe Henderson** *"Song for My Father"* vs. **Clifford Brown** *"I Don't Stand a Ghost of a Chance with You"* → **Clifford Brown**

**Freddie Hubbard** *"Birdlike"* vs. **Miles Davis** *"So What"* → **Freddie Hubbard**

**Clifford Brown** vs. **Freddie Hubbard** → **Clifford Brown**

**John Coltrane** vs. **Clifford Brown** → **John Coltrane**

**Louis Armstrong** vs. **John Coltrane** → **Louis Armstrong**

**Louis Armstrong vs. Charlie Parker**
Bird's solo, from a 1951 live recording, is a brain-bending marvel of speed, soul, and wit – imagine being inside Leonardo DaVinci's brain at the moment he finishes the Mona Lisa's smile. But since none of the rest of the seeds in this draw could possibly have existed without him, Armstrong wins the trophy, now and forever. Take it home, Pops.

**Art Tatum vs. Coleman Hawkins**
After Art Tatum blistered his last piano keyboard, nobody ever played like him again. Once Hawkins's iconic ballad performance started lighting up the juke-boxes of Harlem, nobody didn't play like him, in one way or another. This is the solo that every jazzman learns. Genius plus soul equals a spot in round 3.

THE WINNER

## Louis Armstrong: "West End Blues"

VS

**Clifford Brown vs. Freddie Hubbard**
Two precociously fluent trumpeters go head to head, Freddie with 19 blues choruses that some trumpet player somewhere is guaranteed to be ripping off at this very moment, Clifford with a swoon-inducing ballad that goes from whispering in your ear to shouting from the rooftops. Sweet ain't easy on the trumpet; Clifford wins.

JAZZ, CHARLES MINGUS SAID, IS AMERICA'S ONLY INDIGENOUS ART FORM – that and the atomic bomb. While it's hard to imagine Robret Oppenheimer lighting up the crowd on a Saturday night, jazz musicians have always been happy to turn the bandstand into a zone of armed conflict. More than any other, jazz is an art form you can win. Points are given for spontaneous brilliance, individualism, virtuosity, and sex appeal. Winners stick around to play the late set.

**Sonny Rollins vs. Sonny Stitt**
This one's an actual recorded matchup, from the Dizzy Gillespie record *Sonny Side Up,* on which the two Sonnies take turns doing to the chords of "I've Got Rhythm" (and to each other) something like what Mike Tyson did to Peter McNeeley. Rough, inventive Rollins takes down silky-smooth Stitt.

## Charlie Parker

- Charlie Parker
  - Charlie Parker
    - Charlie Parker
      - McCoy Tyner, *"Passion Dance"*
      - Charlie Parker, *"Lester Leaps In"*
    - Sonny Rollins
      - Sonny Stitt, *"The Eternal Triangle"*
      - Sonny Rollins, *"The Eternal Triangle"*
  - Illinois Jacquet
    - Illinois Jacquet
      - Illinois Jacquet, *"Flying Home"*
      - Paul Gonsalves, *"Diminuendo and Crescendo in Blue"*
    - Thelonious Monk
      - Thelonious Monk, *"Functional"*
      - Oscar Peterson, *"52nd Street Theme"*
- Herbie Hancock
  - Ornette Coleman
    - Kenny Garrett
      - Kenny Garrett, *"Human Nature"*
      - Michael Brecker, *"Syzygy"*
    - Ornette Coleman
      - Paul Chambers, *"Straight, No Chaser"*
      - Ornette Coleman, *"Peace"*
  - Herbie Hancock
    - Keith Jarrett
      - Keith Jarrett, *"Too Young to Go Steady"*
      - JJ Johnson, *"Crazy Rhythm"*
    - Herbie Hancock
      - Bud Powell, *"So Sorry Please"*
      - Herbie Hancock, *"All of You"*

**Illinois Jacquet vs. Paul Gonsalves**
According to legend, Gonsalves's side-splitting 27-chorus solo was thrust upon him by bandleader Duke Ellington as punishment for showing up to the gig at Newport too drunk to stand up right. Given the advantage of (relative) sobriety, the ferociously entertaining Jacquet moves on.

**Ornette Coleman vs. Herbie Hancock**
Ornette's free improvisation is a masterwork of melodic beauty (and also probably the best piece of evidence that he actually knows what the hell he's doing). But Herbie live at the Plugged Nickel is like Federer at the U.S. Open – cool, graceful, wickedly smart, and transportingly able to do anything he wants.

# Romantic Comedies

**By David Denby**

David Denby, a film critic and staff writer at *The New Yorker* since 1998, is the author of *Great Books, American Sucker,* and *Snark.*

*His Girl Friday* (1940)
*When Harry Met Sally* (1989)
*His Girl Friday*

*Bringing Up Baby* (1938)
*Adam's Rib* (1949)
*Adam's Rib*

*His Girl Friday*

*Holiday* (1938)
*Superbad* (2007)
*Superbad*

*Born Yesterday* (1950)
*Sabrina* (1954)
*Born Yesterday*

*Bombshell* (1933)
*The Awful Truth* (1937)
*The Awful Truth*

*Pat and Mike* (1952)
*Midnight* (1939)
*Pat & Mike*

*20th Century* (1934)
*The Shop Around the Corner* (1940)
*20th Century*

*It Happened One Night* (1934)
*Hands Across the Table* (1935)
*It Happened One Night*

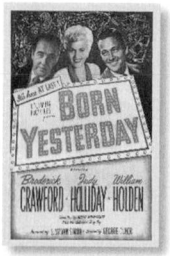


***His Girl Friday* vs. *Born Yesterday***
*His Girl Friday* is Howard Hawks's remake of Ben Hecht and Charles MacArthur's rowdy play (and movie) about yellow journalism, *"The Front Page,"* but this time the editor and reporter are not two men but a former husband and wife (Cary Grant, Rosalind Russell). They go at each other with a speed and ferocity that is still unbelievable. *Born Yesterday,* George Cukor's sly comedy about a not-so-dumb broad (Judy Holliday) whose wealthy lover hires a journalist (William Holden) to teach her "couth," is gentler, slower, more insinuating. It simply can't keep up.

THE WINNER

## *His Girl Friday*

VS

***The Awful Truth* vs. *It Happened One Night***
*The Awful Truth* is the perfect "comedy of re-marriage," as Stanley Cavell called movies in which couples part (in this case Irene Dunne and Cary Grant fully playing Cary Grant for the first time). *It Happened One Night,* directed by Frank Capra, more or less invented the genre back in 1934, with Clark Gable's free-wandering reporter taking charge of Claudette Colbert's spoiled runaway heiress. It wins on sheer charm.

A GREAT ROMANTIC COMEDY IS ABOUT EQUALITY – of looks, temperament, or brains. The man and woman meet, quarrel, part, tentatively reunite, fight again, and finally become a couple in a courtship dance conducted with wit, invention, tooth, claw, romantic seduction. Despite all the anger, the conclusion is as fated as the two halves of a drawbridge falling into place. If there's been a drop-off in recent years, it's because loutish young men have been paired up with hard-driving women, and the genre's beautiful balance has been shattered. These movies all have that balance, some more than others.

***My Man Godfrey* vs. *Some Like It Hot***
Carol Lombard's giddy speed as another heiress who hires what she takes to be a bum (William Powell) as an East Side butler brings *My Man Godfrey* to life. *Some Like It Hot* is Billy Wilder's drag comedy in which Tony Curtis, imitating Grant, winds up with Marilyn and Jack Lemmon winds up with the elderly swain Joe E. Brown. It has the best last line ("Nobody's perfect"), but *Godfrey*, with its perfect balance of silliness and Depression-era blues, wins.

# Annie Hall

***His Girl Friday* vs. *Annie Hall***
*His Girl Friday* is about work – there's a roaring satire of corrupt journalistic technique in the middle of it – and *Annie Hall* is more about taste, which is the way Woody's urbanites send signals to each other. The working battle brings out the equality of editor and writer as a couple, and since equality is my chief criterion for successful romantic comedy, *His Girl Friday* wins. It goes at such a clip that you don't know how the microphones kept up. The actors don't blanket each other; all the gags come through. For sheer momentum, there's nothing like it. Even when Grant and Russell realize they need each other, the movie pauses only briefly. Combat, of course, is their form of romance. It's sexier than sex.

- *My Man Godfrey*
  - *My Man Godfrey*
    - *My Man Godfrey* (1936)
    - *Clueless* (1995)
  - *Tootsie*
    - *Tootsie* (1982)
    - *Knocked Up* (2007)
- *Some Like It Hot*
  - *Philadelphia Story*
    - *The Philadelphia Story* (1940)
    - *Pretty Woman* (1990)
  - *Some Like It Hot*
    - *Some Like It Hot* (1959)
    - *Something's Gotta Give* (2003)
- *Annie Hall*
  - *Smiles of a Summer Night*
    - *Moonstruck*
      - *Moonstruck* (1987)
      - *Mystic Pizza* (1988)
    - *Smiles of a Summer Night*
      - *Smiles of a Summer Night** (1955)
      - *You've Got Mail* (1998)
  - *Annie Hall*
    - *Roman Holiday*
      - *The Lady Eve* (1941)
      - *Roman Holiday* (1953)
    - *Annie Hall*
      - *Woman of the Year* (1942)
      - *Annie Hall* (1977)

***Smiles of a Summer Night* vs. *Annie Hall***
Ingmar Bergman's *Smiles of a Summer Night* is not American, but willfully included here as necessary contrast. A sublime period piece set among aristocrats at a country house, it's more elegant and nostalgic than any of the American films but still a romantic comedy. *Annie Hall* is Woody Allen's "nervous romance" about a midwestern WASP (Diane Keaton) and the intellectual New York Jew (Woody) who tries to contol her and loses her. Nod to Woody for perfectly capturing a contemporary mood with bittersweet lyricism.

# Cats and Dogs

**By Lon Tweeten**

Lon Tweeten, a wildly unsuccessful cartoonist working in NYC, has shared residence with over 20 cats and dogs over the years, though only once simultaneously . . . it ended badly.

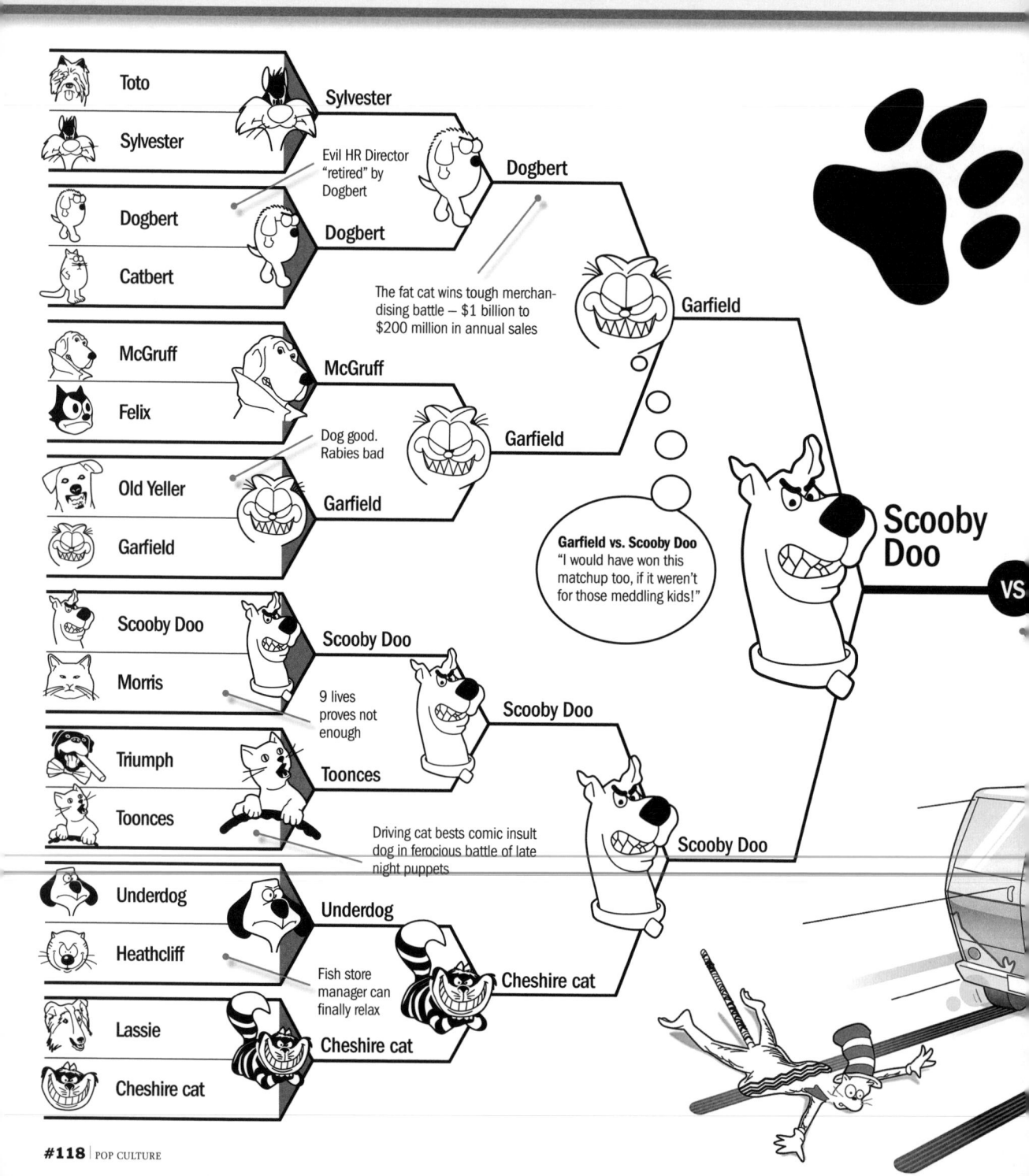

MAN'S FAVORITE DOMESTICATED ANIMALS – *Felis Catus* and *Canis Lupus Familiaris* – share a deep genetic hatred for one another. With the world's cat and dog population estimated at over 500 million and growing, escalation of skirmishes is inevitable.

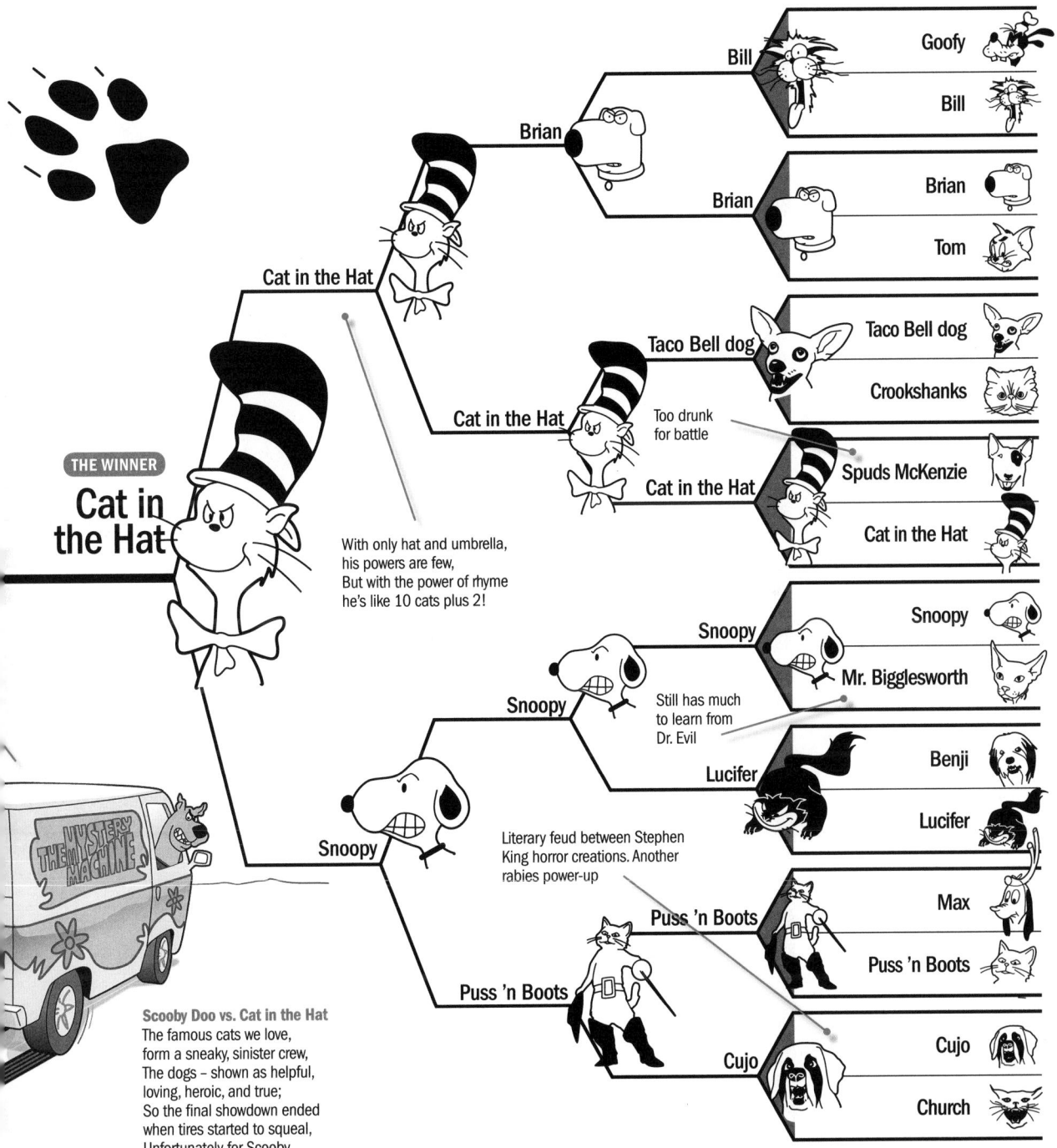


**Scooby Doo vs. Cat in the Hat**
The famous cats we love,
form a sneaky, sinister crew,
The dogs – shown as helpful,
loving, heroic, and true;
So the final showdown ended
when tires started to squeal,
Unfortunately for Scooby,
Toonces was at the wheel.

*NOTE: No dogs or cats were harmed in the making of this bracket.*

# Clint Eastwood Films

**By Manohla Dargis**

Manohla Dargis reviews films for the *New York Times*. She lives in Los Angeles and does not own a gun.

*A Fistful of Dollars* (1964)

*High Plains Drifter* (1973)

*The Good, the Bad and the Ugly* (1966)

*Unforgiven* (1992)

*Hang 'Em High* (1968)

*The Outlaw Josey Wales* (1976)

*Coogan's Bluff* (1968)

*Pale Rider* (1985)

*Where Eagles Dare* (1968)

*Letters from Iwo Jima* (2006)

*Two Mules for Sister Sara* (1970)

*Play Misty for Me* (1971)

*Kelly's Heroes* (1970)

*Gran Torino* (2008)

*Dirty Harry* (1971)

*Mystic River* (2003)

*High Plains Drifter*

*Unforgiven*

*Josey Wales*

*Pale Rider*

*Iwo Jima*

*Play Misty for Me*

*Gran Torino*

*Dirty Harry*

*Unforgiven*

*Josey Wales*

*Iwo Jima*

*Dirty Harry*

*Unforgiven*

***A Fistful of Dollars* vs. *High Plains Drifter***
In *High Plains Drifter*, first-time director Eastwood riffed on the spaghetti Westerns of Sergio Leone, like *A Fistful of Dollars*, which made him a star. Eastwood not only dished up plenty of red sauce in his debut, he also put Leone's name on a gravestone, saying later, "I buried my directors."

***Gran Torino* vs. *Dirty Harry***
In *Gran Torino*, Eastwood plays a retired Detroit auto worker and grumpy old racist who befriends and then defends his Hmong neighbors from local gangbangers. Decades after throwing his badge away in *Dirty Harry*, Eastwood picks it up again to defend a pluralistic neighborhood that looks a lot like America.

***Unforgiven* vs. *Dirty Harry***
*Unforgiven* isn't just a revisionist Western, it is also revisionist Eastwood and a coda to *Dirty Harry*'s law of the gun. "It's a hell of a thing, killing a man," Eastwood's avenging gunslinger says in *Unforgiven*, with a dead-eyed embrace of death. "Deserve's got nothing to do with it."

CLINT EASTWOOD is to the last half of the 20th century what John Wayne was to the first: the embodiment of American radical individualism, plus guns. As the self-styled Hollywood outsider who has made some of its greatest films, Eastwood has spent much of his bifurcated career as an actor-turned-director reconsidering, reconceptualizing, and radically revising his own screen identity. His great subject is masculinity and its discontents, a gift that keeps on giving.

***Unforgiven* vs. *Million Dollar Baby***
His late-life masterpiece, *Million Dollar Baby*, is the summation of all the great questions – What does it mean to be a good man? A decent father? – that have preoccupied Eastwood for a half-century. This is the same artist who made *Unforgiven*, but he has traded in his gun and nihilism for a tender love story about a man and the surrogate daughter who saves him.

**THE WINNER**

## *Million Dollar Baby* (2004)

***Million Dollar Baby* vs. *Perfect World***
The sins of fathers weigh heavily on Eastwood, who has played the on- and offscreen guiding patriarch for younger actors like Kevin Costner in *A Perfect World* and Hilary Swank in *Million Dollar Baby*. Eastwood shoulders that weight himself in *Million Dollar Baby* as the initially reluctant, unconditionally loving father figure to Swank's young boxer.

- *Million Dollar Baby*
  - *Honkytonk Man*
    - *Honkytonk Man*
      - *Sudden Impact*
        - *Magnum Force* (1973)
        - *Sudden Impact* (1983)
      - *Honkytonk Man*
        - *Thunderbolt and Lightfoot* (1974)
        - *Honkytonk Man* (1982)
    - *Bronco Billy*
      - *The Gauntlet*
        - *The Enforcer* (1976)
        - *The Gauntlet* (1977)
      - *Bronco Billy*
        - *Every Which Way But Loose* (1978)
        - *Bronco Billy* (1980)
  - *Million Dollar Baby*
    - *Million Dollar Baby*
      - *White Hunter*
        - *Escape from Alcatraz* (1979)
        - *White Hunter, Black Heart* (1990)
      - *Million Dollar Baby*
        - *Tightrope* (1984)
        - *Million Dollar Baby* (2004)
    - *A Perfect World*
      - *Bridges*
        - *Pink Cadillac* (1989)
        - *The Bridges of Madison County* (1995)
      - *A Perfect World*
        - *In the Line of Fire* (1993)
        - *A Perfect World* (1993)

# Comedy Teams

**By Robert Wuhl**

Robert Wuhl is a two-time Emmy Award–winning writer. Whether he's funny is, of course, based on one's point of view.

The Three Stooges
Lucille Ball and Vivian Vance
The Three Stooges

Penn and Teller
The Little Rascals
The Little Rascals

Three Stooges

Gleason and Carney
Rowan and Martin
Gleason & Carney

Lemmon and Matthau
Klugman and Randall
Lemmon and Matthau

Gleason & Carney

Gleason & Carney

The Smothers Brothers
Burns and Schreiber
Smothers Bros.

Tracy and Hepburn
The Marx Brothers
Marx Bros.

Marx Bros.

Marx Bros.

Rock Hudson and Doris Day
William Powell and Myrna Loy
Hudson & Day

Nichols and May
Stiller and Meara
Nichols & May

Hudson & Day

**The Three Stooges vs. Lucy & Ethel**
I don't love Lucy, regardless of the popularity of her first and best sitcom. She was a talented and sma woman who ruled the airwaves (and the chocolate assembly line with Ethel), but the Stooges often advanced beyond their beautifully choreographed slapstick and into satire – just watch them parody Hitler and Mussolini and you'll understand why I love Moe (and Larry and Curly).

**Three Stooges vs. Gleason & Carney**
Gleason and Carney were great actors who coaxed grand comedy out of the poor, lower-class conditions of their minimalist Brooklyn apartments and blue-collar jobs. Gleason recognized that the blustery Kramden needed the naïve gentility the stage-trained Carney brought to Norton – and that Carney deserved the funniest lines. And it is their brilliant verbal camaraderie that elevates them above the Stooges' zany physicality.

THE WINNER

## The Marx Brothers

VS

**Hudson & Day vs. Nichols & May**
For the comedy intelligentsia, giving Rock and Doris the nod over Nichols and May might seem like heresy. But *Pillow Talk* and (especially) *Lover Come Back* are terrifically crafted romantic satirical comedies, and contain something that the brilliantly verbal Nichols and May bits never contained – sexual tension.

COMEDY IS DIFFICULT ENOUGH TO ACHIEVE, but try doing it night after night, film after film, or episode after episode. When it works — when it is delightfully artful, witty, silly, smart, or physical – it is a combination of music, rhythm, and choreography between two or more artists. What happens in the space between the players generates the chemistry we see, and for us, magic is made. It is very difficult to produce, and even more difficult to maintain. The greatest teams cross generations to create that most involuntary of human responses – making us laugh.

# Abbott & Costello

**Abbott and Costello vs. The Marx Brothers**
No team has ever approached the wit, style, and double-entendred anarchy of Groucho, Chico, and Harpo. Three brothers with three very distinct personalities gave the Marxes an advantage, as did the comic lust factor: Lou was often smitten by a female, but there was always the belief that nothing would actually happen if he got the girl. Not so with Groucho, Chico, or Harpo.

- Abbott & Costello
  - Burns & Allen
    - Burns & Allen
      - Burns and Allen
      - Carol Burnett and Vicki Lawrence
    - Belushi & Aykroyd
      - Belushi and Aykroyd
      - David Spade and Chris Farley
  - Abbott & Costello
    - Abbott & Costello
      - Abbott and Costello
      - Spinal Tap
    - Korman & Conway
      - Korman and Conway
      - Kathy and Mo
- Laurel & Hardy
  - Hope & Crosby
    - Martin & Lewis
      - Martin and Lewis
      - The Ritz Brothers
    - Hope & Crosby
      - Hope and Crosby
      - Cheech and Chong
  - Laurel & Hardy
    - The Bowery Boys
      - Wilder and Pryor
      - The Bowery Boys
    - Laurel & Hardy
      - Laurel and Hardy
      - Sid Caesar and Imogene Coca

**Abbott & Costello vs. Laurel & Hardy**
No doubt from a pure physical comedy viewpoint, Stan and Ollie are difficult to beat. But Bud Abbott was the greatest straight man of all time (with a nod to Dean Martin) and Lou Costello was the best ever at the double-take. And Abbott and Costello had the greatest verbal comedy bit of all time: "Who's on First?"

# Comic Book Superpowers

**By Peter Coogan**

Dr. Peter Coogan is co-chair of the Comics Arts Conference (held at the San Diego Comic-Con International).

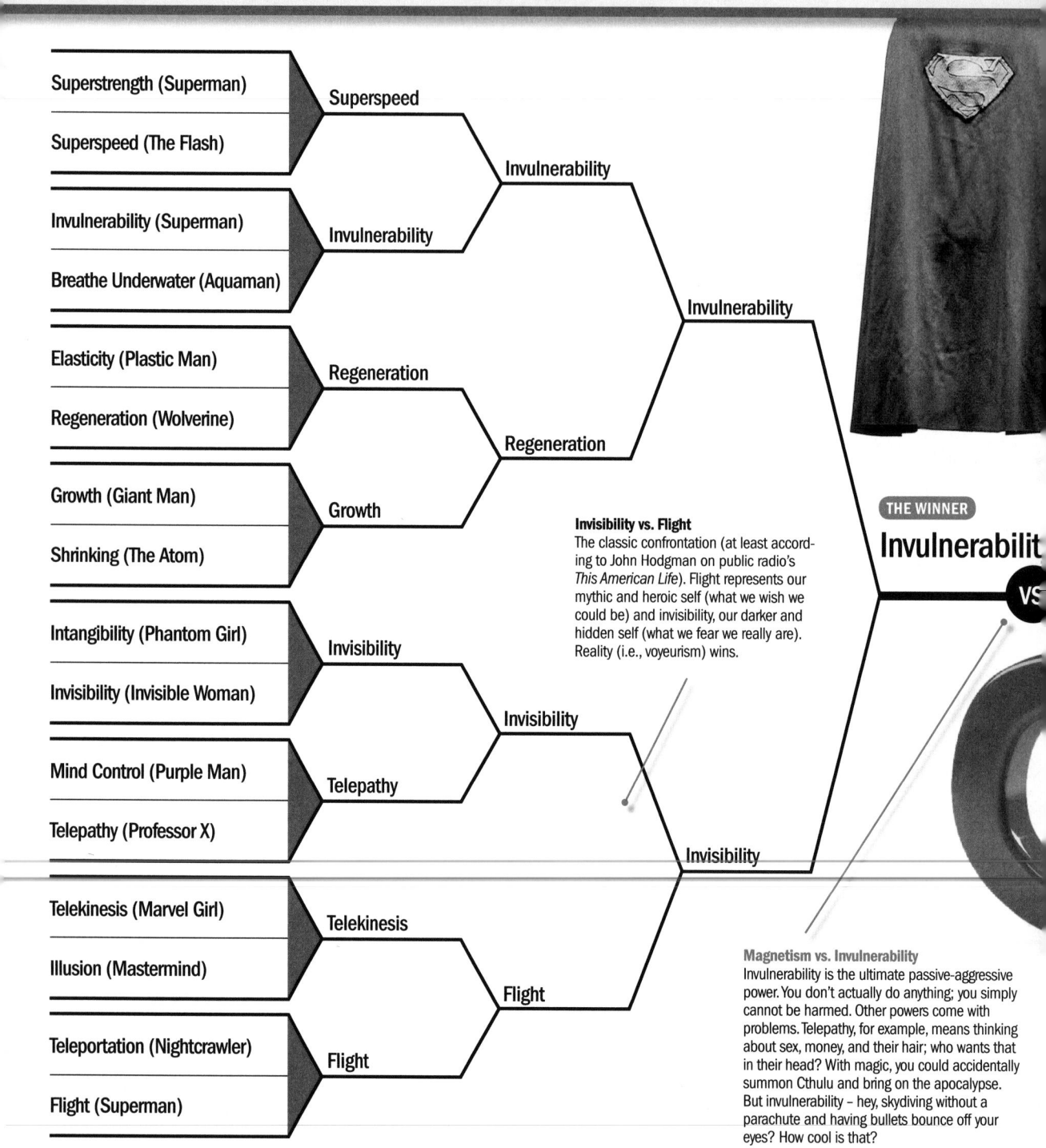


**Invisibility vs. Flight**
The classic confrontation (at least according to John Hodgman on public radio's *This American Life*). Flight represents our mythic and heroic self (what we wish we could be) and invisibility, our darker and hidden self (what we fear we really are). Reality (i.e., voyeurism) wins.

**Magnetism vs. Invulnerability**
Invulnerability is the ultimate passive-aggressive power. You don't actually do anything; you simply cannot be harmed. Other powers come with problems. Telepathy, for example, means thinking about sex, money, and their hair; who wants that in their head? With magic, you could accidentally summon Cthulu and bring on the apocalypse. But invulnerability – hey, skydiving without a parachute and having bullets bounce off your eyes? How cool is that?

THIS BRACKET STEMS FROM CHILDHOOD FANTASY, when we debated which is the best power to have, either in daily life or for fighting crime. I think we can admit now that none of us really wanted to dress up like a bat and spend our nights on patrol. It wasn't the costume; it's the actual superpower that's cool and fun. Ever since Gilgamesh went looking for immortality, people have dreamed of having superpowers to escape the monotony of mundane existence. But if you could only have one power – whether it's physical, mental, or meta – which would it be?

**Dial a Power vs. Reality Warping**
Having access to every superpower sounds great, right? But then come the rules like you can use each power only once or once a year. All that record keeping is such a headache. And the research: always having to look for new heroes and new powers? Who wants that? Superpowers should be fun, not homework. Decision: Reality Warping.

**Reality Warping vs. Magnetism**
Sure, controlling reality seems like the best power, but your every thought becomes reality. This is particularly dangerous if you have any attention-deficit issues. A stray intrusive thought, however quick and harmless inside the mind, can create havoc. But magnetism represents the ultimate vanity: everything can be attracted to you. Magnetism wins.

**Turn into a Wall vs. Body Part Separation**
These comic-book superpowers are so stupid and useless that the contest is a draw – and they present a virtual bye for omnivory in round two. With omnivory (the ability to eat anything – bricks, prison-robot fingers, iron chains – that taste like chocolate cake), at least you can make a living as an "anything for a dollar" geek.

- Magnetism
  - Reality Warping
    - Reality Warping
      - Dial a Power
        - Dial a Power (Kid Eternity)
        - Superpower Mimicry (The Mimic)
      - Reality Warping
        - Time Stopping (Hourman)
        - Reality Warping (Proteus)
    - Magic
      - Magic
        - Magic (Dr. Strange)
        - Weather Control (Storm)
      - Explosion
        - Eye Blasts (Cyclops)
        - Explosion (Human Bomb)
  - Magnetism
    - Magnetism
      - Pyrokinesis
        - Cyrokinesis (Iceman)
        - Pyrokinesis (Human Torch)
      - Magnetism
        - Magnetism (Magneto)
        - Electricity (Electro)
    - Omnivory
      - Omnivory
        - Superventriloquism (Superman)
        - Omnivory (Matter Eater Lad)
      - Bye
        - Turn into a Wall (Blockade Boy)
        - Body Part Separation (MFE Captain Marvel)

# NATURE

**Fears and Phobias** *by Roz Chast* **122**
**National Parks** *by Scott Kirkwood* **123**
**Dangerous Animals** *by Chris Jenkins* **124**
**Best Ski Runs** *by Steve Cohen* **125**
**Nothing but the Tooth** *by James Hudson, D.M.D.* **126**
**Fish Tales** *by Peter Kaminsky* **127**
**Energy Alternatives** *by Gwyneth Cravens* **128**
**My Prized Feathers** *by Luke Dempsey* **129**
**Looking Younger** *by David Leffell, M.D.* **130**

# Fears and Phobias

**By Roz Chast**
Roz Chast is a cartoonist for *The New Yorker* magazine.

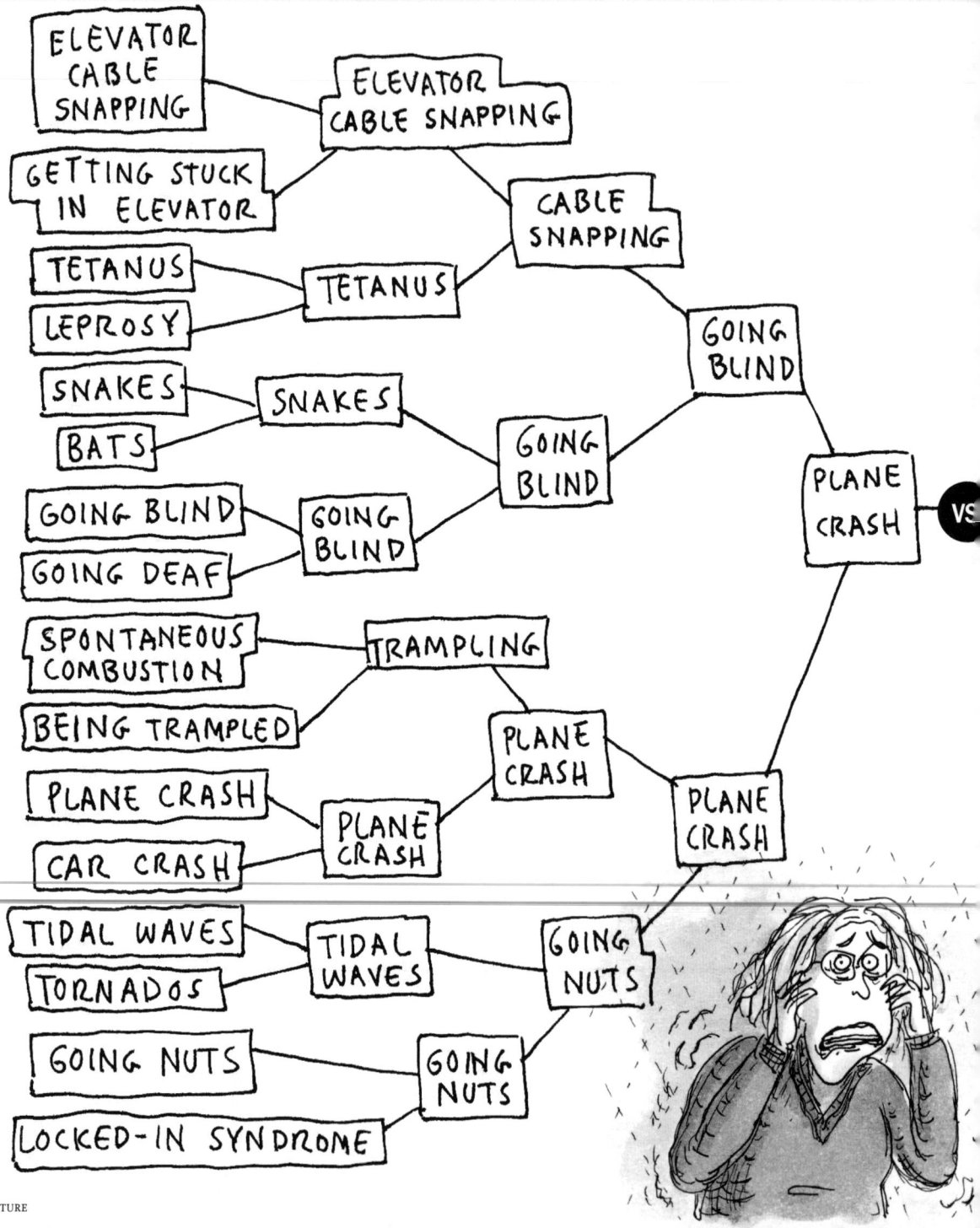

EVER SINCE I WAS LITTLE, I have always had a lot of phobias. When I was a kid, the main ones were appendicitis (thank you, Ludwig Bemelmans); going blind; going cross-eyed; nightmares; losing my permanent teeth; kites; leprosy; spontaneous combustion; and balloons. I have outgrown most of these but not all. The bad news is that as I get older, I accumulate new ones.

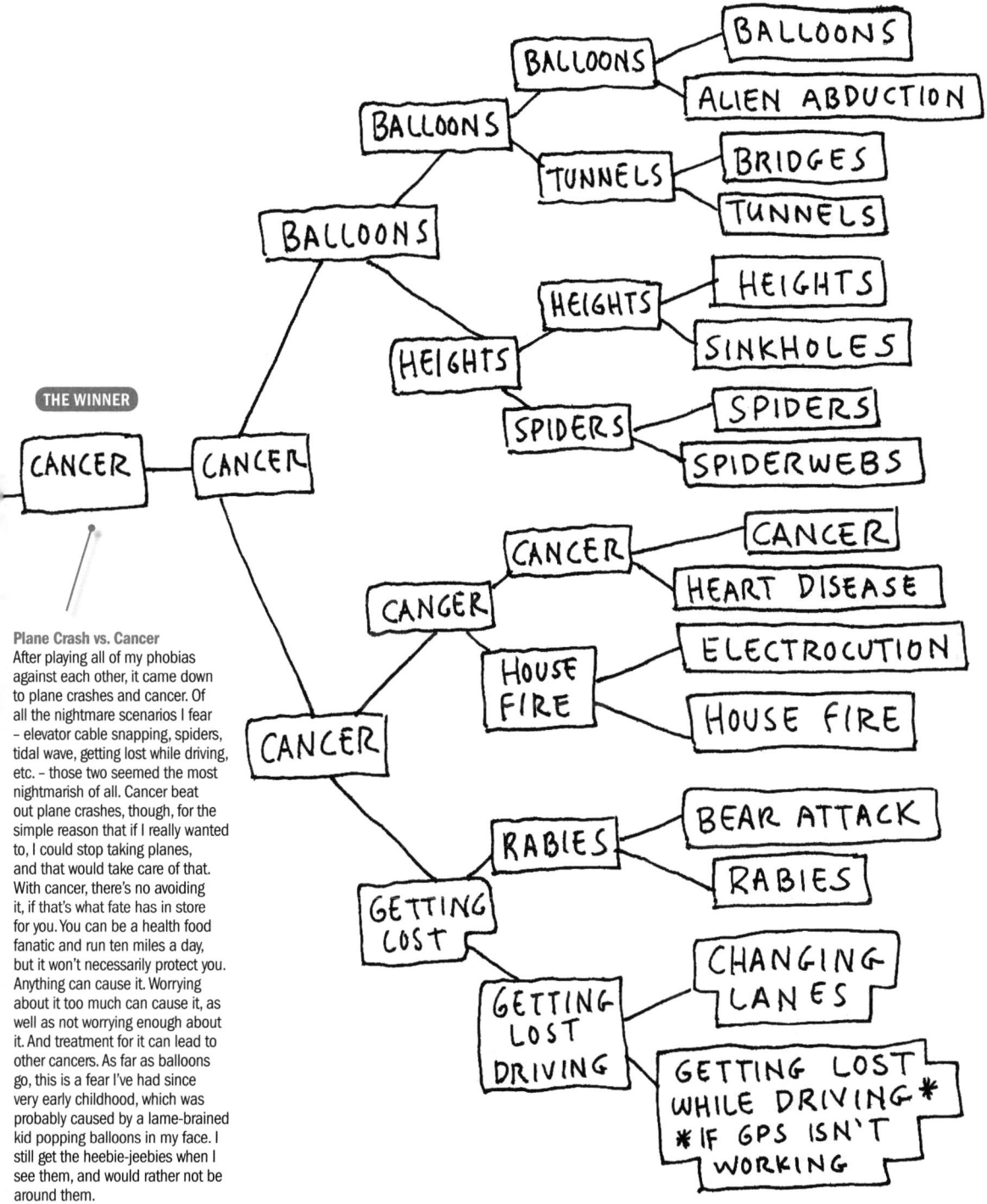


**Plane Crash vs. Cancer**
After playing all of my phobias against each other, it came down to plane crashes and cancer. Of all the nightmare scenarios I fear – elevator cable snapping, spiders, tidal wave, getting lost while driving, etc. – those two seemed the most nightmarish of all. Cancer beat out plane crashes, though, for the simple reason that if I really wanted to, I could stop taking planes, and that would take care of that. With cancer, there's no avoiding it, if that's what fate has in store for you. You can be a health food fanatic and run ten miles a day, but it won't necessarily protect you. Anything can cause it. Worrying about it too much can cause it, as well as not worrying enough about it. And treatment for it can lead to other cancers. As far as balloons go, this is a fear I've had since very early childhood, which was probably caused by a lame-brained kid popping balloons in my face. I still get the heebie-jeebies when I see them, and would rather not be around them.

# National Parks

**By Scott Kirkwood**

Scott Kirkwood is the editor of *National Parks* magazine, published by the National Parks Conservation Association, a nonprofit group that fights to make sure all 391 park units are around for your kids and your kids' kids.

Yellowstone (ID, MT & WY) — Antietam (MD) → Yellowstone

Mt. Rainier (WA) — Sequoia (CA) → Mt. Rainier

Yellowstone — Mt. Rainier → Yellowstone

Gettysburg (PA) — Denali (AK) → Denali

Olympic (WA) — Canyon de Chelly (AZ) → Olympic

Denali — Olympic → Denali

Yellowstone — Denali → Yellowstone

Glacier (MT) — Mount Rushmore (SD) → Glacier

Virgin Islands (VI) — Alcatraz (CA) → Alcatraz

Glacier — Alcatraz → Glacier

Yellowstone — Glacier → Glacier

Yosemite (CA) — Statue of Liberty (NY) → Yosemite

Everglades (FL) — Petrified Forest (AZ) → Everglades

Yosemite — Everglades → Yosemite

Glacier — Yosemite → Glacier

**Gettysburg vs. Denali**
Our Civil War battlefields are sacred places where our nation's story unfolded in the most dramatic way imaginable. But, given the choice, I'd read a book about Gettysburg and visit Denali rather than the other way around. Unless you're a die-hard history buff, rolling hills and stone markers just don't compare to the site of the the continent's highest peak piercing the clouds.

**Zion vs. Glacier**
Clinging to the chains bolted to the peak of Angel's Landing and walking through the canyons of the Virgin River are life-changing experiences that make Zion a favorite. But with 13 campgrounds and 700 miles of trails covering its 1 million acres, Glacier would take seven lifetimes to explore from top to bottom. Not a hiker? World-class couch potatoes love the sprawling Many Glacier Hotel, where you can enjoy the views of Swiftcurrent Lake, try to spot grizzlies from the balcony, or just plop down in front of the biggest fireplace you've ever seen, with a hot chocolate in each hand.

THE WINNER

## Glacier National Park
(Montana)

VS

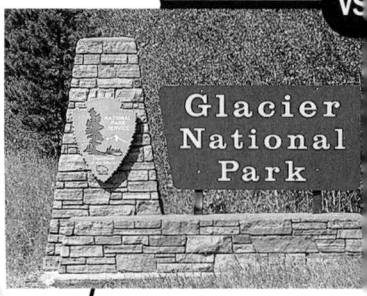

**Yellowstone vs. Glacier**
The grizzlies, bison, and hot springs at our first national park are American icons, but Old Faithful is overrated. (Sorry, somebody had to say it.) Glacier has the grizzlies, the wolves, and the moose. It's got the vintage 1930s red buses with the canvas tops that come off on a July day. And it's got Going-to-the-Sun Road for jaw-dropping views of Lake McDonald and Logan Pass, where you're eye-to-eye with mountain goats and bighorn sheep.

ASK ANYONE WHO'S VISITED A HANDFUL of national parks to pick a favorite, and they'll tell you it's impossible. But as you can see, they're all wrong. Just like every parent secretly has a favorite child, we all find that one national park leaves us with a lasting impression. Whether it's the majestic wildlife, the stunning landscapes, or that tingling feeling that comes when you touch your own country's history, one of these spots will compel you to take dozens of mediocre photos and buy a horrible T-shirt. And go back again and again.

**Glacier Bay vs. Hawaii Volcanoes**
Water snuffs out fire every time. While volcanoes slowly increases its own acreage a little bit every day, climate change means Glacier Bay's namesakes are destined to melt away bit by bit – reason enough to put the park on a list of must-sees.

- Zion
  - Glacier Bay
    - Glacier Bay
      - Glacier Bay (AK)
      - Isle Royale (MI)
    - Hawaii Volcanoes
      - Valley Forge (PA)
      - Hawaii Volcanoes (HI)
  - Zion
    - Joshua Tree
      - Mesa Verde (CO)
      - Joshua Tree (CA)
    - Zion
      - Rocky Mountains (CO)
      - Zion (UT)
  - Acadia
    - Grand Canyon
      - Big Bend
        - Great Smokies (NC & TN)
        - Big Bend (TX)
      - Grand Canyon
        - Grand Canyon (AZ)
        - Arches (UT)
    - Acadia
      - National Mall
        - National Mall (DC)
        - Shenandoah (VA)
      - Acadia
        - Acadia (ME)
        - USS Arizona (HI)

# Zion

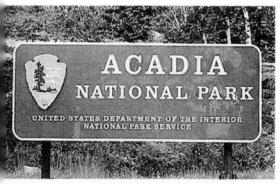


**Acadia vs. Grand Canyon**
No doubt, the Big Ditch is impressive, but Acadia is the little park that could. When you hike its trails, kayak along its rocky coast with harbor seals, and pedal the carriage roads carved out by the Rockefellers, it feels like your own little retreat tucked away in a corner of the country where no one else will ever find it.

# Dangerous Animals

**By Chris Jenkins**

Chris Jenkins is a wildlife biologist working with "dangerous" animals, primarily venomous snakes, and helping people to let go of some of their greatest fears.

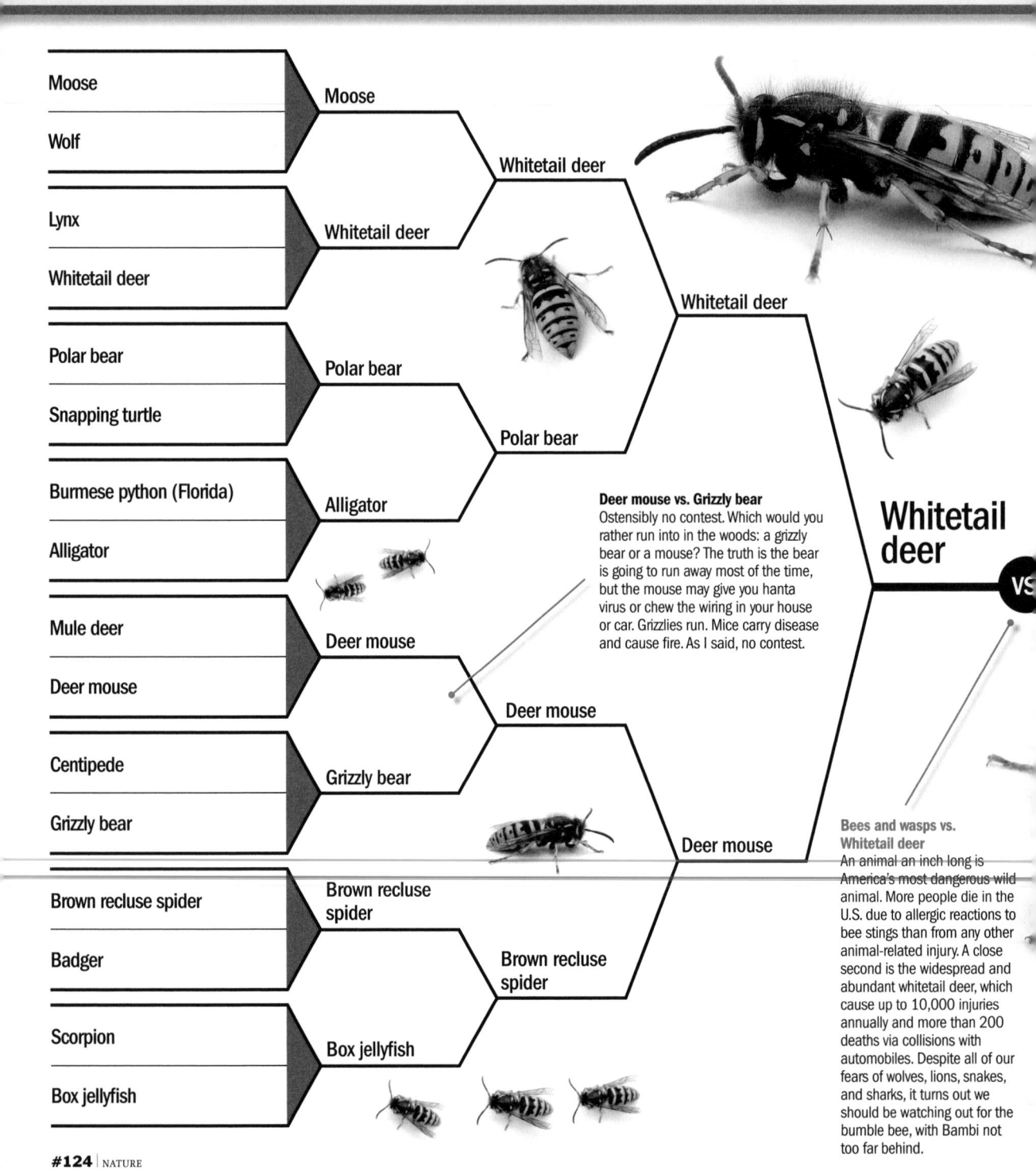


**Deer mouse vs. Grizzly bear**
Ostensibly no contest. Which would you rather run into in the woods: a grizzly bear or a mouse? The truth is the bear is going to run away most of the time, but the mouse may give you hanta virus or chew the wiring in your house or car. Grizzlies run. Mice carry disease and cause fire. As I said, no contest.

**Bees and wasps vs. Whitetail deer**
An animal an inch long is America's most dangerous wild animal. More people die in the U.S. due to allergic reactions to bee stings than from any other animal-related injury. A close second is the widespread and abundant whitetail deer, which cause up to 10,000 injuries annually and more than 200 deaths via collisions with automobiles. Despite all of our fears of wolves, lions, snakes, and sharks, it turns out we should be watching out for the bumble bee, with Bambi not too far behind.

LET'S BEGIN WITH THE FACT that the most dangerous animals in the world are humans. Only then can we understand America's most dangerous wild animals. They range from those that can strike fear in our hearts, such as snakes and wolves, to animals that we don't typically think of as dangerous, such as mice. The criterion here is the animal's chance of causing human injury or death – and the element of surprise when we realize which animals are really scary and which are not.

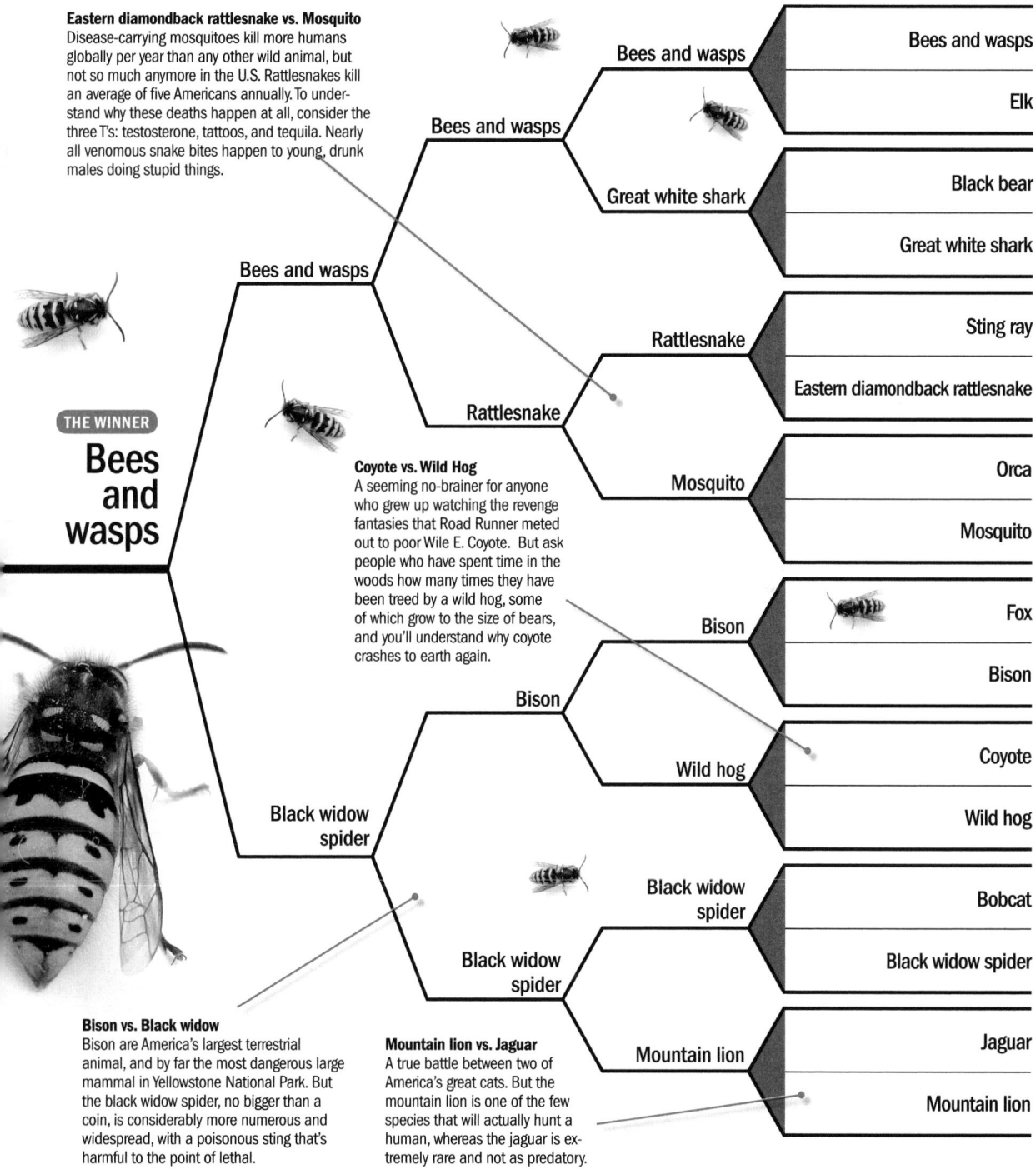


THE WINNER

# Bees and wasps

**Eastern diamondback rattlesnake vs. Mosquito**
Disease-carrying mosquitoes kill more humans globally per year than any other wild animal, but not so much anymore in the U.S. Rattlesnakes kill an average of five Americans annually. To understand why these deaths happen at all, consider the three T's: testosterone, tattoos, and tequila. Nearly all venomous snake bites happen to young, drunk males doing stupid things.

**Coyote vs. Wild Hog**
A seeming no-brainer for anyone who grew up watching the revenge fantasies that Road Runner meted out to poor Wile E. Coyote. But ask people who have spent time in the woods how many times they have been treed by a wild hog, some of which grow to the size of bears, and you'll understand why coyote crashes to earth again.

**Bison vs. Black widow**
Bison are America's largest terrestrial animal, and by far the most dangerous large mammal in Yellowstone National Park. But the black widow spider, no bigger than a coin, is considerably more numerous and widespread, with a poisonous sting that's harmful to the point of lethal.

**Mountain lion vs. Jaguar**
A true battle between two of America's great cats. But the mountain lion is one of the few species that will actually hunt a human, whereas the jaguar is extremely rare and not as predatory.

# Best Ski Runs

**By Steve Cohen**

Steve Cohen is the former editor of *Ski* magazine. He has skied at more than 130 resorts on four continents and, unlike his Euro-sycophant peers, prefers North American skiing. Although his office desk's messiness doesn't show it, he adores the orderliness of American lift lines.

**Mystic Pines** – The Canyons, UT
**Body Bag Glades** – Crested Butte, CO
→ **Body Bag**

**Here Be Dragons** – Solitude, UT
**Shadows** – Steamboat Springs, CO
→ **Here Be Dragons**

→ **Here Be Dragons**

**A to Z Trees** – Telluride, CO
**Temerity to Canopy Glades** – Aspen Highlands, CO
→ **A to Z**

**Staircase** – Jay Peak, VT
**Skiway Glades** – Heavenly, CA
→ **Skiway Glades**

→ **A to Z**

→ **A to Z**

**Corbet's Couloir** – Jackson Hole, WY
**Chute 75 off KT 22** – Squaw Valley, CA
→ **Corbet's**

**The Slides** – Whiteface Mt., NY
**Two Smokes** – Silverton, CO
→ **Two Smokes**

→ **Corbet's**

→ **Corbet's**

**Goat** – Stowe, VT
**Big Couloir** – Big Sky, MT
→ **Big Couloir**

**Eagle's Nest** – Breckenridge, CO
**Heart Chute** – Kirkwood, CA
→ **Eagle's Nest**

→ **Big Couloir**

→ **Corbet's**

**Body Bag Glades vs. Here Be Dragons**
Dodging trees is dicey enough, but the ultra-steep (55-degree) Body Bag Glades are peppered with rocks and 20-foot cliff drops. Here Be Dragons is quite steep, too, but the netherworld qualities of its deceased, gnarled, rusty-colored Limber pines – which do resemble dragons – make it a peacock among America's glades.

**Corbet's vs. A to Z**
Corbet's is the steep everyone comes to ski, but many just see it. Nearly vertical at the top; the only way in requires a leap of faith. The slope then "flattens" to 50 degrees for 500 exhilarating feet. A to Z Trees is always powder-chocked, and the spacing of the trees allows consistent radius turns from top to bottom. Lots of fun but conquering the Corbet's monster is far more satisfying.

**Corbet's vs. Warm Springs**
Any competent intermediate skier can ski great cruisers like Warm Springs if they go slowly enough. So the winner has to be a run that hardly anybody can ski. Experience, skills, knowledge, and pure guts form a powerful compact on Corbet's when you slide down a face so sheer Spider-Man would shudder. There isn't a skier in America who deep down doesn't ache to make the artery-pounding leap into Corbet's.

THE WINNER

## Corbet's Couloir, Jackson Hole, WY

SERIOUS SKIERS CARE MOST ABOUT THE TERRAIN that challenges them mentally and physically or lets them approach speeds that would get them pulled over on the Interstate. These desires are fulfilled on high-speed cruisers, moguls, glades, and steeps – ski runs that are defined by trees, rocks, or some other topographical feature. One rule is enforced here: no schlepping required. If you can't get off a lift and ski down without going up or sideways, it wasn't considered. Sure, that eliminates some great runs, but how do you rate oblivion?

**Poppyfields vs. Warm Springs**
Poppyfields is groomed every mid-morning by a Panzer wedge of snowcats, and if you time it right, you can tear fresh corduroy four or five times down its 1,500-foot length. But Warm Springs is the classic high-speed thigh burner: nearly two miles long with a ridiculously consistent 35-degree pitch. And if you know how to turn 'em, the ski patrollers will look away.

**Al's Run vs. Great Scott**
It's hard not to be intimidated by Al's giant moguls, that will cause you physical and psychological pain if you fail to find a successful zipper line. But Great Scott is the Bo Jackson of ski runs: not only is it pocked with well-formed bumps, and hellaciously steep, but the slope seems to fall away for an eternity on every turn. The movements of those who have come before set a beat that propels you downhill without the thuds usually associated with mogul runs.

# Warm Springs

- Warm Springs
  - Perry Merrill
    - Cow's Face
      - Ruthie's Run, Aspen, CO
      - Cow's Face, Mt. Bachelor, OR
    - Perry Merrill
      - Perry Merrill, Stowe, VT
      - Stein's Way, Deer Valley, UT
  - Warm Springs
    - Lynx
      - Narrow Gauge, Sugarloaf, ME
      - Lynx, Wildcat, NH
    - Warm Springs
      - Poppyfields, Vail, CO
      - Warm Springs, Sun Valley, ID
- Great Scott
  - Al's Run
    - Al's Run
      - Al's Run, Taos, NM
      - High Rustler, Alta, UT
    - Champion's Run
      - National, Stowe, VT
      - Champion's Run, Deer Valley, UT
  - Great Scott
    - Great Scott
      - Outhouse, Winter Park, CO
      - Great Scott, Snowbird, UT
    - Outer Limits
      - Outer Limits, Killington, VT
      - Stein's Run, Sugarbush, VT

# Nothing but the Tooth

**By James Hudson, D.M.D.**

Dr. James Hudson has a private dental practice in New York City and serves as deputy chief forensic dentist for the city's office of Chief Medical Examiner. He, his wife, four children, and two dogs have a combined 244 teeth to care for daily.

Upper Right First Molar (#3) vs. Upper Left Second Premolar (#13) → Upper Right First Molar (#3)

Lower Right Central Incisor (#25) vs. Upper Right Second Molar (#2) → Lower Right Central Incisor (#25)

Upper Right First Molar (#3) vs. Lower Right Central Incisor (#25) → Upper Right First Molar (#3)

Upper Right Central Incisor (#8) vs. Lower Left Wisdom Tooth (#17) → Upper Right Central Incisor (#8)

Upper Right Canine (#6) vs. Lower Left Second Molar (#18) → Upper Right Canine (#6)

Upper Right Central Incisor (#8) vs. Upper Right Canine (#6) → Upper Right Canine (#6)

Upper Right Canine (#6) vs. Upper Right First Molar (#3) → Upper Right Canine (#6)

Lower Right First Molar (#30) vs. Lower Left Second Premolar (#20) → Lower Right First Molar (#30)

Lower Left Central Incisor (#24) vs. Upper Right First Premolar (#5) → Lower Left Central Incisor (#24)

Lower Right First Molar (#30) vs. Lower Left Central Incisor (#24) → Lower Right First Molar (#30)

Upper Left Lateral Incisor (#10) vs. Lower Right First Premolar (#28) → Upper Left Lateral Incisor (#10)

Lower Right Canine (#27) vs. Lower Right Second Molar (#31) → Lower Right Canine (#27)

Lower Right Canine (#27) vs. Lower Right Canine (#27) → Lower Right Canine (#27)

Lower Right Canine (#27) vs. Lower Right Canine (#27) → Lower Right Canine (#27)

**Upper Right First Molar (#3) vs. Lower Right Central Incisor (#25)**
You need your incisors, the upper for biting, the bottom to assist chewing. And of course, there are aesthetic considerations: lose any of your upper and lower front teeth and you've lost your smile. But molars are essential for providing support at the back of the mouth (a.k.a. "posterior stability"). #25 drops out, #3 moves on.

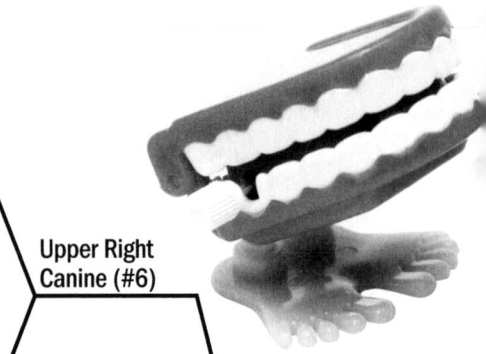

## Lower Right Canine (#27) VS

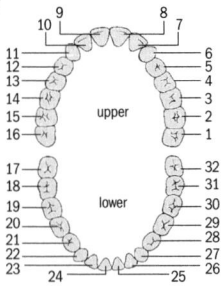


**Lower Left Canine (#22) vs. Lower Right Canine (#27)**
A dead heat, since these two finalists are mirror images of each other. It makes sense that the lower canines go all the way. They're the teeth with the deepest roots and, thus, the greatest strength, stability, and durability. They're the anchors of your mouth. Plus, their strategic position at the corners of the mouth allow for the best retention for any restorations. Still, somebody has to win. So, as a right-handed dentist who knows it's easier to work on the left tooth, I crown #22 the champ.

MOST OF US HAVE 32 TEETH, suggesting that the Intelligent Designer was the first bracketologist. But if you could keep only one tooth, which would it be? And what are your criteria? Aesthetics is important (as vanity is a prime motivator for seeking dental care). But there's no way that retaining only one tooth, or two or three for that matter, could ever look good. So functionality is important, too. Then there's the matter of whether that lone tooth can be a sound building block for future dental work that rebuilds a mouthful of teeth. Now, open your mouth please.

THE WINNER

# Lower Left Canine (#22)

- Upper Left Canine (#11)
  - Upper Left First Molar (#14)
    - Upper Left First Molar (#14)
    - Upper Left Wisdom Tooth (#16)
  - Upper Right Lateral Incisor (#7)
    - Upper Right Lateral Incisor (#7)
    - Lower Right Wisdom Tooth (#32)
  - Upper Left Canine (#11)
    - Lower Left Lateral Incisor (#23)
      - Lower Left Lateral Incisor (#23)
      - Lower Right Second Premolar (#29)
    - Upper Left Canine (#11)
      - Upper Left Canine (#11)
      - Lower Left First Premolar (#21)
- Lower Left Canine (#22)
  - Lower Left First Molar (#19)
    - Lower Left First Molar (#19)
      - Lower Left First Molar (#19)
      - Upper Right Second Premolar (#4)
    - Lower Right Lateral Incisor (#26)
      - Lower Right Lateral Incisor (#26)
      - Upper Left First Premolar (#12)
  - Lower Left Canine (#22)
    - Upper Left Central Incisor (#9)
      - Upper Left Central Incisor (#9)
      - Upper Left Second Molar (#15)
    - Lower Left Canine (#22)
      - Upper Right Wisdom Tooth (#1)
      - Lower Left Canine (#22)

**Upper Left Canine (#11) vs. Lower Left Canine (#22)**
Well, we're down to my favorite teeth, the canines. If your mouth was a theater seating chart, they'd be in the front row, but three seats off the center, meaning they're valuable aesthetically. Choosing between upper and lower is simple. If you lost all your upper teeth, I could still fabricate a complete upper denture that provides good retention. Fabricating a good lower denture is harder because the tongue is in the way, meaning you have to save the lower teeth at all costs. #11 loses, #22 goes on.

**Lower Left First Molar (#19) vs. Upper Right Second Molar (#4)**
In the Universal Numbering System used here, teeth make a round trip from #1 to #32 beginning with the upper right third molar (or wisdom tooth) to the upper left molar, then back from lower left to lower right third molar (#32). #19 is a first (or six-year) molar that's critical for an adult's bite. The position of this and a couple of other teeth determines whether braces will be needed. The molar thrashes #4, a smaller tooth with little function (but that doesn't mean you should stop flossing or brushing around it).

**Lower Left Canine (#22) vs. Upper Right Wisdom Tooth (#1)**
#1 is a wisdom tooth, which can often erupt (or worse, fail to erupt, creating the possibly painful "impacted" tooth) into a poor position that provides little function for most people. On an evolutionary scale, wisdom teeth are fading as our jaws have gotten smaller and our diets more refined. In another million years no one will have them. The future champ advances.

# Fish Tales

**By Peter Kaminsky**

Peter Kaminsky's many fishing books include *The Moon Pulled Up an Acre of Bass* and *The Flyfisherman's Guide to the Meaning of Life.*

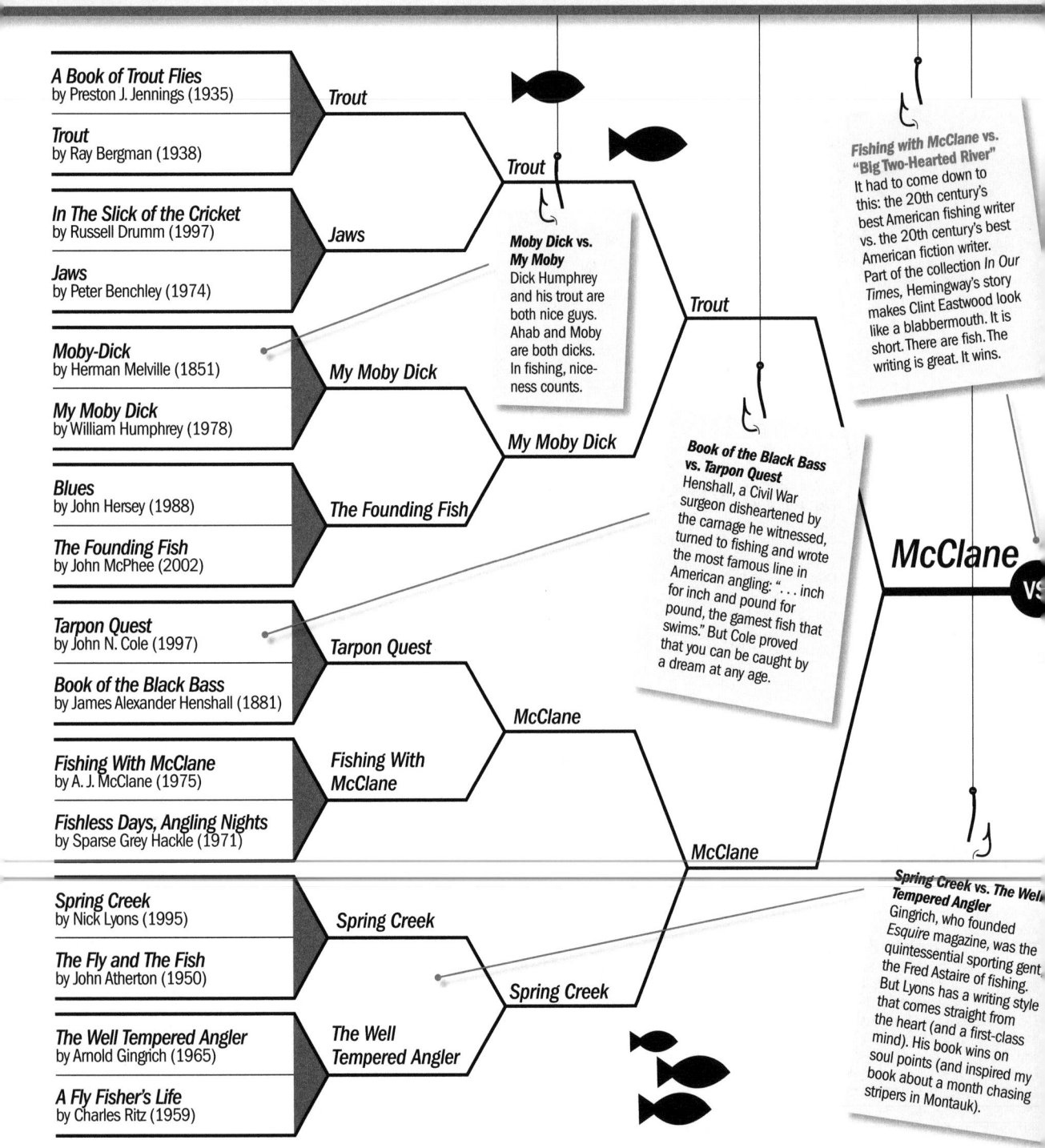

WITH THE POSSIBLE EXCEPTION OF GOLF, FISHING IS THE WORDIEST SPORT. But not all words are created equal. Great fishing writing should enchant, seduce, excite, instruct, induce hunger, and most of all, make you want to grab a rod and get near water. Perhaps because it is a solitary sport (except on ESPN), the best fishing writing puts the reader in the soul and the world of the angler. In that sense, this bracket is about fishing as literature (and vice versa).

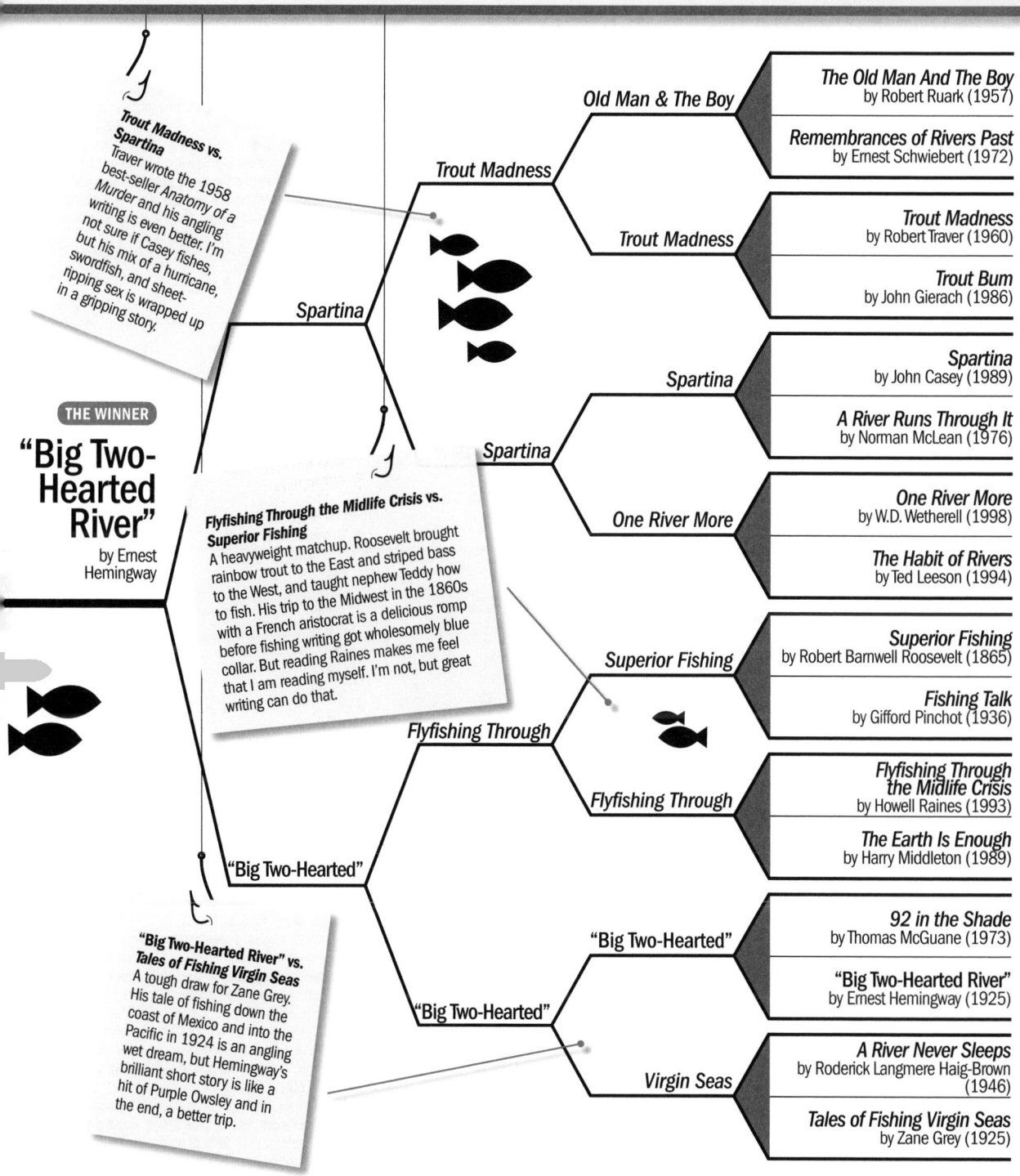

# Energy Alternatives

**By Gwyneth Cravens**

Gwyneth Cravens is the author of *Power to Save the World: The Truth About Nuclear Energy.* She has published five novels. Her fiction and nonfiction have appeared in *Harper's* and *The New Yorker,* where she also worked as a fiction editor.

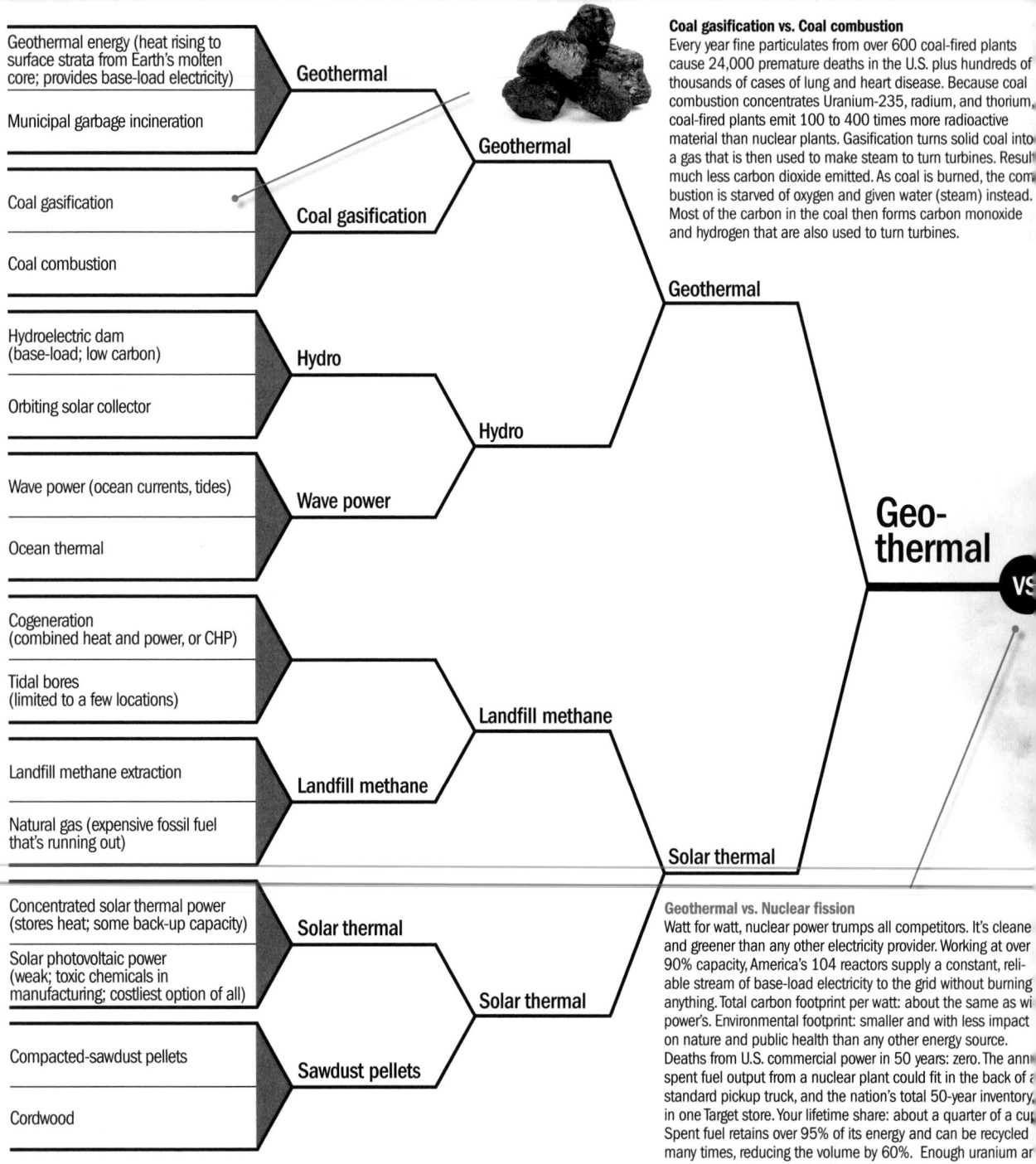


**Coal gasification vs. Coal combustion**
Every year fine particulates from over 600 coal-fired plants cause 24,000 premature deaths in the U.S. plus hundreds of thousands of cases of lung and heart disease. Because coal combustion concentrates Uranium-235, radium, and thorium, coal-fired plants emit 100 to 400 times more radioactive material than nuclear plants. Gasification turns solid coal into a gas that is then used to make steam to turn turbines. Resul much less carbon dioxide emitted. As coal is burned, the com bustion is starved of oxygen and given water (steam) instead. Most of the carbon in the coal then forms carbon monoxide and hydrogen that are also used to turn turbines.

**Geothermal vs. Nuclear fission**
Watt for watt, nuclear power trumps all competitors. It's cleane and greener than any other electricity provider. Working at over 90% capacity, America's 104 reactors supply a constant, reli- able stream of base-load electricity to the grid without burning anything. Total carbon footprint per watt: about the same as wi power's. Environmental footprint: smaller and with less impact on nature and public health than any other energy source. Deaths from U.S. commercial power in 50 years: zero. The ann spent fuel output from a nuclear plant could fit in the back of a standard pickup truck, and the nation's total 50-year inventory, in one Target store. Your lifetime share: about a quarter of a cu Spent fuel retains over 95% of its energy and can be recycled many times, reducing the volume by 60%. Enough uranium ar thorium exist to run reactors for thousands of years.

FOR MILLENNIA, HUMANS HAVE FIGURED OUT HOW TO AVOID HARD WORK by exploiting the energy stored in other humans, animals, falling water, wind, wood, fossil fuels, and 70 years ago, the atomic nucleus. Fossil fuels – coal, oil, and gas – supply 73% of U.S. electricity, and their waste, which is stored in air, water, soil, and lungs, accounts for almost all human-caused greenhouse gases as well as toxic heavy metal and chemical pollution. But supplies are limited. What's the most efficient energy alternative that's also kind to our planet and health? Bracketology demands a single winner, but in reality there are many options.

**Algae-produced fuels vs. Ethanol**
To replace less than 1% of our gasoline consumption with ethanol requires about 5 million acres of land that might otherwise provide food for the hungry. In 2006 U.S. taxpayers spent $5.6 billion on ethanol production that reduced U.S. greenhouse gases by one-nineteenth of 1%. On the other hand, oil-producing micro-algae can be farmed in a nontoxic fashion – and cheaply provide about 20 to 80 times more biofuel per acre than corn or soybeans, which rely on petroleum-based fertilizers and pesticides. It would take an algae farm bigger than the state of Maryland to make all the gasoline the U.S. consumes. But can this much oil be extracted efficiently, and if so, by when?

**Unobtainium vs. Hydrogen**
Unobtainium is a term used by scientists to describe that mysterious energy source, substance, or device that's supposed to drive a space ship faster than light-speed, or provide power to a promising invention, or fill in the blanks of a newfangled energy scheme that looks great on paper but has yet to make it to the real world. In other words, it's fantasy – and loses.

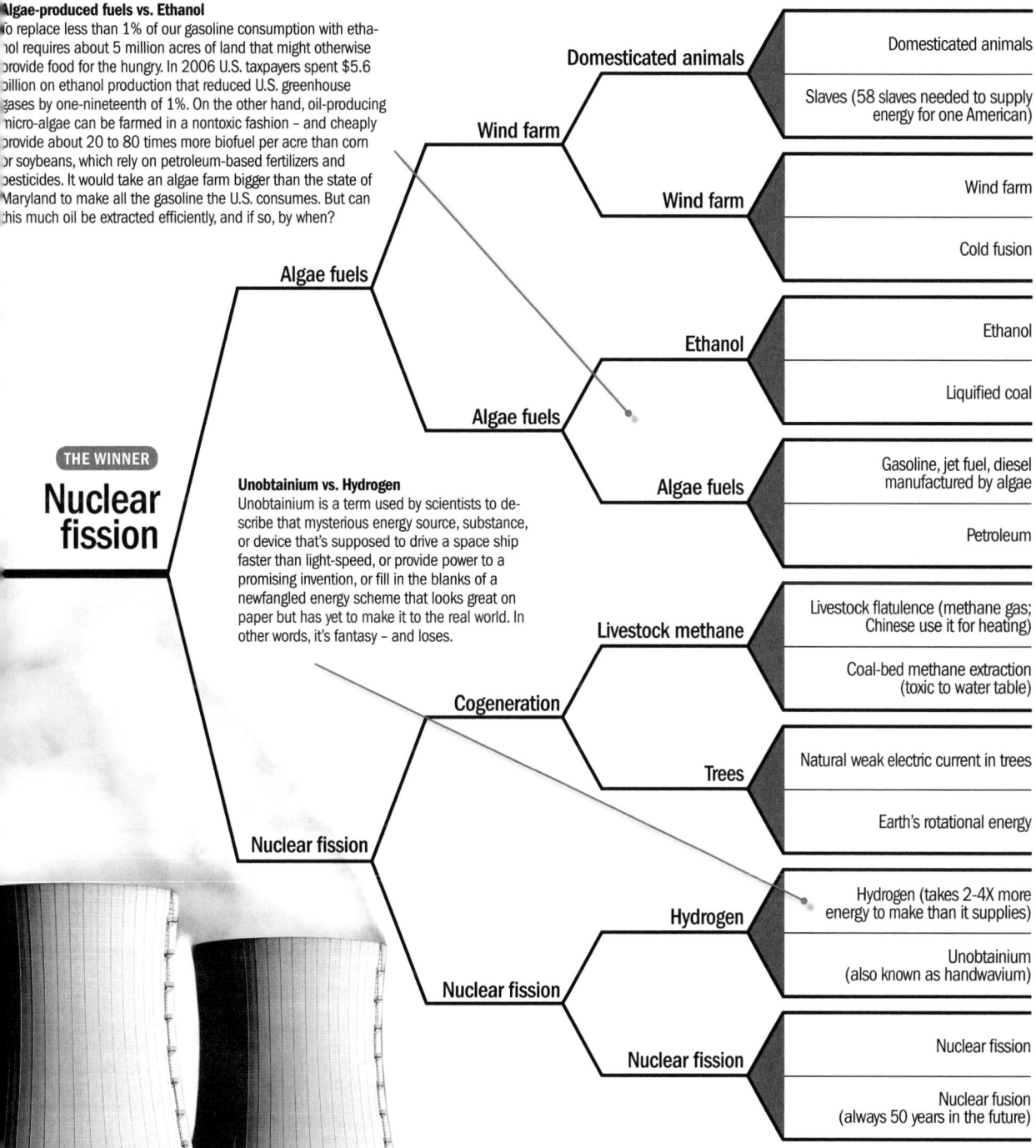

# My Prized Feathers

**By Luke Dempsey**

Luke Dempsey is the author of *A Supremely Bad Idea: Three Mad Birders and Their Quest to See It All,* as well as "Paul Simon Songs" in *The Enlightened Bracketologist.*

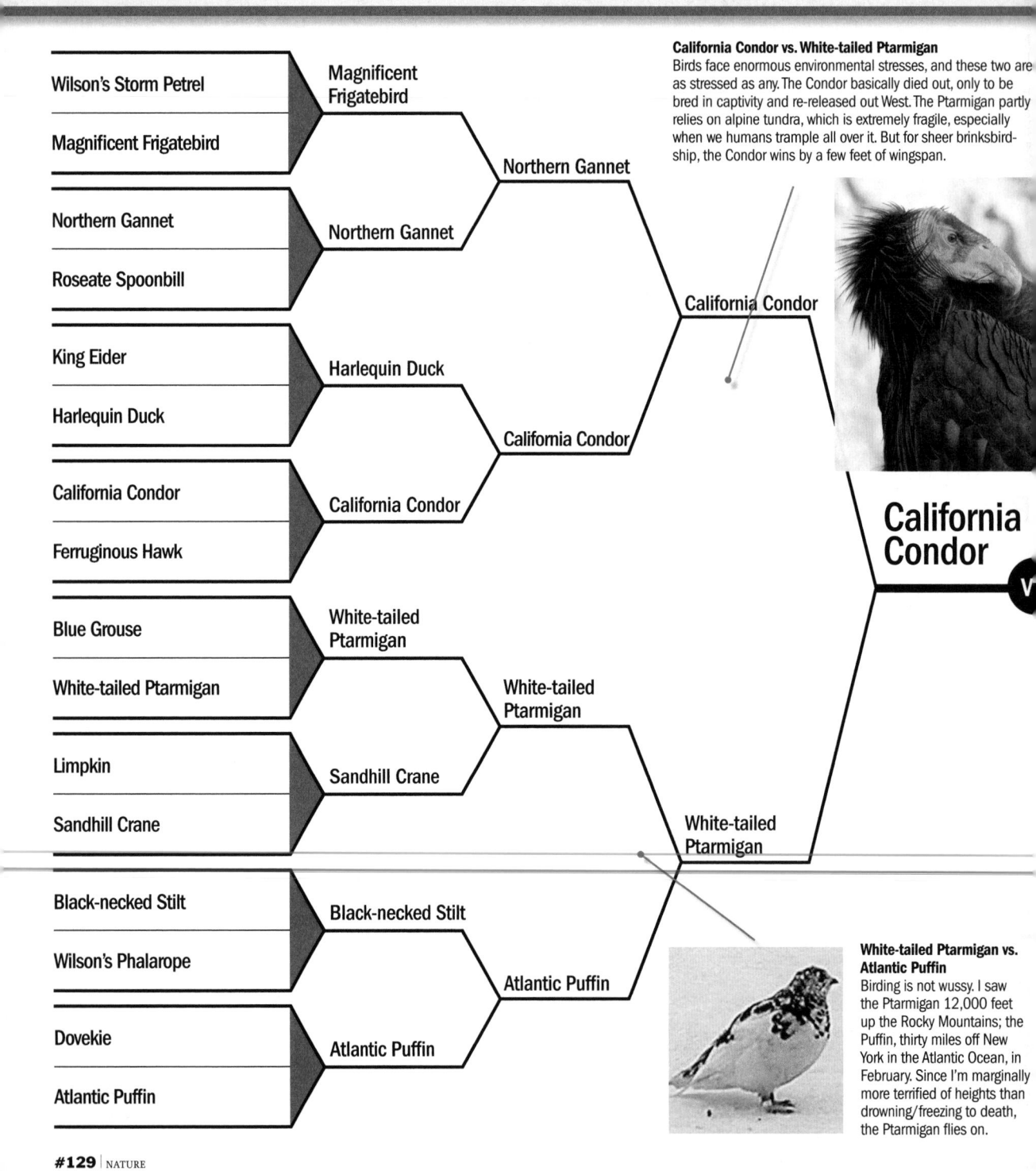


**California Condor vs. White-tailed Ptarmigan**
Birds face enormous environmental stresses, and these two are as stressed as any. The Condor basically died out, only to be bred in captivity and re-released out West. The Ptarmigan partly relies on alpine tundra, which is extremely fragile, especially when we humans trample all over it. But for sheer brinksbirdship, the Condor wins by a few feet of wingspan.

**White-tailed Ptarmigan vs. Atlantic Puffin**
Birding is not wussy. I saw the Ptarmigan 12,000 feet up the Rocky Mountains; the Puffin, thirty miles off New York in the Atlantic Ocean, in February. Since I'm marginally more terrified of heights than drowning/freezing to death, the Ptarmigan flies on.

LONG AGO I KNEW NOTHING ABOUT BIRDS. Then I started looking, and I haven't looked back. If I could turn back time, I would make a list of all the birds in North America that I must see. The list would include the beautiful, the hard to find, the endangered – and could only make sense if I knew something about birds, as I do now. This bracket is the list I would have made if I knew then what I know now. For the record, I've "gotten" all the birds here except the two finalists. One of them is barely alive; the other, so dazzling it makes your eyes hurt. (Or will, if I ever see it. That's why we bird.)

**Northern Hawk Owl vs. Elegant Trogon**
I have a saying: A bird seen by any of us is better if seen by all, "all" being my two birding homies, Don and Donna Graffiti. In early 2009 in northern New York I saw a Northern Hawk Owl, a bird that if it appears anywhere south of the Canadian border is big news. Don and Donna were birding in Honduras at the time. Thus, the Elegant Trogon in Arizona together a few years earlier gets the edge.

**Pileated Woodpecker vs. Scissor-tailed Flycatcher**
I wanted to include the Ivory-billed Woodpecker – a bit bigger than the Pileated, and the Lord Lucan of birds -- but like Lucan, it's probably dead forever.

THE WINNER

# Red-faced Warbler

**Kirtland's Warbler vs Olive Warbler**
To see a Kirtland's – one of the most endangered/rarest birds in North America – you have to go to northern Michigan and get on a government-guided tour. To see an Olive Warbler, you have to be lucky and more than 7,000 feet up a mountain in southeast Arizona. Chance earns the victory here.

**California Condor vs. Red-faced Warbler**
For all our fears for birds' survival, their beauty is enduring, in the flesh or in our hopes. In this final beak-off, the Red-faced Warbler wins because it boasts a gorgeously bright red face and a black helmet. Its numbers are declining, sadly, but while it's still around, head to the mountains of Arizona or New Mexico, and wait. If you see there a short bald man bedecked in binoculars and a big smile, feel free to say hello.

- Elegant Trogon
  - Elegant Trogon
    - Northern Hawk-Owl
      - Snowy Owl
      - Northern Hawk-Owl
    - Elegant Trogon
      - Anna's Hummingbird
      - Elegant Trogon
  - Scissor-tailed Flycatcher
    - Pileated Woodpecker
      - Red-Headed Woodpecker
      - Pileated Woodpecker
    - Scissor-tailed Flycatcher
      - Vermillion Flycatcher
      - Scissor-tailed Flycatcher
- Red-faced Warbler
  - Red-faced Warbler
    - Red-faced Warbler
      - Cerulean Warbler
      - Red-faced Warbler
    - Olive Warbler
      - Kirtland's Warbler
      - Olive Warbler
  - Flame-colored Tanager
    - Flame-colored Tanager
      - Scarlet Tanager
      - Flame-colored Tanager
    - Bobolink
      - Painted Bunting
      - Bobolink

# Looking Younger

**By David J. Leffell, M.D.**

Dr. David J. Leffell is the David Paige Smith Professor of Dermatology & Surgery at the Yale School of Medicine and author of *Total Skin*.

THINGS YOU CAN'T DO YOURSELF

- Microdermabrasion
- Fat transplant
- Chemical peel
- Photodynamic therapy
- Makeup applied by a professional
- Botox
- Fractionated laser
- Eyelift
- Spa facials
- Soft-tissue fillers
- Facelift
- Necklift
- Silicone Implants
- Laser ablation
- Intense pulsed light therapy
- Fat transfer to your hands

**Microdermabrasion vs. Fat transplant**
Stay away from anything micro. If it's micro, you won't see it.

**Fat transplant vs. Chemical peel**
Your hands are the ultimate giveaway of disappearing youth. Old hands can look younger if you replace the fat that disappears on the backs of your hands. It doesn't last and you can only hope people notice. Chemical peels, done by a pro, can stimulate fresh new skin. But you need a series of three or four treatments for best results.

**Botox vs. Facelift**
If a facelift is too much to ponder, go with the next best thing. Botox injections work and they're not permanent. If you get a little too much, it will fade over time and you can wink again.

**Facelift vs. Necklift**
Why stop at the neck, which you can hide with a turtleneck? A facelift is the Big Kahuna of anti-aging. If it's done right, even your ex-husband won't recognize you. Find a board-certified plastic surgeon who does the procedure every day.

**Sun protection vs. Botox**
It's not sexy, it's not instant, and it won't reverse the errors of youth. But since about 90 percent of skin aging (looking older than you are) comes from sun exposure, the sooner you wear sunscreen and follow a good sun protection program, the sooner you will protect the skin you have to keep your face smooth and wrinkle free. Botox can fix some lines that come from facial expression. It works. It's fast. It's reversible. But sun protection will also prevent irregular sun spots and liver spots, not to mention skin cancer.

THE DESIRE FOR IMMORTALITY is followed closely by the desire to appear immortal, to look young as the calendar pages peel off and fly away. More than $30 billion is spent in the United States annually on potions, creams, pills, and every manner of device and insertable creation – all intended to make you look younger than you are. Most of the products should be tossed into the closet where the "Emperor's New Clothes" hang, but some things can make a big difference, whether you do them to yourself or let others do them to you.

**No smoking vs. Sun protection**
Smoking not only causes the deep vertical lines on the lips, from holding and sucking on a cigarette, but the smoke itself stimulates enzymes in the skin to break down precious collagen, leading to wrinkles all over your face. A good dermatologist can spot a smoker from the door. Fortunately more than 80 percent of Americans get it. Not so with avoiding harmful sun.

THE WINNER

## Sun protection

**Retin-A vs. Sun protection**
Also known as tretinoin, Retin-A is the only proven topical agent that can cause new collagen to grow and replace the sun-damaged dermis that leads to wrinkles. But it requires consistency, commitment, and moisturizer, whereas sun protection just requires shade – via a hat, an umbrella, sunblock, or staying indoors.

**Daily moisturizer vs. Exfoliation**
You have a choice: in one you add something, in another you try to remove it. Always add. Moisturize your skin and make your fine lines appear so fine you can't see them. Exfoliation will make the skin feel smooth, but for convenience and skin health, daily moisturizing is the way to go.

- Sun protection
  - Sun protection
    - Vitamin C serum
      - Plant stem cell serum
      - Vitamin C serum
    - Sun protection
      - Sun protection
      - Low-sugar diet
  - No smoking
    - No smoking
      - Human growth hormone (HGH)
      - No smoking
    - Makeup
      - Makeup
      - Green tea extract
- Retin-A
  - Daily moisturizer
    - Daily moisturizer
      - Extract of sea creature cream
      - Daily moisturizer
    - Exfoliation
      - Exfoliation
      - Electrostimulation
  - Retin-A
    - Retin-A
      - Tea bag soaks
      - Tretinoin (Retin-A)
    - Alpha Hydroxy acid cream
      - Alpha Hydroxy acid cream
      - Eye of newt extract

**Low sugar diet vs. Sun protection**
There are plenty of reasons to cut the sucrose and load up on the Splenda, but disappearing wrinkles is not one of them. If it sounds ridiculous it probably is.

**Green tea extract vs. Makeup**
Green tea extract is a classic well-documented antioxidant. Extract applied to the skin or the beverage consumed in the Asian fashion will have a documented effect on skin health. But will anyone notice? Makeup, on the other hand, works.

A B C D
E F G H
I J K L
M N O P
Q R S T
U V W X

# WORDS

**Fatherly Advice** *by Jancee Dunn* **131**
**Motherly Advice** *by Mark Reiter* **132**
**Acronyms** *by Stefan Fatsis* **133**
**Lazy Wit** *by Adi Ignatius* **134**
**Texas Sayings** *by Anne Dingus* **135**
**Seductive Foreign Accents** *by Asif Eydohno* **136**
**Yogi Berra Wisdom** *by Dave Kaplan* **137**
**Fortune Cookies** *by Jennifer 8. Lee* **138**
**All-Purpose Banalities** *by Joe Queenan* **139**
**Deadly Sins of Emailing** *by David Shipley and Will Schwalbe* **140**
**Politically Correct Terms** *by Henry Beard and Christopher Cerf* **141**
**Woody Allen Wisdom** *by Eric Lax* **142**

# Fatherly Advice

**By Jancee Dunn**

Jancee Dunn writes for the *New York Times, Vogue,* and *O, The Oprah Magazine.* Her third book is an essay collection, *Why Is My Mother Getting a Tattoo?*

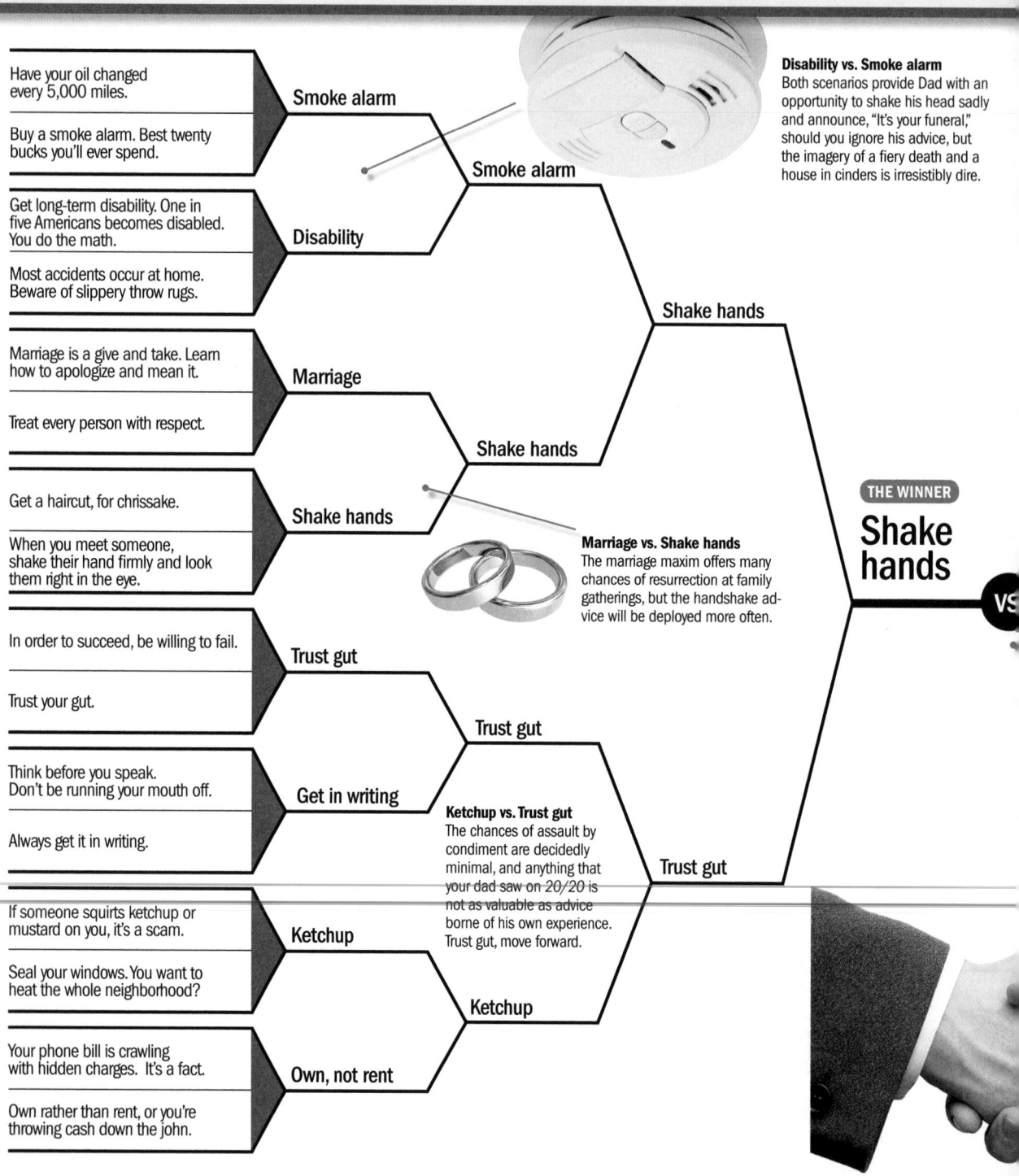

I'VE NEVER HAD AN EXTENDED CONVERSATION WITH MY DAD that didn't end on some sort of teachable moment. Like many fathers, he just couldn't help himself: solicited or not, I was going to learn something. Over the years I've found that standard-issue Dad Wisdom contains one of three elements: preparedness (advice on financial planning, all forms of insurance, termite control), paranoia (potential health hazards, pyramid schemes, identity theft), and personal conduct (your word is your bond.)

**Education vs. Don't overthink**
It is here that any counsel that can be supplemented with a sheaf of research torn from *Consumer Reports* is eliminated. No more tips on cost-cutting and home weatherproofing; only the most elemental guidance remains.

# Education

**Shake hands vs. Education**
Shaking hands is the clear winner. Every time you meet someone for the rest of your life, your father's advice will pop, unbidden, into your head. Depending on how gregarious you are, you will hear his words hundreds of times – perhaps thousands, if you're in politics or sales.

- Education
  - Education
    - Education
      - Don't smoke like your old man did.
      - Get a good education. This is not up for discussion.
    - Retirement fund
      - It's never too early to start a retirement fund. Don't die broke.
      - You think flood insurance is a joke? Wait until the next big storm. Then you won't be laughing.
  - Bulk
    - Buy in bulk
      - Buy in bulk. You know how much I save on toilet paper alone?
      - Get a hand-cranked radio. Say there's an emergency, and the power goes out. How are you supposed to get information?
    - Do not call
      - Set your lights on timers. Mine go out right after Leno.
      - You're on the National 'Do Not Call' list, right? No? Well, then, I guess you like talking to telemarketers.
- Overthink
  - Overthink
    - Flare lights
      - Keep flare lights in the trunk of your car.
      - The people you meet on the way up are the same ones you'll see on the way down.
    - Overthink
      - You can't go wrong if you order the steak.
      - Don't overthink everything. Your generation thinks too much.
  - Kids
    - Buying car
      - Be prepared to walk out when you're buying a car.
      - Bottled water is for suckers. It costs more than Scotch!
    - Kids
      - You might want to get that driveway sealed before the asphalt buckles, or you're looking at some serious damage.
      - I'll tell you, having kids was the best thing I ever did.

# Motherly Advice

**By Mark Reiter**

Mark Reiter, the co-editor of this book, has a mother who has very interesting theories about sleep, electric typewriters, QuickBooks, and automobiles painted red.

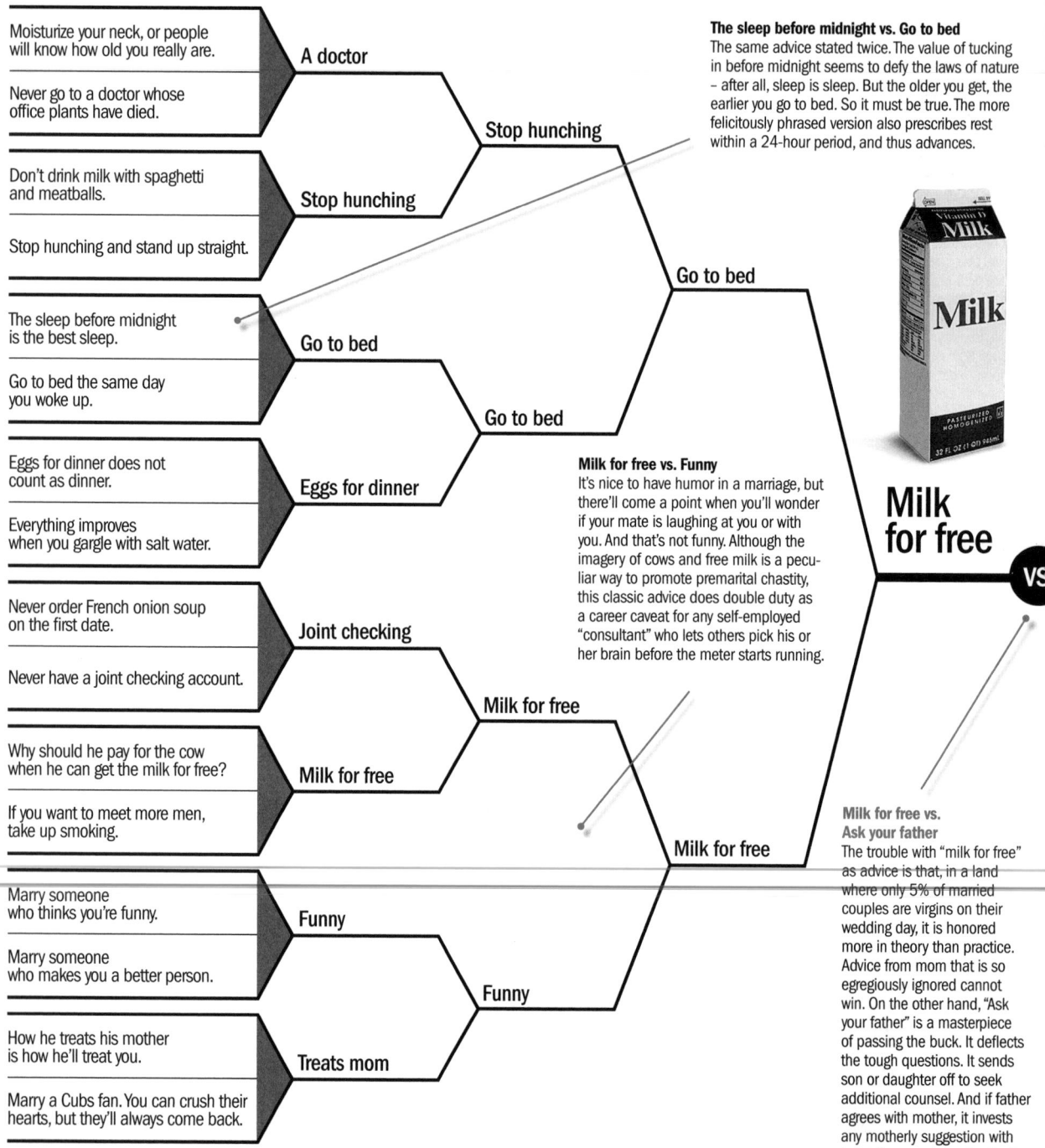


**The sleep before midnight vs. Go to bed**
The same advice stated twice. The value of tucking in before midnight seems to defy the laws of nature – after all, sleep is sleep. But the older you get, the earlier you go to bed. So it must be true. The more felicitously phrased version also prescribes rest within a 24-hour period, and thus advances.

**Milk for free vs. Funny**
It's nice to have humor in a marriage, but there'll come a point when you'll wonder if your mate is laughing at you or with you. And that's not funny. Although the imagery of cows and free milk is a peculiar way to promote premarital chastity, this classic advice does double duty as a career caveat for any self-employed "consultant" who lets others pick his or her brain before the meter starts running.

**Milk for free vs. Ask your father**
The trouble with "milk for free" as advice is that, in a land where only 5% of married couples are virgins on their wedding day, it is honored more in theory than practice. Advice from mom that is so egregiously ignored cannot win. On the other hand, "Ask your father" is a masterpiece of passing the buck. It deflects the tough questions. It sends son or daughter off to seek additional counsel. And if father agrees with mother, it invests any motherly suggestion with twice the parental authority. As advice, it's a twofer – and wins.

UNLIKE FATHERLY ADVICE, which tends toward the protective, motherly advice is all about creating a prettier, smarter, longer-living, more successful you. In other words, dads play defense, moms play offense. Moms want us to marry well and happily ever after. They think they know what we should put in our mouths. And they usually see our career paths more clearly than we do. Memorability and pithiness are the main criteria here, with bonus points for real-life effectiveness or absurdity. P.S. All variations on the Golden Rule ("Do unto others . . .") have been banned here, or else there would be no contest.

# Thank You

**"Thank you" vs. Ask your father**
Of all the gems here, saying "Thank you" to a compliment is the easiest to do. You just put your lips together and say it. But it doesn't stand a chance against the mother of all delegating lines.

THE WINNER

## Ask your father

- Ask your father
  - Ask your father
    - Ask your father
      - You can always make new friends, but old friends are good as gold.
      - Ask your father.
    - Nobody will ever
      - Nobody will ever love you like your mother.
      - Tell your mother you'll visit her grave. She'll never know, but the promise will make her feel better.
  - "Thank you"
    - "Thank you"
      - Never refuse a hug from a person just because his hands are dirty.
      - When someone pays you a compliment, first say "Thank you."
    - By in an instant
      - What goes around comes around.
      - It all goes by in an instant.
- A movie alone
  - Don't be cheap
    - Don't be cheap
      - The A's and B's always end up working for the C's and D's.
      - Don't be cheap about meat, Champagne, and leather.
    - Forecheck
      - Forecheck, backcheck, paycheck.
      - What comes easy isn't worth having.
  - A movie alone
    - A movie alone
      - Never assume people are too busy. Pick up the phone. Even Marilyn Monroe sat home Saturday nights waiting for a call.
      - There's nothing wrong with seeing a movie alone.
    - Choose pleasant
      - If it's a choice between being smart or pleasant, choose pleasant.
      - If it's attention you want, pee in the street. Someone will always see you.

**Don't be cheap vs. A movie alone**
Life really is better when you're wearing fine leather and drinking great Champagne over an expensive slab of beef. But it's not a foolproof strategy, not if your boss is a PETA-loving alcoholic vegan. The obvious benefits of seeing a movie alone include never having to share your popcorn or sit through all the credits. And you can walk out anytime, no explaining needed. Plus, solitary moviegoers build up rugged independence the way fitness freaks build muscle – and that indy streak sustains through the bleakest personal trials as well as the lamest indy films.

**Forecheck vs. What comes easy**
Obviously, one of these is from a hockey mom, and its life application is limited: you can only go so far brutalizing people behind and ahead of you and expecting to be rewarded for it. But it's short if not sweet, and moves on.

# Acronyms

**By Stefan Fatsis**

Stefan Fatsis is the author of *Word Freak: Heartbreak, Triumph, Genius, and Obsession in the World of Competitive Scrabble Players* and *A Few Seconds of Panic: A 5-foot-8, 170-Pound, 43-Year-Old Sportswriter Plays in the NFL.* A former reporter for the *WSJ,* Fatsis talks on NPR and writes for the *NYT, SI,* et al.

**ASAP**
(As Soon As Possible, 1955)

**IMHO**
(In My Humble Opinion, c. 1980s)

**SWAT**
(Special Weapons and Tactics, 1967)

**AWOL**
(Absent Without Leave, 1919)

**WASP**
(White, Anglo-Saxon Protestant, 1957)

**yuppie**
(Young Urban Professional, 1983)

**POTUS**
(President of the United States, 1925)

**TARP**
(Troubled Asset Relief Program, 2008)

**FUBAR**
(Fucked Up Beyond All Recognition, 1944)

**snafu**
(Situation Normal, All Fucked Up, c. 1940)

**Nabisco**
(National Biscuit Company, 1906)

**FAQ**
(Frequently Asked Questions, c. 1980s)

**radar**
(Radio Detection and Ranging, 1941)

**UNIVAC**
(Universal Automatic Computer, 1951)

**scuba**
(Self-Contained Underwater Breathing Apparatus, 1952)

**MADD**
(Mothers Against Drunk Driving, 1980)

ASAP
AWOL
WASP
POTUS
snafu
FAQ
radar
scuba

AWOL
WASP
snafu
scuba

WASP

**AWOL vs. ASAP**
From Orwell's Ingsoc to Bush's USA PATRIOT Act, government bureaucracies are breeding grounds for acronyms, none more than the armed forces. AWOL and ASAP both began as Army slang before invading the daily language. The winner: AWOL, to honor its legacy as one of America's first acronyms.

**scuba vs. snafu**
Scuba and snafu were birthed in acronymic hotbeds (science and the military), assimilated into pop culture, and matured lexicographically into lowercase words. They're so evolved that people don't even know that they're acronyms. Snafu, though, like its WWII partner, FUBAR, is feeling its age. Scuba to the Final Four.

WASP

VS

**WASP vs. AIDS**
As America's dominant social, political, and economic elite, the WASP is dead. As an acronym, though, it remains close to perfect: straightforward, sharp, evocative, funny, unforgettable. But AIDS is the champion. Three decades on, it reminds us of the power of a few common letters.

JOINING THE FIRST LETTER OR FIRST FEW LETTERS of multiple words into a single word is a 20th-century phenomenon, and a distinctly American one; the word "acronym" itself was coined at Bell Laboratories in 1943, from the Greek for "extreme" and "name." While some linguistic permissives consider initialisms – USA, BYOB, WWJD – to be acronyms, for our purposes an acronym has to be a pronounceable word. And real. Memo to KISS fans: your heroes are not Knights in Satan's Service.

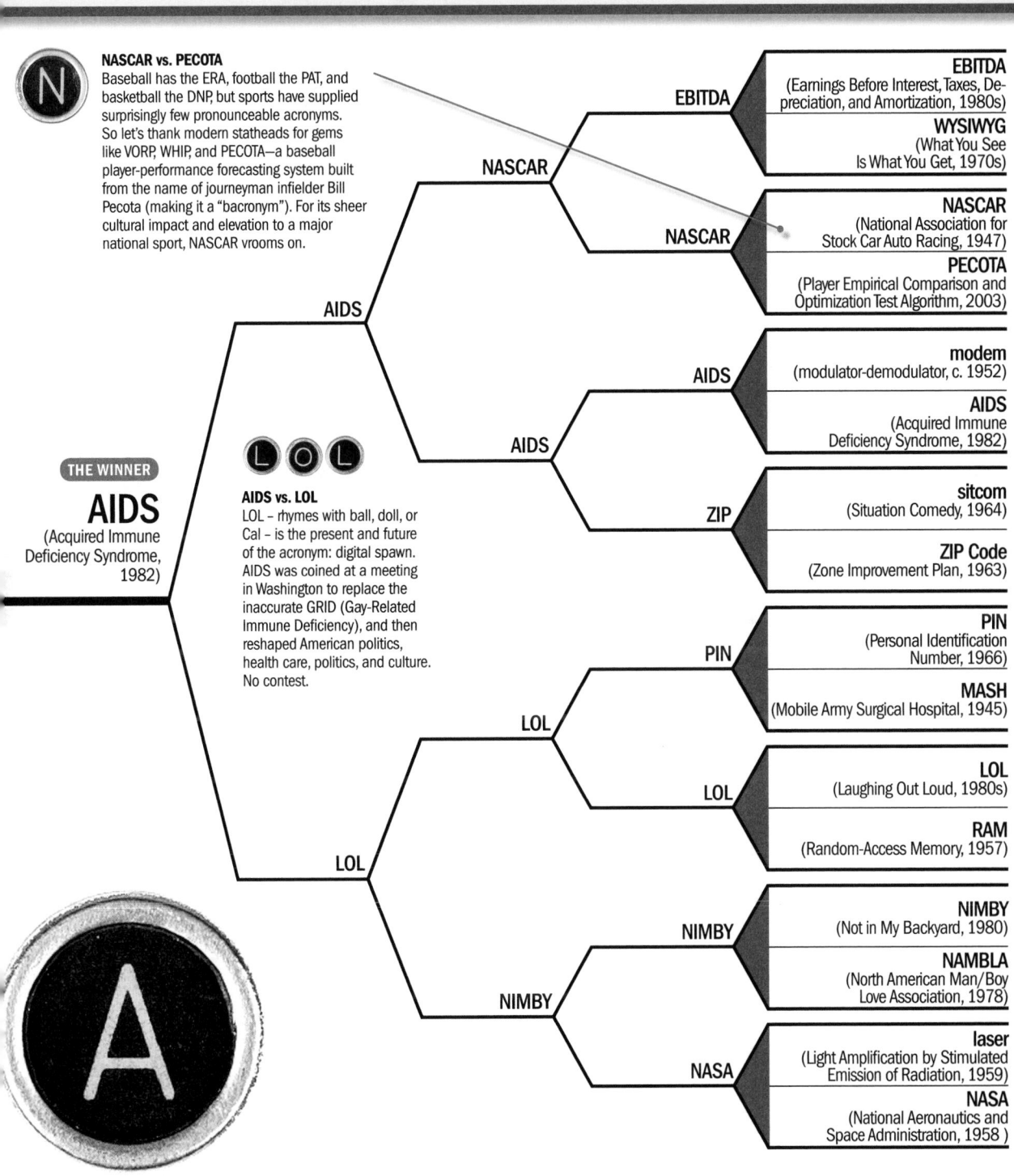

# Lazy Wit

**By Adi Ignatius**

Adi Ignatius, a journalist, relies on most of these lines to get through the day.

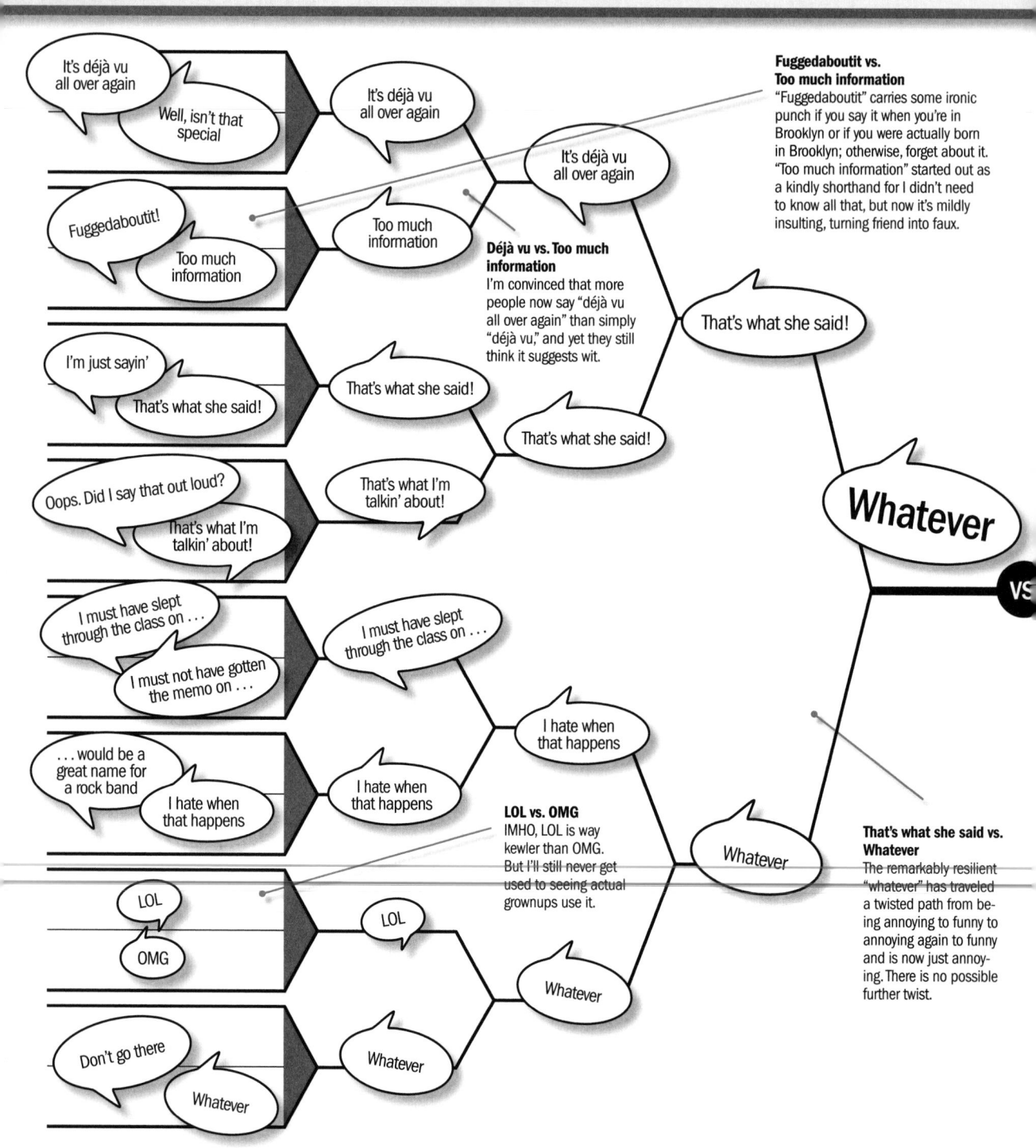


**Fuggedaboutit vs. Too much information**
"Fuggedaboutit" carries some ironic punch if you say it when you're in Brooklyn or if you were actually born in Brooklyn; otherwise, forget about it. "Too much information" started out as a kindly shorthand for I didn't need to know all that, but now it's mildly insulting, turning friend into faux.

**Déjà vu vs. Too much information**
I'm convinced that more people now say "déjà vu all over again" than simply "déjà vu," and yet they still think it suggests wit.

**LOL vs. OMG**
IMHO, LOL is way kewler than OMG. But I'll still never get used to seeing actual grownups use it.

**That's what she said vs. Whatever**
The remarkably resilient "whatever" has traveled a twisted path from being annoying to funny to annoying again to funny and is now just annoying. There is no possible further twist.

WE'VE ALL HEARD THEM. MOST OF US HAVE PROBABLY USED THEM: those handy catchphrases you store up and blurt out at opportune times with a twinkle in your eyes, as if you've just come up with a stunningly clever line. Only in truth, these phrases are used by everyone, of all ages, all the time. If they ever were witty, they certainly aren't by now. Which is the most expired? Follow the bracket.

**Been there, done that vs. Rocket science**
The optional T-shirt add-on gives the first phrase a tiny bit of variety, and it can still be funny when someone describes actual rocket science as not exactly rocket science. But both clichés are way past their sell-by dates.

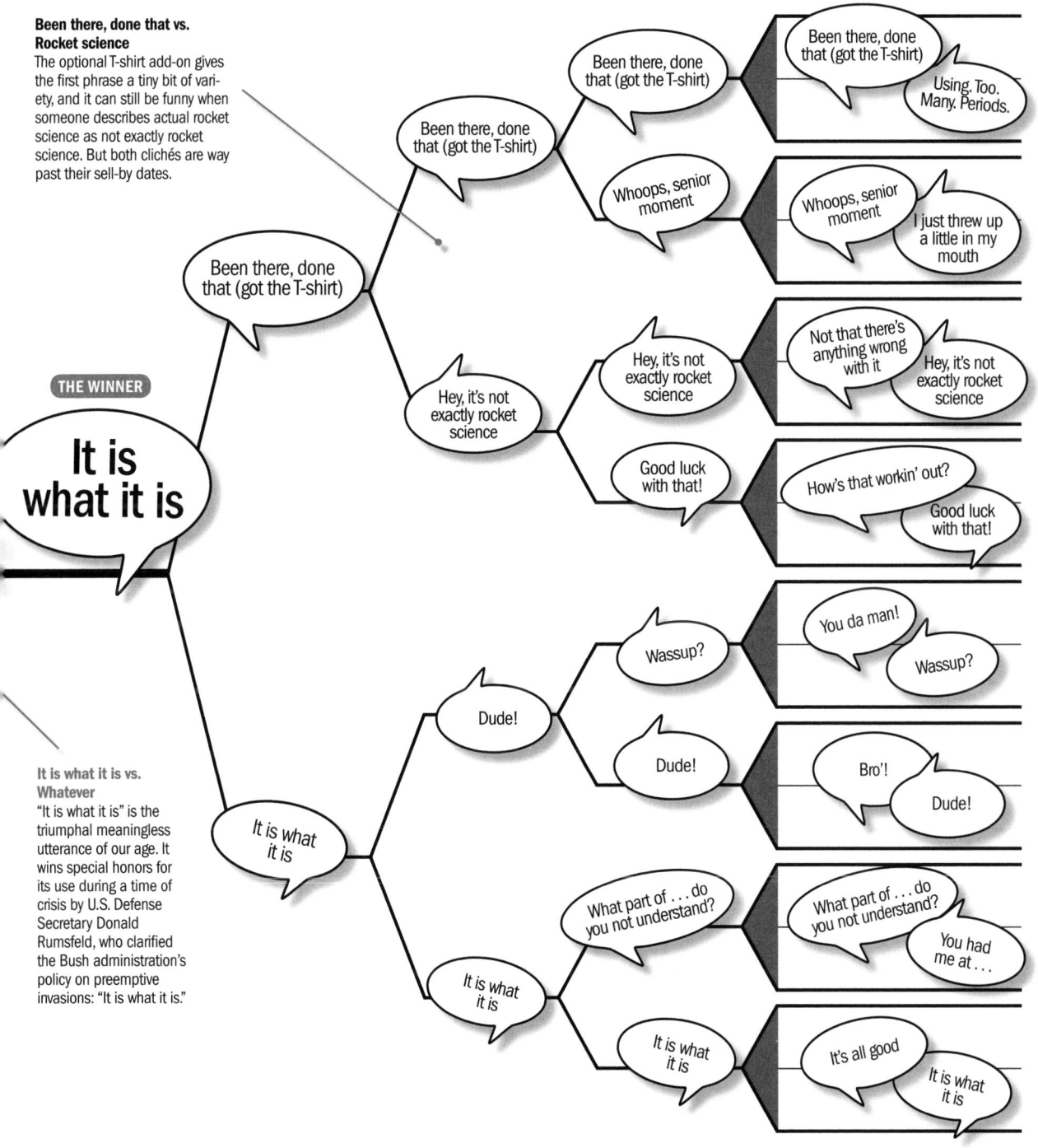


**It is what it is vs. Whatever**
"It is what it is" is the triumphal meaningless utterance of our age. It wins special honors for its use during a time of crisis by U.S. Defense Secretary Donald Rumsfeld, who clarified the Bush administration's policy on preemptive invasions: "It is what it is."

# Texas Sayings

**By Anne Dingus**

Anne Dingus, a former columnist for *Texas Monthly,* is the author of *More Texas Sayings Than You Can Shake a Stick At.* She lives in Austin.

**BIG REGIONAL**

- "Big enough for twins."
- "Big as all hell and half of Texas."
- "So big he looks like he ate his brother."
- "Warm in winter, shady in summer [fat]."

**DUMB REGIONAL**

- "If dumb was dirt, he'd cover about an acre."
- "So dumb that if you hit him with a tire iron, he won't yell till morning."
- "So dumb he couldn't pour piss out of a boot with a hole in the toe and directions on the heel."
- "If brains were leather, he couldn't saddle a flea."

**MEAN REGIONAL**

- "He's such a liar, he'd beat you senseless and tell God you fell off a horse."
- "He's a spherical SOB [an SOB any way you look at him]."
- "I'll whip you like a red-headed stepchild."
- "I'll knock a hole in him you can throw a cat through."

**RICH REGIONAL**

- "Rich as feedlot dirt."
- "They didn't come to town two to a mule."
- "She took rich from her mama and daddy."
- "In tall cotton."

"Big enough for twins."

"Big as all hell and half of Texas."

"Ate his brother"

"So big he looks like he ate his brother." / "Warm in winter, shady in summer [fat]."

"If dumb was dirt"

"If dumb was dirt, he'd cover about an acre." / "So dumb that if you hit him with a tire iron, he won't yell till morning."

"So dumb he couldn't"

"So dumb he couldn't pour piss out of a boot with a hole in the toe and directions on the heel." / "If brains were leather, he couldn't saddle a flea."

"He's such a liar"

"He's such a liar, he'd beat you senseless and tell God you fell off a horse." / "He's a spherical SOB [an SOB any way you look at him]."

"I'll whip you"

"I'll whip you like a red-headed stepchild." / "I'll knock a hole in him you can throw a cat through."

"Two to a mule"

"Rich as feedlot dirt." / "They didn't come to town two to a mule."

"In tall cotton"

"She took rich from her mama and daddy." / "In tall cotton."

"Ate his brother"

"So dumb he couldn't"

"He's such a liar"

"Two to a mule"

"So dumb he couldn't"

"He's such a liar"

**THE WINNER**

**"So dumb he couldn't pour piss out of a boot with a hole in the toe and directions on the heel."**

**VS**

**"So big he looks like he ate his brother" vs. "Big as all hell and half of Texas"**
Both of these lines convey the same idea, but "ate his brother" merely conjures up a perverse unappetizing visual while "Big as all hell" invokes Texas's fabled size. We're suckers for any reference to big-big-big, even half a century after losing our number-one status to Alaska. You betcha'.

**"So dumb that if you hit him with a tire iron, he won't yell till morning" vs. "If dumb was dirt, he'd cover about an acre"**
A duel of classic "dumb" locutions. The loser follows a now-standard construction that smacks of modern stand-up comedy. But the winner – "If dumb was dirt, he'd cover about an acre" – is more than a one-line rip about diminished intelligence. In Texas, an acre is considered a piddling piece of land, so the line is doubly insulting.

**"In tall cotton" vs. "Two to a mule"**
"In tall cotton" has brevity and politeness going for it. "They didn't come to town two to a mule," however, conveys wealth with a sly, understated, mule-scented charm. It conveys admiration, but it has the potential to be snarky, too.

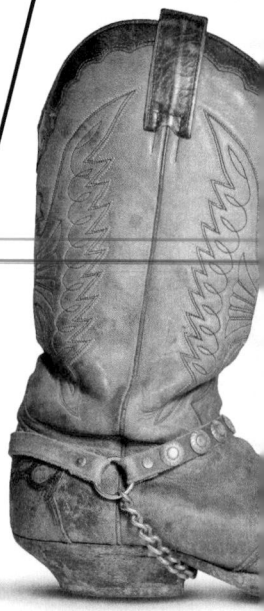

WE TEXANS JUST LOVE TO HEAR OURSELVES TALK. No surprise, then, that we never settle for wimpy little adjectives or repressed ladylike exclamations. We prefer similes, metaphors, and colorful humor that channels Davy Crockett and Pecos Bill. We laugh at ourselves (and you, most likely), and we brag about everything from oil wells and pretty belles to at least one Texas president. Our sense of humor is big, rich, loud, hot, and occasionally dumb and mean, just like Texas. But always sprawling, out-size funny. Y'all talk back now, hear?

# "Trees are bribing the dogs"

- "Sorts bobcats for a living"
  - "Sorts bobcats for a living"
    - "Sorts bobcats for a living"
      - "She looks like the wrath of God."
      - "He looks like he sorts bobcats for a living."
    - "Tide wouldn't take her"
      - "He looks like he was inside the outhouse when the lightning struck."
      - "She's so ugly the tide wouldn't take her out."
  - "Boomtown whore"
    - "Boomtown whore"
      - "Busier than a funeral-home fan in July."
      - "Busier than a boomtown whore."
    - "I got to slop the hogs"
      - "Busy as grease on a hot skillet."
      - "I got to slop the hogs, dig the well, and plow the south forty before breakfast."
- "Trees are bribing the dogs"
  - "Trees are bribing the dogs"
    - "Trees are bribing the dogs"
      - "Cold as a cast-iron commode."
      - "So dry the trees are bribing the dogs."
    - "So hot I saw a dog chasin'"
      - "So dry the Baptists are sprinkling, the Methodists are spitting, and the Catholics are giving rainchecks."
      - So hot I saw a dog chasin' a cat, and him a-walkin'.
  - "Might as well. Can't dance"
    - "Better than a poke"
      - "Better than a poke in the eye with a sharp stick."
      - "The Lord throws a mighty wide loop."
    - "Might as well. Can't dance"
      - "Might as well. Can't dance, never could sing, and it's too wet to plow."
      - "Pigs get fat; hogs get slaughtered."

UGLY REGIONAL

BUSY REGIONAL

WEATHER REGIONAL

GENERAL ADVICE REGIONAL

**"Boomtown whore" vs. "Sorts bobcats for a living"**
Texas has a long history of boomtowns (and boom-boom), but the "ugly" line prompts a brief pause before the bobcat humor pounces. Beautiful!

**"Might as well. Can't dance" vs. "Trees are bribing the dogs"**
The former is a funny but long-winded way to say "Yeah, okay," whereas the second zinger provides, along with a how's-the-weather comment, a great visual image.

**"Trees are bribing the dogs" vs. "So dumb he couldn't"**
How about that? Two tropes involving micturation. The runner-up isn't a whit less witty, but the piss-pouring line involves a classic Texas icon – the boot – and the oral-history embellishments don't weaken the insult but actually reinforce it. And hey – how did the piss get in the boot in the first place? No doubt because of some rich, ugly spherical SOB.

# Seductive Foreign Accents

**By Asif Eydohno**

Asif Eydohno is a guest editor of this book. His native tongue is Hebrew, and he regards English as his most seductive foreign accent.

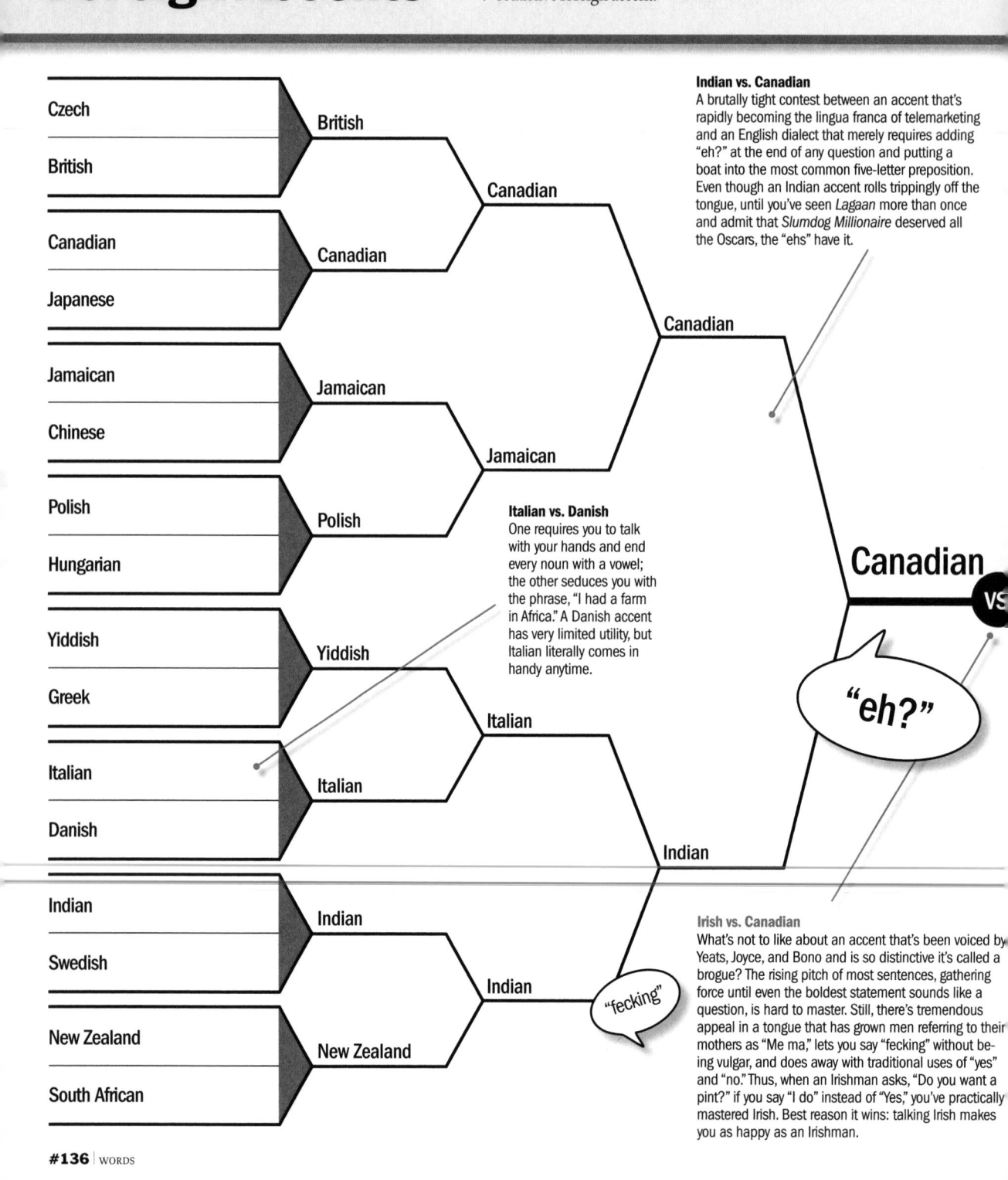


**Indian vs. Canadian**
A brutally tight contest between an accent that's rapidly becoming the lingua franca of telemarketing and an English dialect that merely requires adding "eh?" at the end of any question and putting a boat into the most common five-letter preposition. Even though an Indian accent rolls trippingly off the tongue, until you've seen *Lagaan* more than once and admit that *Slumdog Millionaire* deserved all the Oscars, the "ehs" have it.

**Italian vs. Danish**
One requires you to talk with your hands and end every noun with a vowel; the other seduces you with the phrase, "I had a farm in Africa." A Danish accent has very limited utility, but Italian literally comes in handy anytime.

**Irish vs. Canadian**
What's not to like about an accent that's been voiced by Yeats, Joyce, and Bono and is so distinctive it's called a brogue? The rising pitch of most sentences, gathering force until even the boldest statement sounds like a question, is hard to master. Still, there's tremendous appeal in a tongue that has grown men referring to their mothers as "Me ma," lets you say "fecking" without being vulgar, and does away with traditional uses of "yes" and "no." Thus, when an Irishman asks, "Do you want a pint?" if you say "I do" instead of "Yes," you've practically mastered Irish. Best reason it wins: talking Irish makes you as happy as an Irishman.

EVER WATCH A CHARLES BOYER FILM and walk out of the theater talking like Pepe Le Pew? Or go to a Bengali restaurant and against every instinct of polite public behavior, order from the menu with a newfound Indian accent? Do you watch *Sophie's Choice* or *Out of Africa* and think "I could do what Meryl does." If so, this bracket's for you. A tournament to determine the most seductive (and maybe politically incorrect) foreign accent adopted by everyday Americans.

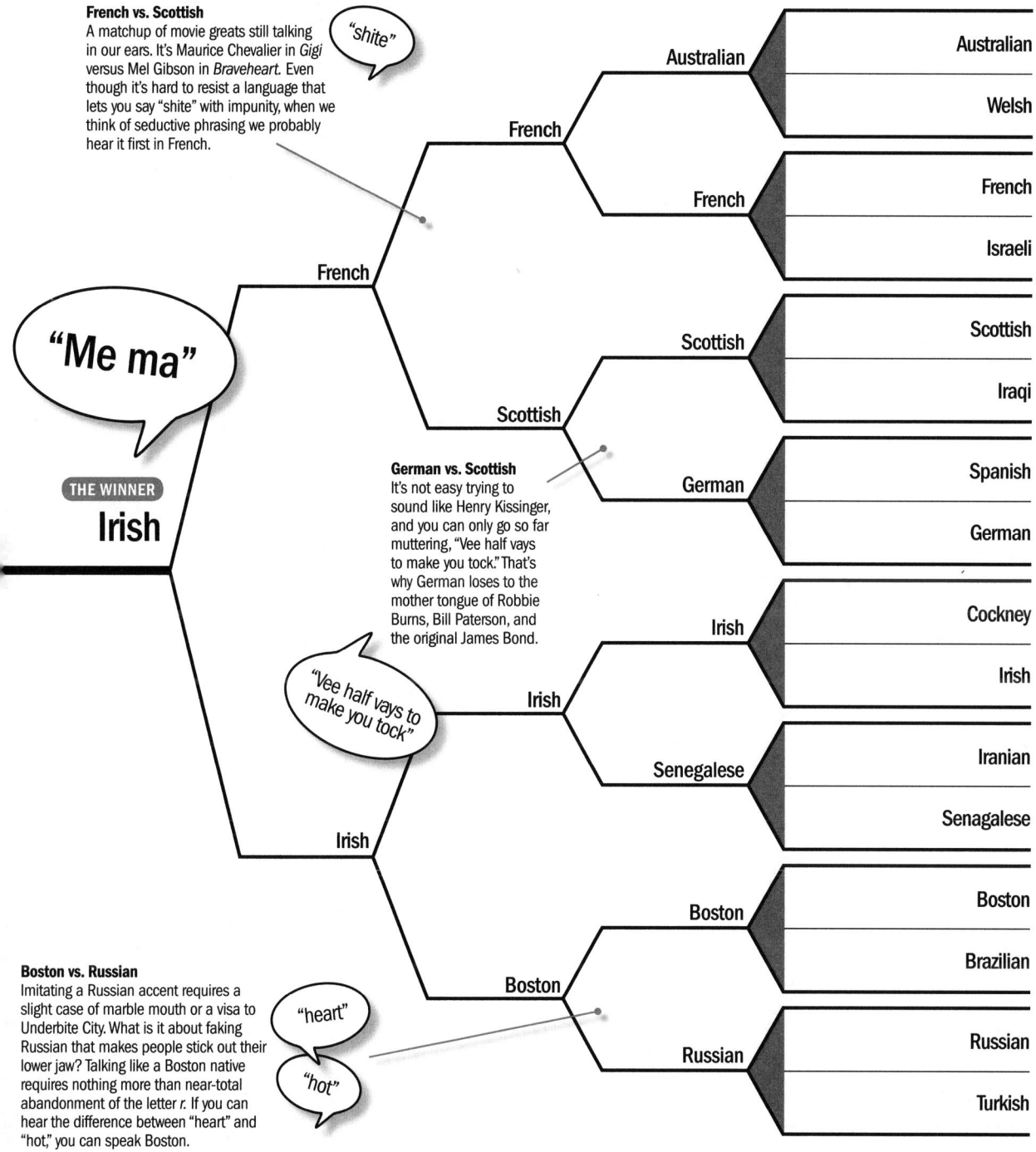


**French vs. Scottish**
A matchup of movie greats still talking in our ears. It's Maurice Chevalier in *Gigi* versus Mel Gibson in *Braveheart.* Even though it's hard to resist a language that lets you say "shite" with impunity, when we think of seductive phrasing we probably hear it first in French.

**German vs. Scottish**
It's not easy trying to sound like Henry Kissinger, and you can only go so far muttering, "Vee half vays to make you tock." That's why German loses to the mother tongue of Robbie Burns, Bill Paterson, and the original James Bond.

**Boston vs. Russian**
Imitating a Russian accent requires a slight case of marble mouth or a visa to Underbite City. What is it about faking Russian that makes people stick out their lower jaw? Talking like a Boston native requires nothing more than near-total abandonment of the letter *r.* If you can hear the difference between "heart" and "hot," you can speak Boston.

# Yogi Berra Wisdom

**By Dave Kaplan**

Dave Kaplan is the founding director of the Yogi Berra Museum & Learning Center on the campus of Montclair State (NJ) University. He has collaborated with Yogi on four books, including the bestselling *When You Come to a Fork in the Road, Take It!*

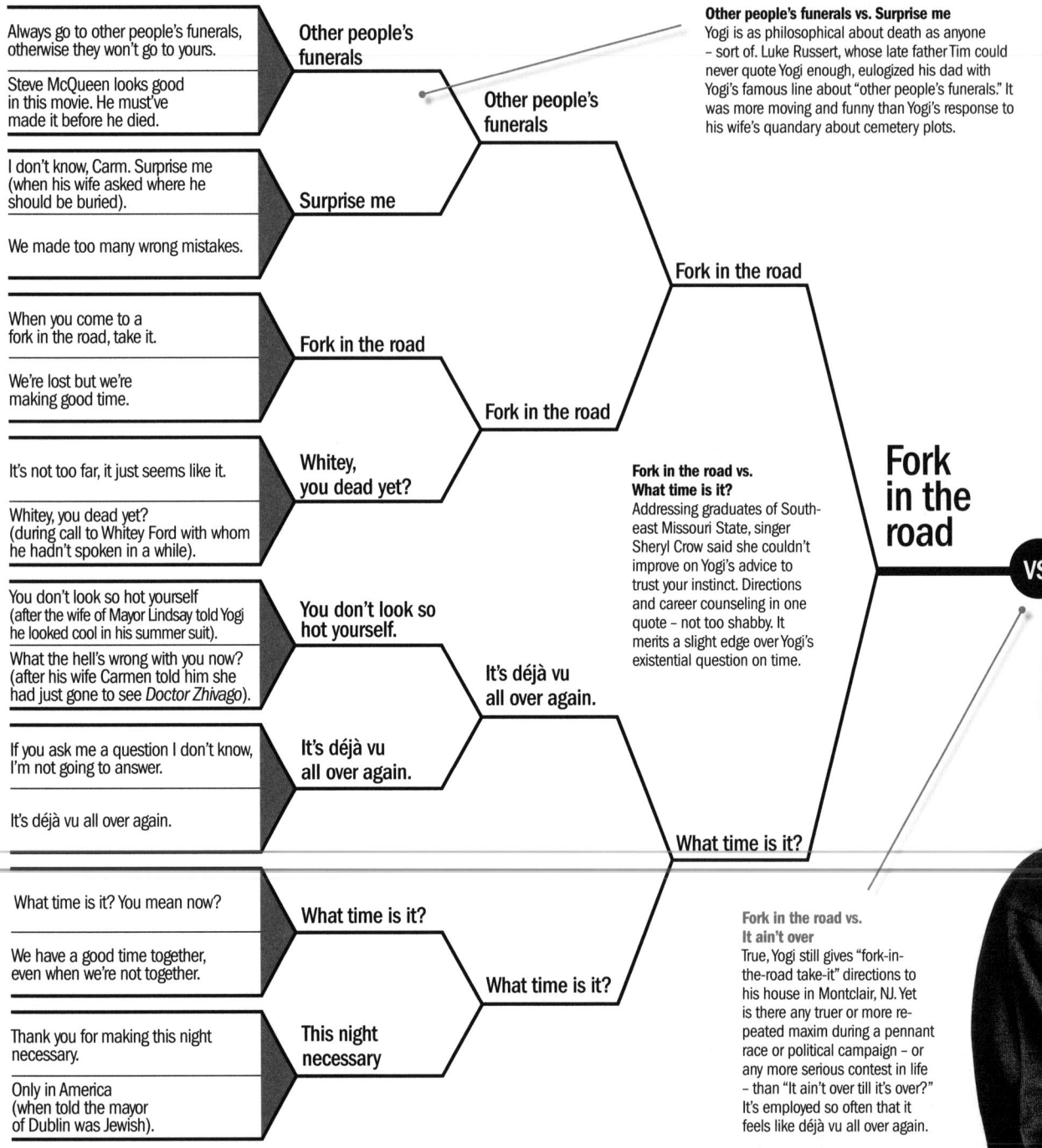


**Other people's funerals vs. Surprise me**
Yogi is as philosophical about death as anyone – sort of. Luke Russert, whose late father Tim could never quote Yogi enough, eulogized his dad with Yogi's famous line about "other people's funerals." It was more moving and funny than Yogi's response to his wife's quandary about cemetery plots.

**Fork in the road vs. What time is it?**
Addressing graduates of Southeast Missouri State, singer Sheryl Crow said she couldn't improve on Yogi's advice to trust your instinct. Directions and career counseling in one quote – not too shabby. It merits a slight edge over Yogi's existential question on time.

**Fork in the road vs. It ain't over**
True, Yogi still gives "fork-in-the-road take-it" directions to his house in Montclair, NJ. Yet is there any truer or more repeated maxim during a pennant race or political campaign – or any more serious contest in life – than "It ain't over till it's over?" It's employed so often that it feels like déjà vu all over again.

YOGI BERRA SEES THINGS DIFFERENTLY. Actually, he says things differently. Yet his inadvertent insights on baseball and life have a special logic. As the winner of 10 World Series rings with the Yankee dynasties of the late 1940s to early '60s and a three-time MVP on teams with DiMaggio and Mantle, he's not a Zen Master. He's simply Yogi. The winner here is the casual Berra brilliance that has most effectively wedged itself into America's conversation as all-purpose wisdom and truth.

**Nobody goes there vs. A nickel**
Yogi's observation about flocking behavior at Ruggeri's restaurant in St. Louis, where he was once the head waiter, applies to any over-trafficked destination – and stands as exquisite sociology. Hence, it is more useful than his economist's pronouncement about constant inflation and devaluation.

THE WINNER

## It ain't over till it's over.

**You can't think vs. You can observe a lot**
As a rookie in 1947, Yogi knew that over-analysis would cause paralysis (and maybe inspired Nike's "Just do it" slogan). Yet as a catcher, coach, and manager, Yogi became the savant of watching; he was a one-man focus group. Where would trend forecasters be if they didn't observe a lot by watching?

- It ain't over till it's over.
  - Nobody goes there
    - Nobody goes there
      - Nobody goes there anymore, it's too crowded.
      - A nickel ain't worth a dime anymore.
    - 90% is half mental
      - If the world were perfect, it wouldn't be.
      - 90% of the game is half mental.
  - It ain't over till it's over
    - It ain't over till it's over
      - It ain't over till it's over.
      - It gets late early out there.
    - If people don't want
      - If people don't want to come to the ballpark, how are you going to stop them?
      - We have deep depth.
- You can observe
  - You can't think and hit
    - If you can't imitate him
      - If you can't imitate him, don't copy him.
      - If I didn't wake up, I'd still be sleeping.
    - You can't think and hit
      - You can't think and hit at the same time.
      - Never answer an anonymous letter.
  - You can observe
    - Why buy good luggage
      - Why buy good luggage; you only use it when you travel.
      - Slump? I ain't in no slump, I'm just not hitting.
    - You can observe
      - It was impossible to get a conversation going, everybody was talking too much.
      - You can observe a lot by watching.

# Fortune Cookies

## By Jennifer 8. Lee

Jennifer 8. Lee, a *New York Times* reporter, traced the elusive history of the fortune cookie in her book, *The Fortune Cookie Chronicles: Adventures in the World of Chinese Food.*

Simplicity and clarity should be your theme in dress.

You lead by example which inspires others.

You lead by example which inspires others.

Happiness is all in the mind.

Happiness is all in the mind.

You are filled with a sense of urgency. Be patient or you will end up confused.

Happiness is all in the mind.

Happiness is all in the mind.

You are talented in many ways.

Pursue your wishes aggressively.

You are talented in many ways.

You are talented in many ways.

You will be hungry soon. Order take out.

Today you should spend some time to search in yourself.

You will be hungry soon. Order take out.

**You will be hungry soon vs. Talented in many ways**
In this battle of declarations, "You will be hungry soon" not only pokes fun at Chinese food's reputation for short-lived satiety but highlights the restaurant owner's entrepreneurship. Its pithiness beats a foe that is blandly exhortative and lacks the detail to make readers feel good about themselves.

Beware of cookies bearing fortunes.

Character is much easier kept than recovered.

Beware of cookies bearing fortunes.

Do or do not. There is no try.

Your love life will be happy and harmonious.

Do or do not. There is no try.

Do or do not. There is no try.

Do or do not. There is no try.

THE WINNER

Do or do not. There is no try.

VS

**Do or do not vs. Many hidden talents**
Both fortunes pass the college ritual of adding "in bed" at the end, thus enriching the originals with new meanings. But as exemplary as "hidden talents" is, "Do or do not" wins with a Zen/New Age aura that mixes the winning philosophy of Vince Lombardi with the mandarin wisdom of *Star Wars'* Yoda (from whence it is lifted). Believe or believe not. There is no doubt.

Opportunities surround you if you know where to look.

Next month is your chance to make headway. So move quickly.

Opportunities surround you if you know where to look.

Your flair for the creative takes an important part in your life.

Confucius say, A man's great possession is a sympathetic wife.

Your flair for the creative takes an important part in your life.

Your flair for the creative takes an important part in your life.

**Flair for the creative vs. sympathetic wife**
Paternal Confucian aphorisms, phased out in the early 1990s, now feel outdated, not to mention that Confucius never said most of the quotes attributed to him in the cookies. But everyone likes being told of their penchant for creativity, a fortune that gets bonus points for projecting the future.

THE "CONFUCIUS SAY" FORTUNE COOKIE PREAMBLE of decades past is deceptive. Fortune cookies were invented by the Japanese, popularized by the Chinese, but are ultimately consumed by Americans by the billions. As such, fortunes today are written by and for Americans seeking uplift with their General Tso's chicken. Writing fortunes is a demanding task: the best ones must be pithy enough to fit on a tiny slip of paper, generalized across a broad swath of the population, and possess a happy tone. Who wants to end dinner on a sour note?

**Inherit a large sum of money vs. Many hidden talents**
While a prediction of great inheritance is pleasing, it also tactlessly implies that "Someone close to you will die soon." The appeal of being told that our hidden talents will reveal themselves is universal. The spotlight that will shine on them is just a moment or day or year away. Who doesn't believe that?

You will soon inherit a large sum of money.

You will soon inherit a large sum of money.

Smile when you are ready.

You will soon inherit a large sum of money.

If you want good advice, consult you mother.

If you want good advice, consult you mother.

A great pleasure in life is doing what others say you can't.

Your many hidden talents will become obvious to those around you.

This could be an almost perfect day. Enjoy it.

Their smart thing is to prepare for the unexpected.

This could be an almost perfect day. Enjoy it.

Your many hidden talents will become obvious to those around you.

Your many hidden talents will become obvious to those around you.

Your many hidden talents will become obvious to those around you.

Friends long absent are coming back to you.

Your many hidden talents will become obvious to those around you.

It's over your head now. Time to get professional help.

You will move to a wonderful new home without the year.

It's over your head now. Time to get professional help.

It's over your head now. Time to get professional help.

You will be free of the heavy burdens you have been carrying.

You will be free of the heavy burdens you have been carrying.

We grow great by dreams. All big men are dreamers.

Turn off the TV and computer and exercise your mind with a good book.

Give a kiss to the person who sits next to you.

Give a kiss to the person who sits next to you.

You display the wonderful traits of charm and courtesy.

Turn off the TV and computer and exercise your mind with a good book.

Turn off the TV and computer and exercise your mind with a good book.

You will be rewarded for your good ideas.

Turn off the TV and computer and exercise your mind with a good book.

**Many hidden talents vs. Turn off the TV**
People who like Chinese food, especially take-out (which is best consumed in front of a TV) do not want to be nagged, even a little, by a contemporary fortune that tells them to tune out and curl up with a novel. It sounds too much like homework. It can't compete with a strong all-around fortune that is inoffensive, widely applicable, and forward-thinking.

# All-Purpose Banalities

**By Joe Queenan**

Joe Queenan is a freelance writer based in Tarrytown, NY. His latest book, *Closing Time,* contains none of the appalling clichés listed here.

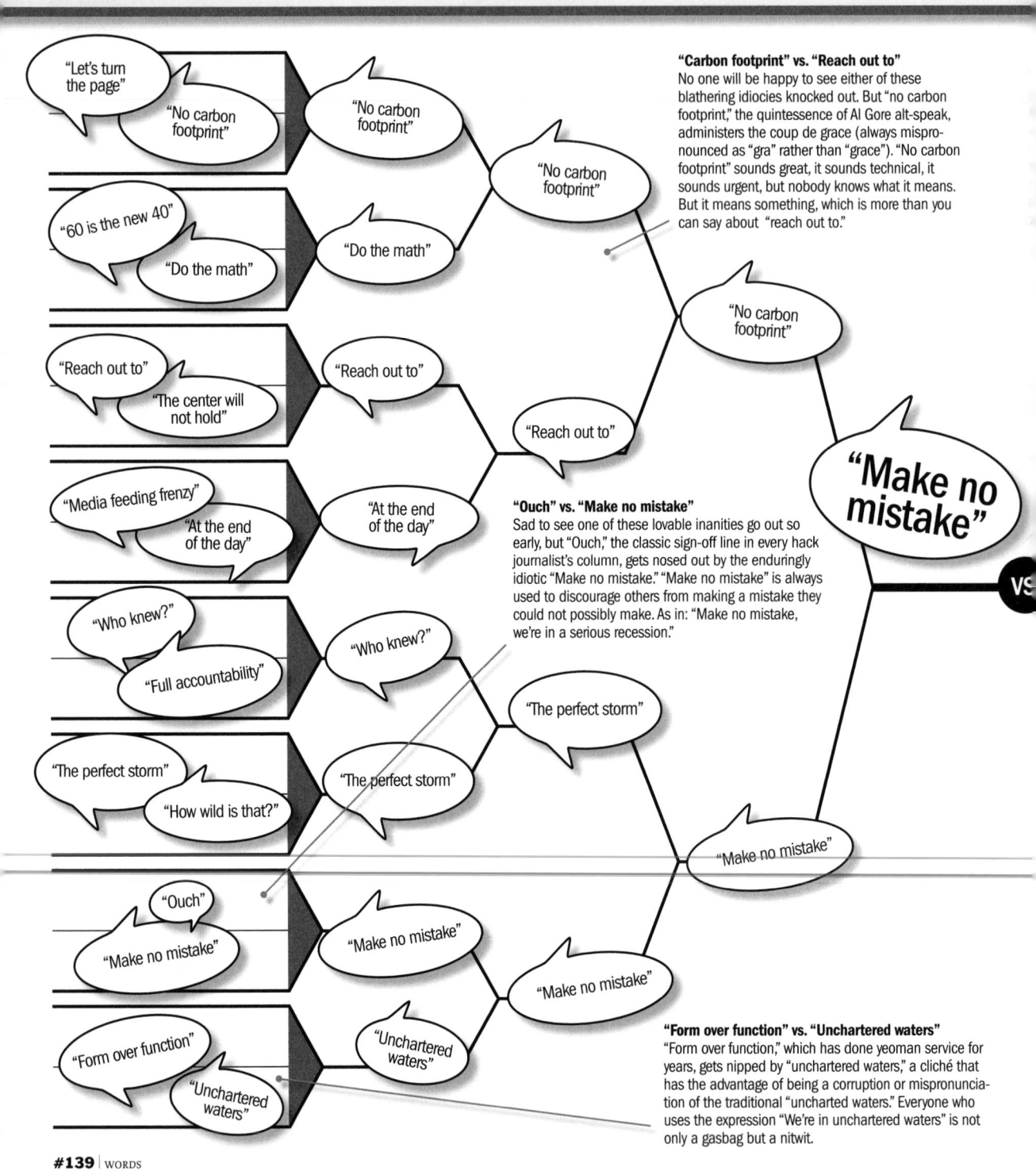


**"Carbon footprint" vs. "Reach out to"**
No one will be happy to see either of these blathering idiocies knocked out. But "no carbon footprint," the quintessence of Al Gore alt-speak, administers the coup de grace (always mispronounced as "gra" rather than "grace"). "No carbon footprint" sounds great, it sounds technical, it sounds urgent, but nobody knows what it means. But it means something, which is more than you can say about "reach out to."

**"Ouch" vs. "Make no mistake"**
Sad to see one of these lovable inanities go out so early, but "Ouch," the classic sign-off line in every hack journalist's column, gets nosed out by the enduringly idiotic "Make no mistake." "Make no mistake" is always used to discourage others from making a mistake they could not possibly make. As in: "Make no mistake, we're in a serious recession."

**"Form over function" vs. "Unchartered waters"**
"Form over function," which has done yeoman service for years, gets nipped by "unchartered waters," a cliché that has the advantage of being a corruption or mispronunciation of the traditional "uncharted waters." Everyone who uses the expression "We're in unchartered waters" is not only a gasbag but a nitwit.

ALL-PURPOSE BANALITIES CONFER A SENSE OF GRAVITAS on the person enunciating them or introduce a sinister, Rosie O'Donnell chumminess into the conversation, assuring the listener that the speaker holds the same salt-of-the-earth values as the common man. To qualify for this bracket, a banality must sound like something Nancy Pelosi would tell Jim Lehrer, something a major pundit might write, or something a White House press secretary would say to avoid talking about the Middle East situation, which is, it goes without saying, dire and fraught with peril.

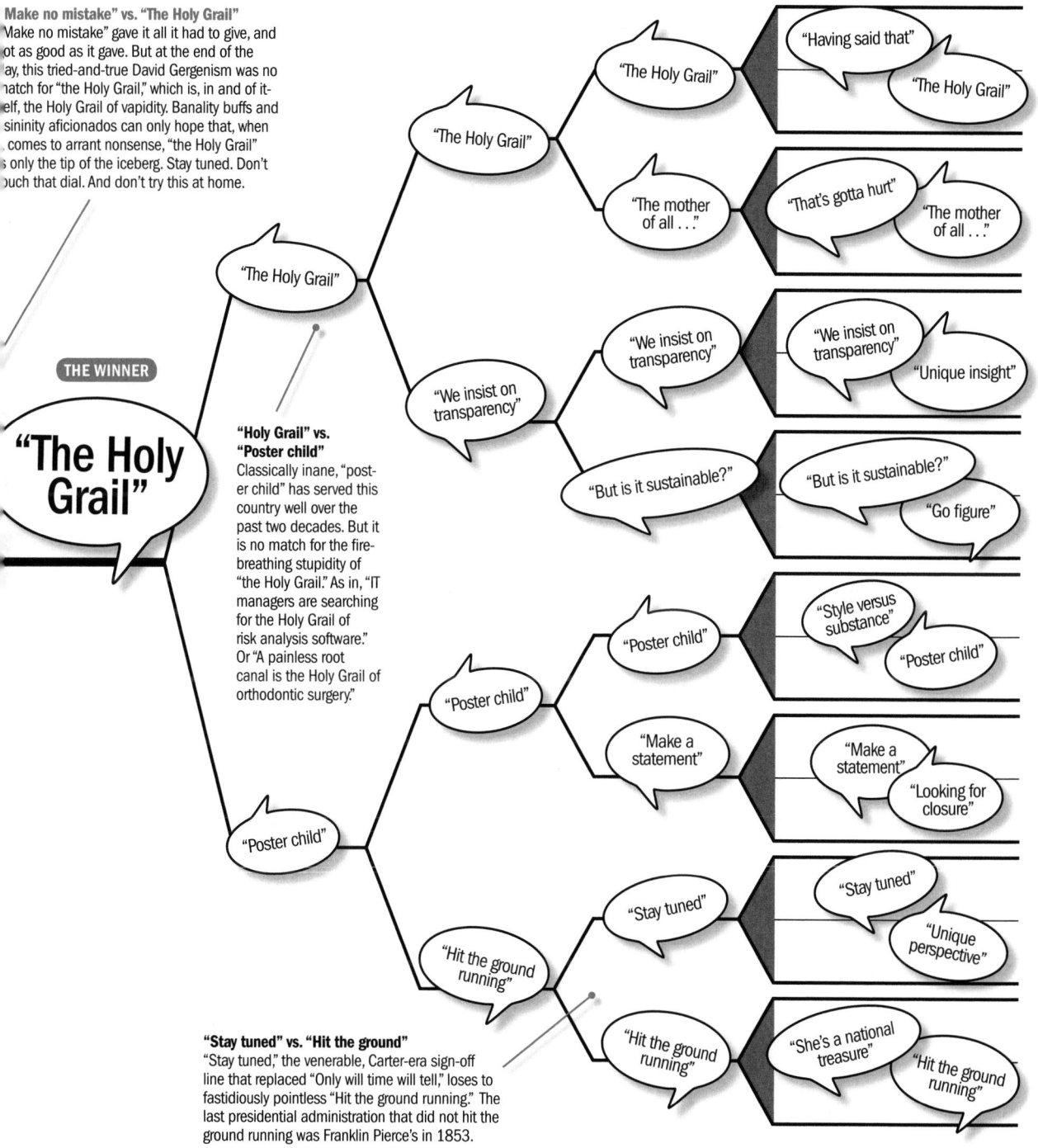

# Deadly Sins of Emailing

**By David Shipley and Will Schwalbe**

David Shipley and Will Schwalbe are the authors of *SEND: Why People Email So Badly and How to Do It Better*. Shipley is the deputy editorial page editor and Op-Ed page editor of the *New York Times*. Schwalbe is the founder and CEO of Cookstr.com.

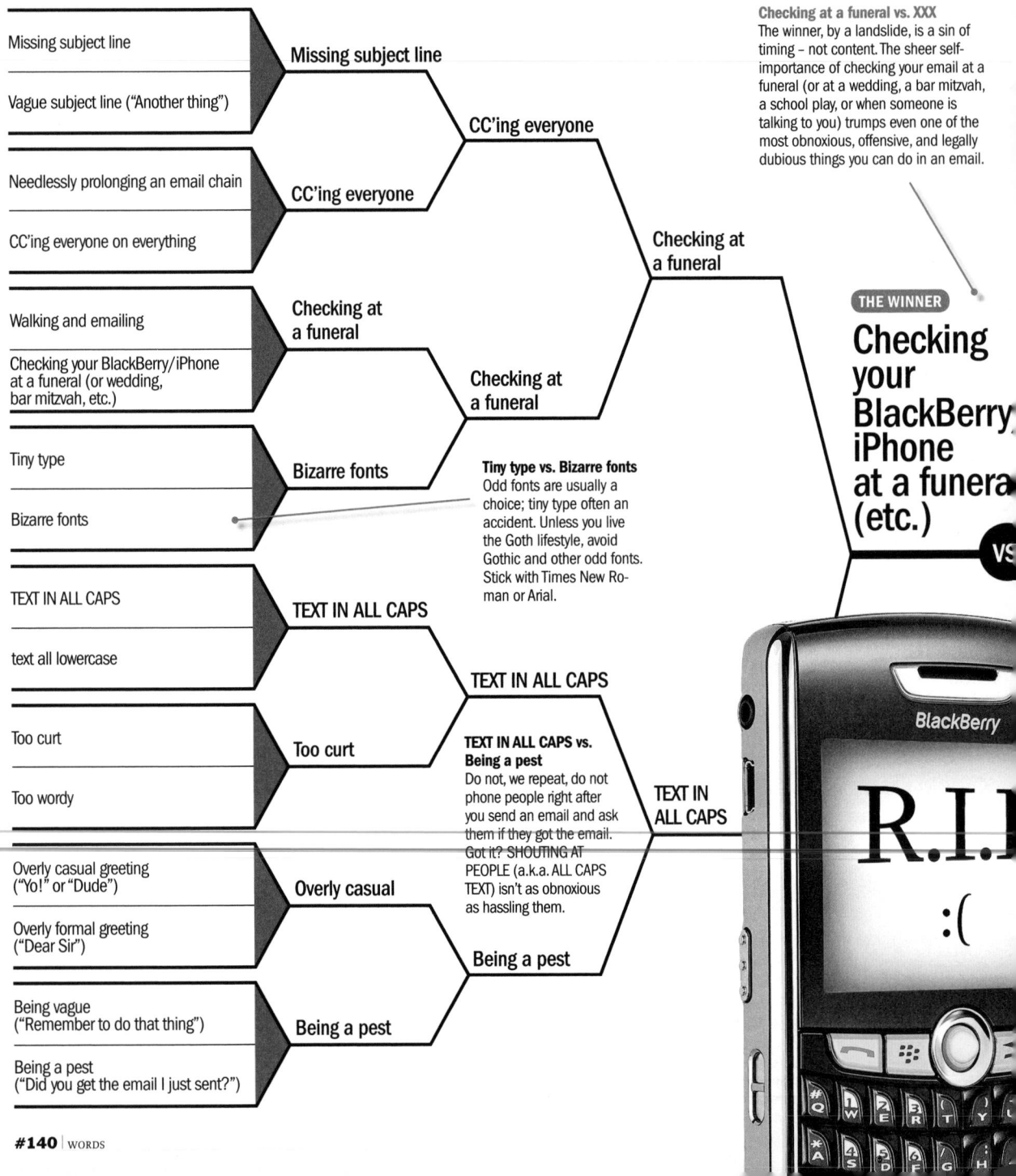

IN NO TIME AT ALL, email has taken over our lives. Don't get us wrong – we love email. But email comes with a host of boorish and terrible behaviors. Some behaviors make email hard to read (that's why missing subject lines, spelling errors, and bizarre fonts are so aggravating). Some are simply tough to take (is there anyone left who doesn't know that ALL CAPS is shouting?). Some are wildly dangerous to send in business ("this might not be legal") or affairs of the heart (emailing while drunk). Some, like our winner, are simply rude.

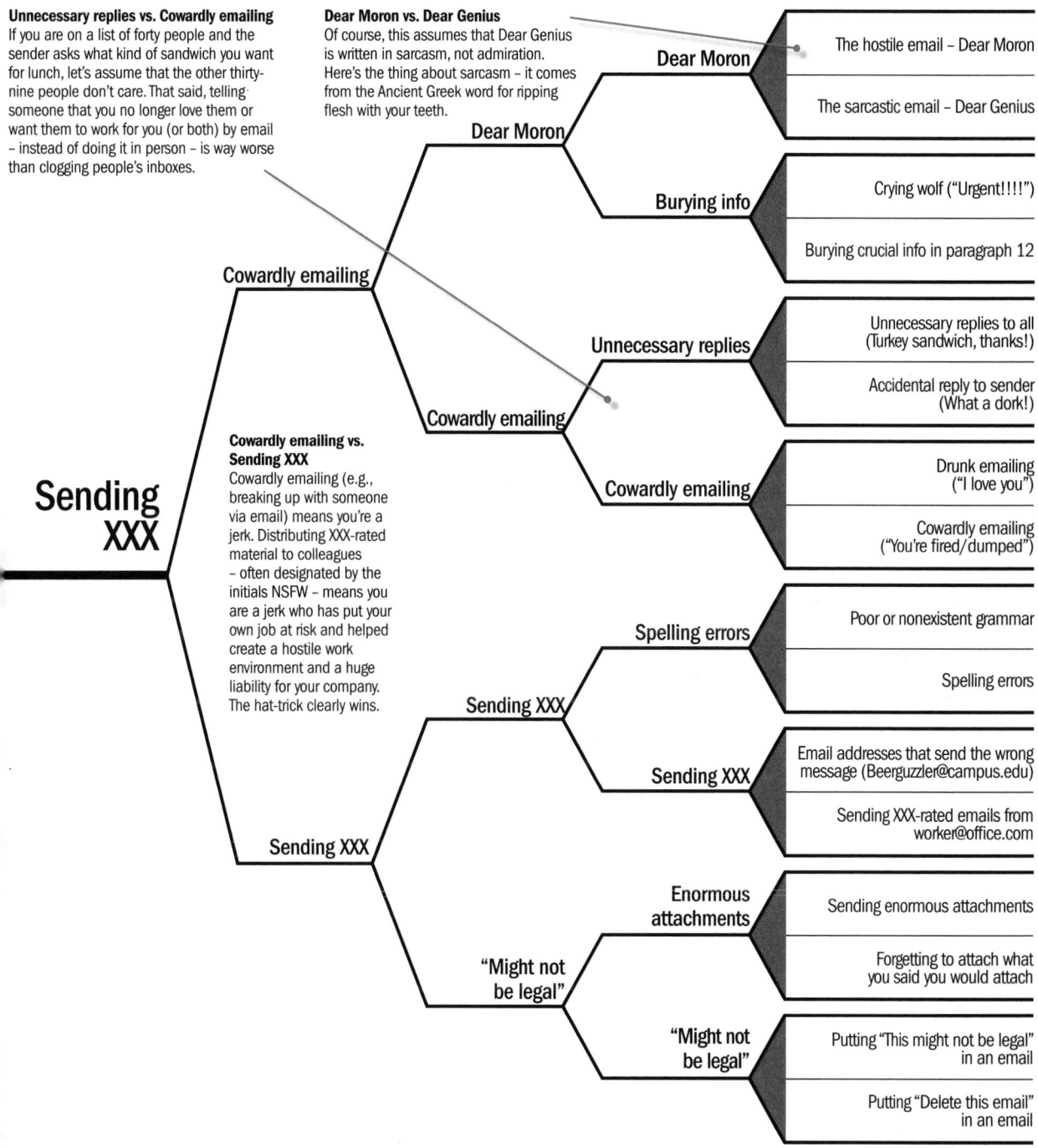

# Politically Correct Terms

**By Henry Beard and Christopher Cerf**

Henry Beard and Christopher Cerf are the co-authors of several processed tree carcasses, including *The Official Politically Correct Dictionary and Handbook* and its companion volume *The Official Sexually Correct Dictionary and Dating Guide.*

Consumer of mental health services (nutcase)

Client of the correctional system (jailbird)

**Mental health consumer**

Processed tree carcass (book)

Scorched animal corpse (meat)

**Tree carcass**

**Tree carcass**

Waitron (waitress)

Animal companion (pet)

**Waitron**

**Waitron**

Nontraditional shopper (looter)

Unpremisesed businessperson (sidewalk peddler)

**Nontraditional shopper**

Femhole (manhole)

Womage (manage)

**Femhole**

**Femhole**

Individual holding a management position in the sexual work force (pimp)

Person presenting herself as a commodity allotment within a business doctrine (prostitute)

**Person presenting herself as an allotment**

Terminally inconvenienced (dead)

Cerebrally challenged (stupid)

**Cerebrally challenged**

**Issue**

Issue (problem)

Least worst (best)

**Issue**

**Issue**

"Houston, we have an issue."

**THE WINNER**

**Issue**
(problem)

VS

**Tree carcass vs. Waitron**
The gender-neutral suffix "tron" is amazingly versatile. Among its many euphonious variations are "actron," "seductron," "temptron," "adultron," "seamstron," and "sorceron."

**Issue vs. Lookism survivor**
This little shift in terminology is far from the most blatant PC usage, but it is creepy how thoroughly it has insinuated itself into our everyday speech. In usurping the concept of a problem as something that needs to be addressed and for which someone bears responsibility, "issue" now renders all troubling circumstances as subjects for discussion or rueful acceptance, like the weather. In this subtly altered moral environment, the desperate *Apollo 13* astronauts would have radioed back to Earth, "Houston, we have an issue."

POLITICALLY CORRECT SPEECH is not exclusively American, but we excel at it. The PC kerfuffle is a straw man – oops, "a person of straw" – for liberal-bashers desperate to portray any marginal movement as a vast conspiracy of behavior modification. That said, the idea of self-censorship has a disturbingly Orwellian Big Brother – er, Big Sibling – quality. Choosing a favorite implies winners and losers, which is a no-no because even the clunkiest turn of phrase is elegant in its own special way. Blame it on the bracketological tyranny of a male-dominant culture of sports hierarchicalism.

**Person of size vs. Person of differing sobriety**
The "person of" formulation is preferred in liberation politics circles because it "puts people first," emphasizing the identity and importance of the individual before adding any descriptions or qualifications. Still, the second syllable of this wording clearly contains a masculine reference, and so strictly speaking (and after all, isn't that what PC is all about?), the term really should be "perposterity of" or "perprogeny of."

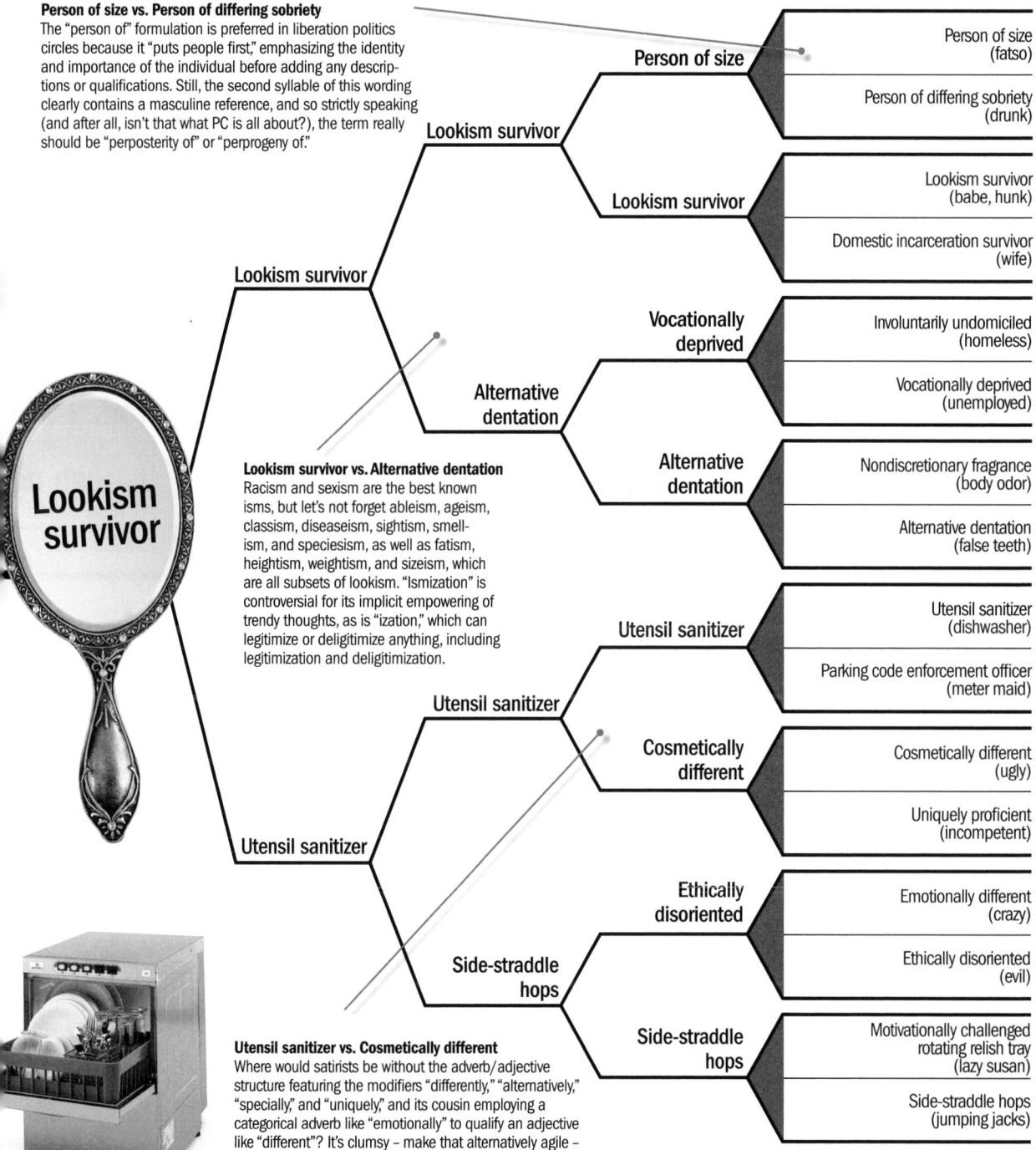


**Lookism survivor vs. Alternative dentation**
Racism and sexism are the best known isms, but let's not forget ableism, ageism, classism, diseaseism, sightism, smellism, and speciesism, as well as fatism, heightism, weightism, and sizeism, which are all subsets of lookism. "Ismization" is controversial for its implicit empowering of trendy thoughts, as is "ization," which can legitimize or deligitimize anything, including legitimization and deligitimization.

**Utensil sanitizer vs. Cosmetically different**
Where would satirists be without the adverb/adjective structure featuring the modifiers "differently," "alternatively," "specially," and "uniquely," and its cousin employing a categorical adverb like "emotionally" to qualify an adjective like "different"? It's clumsy – make that alternatively agile – but it makes up in flexibility what it lacks in felicity.

# Woody Allen Wisdom

**By Eric Lax**

Besides *Woody Allen, a Biography,* and *Conversations with Woody Allen,* Eric Lax's books include *The Mold in Dr. Florey's Coat, Life and Death on 10 West,* and *On Being Funny.*

It seemed the world was divided into good and bad people. The good ones slept better . . . while the bad ones seemed to enjoy the waking hours more. ("The Condemned," *Side Effects*)

A relationship, I think, is like a shark. You know, it has to constantly move forward or it dies. And I think what we've got on our hands is a dead shark. *(Annie Hall)*

**A relationship is like a shark**

Not only is there no God, but try getting a plumber on weekends. ("My Philosophy," *Getting Even*)

Death is one of the few things that can be done as easily as lying down. ("The Early Essays," *Without Feathers*)

**Death is one . . .**

**A relationship is like a shark**

The most beautiful words in the English language are not "I love you," but "It's benign." *(Deconstructing Harry)*

If God would only give me some clear sign! Like making a large deposit in my name at a Swiss bank. ("The Scrolls," *Without Feathers*)

**The most beautiful words**

Gossip is the new pornography. *(Manhattan)*

It is only we, with our capacity to love, that give meaning to the indifferent universe. *(Crimes and Misdemeanors)*

**It is only we**

**The most beautiful words**

A fast word about oral contraception.
I asked a girl to go to bed with me and she said, "No."
*(Woody Allen: The Nightclub Years 1964–1968,* LP record)

I was thrown out of NYU my freshman year for cheating on my metaphysics final. I looked within the soul of the boy next to me. *(Woody Allen: The Nightclub Years)*

**I was thrown out of NYU**

I don't want to achieve immortality through my work. I want to achieve it through not dying. *(On Being Funny)*

Faith is the path of least resistance. *(Match Point)*

**Immortality**

**Immortality**

The important thing is not to think of death as an end, but rather as a very effective way of cutting down on your expenses. *(Love and Death)*

Sonja: Sex without love is an empty experience.
Boris: Yes, but, as empty experiences go, it's one of the best.
*(Love and Death)*

**Sex without love**

The Lion and the Calf shall lie down together but the calf won't get much sleep. ("The Scrolls," *Without Feathers*)

On Los Angeles; I don't want to live in a city where the only cultural advantage is that you can make a right turn on a red light. *(Annie Hall)*

**I don't want to live**

**I don't want to live**

**A relationship is like a shark vs. Death is one**
The unpredictability of love and the mystery of its departure, like a shark, are steady themes in Woody's work. Love requires effort and emotional energy, which not everyone can manage. But death – everyone can do death, even in their sleep.

**A relationship is like a shark vs. The most beautiful words**
Love is no match for self-preservation. You can't love somebody if you're not alive. Woody's characters often are hypochondriacal in the extreme but he admits what we may not: most of us would rather be well and have the illusion of fending off death than die in a loved one's arms.

**THE WINNER**

**"I don't wan to achieve immortality through my work. I wan to achieve i through not dying."**

(*On Being Funny*)

**A fast word vs. I was thrown out of NYU**
In these "verbal cartoons" that formed much of Woody's stand-up performances, he created two conceptually funny lines that play well on the page and in a nightclub. But the unusual territory for a comedian trumps just saying no to the nebbish character he created. The first line is a play on words but the second is a more complex and rewarding joke.

WOODY ALLEN'S QUIPS AND ONE-LINERS on love, death, sex, and the elusiveness of God combine a comic's insight with a poet's capacity to make the most of every word. His ease with ideas and his understanding of human frailty in films, stand-up comedy, essays, and interviews make for lines that are smart without being pedantic, biting without being rabid, and true in ways we had never considered, which is why they are funny, sage, and memorable.

**If it turns out vs. Rather than live**
God is speculative, death is absolute, as is Woody's desire to avoid it. One reason he is so prolific is that immersion in work distracts him from dwelling on eschatology. A God who lived up to His potential would let Woody live on in his beautiful home.

# Rather than live on

- **If it turns out**
  - **If it turns out**
    - **If it turns out**
      - Sex alleviates tension. Marriage causes it. *(A Midsummer Night's Sex Comedy)*
      - If it turns out there is a God, I don't think that He's evil. I think the worst you can say about Him is that basically He's an underachiever. *(Love and Death)*
    - **Loneliness and misery**
      - Life doesn't imitate art. It imitates bad television. *(Hannah and Her Sisters)*
      - [Life] is full of loneliness and misery and suffering and unhappiness, and it's all over much too quickly. *(Annie Hall)*
  - **Showing up is 80 percent**
    - **Showing up is 80 percent**
      - Showing up is 80 percent of life. (The *New York Times*, Dec. 1, 1975)
      - [Intellectuals are] like the Mafia. They only kill their own. *(Stardust Memories)*
    - **I am two with nature**
      - It's not that I'm afraid to die, I just don't want to be there when it happens. ("Death (A Play)," *Without Feathers)*
      - I am two with nature. *(Woody Allen: The Nightclub Years 1964–1968* (LP record))
- **Rather than live on**
  - **Rather than live on**
    - **Rather than live on**
      - Rather than live on in the hearts and minds of my fellow man, I'd prefer to live on in my apartment. *(Conversations With Woody Allen)*
      - My one regret in life is that I'm not someone else. *(Getting Even)*
    - **Tradition is . . .**
      - To you, I'm an atheist; to God, I'm the loyal opposition. *(Stardust Memories)*
      - Tradition is the illusion of permanence. *(Deconstructing Harry)*
  - **"Cynicism"**
    - **Love is the answer**
      - Is sex dirty? Only when it's being done right. (To Johnny Carson on *The Tonight Show)*
      - Love is the answer, but while you're waiting for the answer, sex raises some good questions. *(Time,* Sept. 15, 1975)
    - **"Cynicism"**
      - You're God's answer to Job. *(Manhattan)*
      - "Cynicism" is just an alternative spelling of "reality." (Answer to an interviewer at the Cannes Film Festival)

**ather than live on vs. don't want to achieve**
he runner-up politely euphemizes eath; the winner addresses it by name. Woody can give his characters sparkling nes but what he wants more than nything is beyond his words or imagiation. It's the nub of it all for Woody: o matter how much you accomplish, eath awaits. He once told me: "I'm firm believer that when you're dead, aming a street after you doesn't help our metabolism. I saw what happened Rembrandt and Plato and all those ther nice people. They just lie there."

# FOOD & DRINK

**It's Better with Bacon** *by Peter Kaminksy* **143**
**Cocktails** *by Jonathan Miles* **144**
**Breakfast Cereals** *by Drew Magary* **145**
**Domestic Beers** *by Maureen Ogle* **146**
**Artisan Cheeses** *by Max McCalman and David Gibbons* **147**
**Regional Soda Pop** *by Bob Roe* **148**
**American Wines** *by Joseph S. Ward* **149**
**Classic Cookbooks** *by Katie Workman* **150**

# It's Better with Bacon

**By Peter Kaminsky**

Peter Kaminsky is the author of *Pig Perfect: Encounters With Remarkable Swine,* and one of the world's leading hamthropologists.

**Baked Beans**
**Mashed Potatoes and Bacon**

**BLT** (on white toast, don't hold the mayo)
**BBLT** (Bass, Bacon, Lettuce, and Tomato)

**Grilled Cheese and Bacon**
**Bacon and Eggs** (Sunny Side Up, Runny Yolks)

**Beggin' Strips**
**Brunswick Stew with Fresh-Killed Squirrel**

**Bacon-Wrapped Prunes** (appetizer)
**Hamantashen with Bacon** (a.k.a. Purim Tart with Bacon, not kosher but good)

**Succotash**
**Collards**

**Bacon Cheeseburger**
**Bacon Beef Burger** (from John T. Edge: chopped-up bacon and ground beef)

**Beverly Hills Hotel Cardio Dog** (hot dog with melted cheese wrapped in bacon)
**Bacon Explosion**

**Baked Beans**
**BLT**
**Bacon and Eggs**
**Beggin' Strips**
**Purim Tart**
**Succotash**
**Bacon Cheeseburger**
**Cardio Dog**

**BLT**
**Bacon and Eggs**
**Purim Tart**
**Bacon Cheeseburger**

**BLT**
**Bacon Cheeseburger**

**THE WINNER**
**BLT**

**BLT vs. Bacon Ice Cream**
The old champ versus the new kid on the block. Bottom line, a bacon, lettuce, and tomato sandwich is the one thing you can order anyplace in America that is impossible to screw up, with the exception of hospital commissaries, airlines, and my late aunt Celia Weiner. Still, that a better batting average than Hank Greenberg had. BLT rules.

**Beggin' Strips vs. Bacon and Eggs**
Yes, Beggin' Strips is dog food, and under normal circumstances disqualified. But with a nice beer, you could easily serve this to friends during an exciting football game, and they'd like it. Still, it's for pets. The classic B&E breakfast, on more menus in the 50 states than any other item, cannot lose.

**Purim Tart vs. Bacon Cheeseburger**
For those who don't know, hamantash is a three-sided pastry, filled with fruits, that is served during the Jewish holiday of Purim. The big surprise is that a dish inspired by the Old Testament could go so deep into this Tournament of Treyf. What's next? Bacon on Matzoh? (Not a bad idea.) But beat a bacon cheeseburger? Maybe next year in Jerusalem.

**Beverly Hills Hotel Cardio Dog vs. Bacon Explosion**
Brought to you by the American Academy of Cardiologists. Keep eating these and they'll stay in business. Good for Lipitor's manufacturer, too. Buddy Hackett once ate two of these dogs at the hotel pool, then dozed off during an intense game of pinochle. But the Explosion is the hottest bacon invention of the century. Google it.

THE HUMORIST SEAN KELLY CLAIMS that any literary work sounds funny when you insert the word "pork" into the title, as in "To Pork and Pork Not," "Gone with the Pork," or "The Porking Point." Likewise, there isn't a food on earth that isn't improved by the addition of bacon. Salty, crispy, fatty, meaty, funky – bacon is irresistible, which explains why I enjoy watching as one vegetarian after another steps on the steep slope that takes him from a first nibble of bacon in the morning to a bloody Porterhouse by dinner time. Bacon is the ultimate gateway drug.

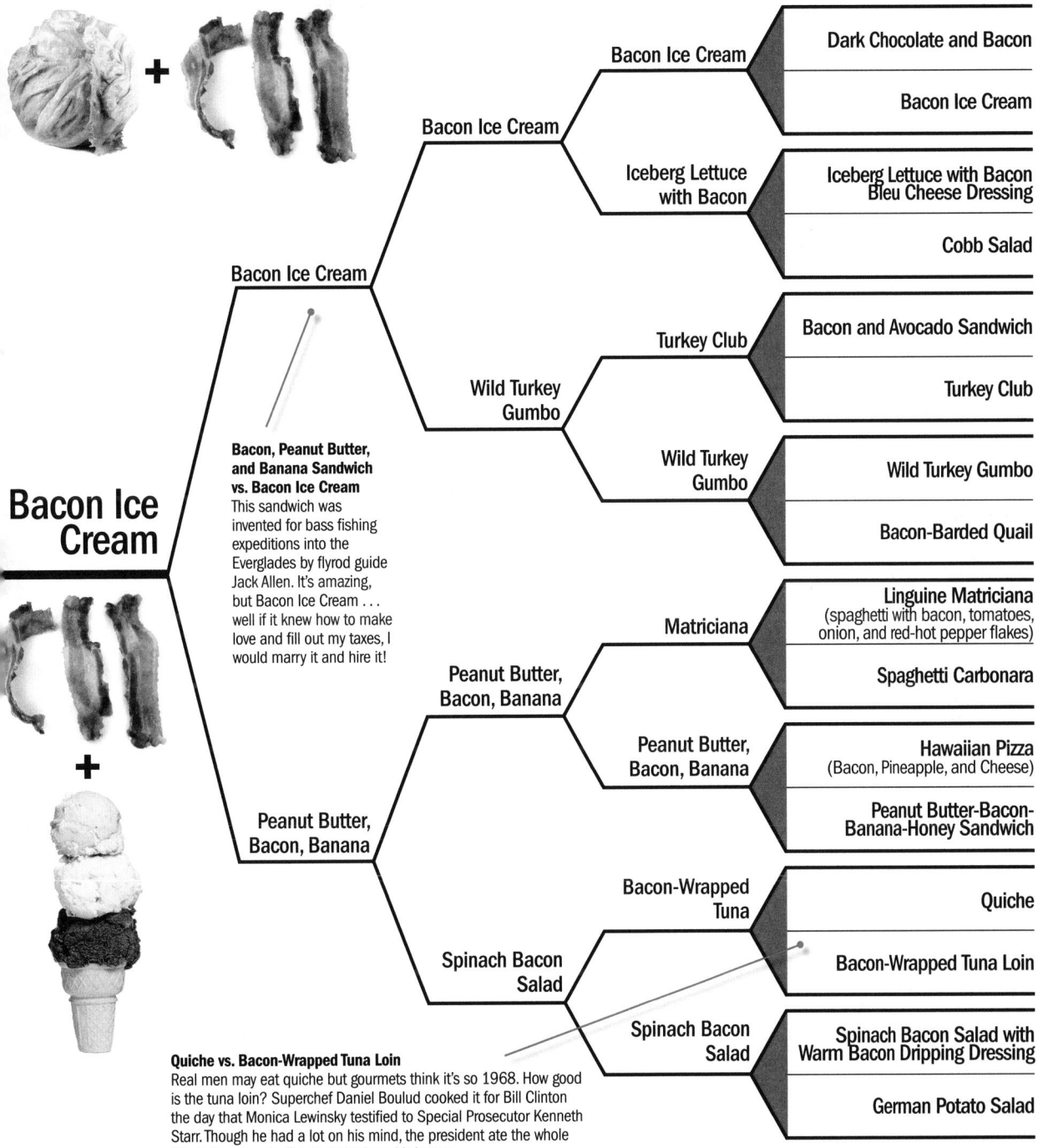


**Bacon, Peanut Butter, and Banana Sandwich vs. Bacon Ice Cream**
This sandwich was invented for bass fishing expeditions into the Everglades by flyrod guide Jack Allen. It's amazing, but Bacon Ice Cream . . . well if it knew how to make love and fill out my taxes, I would marry it and hire it!

**Quiche vs. Bacon-Wrapped Tuna Loin**
Real men may eat quiche but gourmets think it's so 1968. How good is the tuna loin? Superchef Daniel Boulud cooked it for Bill Clinton the day that Monica Lewinsky testified to Special Prosecutor Kenneth Starr. Though he had a lot on his mind, the president ate the whole thing! Stress eating? I don't think so. It's bacon.

# Cocktails

**By Jonathan Miles**

Jonathan Miles writes the "Shaken and Stirred" column for the Sunday Styles section of the *New York Times,* and is the author of a novel, *Dear American Airlines.*

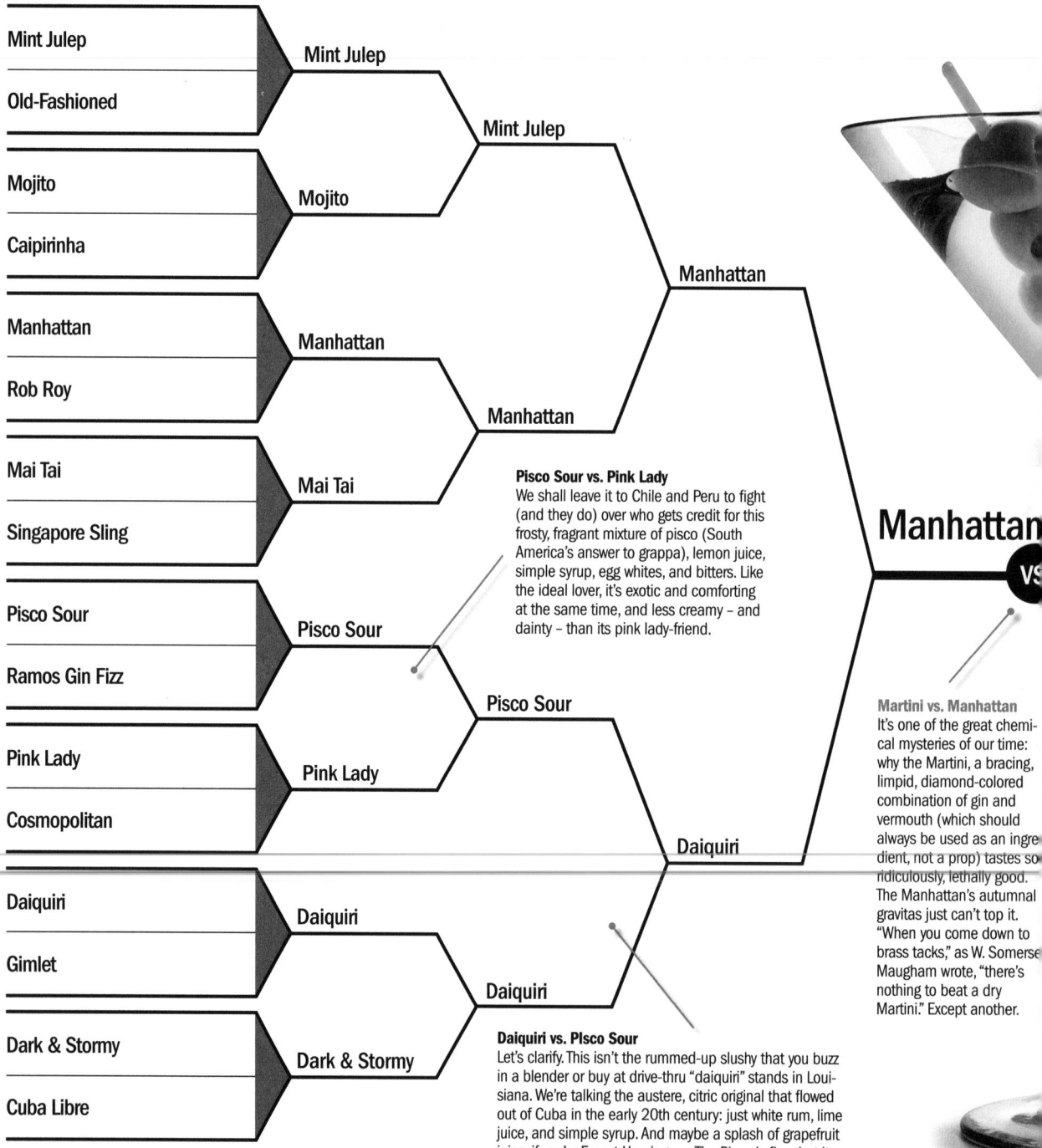


**Pisco Sour vs. Pink Lady**
We shall leave it to Chile and Peru to fight (and they do) over who gets credit for this frosty, fragrant mixture of pisco (South America's answer to grappa), lemon juice, simple syrup, egg whites, and bitters. Like the ideal lover, it's exotic and comforting at the same time, and less creamy – and dainty – than its pink lady-friend.

**Daiquiri vs. Pisco Sour**
Let's clarify. This isn't the rummed-up slushy that you buzz in a blender or buy at drive-thru "daiquiri" stands in Louisiana. We're talking the austere, citric original that flowed out of Cuba in the early 20th century: just white rum, lime juice, and simple syrup. And maybe a splash of grapefruit juice, if you're Ernest Hemingway. The Pisco is fine, but it didn't have Papa for a spokesman.

**Martini vs. Manhattan**
It's one of the great chemical mysteries of our time: why the Martini, a bracing, limpid, diamond-colored combination of gin and vermouth (which should always be used as an ingredient, not a prop) tastes so ridiculously, lethally good. The Manhattan's autumnal gravitas just can't top it. "When you come down to brass tacks," as W. Somerset Maugham wrote, "there's nothing to beat a dry Martini." Except another.

THE COCKTAIL IS NOT ONLY AN AMERICAN INVENTION. It is, like jazz, an American symbol: the shaking and stirring of disparate components, many of them imports, to produce something greater than the sum of the parts. We herald our country as a "melting pot," but what the heck is a melting pot anyway and when might I have seen one? No, my country 'tis of thee is a cocktail shaker. The judging here was based on historical significance, lore and legend, and a prodigious series of semi-scientific tastings. Now if someone will just tell me on what page I can find the bracket for hangover remedies.

**Bloody Mary vs. Michelada**
This is the one drink for which every American is allowed to claim a "secret recipe." Just about everything has been wedged into this tailgate and brunch standard – from pickled oysters to okra, and that's just the O's – with varying degrees of success. The beer-based Michelada is another kitchen-sink of a drink, but not quite so all-purpose. You wouldn't want one for breakfast.

THE WINNER
**Martini**

**Aviation vs. French 75**
Credit the Internet for this archeological find. Online cocktail geeks rescued this sublime, Prohibition-era fusion of gin, maraschino liqueur, and lemon juice (and Créme de Violette, if you want to stay true to the original recipe) from undeserved obscurity. Like the French 75, it's now an iconic fixture at haute cocktaileries, but it's a more streamlined concoction, and packs a higher coolness quotient.

**Hurricane vs. Long Island Iced Tea**
This is where memories of a trip to New Orleans go to die: at the tail-end of a 29-ounce Hurricane at Pat O'Brien's French Quarter bar. The Hurricane can be a splendid drink if you ditch the souvenir powdered premix and mix it from scratch. The present revival of Tiki drinks may bring this mindblower some kitschy respect. Long Island Iced Tea, on the other hand, will always be the Amy Fisher of drinks.

- Martini
  - Martini
    - Martini
      - Martini
      - Sazerac
    - Blood Mary
      - Bloody Mary
      - Michelada
  - Aviation
    - Aviation
      - Aviation
      - Vesper
    - French 75
      - French 75
      - Champagne Cocktail
- Margarita
  - Margarita
    - Margarita
      - Margarita
      - Sidecar
    - Hurricane
      - Hurricane
      - Long Island Iced Tea
  - Negroni
    - Negroni
      - Negroni
      - Pimm's Cup
    - Pina Colada
      - White Russian
      - Pina Colada

# Breakfast Cereals

**By Drew Magary**

Drew Magary is the author of *Men with Balls: The Professional Athlete's Handbook*, and the co-founder of Kissing Suzy Kolber. He has eaten cereal for dinner more often than he has eaten real food for dinner.

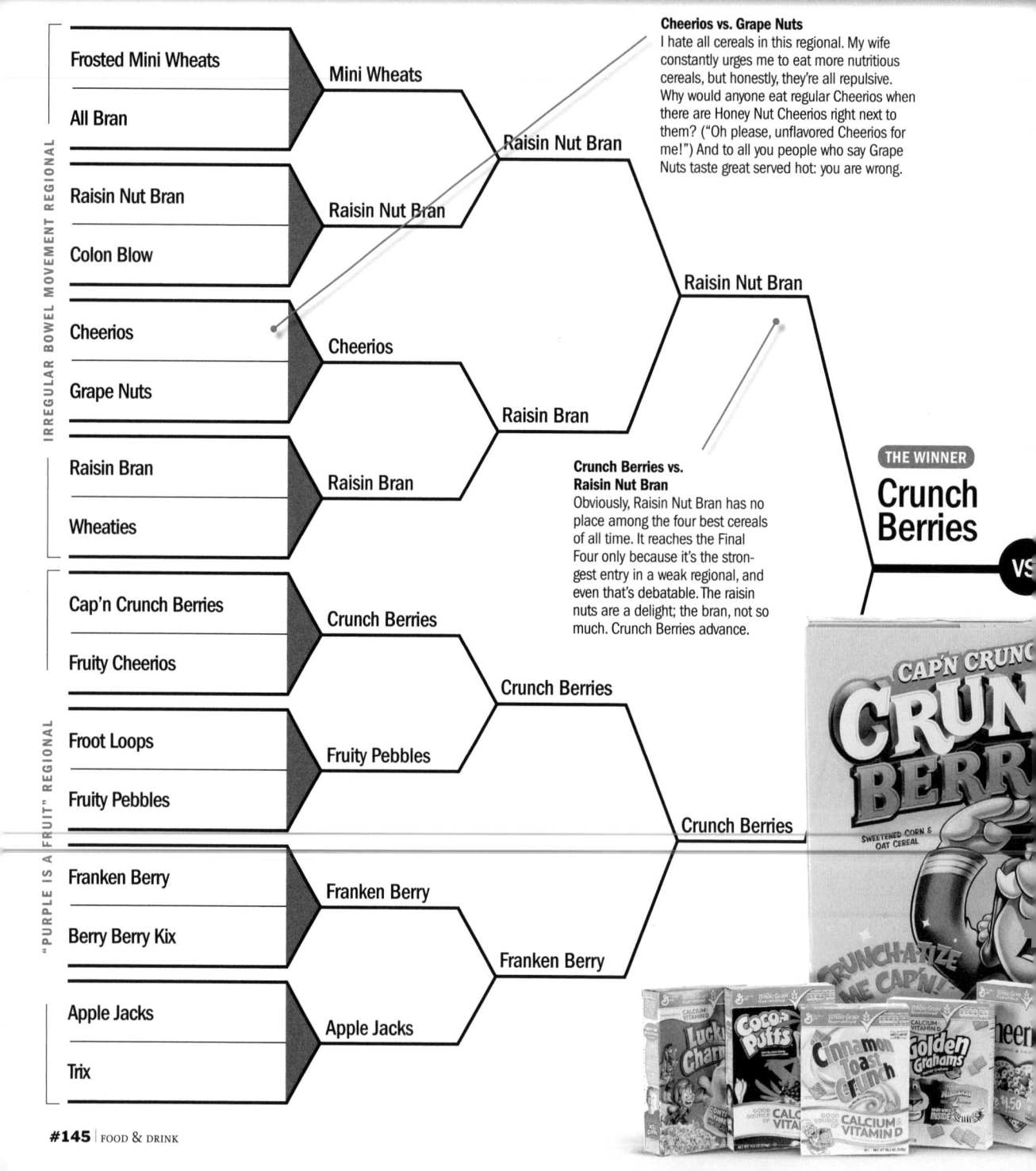


**Cheerios vs. Grape Nuts**
I hate all cereals in this regional. My wife constantly urges me to eat more nutritious cereals, but honestly, they're all repulsive. Why would anyone eat regular Cheerios when there are Honey Nut Cheerios right next to them? ("Oh please, unflavored Cheerios for me!") And to all you people who say Grape Nuts taste great served hot: you are wrong.

**Crunch Berries vs. Raisin Nut Bran**
Obviously, Raisin Nut Bran has no place among the four best cereals of all time. It reaches the Final Four only because it's the strongest entry in a weak regional, and even that's debatable. The raisin nuts are a delight; the bran, not so much. Crunch Berries advance.

I AM 32 YEARS OLD AND HAVE EATEN EVERY BREAKFAST CEREAL known to mankind. Ever have C3PO's? I have. Ever moan in ecstasy at the sight of a box of Oreo O's, which were discontinued in 2007 because they may or may not have caused instadiabetes in toddlers? I do. The best cereals stay crunchy in milk; leave tasty-flavored milk at the end; have enough sugar to destroy your pancreas; and have not-too-challenging mazes on the backs of their boxes.

**Crunch Berries vs. Cinnamon Toast Crunch**
In seventh grade, a friend of mine conducted a science experiment to determine which cereal stayed crunchy in milk the longest. All Cap'n Crunch varieties won by a mile. Unlike Cinnamon Toast Crunch, which de-crunches faster than I like, you could leave Crunch Berries in battery acid for a week and they'd still be intact – and they'd leave behind strawberry milk. If you don't think that's a great way to start a morning, I don't want to know you. You probably eat All Bran.

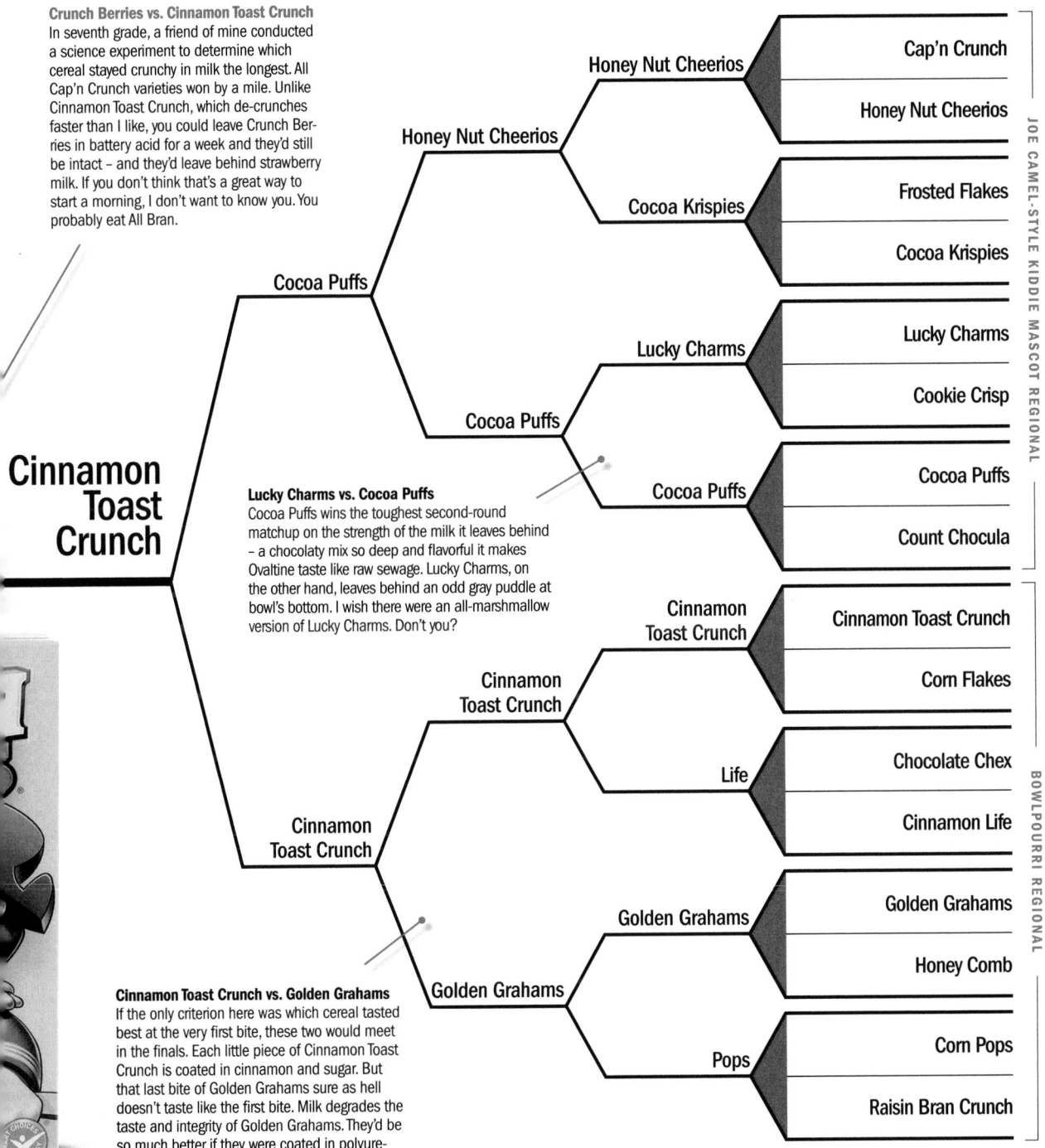


**Lucky Charms vs. Cocoa Puffs**
Cocoa Puffs wins the toughest second-round matchup on the strength of the milk it leaves behind – a chocolaty mix so deep and flavorful it makes Ovaltine taste like raw sewage. Lucky Charms, on the other hand, leaves behind an odd gray puddle at bowl's bottom. I wish there were an all-marshmallow version of Lucky Charms. Don't you?

**Cinnamon Toast Crunch vs. Golden Grahams**
If the only criterion here was which cereal tasted best at the very first bite, these two would meet in the finals. Each little piece of Cinnamon Toast Crunch is coated in cinnamon and sugar. But that last bite of Golden Grahams sure as hell doesn't taste like the first bite. Milk degrades the taste and integrity of Golden Grahams. They'd be so much better if they were coated in polyurethane. I'm willing to accept the risks involved.

# Domestic Beers

**By Maureen Ogle**

Maureen Ogle is the author of *Ambitious Brew: The Story of American Beer.* Beer, she has decided in middle age, is a portal to the meaning of life.

Leinenkugel Sunset Wheat
Coors Blue Moon Belgian White
Coors Blue Moon Belgian White
New Belgium Mothership Wit
Widmer Hefeweizen
Anheuser-Busch InBev Budweiser
Leinenkugel's Original
Pabst Blue Ribbon
Miller High Life
Schlitz (Classic '60s Formula)
Coors Banquet
Anchor Steam Beer
Saranac Adirondack Lager
Abita Amber Lager
Bell's Amber Ale
Sam Adams Lager
Schell FireBrick

Coors Blue Moon Belgian White
Widmer Hefeweizen
Leinenkugel's Original
Pabst Blue Ribbon
Coors Banquet
Saranac Adirondack Lager
Abita Amber Lager
Sam Adams Lager

Widmer Hefeweizen
Leinenkugel's Original
Saranac Adirondack Lager
Abita Amber Lager

Widmer Hefeizen
Abita Amber Lager

**New Belgium Mothership Wit vs. Widmer Hefeweizen**
Widmer is one of the original microbreweries, now partly owned by Anheuser-Busch InBev. New Belgium is a family-owned regional craft powerhouse. Both of these examples of the "new" American wheat beers are scrumptious. But Widmer's more nuisanced spice carried the day.

**Abita Amber Lager vs. Abita Turbodog**
This is like having UNC-Chapel Hill and UNC-Greensboro reach the NCAA finals. What's up with these guys from Louisiana? Frankly, Turbodog trounced its Amber brother, but the fact that both made it this far . . . well, apparently the South rises again. Zymotechnically speaking, that is.

**Saranac Adirondack Lager vs. Abita Amber Ale**
The headline-grabbing upset. In 2007's *The Enlightened Bracketologist* tournament, Saranac took home the trophy. But having captured my tongue and nose in Round 2, Abita Amber refused to retreat.

**Abita Amber Lager vs. Sam Adams Lager**
Sam Adams is a superb American beer. Bright and shiny as a new coin, with dark flavors that give it gravitas. Brewer Jim Koch uses nothing but the finest ingredients and top-notch talent in his brewhouse. So, remind me: Who are these Abita people?

Abita Amber Lager

VS

LAST TIME I TRIED THIS, Saranac Adirondack Lager won. Hey, life is about change, but the rules remain the same: American beers only (au revoir, Stella), available year-round (no pumpkin ales or other seasonals), and sold in Ames, Iowa, where I live. That narrowed the field because the vast majority of American beers are distributed locally; if I'd been sitting in Utah or Pennsylvania, I'd be bracketing different beers. Yes, the rule favors breweries with national distribution. But it's beer, right? It's all good!

**Budweiser American Ale vs. Anchor Liberty Ale**
Bud Ale is a newcomer to the community of American craft beers. The folks in St. Louis poured their hearts into this all-malt ale, but they're not quite ready to compete with the masters-of-all-malt at Anchor.

**Abita Turbodog vs. Leinenkugel's Creamy Dark**
Leinie Dark is a near-perfect Northern lager, with a slightly smoky body that hangs on the tongue. But Turbodog is a brew of destiny, it seems, with an astonishing bouquet and bold bundle of flavors in every sip (or gulp). Serious contenders, the two of them: full-bodied, complex, luscious. I spun the bottle and it pointed to the Southerner.

THE WINNER

**Abita Turbodog**

- Abita Turbodog
  - Abita Turbodog
    - Abita Turbodog
      - Sam Adams Brown Ale
      - Abita Turbodog
    - Anchor Liberty Ale
      - Anheuser-Busch InBev Budweiser American Ale
      - Anchor Liberty Ale
  - Sam Adams Boston Ale
    - Sam Adams Boston Ale
      - Sam Adams Boston Ale
      - Saranac Brown Ale
    - Sierra Nevada Pale Ale
      - Sierra Nevada Pale Ale
      - Saranac Pale Ale
- Leinenkugel's Creamy Dark
  - Leinenkugel's Creamy Dark
    - Michelob AmberBock
      - Anheuser-Busch InBev Michelob AmberBock
      - Shiner Bock
    - Leinenkugel's Creamy Dark
      - Leinenkugel's Creamy Dark
      - Saranac Black Forest
  - Bell's Stout
    - Bell's Stout
      - Sam Adams Cream Stout
      - Bell's Stout
    - Breckenridge Oatmeal Stout
      - Goose Island Oatmeal Stout
      - Breckenridge Oatmeal Stout

# Artisan Cheeses

**By Max McCalman and David Gibbons**

Max McCalman and David Gibbons are authors of *The Cheese Plate and Cheese: A Connoisseur's Guide to the World's Best,* which won a James Beard Award. Their third book, *Mastering Cheese,* is a compilation of nearly two decades of cheese tastings and research.

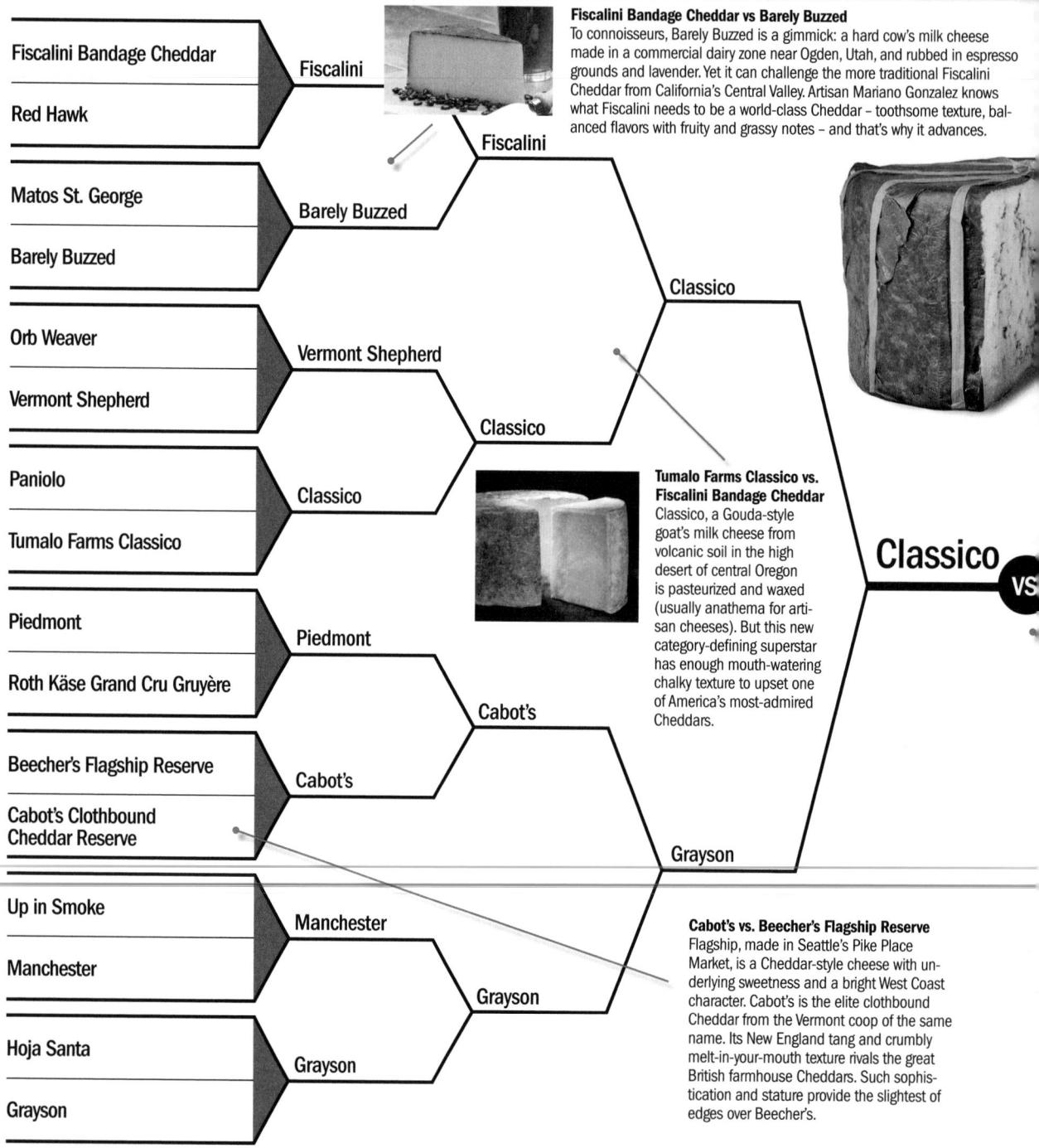


**Fiscalini Bandage Cheddar vs Barely Buzzed**
To connoisseurs, Barely Buzzed is a gimmick: a hard cow's milk cheese made in a commercial dairy zone near Ogden, Utah, and rubbed in espresso grounds and lavender. Yet it can challenge the more traditional Fiscalini Cheddar from California's Central Valley. Artisan Mariano Gonzalez knows what Fiscalini needs to be a world-class Cheddar – toothsome texture, balanced flavors with fruity and grassy notes – and that's why it advances.

**Tumalo Farms Classico vs. Fiscalini Bandage Cheddar**
Classico, a Gouda-style goat's milk cheese from volcanic soil in the high desert of central Oregon is pasteurized and waxed (usually anathema for artisan cheeses). But this new category-defining superstar has enough mouth-watering chalky texture to upset one of America's most-admired Cheddars.

**Cabot's vs. Beecher's Flagship Reserve**
Flagship, made in Seattle's Pike Place Market, is a Cheddar-style cheese with underlying sweetness and a bright West Coast character. Cabot's is the elite clothbound Cheddar from the Vermont coop of the same name. Its New England tang and crumbly melt-in-your-mouth texture rivals the great British farmhouse Cheddars. Such sophistication and stature provide the slightest of edges over Beecher's.

AMERICAN CHEESE HAS COME A LONG WAY since the year 2000, when barely 20 U.S. farmstead cheesemakers qualified for world-class status. Now more than five dozen artisans rank with the best. The cradles of artisan cheese used to be Vermont and California (and nine of the 32 entrants are from those two states). But eleven other states are represented, most impressively Oregon, which is eco-friendly and supportive of its small sustainable dairy farming and creamery operators – and performs well and deep into our tournament.

**Hooligan vs. Great Hill Blue**
Great Hill Blue shows its Southern Massachusetts roots with hints of the briny breezes off nearby Buzzard's Bay. Hooligan lived up to its name when it first burst onto the scene in 2001: wild and erratic. A washed-rind cow's milk cheese made at Connecticut's Cato Corner Farm in the style of the Belgian Chimay, Hooligan has been tamed and now surpasses its European forebears with its rich mouth feel and balance of salty and sour flavors.

THE WINNER

# Rogue River Blue

**Wimer Winter vs. Pleasant Ridge Reserve**
Uplands Cheese Company's Pleasant Ridge Reserve packs a tremendous amount of Wisconsin raw cow's milk goodness into an alluring package. Wimer Winter is a raw goat's milk, washed-rind, moderately stinky cheese from the hotbed of Oregon's Rogue River Valley. This is not an easy format to corral but gifted cheesemaker (and goat breeder) Gianaclis Caldwell pulls it off. Her secret weapon is the milk of her Nigerian Dwarf goats, which imparts wonderful nut-like notes – and not a hint of gamey or goaty flavor.

**Tumalo Farms Classico vs. Rogue River Blue**
A past winner of "Best Blue in the World," Rogue River has become America's international ambassador. Like all great blues, its bite merely serves to focus and enhance the flavors of its delicious raw milk, accented by its wrapping in pear brandy-soaked syrah grape vine leaves, an ancient ripening touch that transmits a triple-whammy of Oregon terroir. There's no shame for Classico to succumb to this multi-faceted champion.

- Rogue River
  - Wimer
    - Pleasant Ridge
      - Pleasant Ridge
        - Cave Aged Marisa
        - Pleasant Ridge Reserve
      - Hooligan
        - Great Hill Blue
        - Hooligan
    - Wimer Winter
      - Tarentaise
        - Ocooch Mountain Cheese
        - Tarentaise
      - Wimer Winter
        - Odessa Blue
        - Wimer Winter
  - Rogue River
    - Winnimere
      - Winnimere
        - Winnimere
        - Hudson Valley Camembert
      - Mont St. Francis
        - Bonne Bouche
        - Mont St. Francis
    - Rogue River
      - Redmondo
        - Humboldt Fog
        - Redmondo
      - Rogue River
        - Rogue River Blue
        - Vella Special Dry Jack

# Regional Soda Pop

**By Bob Roe**

Bob Roe grew up in Southern California, fueled mainly by Wampums (imagine a bag of Fritos with some hair on its chest) washed down with Bubble-Up. His beverage of choice these days is a Chinotto, an Italian soda that his wife says tastes like cough medicine.

EAST

- Moxie
- Manhattan Special
- Polar Orange Dry
- Frostie Cherry LimeAde
- Tom Tucker Mint Ginger Ale
- Hosmer Mountain Dangerous Ginger Beer
- Frank's Black Cherry Wishniak
- A-Treat Sarsaparilla

MIDWEST

- Vernor's Ginger Ale
- Green River
- Cherikee Red
- Cherry Lemon Sundrop
- Vess Whistle Orange Soda
- Fitz's Root Beer
- DANG! That's Good Butterscotch Root Beer
- Sprecher's RAVIN' RED

Moxie

Frostie Cherry LimeAde

Tom Tucker Mint Ginger Ale

Frank's Black Cherry Wishniak

Vernor's Ginger Ale

Cherry Lemon Sundrop

Vess Whistle Orange Soda

DANG!

Moxie

Frank's Wishniak

Vernor's Ginger Ale

DANG!

Moxie

DANG!

THE WINNER

**Moxie**

VS

**Tom Tucker Mint Ginger Ale vs. Frank's Black Cherry Wishniak**
A bruising intra-state rivalry between Pittsburgh's Tom Tucker (what's with the top hat you're wearing on the label, TT?) and a Philly pop icon, which is an impressive accomplishment given the large number (and variety) of sodas born and bubbled in that city. P.S., "Wishniak" is not Frank's last name – it's a type of cherry used in Eastern Europe for wines and liqueurs.

**Vernor's Ginger Ale vs. Cherry Lemon Sundrop**
A true David vs. Goliath chug-fest, since Vernor's may be the oldest soft drink in the country; the distinctive vanilla nose of this Detroit juggernaut makes it unlike other ginger ales (some detractors compare it to "urine," although no one explains how that taste test was conducted). The loser made it a close contest by having the best – and most disconcerting – slogan in the field: "Feel the burn."

**Cheerwine vs. Moxie**
Moxie's strength comes from its longevity (some claim it was the first soda), how poorly it "travels" (try to find one outside New York), and its contribution to slang. Also, how can you not feel protective about a soda that is so loved and hated? Devotees are almost religious in their fanaticism; first-time sippers often describe it as "disgusting."

IF YOU ONLY DRINK COKE OR PEPSI, you need more fizz in our life. America has a long, often goofy legacy of regional sodas that stretches back to the 1890s. In judging the best regional pops today, points were awarded for longevity, quality, uniqueness, and a defiantly regional appeal – in other words, a "brew" that might taste odd to someone who hadn't been weaned on it. As has happened in March Madness, the West was so weak that powerhouses from other areas had to be imported to fill out the regional.

**Cheerwine vs. Ale-8-One**
This king of the Carolinas is a cherry soda that defies comparison (is there a hint of almond in there?) and it got bonus points for being family-O&O since 1917. The loser here is Kentucky's finest; mix it with (surprise!) bourbon and you get a "Kentucky Speed Ball." And no, Cheerwine is not a wine, any more than root beer is a beer. It just looks like a burgundy in those sexy, retro tall-necks.

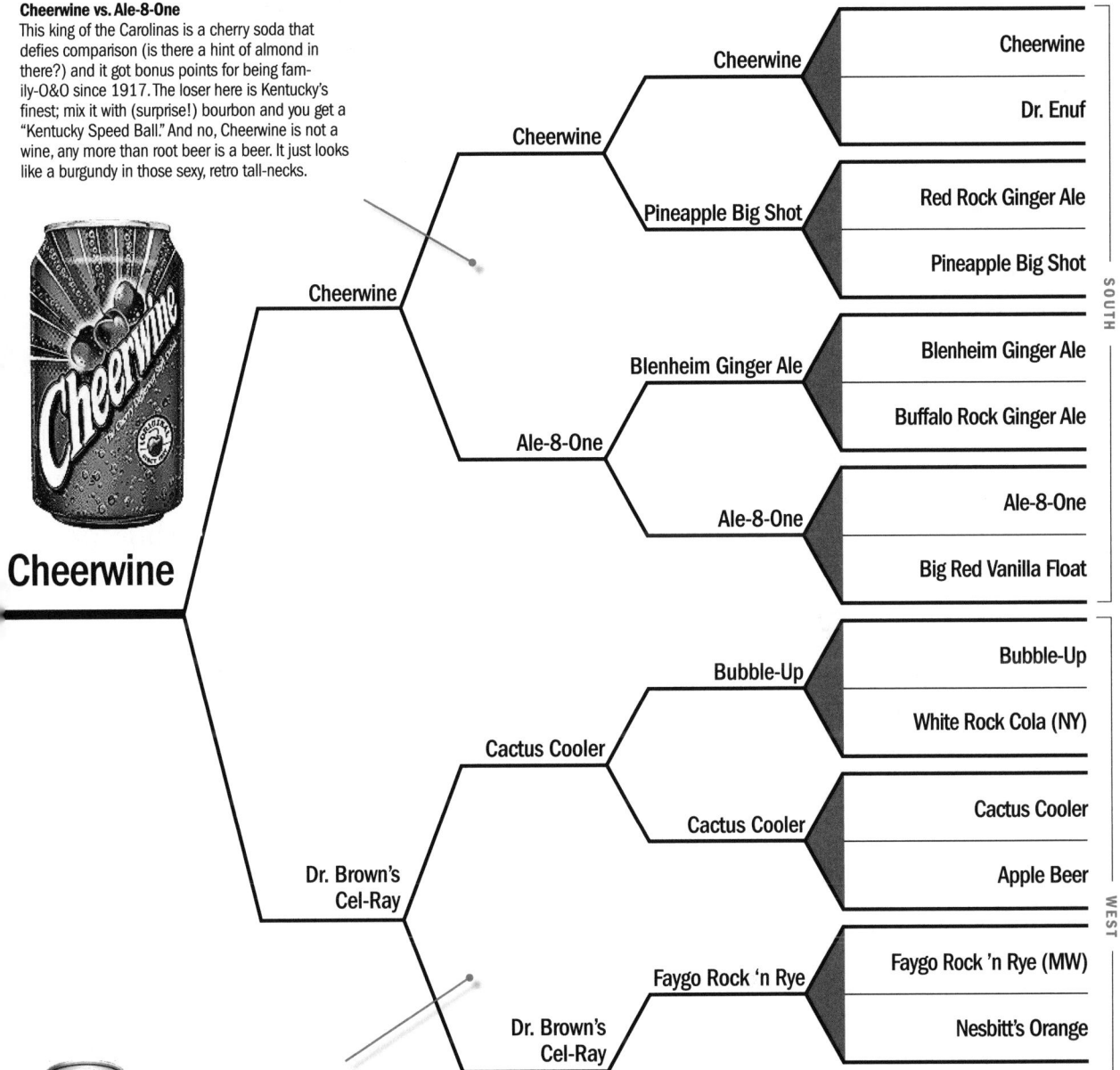


**Cactus Cooler vs. Dr. Brown's Cel-Ray Green**
Power can only take you so far. Dr. Brown's entrant is the only contender here based on a vegetable . . . we hope. The conceit of mixing a bitter vegetal taste with sugar is bold (and perverse) enough to score it big points, but not enough to make up for the fact that most of its fans drink it in delis, in order to cut through the grease dripping from their pastrami sandwiches.

# American Wines

**By Joseph S. Ward**

Joseph S. Ward is the wine editor for *Condé Nast Traveler* and the co-author, with Steven Spurrier, of *How to Buy Fine Wines: Practical Advice for the Investor and Connoisseur.*

RED REGIONAL

Chateau Montelana Estate Cabernet Sauvignon (Napa)
Williams-Selyem Pinot Noir Allen Vineyard (Russian River Valley)
**Ch. Montelena**

Screaming Eagle Cabernet Sauvignon (Napa)
Rochioli Pinot Nor West Block (Russian River Valley)
**Screaming Eagle**

Pax Syrah Alder Springs Vineyard "The Terraces" (Mendocino)
Beringer Private Reserve Cabernet Sauvignon (Napa)
**Beringer**

Quilceda Creek Cabernet Sauvignon (Columbia Valley)
Caymus Special Selection (Napa)
**Quilceda**

Dominus (Napa)
Marcassin Pinot Noir "Marcassin Vineyard" (Sonoma Coast)
**Marcassin Pinot**

Harlan Estate (Napa)
Ridge Montebello (Santa Cruz Mountains)
**Harlan Estate**

Martinelli Zinfandel Jackass Hill (Russian River Valley)
Thomas Pinot Noir (Dundee Hills)
**Martinelli Jackass Hill**

Shafer Vineyards Cabernet Sauvignon Hillside Select (Stags Leap)
Colgin IX Proprietary Red (Napa)
**Shafer Hillside Select**

**Ch. Montelena**

**Quilceda Creek**

**Marcassin Pinot**

**Shafer Hillside Select**

**Ch. Montelena**

**Shafer Hillside Select**

**Quilceda vs. Beringer**
Before there were cult Cabs, Beringer Private Reserve pioneered the big ultra-rich style and it still soars. Quilceda Creek, from Washington's Columbia Valley, is the greatest Cab not from California – an achievement that wins this round.

**Martinelli Jackass Hill vs. Shafer Hillside Select**
Zinfandel is California's native grape. Though it lacks the glamour of other varietals, in the right hands it can be special, none more so than from the old vines on Martinelli's steep hillside in Sonoma. That's not enough, however, to beat Shafer.

**Marcassin Pinot vs. Shafer Hillside Select**
A brutal matchup, since I'm a Pinot man and this Marcassin bottling is America's best Pinot. But no California Cab has produced as many stunning vintages since the early 1990s as Shafer Hillside Select. It's the benchmark of Napa's Stag's Leap district.

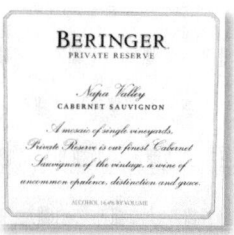

AMERICAN WINEMAKERS haven't had an inferiority complex for decades now. The 16 reds and 16 whites here certainly don't. The main criterion in this tournament, high quality and consistency being givens, is a wine that not only matches the Old World classics but creates a new archetype that stands on its own. From vintage to vintage, it is the benchmark other Americans aim for. If you see any of these on a wine list (and can handle the price), order a bottle.

**Peter Michael Inidgene vs. Marcassin "Marcassin"**
A rematch of sorts. Marcassin's Helen Turley made her reputation in the 1980s with brilliant Chardonnays at Peter Michael. With husband John Wetlaufer, she planted her first grapes in their small "Marcassin" vineyard in the early 1990s. In short time, it's become the California benchmark for Chardonnay. Marcassin by a nose.

THE WINNER

# Marcassin hardonnay "Marcassin Vineyard"

(Sonoma Coast)

**hafer Hillside Select vs. larcassin "Marcassin"**
aving conquered the warm, ark fruit style of Chateau Iontelena, Shafer reigns as merica's greatest red. But ven the savviest winemakers f Burgundy would be hard ressed to match Marcassin (or ur Final Four's Kistler) for con-istent excellence. People who ay they don't like Chardonnay ave never tasted the Marcassin ineyard bottling – our champ.

**Aubert vs. Konsgaard Vio Rous**
Mark Aubert makes intensely rich Chardonnays from cool sites along the Sonoma Coast. But John Konsgaard gets bonus points for making a great Rhone blend of Viognier and Roussanne that is the only non-Chardonnay among the great whites.

**Williams-Selyem vs. Mount Eden**
Williams-Selyem is one of only two sites to have invites to both sides of the draw. But Mount Eden has been making great Chardonnay longer than anyone. It's often taken for granted, but not here.

- Marcassin "Marcassin"
  - Peter Michael Indegene
    - Ramey Ritchie Vineyard
      - David Ramey Chardonnay Ritchie Vineyard (Russian River Valley)
      - J. Rochioli Chardonnay River Block (Russian River Valley)
    - Peter Michael Indegene
      - Peter Michael Chardonnay Cuvee Indigene (Alexander Mountain)
      - Paul Hobbs Chardonnay Richard Dinner Vineyard (Sonoma Mtn.)
  - Marcassin "Marcassin"
    - Konsgaard Vio Rous
      - Aubert Chardonnay Reuling Vineyard (Sonoma Coast)
      - Konsgaard Vio Rous (Napa Valley)
    - Marcassin "Marcassin"
      - Marcassin Chardonnay "Marcassin Vineyard" (Sonoma Coast)
      - Ramey Chardonnay Hyde Vineyard (Carneros)
- Kistler "Kistler"
  - Mount Eden
    - Kistler "Vine Hill"
      - Kistler Chardonnay Vine Hill Vineyard (Russian River Valley)
      - DuMol Chardonnay Chloe (Russian River Valley)
    - Mount Eden
      - Williams-Selyem Chardonnay Allen Vineyard (Russian River Valley)
      - Mount Eden Vineyards Chardonnay (Santa Cruz Mountain)
  - Kistler "Kistler"
    - Marcassin "Three Sisters"
      - Konsgaard Chardonnay The Judge (Napa)
      - Marcassin Chardonnay "Three Sisters Vineyard" (Russian River Valley)
    - Kistler "Kistler"
      - Peter Michael Chardonnay Mon Plaisir (Alexander Mountain)
      - Kistler Chardonnay "Kistler Vineyard" (Sonoma Valley)

WHITE REGIONAL

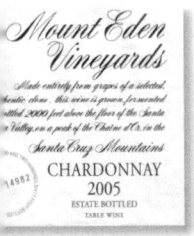

# Classic Cookbooks*

**By Katie Workman**

Katie Workman is the editor in chief and chief marketing officer of Cookstr.com, a recipe site dedicated to great recipes from respected cookbook authors and chefs.

***by authors who are no longer with us**

*Mastering the Art of French Cooking* by Julia Child (1961)

*New York Times Bread and Soup Cookbook* by Yvonne Young Tarr (1972)

Julia Child

*The Simpler the Better* by Leslie Revsin (2004)

*Alice B. Toklas Cookbook* by Alice B. Toklas (1954)

Leslie Revsin

Julia Child

*The New Making of a Cook* by Madeline Kamman (1997)

*Lee Bailey's Country Weekends* by Lee Bailey (1983)

Madeline Kamman

Madeline Kamman

*Eula Mae's Cajun Kitchen* by Eula Mae Dore (2007)

*Home Cooking* by Laurie Colwin (1988)

Laurie Colwin

Julia Child

*China Moon* by Barbara Tropp (1992)

*The Original Boston Cooking School Book* by Fannie Farmer

Fannie Farmer

Edna Lewis

*The Food of France* by Waverly Root (1966)

*The Taste of Country Cooking* by Edna Lewis (1976)

Edna Lewis

Craig Claiborne

*Mrs. Lincoln's Boston Cook Book* by Mary Johnson Lincoln (1883)

*The New York Times Cookbook* by Craig Claiborne (1961)

Craig Claiborne

Craig Claiborne

*The Korean Kitchen* by Copeland Marks (1993)

*Cooking with Patrick Clark* by Patrick Clark et al (1999)

Copeland Marks

**Edna Lewis vs. Fannie Farmer**
Like many renowned cookbooks, *Fannie Farmer's* is simply called by its author's name. But Edna Lewis, who is survived by her friend and co-author Scott Peacock, gets the edge for introducing the regional cuisine of the South to the rest of us in an honest and dignified way.

***Joy of Cooking* vs. Julia Child**
Was there any doubt that these two would meet in the finals? But the crown goes to Julia Child's high-impact opening statement from 1961, which rocked the American world of home cooking. Not just for the book, but because she started her work later than most, and because she kept at it wonderfully for the rest of her life.

THE WINNER

***Mastering the Art of French Cooking***
**by Julia Child (1961)**

VS

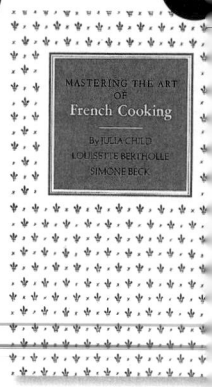

COOKBOOKS CAN BE CLASSICS while their authors are still living. But they take on mythic stature after their authors pass on. Comparing the ur-texts written by the late and great of American cookery collected here is not an apples-to-apples thing; it's more like apples to rambutans. Some are broad in scope, others very specific, but they all aim to stir excitement in your kitchen. The greater the impact, the further they go.

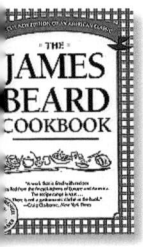


**James Beard vs. *Joy of Cooking***
A battle of titans that could be argued either way. James Beard was a genius who force-fed the media and the masses to appreciate American cooking. *Joy of Cooking* was self-published by a newly widowed woman in 1931 and became the go-to book for tens of millions of people. It still lives on in big-selling updates, and merits the label "bible."

**Richard Olney vs. Richard Sax**
Richard Sax published his brilliant dessert book the year before he died, and using the word "classic" in the title is neither braggadocio nor understatement. Sax was a cooking teacher who knew how to make people feel confident in the kitchen. That talent comes through in all of his cookbooks, but nowhere better than his last.

**Richard Olney vs. Michael McLaughlin**
A matchup, where the most evocative prose wins the day. If Richard Olney's sensuous, marvelously bossy language doesn't make you want to get into the kitchen, then you should call it a day and order take-out.

**M.F.K. Fisher vs. *Vogue***
M.F.K. Fisher was clearly more about the food writing than the recipes, but she can take a lot of the credit for making us all realize that food prose was something to be taken seriously.

# *Joy of Cooking*

- *Joy of Cooking*
  - *Joy of Cooking*
    - *Joy of Cooking* by Irma S. Rombauer, Marion Rombauer Becker, and Ethan Becker (1931)
    - *Parisian Home Cooking* by Michael Roberts (1999)
  - *Good Housekeeping*
    - *How America Eats* by Clementine Paddleford (1960)
    - *The Good Housekeeping Cookbook* by the Editors of Good Housekeeping (1903)
- Richard Sax
  - Richard Sax
    - *The Settlement Cookbook* by Mrs. Simon [Lillian] Kander (1903)
    - *Classic Home Desserts* by Richard Sax (1994)
  - Richard Olney
    - *Simple French Food* by Richard Olney (1974)
    - *Manhattan Chili Company Southwest American Cookbook* by Michael McLaughlin (1986)
- James Beard
  - James Beard
    - Better Homes & Gardens Cookbook (1930)
    - *The James Beard Cookbook* by James Beard (1959)
  - *American Heritage*
    - *The American Heritage Cookbook* by The American Heritage Editors (1964)
    - *The I Hate to Cook Book* by Peg Bracken (1965)
- Bert Greene
  - Bert Greene
    - *Greene on Greens* by Bert Greene (1984)
    - *Mostly Muffins* by Barbara Albright (1984)
  - M.F.K. Fisher
    - *The Art of Eating* by M.F.K. Fisher (1954)
    - *The Vogue Book of Menus and Recipes* by Jessica Daves (1964)

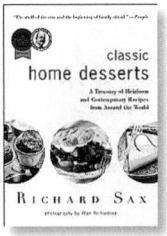

*Name of Bracket*

*Your Name*

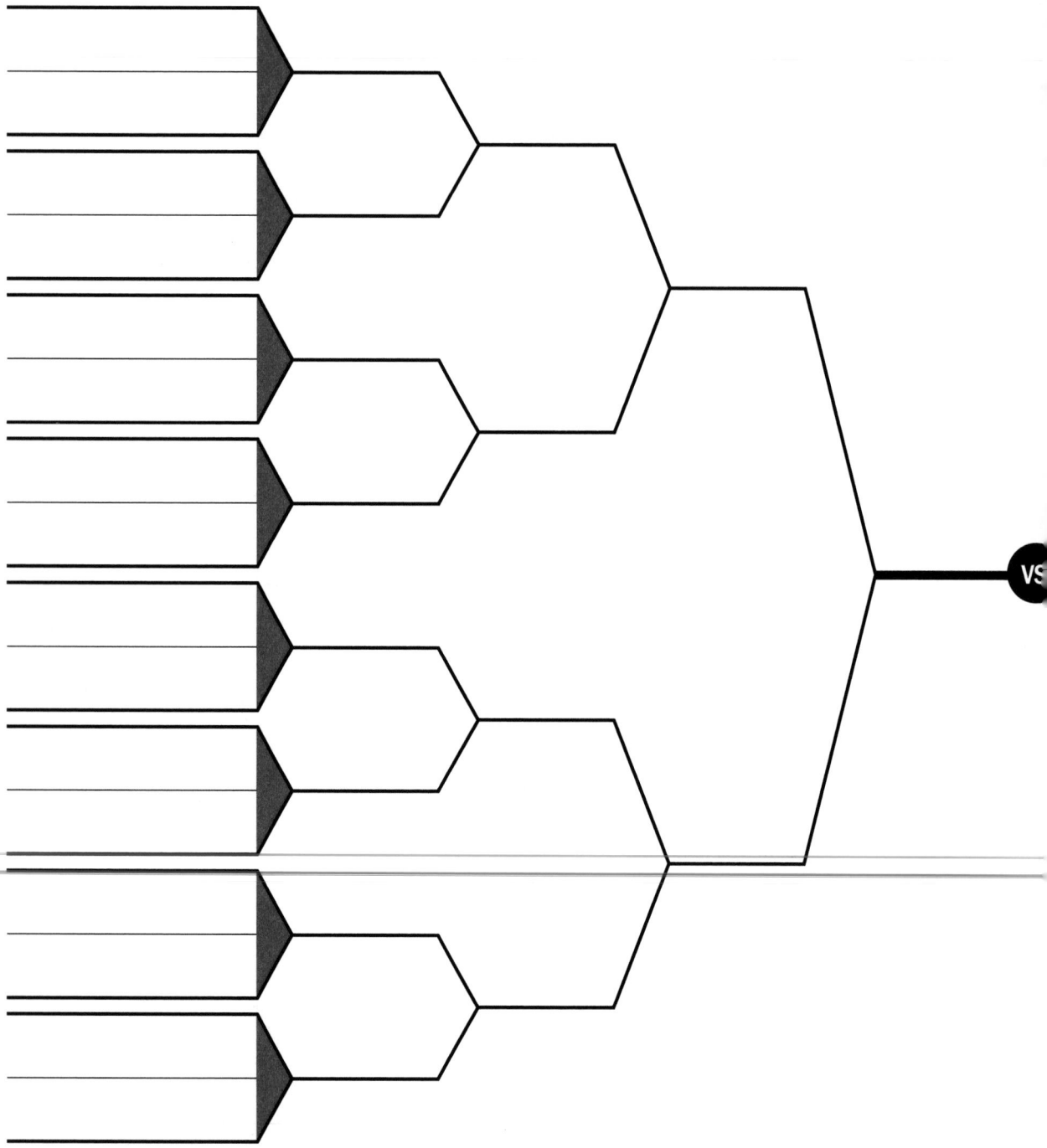

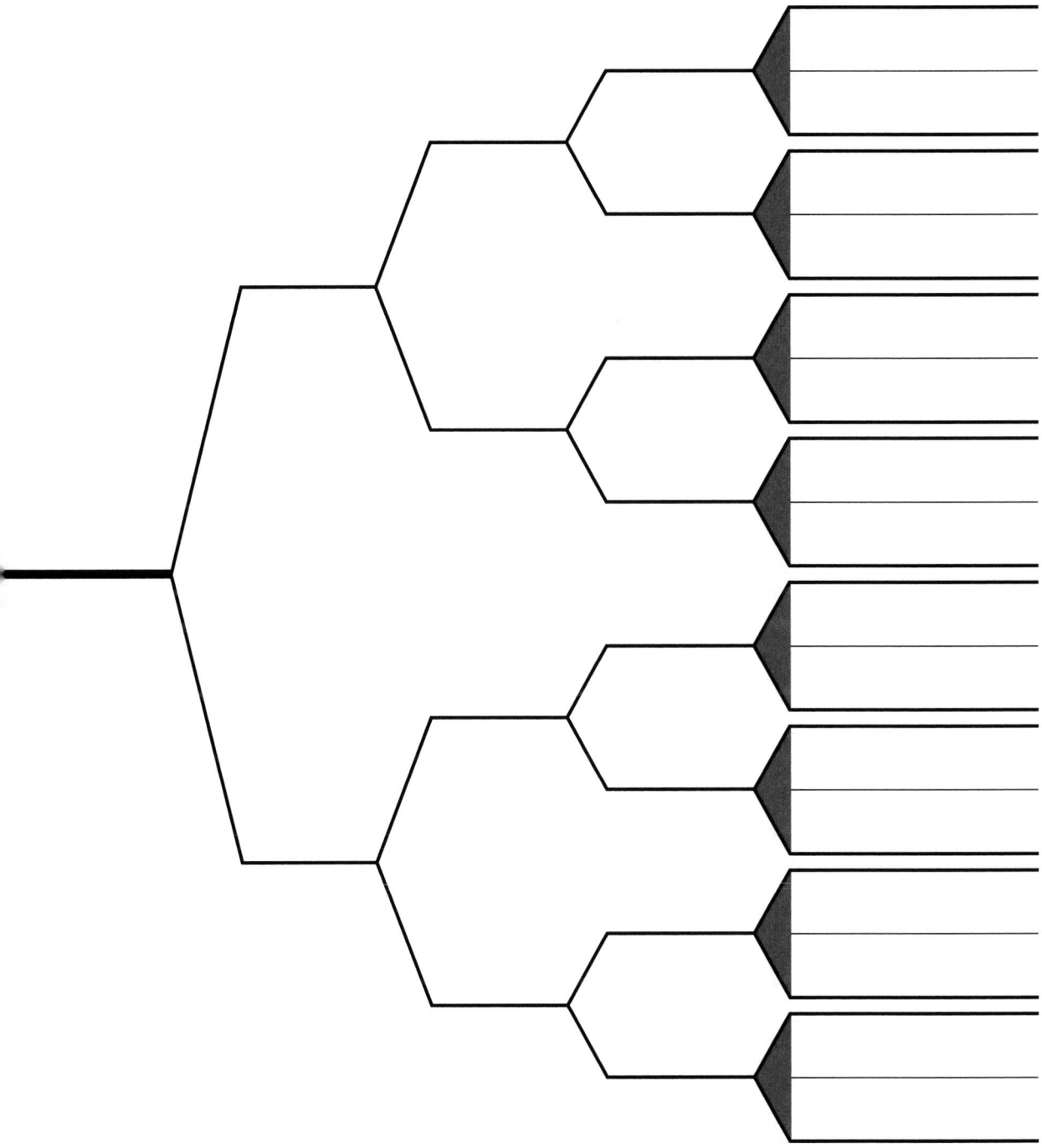

# Acknowledgments

**The Final Four of Everything**


## Our heartfelt thanks go to:

**Our contributors,** for getting the idea, dropping what they were doing, and jumping in with unbridled enthusiasm. When their brackets started coming in, every day seemed like Christmas.

**Our publisher** David Rosenthal, for getting the ball rolling with a simple but shrewd tweak.

**Our editor** Priscilla Painton, for her brilliant suggestions and steady hand on a project that resembles herding cats – and for bringing our attention to . . .

**Our designer** D.W. Pine, who got the concept immediately and then took it further than we imagined.

**Our picture editor** Skye Gurney, whose cleverness and work ethic are humbling.

**Our fact-man** Will Reiter, for checking the results.

**Our web gurus** Nina Schwartz and Michael Szczerban, for their proactive belief in the e-potential of brackets.

**Our Simon & Schuster production team,** for their infinite patience.

**And for their ideas, connective tissue, and support:** David McCormick, Annik Lafarge, David Hirshey, Ted Shaker, Sheryl Shaker, Zoe Pagnamenta, Theresa Park, Candy Lee, Susan Bolotin, Susan Mercandetti, Rachel Klayman, Susan Reed, Michael Solomon, Emily Sklar, Lisa Queen, Ben Adams, Dan Cabrera, Nick Reiter, Vince Wladika, Stefan Fatsis, Chris LaPlaca, Mark Mandel, Tom Jolly, Sandy Keenan, Will Leitch, Alan Schwarz, and our dear friend, Wikipedia.

**To our spouses,** Marie Rama and Griffin Miller, who moved easily into the finals of the Great Wives bracket.

# Photo Credits

## The Final Four of Everything

**Introduction:** Mugshot: www.thesmokinggun.com; Michael Jordan © Joshua Massel; Mary Tyler Moore: AP; George Carlin: Bonnie Murphy; William Shatner: David Gabber/PR Photos

**Americana:** #3: AP; #6 iStockPhoto; #7 www.15q.net; #8 Bluebird: Elaine R. Wilson; pelican: Calibus; oriole: Mdf; #10 "Moonrise, Hernandez, 1941": Photograph by Ansel Adams. © 2009 The Ansel Adams Publishing Rights Trust; #11 Jar of hair: © 2009 MastroAuctions.com; Buddy Holly: AP ;#14 All photographs courtesy of Scott Rutherford; #15 Water bottle: Answer sheet; alarm clock: iStockPhoto; #16 John Wayne: courtesy of www.doctormacro1.info

**History & Politics:** #18 Foam finger: iStockPhoto; #23 Cathode ray tube: iStockPhoto; #31 Jerry Falwell: Liberty University

**People:** Opener: Rita Hayworth: AP; #33 All photographs: NASA; #34 Cindy Crawford: Terry Thompson/PR photos; Dell'Orefice: The Heart Truth; Lauren Hutton: Lauren Hutton; Dovima: David Clarkson McJonathan-Swarm; #35. All photographs courtesy of www.thesmokinggun.com; #36 Mary Tyler Moore: AP; Mary Wilson: Jay D. Schwartz; #37 Michael Jordan © Joshua Massel; #38 Cat in the Hat © Dr. Seuss Enterprises, L.P.; lightbulb, chess pieces, and Monticello: iStockPhoto; #39 Moxie CrimeFighter Jillette courtesy of her parents; apple, peanut, and block: iStockPhoto; #40 Otis Redding: AP; #41 David Letterman: AP; David Axelrod: Newshour; David Ortiz: Aaron Donovan; David Wells: imagesbyferg/Ferguson; #43 John Edwards: David Victor Feldman; #44 William Shatner: David Gabber/PR Photos; William Perry: AP; #46 Richard Pryor: Alan Light; Dick Cavett: Christopher Peterson; #47 Rita Hayworth: AP; #49 Baldwins: AP; Wrights: AP; Coens: Rita Molnar; #50 Tommy Lee Jones: Jay Kravetz/PR Photos

**Sports:** #52 Michael Phelps: Bryan Allison; #54 Roger Staubach: AP; all other photographs courtesy of George Kitrinos; #55 Personal collection; #56 George Blanda: AP; #58 Y.A.Tittle: AP; Elgin Baylor: AP ; #59 Pinehurst No. 2 © Pinehurst, LLC 2007; #60 Chris Chelios: Dan4th Nicholas; Mike Modano: Elliot Lowe; puck: Tait Lifto; #61 iStockPhoto; #63 © YouTube; #65 Bosox: Leif Hedstrom; Joe DiMaggio by Gallerygal, available from geringlopez.com; #66 Polar bear: Ken Colwell; Nads: Jeffrey Daniel; #67 iStockPhoto; #69 Arnold Schwarzenegger: AP; Burt Reynolds: Alan Light; Mark Harmon: Jerry Avenaim; #70 Jim McKay: AP; Vin Scully: Dennis Ralutin; inset of Vin Scully: Craig Y. Fujii; #71 Tim Tebow: AP; Pete Maravich: AP; Gwen Torrence: courtesy of UGA Sports; #72 Joe Louis: Carl Van Vechten; ticket images courtesy of www.championsofthering.com; #73 Courtesy of Micah Larsen; #74 Personal collection; #75 Babe Ruth: AP; Jackie Robinson: AP; John McEnroe: Brett Weinstein; #76 Ted Williams: AP; Tom Brady: AP ; #77 AP

**Pop Culture:** Opener: Paul Newman: AP; #81 All photographs © YouTube; #82-#86 All photographs: AP; #88 film strip: iStockPhoto; #92 All photographs: AP; #94 Jeff Foxworthy: AP; Chris Rock: AP; Richard Pryor: Alan Light; #96 Top: Kevin Armstrong; bottom two photographs: Bonnie Murphy; #97 All images: iStockPhoto; #98 Omarosa: Glenn Francis; Paris Hilton and Nicole Richie: AP; Flavor Flav: PR Photos; #99 Atticus Finch: AP; gavel: iStockphoto; #100 All photographs: AP; #105 TV: iStockPhoto; #106 Will Smith: AP; Sylvester Stallone: AP; John Malkovich: Victor Felder; #107 Howard Stern: AP; #108 Shirley Temple: AP; Patty Duke: AP; #110 Maria Callas: AP; Nina Simone: Roland Godefroy; #112 Bill Cullen and Tom Kennedy: Adam Nedeff, GameShowUtopia.net; Pat Sajak: AP; #115 All photographs: AP; #116 Charlie Parker: AP; #118 Lon Tweeten; #119 AP; #120 Abbott and Costello: AP; #121 Magnet: iStockPhoto

**Nature:** Opener: iStockPhoto; #122 Roz Chast; #124 Trounce–Wikimedia; #125 Courtesy of Alan Ng; #126 Teeth: iStockPhoto; #128 All photographs: iStockPhoto; #129 Condor: Cszmurlo; trogon: Dominic Sherony; #130 syringe and lotion: iStockPhoto

**Words:** Opener: iStockPhoto; #131 All photographs: iStockPhoto; #133 iStockPhoto; #135 All photographs: iStockPhoto; #137 Courtesy of the Yogi Berra Museum & Learning Center; #138 iStockPhotos; #141 Mirror and waitress: iStockPhoto; #142 All photographs: PR Photos

**Food & Drink:** Opener: Courtesy of Rogue Creamery; #143 All photographs: iStockPhoto; #144: iStockPhoto